KU-033-234

# Complete Family Food

FLAME TREE
PUBLISHING

**HEALTH RATING**

Throughout the book, you will see a Health Rating on each page featuring this symbol: 

Quite simply, the more apples a recipe has, the healthier it is, giving you a rough guide to helping your family follow a healthy lifestyle.

= Not very healthy
= Very healthy

Publisher and Creative Director: Nick Wells
General Editor: Gina Steer
Project Editor: Sarah Goulding
Picture Research: Melinda Révèsz
Art Director: Mike Spender
Digital Design and Production: Chris Herbert
Layout Design: Cliff O'Dea

Authors: Catherine Atkinson, Juliet Barker, Liz Martin, Vicki Smallwood, Gina Steer, Kathy Steer, Carol Tennant, Mari Mererid Williams, Elizabeth Wolf-Cohen and Simone Wright
Photography: Colin Bowling, Paul Forrester and Stephen Brayne
Home Economists and Stylists: Jacqueline Bellefontaine, Mandy Phipps, Vicki Smallwood and Penny Stephens

All props supplied by Barbara Stewart at Surfaces

07 09 11 10 08

1 3 5 7 9 10 8 6 4 2

First published in 2004

This edition first published 2007 by
**FLAME TREE PUBLISHING**
Crabtree Hall, Crabtree Lane
Fulham, London SW6 6TY
United Kingdom

www.flametreepublishing.com

Flame Tree Publishing is part of the Foundry Creative Media Co. Ltd.



ISBN 978-1-84451-935-4

A CIP record for this book is available from the British Library upon request.



Printed in China

# Foreword

Juggling today's busy lifestyle of family, home and work is hard enough, and when you add to that having to provide a meal every night, the task can be quite daunting. This is where a reliable cookbook is an absolute must – one that will provide recipes suitable for any occasion, whether it is a simple, speedy supper or an extra-special dessert for entertaining friends. This book will answer all your needs, providing easy-to-follow recipes to suit any occasion, with helpful suggestions or alternatives, accompaniments, starters or puddings on every page.

Over the years, food and cooking has changed radically. The ease of travelling has widened horizons and brought foods previously regarded as exotic into everyday life. These can now be transported from all over the world, offering a vast array of exciting and delicious ingredients that excite the taste buds and expand the range of dishes on offer both at home and in restaurants. Food has expanded to embrace all manner of different cuisines. Dishes have mingled together, creating a host of new, exciting and innovative recipes that can take their origins from the Far East, from Thailand, Australia and India, from the Caribbean Islands and the Americas, producing Cajun, Creole and Fusion dishes which broaden our food horizons enormously. *Complete Family Food* offers a wide range of these dishes, as well as classics such as lasagne, shepherd's pie, roast chicken and treacle tart. Salads, once considered boring and dull – limp lettuce, halved tomatoes and flabby cucumber – have also been re-invigorated and now come in many different guises, from warm salads full of plump Mediterranean vegetables such as peppers and vine-ripened tomatoes, bursting with flavour and garlic, to an array of salad leaves ranging from the bitter red radicchio, rocket, crisp curly endive, the attractive lollo rosso, tinged with red, and the crisp Romaine lettuce ideal for a classic Caesar Salad.

We have also included a wide array of tempting vegetarian dishes, along with recipes ideal for serving to children. If you're watching your diet, not only will you find low fat alternatives throughout the book, but each main recipe also features a simple health rating.

Even the most experienced cook sometimes needs a little help, so this book also offers a reminder to the experienced and help for beginners with a comprehensive section of basic recipes. These include classic sweet and savoury sauces, how to make your own pastry, creating meat, poultry, fish and vegetable stocks, whipping up your own creamy homemade mayonnaise, how to make meringues and poach fruit, and everything you ever need to know about eggs, whether boiled, fried, poached, scrambled or made into omelettes. There is also the definitive section on how to prepare different cuts of meat, poultry and fish, plus helpful hints and tips for cooking them – in fact, everything a busy cook needs, including an essential metric conversion table. So look no further for your cookery Bible and happy cooking!

Gina Steer
**General Editor**

# Contents

Whether you've been cooking for years and just need a reminder, or you're a complete beginner and need help with the basics, this section tells you everything you need to know about cooking for a family. From how to make pastry and a basic white sauce, to cuts of meat, how to cook them and hygiene in the kitchen, your introduction to cooking starts here.

Nothing says comfort food quite like a delicious, homemade soup, and nothing could be simpler with these straightforward, step-by-step recipes. Starters are also made easy with something for every member of the family. Each recipe features two alternatives, covering everything from low fat and vegetarian options to suggested accompaniments and even entertaining versions.

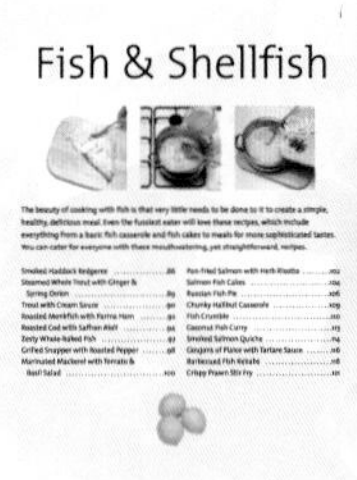

The beauty of cooking with fish is that very little needs to be done to it to create a simple, healthy, delicious meal. Even the fussiest eater will love these recipes, which include everything from a basic fish casserole and fish cakes to meals for more sophisticated tastes. You can cater for everyone with these mouthwatering, yet straightforward, recipes.

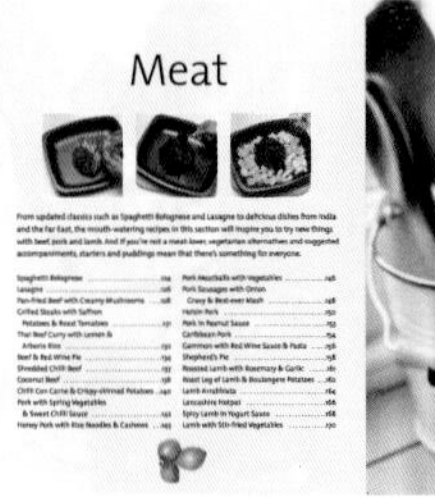


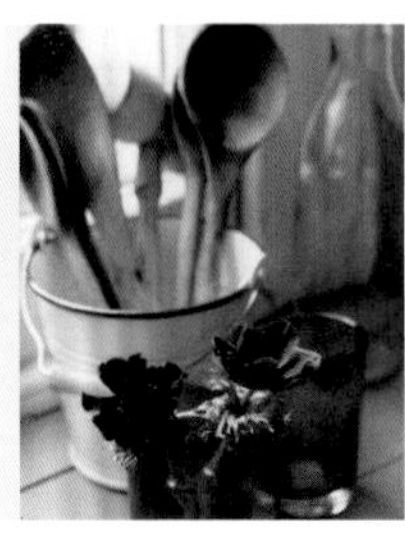



From updated classics such as Spaghetti Bolognese and Lasagne to delicious dishes from India and the Far East, the mouth-watering recipes in this section will inspire you to try new things with beef, pork and lamb. And if you're not a meat-lover, vegetarian alternatives and suggested accompaniments, starters and puddings mean that there's something for everyone.

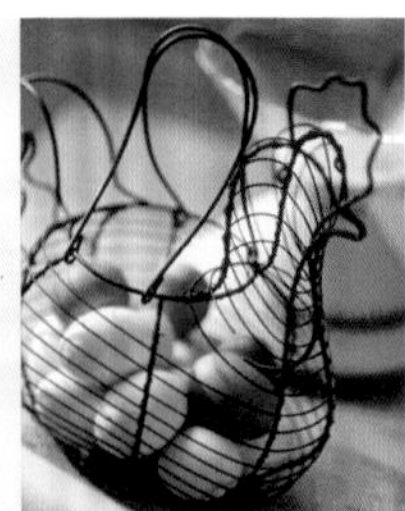



Whatever you need inspiration for, whether it's a traditional Sunday roast or something that little bit different for a dinner party, you'll find it amongst these delicious, easy-to-follow recipes. Tackling everything from chicken and turkey to duck, pheasant and even rabbit, these recipes give old favourites a fresh twist and introduce some new ideas that the whole family will love.

You don't have to be vegetarian to appreciate these mouthwatering recipes, but if you are, you're in for a real treat. With lots of delicious main meals as well as lots of accompaniments and starters, these endlessly adaptable recipes will suit any occasion. From summer salads to winter warmers, even the meat-lovers in your family won't be able to resist.

Endlessly versatile as an accompaniment, a meal in it's own right or even a pudding, rice forms the basis of these delicious recipes. From Risottos, Paella and Egg Fried Rice, to Thai Rice Cakes, Rice-filled Peppers and even Rice Soup, your family will love these tasty dishes. And for those with a sweet tooth, there's a Chocolate Rice Pudding that will banish school meal memories forever.

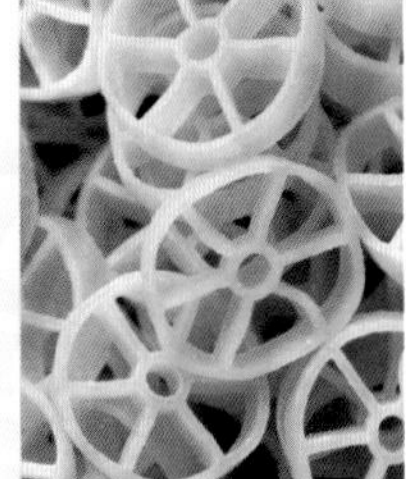

When it comes to quick and simple dishes, nothing beats pasta for speed and convenience. You'll find something to tempt everyone here, from delicious family favourites such as Macaroni Cheese and Spaghetti with Meatballs, to the more sophisticated Parma Ham-wrapped Chicken with Ribbon Pasta and Fettuccini with Wild Mushrooms & Prosciutto.

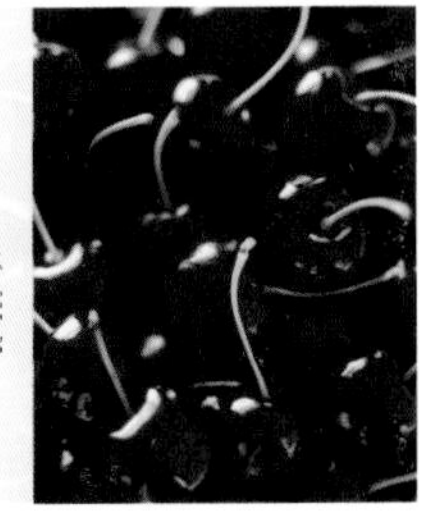

No matter how good the main course, there's always room for pudding! With these delicious recipes, old-fashioned favourites such as Jam Roly Poly are made easy, and no one will be able to resist Chocolate Sponge Pudding with Fudge Sauce. Dieters need not despair, though – low fat recipes such as Summer Pavlova and Oaty Fruit Puddings mean that everyone can indulge.



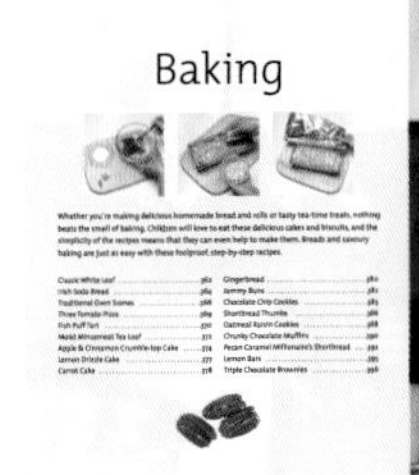

Whether you're making delicious homemade bread and rolls or tasty tea-time treats, nothing beats the smell of baking. Children will love to eat these delicious cakes and biscuits, and the simplicity of the recipes means that they can even help to make them. Breads and savoury baking are just as easy with these foolproof, step-by-step recipes.

If you're hosting a dinner party and are cooking to impress, or you're just having a few friends round and want to cook something special, these recipes will help you create a delicious meal. Covering everything from starters and main courses to puddings and drinks, whatever the occasion, you'll be ready for anything.

# Basic Recipes

Whether you've been cooking for years and just need a reminder, or you're a complete beginner and need help with the basics, this section tells you everything you need to know about cooking for a family. From how to make pastry and a basic white sauce, to cuts of meat, how to cook them and hygiene in the kitchen, your introduction to cooking starts here.

# Basic Recipes: Eggs

## Boiled Eggs

Eggs should be boiled in gently simmering water. Remove the egg from the refrigerator at least 30 minutes before cooking. Bring a pan of water to the boil, then once boiling lower the heat to a simmer. Gently lower the egg into the water and cook for 3 minutes for lightly set, or 4 minutes for a slightly firmer set. Remove and lightly tap to stop the egg continuing to cook. Hard boiled eggs should be cooked for 10 minutes then plunged into cold water and left until cold before shelling. Serve lightly boiled eggs with toast or buttered bread cut into fingers to use as dippers.

## Fried Eggs

Place a little sunflower oil or butter in a frying pan until hot. Break an egg into a cup or small jug and carefully slip into the pan. Cook, spooning the hot oil or fat over the egg for 3–4 minutes or until set to personal preference. Remove with a palette knife or fish slice and serve with freshly grilled bacon or sausages or on fried bread with baked beans and tomatoes.

# Poached Eggs

Half-fill a frying pan with water and bring to a gentle boil, then reduce the heat to a simmer. Add either a little salt or a few drops of vinegar or lemon juice – this will help the egg retain its shape. Break the egg into a cup or small jug and carefully slip into the simmering water. Lightly oiled round, plain pastry cutters can be used to contain the eggs if preferred. Cover the pan with a lid and cook for 3–4 minutes or until set to personal preference. Once cooked, remove by draining with a slotted draining spoon or fish slice and serve. Alternatively, special poaching pans are available if preferred. With these, half-fill the pan with water and place the tray with the egg containers on top. Place a little butter in the cups and bring to the boil. Swirl the melted butter around and carefully slip in the eggs. Cover with the lid and cook for 3–4 minutes. Serve either on hot buttered toast or on top of sliced ham or freshly cooked spinach.

# Scrambled Eggs

Melt 15 g/½ oz butter in a small pan. Allowing two eggs per person, break the eggs into a small bowl and add 1 tablespoon of milk and seasoning to taste. Whisk until blended with a fork, then pour into the melted butter. Cook over a gentle heat, stirring with a wooden spoon, until set and creamy. Serve on hot buttered toast with smoked salmon or stir in some freshly snipped chives or chopped tomatoes.

# Omelette

Allow two eggs per person. Break the eggs into a small bowl, add seasoning to taste and 1 tablespoon of milk. Whisk with a fork until frothy. Heat 2 teaspoons of olive oil in a frying pan, and, when hot, pour in the egg mixture. Cook gently, stirring with the fork, and bringing the mixture from the edges of the pan to the centre. Allow the uncooked egg mixture to flow to the edges. When the egg has set, cook without stirring for an extra minute before folding the omelette into three and gently turning out onto a warmed serving plate. Take care not to overcook.

# Cheese Omelette

Proceed as before, then sprinkle 25–40 g/1–1 ½ oz grated mature Cheddar cheese on top of the lightly set omelette. Cook for a further 2 minutes or until the cheese has begun to melt. If liked, place under a preheated grill for 2–3 minutes or until golden, fold over and serve.

# Tomato Omelette

Proceed as for a plain omelette and after 2 minutes of cooking time, add 1 medium chopped tomato on top of the omelette and cook as above until set.

# Fine Herbs Omelette

Stir in 1 tablespoon of finely chopped, fresh mixed herbs into the beaten eggs before cooking. Proceed as for a plain omelette.

# Mushroom Omelette

Wipe and slice 50 g/2 oz button mushrooms. Heat 15 g/½ oz of butter in a small pan and cook the mushrooms for 2–3 minutes, drain and reserve. Cook omelette as above, adding the cooked mushrooms once it is lightly set.

# Basic Recipes: Pastry

## Shortcrust Pastry

**Makes 225 g/8 oz**

225 g/8 oz plain white flour
pinch of salt
50 g/2 oz white vegetable fat or lard
50 g/2 oz butter or block margarine

Sift the flour and salt into a mixing bowl. Cut the fats into small pieces and add to the bowl. Rub the fats into the flour using your fingertips until the mixture resembles fine breadcrumbs. Add 1–2 tablespoons of cold water and mix to form a soft, pliable dough. Knead gently on a lightly floured surface until smooth and free from cracks, then wrap and chill for 30 minutes before rolling out on a lightly floured surface. Use as required. Cook in a preheated hot oven (200°C/400°F/Gas Mark 6).

## Sweet Shortcrust Pastry (Pâte Sucrée)

**Makes 225 g/8 oz**

225 g/8 oz plain white flour
150 g/5 oz unsalted butter, softened
2 tbsp caster sugar
1 medium egg yolk

Sift the flour into a mixing bowl, cut the fat into small pieces, add to the bowl and rub into the flour. Stir in the sugar, then mix to form a pliable dough with the egg yolk and about 1 tablespoon of cold water. Wrap, chill and use as required.

## Cheese Pastry

Follow the recipe for sweet shortcrust pastry, but omit the sugar and add 1 teaspoon of dried mustard powder and 50 g/2 oz of mature grated Cheddar cheese.

## Rough Puff Pastry

**Makes 225 g/8 oz**

225 g/8 oz plain white flour
pinch of salt
150 g/5 oz butter, block margarine or lard
squeeze of lemon juice

Sift the flour and salt together in a mixing bowl. Cut the fat into small pieces and add to the bowl. Add the lemon juice and sufficient cold water, about 6–7 tablespoons, and mix with a fork until you have a fairly stiff mixture. Turn out on to a lightly floured surface and roll into an oblong. Fold the bottom third up to the centre and bring the top third down to the centre. Gently press the edges together. Give the pastry a half turn then roll the pastry out again into an oblong. Repeat the folding, turning and rolling at least four more times, then wrap and leave to rest in a cool place for at least 30 minutes. Use as required. To cook, place in a preheated oven at 220°C/425°F/Gas Mark 7.

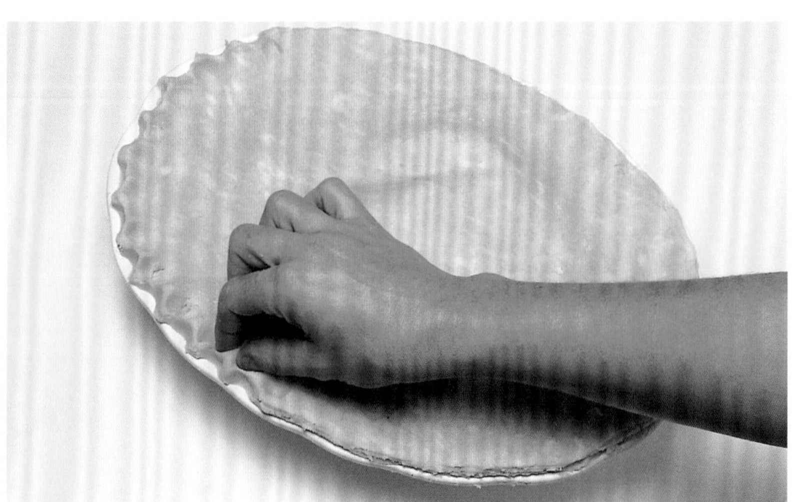

# Choux Pastry

**Makes 225 g/8 oz**

75 g/3 oz plain white flour

pinch salt

50 g/2 oz butter

2 medium eggs, beaten

Place the butter and 150 ml /¼ pt water in a heavy-based saucepan. Heat gently, stirring until the butter has melted, and bring to the boil. Draw off the heat and add the flour all at once. Beat with a wooden spoon until the mixture forms a ball in the centre. Cool for five minutes. Gradually add the eggs, beating well after each addition until a stiff mixture is formed. Either place in a piping bag fitted with a large nozzle, or shape using two spoons. Cook in a preheated oven at 200°C/400°F/Gas Mark 6 for 15–25 minutes, depending on size. Remove and make a small slit in the side (see below), then return to the oven and cook for a further five minutes. Remove and leave until cold before filling.

# Hot Water Crust Pastry

**Makes 450 g/1 lb**

450 g/1 lb plain white flour

1 tsp salt

100 g/4 oz lard or white vegetable fat

150 ml/¼ pt milk and water, mixed

Sift the flour and salt together and reserve. Heat the lard or white vegetable fat until melted and bring to the boil. Pour immediately into the flour and using a wooden spoon, mix together and beat until the mixture comes together and forms a ball.

When cool enough to handle, knead lightly until smooth and pliable. Use as required, covering the dough with a clean cloth before use. Bake in a preheated oven at 220°C/425°F/Gas Mark 7, or as directed.

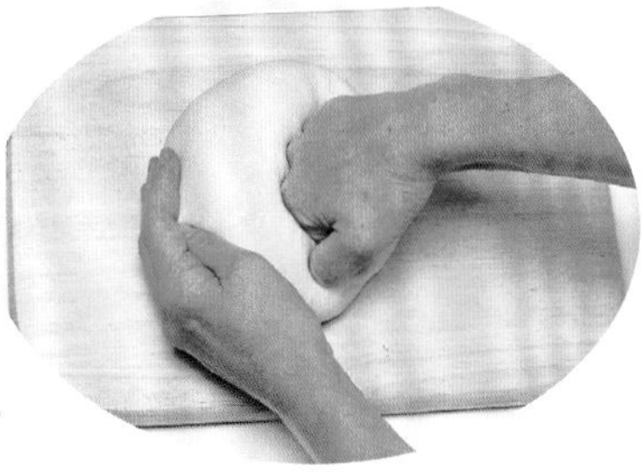

# Basic Recipes: Vegetables

## Blanched Vegetables

Vegetables are often blanched to preserve their colour or to speed up the cooking process. This technique is normally used for green vegetables and peppers. Trim or peel the vegetable, according to each variety, and cut into small pieces or as directed in the recipe. Rinse well. Bring a pan of lightly salted water to the boil, add the vegetables, cover with a lid, reduce the heat and simmer for 2–4 minutes or as directed. Remove, drain and plunge the vegetables immediately into cold water. Leave until cold, then drain and use.

## Blanched Chips

Peel some even-sized potatoes and cut into either thin or chunky chips as desired. Cover in cold water and soak for at least 10 minutes to remove the starch, then drain thoroughly and dry on a clean tea towel. Cover a chip basket with a layer of chips, and heat a deep-fat fryer half-filled with oil to a temperature of 180°C/350°F. Plunge the chips into the oil and cook for 3–4 minutes or until soft but not coloured. Drain and place on a tray. Repeat with the remaining chips. When ready to fry, heat the oil to 190°C/375°F, arrange a layer of chips in the chip basket and carefully lower into the hot oil. Cook for 3–5 minutes or until crisp and golden. Drain on absorbent paper and repeat with remaining chips.

## Par-boiled Potatoes and Parsnips

Peel and trim the potatoes and parsnips, discarding any eyes or damaged vegetables. Cut into even-sized pieces. Place separately in large saucepans, add a little salt and cover with cold water. Bring to the boil, cover with lids, reduce the heat and simmer for 5 minutes. Drain, return the vegetables to the saucepans and cover with the lids. Heat gently for about 5 minutes, shaking the pans so as to slightly break up the surface of the vegetables. Use as required.

## Roasted Potatoes

Par-boil potatoes as previously directed. For 450 g/1 lb potatoes, pour 1–2 tablespoons of sunflower or olive oil into a roasting tin and heat in a preheated hot oven at 200°C/400°F/Gas Mark 6 for 5–8 minutes or until really hot. Add the potatoes to the tin and turn in the hot oil. Cook for 50 minutes to 1 hour or until crisp and golden. Turn occasionally during roasting.

Parsnips can be roasted in the same way and can, if liked, be cooked with the potatoes.

# Roasted Vegetables

Clean, trim and peel the vegetables, discarding any seeds or stalks. Cut into even-sized pieces. Place in a roasting tin and pour over 2–3 tablespoons of olive oil. Peel and cut 2–3 garlic cloves into thick slices and scatter over the vegetables. Season to taste and add a few sprigs of fresh rosemary, thyme or oregano. Roast in a preheated oven at 200°C/400°F/Gas Mark 6 for 40–45 minutes or until tender and beginning to char around the edges. Turn occasionally during cooking.

Vegetables suitable for roasting include onions, cut into wedges, assorted coloured peppers, courgettes, aubergines and carrots. Tomatoes and mushrooms will take less time to roast, about 20 minutes.

# Frying Onions

Peel 450 g/1 lb onions, keeping the base of each onion intact (this will help to prevent 'crying' while peeling the onions). Heat 2–3 tablespoons of olive or sunflower oil in a large, heavy-based frying pan. Add the onions and sauté gently, stirring for 10–12 minutes or until the onions are soft but still retain a bite.

# Caramelising Onions

Cook as above and after 10 minutes, sprinkle in 2 teaspoons of light muscovado sugar and continue to cook, stirring frequently for a further 10–15 minutes or until golden.

# Basic Recipes: Sauces

## White Pouring Sauce

**Makes 300 ml/½ pt**

15 g/½ oz butter or margarine

2 tbsp plain white flour

300 ml/½ pt milk

salt and freshly ground black pepper

Melt the butter or margarine in a small saucepan and stir in the flour. Cook, stirring over a gentle heat for 2 minutes, then draw off the heat and gradually stir in the milk. Return to the heat and cook, stirring with a wooden spoon until the sauce thickens and coats the back of the spoon. Add seasoning to taste and use as required.

For a coating sauce, use 25 g/1 oz of butter or margarine and 3 tablespoons of plain white flour to 300 ml/½ pt liquid and proceed as above.

For a binding sauce, use 50 g/2 oz butter or margarine and 50 g/2 oz plain white flour to 300 ml/½ pint liquid and proceed as above

## Cheese Sauce

Proceed as before, depending on which consistency is required, stirring in 1 tsp dried mustard powder with the flour. When the sauce has thickened, remove from the heat and stir in 50 g/2 oz mature Cheddar cheese, or any other cheese of choice. Stir until melted.

## Herb Sauce

Make a white sauce as before, then stir in 1 tbsp freshly chopped herbs such as parsley, basil, oregano or a mixture of fresh herbs.

## Mushroom Sauce

Make as before and lightly sauté 50 g/2 oz sliced mushrooms in 1 tablespoon of butter for 3 minutes or until tender. Drain and stir into the prepared white sauce.

## Bechamel Sauce

**Makes 300 ml/½ pint**

Peel 1 small onion and place in a small saucepan together with a small piece of peeled carrot, a small celery stick, 3 whole cloves and a few black peppercorns. Add 300 ml/½ pint milk and bring slowly to just below boiling point. Remove from the heat, cover with a lid and leave to infuse for at least 30 minutes. When ready to use, strain off the milk and use to make a white sauce as before. If liked, 1–2 tablespoons of single cream can be stirred in at the end of cooking.

# Gravy

**Makes 300 ml/½ pint**

When roasting meat, once the meat is cooked, remove from the roasting tin, cover and keep warm. Pour off all but 2–3 tablespoons of the meat juices and heat on the hob. Stir in 2 tablespoons of plain white flour and cook for 2 minutes, stirring the sediment that is left in the tin into the gravy. Draw off the heat and gradually stir in 300 ml/½ pint of stock, according to the flavour of the meat. Return to the heat and cook, stirring until the gravy comes to the boil and thickens. Add seasoning to taste and, if liked, a little port, wine or redcurrant jelly. Gravy browning can be added if desired to give a darker colour.

If no meat juices are available, heat 2 tablespoons of oil and stir in 1–2 tablespoons of flour. Cook for 2 minutes then draw off the heat and stir in 300 ml/½ pint of stock of your choice. Return to the heat and cook, stirring until thickened. Add seasoning, flavourings and gravy browning according to personal preference.

# Tomato Sauce

**Makes 450 ml/¾ pint**

1 tbsp olive or sunflower oil
1 small onion, peeled and finely chopped
1–2 garlic cloves, peeled and crushed
50 g/2 oz streaky bacon, optional
450 g/1 lb ripe tomatoes, peeled if preferred and chopped or
400 g can chopped tomatoes
1–2 tbsp tomato purée
150 ml/¼ pint vegetable stock
salt and freshly ground pepper
1 tbsp freshly chopped oregano, marjoram or basil

Heat the oil in a saucepan and sauté the onion, garlic and bacon, if using, for 5 minutes. Add the chopped tomatoes and sauté for a further 5 minutes, stirring occasionally. Blend the tomato purée with the stock then pour into the pan, add seasoning and herbs and bring to the boil. Cover with a lid, reduce the heat and simmer for 12–15 minutes or until a chunky sauce is formed. Blend in a food processor to form a slightly less chunky sauce, or if a smoother sauce is preferred then rub through a fine sieve. Adjust seasoning and use as required.

# Curry Sauce

**Makes 300 ml/½ pint**

1 tbsp sunflower oil
1 medium onion, peeled and chopped
2–4 garlic cloves, peeled and crushed
1 celery stick, trimmed and chopped
1–2 red chillies, deseeded and chopped
1 tsp ground coriander
1 tsp ground cumin
½ tsp turmeric
1 tbsp plain white flour
450 ml/¾ pt vegetable stock
salt and freshly ground black pepper
1 tbsp freshly chopped coriander, optional

Heat the oil in a saucepan and sauté the onion, garlic, celery and chillies for 5–8 minutes or until softened. Add the spices and continue to sauté for a further 3 minutes, stirring frequently. Sprinkle in the flour, cook for 2 minutes, then slowly add the stock and bring to the boil. Cover with a lid, reduce the heat and simmer for 15 minutes, stirring occasionally. Add seasoning to taste and stir in the chopped coriander if using. Use as required.

# Apple Sauce

**Makes 300 ml/½ pint**

450 g/1 lb Bramley cooking apples, peeled, cored and chopped

1 tbsp butter

25–40 g/1 ½–2 oz sugar

Place all the ingredients with 2 tablespoons of water in a saucepan and cook over a gentle heat for 10 minutes, or until the apples are tender, stirring occasionally. Take care that the apples do not burn on the base of the pan. Remove from the heat and either rub through a sieve to form a smooth purée or beat with the spoon to give a chunkier sauce. The apple sauce can be flavoured with 1 tablespoon of finely grated orange or lemon rind and 2–3 whole cloves, which you should remove before serving. Alternatively, add 1 lightly bruised cinnamon stick (remove before serving).

# Mint Sauce

**Makes 120 ml/4 fl oz**

15 g/½ oz fresh mint

1 tbsp caster sugar

3–4 tbsp white wine vinegar or other vinegar of choice

Discard the stalks from the mint, rinse the leaves and dry. Finely chop and place in a sauceboat or small bowl. Pour over 3–4 tablespoons of hot but not boiling water, then stir in the sugar until dissolved. Stir in the vinegar and use as required.

# Cranberry Sauce

**Makes 450 g/1 lb**

450 g/1 lb fresh or thawed frozen cranberries

150 ml/¼ pt orange juice

50 g/2 oz light muscovado sugar, or to taste

1–2 tbsp port, optional

Rinse the cranberries and place in a saucepan with the orange juice and sugar. Place over a gentle heat and cook, stirring occasionally for 12–15 minutes or until the cranberries are soft and have 'popped'. Remove from the heat and stir in the port, if using. Use as required.

# French Dressing

**Makes 120 ml/4 fl oz**

½ tsp dry mustard powder

½-1 tsp caster sugar, or to taste

salt and freshly ground black pepper

3 tbsp white wine vinegar

120 ml/4 fl oz extra virgin olive oil

Place all the ingredients in a screw top jar and shake vigorously. Use as required.

Other flavours can be made by substituting the vinegar: try raspberry, cider or balsamic vinegar with a little clear honey in place of the sugar. Replace the dry mustard powder with 1 teaspoon of wholegrain mustard. Freshly chopped herbs can also be added to the dressing.

# Mayonnaise

**Makes 150 ml/¼ pint**

1 medium egg yolk

¼ tsp dry mustard powder

salt and freshly ground black pepper

½ tsp caster sugar

150 ml/¼ pt extra virgin olive oil

1 tbsp white wine vinegar or lemon juice

Place the egg yolk in a bowl and stir in the mustard powder with a little seasoning and the sugar. Beat with a wooden spoon until blended then gradually add the oil, drop by drop, stirring briskly with either a whisk or wooden spoon. If the mixture becomes too thick, beat in a little of the vinegar or lemon juice. When all the oil has been added, stir in the remaining vinegar or lemon juice and adjust the seasoning. Store covered in the refrigerator until required.

If the mayonnaise should curdle whilst making, place a further egg in a separate bowl then slowly beat into the curdled mixture.

# Tartare Sauce

**Makes 150 ml/¼ pint**

150 ml/¼ pt prepared mayonnaise

1 tbsp freshly chopped tarragon

1 tbsp freshly chopped parsley

1 tbsp capers, rinsed and chopped

1 tbsp gherkins, finely chopped

1 tbsp lemon juice

Mix all the ingredients together. Place in a small bowl, cover and leave for at least 30 minutes for the flavours to blend.

# Chocolate Sauce

**Makes 150 ml/¼ pint**

100 g/4 oz plain dark chocolate

1 tbsp butter

1 tsp golden syrup

75 ml/3 fl oz semi-skimmed milk

Break the chocolate into small pieces and place in a small, heavy-based saucepan. Add the remaining ingredients and place over a gentle heat, stirring occasionally until smooth. Pour into a small jug and use as required.

# Butterscotch Sauce

**Makes 300 ml/½ pint**

75 g/3 oz light muscovado sugar

1 tbsp golden syrup

50 g/2 oz butter

200 ml/7 fl oz single cream

Place the sugar, syrup and butter in a heavy-based saucepan and heat gently, stirring occasionally until blended. Stir in the cream and continue to heat, stirring until the sauce is smooth. Use as required.

# Syrup Sauce

**Makes 150 ml/¼ pint**

5 tbsp golden syrup

2 tbsp lemon juice

1 tbsp arrowroot

Pour the syrup and lemon juice into a small pan and add 3 tablespoons of water. Bring to the boil. Blend the arrowroot with 1 tablespoon of water, then stir into the boiling syrup. Cook, stirring, until the sauce thickens and clears. Serve.

# Lemon Sauce

**Makes 150 ml/¼ pint**

Grated rind of 1 large lemon, preferably unwaxed

75 ml/3 fl oz fresh lemon juice, strained

2 tbsp caster sugar

1 tbsp arrowroot

2 tsp butter

Place the grated lemon rind with the juice in a saucepan with 4 tablespoons of water. Stir in the sugar and heat, stirring until the sugar has dissolved. Bring to the boil. Blend the arrowroot with 1 tablespoon of water then blend into the boiling sauce. Cook, stirring until the sauce thickens and clears. Add the butter and cook for a further 1 minute. Oranges can be used in place of the lemon, or a combination of the two.

# Melba Sauce

**Makes 300 ml/½ pint**

350 g/12 oz fresh or thawed frozen raspberries

40 g/1 ½ oz sugar or to taste

1 tbsp lemon or orange juice

Clean the raspberries if using fresh, then place all the ingredients and 4 tablespoons of water in a heavy-based saucepan and place over a gentle heat. Bring to the boil, then reduce the heat and simmer for 5–8 minutes or until the fruits are really soft. Remove from the heat, cool slightly, then blend in a food processor to form a purée. Rub through a fine sieve to remove the pips and use as required.

# Jam Sauce

**Makes 150 ml/¼ pt**

4 tbsp jam, such as raspberry, apricot, strawberry or marmalade

150 ml/¼ pt fruit juice or water

1 tbsp arrowroot

1 tbsp lemon juice

Place the jam and the fruit juice or water in a small pan and heat, stirring until blended. Rub through a fine sieve to remove any pips, return to the pan and bring to the boil. Blend the arrowroot with the lemon juice and stir into the sauce. Cook, stirring until the sauce thickens and clears. If a thicker sauce is required, use half the amount of fruit juice or water.

# Custard

**Makes 300 ml/½ pint**

300 ml/½pt milk

2 tbsp plain white flour

1 medium egg

few drops vanilla extract

1 tbsp butter

1–2 tbsp caster sugar or to taste

Heat the milk to blood heat. Sift the flour into a bowl, make a well in the centre and add the egg. Beat the egg into the flour, drawing the flour in from the sides of the bowl and slowly adding half the warmed milk. When all the flour has been incorporated, beat well to remove any lumps then stir in the remaining milk. Strain into a clean saucepan and place over a gentle heat and cook, stirring until the sauce thickens and coats the back of the wooden spoon. Stir in the vanilla extract, butter and sugar to taste. Stir until blended and use as required.

# Basic Recipes: Stocks

## Chicken Stock

**Makes 900 ml/1 ½ pints**

1 cooked chicken carcass

1 medium onion, peeled and cut into wedges

1 large carrot, peeled and chopped

1 celery stick, trimmed and chopped

1 bouquet garni

10 peppercorns

4 whole cloves

salt to taste

Remove any large pieces of meat from the carcass and use as required. Break the carcass into small pieces and place in a large saucepan. Add the vegetables, bouquet garni and spices with 1.2 litres/2 pints of water and bring to the boil. Cover with a lid, reduce the heat and simmer for 2 hours. If the liquid is evaporating too quickly, reduce the heat under the pan. Cool, strain and allow to cool fully before storing covered in the refrigerator. Store for up to 3 days. Bring to the boil and simmer for 5 minutes before re-using. Freeze if desired in small, freezer-safe tubs.

## Beef Stock

**Makes 900 ml/1 ½ pints**

450 g/1 lb beef bones, chopped into small chunks

250 g/12 oz shin of beef, fat discarded and cut into small chunks

1 onion, peeled and cut into wedges

1 large carrot, peeled and cut into chunks

1 celery stick, trimmed and chopped

1 bouquet garni

12 black peppercorns

salt to taste

Place the bones and beef in a roasting tin and cook in an oven preheated to 200°C/400°F/Gas Mark 6 for 20 minutes or until sealed and browned. Remove and place in a large saucepan with the remaining ingredients and 1.2 litres/2 pints of water. Bring to the boil, cover with a lid, reduce the heat and simmer very gently for 4 hours. Strain and add salt to taste. Cool, then skim off any fat that rises to the surface. Store in the refrigerator for up to 3 days, boiling for 5 minutes before using. Alternatively, freeze in small, freezer-safe tubs, covered and labelled.

# Vegetable Stock

**Makes 900 ml/1 ½ pints**

1 tbsp sunflower oil

1 medium onion, peeled and cut into wedges

1 large carrot, peeled and chopped

2 celery sticks, trimmed and chopped

1 small turnip, peeled and chopped, optional

2 bay leaves

10 black peppercorns

3 whole cloves

salt to taste

Heat the oil in a large saucepan and sauté the vegetables for 8 minutes, stirring frequently. Add the bay leaves with the spices and 1.2 litres/2 pints of water and bring to the boil. Cover with a lid, reduce the heat and simmer for 40 minutes. Strain the stock and add salt to taste. Cool, cover and store in the refrigerator for up to 3 days. Alternatively, pour into small, freezer-safe tubs, cover, label and freeze for up to 1 month.

# Bouquet Garni

1 celery stick

2 bay leaves

2 sprigs of parsley

1 sprig of thyme

1 sprig of sage

Cut the celery stick in half and rinse the herbs. Place the herbs on top of one piece of celery and place the second piece of celery on top. Tie securely and use as required.

# Fish Stock

**Makes 600 ml/1 pint**

Fish bones or 1 cod's head

1 onion, peeled and cut into wedges

1 celery stick, trimmed and chopped

1 bouquet garni

salt and freshly ground black pepper

Thoroughly wash the fish bones or cod's head and place in a large saucepan with the vegetables and bouquet garni. Add 900 ml/1½ pints of water and bring to the boil. Cover with a lid, reduce the heat and simmer for 30 minutes. Strain and add seasoning to taste, then cool and store in the refrigerator. Use within 2 days, bringing to the boil and simmering steadily for 5 minutes before using. If desired, freeze in small, freezer-safe tubs, covered and labelled.

# Basic Recipes: Cooking Fish

## Poached Fish

Clean the fish, remove scales if necessary and rinse thoroughly. Place in a large frying pan with 1 small peeled and sliced onion and carrot, 1 bay leaf, 5 peppercorns and a few parsley stalks. Pour over sufficient cold water to barely cover, then bring to the boil over a medium heat. Reduce the heat to a simmer, cover and cook gently for 8–10 minutes for fillets and 10–15 minutes for whole fish.

This method is suitable for fillets and small whole fish. When the fish is cooked, the flesh should yield easily when pierced with a round bladed knife, and the fish should look opaque.

## Grilled Fish

Line a grill rack with tin foil and preheat the grill to medium high just before grilling. Lightly rinse the fish, pat it dry and place on the foil-lined grill rack. Season with salt and pepper and brush lightly with a little oil. Cook under the grill for 8–10 minutes or until cooked, turning the heat down if the fish is cooking too quickly. Sprinkle with herbs or pour over a little melted butter or herb-flavoured olive oil to serve.

This method is suitable for fresh fish fillets (not smoked), sardines and other small whole fish. Make 3 slashes across whole fish before grilling.

## Griddled Fish

Rinse the fish fillet, pat dry and, if desired, marinate in a marinade of your choice for 30 minutes. Heat a griddle pan until smoking and add the fish, skin side down. Cook for 5 minutes, pressing the fish down with a fish slice. Turn the fish over and continue to cook for a further 4–5 minutes or until cooked to personal preference.

# Basic Recipes: Grilling

## Grilled Chicken

Line a grill rack with tin foil and preheat the grill to medium high just before cooking. Lightly rinse the chicken piece and pat dry. If wanted, marinate for 30 minutes before cooking. Drain the chicken from the marinade, if using, and place on the foil-lined grill rack. Cook under the preheated grill for 4 minutes on each side. Reduce the heat to medium and continue to cook for a further 10–12 minutes or until thoroughly cooked and the juices run clear. Serve.

This method is suitable for boneless, skinless chicken breast portions, which may cook in a slightly shorter time, and also for chicken secured on skewers, thighs, drumsticks, wings and quarters. Small cuts of chicken and spatchcocked poussin will also work well with this method.

It is vital that all poultry is thoroughly cooked. All juices should run clear and the flesh should not show any pink. If in doubt, remove from the heat and cut through into the centre with a small sharp knife – if still slightly pink, return to the heat and cook a little longer.

## Grilled Sausages

Line a grill rack with tin foil and preheat the grill to high just before cooking. Prick the sausages all over with the tines of a fork and place on the foil-lined grill rack. Place under the preheated grill and cook for 12–18 minutes, turning frequently, until golden brown all over. Turn the heat down halfway through the cooking time.

Chipolata sausages will cook in about 12 minutes, whilst large sausages cook under the grill in about 18 minutes.

## Cheese on Toast

Preheat the grill to high. Spread freshly-made and buttered toast with a little pickle or ready-made mustard. Finely grate 25 g/1 oz of cheese and pile on top of the toast. Place under the grill and cook for 2–3 minutes or until golden and bubbling. Cut into fingers to serve

If liked, thinly sliced tomatoes or very thinly sliced onion could be placed under the cheese before grilling. Alternatively, mix the grated cheese with finely chopped spring onions.

## Welsh Rarebit

225 g/8 oz mature Cheddar cheese, grated
25 g/1 oz butter
1 tsp dry mustard powder
salt and freshly ground black pepper
few drops Worcestershire sauce
4 tbsp brown ale
freshly-made buttered toast to serve
parsley sprigs to garnish

Preheat the grill to high just before serving. Place all the ingredients in a heavy-based saucepan and heat gently, stirring occasionally until melted and creamy. Spoon the mixture onto toast and cook under the preheated grill for 3 minutes or until golden and bubbling. Garnish with parsley and serve immediately.

### Salsa (to accompany the Welsh Rarebit)

1 red chilli, deseeded and finely chopped
4 spring onions, trimmed and finely chopped
3 ripe tomatoes, peeled, seeded and finely chopped
1 small ripe avocado, pitted, peeled and finely chopped
1 tbsp finely grated lemon rind
salt and freshly ground black pepper
2 tsp clear honey, warmed
1 tbsp freshly chopped coriander

Mix all the ingredients together, cover and leave for the flavours to infuse for at least 30 minutes. Use as required. Other ingredients can be used to make salsas – try finely diced fruits such as mango, papaya and apple, chopped red onion, chopped skinned peppers, celery, crushed garlic or some chopped dried fruits, such as ready-to-eat apricots, dried cranberries or raisins.

# Basic Recipes: Baking

## Pouring Batter/ Yorkshire Puddings

100 g/4 oz plain white flour
pinch of salt
2 medium eggs
300 ml/½ pt whole milk and water mixed

Sift the flour and salt into a mixing bowl and make a well in the centre. Drop the eggs into the well with a little milk. Beat the eggs into the flour, gradually drawing the flour in from the sides of the bowl. Once half the milk has been added, beat well until smooth and free from lumps. Stir in the remaining milk and leave to stand for 30 minutes. Stir before using. Heat 1 tablespoon of oil in a roasting tin or individual Yorkshire Pudding tins in an oven preheated to 220°C/425°F/Gas Mark 7. When the oil is almost smoking, stir the batter then pour into the hot oil. Cook for 30–40 minutes for a large pudding and 18–20 minutes for individual puddings.

This batter can also be used for pancakes and, if liked, 25 g/1 oz caster sugar can be added.

## Coating Batter/Fritters

100 g/4 oz plain white flour
pinch of salt
1 tbsp sunflower oil
150 ml/¼ pint water
2 medium egg whites

Sift the flour and salt into a mixing bowl and make a well in the centre. Add the oil and half the water and beat until smooth and free from lumps. Gradually beat in the remaining water. Just before using, whisk the egg whites until stiff then stir into the batter and use immediately.

# Meringues

Meringue is made from egg whites and sugar, normally caster sugar. As a general rule, allow 1 medium egg white to 50 g/2 oz caster sugar. If liked, a pinch of salt can be added at the beginning of whisking.

Place the egg whites in a clean mixing bowl (any grease in the bowl will prevent the egg white from whisking). Use a balloon or wire whisk, if whisking by hand, or an electric mixer fitted with the balloon wire whisk if not. Whisk the egg whites until stiff. To test if they are stiff enough, turn the bowl upside down – if the egg white does not move, it is ready. Slowly add half the sugar, 1 teaspoon at a time and whisking well after each addition. Once half the sugar has been added, add the remaining sugar and gently stir it in with a metal spoon. Take care not to over-mix.

## Whipped Cream (to accompany the Meringues)

Whipping cream, double cream or a combination of single cream and double cream will all whip. If using single and double cream, use one-third single and two-thirds double cream.

Place the cream in a mixing bowl and use a balloon whisk, wire whisk or electric mixer fitter with the balloon whisk attachment. Place the bowl on a damp cloth if whipping by hand. Whip until thickened and soft peaks are formed – this is when the whisk is dragged gently through the cream and lifted out leaving soft peaks in the cream. Whipped cream is ideal for using in soufflés, mousses and other cream desserts. For piping and to use as a filling, whip for a little longer and until cream is slightly stiffer. Take care if using only double cream that you do not over-whip as it will curdle.

# Basic Recipes: Chocolate & Icing

## Chocolate

When cooking with chocolate, always use the best chocolate available. The higher the cocoa butter content, the better the flavour and the performance will be.

### Melting Chocolate over Water

Break the chocolate into small pieces and place in a small heat-proof bowl. Place over a pan of gently simmering water, taking care that the base of the bowl does not touch the simmering water. Heat gently, stirring occasionally until melted. Once melted, remove from the saucepan, stir until smooth, then cool and use as required.

Add any liquid to the chocolate when using this method before commencing to heat. If adding butter, however, add it after melting but before stirring.

### Melting Chocolate in a Microwave (650 or 750 watt)

Break the chocolate into small pieces and place in a microwaveable bowl. Heat on 50 per cent heat for 1 ½ minutes, remove and stir. Continue to heat for 30 seconds each time and stirring until thoroughly melted.

### Melting Chocolate in a Saucepan

Break the chocolate into small pieces and place in a heavy-based saucepan. Add either cream or milk with a little butter or liqueur (optional). Heat gently, stirring frequently until the chocolate has melted. Remove and stir until smooth.

If the chocolate becomes hard and grainy during any of these methods due to over-heating, add 1 teaspoon of vegetable fat for every 75 g/3 oz of chocolate and stir until the chocolate becomes soft and smooth. Do not use butter, margarine or oil. Take care that water does not touch the chocolate when melting either in a bowl over water or in the microwave.

## Making Caramel

Place 100 g/4 oz granulated sugar in a medium sized, heavy-based saucepan. Add 150 ml/¼ pint water and place over a gentle heat. Stir until the sugar has dissolved, then bring to the boil. Boil steadily without stirring for 6–8 minutes or until the sugar becomes golden in colour. Remove and use as required. Plunge the base of the saucepan into cold water to stop the sugar from caramelising further. Take care as the caramel is extremely hot and may spit slightly.

## Poaching Fruit

Place 75 g/3 oz sugar in a heavy-based saucepan with 150 ml/¼ pint water. Place over a gentle heat and stir occasionally until the sugar has dissolved. Bring to the boil and boil steadily for 5 minutes or until a syrup is formed. Pour into a frying pan, or if the pan is large enough, keep the

syrup in the pan. Prepare the fruit to be poached by rinsing and cutting in half and discarding the stones. Add to the syrup and poach gently for 8–10 minutes or until just cooked. Remove from the heat and gently transfer to a serving dish.

This method is suitable for plums, apricots, damsons, greengages, peaches, nectarines, cherries, raspberries, strawberries, blackberries and currants, cored and sliced cooking apples, peeled and cored pears and rhubarb

Alternatively the fruits can be gently poached without sugar. Simply prepare as required and rinse lightly. Half-fill a frying pan with water or a mixture of orange juice and water and bring to the boil. Reduce the heat to a simmer, then add the fruits and cook for 5–10 minutes or until just tender.

## Butter Cream Icing

100 g/4 oz softened, unsalted butter or margarine
1 tsp vanilla extract
225 g/8 oz icing sugar, sifted

Cream the butter or margarine with the vanilla extract until soft and creamy. Add the icing sugar, 1 tablespoon at a time, and beat well. Continue until all the icing sugar is incorporated. Beat in 1– 2 tablespoons of slightly cooled boiled water or fruit juice to give a smooth, spreadable consistency.

## Chocolate Butter Cream

Melt 50 g/2 oz plain dark chocolate and stir into the prepared butter cream, omitting the hot water. Or if preferred, replace 1 tablespoon of the icing sugar with 1 tablespoon of cocoa powder.

## Orange/Lemon Butter Cream

Beat 1 tablespoon of finely grated orange or lemon rind into the butter cream and replace the water with fruit juice.

## Coffee Butter Cream

Dissolve 1 tablespoon of coffee granules in a little very hot water. Omit the vanilla extract and stir in the dissolved coffee in place of the hot water.

## Mocha Butter Cream

Make the coffee butter cream as above and replace 1 tablespoon of the icing sugar with 1 tablespoon of cocoa powder or use melted chocolate.

## Glacé Icing

Sift 225 g/8 oz icing sugar into a mixing bowl, then slowly stir in 2–3 tablespoons of hot water and blend to form a spreadable consistency – the icing should coat the back of a wooden spoon.

Other flavours can be made by simply adding 1 tablespoon of cocoa powder to the icing sugar or 1 tablespoon of coffee granules, dissolved in hot water. Fruit-flavoured icing can be made by using orange or lemon juice. To make a coloured icing, simply add a few drops of food colouring.

# Guidelines for Different Age Groups

**Good food plays such an important role in everyone's life. From infancy through to adulthood, a healthy diet provides the body's foundation and building blocks and teaches children healthy eating habits. Studies have shown that these eating habits stay with us into later life helping us to maintain a healthier lifestyle as adults. This reduces the risk of illness, disease and certain medical problems.**

Striking a healthy balance is important and at certain stages in life, this balance may need to be adjusted to help our bodies cope. As babies and children, during pregnancy and in later life, our diet assists us in achieving optimal health. How do we go about achieving this?

We know that foods such as oily fish, for example, are advantageous to everyone, as they is rich in Omega-3 fatty acids which have been linked with more efficient brain functioning and better memory. They can also help lower the risk of cancer and heart disease. But are there any other steps we can take to maximise health benefits through our diet?

## Babies and Young Children

Babies should not be given solids until they are at least six months old, then new tastes and textures can be introduced to their diets. Probably the easiest and cheapest way is to adapt the food that the rest of the family eat. Babies under the age of one should be given breast milk or formula milk. From the age of one to two, whole milk should be given and from two to five semi-skimmed milk can be given. From then on, skimmed milk can be introduced if desired.

The first foods for babies under six months should be of a purée-like consistency, which is smooth and fairly liquid, therefore making it easy to swallow. This can be done using an electric blender, a hand blender or just by pushing foods through a sieve to remove any lumps. Remember, however, babies still need high levels of milk.

Babies over six months old should still be having puréed food, but the consistency of their diet can be made progressively lumpier. Around the 10-month mark, most babies are able to manage food cut up into small pieces.

So, what food groups do babies and small children need? Like adults, a high proportion of their diet should contain grains such as cereal, pasta, bread and rice. Be careful, however, as babies and small children cannot cope with too much high-fibre food in their diet.

Fresh fruits and vegetables should be introduced, as well as a balance of dairy and meat proteins and only a small proportion of fats and sweets. Research points out that delaying the introduction of foods which could cause allergies during the first year (such as cow's milk, wheat, eggs, cheese, yogurt and nuts) can significantly reduce the risk of certain food allergies later on in life. Peanuts should never be given to children under five years old.

Seek a doctor or health visitor's advice regarding babies and toddlers. Limit sugar in young children's diets, as sugar provides only empty calories. Use less processed sugars (muscovado is very sweet, so the amount used can be

reduced) or incorporate less-refined alternatives such as dried fruits, dates, rice syrup or honey, although honey should not be given to infants under one year of age.

As in a low-fat diet, it is best to eliminate fried foods and avoid adding salt – especially for under one-year-olds and young infants. Instead, introduce herbs and gentle spices to make food appetising. The more varied the tastes that children experience in their formative years, the wider the range of foods they will accept later in life.

## Pregnancy

During pregnancy, women are advised to take extra vitamin and mineral supplements. Pregnant women benefit from a healthy balanced diet, rich in fresh fruit and vegetables, and full of essential vitamins and minerals. Occasionally eating oily fish, such as salmon, not only gives the body essential fats but also provides high levels of bio-available calcium.

Certain food groups, however, hold risks during pregnancy. This section gives advice on everyday foods and those that should be avoided.

### Cheese

Pregnant women should avoid all soft, mould-ripened cheese such as Brie. Also if pregnant, do not eat cheese such as Parmesan or blue-veined cheese like Stilton as they carry the risk of listeria. It is fine for pregnant women to carry on eating hard cheese like Cheddar, as well as cottage cheese.

### Eggs

There is a slight chance that some eggs will carry salmonella. Cooking the eggs until both the yolk and white are firm will eliminate this risk. However, particular attention should be paid to dishes and products that incorporate lightly cooked or raw eggs – homemade mayonnaise or similar sauces, mousses, soufflés, meringues, ice cream and sorbets. Commercially produced products, such as mayonnaise, which are made with pasteurised eggs, may be eaten safely. If in doubt, play safe and avoid it.

### Ready-made Meals and Ready-to-eat Items

Previously cooked, then chilled meals are now widely available, but those from the chilled counter can contain bacteria. Avoid prepacked salads in dressings and other foods which are sold loose from chilled cabinets. Also do not eat raw or partly cooked meats, pâté, unpasteurised milk and soil-dirty fruits and vegetables as they can cause toxoplasmosis.

### Meat and Fish

Certain meats and poultry carry the potential risk of salmonella and should be cooked thoroughly until the juices run clear and there is no pinkness left.

Pay particular attention when buying and cooking fish (especially shellfish). Buy only the freshest fish which should smell salty but not strong or fishy.

Look for bright eyes and reject any with sunken eyes. The bodies should look fresh, plump and shiny. Avoid any fish with dry, shrivelled or damp bodies.

It is also best to avoid any shellfish while pregnant unless it is definitely fresh and thoroughly cooked. Shellfish also contains harmful bacteria and viruses.

## Later Life

So what about later on in life? As the body gets older, we can help stave off infection and illness through our diet. There is evidence to show that the immune system becomes weaker as we get older, which can increase the risk of suffering from cancer and other illnesses. Maintaining a diet rich in antioxidants, fresh fruits and vegetables, plant oils and oily fish is especially beneficial in order to either prevent these illnesses or minimise their effects. As with all age groups, the body benefits from the five-a-day eating plan – to eat five portions of fruit or vegetables each day. Leafy green vegetables, in particular, are rich in antioxidants. Cabbage, broccoli, Brussels sprouts, cauliflower and kale contain particularly high levels of antioxidants, which lower the risk of cancer.

Foods which are green in colour tend to provide nutrients essential for healthy nerves, muscles and hormones, while foods red in colour protect against cardiovascular disease. Other foods which can also assist in preventing cardiovascular disease and ensuring a healthy heart include vitamins E and C, oily fish and essential fats (such as extra virgin olive oil and garlic). They help lower blood cholesterol levels and clear arteries. A diet high in fresh fruits and vegetables and low in salt and saturated fats can considerably reduce heart disease.

Other foods have recognised properties. Certain types of mushrooms are known to boost the immune system, while garlic not only boosts the immune system but also protects the body against cancer. Live yogurt, too, has healthy properties as it contains gut-friendly bacteria which help digestion.

Some foods can help to balance the body's hormone levels during the menopause. For example, soya regulates hormone levels. Studies have shown that a regular intake of soya can help to protect the body against breast and prostate cancer.

A balanced, healthy diet, rich in fresh fruits and vegetables, carbohydrates, proteins and essential fats and low in saturates, can help the body protect itself throughout your life. It really is worth spending a little extra time and effort when shopping or even just thinking about what to cook.

# Store Cupboard Essentials

## Ingredients for a Healthy Lifestyle

**With the increasing emphasis on the importance of cooking healthy meals for your family, modern lifestyles are naturally shifting towards lower-fat and cholesterol diets. Low-fat cooking has often been associated with the idea that reducing fat reduces flavour, but this simply is not the case, which is great news for those trying to eat healthily. Thanks to the increasing number of lower-fat ingredients now available in shops, there is no need to compromise on the choice of foods we eat.**

The store cupboard is a good place to start when cooking healthy meals. Most of us have fairly limited cooking and preparation time available during the week, and so choose to experiment during weekends. When time is of the essence, or friends arrive unannounced, it is a good idea to have some well thought-out basics in the cupboard, namely foods that are high on flavour whilst still being healthy.

As store cupboard ingredients keep reasonably well, it is worth making a trip to a good speciality grocery shop. Our society's growing interest in recent years with travel and food from around the world has led us to seek out alternative ingredients with which to experiment and incorporate into our cooking. Consequently, supermarket chains have had to broaden their product range and often have a specialist range of imported ingredients from around the world.

If the local grocers or supermarket only carries a limited choice of products, do not despair. The Internet now offers freedom to food lovers. There are some fantastic food sites (both local and international) where food can be purchased and delivery arranged online.

When thinking about essentials, think of flavour, something that is going to add to a dish without increasing its fat content. It is worth spending a little bit more money on these products to make flavoursome dishes that will help stop the urge to snack on fatty foods.

### Store Cupboard Hints

There are many different types of store cupboard ingredients readily available – including myriad varieties of rice and pasta – which can provide much of the carbohydrate required in our daily diets. Store the ingredients in a cool, dark place and remember to rotate them. The ingredients will be safe to use for six months.

**Bulghur wheat** A cracked wheat which is often used in tabbouleh. Bulghur wheat is a good source of complex carbohydrate.

**Couscous** Now available in instant form, couscous just needs to be covered with boiling water then forked. Couscous is a precooked wheat semolina. Traditional couscous needs to be steamed and is available from health food stores. This type of couscous contains more nutrients than the instant variety.

**Dried fruit** The ready-to-eat variety are particularly good as they are plump, juicy and do not need to be soaked. They are fantastic when puréed into a compote, added to water and heated to make a pie filling and when added to stuffing mixtures. They are also good cooked with meats, rice or couscous.

**Flours** A useful addition (particularly cornflour) which can be used to thicken sauces. It is worth mentioning that whole-grain flour should not be stored for too long at room temperature as the fats may turn rancid. While not strictly a flour, cornmeal is a very versatile low-fat ingredient which can be used when making dumplings and gnocchi.

**Noodles** Also very useful and can accompany any Far Eastern dish. They are low-fat and also available in the wholewheat variety. Rice noodles are available for those who have gluten-free diets and, like pasta noodles, provide slow-release energy to the body.

**Pasta** It is good to have a mixture of wholewheat and plain pasta as well as a wide variety of flavoured pastas. Whether fresh (it can also be frozen) or dried, pasta is a versatile ingredient with which to provide the body with slow-release energy. It comes in many different sizes and shapes; from the tiny tubettini (which can be added to soups to create a more substantial dish), to penne, fusilli, rigatoni and conchiglie, up to the larger cannelloni and lasagne sheets.

**Pot and pearl barley** Pot barley is the complete barley grain whereas pearl barley has the outer husk removed. A high cereal diet can help to prevent bowel disorders and diseases.

**Pulses** A vital ingredient for the store cupboard, they are easy to store, have a very high nutritional value and are great when added to soups, casseroles, curries and hot pots. Pulses also act as a thickener, whether flavoured or on their own. They come in two forms; either dried (in which case they generally need to be soaked overnight and then cooked before use – it is important to follow the instructions on the back of the packet), or canned, which is a convenient timesaver because the preparation of dried pulses can take a while. If buying canned pulses, try to buy the variety in water with no added salt or sugar. These simply need to be drained and rinsed before being added to a dish.

Kidney beans, borlotti, cannellini, butter, flageolet beans, split peas and lentils all make tasty additions to any dish. Baked beans are a favourite with everyone and many shops now stock the organic variety, which have no added salt or sugar but are sweetened with fruit juice instead.

When boiling previously dried pulses, remember that salt should not be added as this will make the skins tough and inedible. Puy lentils are a smaller variety. They often have mottled skins and are particularly good for cooking in slow dishes as they hold their shape and firm texture particularly well.

**Rice** Basmati and Thai fragrant rice are well suited to Thai and Indian curries, as the fine grains absorb the sauce and their delicate creaminess balances the pungency of the spices. Arborio is only one type of risotto rice – many are available depending on whether the risotto is meant to accompany meat, fish or vegetable dishes. When cooked, rice swells to create a substantial low-fat dish. Easy-cook American rice, both plain and whole-grain, is great for casseroles and for stuffing meat, fish and vegetables, as it holds its shape and firmness. Pudding rice can be used in a variety of ways to create an irresistible dessert.

**Stock** Good-quality stock is a must in low-fat cooking as it provides a good flavour base for many dishes. Many supermarkets now carry a variety of fresh and organic stocks which although need refrigeration, are probably one of the most time- and effort-saving ingredients available. There is also a fairly large range of dried stock, perhaps the best being bouillon, a high-quality form of stock (available in powder or liquid form) which can be added to any dish whether it be a sauce, casserole, pie or soup.

Many people favour meals which can be prepared and cooked in 30–45 minutes, so helpful ingredients which kick-start a sauce are great. A good-quality **passata sauce** or **canned plum tomatoes** can act as the foundation for any sauce, as can a good-quality **green** or **red pesto**. Other handy store cupboard additions include **tapenade, mustard** and **anchovies**. These ingredients have very distinctive tastes and are particularly flavoursome. **Roasted red pepper sauce** and **sundried tomato purée**, which tends to be sweeter and more intensely flavoured than regular tomato purée, are also very useful.

**Vinegar** is another worthwhile store cupboard essential and with so many uses it is worth splashing out on really good quality balsamic and wine vinegars. **Herbs and spices** are a must, so it is worth taking a look at the section on pages 48–49. Using herbs when cooking at home should reduce the temptation to buy ready-made sauces. Often these types of sauces contain large amounts of sugar and additives.

**Yeast extract** is also a good store cupboard ingredient, which can pep up sauces, soups and casseroles and adds a little substance, particularly to vegetarian dishes.

Eastern flavours offer a lot of scope where low-fat cooking is concerned. Flavourings such as **fish sauce, soy sauce, red** and **green curry paste** and **Chinese rice wine** all offer mouthwatering low-fat flavours to any dish.

For those who are incredibly short on time, or who rarely shop, it is now possible to purchase a selection of readily prepared freshly minced **garlic, ginger** and **chilli** (available in jars which can be kept in the refrigerator).

As well as these store cupboard additions, many shops and especially supermarkets provide a wide choice of foods. Where possible, invest in the leanest cut of meat and substitute saturated fats such as cream, butter and cheese with low-fat or half-fat alternatives.

# Meat

**Both home-grown and imported meat is readily available from supermarkets, butchers, farm shops and markets. Home-grown meat is normally more expensive than imported meat, often brought into the country frozen. Meat also varies in price depending on the cut. The more expensive and tender meats are usually those cuts that exercised less. They need a minimal amount of cooking and are suitable for roasting, grilling, griddling, frying and stir-frying. The cheaper cuts normally need longer, slower cooking and are used in casseroles and for stewing. Meat plays an important part in most people's diet, offering an excellent source of protein, B vitamins and iron.**

When choosing meat, it is important to buy from a reputable source and to choose the correct cut for the cooking method. Look for meat that is lean without an excess of fat, is a good colour and has no unpleasant odour. If in doubt about the suitability of a cut, ask the butcher who should be happy to advise.

If buying frozen meat, allow to thaw before using. This is especially important for both pork and poultry. It is better to thaw meat slowly, lightly covered on the bottom shelf of the refrigerator. Use within 2–3 days of thawing, providing it has been kept in the refrigerator. If buying meat to freeze, do not freeze large joints in a home freezer as it will not be frozen quickly enough.

Store thawed or fresh meat out of the supermarket wrappings, on a plate, lightly covered with greaseproof or baking paper and then wrap with cling film if liked. Do not secure the paper tightly round the meat as it needs to breathe. Ensure that the raw meat juices do not drip on to cooked foods. The refrigerator needs to be at a temperature of 5°C. Fresh meat such as joints, chops and steaks can be stored for up to three days. Mince, sausages and offal should be stored for only one day.

Different cultures and religion affect the way the meat has been killed and the carcass cut. The following is a description of different cuts of meat. They may be called by different names in different parts of the country.

## Beef

When choosing beef, look for meat that is a good colour, with creamy yellow fat. There should be small flecks of fat (marbling) throughout, as this helps the meat to be tender. Avoid meat with excess gristle. Bright red beef means that the animal has been butchered recently, whereas meat that has a dark, almost purple, tinge is from meat that has been hung in a traditional manner. The darker the colour, especially with roasting joints, the more tender and succulent the beef will be.

**Rib or fore rib (1)** – suitable for roasting. Sold either on or off the bone. Look for meat that is marbled for tenderness and succulence.

**Topside (2)** – suitable for pot roasting, roasting or braising. A lean, tender cut from the hindquarter.

**Sirloin** – suitable for roasting, grilling, frying, barbecuing or griddling. Sold boned or off the bone. A lean and tender cut from the back.

**T-bone steak** – suitable for grilling, griddling, barbecuing or roasting. A tender, succulent cut taken from the fillet end of the sirloin.

**Top rib** – suitable for pot roasting or braising. Sold on or off the bone.

**Fillet steak** – suitable for grilling, frying, barbecuing or griddling. A whole fillet is used to make Châteaubriand, some say the best of all cuts. The most tender and succulent cut with virtually no fat. Comes from the centre of the sirloin.

**Rump (3)** – suitable for grilling, frying, griddling or barbecuing. Not as tender as fillet of sirloin, but reputed to have more flavour.

**Silverside (4)** – suitable for boiling and pot roasts. Used to be sold ready-salted but is now normally sold unsalted.

**Flash-fry steaks (5)** – suitable for grilling, griddling or frying. Cut from the silverside, thick flank or topside.

**Braising steak (6)** – chuck, blade or thick rib, ideal for all braising or stews. Sold either in pieces or ready diced.

**Flank (7)** – suitable for braising or stewing. A boneless cut from the mid- to hindquarter

**Minute steaks** – suitable for grilling or griddling. Cut from the flank, a thin steak and beaten to flatten.

**Skirt** – suitable for stewing or making into mince. A boneless, rather gristly cut.

**Brisket** – suitable for slow roasting or pot roasting. Sold boned and rolled and can be found salted.

**Mince** – suitable for meat sauces such as bolognese, also burgers, shepherd's pie and moussaka. Normally cut from clod, skirt, neck, thin rib or flank. Can be quite fatty. Steaks can also be minced if preferred to give a leaner mince. Sometimes referred to as ground beef.

**Ox kidney** – suitable for casseroles and stews. Strong flavour with hard central core that is discarded.

**Oxtail** – suitable for casseroles or braising. Normally sold cut into small pieces.

## Lamb

Lamb is probably at its best in the Spring, when the youngest lamb is available. It is tender to eat with a delicate flavour, and its flesh is a paler pink than the older lamb where the flesh is more red. The colour of the fat is also a good indication of age: young lamb fat is a very light, creamy colour. As the lamb matures, the fat becomes whiter and firmer. Imported lamb also has firmer, whiter fat. Lamb can be fatty so take care when choosing.

It used to be possible to buy mutton (lamb that is at least one year old), but this now tends to be available only in specialist outlets. It has a far stronger, almost gamey flavour and the joints tend to be larger.

**Leg (1)** – suitable for roasting. Often sold as half legs and steaks cut from the fillet end. These can be grilled, griddled or barbecued. Steaks are very lean and need a little additional oil to prevent the meat from drying out.

**Shank** – suitable for braising. A cut off the leg.

**Shoulder (2)** – suitable for roasting. Can be sold boned, stuffed and rolled. Is fattier than the leg and has more flavour.

**Loin (3)** – suitable for roasting. Sold on or off the bone, and can be stuffed and rolled. Can also be cut into chops, often as double loin chops which are suitable for grilling, griddling and barbecuing.

**Noisette** – suitable for grilling, griddling or barbecuing. A small boneless chop cut from the loin.

**Valentine steak** – suitable for grilling, griddling or barbecuing. Cut from a loin chop.

**Chump chop (4)** – suitable for grilling, griddling or barbecuing. Larger than loin chops and can be sold boneless.

**Best end of neck (5)** – suitable for roasting, grilling or griddling. Sold as a joint or cutlets.

**Neck fillet** – suitable for grilling or griddling. Sold whole or diced.

**Middle and scrag end (6)** – suitable for pot roasting, braising or stewing. A cheaper cut with a high ratio of fat and bone.

**Breast (7)** – suitable for pot roast if boned, stuffed and rolled. Can be marinated and grilled or barbecued.

**Mince** – suitable for burgers, pies, meat balls and for stuffing vegetables such as peppers. From various cuts and is often fatty.

**Liver** – suitable for pan frying or grilling. Milder than ox or pig liver and cheaper than calves' liver.

**Kidney** – suitable for grilling, pan frying or casserole. Milder than ox or pig liver and normally sold encased in suet that is discarded.

## Pork

Pork should be pale pink in colour and slightly marbled with small flecks of fat. There should be a good layer of firm white fat with a thin elastic skin (rind) which can be scored before roasting to provide crackling. All cuts of pork are normally tender, as the pigs are slaughtered at an early age and nowadays are reared to be lean rather than fatty.

Pork used to be well-cooked, if not over-cooked, due to the danger of the parasite trichina. This no longer applies, however, and it is now recommended that the meat is cooked less to keep it moist and tender.

**Leg (1)** – suitable for roasting. Sold either on the bone or boned. Can be cut into chunks and braised or casseroled.

**Steaks (2)** – suitable for grilling, frying, griddling or barbecue. A lean cut from the leg or the shoulder. Very tender but can be dry.

**Fillet** – sometimes called tenderloin and suitable for roasting, pan frying, griddling or barbecuing. A tender cut, often sold already marinated

**Loin (3)** – suitable for roasting as a joint or cut into chops. Often sold with the kidney intact.

**Shoulder (4)** – suitable for roasting. Often referred to as hand and spring, and sold cubed for casseroles and stews. A fatty cut.

**Spare ribs** – suitable for barbecuing, casseroles and roasting. Sold either as 'Chinese' where thin ribs are marinated then cooked, or 'American Style' ribs which are larger.

**Escalope** – suitable for grilling, frying, griddling or barbecuing. Very lean and tender and requires very little cooking.

**Mince** – suitable for burgers, meat balls or similar recipes. Can be from several different cuts, but is often from the cheaper cuts and can be fatty.

**Belly (5)** – suitable for grilling or roasting. Can be salted before cooking. Is generally used to provide streaky bacon and is perhaps the fattiest cut of all.

**Liver** – suitable for casseroles or frying. Stronger than lamb or calves' liver.

**Kidney** – suitable for casseroles or frying. Often sold as part of a loin chop. Stronger than lambs' kidneys.

# Useful Conversions

## Liquid Measures

Metric/Imperial

|  |  |
|---|---|
| 2.5 ml | ½ teaspoon |
| 5 ml | 1 teaspoon |
| 15 ml | 1 tablespoon |
| 25 ml | 1 fl oz |
| 50 ml | 2 fl oz |
| 65 ml | 2½ fl oz |
| 85 ml | 3 fl oz |
| 100 ml | 3½ fl oz |
| 120 ml | 4 fl oz |
| 135 ml | 4½ fl oz |
| 150 ml | ¼ pint (5 fl oz) |
| | 8 tablespoons |
| 175 ml | 6 fl oz |
| 200 ml | 7 fl oz (1/3 pint) |
| 250 ml | 8 fl oz |
| 275 ml | 9 fl oz |
| 300 ml | ½ pint (10 fl oz) |
| 350 ml | 12 fl oz |
| 400 ml | 14 fl oz |
| 450 ml | ¾ pint (15 fl oz) |
| 475 ml | 16 fl oz |
| 500 ml | 18 fl oz |
| 600 ml | 1 pint (20 fl oz) |
| 750 ml | 1¼ pints |
| 900 ml | 1½ pints |
| 1 litre | 1¾ pints |
| 1.2 litres | 2 pints |
| 1.25 litres | 2¼ pints |
| 1.5 litres | 2½ pints |
| 1.6 litres | 2¾ pints |
| 1.7 litres | 3 pints |
| 2 litres | 3½ pints |
| 2.25 litres | 4 pints |
| 2.5 litres | 4½ pints |
| 2.75 litres | 5 pints |

## Temperature Conversion

|  |  |
|---|---|
| –4°F | –20°C |
| 5°F | –15°C |
| 14°F | –10°C |
| 23°F | –5°C |
| 32°F | 0°C |
| 41°F | 5°C |
| 50°F | 10°C |
| 59°F | 15°C |
| 68°F | 20°C |
| 77°F | 25°C |
| 86°F | 30°C |
| 95°F | 35°C |
| 104°F | 40°C |
| 113°F | 45°C |
| 122°F | 50°C |
| 212°F | 100°C |

## Dry Weights

Metric/Imperial

|  |  |
|---|---|
| 10 g | ¼ oz |
| 15 g | ½ oz |
| 20 g | ¾ oz |
| 25 g | 1 oz |
| 40 g | 1½ oz |
| 50 g | 2 oz |
| 65 g | 2½ oz |
| 75 g | 3 oz |
| 90 g | 3½ oz |
| 100 g | 4 oz |
| 120 g | 4½ oz |
| 150 g | 5 oz |
| 165 g | 5½ oz |
| 175 g | 6 oz |
| 185 g | 6½ oz |
| 200 g | 7 oz |
| 225 g | 8 oz |
| 250 g | 9 oz |
| 300 g | 10 oz |
| 325 g | 11 oz |
| 350 g | 12 oz |
| 375 g | 13 oz |
| 400 g | 14 oz |
| 425 g | 15 oz |
| 450 g | 1 lb (16 oz) |

## Oven Temperatures

|  |  |  | |
|---|---|---|---|
| 110°C | 225°F | Gas Mark ¼ | Very slow oven |
| 120/130°C | 250°F | Gas Mark ½ | Very slow oven |
| 140°C | 275°F | Gas Mark 1 | Slow oven |
| 150°C | 300°F | Gas Mark 2 | Slow oven |
| 160/170°C | 325°F | Gas Mark 3 | Moderate oven |
| 180°C | 350°F | Gas Mark 4 | Moderate oven |
| 190°C | 375°F | Gas Mark 5 | Moderately hot oven |
| 200°C | 400°F | Gas Mark 6 | Moderately hot oven |
| 220°C | 425°F | Gas Mark 7 | Hot oven |
| 230°C | 450°F | Gas Mark 8 | Hot oven |
| 240°C | 475°F | Gas Mark 9 | Very hot oven |

# Poultry & Game

Poultry relates to turkey, chicken, poussin, duck and geese. Most poultry is sold plucked, drawn and trussed. Due to extensive farming since the war, chicken in particular offers a good source of cheap meat. However, there is a growing movement to return to the more traditional methods of farming. Organically-grown chickens offer a far more succulent bird with excellent flavour, although they tend to be a little more expensive. Both home-grown and imported poultry, fresh and frozen are available. When buying fresh poultry, look for plump birds with a flexible breast bone, and no unpleasant odour or green tinge.

Frozen poultry should be rock hard with no ice crystals, as this could mean that the bird has thawed and been re-frozen. Avoid any produce where the packaging is damaged. When thawing, place in the refrigerator on a large plate and ensure that none of the juices drip on to other foods. Once thawed, remove all packaging, remove the giblets, if any, and reserve separately. Place on a plate and cover. Use within two days and ensure that the meat is thoroughly cooked and the juices run clear. Rest for 10 minutes before carving.

When storing fresh poultry, place on a plate and cover lightly, allowing air to circulate. Treat as thawed poultry: store for no longer than two days in the refrigerator, storing the giblets separately, and ensure that it is thoroughly cooked. Use within two days of cooking.

Poultry and game are low in saturated fat and provide a good source of protein as well as selenium, an antioxodant mineral. Remove the skin from poultry before eating if following a low-fat diet.

## Poultry

**Turkey** – whole birds are suitable for roasting. Traditionally served at Christmas, although with all the different cuts now available, turkey is eaten throughout the year.

**Crown** – the whole bird with the legs removed.

**Saddle** – two turkey breast fillets, boned with the wings inserted.

**Butterfly** – the two breast fillets.

**Breast roll** – boned breast meat, rolled and tied or contained in a net.

**Turkey portions** are also available, ranging from breast steaks, diced thigh, escalopes, small whole breast fillets, drumsticks, wings and mince.

**Chicken** – suitable for all types of cooking: roasting, grilling, griddling, stewing, braising, frying and barbecuing. Also available in many different breeds and varieties, offering a good choice to the consumer. There are many cuts of chicken readily available: breast, wing and leg quarters which are still on the bone, drumsticks, thighs, breast fillets, escalopes (boneless, skinless portions), diced and stir-fry strips as well as mince.

**Capon** – suitable for roasting. These are young castrated cockerels and are normally bred for their excellent flavour.

**Broilers** – these are older chickens which would be too tough to roast. Normally quite small birds about 1.6 kg/3 ½ lbs.

**Poussin** – suitable for roasting, grilling or casseroles. These are spring chickens and are 4–6 weeks old. They can be bought whole or spatchcocked – this is where the bird is split through the breast, opened up and secured on skewers. Normally serve two per person if small (450 g/1 lb) or one if larger (900 g/2 lb).

**Guinea fowl** – suitable for roasting or casseroles. Available all year round and about the same size as a pheasant, with a slightly gamey flavour. Most guinea fowl have already been hung and are sold ready for the table. When roasting, use plenty of fat or bacon as they can be dry.

**Goose** – suitable for roasting and often served as an alternative to turkey. Once dressed for the table, a goose will weigh around 4.5 kg/10 lb, but there is not much meat and this will serve around 6–8 people. It is very fatty, so pierce the skin well and roast on a trivet so the fat can be discarded or used for other cooking. Has a rich flavour, slightly gamey and a little like duck. Goose liver is highly prized and is used for foie gras.

**Duck** – suitable for roasting, grilling, griddling and casseroles. Ducklings are normally used for the table and are between six weeks to three months old; ducks are not normally eaten. Duck has an excellent flavour but it is a fatty bird, so cook on a trivet as for goose. Available fresh or frozen and on average weighs 1.75–2.75 kg/ 4–6 lb. Also available in cuts, as boneless breast fillets, ideal for grilling or griddling, and leg portions, suitable for casseroles. The meat is also used to make pâté. There are quite a few varieties available, with perhaps the best well-known being the Aylesbury. Long Island, Peking and Barbary are also popular varieties.

## Game

Game describes birds or animals which are hunted, not farmed, although some, such as pheasant, quails and rabbits, are now being reared domestically. Most game has a stronger flavour than poultry and some is at it's best when 'high' and smelling quite strong. Game is not as popular as most meat or poultry and is an acquired taste. When buying game, it is important to know its age, as this dictates the method of cooking. Normally sold oven-ready, it is advisable to buy from a reputable source who can guarantee the quality.

**Pigeon** – suitable for casseroles or stews, although the breast from young pigeons can be fried or grilled. Sometimes classified as poultry. Not widely available, mainly from licensed game sources.

**Pheasant** – suitable for roasting or casseroles. Breast, which can be grilled, is also available. Pheasant needs to be well hung to give the best flavour.

**Rabbit** – suitable for casseroles, stews and can be roasted, or if young, fried. Also makes excellent pies and fricassée. Sold whole or in portions, both with and without the bone, and available both fresh and frozen. Frozen rabbit often comes from China. If a milder flavour is preferred, soak in cold salted water for two hours before using. Generally regarded as country food and not served as haute cuisine.

**Hare** – suitable for casseroles. The most well-known recipe is Jugged Hare, where the blood is used to thicken the dish. Has a strong, gamey flavour. If a milder flavour is preferred, soak in cold water for up to 24 hours. Available from reputable game dealers.

**Venison** – suitable for roasting, grilling, casseroles or making into sausages. The best joints for roasting are the saddle, haunch and shoulder, although the loin and fillet can also be used. All cuts benefit from marinating to help tenderise.

Other game which is less widely available includes partridge, grouse, quail, snipe and boar.

# Fish

Requiring only minimal cooking, all fish is an excellent choice for speedy and nutritious meals. There are two categories of fish: white and oily. White fish such as cod, haddock, plaice or coley are an excellent source of protein and have a low fat content. They also contain vitamin B12 and niacin, plus important minerals such as phosphorous, iodine, selenium and potassium. Oily fish such as sardines, mackerel, salmon and herring have a higher fat content but are an excellent source of Omega 3 polyunsaturated fatty acids, important in fighting heart disease, cancers and arthritis. Oily fish also contain niacin, B6, B12 and D vitamins and selenium, iodine, potassium and phosphorous minerals. It is recommended that at least one portion of oily fish should be eaten each week.

## Cleaning Fish

When cleaning whole fish, first remove the scales. Using a round bladed knife, gently scrape the knife along the fish starting from the tail towards the head. Rinse frequently.

To clean round fish, make a slit along the abdomen from the gills to the tail using a small, sharp knife and scrape out the innards. Rinse thoroughly.

For flat fish, open the cavity under the gills and remove the innards. Rinse. Remove the gills and fins and, if preferred, the tail and head. Rinse thoroughly in cold water and pat dry.

Cutlet and fillets simply need lightly rinsing in cold water and patting dry.

## Skinning Fish

For whole flat fish, clean and remove the fins as before. Make a small cut on the dark side of the fish across the tail and slip your thumb between the skin and flesh. Loosen the skin along the side. Holding the fish firmly with one hand, rip the skin off with the other. The white skin can be removed in the same way.

Round fish are normally cooked with the skin on, but if you do wish to skin them, start from the head and cut a narrow strip of skin along the backbone. Cut below the head and loosen the skin with the point of the knife. Dip your fingers in salt for a better grip and gently pull the skin down towards the tail. Take care not to break the flesh.

## Filleting Fish

To fillet flat fish, use a sharp knife and make a cut along the line of bones. Insert the knife under the flesh and carefully cut it with long sweeping strokes. Cut the first fillet from the left-hand side, working from head to tail. Turn the fish round and repeat, this time cutting from tail to head. Turn the fish over and repeat on this side.

For round fish, cut along the centre of the back to the bone and then cut along the abdomen. Cleanly remove the flesh with short, sharp strokes from the head downwards pressing the knife against the bones. Turn the fish over and repeat. This is suitable for larger fish such as salmon.

To fillet herring and mackerel, discard the head, tail and fins and clean, reserving any roe if

applicable. Place on a chopping board and gently press along the backbone to open fully and loosen the bone. Turn the fish over, ease the backbone up and remove, taking as many of the small bones as possible at the same time.

## White Fish

Sold fresh or frozen as small whole fish, fillets or cutlets. Store as soon as possible in the refrigerator. Remove from the wrappings, place on a plate, cover lightly and store towards the top. Use within one day of purchase. If using frozen, thaw slowly in the refrigerator and use within one day of thawing. Requires minimal amount of cooking for best results.

**Bass** Sea fish, suitable for grilling or frying. Large bass can be poached whole. Has very white flesh. At its best from May to August.

**Sea bream** Sea fish, suitable for grilling, poaching and frying, can also be stuffed and baked or poached. Has white firm flesh with a delicate flavour. At its best from June to December.

**Brill** Sea fish, suitable for grilling, baking or

poaching and serving cold. Has firm flesh with a slight yellow tinge. At its best from April to August, but available all year.

**Cod** Sea fish, also available smoked. Suitable for all types of cooking. Perhaps the most popular and versatile of all fish, with white flesh and a very delicate flavour. At its best from October to May but available all year round.

**Coley** Sea fish, suitable for all types of cooking. One of the cheaper varieties of fish. Has a greyish-coloured flesh which turns slightly white on cooking. Available all year round.

**Haddock** Sea fish, also available smoked. Suitable for all types of cooking. Has a firm, white flesh with a slightly stronger flavour than cod. At its best from September to February, but available all year round.

**Hake** Sea fish, suitable for all methods of cooking. Has a firm, close-textured white flesh and is considered to have a better flavour than cod. At its best from June to January, but available all year round.

**Halibut** Sea fish, suitable for all methods of cooking except deep frying. A large flat fish with excellent flavour. At its best from August to April but available all year round.

**John Dory** Sea fish, suitable for poaching or baking whole, or fillets can be cooked as for sole. Has a firm, white flesh with good flavour. Can be difficult to find. At its best from October to December.

**Monkfish** Sea fish, suitable for all methods of cooking including roasting. A firm, white fish with 'meaty' texture. A good substitute for lobster. Only the tail is eaten – the central bone is normally discarded and the two fillets are used. Available all year round.

**Plaice** Sea fish. The whole fish is suitable for grilling and pan frying, whilst fillets can be steamed, stuffed and rolled or used as goujons. A flat fish with distinctive dark grey/black skin with red spots. Has soft, white flesh with a very delicate flavour. Available all year round.

**Skate** Sea fish, suitable for grilling, frying or poaching. Only the wings are eaten and the bones are soft and gelatinous. A white fish with a delicate flavour. At its best from September to April.

**Sole** Sea fish, suitable for frying or grilling. Has a firm, yet delicate white skin with a delicious flavour. Available all year round. Dover sole is recognised by its dark grey/black skin and is considered by many to be the finest of the sole varieties. Lemon sole, which is more pointed, witch and Torbay soles have the same qualities but the flavour is not as good.

**Turbot** Sea fish, suitable for grilling or baking. Normally sold in cutlets, it has a creamy, white flesh with a delicious flavour which is reputed to be the best of all flat fish. At its best from March to August.

**Whiting** Sea fish, suitable for all methods of cooking. Cooked whole or in fillets, it has a white, delicately-flavoured flesh. Available all year round.

## Oily Fish

Oily fish have a higher fat content and a darker flesh than white fish. The flavour is stronger and more robust, enabling stronger flavours such as chilli and garlic to be used. They provide an excellent source of protein as well as vitamins, minerals and Omega 3 fatty acids. Buy and store as for white fish.

**Herring** Sea fish, suitable for frying, grilling or preserving in vinegar to make rollmops. A small fish with creamy-coloured flesh and fairly strong flavour, herring contain many bones. At its best from June to December

**Mackerel** Sea fish, suitable for grilling and frying, whilst whole fish can be stuffed or baked. Have a distinctive bluish-coloured skin with blue/black lines and a creamy underside. At its best from April to June.

**Pilchard** Sea fish, normally sold canned but fresh pilchards are sometimes available. Similar to herring but smaller. Caught off the Cornish coast all year round.

**Red mullet** Sea fish, suitable for grilling, frying or baking. Has a firm, white flesh and red skin. At its best from May to September.

**Salmon** Freshwater fish. The whole fish is suitable for poaching or baking to serve hot or cold. Fillets or cutlets can be fried, grilled, baked, steamed or barbecued. Farmed salmon has a milder flavour than wild, and the deep pink flesh is not as firm as that of wild salmon. The smaller wild salmon is much paler in colour, with a far-superior flavour and texture. Nowadays farmed salmon is available all year round – wild salmon is at its best from February to August.

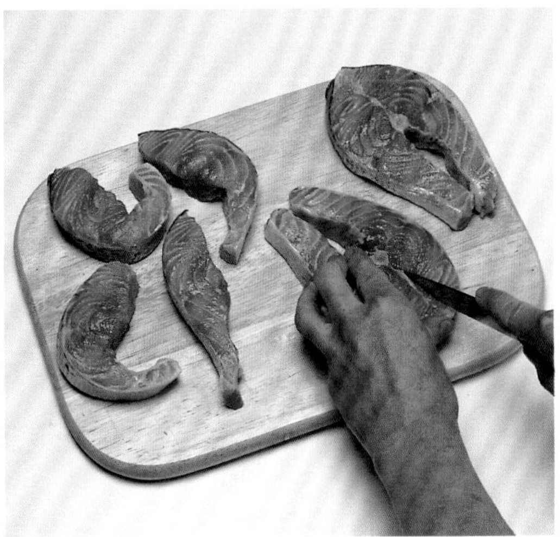

**Sardine** Sea fish, suitable for grilling or frying. Sardines are young pilchards, sprats or herrings. Available all year round.

**Sprat** Sea fish, suitable for frying or grilling. A small fish similar to herring and at its best from November to March.

**Brown trout** Freshwater fish, suitable for grilling or frying. The darker pink/red flesh is considered to be better than that of rainbow trout. At its best from March to September.

**Rainbow trout** Freshwater fish, suitable for grilling, frying, poaching and baking. Can be cooked whole or in fillets. Has a delicate pale pink flesh. Available all year round.

**Salmon trout** Freshwater fish, suitable for poaching or baking whole. Cutlets or fillets can be fried, grilled or griddled. At its best from March to August. Treat as for salmon. Has a pinker flesh than salmon and the flavour is not as good.

## Seafood

Seafood can be divided into three categories: shellfish, crustaceans and molluscs. Crustaceans, such as lobsters, have hard shells which they shed and replace during their life-time. Molluscs are animals that have hinged shells, such as scallops, or single shells, such as whelks. This term also includes cephalopods such as squid, cuttlefish and octopus.

Seafood should be eaten as fresh as possible. Live seafood gives the best flavour, as long as it is consumed on the day of purchase. If live is not available, buy from a reputable source and eat on the day of purchase, refrigerating until required. Clean all seafood thoroughly and with mussels and clams, discard any that do not close when tapped lightly before cooking. After cooking, discard any that have not opened.

**Clam** Available all year round but best in September. Usually eaten raw like oysters, or cook as for mussels.

**Cockles** Available all year round, but best in September. Normally eaten cooked. Eat plain with vinegar or use in recipes such as paella.

**Crab** Best from May to August, but also available canned and frozen. Normally sold ready-cooked either whole or as dressed crab.

**Crawfish** Also known as langoustines. Available all year round, usually imported frozen. Has no claws and is the size of a small lobster.

**Crayfish** Available from September to April. Resemble mini-lobsters and have a delicate flavour.

**Mussels** Best from September to March, but available most of the year due to farming. Normally sold live and can be eaten raw or cooked.

**Oysters** Available from September to April. Usually eaten raw on day of purchase, but can be cooked. Must be eaten absolutely fresh.

**Dublin Bay Prawns** Available all year round. Sold live or cooked. Other large prawns are often confused for them.

**Tiger prawns** Available all year round, raw or cooked. Just one of many varieties of large prawns that are now imported. They are grey when raw and turn pink once cooked. Use within one day of purchasing if live or thawed.

**Shrimp/prawns** Available all year round, fresh or frozen. Shrimp are the smaller of the two and are not used as much in everyday cooking. Shrimp are brown in colour prior to cooking and prawns are grey, both tuning pink once cooked.

**Scallops** Best from October to March, but available frozen all year. Usually sold live on the shell, but can be bought off the shell, often frozen. Scallops have a bright orange core which is edible. Serve cooked.

**Squid/octopus** Available all year round, sold fresh but previously frozen. Their black ink is often used in sauces, and is also used to make black pasta.

**Whelks** Best from September to February. Usually sold cooked and shelled and served with vinegar.

**Winkles** Best from October to May. Can be sold cooked or raw. Normally served cooked and with vinegar.

# Vegetables & Salads

Vegetables add colour, texture, flavour and valuable nutrients to a meal. They play an important role in the diet, providing necessary vitamins, minerals and fibre. Vegetables are versatile: they can be served as an accompaniment to other dishes – they go well with meat, poultry and fish – or they can be used as the basis for the whole meal. There is a huge range of fresh vegetables on sale today in supermarkets, greengrocers and local markets. Also available is a growing selection of fresh organic produce, plus a wide variety of seasonal pick-your-own vegetables from specialist farms. For enthusiastic gardeners, a vast range of vegetable seeds are available. In addition, the increase of ethnic markets has introduced an extensive choice of exotic vegetables, such as chayote and breadfruit. With improved refrigeration and transport networks, vegetables are now flown around the world resulting in year-round availability

Vegetables are classified into different groups: leaf vegetables; roots and tubers; beans, pods and shoots; bulb vegetables; fruit vegetables; brassicas; cucumbers and squashes; sea vegetables; and mushrooms.

## Leaf Vegetables

This includes lettuce and other salad leaves, such as oakleaf, frisée, radicchio, lamb's lettuce and lollo rosso as well as rocket, spinach, Swiss chard and watercress. These are available all year round as most are now grown under glass. Many leaf vegetables, such as watercress and spinach, are delicious cooked and made into soups.

## Roots and Tubers

This group includes beetroot, carrots, celeriac, daikon, Jerusalem artichokes, parsnips, potatoes, radish, salsify, scorzonera, sweet potatoes, swede, turnip and yam. Most are available all year round.

## Beans, Pods and Shoots

This category includes all the beans, such as broad beans, French beans, mangetout and runner beans as well as peas, sugar snap peas and sweetcorn, baby corn and okra. Shoots include asparagus, bamboo shoots, celery, chicory, fennel, globe artichokes and palm hearts. The majority are available all year round.

## Bulb Vegetables

This is the onion family and includes all the different types of onion, from the common brown-skinned globe onion, Italian red onion and Spanish onion to shallots, pickling onions, pearl onions and spring onions. This category also includes leeks, chives and garlic. All are available throughout the year.

## Fruit Vegetables

This group originates from hot climates like the Mediterranean and includes aubergines, avocados, chilli peppers, sweet peppers and tomatoes. These are available all year round but are more plentiful in the summer.

## Brassicas

This is the cabbage family and includes all the different types of cabbage, broccoli, Brussels sprouts, cauliflower, curly kale, Chinese cabbage, pak choi, purple sprouting broccoli and bok choy. Some of the cabbages are only seasonal, such as Savoy cabbage and red cabbage, while summer cabbages are available only during the summer months.

## Cucumbers and Squashes

These vegetables are members of the gourd family and include cucumbers, gherkins, pumpkins and other squashes. There are two types of squash – summer squashes, which include courgettes, marrows, and pattypan squashes, and winter squashes such as pumpkins and butternut, acorn, gem and spaghetti squashes. Courgettes and cucumbers are available throughout the year but pumpkins and other winter squashes and marrow are seasonal.

## Sea Vegetables

The vegetables from this group may be quite difficult to find in supermarkets. The most readily available are seaweed (normally available dried) and sea kale.

## Mushrooms and Fungi

This category includes all the different types of mushroom: the cultivated button mushrooms, chestnut mushrooms, large portobello or flat mushrooms and oyster and shiitake mushrooms, as well as wild mushrooms such as ceps, morels, chanterelles and truffles. Cultivated mushrooms are available throughout the year but wild ones are only around from late summer. If you collect your own wild mushrooms, make sure you correctly identify them before picking as some are very poisonous and can be fatal if eaten. Dried mushrooms are also available, including ceps, morels and oyster mushrooms. They add a good flavour to a dish, but need to be re-constituted before use.

## Buying and Storage

When buying fresh vegetables, always look for ones that are bright and feel firm to the touch, and avoid any that are damaged or bruised. Choose onions and garlic that are hard and not sprouting and avoid ones that are soft as they may be damaged. Salad leaves and other leaf vegetables should be fresh, bright and crisp – do not buy any that are wilted, look limp or have yellow leaves. Vegetables like peas and beans do not keep for very long, so try to eat them as soon as possible after buying or picking. Most vegetables can be stored in a cool, dry place that is frost-free, such as the larder or garage. Green vegetables, fruit vegetables and salad leaves should be kept in the salad drawer of the refrigerator, while root vegetables, tuber vegetables and winter squashes should be kept in a cool, dark place. Winter squashes can be kept for several months if stored correctly.

## Preparation

Always clean vegetables thoroughly before using. Brush or scrape off any dirt and wash well in cold water. Wash lettuce and other salad leaves gently under cold running water and tear

rather than cut the leaves. Dry thoroughly in a salad spinner or on kitchen paper before use, otherwise the leaves tend to wilt. Spinach should be washed thoroughly to remove all traces of dirt, and you should cut off and discard any tough stalks and damaged leaves. Wash leaf vegetables and salad leaves well, then pull off and discard any tough stalks or outer leaves. Leeks need to be thoroughly cleaned before use to remove any grit and dirt. Most mushrooms just need wiping with a damp cloth. Prepare the vegetables just before cooking, as once peeled they lose nutrients. Do not leave them in water, as valuable water-soluble vitamins will be lost.

## Cooking Techniques

Vegetables can be cooked in a variety of different ways, such as baking, barbecuing, blanching, boiling, braising, deep-frying, grilling, roasting, sautéing, steaming and stir-frying.

**Boiling** Always cook vegetables in a minimum amount of water and do not over-cook, or valuable nutrients will be lost. It is best to cut vegetables into even-sized pieces and briefly cook them in a small amount of water.

**Blanching** This means lightly cooking raw vegetables for a brief period of time. It is a method used to par-boil potatoes before frying or roasting, cabbage before braising and for cooking leaf vegetables such as spinach. Spinach should be cooked in only the water clinging to its leaves for 2–3 minutes, or until wilted. Blanching is also used to easily remove skins from tomatoes. Cut a small cross in the top of the tomato and place in a heat-proof bowl. Cover with boiling water and leave for a few seconds, then drain and peel off the skin.

**Braising** This method is a slow way of cooking certain vegetables, notably cabbage and leeks. The vegetable is simmered for a long period of time in a small amount of stock or water.

**Deep-frying** This method is suitable for most vegetables except leaf. The vegetables can be cut into small pieces, coated in batter, then deep-fried briefly in hot oil.

**Grilling** When grilling and barbecuing peppers, aubergines and tomatoes, brush them with a little oil first as they quickly dry out. To remove the skins from peppers, cut the pepper in half lengthways and de-seed. Place the peppers skin-side up on the grill rack under a pre-heated hot grill and cook until the skins are blackened and blistered. Remove the peppers with tongs and place in a polythene bag, which will retain moisture. Seal and leave until the peppers are cool enough to handle. Once cool, remove from the bag and carefully peel away the blackened skin.

**Roasting** This method is suitable for vegetables such as fennel, courgettes, pumpkin, squash, peppers, garlic, aubergine and tomatoes. Cut the vegetables into even-sized chunks. Heat some oil in a roasting tin in a preheated oven at 200°C/400°F/Gas Mark 6. Put the vegetables in the hot oil, baste, and roast in the oven for 30 minutes. Garlic can be split into different cloves or whole heads of garlic can be roasted. It is best not to peel them until after cooked.

**Steaming** This is a great way to cook vegetables such as broccoli, cauliflower, beans, carrots, parsnips and peas. Fill a large saucepan with about 5 cm/2 inches of water. Cut the vegetables into even-sized pieces, place in a metal steamer or on a plate and lower into the saucepan, then cover and steam until tender. Do not let the water boil – it should be just simmering. Once tender, refresh under cold running water. Asparagus is best steamed and is traditionally cooked in an asparagus steamer.

## Health and Nutrition

Vegetables contain many essential nutrients and are especially high in vitamins A, B and C. They contain important minerals, in particular iron and calcium, and are also low in fat, high in fibre and have low cholesterol value. Red and orange vegetables, such as peppers and carrots, and dark green vegetables, such as broccoli, are an essential part of the diet as they contain excellent anti-cancer properties as well as helping to prevent heart disease. Current healthy eating guidelines suggest that five portions of fruit and vegetables should be eaten per day, with vegetables being the more essential.

# Rice

## Varieties

Rice is the staple food of many countries throughout the world. Every country and culture has its own repertoire of rice recipes – India, for example, has the aromatic biryani, Spain has the saffron-scented paella, and Italy has the creamy risotto. Rice is grown on marshy, flooded land where other cereals cannot thrive and because it is grown in so many different areas, there is a huge range of rice types.

**Long-grain white rice** Probably the most widely used type of rice. Long-grain white rice has been milled so that the husk, bran and germ is removed. Easy-cook long-grain white rice has been steamed under pressure before milling. Pre-cooked rice, also known as par-boiled or converted rice, is polished white rice which is half-cooked after milling, then dried again. It is quick to cook but has a bland flavour.

**Long-grain brown rice** Where the outer husk is removed, leaving the bran and germ behind. This retains more of the fibre, vitamins and minerals. It has a nutty, slightly chewy texture and takes longer to cook than white rice.

**Basmati rice** This slender long-grain rice, which may be white or brown, is grown in the foothills of the Himalayas. After harvesting, it is allowed to mature for a year, giving it a unique aromatic flavour, hence its name, which means fragrant.

**Risotto rice** Grown in the north of Italy, this is the only rice that is suitable for making risotto. The grains are plump and stubby and have the ability to absorb large quantities of liquid without becoming too soft, cooking to a creamy texture with a slight bite. There are two grades of risotto rice: superfino and fino. Arborio rice is the most widely sold variety of the former, but you may also find carnaroli, Roma and baldo in Italian delicatessens. Fino rice such as vialone nano has a slightly shorter grain, but the flavour is still excellent.

**Valencia rice** Traditionally used for Spanish paella, Valencia rice is soft and tender when ready. The medium-sized grains break down easily, so should be left unstirred during cooking to absorb the flavour of the stock and other ingredients.

**Jasmine rice** Also known as Thai fragrant rice, this long-grain rice has a delicate, almost perfumed aroma and flavour and has a soft, sticky texture.

**Japanese sushi rice** This is similar to glutinous rice in that it has a sticky texture. When mixed with rice vinegar it is easy to roll up with a filling inside to make sushi.

**Pudding rice** This rounded, short-grain rice is ideal for rice desserts. The grains swell and absorb large quantities of milk during cooking, giving puddings a rich, creamy consistency.

**Wild rice** This is an aquatic grass grown in North America rather than a true variety of rice. The black grains are long and slender and after harvesting and cleaning they are toasted to remove the chaff and intensify the nutty flavour and slight chewiness. It is often sold as a mixture with long-grain rice.

**Rice flour** Raw rice can be finely ground to make rice flour, which may be used to thicken sauces (1 tablespoon will thicken 300 ml/½ pint of liquid) or in Asian desserts. It is also used to make rice noodles.

## Buying and Storing Rice

Rice will keep for several years if kept in sealed packets. However, it is at its best when fresh. To ensure freshness, always buy rice from reputable shops with a good turnover and buy in small quantities. Once opened, store the rice in an airtight container in a cool, dry place to keep out moisture. Most rice (but not risotto) benefits from washing before cooking – tip into a sieve and rinse under cold running water until the water runs clear. This removes any starch still clinging to the grains.

Cooked rice will keep for up to two days if cooled and stored in a covered bowl in the refrigerator. If eating rice cold, serve within 24 hours – after this time it should be thoroughly re-heated.

## Cooking Techniques

There are countless ways to cook rice, but much depends on the variety of rice being used, the dish being prepared and the desired results. Each variety of rice has its own characteristics. Some types of rice cook to light, separate grains, some to a rich, creamy consistency and some to a consistency where the grains stick together. Different types of rice have different powers of absorption. Long-grain rice will absorb three times its weight in water, whereas 25 g/1 oz of short-grain pudding rice can soak up a massive 300 ml/½ pint of liquid.

### Cooking Long-grain Rice

The simplest method of cooking long-grain rice is to add it to plenty of boiling, salted water in a large saucepan. Allow 50 g/2 oz of rice per person when cooking as an accompaniment. Rinse under cold running water until clear then tip into rapidly boiling water. Stir once, then when the water returns to the boil, reduce the heat and simmer uncovered. Allow 10–12 minutes for white rice and 30–40 minutes for brown – check the packet for specific timings. The easiest way to test if rice is cooked is to bite a couple of grains – they should be tender but still firm. Drain immediately, then return to the pan with a little butter and herbs if liked. Fluff up with a fork and serve. To keep the rice warm, put it in a bowl and place over a pan of barely simmering water. Cover the top of the bowl with a tea towel until ready to serve.

### Absorption Method

Cooking rice using the absorption method is also simple. Weigh out the quantity, then measure it by volume in a measuring jug – you will need 150 ml/¼ pint for two people. Rinse the rice then tip into a large saucepan. If liked, cook the rice in a little butter or oil for 1 minute. Pour in two parts water or stock to one part rice, season with salt and bring to the boil. Cover, then simmer gently until the liquid is absorbed and the rice is tender. White rice will take 15 minutes to cook, whereas brown rice will take 35 minutes. If there is still a little liquid left when the rice is tender, uncover and cook for 1 minute until evaporated. Remove from the heat and leave, covered, for 4–5 minutes then fluff up before serving. This method is good for cooking Jasmine and Valencia rice.

### Oven-Baked Method

The oven-baked method also works by absorption, but takes longer than cooking on the hob. To make oven-baked rice for two people, fry a chopped onion in 1 tablespoon olive oil in a 1.1 litre/2 pint flameproof casserole until soft and golden. Add 75 g/3 oz long-grain rice and cook for 1 minute, then stir in 300 ml/½ pint of stock – add a finely pared strip of lemon rind or bay leaf if liked. Cover and bake in a preheated oven at 180°C/350°F/Gas Mark 4 for 40 minutes, or until the rice is tender and all the stock has been absorbed. Fluff up before serving.

### Cooking in the Microwave

Place rinsed long-grain rice in a large, heatproof bowl. Add boiling water or stock, allowing 300 ml/½ pint for 100 g/4 oz rice and 550 ml/18 fl oz for 225 g/8 oz rice. Add a pinch of salt and a knob of butter, if desired. Cover with clingfilm which has been pierced and cook on high for 3 minutes. Stir, re-cover and cook on medium for 12 minutes for white rice and 25 minutes for brown. Leave, covered, for 5 minutes before fluffing up and serving.

### In a Pressure Cooker

Follow the quantities given for the absorption method and bring to the boil in the pressure cooker. Stir, cover and bring to a high 6.8 kg/15 lb pressure. Lower the heat and cook for 5 minutes if white rice or for 8 minutes for brown.

### In a Rice Cooker

Follow the quantities given for the absorption method. Put the rice, salt and boiling water or stock in the cooker, return to the boil and cover. When all the liquid has been absorbed the cooker will turn off automatically.

## Health and Nutrition

Rice is low in fat and high in complex carbohydrates, which are absorbed slowly and help to maintain blood sugar levels. It is also a reasonable source of protein and provides many B vitamins and the minerals potassium and phosphorus. It is a gluten-free cereal, making it suitable for coeliacs. Brown rice is richer in nutrients and fibre than refined white rice.

# Pasta

## How to Make Pasta

**Home-made pasta has a light, almost silky texture and is different from the fresh pasta that you can buy vacuum-packed in supermarkets. It is also easy to make and little equipment is needed, just a rolling pin and a sharp knife. If you make pasta regularly it is perhaps worth investing in a pasta machine.**

### Basic Egg Pasta Dough

225 g/8 oz type '00' pasta flour, plus extra for dusting
1 tsp salt
2 eggs, plus 1 egg yolk
1 tbsp olive oil
1–3 tsp cold water

Sift the flour and salt into a mound on a work surface and make a well in the middle, keeping the sides high so that the egg mixture will not trickle out when added. Beat the eggs, yolk, oil and 1 teaspoon of water together. Add to the well, then gradually work in the flour, adding extra water if needed, to make a soft, not sticky dough. Knead on a lightly floured surface for 5 minutes, or until the dough is smooth and elastic. Wrap in clingfilm and leave for 20 minutes at room temperature.

### Using a Food Processor

Sift the flour and salt into a food processor fitted with a metal blade. Add the eggs, yolk, oil and water and pulse-blend until mixed and the dough begins to come together, adding extra water if needed. Knead for 1–2 minutes, then wrap and rest as before.

### Rolling Pasta by Hand

Unwrap the pasta dough and cut in half. Work with just half at a time and keep the other half wrapped in clingfilm. Place the dough on a lightly-floured work surface, then flatten and roll out. Always roll away from you, starting from the centre and giving the dough a quarter turn after each rolling. Sprinkle a little more flour over the dough if it starts to get sticky. Continue rolling and turning until the dough is as thin as possible, ideally 3 mm/⅛ inch thick.

### Rolling Pasta by Machine

Always refer to the manufacturers' instructions before using. Clamp the machine securely and attach the handle. Set the rollers at their widest setting and sprinkle with flour. Cut the pasta dough into four pieces. Wrap three of them in clingfilm and reserve. Flatten the unwrapped dough slightly, then feed it through the rollers. Fold the strip of dough in three, rotate and feed through the rollers a second time. Continue to roll the dough, narrowing the roller setting by one notch every second time and flouring the rollers if the dough starts to get sticky. Only fold the dough the first time it goes through each roller width. If it gets too difficult to handle, cut the strip in half and work with one piece at a time. Fresh pasta should be dried slightly before cutting. Either drape over a wooden pole for five minutes or place on a tea towel sprinkled with a little flour for 10 minutes.

### Shaping Up

When cutting and shaping freshly-made pasta, have several lightly-floured tea towels ready.

**Farfalle** Use a fluted pasta wheel to cut the pasta sheets into rectangles 2.5 x 5 cm/1 x 12 inches. Pinch the long sides of each rectangle in the middle to make a bow. Spread out on a floured tea towel and leave for 15 minutes.

**Lasagne** Trim the pasta sheets until neat and cut into lengths. Spread the sheets on tea towels sprinkled with flour.

**Noodles** If using a pasta machine, use the cutter attachment to produce tagliatelle or use a narrower one for spaghetti. To make by hand, sprinkle the rolled-out pasta with flour, then roll up like a Swiss roll and cut into thin slices. Unravel immediately after cutting. Leave over a wooden pole for five minutes to dry.

**Ravioli** Cut the rolled-out sheet of dough in half widthways. Cover one half. Brush the other sheet of dough with beaten egg. Place 1 teaspoon of filling in even rows, spacing them at 4 cm/1½ inch intervals. Remove the clingfilm from the reserved pasta sheet and, using a rolling pin, lift over the dough with the filling. Press down between the pockets to push out any air. Cut into squares. Leave on a floured tea towel for 45 minutes before cooking.

### Variations

Flavoured pastas are simple and there are dozens of ways that you can change the flavour

and colour of pasta.
**Chilli** Add 2 teaspoons of crushed, dried red chillies to the egg mixture.
**Herb** Stir 3 tablespoons of chopped fresh herbs into the flour.
**Olive** Blend 2 tablespoons of black olive paste with the egg mixture and omit the water.
**Porcini** Soak 15 g/½ oz dried porcini mushrooms in boiling water for 20 minutes. Drain and squeeze out as much water as possible, then chop finely. Add to the egg mixture.
**Spinach** Chop 75 g/3 oz cooked fresh spinach finely. Add to the egg mixture.

## Dried Pasta Varieties

**Buckwheat** A gluten-free pasta made from buckwheat flour.
**Coloured and flavoured pasta** Varieties are endless, the most popular being spinach and tomato. Others include beetroot, herb, garlic, chilli, mushroom and black ink.
**Durum wheat pasta** Most readily available and may be made with or without eggs. Look for 'durum wheat' or 'pasta di semola di grano duro' on the packet, as pastas made from soft wheat tend to become soggy when cooked.
**Wholewheat pasta** Made with wholemeal flour, this has a higher fibre content than ordinary pasta. Wholewheat pasta takes longer to cook than the refined version.

## Pasta Shapes

### Long Pasta

**Spaghetti** Probably the best known type of pasta, spaghetti derives its name from the word 'spago' meaning string, which describes its round, thin shape perfectly.

**Tagliatelle** Most common type of ribbon noodle pasta. It is traditionally from Bologna where it accompanies bolognaise sauce (rather than spaghetti). Fettuccine is the Roman version of tagliatelle and is cut slightly thinner.

### Short Pasta

There are two types of short pasta: 'secca' is factory-made from durum wheat and water and 'pasta all'uovo' is made with eggs. There are numerous different shapes and some of the most popular ones are listed below.

**Conchiglie** Pasta shapes resembling conch shells. Sizes vary from tiny to large. They may be smooth or ridged conchiglie rigate.

**Eliche and fusilli** These are twisted into the shape of a screw.

**Farfalle** Bow or butterfly shaped, often with crinkled edges.

**Macaroni** Known as elbow macaroni or maccheroni in Italy. A thin, quick-cook variety is also available.

**Penne** Slightly larger than macaroni, the ends of these hollow tubes are cut diagonally and are pointed like quills.

**Pipe** Curved, hollow pasta and often sold ridged as pipe rigate.

**Rigatoni** Substantial, chunky, tubular pasta and often used for baking.

**Rotelle** Thin, wheel-shaped pasta, often sold in packets of two or three colours.

### Stuffed Pasta

**Tortellini** The most common variety, consisting of tiny, stuffed pieces of pasta. Larger ones are called tortelloni. Cappelletti, ravioli and agnalotti are sometimes sold dried, but are more often available fresh.

### Fresh Pasta

Fresh pasta can be found in supermarkets and specialist shops. It is generally available in the same shapes as dried pasta.

## How to Cook Perfect Pasta

Follow a few simple rules to ensure that your pasta is cooked to perfection every time:

1 Choose a large saucepan – there needs to be plenty of room for the pasta to move around so it does not stick together.

2 Cook the pasta in a large quantity of fast-boiling, well-salted water; ideally 4 litres/7 pints water and 1½–2 tablespoons of salt for every 350–450 g/12 oz–1 lb of pasta.

3 Tip in the pasta all at once, stir and cover. Return to a rolling boil, then remove the lid. Once it is boiling, lower the heat to medium-high and cook the pasta for the required time. It should be 'al dente' or tender, but still firm to the bite.

4 Drain, reserving a little of the cooking water to stir into the pasta. This helps to thin the sauce, if necessary, and helps prevent the pasta sticking together as it cools.

## Serving Quantities

As an approximate guide, allow 75–100 g (3–4 oz) uncooked pasta per person. The amount will depend on whether the pasta is being served for a light or main meal and the type of sauce that it is being served with.

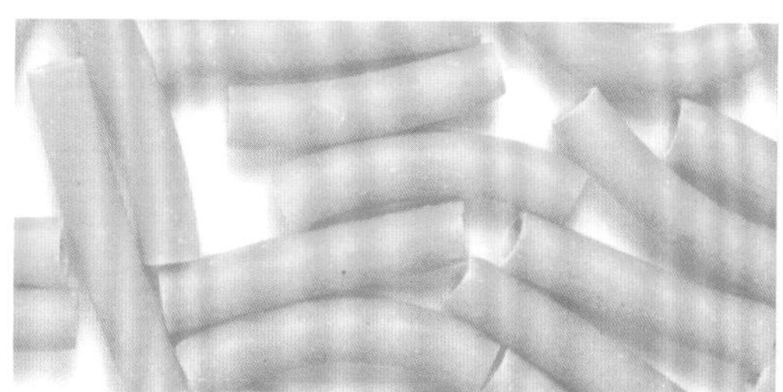

# Herbs & Spices

**In a culture where fast food, ready-made meals and processed foods are popular, homemade food can sometimes taste bland by comparison, due to the fact that the palate can quickly become accustomed to additives and flavour enhancers. The use of herbs and spices, however, can make all the difference in helping to make delicious homemade dishes.**

Herbs are easy to grow and a garden is not needed as they can easily thrive on a small patio, window box or even on a windowsill. It is worth the effort to plant a few herbs as they do not require much attention or nurturing. The reward will be a range of fresh herbs available whenever needed and fresh flavours which cannot be beaten to add to any dish that is being prepared.

While fresh herbs should be picked or bought as close as possible to the time of use, freeze-dried and dried herbs and spices will usually keep for around six months.

The best idea is to buy little and often, and to store the herbs in airtight jars in a cool, dark cupboard. Fresh herbs tend to have a milder flavour than dried and equate to around one level tablespoons of fresh to one level teaspoon of dried. As a result, quantities used in cooking should be altered accordingly. A variety of herbs and spices and their uses are listed below.

**Allspice** The dark allspice berries come whole or ground and have a flavour similar to that of cinnamon, cloves and nutmeg. Although not the same as mixed spices, allspice can be used with pickles, relishes, cakes and milk puddings, or whole in meat and fish dishes.

**Aniseed** Comes in whole seeds or ground. It has a strong aroma and flavour and should be used sparingly in baking and salad dressings.

**Basil** Best fresh but also available in dried form, basil can be used raw or cooked and works well in many dishes but is particularly well-suited to tomato-based dishes and sauces, salads and Mediterranean dishes.

**Bay leaves** Available in fresh or dried form as well as ground. They make up part of a bouquet garni and are particularly delicious when added to meat and poultry dishes, soups, stews, vegetable dishes and stuffing. They also impart a spicy flavour to milk puddings and egg custards.

**Caraway seeds** These have a warm, sweet taste and are often used in breads and cakes, but are also delicious with cabbage dishes and pickles.

**Cayenne** The powdered form of a red chilli pepper said to be native to Cayenne. It is similar in appearance to paprika and can be used sparingly to add a fiery kick to many dishes.

**Cardamom** Has a distinctive sweet, rich taste and can be bought whole in the pod, in seed form or ground. This sweet aromatic spice is delicious in curries, rice, cakes and biscuits and is great served with rice pudding and fruit.

**Chervil** Reminiscent of parsley and available either in fresh or dried form, chervil has a faintly sweet, spicy flavour and is particularly good in soups, cheese dishes, stews and with eggs.

**Chilli** Available whole, fresh, dried and in powdered form, red chillies tend to be sweeter in taste than their green counterparts. They are particularly associated with Spanish and Mexican-style cooking and curries, but are also delicious with pickles, dips, sauces and in pizza toppings.

**Chives** Best used when fresh but also available in dried form, this member of the onion family is ideal for use when a delicate onion flavour is required. Chives are good with eggs, cheese, fish and vegetable dishes. They also work well as a garnish for soups, meat and vegetable dishes.

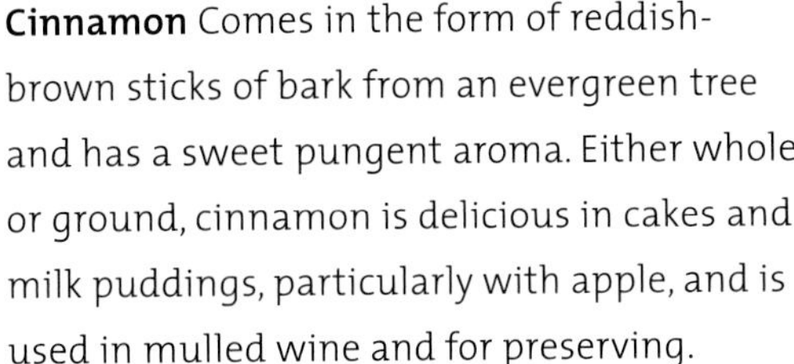

**Cinnamon** Comes in the form of reddish-brown sticks of bark from an evergreen tree and has a sweet pungent aroma. Either whole or ground, cinnamon is delicious in cakes and milk puddings, particularly with apple, and is used in mulled wine and for preserving.

**Cloves** Mainly used whole although available ground, cloves have a very warm, sweet, pungent aroma and can be used to stud roast ham and pork, in mulled wine and punch and when pickling fruit. When ground, they can be used in making mincemeat and in Christmas puddings and biscuits.

**Coriander** Coriander seeds have an orangey flavour and are available whole or ground. Coriander is particularly delicious (whether whole or roughly ground) in casseroles, curries and as a pickling spice. The leaves are used both to flavour spicy aromatic dishes as well as a garnish.

**Cumin** Also available ground or as whole seeds, cumin has a strong, slightly bitter flavour. It is one of the main ingredients in curry powder and compliments many fish, meat and rice dishes.

**Dill** These leaves are available fresh or dried and have a mild flavour, while the seeds are slightly bitter. Dill is particularly good with salmon, new potatoes and in sauces. The seeds are good in pickles and vegetable dishes.

**Fennel** Whole seeds or ground, fennel has a fragrant, sweet aniseed flavour and is sometimes known as the fish herb because it compliments fish dishes so well.

**Ginger** Comes in many forms but primarily as a fresh root and in dried, ground form, which can be used in baking, curries, pickles, sauces and Chinese cooking.

**Lemon grass** Available fresh and dried, with a subtle, aromatic, lemony flavour, lemon grass is essential to Thai cooking. It is also delicious when added to soups, poultry and fish dishes.

**Mace** The outer husk of nutmeg has a milder nutmeg flavour and can be used in pickles, cheese dishes, stewed fruits, sauces and hot punch.

**Marjoram** Often dried, marjoram has a sweet, slightly spicy flavour, which tastes fantastic when added to stuffing, meat or tomato-based dishes.

**Mint** Available fresh or dried, mint has a strong, sweet aroma which is delicious in a sauce or jelly to serve with lamb. It is also great with fresh peas and new potatoes and is an essential ingredient in Pimms.

**Nutmeg** The large, whole seeds have a warm, sweet taste and compliment custards, milk puddings, cheese dishes, parsnips and creamy soups.

**Oregano** These strongly flavoured dried leaves are similar to marjoram and are used extensively in Italian and Greek cooking.

**Paprika** Often comes in two varieties. One is quite sweet and mild and the other has a slight bite to it. Paprika is made from the fruit of the sweet pepper and is good in meat and poultry dishes as well as a garnish. The rule of buying herbs and spices little and often applies particularly to paprika as unfortunately it does not keep particularly well.

**Parsley** The stems as well as the leaves of parsley can be used to compliment most savoury dishes as they contain the most flavour. They can also be used as a garnish.

**Poppy seeds** These small, grey-black coloured seeds impart a sweet, nutty flavour when added to biscuits, vegetable dishes, dressings and cheese dishes.

**Rosemary** Delicious fresh or dried, these small, needle-like leaves have a sweet aroma which is particularly good with lamb, stuffing and vegetables dishes. Also delicious when added to charcoal on the barbecue to give a piquant flavour to meat and corn on the cob.

**Saffron** Deep orange in colour, saffron is traditionally used in paella, rice and cakes but is also delicious with poultry. Saffron is the most expensive of all spices.

**Sage** These fresh or dried leaves have a pungent, slightly bitter taste which is delicious with pork and poultry, sausages, stuffing and with stuffed pasta when tossed in a little butter and fresh sage.

**Sesame** Sesame seeds have a nutty taste, especially when toasted, and are delicious in baking, on salads, or with Far Eastern cooking.

**Tarragon** The fresh or dried leaves of tarragon have a sweet aromatic taste, which is particularly good with poultry, seafood, fish, creamy sauces and stuffing.

**Thyme** Available fresh or dried, thyme has a pungent flavour and is included in bouquet garni. It compliments many meat and poultry dishes and stuffing.

**Turmeric** Obtained from the root of a lily from southeast Asia. This root is ground and has a brilliant yellow colour. It has a bitter, peppery flavour and is often combined for use in curry powder and mustard. Also delicious in pickles, relishes and dressings.

# Entertaining

There are many ways of entertaining friends and family, and whether it's an informal or formal occasion, there are some rules that can be applied to all entertaining that will help make life easy for the host and hostess.

First of all, decide what kind of entertaining you wish to do: dinner party, supper, barbecue, picnic, cheese and wine or even a disco. This will dictate how formal the event will be, These days parties tend to be far more informal and relaxed, but even so it is still advisable to be guided by a few rules.

## Make Life Easy

- Decide how many guests to invite and check their dietary requirements – are they vegetarian, do they have allergies to certain foods or have specific likes or dislikes?

- Choose the venue and menu and decide on the drinks to serve, ensuring that there are plenty of soft drinks for those driving.

- Make a shopping list ahead of time. This will allow for non-perishable foods to be bought early, as well as leaving time for a change of menu if necessary.

- Check china, cutlery, glasses and table linen. Make sure that it is clean and you have sufficient for all the guests.

- If it helps, work out a time plan early on. This will enable you to cook ahead if possible, thus saving time and effort on the day.

- If trying a new recipe, it is advisable to cook it beforehand to ensure that it works and tastes good.

- Arrange flowers the day before. Ensure you have nibbles and appetisers to serve, and stock up on ice, mixer drinks, lemon and glasses. Make sure you have plenty of coffee, tea or other after-dinner drinks.

## Menu Planning for Different Occasions

### Drinks Parties

These are normally semi-informal, and unless you serve very expensive wines or champagne, relatively cheap. Although food is not served as at an actual meal, it is a good idea to serve some light starters. This will help to offset too much alcoholic drink. People tend to eat more than you might think and it is a good idea to offer at least four or five different snacks as well as the obligatory nuts, crisps and little biscuits. Try to offer at least two vegetarian choices.

Try serving bite-sized vol-au-vents, perhaps filled with peeled prawns in a flavoured mayonnaise or chicken and sweetcorn. Small squares of quiche are good, or try roasted peppers with blue cheese. Smoked salmon and asparagus rolls, in both white and brown bread, cocktail sausages on sticks with a sweet chilli dip and chicken satay on sticks with satay sauces are all fairly straightforward. Hand round either small napkins or plates so guests can take a few at a time and do not spill the food on themselves or your furniture.

Keep drinks simple – do not offer everything. People are quite happy with a limited choice, red or white wine and beer with plenty of soft drinks is perfectly acceptable, or in winter try a warming punch. Pimms in the summer is an ideal choice.

### Formal Dinner Party

These take a little more planning, both in terms of which guests to invite and the food. When working out the invitations, ensure that all your guests will get on well together and that there is at least one thing they have in common. Always remember to check their dietary requirements. Dinner parties can consist of as many courses as wished. If offering more than three, ensure that all the courses compliment each other and that the portions are not too large. Invite guests to arrive at least 30 minutes before you hope to sit down – this allows for guests arriving late.

Menus should be balanced: normally the dinner should start with a soup or small appetiser, and fish can be served either as the main course or as a second course as a prelude to the meat or poultry . Cheese and dessert are served after the main course; it is a matter of personal preference which is served first.

### Supper, Lunch or Brunch Parties

These are normally much more informal and spur-of-the-moment events. However, a little planning is an excellent idea so that the host or hostess does not spend the entire time dashing around, making both themselves and the guests stressed trying to ensure that everyone enjoys the occasion.

Obviously, the menu will depend on the time of year and the ages of those involved. Younger people are more than happy with fast food such as pizza or baked chicken pieces, with plenty of crisps and oven baked chips or a large bowl of pasta.

Try a theme for your party such as Italian or Oriental. There are many excellent Chinese and pasta dishes in this book to choose from.

### Barbecue Parties

In this county, because of the weather, barbecues have to be fairly impromptu, meaning that the food needs to be simple and adaptable. Depending on tastes, keep the food quick and easy to prepare – the best choices are steak, chicken pieces, small whole fish such as sardines, and sausages, all of which can be cooked whole or cut into cubes and skewered and marinated to make kebabs. These cook quickly and will be ready in a very short time. Serve plenty of salads and bread. If cooking chicken portions which still contain the bones, it is advisable to cook them in the oven first and finish them on the barbecue to ensure that the chicken is thoroughly cooked through.

When barbecuing, it is vital that the food is cooked properly – semi-cooked sausages and chicken are one of the main causes of stomach upsets. If using a barbecue that uses coal, light it in plenty of time (at least 20 minutes before required) to allow the coals to reach the correct temperature before commencing to cook. The coals should be white/grey in colour and coated in ash, and the flames should have died down to give a good, steady heat.

Eating outside often sharpens the appetite, so along with the meats serve plenty of bread or potatoes with assorted salads. Coleslaw and rice and pasta salads all work well. Keep desserts and drinks simple: fresh fruit, ice cream or cheese with wine or beer to drink.

### Children's Parties

The highlight of any child's year is their birthday party, and to avoid tears, a little planning is a good idea. Many companies now offer a complete service so that the children can participate in an activity, such as skating, football or swimming, then the birthday tea is provided and all that is expected of the parents is to take and collect. This is by far one of the easiest and least stressful ways to celebrate their day, but can be expensive.

If that is not for you, above all keep it simple, whether you hold the party at home or in a local hall. First, decide on a date and venue and how long the party will be. Send out the invitations in plenty of time, stating clearly what time it will finish – most important for your sanity. Enlist the help of at least two other adults who are used to dealing with tears and tantrums. Decide on a few games, depending on age, such as pass the parcel, pin the tail on the donkey, musical chairs or blind man's bluff. Clear away furniture and any breakable ornaments and ensure that no sharp objects are in easy reach of little fingers.

Serve the food in a separate room and keep it fairly plain. Too much rich food could result in a few children being ill. Go for simple sandwiches, small pieces of cheese with grapes, sausages, sausage rolls, crisps, fairy cakes and, of course, a birthday cake. Serve squash to drink.

Many parties finish with the guests being issued with a goody bag to take home. If you do this, keep it simple: a few sweets, a piece of birthday cake and two or three very small gifts is perfectly acceptable. There is no need to spend a lot on these.

# Wines

There are many different and excellent wines to choose from: white, red or rosé, sweet, medium or dry coming from all parts of the world. When choosing wines for a special occasion there are few points to bear in mind.

• Work out how many bottles you require. Allow 5–6 glasses from each bottle of wine; for fortified wines, sherry, Madeira and port allow 12–16 glasses. Champagne also yields between 5–6 glasses.

• Choose wines that are of medium price. Cheap wines taste cheap and your guests will not be impressed; expensive wines, on the other hand, will most probably not be appreciated in the general chat and movement.

• White wine is best served chilled. Place in the refrigerator at least the day before. If space is short, arrange for some ice for the day, place in a wine bucket or any clean container and chill the wine in this.

• Red wine should be served at room temperature, so if stored in a cool place, bring into another room and allow to come to room temperature. Open about 1–2 hours before serving. There is no need to decant either white or red wine, but it does look good and also allows red wine to breathe more easily. For wine with a heavy sediment it is advisable to decant it.

• For the greatest appreciation, red wine glasses should be wide-necked, allowing the bouquet to be enjoyed. White wine glasses are narrow at the neck. All should have a stem so that the glasses can be swirled in order to release the fragrance.

## Know Your Wine

### France

Renowned for its fine wines, Champagnes and excellent table wines. The Appellations d'Origines Contrôlées (A.O.C.) is a system that signifies if a wine comes from a fine wine region. Indicating different grades of quality, these appellations go in stages from simple wines to prized wines such as Beaune, Chateau Neuf du Pape and Sancerre. Simple vins des tables are blended wines that generally offer excellent value for money

### Germany

German wines have improved considerably over the last 40 years. Gone, in the main, are the sweet white wines and heavy, rough reds. In their place are delicate, crisp wines from the Moselle and Rhine using the Riesling grape, and others such as Traminer, Sylvaner and other varieties blended together. Hock is perhaps one of the most well-known wines and comes from the four main regions in the Rhine. There are many fine wines, which carry the name of the grape.

### Italy

Most of the regions of Italy produce wine, as do Sardinia and Sicily. When buying Italian wines, look for D.O.C. on the label. They produce both white and red, perhaps the most well-known of which is Chianti. This wine comes from Tuscany and is a fruity and robust wine and goes well with all red meats and game. Other red wines include Barolo from Piedmont and Valpolicella from the Veneto region. There are other excellent red wines from the north made from the Cabernet, Pinot and Merlot grapes.

Italy also produces some excellent white wines, ranging from Soave, Verdicchio, Frascati and Pinot Grigio – all have their own distinct style ranging from very dry, light wine to a heavier, sweeter wine.

### Spain

Although Spain is world-famous for sherry, it also produces some excellent wines. The best-known is probably Rioja, which is produced both as white and red. This wine is produced throughout the whole of Spain, with the red Rioja coming in two styles, one being drier than the other, and the white tending to be full-bodied and dry.

### New World

There are now some serious contenders to 'Old World' wines coming from as far afield as Australia – known as a 'New World' wine producer. Australia, South Africa, Chile and California all produce excellent wines that seriously challenge the established wine-growers. Growers from these countries have taken on-board all the established guidelines and knowledge and have expanded it to produce wines that are every bit as good. When buying New World wine, apply the same guidelines as for the established wines.

# Good Cooking Rules

**When handling and cooking foods, there are a few rules and guidelines that should be observed so that food remains fit to eat and uncontaminated with the bacteria and bugs that can result in food poisoning.**

## Good Hygiene Rules

- Personal hygiene is imperative when handling food. Before commencing any preparation, wash hands thoroughly with soap, taking particular care with nails. Always wash hands after going to the toilet. Wash again after handling raw foods, cooked meats or vegetables. Do not touch any part of the body or handle pets, rubbish or dirty washing during food preparation.
- Cuts should be covered with a waterproof plaster, preferably blue so it can be easily seen if lost.
- Do not smoke in the kitchen.
- Keep pets off all work surfaces and out of the kitchen if possible. Clean surfaces with an anti-bacterial solution. Wash their eating bowls separately.
- Ensure that hair is off the face and does not trail into food or machinery.
- Use a dishwasher wherever possible and wash utensils and equipment in the very hot, soapy water.
- Use clean dish cloths and tea towels, replacing regularly. Boil them to kill any bacteria, and use absorbent kitchen paper where possible to wipe hands and equipment.
- Chopping boards and cooking implements must be clean. Boards should either be washed in a dishwasher or scrubbed after each use. Keep a separate board for meat, fish and vegetables and wash knives before using on different types of food. Do not use the same board for raw and cooked food: wash in-between, or better still, use a different board.
- Use dustbin liners for rubbish and empty regularly, cleaning your bin with disinfectant. Dustbins should be outside.

## Guidelines for Using a Refrigerator

- Ensure that the refrigerator is situated away from any equipment that gives off heat, such as the cooker, washing machine or tumble drier, to ensures the greatest efficiency. Ensure that the vents are not obstructed.
- If not frost-free, defrost regularly, wiping down with a mild solution of bicarbonate of soda dissolved in warm water and a clean cloth.
- Close the door as quickly as possible so that the motor does not have to work overtime to keep it at the correct temperature.
- Ensure that the temperature is 5°C. A thermometer is a good investment.
- Avoid over-loading – this just makes the motor work harder.
- Cool food before placing in the refrigerator and always cover to avoid any smells or transference of taste to other foods.

## Stacking Your Refrigerator

- Remove supermarket packaging from raw meat, poultry and fish, place on a plate or dish, cover loosely and store at the base of the refrigerator to ensure that the juices do not drip on other foods.
- Store cheese in a box or container, wrapped to prevent the cheese drying out.
- Remove food to be eaten raw 30 minutes before use so it can return to room temperature.
- Cooked meats, bacon and all cooked dishes should be stored at the top – this is the coldest part.
- Store eggs in the egg compartment and remove 30 minutes before cooking in order to return them to room temperature.
- Butter and all fats can be stored on the door, as can milk, cold drinks, sauces, mayonnaise and preserves with low sugar content.
- Cream and other dairy products, as well as pastries such as chocolate éclairs, should be stored on the middle shelf.
- Vegetables, salad and fruit should be stored in the salad boxes at the bottom of the refrigerator.
- Soft fruits should be kept in the salad box along with mushrooms, which are best kept in paper bags.
- To avoid cross-contamination, raw and cooked foods must be stored separately.
- Use all foods by the sell-by date – once opened, treat as cooked foods and use within two days.

## General Rules

- Use all foods by the use-by date and store correctly. This applies to all foods: fresh, frozen, canned and dried. Potatoes are best if removed from polythene, stored in brown paper and kept in the cool and dark.
- Ensure that all food is thoroughly thawed before use, unless meant to be cooked from frozen.
- Cook all poultry thoroughly at the correct temperature (190°C/375°F/Gas Mark 5) ensuring that the juices run clear.
- Leave foods to cool as quickly as possible before placing in the refrigerator, and cover while cooling.
- Do not re-freeze any thawed frozen foods unless cooked first.
- Date and label frozen food and use in rotation.
- Re-heat foods thoroughly until piping hot. Remember to allow foods to stand when using the microwave and stir to distribute the heat.
- Microwaves vary according to make and wattage – always refer to manufacturer's instructions.
- Only re-heat dishes once and always heat until piping hot.
- Ensure that eggs are fresh. If using for mayonnaise, soufflés or other dishes that use raw or semi-cooked egg, do not give to the vulnerable – the elderly, pregnant women, those with a recurring illness, toddlers and babies.
- When buying frozen foods, transport in freezer-insulated bags, placing in the freezer as soon as possible after purchase.
- Chilled foods, such as cold meats, cheese, fresh meat, fish and dairy products should be bought, taken home and placed in the refrigerator immediately. Do not keep in a warm car or room.
- Avoid buying damaged or unlabelled canned goods. Keep store cupboards clean, wiping down regularly and rotating the food.
- Flour, nuts, rice, pulses, grains and pasta should be checked regularly and once opened, placed in airtight containers.
- Do not buy eggs or frozen or chilled foods that are damaged in any way.
- Keep dried herbs and ready-ground spices in a cool, dark place, not in a spice rack on the work surface. They quickly lose their pungency and flavour when exposed to light.

# Soups & Starters

Nothing says comfort food quite like a delicious, homemade soup, and nothing could be simpler with these straightforward, step-by-step recipes. Starters are also made easy with something for every member of the family. Each recipe features two alternatives, covering everything from low fat and vegetarian options to suggested accompaniments and even entertaining versions.

# Potato, Leek & Rosemary Soup

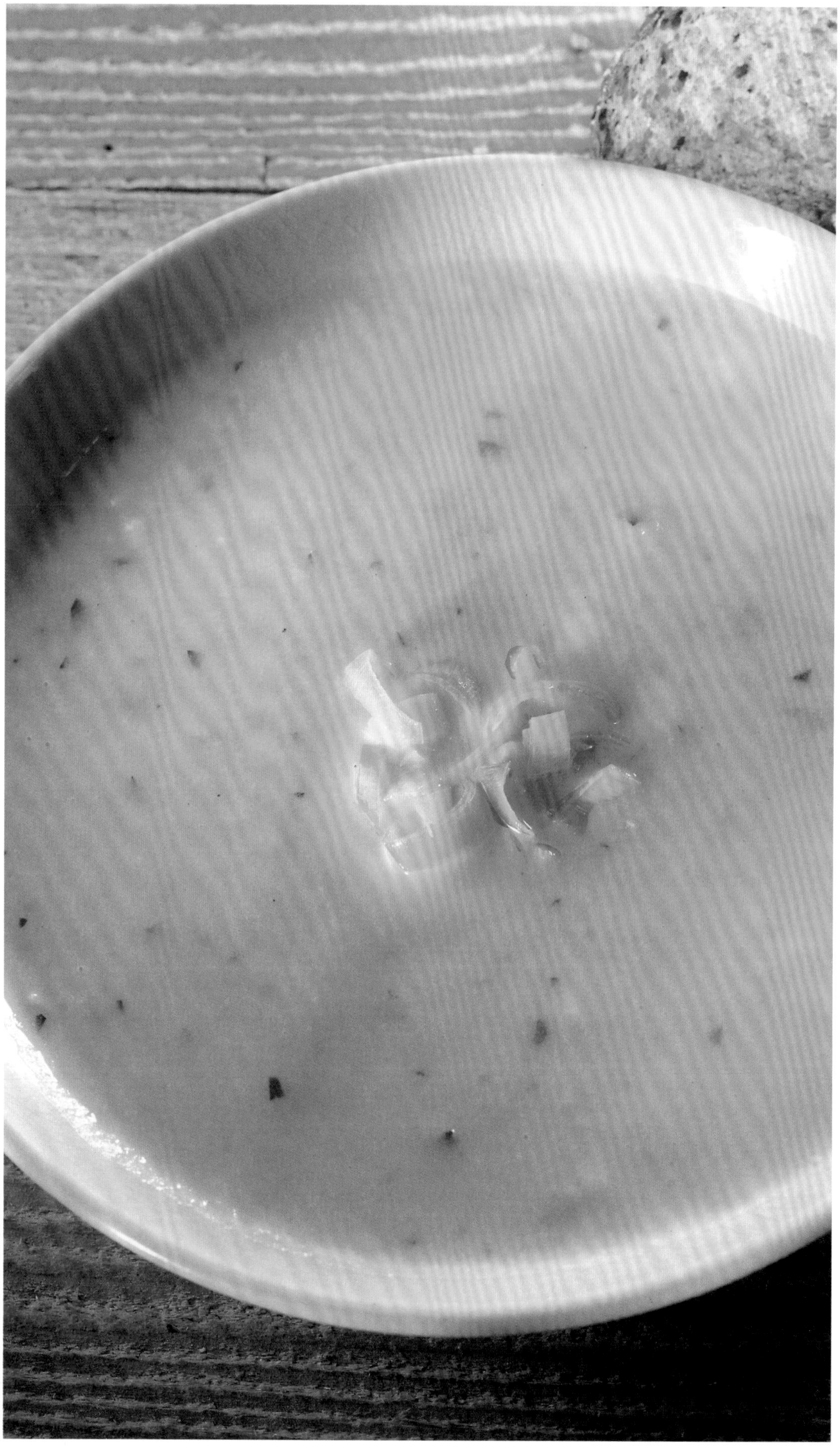

INGREDIENTS **Serves 4**

50 g/2 oz butter
450 g/1 lb leeks, trimmed and finely sliced
700 g/1½ lb potatoes, peeled and roughly chopped
900 ml/1½ pints vegetable stock
4 sprigs of fresh rosemary
450 ml/¾ pint full-cream milk
2 tbsp freshly chopped parsley
2 tbsp crème fraîche
salt and freshly ground black pepper
wholemeal rolls, to serve

Melt the butter in a large saucepan, add the leeks and cook gently for 5 minutes, stirring frequently. Remove 1 tablespoon of the cooked leeks and reserve for garnishing.

Add the potatoes, vegetable stock, rosemary sprigs and milk. Bring to the boil, then reduce the heat, cover and simmer gently for 20–25 minutes, or until the vegetables are tender.

Cool for 10 minutes. Discard the rosemary, then pour into a food processor or blender and blend well to form a smooth-textured soup.

Return the soup to the cleaned saucepan and stir in the chopped parsley and crème fraîche. Season to taste with salt and pepper. If the soup is too thick, stir in a little more milk or water. Reheat gently without boiling, then ladle into warm soup bowls. Garnish the soup with the reserved leeks and serve immediately with wholemeal rolls.

## HEALTH RATING ●●●

**LOW FAT ALTERNATIVE**
Tomato & Basil Soup

**ENTERTAINING ALTERNATIVE**
Cream of Spinach Soup

LOW FAT ALTERNATIVE
## Tomato & Basil Soup

INGREDIENTS **Serves 4**

- 1.1 kg/2½ lb ripe tomatoes, cut in half
- 2 garlic cloves
- 1 tsp olive oil
- 1 tbsp balsamic vinegar
- 1 tbsp dark brown sugar
- 1 tbsp tomato purée
- 300 ml/½ pint vegetable stock
- 6 tbsp low-fat natural yogurt
- 2 tbsp freshly chopped basil
- salt and freshly ground black pepper
- small basil leaves, to garnish

Preheat the oven to 200°C/400°F/Gas Mark 6. Evenly spread the tomatoes and unpeeled garlic in a single layer in a large roasting tin.

Mix the oil and vinegar together. Drizzle over the tomatoes and sprinkle with the dark brown sugar.

Roast the tomatoes in the preheated oven for 20 minutes until tender and lightly charred in places.

Remove from the oven and allow to cool slightly. When cool enough to handle, squeeze the softened flesh of the garlic from the papery skin. Place with the charred tomatoes in a nylon sieve over a saucepan.

Press the garlic and tomato through the sieve with the back of a wooden spoon.

When all the flesh has been sieved, add the tomato purée and vegetable stock to the pan. Heat gently, stirring occasionally.

In a small bowl beat the yogurt and basil together and season to taste with salt and pepper. Stir the basil yogurt into the soup. Garnish with basil leaves and serve immediately.

ENTERTAINING ALTERNATIVE
## Cream of Spinach Soup

INGREDIENTS **Serves 6–8**

- 1 large onion, peeled and chopped
- 5 large plump garlic cloves, peeled and chopped
- 2 medium potatoes, peeled and chopped
- 750 ml/1¼ pints cold water
- 1 tsp salt
- 450 g/1 lb spinach, washed and large stems removed
- 50 g/2 oz butter
- 3 tbsp flour
- 750 ml/1¼ pints milk
- ½ tsp freshly grated nutmeg
- freshly ground black pepper
- 6–8 tbsp crème fraîche or soured cream
- warm foccacia bread, to serve

Place the onion, garlic and potatoes in a large saucepan and cover with the cold water. Add half the salt and bring to the boil. Cover and simmer for 15–20 minutes, or until the potatoes are tender. Remove from the heat and add the spinach. Cover and set aside for 10 minutes.

Slowly melt the butter in another saucepan, add the flour and cook over a low heat for about 2 minutes. Remove the saucepan from the heat and add the milk, a little at a time, stirring continuously. Return to the heat and cook, stirring continuously, for 5–8 minutes, or until the sauce is smooth and slightly thickened. Add the freshly grated nutmeg to taste.

Blend the cooled potato and spinach mixture in a food processor or blender to a smooth purée, then return to the saucepan and gradually stir in the white sauce. Season to taste with salt and pepper and gently reheat, taking care not to allow the soup to boil.

Ladle into soup bowls and top with spoonfuls of crème fraîche or soured cream. Serve immediately with warm foccacia bread.

# Bacon & Split Pea Soup

INGREDIENTS **Serves 4**

50 g/2 oz dried split peas
25 g/1 oz butter
1 garlic clove, peeled and finely chopped
1 medium onion, peeled and thinly sliced
175 g/6 oz long-grain rice
2 tbsp tomato purée
1.1 litres/2 pints vegetable or chicken stock
175 g/6 oz carrots, peeled and finely diced
125 g/4 oz streaky bacon, finely chopped
salt and freshly ground black pepper
2 tbsp freshly chopped parsley
4 tbsp single cream
warm crusty garlic bread, to serve

Cover the dried split peas with plenty of cold water, cover loosely and leave to soak for a minimum of 12 hours, preferably overnight.

Melt the butter in a heavy-based saucepan, add the garlic and onion and cook for 2–3 minutes, without colouring. Add the rice, drained split peas and tomato purée and cook for 2–3 minutes, stirring constantly to prevent sticking. Add the stock, bring to the boil, then reduce the heat and simmer for 20–25 minutes, or until the rice and peas are tender. Remove from the heat and leave to cool.

Blend about three-quarters of the soup in a food processor or blender to form a smooth purée. Pour the purée into the remaining soup in the saucepan. Add the carrots to the saucepan and cook for a further 10–12 minutes, or until the carrots are tender.

Meanwhile, place the bacon in a non-stick frying pan and cook over a gentle heat until the bacon is crisp. Remove and drain on absorbent kitchen paper.

Season the soup with salt and pepper to taste, then stir in the parsley and cream. Reheat for 2–3 minutes, then ladle into soup bowls. Sprinkle with the bacon and serve immediately with warm garlic bread.

HEALTH RATING 🍎🍎🍎

**VEGETARIAN ALTERNATIVE**
Swede, Turnip, Parsnip & Potato Soup

**LOW FAT ALTERNATIVE**
Roasted Red Pepper, Tomato & Red Onion Soup

**VEGETARIAN ALTERNATIVE**
## Swede, Turnip, Parsnip & Potato Soup

INGREDIENTS **Serves 4**

2 large onions, peeled
25 g/1 oz butter
2 medium carrots, peeled and roughly chopped
175 g/6 oz swede, peeled and roughly chopped
125 g/4 oz turnip, peeled and roughly chopped
125 g/4 oz parsnips, peeled and roughly chopped
175 g/6 oz potatoes, peeled
1 litre/1¾ pints vegetable stock
½ tsp freshly grated nutmeg
salt and freshly ground black pepper
4 tbsp vegetable oil, for frying
125 ml/4 fl oz double cream
warm crusty bread, to serve

Finely chop 1 onion. Melt the butter in a large saucepan and add the onion, carrots, swede, turnip, parsnip and potatoes. Cover and cook gently for about 10 minutes, without colouring. Stir occasionally during this time.

Add the stock and season to taste with the nutmeg, salt and pepper. Cover and bring to the boil, then reduce the heat and simmer gently for 15–20 minutes, or until the vegetables are tender. Remove from the heat and leave to cool for 30 minutes.

Heat the oil in a large, heavy-based frying pan. Finely chop the remaining onion, add to the frying pan and cook over a medium heat for about 2–3 minutes, stirring frequently, until golden brown. Remove the fried onions with a slotted spoon and drain well on absorbent kitchen paper. As they cool, they will turn crispy.

Pour the cooled soup into a food processor or blender and process to form a smooth purée. Return to the cleaned pan, adjust the seasoning, then stir in the cream. Gently reheat and top with the crispy onions. Serve immediately with chunks of bread.

**LOW FAT ALTERNATIVE**
## Roasted Red Pepper, Tomato & Red Onion Soup

Preheat the oven to 190°C/375°F/Gas Mark 5. Spray a large roasting tin with the oil and place the peppers and onion in the base. Cook in the oven for 10 minutes. Add the tomatoes and cook for a further 20 minutes or until the peppers are soft.

Cut the bread into 1 cm/½ inch slices. Cut the garlic clove in half and rub the cut edge of the garlic over the bread.

Place all the bread slices on a large baking tray, and bake in the preheated oven for 10 minutes, turning halfway through, until golden and crisp.

Remove the vegetables from the oven and allow to cool slightly, then blend in a food processor until smooth. Strain the vegetable mixture through a large nylon sieve into a saucepan, to remove the seeds and skin. Add the stock, season to taste with salt and pepper and stir to mix. Heat the soup gently until piping hot.

In a small bowl beat together the Worcestershire sauce with the fromage frais. Pour the soup into warmed bowls and swirl a spoonful of the fromage frais mixture into each bowl. Serve immediately with the garlic toast.

INGREDIENTS **Serves 4**

fine spray of oil
2 large red peppers, deseeded and roughly chopped
1 red onion, peeled and roughly chopped
350 g/12 oz tomatoes, halved
1 small crusty French loaf
1 garlic clove, peeled
600 ml/1 pint vegetable stock
salt and freshly ground black pepper
1 tsp Worcestershire sauce
4 tbsp fromage frais

**VEGETARIAN ALTERNATIVE**
## Mushroom & Sherry Soup

Preheat the oven to 180°C/350°F/Gas Mark 4. Remove the crusts from the bread and cut the bread into small cubes.

In a large bowl toss the cubes of bread with the lemon rind and juice, 2 tablespoons of water and plenty of freshly ground black pepper. Spread the bread cubes on to a lightly oiled, large baking tray and bake for 20 minutes until golden and crisp. If the wild mushrooms are small, leave some whole. Otherwise, thinly slice all the mushrooms and reserve.

Heat the oil in a saucepan. Add the garlic and spring onions and cook for 1–2 minutes. Add the mushrooms and cook for 3–4 minutes until they start to soften. Add the chicken stock and stir to mix. Bring to the boil, then reduce the heat to a gentle simmer. Cover and cook for 10 minutes.

Stir in the sherry, and season to taste with a little salt and pepper. Pour into warmed bowls, sprinkle over the chives, and serve immediately with the lemon croûtons.

INGREDIENTS **Serves 4**

4 slices day old white bread
zest of ½ lemon
1 tbsp lemon juice
salt and freshly ground black pepper
125 g/4 oz assorted wild mushrooms, lightly rinsed
125 g/4 oz baby button mushrooms, wiped
2 tsp olive oil
1 garlic clove, peeled and crushed
6 spring onions, trimmed and diagonally sliced
600 ml/1 pint chicken stock
4 tbsp dry sherry
1 tbsp freshly snipped chives, to garnish

**SUGGESTED ACCOMPANIMENT**
## Sweet Potato Baps

INGREDIENTS **Makes 16**

225 g/8 oz sweet potato
15 g/½ oz butter
freshly grated nutmeg
about 200 ml/7 fl oz milk
450 g/1 lb strong white flour
2 tsp salt
7 g/¼ oz sachet easy-blend yeast
1 medium egg, beaten

**To finish:**

beaten egg, to glaze
1 tbsp rolled oats

Preheat the oven to 200°C/400°F/Gas Mark 6, 15 minutes before baking. Peel the sweet potato and cut into large chunks. Cook in a saucepan of boiling water for 12–15 minutes, or until tender. Drain well and mash with the butter and nutmeg. Stir in the milk, then leave until barely warm.

Sift the flour and salt into a large bowl. Stir in the yeast. Make a well in the centre, then add the mashed sweet potato and beaten egg and mix to a soft dough. Add a little more milk if needed, depending on the moisture in the sweet potato.

Turn out the dough on to a lightly floured surface and knead for about 10 minutes, or until smooth and elastic. Place in a lightly oiled bowl, cover with clingfilm and leave in a warm place to rise for about 1 hour, or until the dough doubles in size. Turn out the dough and knead for a minute or two until smooth. Divide into 16 pieces, shape into rolls and place on a large, oiled baking sheet. Cover with oiled clingfilm and leave to rise for 15 minutes.

Brush the rolls with beaten egg, then sprinkle half with rolled oats and leave the rest plain. Bake in the preheated oven for 12–15 minutes, or until they are well risen, lightly browned and sound hollow when the bases are tapped. Transfer to a wire rack and immediately cover with a clean tea towel to keep the crusts soft.

# Clear Chicken & Mushroom Soup

INGREDIENTS **Serves 4**

2 large chicken legs, about 450 g/1 lb total weight
1 tbsp groundnut oil
1 tsp sesame oil
1 onion, peeled and very thinly sliced
2.5 cm/1 inch piece root ginger, peeled and very finely chopped
1.1 litres/2 pints clear chicken stock
1 lemon grass stalk, bruised
50 g/2 oz long-grain rice
75 g/3 oz button mushrooms, wiped and finely sliced
4 spring onions, trimmed, cut into 5 cm/2 inch pieces and shredded
1 tbsp dark soy sauce
4 tbsp dry sherry
salt and freshly ground black pepper

Skin the chicken legs and remove any fat. Cut each in half to make 2 thigh and 2 drumstick portions and reserve. Heat the groundnut and sesame oils in a large saucepan. Add the sliced onion and cook gently for 10 minutes, or until soft but not beginning to colour.

Add the chopped ginger to the saucepan and cook for about 30 seconds, stirring all the time to prevent it sticking, then pour in the stock. Add the chicken pieces and the lemon grass, cover and simmer gently for 15 minutes. Stir in the rice and cook for a further 15 minutes or until the chicken is cooked.

Remove the chicken from the saucepan and leave until cool enough to handle. Finely shred the flesh, then return to the saucepan with the mushrooms, spring onions, soy sauce and sherry. Simmer for 5 minutes, or until the rice and mushrooms are tender. Remove the lemon grass.

Season the soup to taste with salt and pepper. Ladle into warmed serving bowls, making sure each has an equal amount of shredded chicken and vegetables and serve immediately.

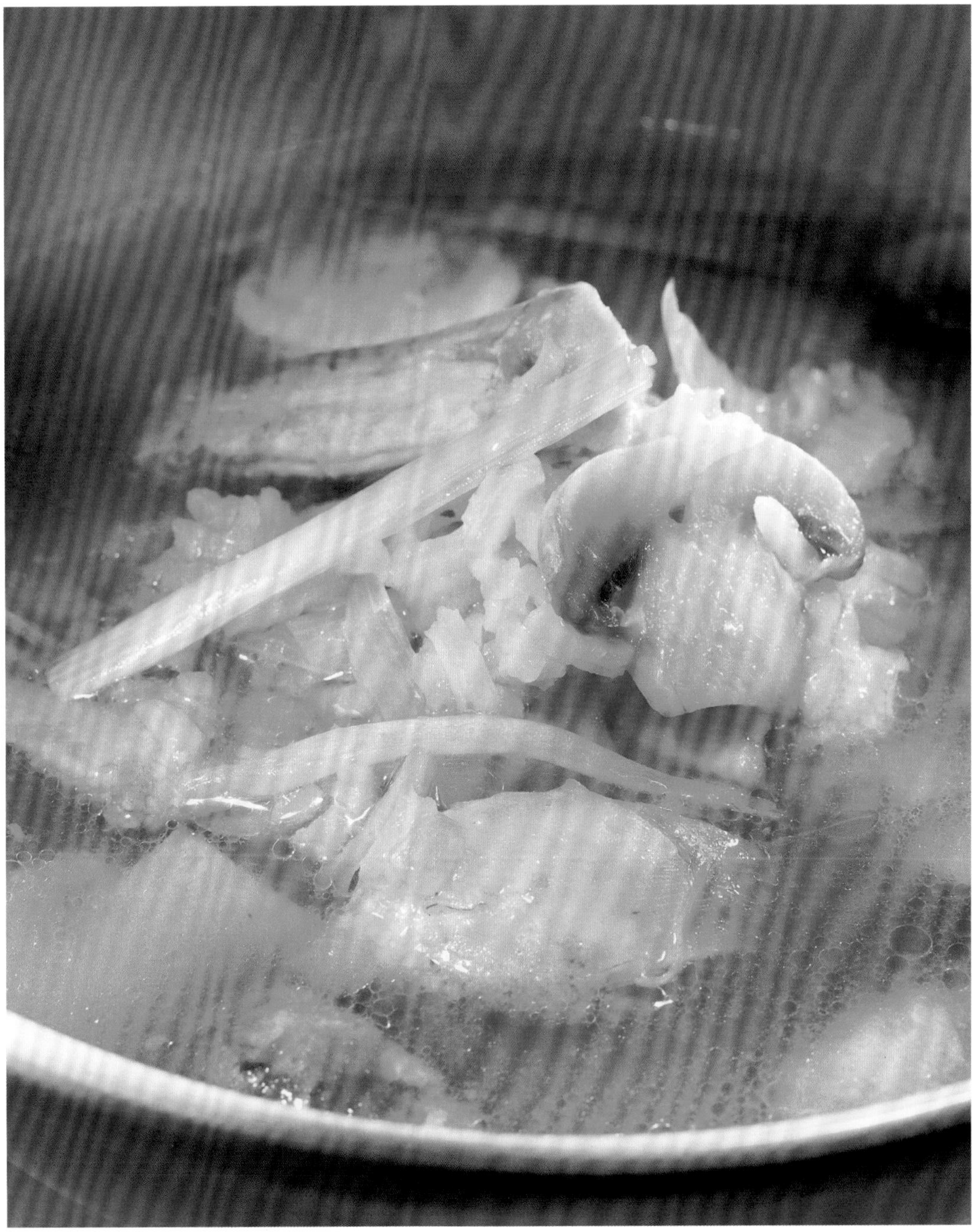

## HEALTH RATING ❦❦❦❦

**VEGETARIAN ALTERNATIVE**
Mushroom & Sherry Soup

**SUGGESTED ACCOMPANIMENT**
Sweet Potato Baps

# Classic Minestrone

INGREDIENTS **Serves 6–8**

25 g/1 oz butter
3 tbsp olive oil
3 rashers streaky bacon
1 large onion, peeled
1 garlic clove, peeled
1 celery stick, trimmed
2 carrots, peeled
400 g can chopped tomatoes
1.1 litre/2 pints chicken stock
175 g/6 oz green cabbage, finely shredded
50 g/2 oz French beans, trimmed and halved
3 tbsp frozen petits pois
50 g/2 oz spaghetti, broken into short pieces
salt and freshly ground black pepper
Parmesan cheese shavings, to garnish
crusty bread, to serve

HEALTH RATING

**ORIENTAL ALTERNATIVE**
Wonton Noodle Soup

**SUGGESTED ACCOMPANIMENT**
Wok-fried Snacks

Heat the butter and olive oil together in a large saucepan. Chop the bacon and add to the saucepan. Cook for 3–4 minutes, then remove with a slotted spoon and reserve.

Finely chop the onion, garlic, celery and carrots and add to the saucepan, one ingredient at a time, stirring well after each addition. Cover and cook gently for 8–10 minutes, until the vegetables are softened.

Add the chopped tomatoes, with their juice and the stock, bring to the boil then cover the saucepan with a lid, reduce the heat and simmer gently for about 20 minutes.

Stir in the cabbage, beans, peas and spaghetti pieces. Cover and simmer for a further 20 minutes, or until all the ingredients are tender. Season to taste with salt and pepper.

Return the cooked bacon to the saucepan and bring the soup to the boil. Serve the soup immediately with Parmesan cheese shavings sprinkled on the top and plenty of crusty bread to accompany it.

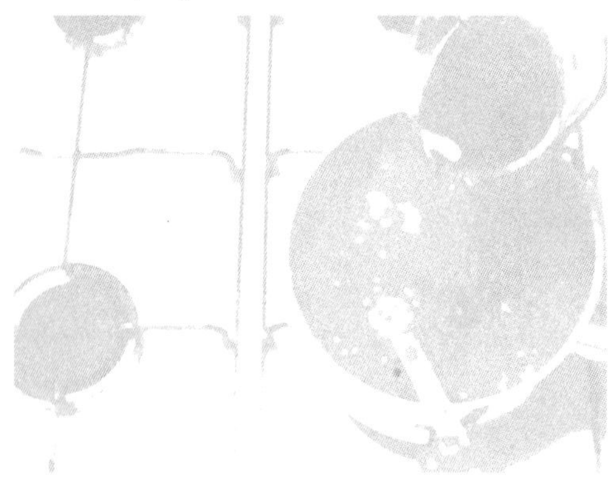

INGREDIENTS **Serves 4**

4 Chinese (shiitake) mushrooms, wiped
125 g/4 oz raw prawns, peeled and finely chopped
125 g/4 oz pork mince
4 water chestnuts, finely chopped
4 spring onions, trimmed and finely sliced
1 medium egg white
salt and freshly ground black pepper
1½ tsp cornflour
1 packet fresh wonton wrappers
1.1 litres/2 pints chicken stock
2 cm/¾ inch piece root ginger, peeled and sliced
75 g/3 oz fine egg noodles
125 g/4 oz pak choi, shredded

**ORIENTAL ALTERNATIVE**

## Wonton Noodle Soup

Place the mushrooms in a bowl, cover with warm water and leave to soak for 1 hour. Drain, remove and discard the stalks and finely chop the mushrooms. Return to the bowl with the prawns, pork, water chestnuts, 2 of the spring onions and egg white. Season to taste with salt and pepper. Mix well.

Mix the cornflour with 1 tablespoon of cold water to make a paste. Place a wonton wrapper on a board and brush the edges with the paste. Drop a little less than 1 teaspoon of the pork mixture in the centre then fold in half to make a triangle, pressing the edges together. Bring the 2 outer corners together, fixing together with a little more paste. Continue until all the pork mixture is used up; you should have 16–20 wontons.

Pour the stock into a large, wide saucepan, add the ginger slices and bring to the boil. Add the wontons and simmer for about 5 minutes. Add the noodles and cook for 1 minute. Stir in the pak choi and cook for a further 2 minutes, or until the noodles and pak choi are tender and the wontons have floated to the surface and are cooked through.

Ladle the soup into warmed bowls, discarding the ginger. Sprinkle with the remaining sliced spring onion and serve immediately.

INGREDIENTS **Serves 4–6**

**For the popcorn:**
75 ml/3 fl oz vegetable oil
75 g/3 oz unpopped popcorn
½ tsp garlic salt
1 tsp hot chilli powder

**For the pecans:**
50 g/2 oz sugar
½ tsp ground cinnamon
½ tsp ground Chinese five spice powder
¼ tsp salt
¼ tsp cayenne pepper
175 g/6 oz pecan or walnut halves
sesame seeds for sprinkling

**SUGGESTED ACCOMPANIMENT**

## Wok-fried Snacks – Popcorn & Sesame-coated Pecans

For the popcorn, heat half the oil in a large wok over a medium-high heat. Add 2–3 kernels and cover with a lid. When these kernels pop, add all the popcorn and cover tightly. Cook until the popping stops, shaking from time to time.

When the popping stops, pour the popped corn into a bowl and immediately add the remaining oil to the wok with the garlic salt and chilli powder. Stir-fry for 30 seconds, or until blended and fragrant. Return the popcorn to the wok, stir-fry and toss for a further 30 seconds, or until coated. Pour into the bowl and serve warm or at room temperature.

For the pecans, put the sugar, cinnamon, Chinese five spice powder, salt and cayenne pepper into a large wok and stir in 50 ml/2 fl oz water. Bring to the boil over a high heat, then simmer for 4 minutes, stirring frequently.

Remove from the heat and stir in the pecans or walnuts until well coated. Turn onto a lightly oiled, non-stick baking sheet and sprinkle generously with the sesame seeds.

Working quickly with 2 forks, separate the nuts into individual pieces or bite-sized clusters. Sprinkle with a few more sesame seeds and leave to cool completely. Carefully remove from the baking sheet, breaking into smaller pieces if necessary.

# Cream of Pumpkin Soup

INGREDIENTS **Serves 4**

900 g/2 lb pumpkin flesh (after peeling and discarding the seeds)
4 tbsp olive oil
1 large onion, peeled
1 leek, trimmed
1 carrot, peeled
2 celery sticks
4 garlic cloves, peeled and crushed
1.7 litres/3 pints water
salt and freshly ground black pepper
¼ tsp freshly grated nutmeg
150 ml/¼ pint single cream
¼ tsp cayenne pepper
warm herby bread, to serve

Cut the skinned and de-seeded pumpkin flesh into 2.5 cm/1 inch cubes. Heat the olive oil in a large saucepan and cook the pumpkin for 2–3 minutes, coating it completely with oil. Chop the onion and leek finely and cut the carrot and celery into small chunks.

Add the vegetables to the saucepan with the garlic and cook, stirring for 5 minutes or until they have begun to soften. Cover the vegetables with the water and bring to the boil. Season with plenty of salt and pepper and the nutmeg, cover and simmer for 15–20 minutes, or until all of the vegetables are tender.

When the vegetables are tender, remove from the heat, cool slightly then pour into a food processor or blender. Liquidise to form a smooth purée then pass through a sieve into a clean saucepan.

Adjust the seasoning to taste and add all but 2 tablespoons of the cream and enough water to obtain the correct consistency. Bring the soup to boiling point, add the cayenne pepper and serve immediately swirled with cream and accompanied by warm herby bread.

HEALTH RATING 🍎🍎🍎

**MEAT ALTERNATIVE**

White Bean Soup with Parmesan Croûtons

**ENTERTAINING ALTERNATIVE**

Rocket & Potato Soup with Garlic Croûtons

**MEAT ALTERNATIVE**
## White Bean Soup with Parmesan Croûtons

INGREDIENTS **Serves 4**

- 3 thick slices of white bread, cut into 1 cm/½ inch cubes
- 3 tbsp groundnut oil
- 2 tbsp Parmesan cheese, finely grated
- 1 tbsp light olive oil
- 1 large onion, peeled and finely chopped
- 50 g/2 oz unsmoked bacon lardons (or thick slices of bacon, diced)
- 1 tbsp fresh thyme leaves
- 2 x 400 g cannellini beans, drained
- 900 ml/1½ pints chicken stock
- salt and freshly ground black pepper
- 1 tbsp prepared pesto sauce
- 50 g/2 oz piece of pepperoni sausage, diced
- 1 tbsp fresh lemon juice
- 1 tbsp fresh basil, roughly shredded

Preheat the oven to 200°C/400°F/Gas Mark 6. Place the cubes of bread in a bowl and pour over the groundnut oil. Stir to coat the bread, then sprinkle over the Parmesan cheese. Place on a lightly oiled baking tray and bake in the preheated oven for 10 minutes, or until crisp and golden. Reserve.

Heat the olive oil in a large saucepan and cook the onion for 4–5 minutes until softened. Add the bacon and thyme and cook for a further 3 minutes. Stir in the beans, stock and black pepper and simmer gently for 5 minutes.

Place half the bean mixture and liquid into a food processor and blend until smooth.

Return the purée to the saucepan. Stir in the pesto sauce, pepperoni sausage and lemon juice and season to taste with salt and pepper.

Return the soup to the heat and cook for a further 2–3 minutes, or until piping hot. Place some of the beans in each serving bowl and add a ladleful of soup. Garnish with shredded basil and serve immediately with the croûtons scattered over the top.

**ENTERTAINING ALTERNATIVE**
## Rocket & Potato Soup with Garlic Croûtons

INGREDIENTS **Serves 4**

- 700 g/1½ lb baby new potatoes
- 1.1 litres/2 pints chicken or vegetable stock
- 50 g/2 oz rocket leaves
- 125 g/4 oz thick white sliced bread
- 50 g/2 oz unsalted butter
- 1 tsp groundnut oil
- 2–4 garlic cloves, peeled and chopped
- 125 g/4 oz stale ciabatta bread, with the crusts removed
- 4 tbsp olive oil
- salt and freshly ground black pepper
- 2 tbsp Parmesan cheese, finely grated

Place the potatoes in a large saucepan, cover with the stock and simmer gently for 10 minutes. Add the rocket leaves and simmer for a further 5–10 minutes, or until the potatoes are soft and the rocket has wilted.

Meanwhile, make the croûtons. Cut the thick, white sliced bread into small cubes and reserve. Heat the butter and groundnut oil in a small frying pan and cook the garlic for 1 minute, stirring well. Remove the garlic. Add the bread cubes to the butter and oil mixture in the frying pan and sauté, stirring continuously, until they are golden brown. Drain the croûtons on absorbent kitchen paper and reserve.

Cut the ciabatta bread into small cubes and stir into the soup. Cover the saucepan and leave to stand for 10 minutes, or until the bread has absorbed a lot of the liquid.

Stir in the olive oil, season to taste with salt and pepper and ladle into individual bowls with a few of the garlic croûtons scattered over the top and a little grated Parmesan cheese.

# Carrot & Ginger Soup

INGREDIENTS **Serves 4**

4 slices of bread, crusts removed
1 tsp yeast extract
2 tsp olive oil
1 onion, peeled and chopped
1 garlic clove, peeled and crushed
½ tsp ground ginger
450 g/1 lb carrots, peeled and chopped
1 litre/1¾ pint vegetable stock
2.5 cm/1 inch piece of root ginger, peeled and finely grated
salt and freshly ground black pepper
1 tbsp lemon juice

**To garnish:**
chives
lemon zest

Preheat the oven to 180°C/350°F/Gas Mark 4. Roughly chop the bread. Dissolve the yeast extract in 2 tablespoons of warm water and mix with the bread.

Spread the bread cubes over a lightly oiled baking tray and bake for 20 minutes, turning half way through. Remove from the oven and reserve.

Heat the oil in a large saucepan. Gently cook the onion and garlic for 3–4 minutes.

Stir in the ground ginger and cook for 1 minute to release the flavour.

Add the chopped carrots, then stir in the stock and the fresh ginger. Simmer gently for 15 minutes.

Remove from the heat and allow to cool a little. Blend until smooth, then season to taste with salt and pepper. Stir in the lemon juice. Garnish with the chives and lemon zest and serve immediately.

HEALTH RATING ●●●●●

**ENTERTAINING ALTERNATIVE**
Potato & Fennel Soup

**SUGGESTED ACCOMPANIMENT**
Carrot & Parsnip Terrine

**ENTERTAINING ALTERNATIVE**
## Potato & Fennel Soup

INGREDIENTS **Serves 4**

25 g/1 oz butter
2 large onions, peeled and thinly sliced
2–3 garlic cloves, peeled and crushed
1 tsp salt
2 medium potatoes (about 450 g/1 lb in weight), peeled and diced
1 fennel bulb, trimmed and finely chopped
½ tsp caraway seeds
1 litre/1¾ pints vegetable stock
freshly ground black pepper
2 tbsp freshly chopped parsley
4 tbsp crème fraîche
roughly torn pieces of French stick, to serve

Melt the butter in a large, heavy-based saucepan. Add the onions with the garlic and half the salt. Cook over a medium heat, stirring occasionally, for 7–10 minutes or until the onions are very soft and beginning to turn brown.

Add the potatoes, fennel bulb, caraway seeds and the remaining salt. Cook for about 5 minutes, then pour in the vegetable stock. Bring to the boil, partially cover and simmer for 15–20 minutes, or until the potatoes are tender. Stir in the chopped parsley and adjust the seasoning to taste.

For a smooth-textured soup, allow to cool slightly then pour into a food processor or blender and blend until smooth. Reheat the soup gently, then ladle into individual soup bowls. For a chunky soup, omit this blending stage and ladle straight from the saucepan into soup bowls.

Swirl a spoonful of crème fraîche into each bowl and serve immediately with roughly-torn pieces of French stick.

**SUGGESTED ACCOMPANIMENT**
## Carrot & Parsnip Terrine

INGREDIENTS **Serves 8–10**

550 g/1¼ lb carrots, peeled and chopped
450 g/1 lb parsnips, peeled and chopped
6 tbsp half-fat crème fraîche
450 g/1 lb spinach, rinsed
1 tbsp brown sugar
1 tbsp freshly chopped parsley
½ tsp freshly grated nutmeg
salt and freshly ground black pepper
6 medium eggs
sprigs of fresh basil, to garnish

**For the tomato coulis:**
450 g/1 lb ripe tomatoes, deseeded and chopped
1 medium onion, peeled and finely chopped

Preheat the oven to 200°C/400°F/Gas Mark 6. Oil and line a 900 g/2 lb loaf tin with non-stick baking paper. Cook the carrots and parsnips in boiling salted water for 10–15 minutes or until very tender. Drain and purée separately. Add 2 tablespoons of crème fraîche to both the carrots and the parsnips.

Steam the spinach for 5–10 minutes or until very tender. Drain and squeeze out as much liquid as possible, then stir in the remaining crème fraîche. Add the brown sugar to the carrot purée, the parsley to the parsnip mixture and the nutmeg to the spinach. Season all to taste with salt and pepper.

Beat 2 eggs, add to the spinach and turn into the prepared tin. Add another 2 beaten eggs to the carrot mixture and layer carefully on top of the spinach. Beat the remaining eggs into the parsnip purée and layer on top of the terrine.

Place the tin in a baking dish and pour in enough hot water to come halfway up the sides of the tin. Bake in the preheated oven for 1 hour until a skewer inserted into the centre comes out clean. Leave the terrine to cool for at least 30 minutes. Run a sharp knife around the edges. Turn out on to a dish and reserve.

Make the tomato coulis by simmering the tomatoes and onions together for 5–10 minutes until slightly thickened. Season to taste. Blend well in a liquidiser or food processor and serve as an accompaniment to the terrine. Garnish with sprigs of basil and serve with crusty bread.

## VEGETARIAN ALTERNATIVE
# Hot-&-Sour Mushroom Soup

INGREDIENTS **Serves 4**

4 tbsp sunflower oil
3 garlic cloves, peeled and finely chopped
3 shallots, peeled and finely chopped
2 large red chillies, deseeded and finely chopped
1 tbsp soft brown sugar
large pinch of salt
1 litre/1¾ pints vegetable stock
250 g/9 oz Thai fragrant rice
5 kaffir lime leaves, torn
2 tbsp soy sauce
grated rind and juice of 1 lemon
250 g/9 oz oyster mushrooms, wiped and cut into pieces
2 tbsp freshly chopped coriander

**To garnish:**
2 green chillies, deseeded and finely chopped
3 spring onions, trimmed and finely chopped

Heat the oil in a frying pan, add the garlic and shallots and cook until golden brown and starting to crisp. Remove from the pan and reserve. Add the chillies to the pan and cook until they start to change colour.

Place the garlic, shallots and chillies in a food processor or blender and blend to a smooth purée with 150 ml/¼ pint water. Pour the purée back into the pan, add the sugar with a large pinch of salt, then cook gently, stirring, until dark in colour. Take care not to burn the mixture.

Pour the stock into a large saucepan, add the garlic purée, rice, lime leaves, soy sauce and the lemon rind and juice. Bring to the boil, then reduce the heat, cover and simmer gently for about 10 minutes.

Add the mushrooms and simmer for a further 10 minutes, or until the mushrooms and rice are tender. Remove the lime leaves, stir in the chopped coriander and ladle into bowls. Place the chopped green chillies and spring onions in small bowls and serve separately to sprinkle on top of the soup.

## ENTERTAINING ALTERNATIVE
# Thai Hot-&-Sour Prawn Soup

INGREDIENTS **Serves 6**

700 g/1½ lb large raw prawns
2 tbsp vegetable oil
3–4 stalks lemon grass, outer leaves discarded and coarsely chopped
2.5 cm/1 inch piece fresh root ginger, peeled and finely chopped
2–3 garlic cloves, peeled and crushed
small bunch of fresh coriander, leaves stripped and reserved and stems finely chopped
½ tsp freshly ground black pepper
1.8 litres/3¼ pints water
1–2 small red chillies, deseeded and thinly sliced
1–2 small green chillies, deseeded and thinly sliced
6 kaffir lime leaves, thinly shredded
4 spring onions, trimmed and diagonally sliced
1–2 tbsp Thai fish sauce
1–2 tbsp freshly squeezed lime juice

Remove the heads from the prawns by twisting away from the body and reserve. Peel the prawns, leaving the tails on and reserve the shells with the heads. Using a sharp knife, remove the black vein from the back of the prawns. Rinse and dry the prawns and reserve. Rinse and dry the heads and shells.

Heat a wok, add the oil and, when hot, add the prawn heads and shells, the lemon grass, ginger, garlic, coriander stems and black pepper and stir-fry for 2–3 minutes, or until the prawn heads and shells turn pink and all the ingredients are coloured.

Carefully add the water to the wok and return to the boil, skimming off any scum which rises to the surface. Simmer over a medium heat for 10 minutes or until slightly reduced. Strain through a fine sieve and return the clear prawn stock to the wok.

Bring the stock back to the boil and add the reserved prawns, chillies, lime leaves and spring onions and simmer for 3 minutes, or until the prawns turn pink. Season with the fish sauce and lime juice. Spoon into heated soup bowls, dividing the prawns evenly and float a few coriander leaves over the surface.

# Hot-&-Sour Soup

INGREDIENTS **Serves 4–6**

25 g/1 oz dried Chinese (shiitake) mushrooms
2 tbsp groundnut oil
1 carrot, peeled and cut into julienne strips
125 g/4 oz chestnut mushrooms, wiped and thinly sliced
2 garlic cloves, peeled and finely chopped
½ tsp dried crushed chillies
1.1 litres/2 pints chicken stock
75 g/3 oz cooked boneless chicken or pork, shredded
125 g/4 oz fresh bean curd, thinly sliced, optional
2–3 spring onions, trimmed and finely sliced diagonally
1–2 tsp sugar
3 tbsp cider vinegar
2 tbsp soy sauce
salt and freshly ground black pepper
1 tbsp cornflour
1 large egg
2 tsp sesame oil
2 tbsp freshly chopped coriander

Place the dried Chinese (shiitake) mushrooms in a small bowl and pour over enough almost boiling water to cover. Leave for 20 minutes to soften, then gently lift out and squeeze out the liquid. (Lifting out the mushrooms leaves any sand and grit behind.) Discard the stems, thinly slice the caps and reserve.

Heat a large wok and add the oil. When hot, add the carrot strips and stir-fry for 2–3 minutes or until beginning to soften. Add the chestnut mushrooms and stir-fry for 2–3 minutes, or until golden, then stir in the garlic and chillies.

Add the chicken stock to the vegetables and bring to the boil, skimming off any foam which rises to the surface. Add the shredded chicken or pork, bean curd (if using), spring onions, sugar, vinegar, soy sauce and reserved Chinese mushrooms and simmer for 5 minutes, stirring occasionally. Season to taste with salt and pepper.

Blend the cornflour with 1 tablespoon of cold water to form a smooth paste and whisk into the soup. Return to the boil and simmer over a medium heat until thickened.

Beat the egg with the sesame oil and slowly add to the soup in a slow, steady stream, stirring constantly. Stir in the chopped coriander and serve immediately.

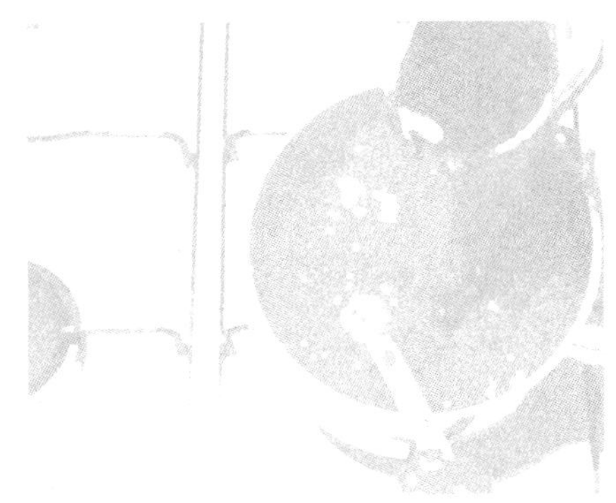

HEALTH RATING 🍎🍎🍎🍎

**VEGETARIAN ALTERNATIVE**
Hot-&-Sour Mushroom Soup

**ENTERTAINING ALTERNATIVE**
Thai Hot-&-Sour Prawn Soup

# Coconut Chicken Soup

INGREDIENTS **Serves 4**

2 lemon grass stalks
3 tbsp vegetable oil
3 medium onions, peeled and finely sliced
3 garlic cloves, peeled and crushed
2 tbsp fresh root ginger, finely grated
2–3 kaffir lime leaves
1½ tsp turmeric
1 red pepper, deseeded and diced
400 ml can coconut milk
1.1 litres/2 pints vegetable or chicken stock
275 g/9 oz easy-cook long-grain rice
275 g/10 oz cooked chicken meat
285 g can sweetcorn, drained
3 tbsp freshly chopped coriander
1 tbsp Thai fish sauce
freshly chopped pickled chillies, to serve

Discard the outer leaves of the lemon grass stalks, then place on a chopping board and, using a mallet or rolling pin, pound gently to bruise; reserve.

Heat the vegetable oil in a large saucepan and cook the onions over a medium heat for about 10–15 minutes until soft and beginning to change colour.

Lower the heat, stir in the garlic, ginger, lime leaves and turmeric and cook for 1 minute. Add the red pepper, coconut milk, stock, lemon grass and rice. Bring to the boil, cover and simmer gently over a low heat for about 10 minutes.

Cut the chicken into bite-sized pieces, then stir into the soup with the sweetcorn and the freshly chopped coriander. Add a few dashes of Thai fish sauce to taste, then reheat gently, stirring frequently. Serve immediately with a few chopped pickled chillies to sprinkle on top.

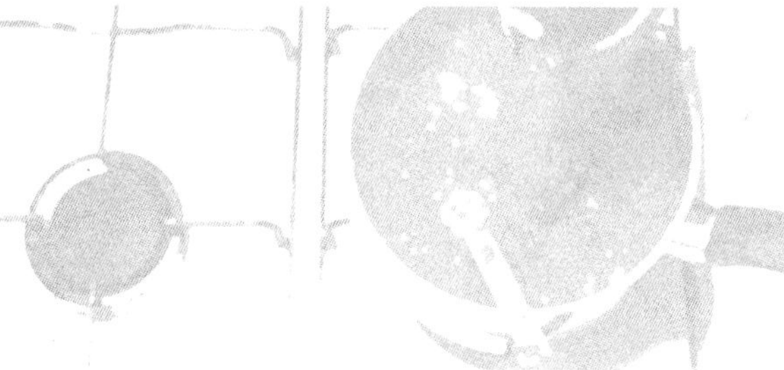

HEALTH RATING

**MILD ALTERNATIVE**
Creamy Chicken & Tofu Soup

**SUGGESTED ACCOMPANIMENT**
Rustic Country Bread

**MILD ALTERNATIVE**
## Creamy Chicken & Tofu Soup

Cut the tofu into 1 cm/½ inch cubes, then pat dry on absorbent kitchen paper. Heat 1 tablespoon of the oil in a nonstick frying pan. Fry the tofu in 2 batches for 3–4 minutes or until golden brown. Remove, drain on absorbent kitchen paper and reserve.

Heat the remaining oil in a large saucepan. Add the garlic, ginger, galangal and lemon grass and cook for about 30 seconds. Stir in the turmeric, then pour in the stock and coconut milk and bring to the boil. Reduce the heat to a gentle simmer, add the cauliflower and carrots and simmer for 10 minutes. Add the green beans and simmer for a further 5 minutes.

Meanwhile, bring a large saucepan of lightly salted water to the boil. Add the noodles, turn off the heat, cover and leave to cook, or cook according to the packet instructions.

Remove the lemon grass from the soup. Drain the noodles and stir into the soup with the chicken and browned tofu. Season to taste with salt and pepper, then simmer gently for 2–3 minutes or until heated through. Serve immediately in warmed soup bowls.

INGREDIENTS **Serves 4–6**

225 g/8 oz firm tofu, drained
3 tbsp groundnut oil
1 garlic clove, peeled and crushed
2.5 cm/1 inch piece root ginger, peeled and finely chopped
2.5 cm/1 inch piece fresh galangal, peeled and finely sliced (if available)
1 lemon grass stalk, bruised
¼ tsp ground turmeric
600 ml/1 pint chicken stock
600 ml/1 pint coconut milk
225 g/8 oz cauliflower, cut into tiny florets
1 medium carrot, peeled and cut into thin matchsticks
125 g/4 oz green beans, trimmed and cut in half
75 g/3 oz fine egg noodles
225 g/8 oz cooked chicken, shredded
salt and freshly ground black pepper

**SUGGESTED ACCOMPANIMENT**
## Rustic Country Bread

Preheat the oven to 220°C/425°F/Gas Mark 7, 15 minutes before baking. For the starter, sift the flour into a bowl. Stir in the yeast and make a well in the centre. Pour in the warm water and mix with a fork. Transfer to a saucepan, cover with a clean tea towel and leave for 2–3 days at room temperature. Stir the mixture and spray with a little water twice a day.

For the dough, mix the flours, salt, sugar and yeast in a bowl. Add 225 ml/8 fl oz of the starter, the oil and the warm water. Mix to a soft dough. Knead on a lightly floured surface for 10 minutes until smooth and elastic. Put in an oiled bowl, cover and leave to rise in a warm place for about 1½ hours, or until doubled in size.

Turn the dough out and knead for a minute or two. Shape into a round loaf and place on an oiled baking sheet. Cover with oiled clingfilm and leave to rise for 1 hour, or until doubled in size.

Dust the loaf with flour, then using a sharp knife make several slashes across the top of the loaf. Slash across the loaf in the opposite direction to make a square pattern. Bake in the preheated oven for 40–45 minutes, or until golden brown and hollow sounding when tapped underneath. Cool on a wire rack and serve.

INGREDIENTS **Makes 1 large loaf**

**Sourdough starter:**
225 g/8 oz strong white flour
2 tsp easy-blend dried yeast
300 ml/½ pint warm water

**Bread dough:**
350 g/12 oz strong white flour
25 g/1 oz rye flour
1½ tsp salt
½ tsp caster sugar
1 tsp dried yeast
1 tsp sunflower oil
175 ml/6 fl oz warm water

**To finish:**
2 tsp plain flour
2 tsp rye flour

# Vietnamese Beef & Rice Noodle Soup

INGREDIENTS **Serves 4–6**

**For the beef stock:**

900 g/2 lb meaty beef bones
1 large onion, peeled and quartered
2 carrots, peeled and cut into chunks
2 celery stalks, trimmed and sliced
1 leek, washed and sliced into chunks
2 garlic cloves, unpeeled and lightly crushed
3 whole star anise
1 tsp black peppercorns

**For the soup:**

175 g/6 oz dried rice stick noodles
4–6 spring onions, trimmed and diagonally sliced
1 red chilli, deseeded and diagonally sliced
1 small bunch fresh coriander
1 small bunch fresh mint
350 g/12 oz fillet steak, very thinly sliced
salt and freshly ground black pepper

Place all the ingredients for the beef stock into a large stock pot or saucepan and cover with cold water. Bring to the boil and skim off any scum that rises to the surface. Reduce the heat and simmer gently, partially covered, for 2–3 hours, skimming occasionally.

Strain into a large bowl and leave to cool, then skim off the fat. Chill in the refrigerator and when cold remove any fat from the surface. Pour 1.7 litres/3 pints of the stock into a large wok and reserve.

Cover the noodles with warm water and leave for 3 minutes, or until just softened. Drain, then cut into 10 cm/4 inch lengths.

Arrange the spring onions and chilli on a serving platter or large plate. Strip the leaves from the coriander and mint and arrange them in piles on the plate. These are to be added to personal taste once served.

Bring the stock in the wok to the boil over a high heat. Add the noodles and simmer for about 2 minutes, or until tender. Add the beef strips and simmer for about 1 minute. Season to taste with salt and pepper. Ladle the soup with the noodles and beef strips into individual soup bowls and serve immediately, each person adding their own spring onions, chilli and herbs to taste.

HEALTH RATING ● ● ● ●

**MILD ALTERNATIVE**

Chinese Leaf & Mushroom Soup

**SUGGESTED ACCOMPANIMENT**

Barbecue Pork Steamed Buns

INGREDIENTS **Serves 4–6**

450 g/1 lb Chinese leaves
25 g/1 oz dried Chinese (shiitake) mushrooms
1 tbsp vegetable oil
75 g/3 oz smoked streaky bacon, diced
2.5 cm/1 inch piece fresh root ginger, peeled and finely chopped
175 g/6 oz chestnut mushrooms, thinly sliced
1.1 litres/2 pints chicken stock
4–6 spring onions, trimmed and cut into short lengths
2 tbsp dry sherry or Chinese rice wine
salt and freshly ground black pepper
sesame oil for drizzling

**MILD ALTERNATIVE**

## Chinese Leaf & Mushroom Soup

Trim the stem ends of the Chinese leaves and cut in half lengthways. Remove the triangular core with a knife, then cut into 2.5 cm/1 inch slices and reserve.

Place the dried Chinese mushrooms in a bowl and pour over enough almost boiling water to cover. Leave to stand for 20 minutes to soften, then gently lift out and squeeze out the liquid. Discard the stems and thinly slice the caps and reserve. Strain the liquid through a muslin-lined sieve or a coffee filter paper and reserve.

Heat a wok over a medium-high heat, add the oil and when hot add the bacon. Stir-fry for 3–4 minutes, or until crisp and golden, stirring frequently. Add the ginger and chestnut mushrooms and stir-fry for a further 2–3 minutes. Add the chicken stock and bring to the boil, skimming any fat and scum that rises to the surface. Add the spring onions, sherry or rice wine, Chinese leaves, sliced Chinese mushrooms and season to taste with salt and pepper. Pour in the reserved soaking liquid and reduce the heat to the lowest possible setting.

Simmer gently, covered, until all the vegetables are very tender – this will take about 10 minutes. Add a little water if the liquid has reduced too much. Spoon into soup bowls and drizzle with a little sesame oil. Serve immediately.

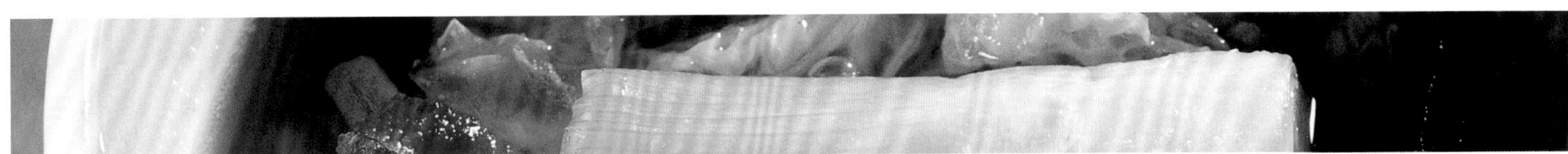

**SUGGESTED ACCOMPANIMENT**

## Barbecue Pork Steamed Buns

Put 75 g/3 oz of the flour in a bowl and stir in the yeast. Heat the milk, oil, sugar and salt in a small saucepan until warm, stirring until the sugar has dissolved. Pour into the bowl and, with an electric mixer, beat on a low speed for 30 seconds, scraping down the sides of the bowl, until blended. Beat at high speed for 3 minutes, then with a wooden spoon stir in as much of the remaining flour as possible until a stiff dough forms. Shape into a ball, place in a lightly oiled bowl, cover with clingfilm and leave for 1 hour in a warm place, or until doubled in size.

To make the filling, heat a wok, add the oil and when hot add the red pepper and garlic. Stir-fry for 4–5 minutes. Add the remaining ingredients and bring to the boil, stir-frying for 2–3 minutes until thick and syrupy. Cool and reserve.

Punch down the dough and turn onto a lightly floured surface. Divide into 12 pieces and shape them into balls, then cover and leave to rest for 5 minutes. Roll each ball to a 7.5 cm/3 inch circle. Place a heaped tablespoon of filling in the centre of each. Dampen the edges, then bring them up and around the filling, pinching together to seal. Place seam-side down on a small square of non-stick baking parchment. Continue with the remaining dough and filling. Leave to rise for 10 minutes.

Bring a large wok half-filled with water to the boil and place the buns in a lightly oiled Chinese steamer, without touching each other. Cover and steam for 20–25 minutes, then remove and cool slightly. Garnish with spring onion tassels and serve with salad leaves.

INGREDIENTS **Serves 12**

**For the buns:**

175–200 g/6–7 oz plain flour
1 tbsp dried yeast
125 ml/4 fl oz milk
2 tbsp sunflower oil
1 tbsp sugar
½ tsp salt
spring onion tassels, to garnish
fresh green salad leaves, to serve

**For the filling:**

2 tbsp vegetable oil
1 small red pepper, deseeded and finely chopped
2 garlic cloves, peeled and finely chopped
225 g/8 oz cooked pork, finely chopped
50 g/2 oz light brown sugar
50 ml/2 fl oz tomato ketchup
1–2 tsp hot chilli powder, or to taste

# Spring Rolls

INGREDIENTS **Makes 26–30 rolls**

**For the filling:**

15 g/½ oz dried Chinese (shiitake) mushrooms
50 g/2 oz rice vermicelli
1–2 tbsp groundnut oil
1 small onion, peeled and finely chopped
3–4 garlic cloves, peeled and finely chopped
4 cm/1½ inch piece fresh root ginger, peeled and chopped
225 g/8 oz fresh pork mince
2 spring onions, trimmed and finely chopped
75 g/3 oz beansprouts
4 water chestnuts, chopped
2 tbsp freshly snipped chives
175 g/6 oz cooked peeled prawns, chopped
1 tsp oyster sauce
1 tsp soy sauce
salt and freshly ground black pepper
spring onion tassels, to garnish

**For the wrappers:**

4–5 tbsp plain flour
26–30 spring roll wrappers
300 ml/½ pint vegetable oil for deep frying

Soak the Chinese mushrooms in almost boiling water for 20 minutes. Remove and squeeze out the liquid. Discard any stems, slice and reserve. Soak the rice vermicelli as per packet instructions.

Heat a large wok and when hot, add the oil. Heat, then add the onion, garlic and ginger and stir-fry for 2 minutes. Add the pork, spring onions and Chinese mushrooms and stir-fry for 4 minutes. Stir in the beansprouts, water chestnuts, chives, prawns and oyster and soy sauces. Season to taste with salt and pepper and spoon into a bowl. Drain the noodles well, add to the bowl and toss until well mixed, then leave to cool.

Blend the flour to a smooth paste with 3–4 tablespoons of water. Soften a wrapper in a plate of warm water for 1–2 seconds, then drain. Put 2 tablespoons of the filling near one edge of the wrapper, fold the edge over the filling, then fold in each side and roll up. Seal with a little flour paste and transfer to a baking sheet, seam-side down. Repeat with the remaining wrappers.

Heat the oil in a large wok to 190°C/375°F, or until a cube of bread browns in 30 seconds. Fry the spring rolls a few at a time, until golden. Remove and drain on absorbent kitchen paper. Arrange on a serving plate and garnish with spring onion tassels. Serve immediately.

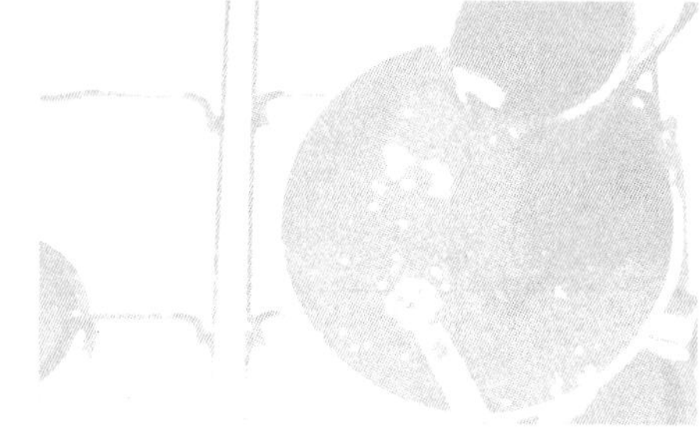

HEALTH RATING

**ENTERTAINING ALTERNATIVE**
Chicken-filled Spring Rolls

**VEGETARIAN ALTERNATIVE**
Vegetable Thai Spring Rolls

**ENTERTAINING ALTERNATIVE**
## Chicken-filled Spring Rolls

INGREDIENTS **Serves 12–14 rolls**

**For the filling:**
1 tbsp vegetable oil
2 slices streaky bacon, diced
225 g/8 oz skinless chicken breast fillets, thinly sliced
1 small red pepper, deseeded and finely chopped
4 spring onions, trimmed and finely chopped
2.5 cm/1 inch piece fresh root ginger, peeled and finely chopped
75 g/3 oz mangetout, thinly sliced
75 g/3 oz beansprouts
1 tbsp soy sauce
2 tsp Chinese rice wine or dry sherry
2 tsp hoisin or plum sauce

**For the wrappers:**
3 tbsp plain flour
12–14 spring roll wrappers
300 ml/½ pint vegetable oil for deep frying
shredded spring onions, to garnish
dipping sauce, to serve

Heat a large wok, add the oil and when hot add the diced bacon and stir-fry for 2–3 minutes, or until golden. Add the chicken and pepper and stir-fry for a further 2–3 minutes. Add the remaining filling ingredients and stir-fry for 3–4 minutes until all the vegetables are tender. Turn into a colander and leave to drain as the mixture cools completely.

Blend the flour with about 1½ tablespoons of water to form a paste. Soften each wrapper in a plate of warm water for 1–2 seconds, then place on a chopping board. Put 2–3 tablespoons of filling on the near edge. Fold the edge over the filling to cover, then fold in each side and roll up. Seal the edge with a little flour paste and press to seal securely. Transfer to a baking sheet, seam-side down.

Heat the oil in a large wok to 190°C/375°F, or until a small cube of bread browns in about 30 seconds. Working in batches of 3–4, fry the spring rolls until they are crisp and golden, turning once (this should take about 2 minutes). Remove and drain on absorbent kitchen paper. Arrange the spring rolls on a serving plate, garnish with spring onion tassels and serve hot with dipping sauce.

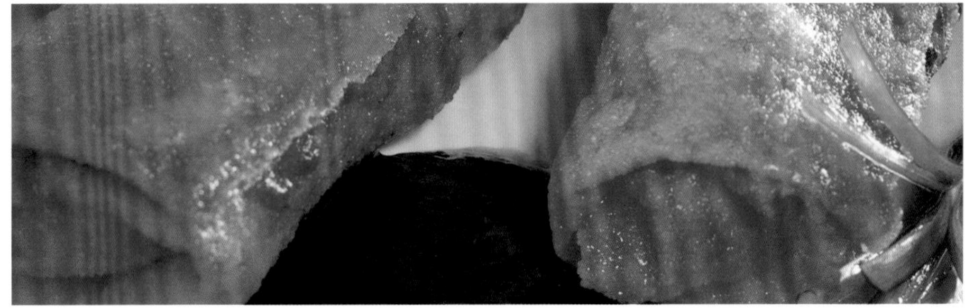

**VEGETARIAN ALTERNATIVE**
## Vegetable Thai Spring Rolls

INGREDIENTS **Serves 4**

50 g/2 oz cellophane vermicelli
4 dried Chinese (shiitake) mushrooms
1 tbsp groundnut oil
2 medium carrots, peeled and cut into fine matchsticks
125 g/4 oz mangetout, cut lengthways into fine strips
3 spring onions, trimmed and chopped
125 g/4 oz canned bamboo shoots, cut into fine matchsticks
1 cm/½ inch piece fresh root ginger, peeled and grated
1 tbsp light soy sauce
1 medium egg, separated
salt and freshly ground black pepper
20 spring roll wrappers, each about 12.5 cm/5 inch square
vegetable oil for deep-frying
spring onion tassels, to garnish

Place the vermicelli in a bowl and pour over enough boiling water to cover. Leave to soak for 5 minutes or until softened, then drain. Cut into 7.5 cm/3 inch lengths. Soak the shiitake mushrooms in almost boiling water for 15 minutes, drain, discard the stalks and slice thinly.

Heat a wok or large frying pan, add the groundnut oil and when hot, add the carrots and stir-fry for 1 minute. Add the mangetout and spring onions and stir-fry for 2–3 minutes or until tender. Tip the vegetables into a bowl and leave to cool.

Stir the vermicelli and shiitake mushrooms into the cooled vegetables with the bamboo shoots, ginger, soy sauce and egg yolk. Season to taste with salt and pepper and mix thoroughly.

Brush the edges of a spring roll wrapper with a little beaten egg white. Spoon 2 teaspoons of the vegetable filling on to the wrapper, in a 7.5 cm/3 inch log shape 2.5 cm/1 inch from one edge. Fold the wrapper edge over the filling, then fold in the right and left sides. Brush the folded edges with more egg white and roll up neatly. Place on an oiled baking sheet, seam-side down and make the rest of the spring rolls.

Heat the oil in a heavy-based saucepan or deep-fat fryer to 180°C/350°F. Deep-fry the spring rolls, six at a time for 2–3 minutes, or until golden brown and crisp. Drain on absorbent kitchen paper and arrange on a warmed platter. Garnish with spring onion tassels and serve immediately.

# Crostini with Chicken Livers

INGREDIENTS **Serves 4**

2 tbsp olive oil
2 tbsp butter
1 shallot, peeled and finely chopped
1 garlic clove, peeled and crushed
150 g/5 oz chicken livers
1 tbsp plain flour
2 tbsp dry white wine
1 tbsp brandy
50 g/2 oz mushrooms, sliced
salt and freshly ground black pepper
4 slices of ciabatta or similar bread

**To garnish:**
fresh sage leaves
lemon wedges

Heat 1 tablespoon of the olive oil and 1 tablespoon of the butter in a frying pan, add the shallot and garlic and cook gently for 2–3 minutes.

Trim and wash the chicken livers thoroughly and pat dry on absorbent kitchen paper as much as possible. Cut into slices, then toss in the flour. Add the livers to the frying pan with the shallot and garlic and continue to fry for a further 2 minutes, stirring continuously.

Pour in the white wine and brandy and bring to the boil. Boil rapidly for 1–2 minutes to allow the alcohol to evaporate, then stir in the sliced mushrooms and cook gently for about 5 minutes, or until the chicken livers are cooked, but just a little pink inside. Season to taste with salt and pepper.

Fry the slices of ciabatta or similar-style bread in the remaining oil and butter, then place on individual serving dishes. Spoon over the liver mixture and garnish with a few sage leaves and lemon wedges. Serve immediately.

HEALTH RATING

**SPEEDY ALTERNATIVE**

Bruschetta with Pecorino, Garlic & Tomatoes

**VEGETARIAN ALTERNATIVE**

Mozzarella Frittata with Tomato & Basil Salad

**SPEEDY ALTERNATIVE**
## Bruschetta with Pecorino, Garlic & Tomatoes

Preheat grill and line the grill rack with tinfoil just before cooking. Make a small cross in the top of the tomatoes, then place in a small bowl and cover with boiling water. Leave to stand for 2 minutes, then drain and remove the skins. Cut into quarters, remove the seeds, and chop the flesh into small cubes.

Mix the tomato flesh with the pecorino cheese and 2 teaspoons of the fresh oregano and season to taste with salt and pepper. Add 1 tablespoon of the olive oil and mix thoroughly.

Crush the garlic and spread evenly over the slices of bread. Heat 2 tablespoons of the olive oil in a large frying pan and sauté the bread slices until they are crisp and golden.

Place the fried bread on a lightly oiled baking tray and spoon on the tomato and cheese topping. Place a little mozzarella on top and place under the preheated grill for 3–4 minutes, until golden and bubbling. Garnish with the remaining oregano, then arrange the bruschettas on a serving plate and serve immediately with the olives.

INGREDIENTS **Serves 4**

6 ripe but firm tomatoes
125 g/4 oz pecorino cheese, finely grated
1 tbsp oregano leaves, chopped
salt and freshly ground black pepper
3 tbsp olive oil
3 garlic cloves, peeled
8 slices of flat Italian bread, such as focaccia
50 g/2 oz mozzarella cheese
marinated black olives, to serve

**VEGETARIAN ALTERNATIVE**
## Mozzarella Frittata with Tomato & Basil Salad

To make the tomato and basil salad, slice the tomatoes very thinly, tear up the basil leaves and sprinkle over. Make the dressing by whisking the olive oil, lemon juice and sugar together well. Season with black pepper before drizzling the dressing over the salad.

To make the frittata, preheat the grill to a high heat, just before beginning to cook. Place the eggs in a large bowl with plenty of salt and whisk. Grate the mozzarella and stir into the egg with the finely chopped spring onions.

Heat the oil in a large, non-stick frying pan and pour in the egg mixture, stirring with a wooden spoon to spread the ingredients evenly over the pan.

Cook for 5–8 minutes, until the frittata is golden brown and firm on the underside. Place the whole pan under the preheated grill and cook for about 4–5 minutes, or until the top is golden brown. Slide the frittata on to a serving plate, cut into six large wedges and serve immediately with the tomato and basil salad and plenty of warm crusty bread.

INGREDIENTS **Serves 6**

**For the salad:**
6 ripe but firm tomatoes
2 tbsp fresh basil leaves
2 tbsp olive oil
1 tbsp fresh lemon juice
1 tsp caster sugar
freshly ground black pepper

**For the frittata:**
7 medium eggs, beaten
salt
300 g/11 oz mozzarella cheese
2 spring onions, trimmed and finely chopped
2 tbsp olive oil
warm crusty bread, to serve

**LOW FAT ALTERNATIVE**
## Hot Herby Mushrooms

INGREDIENTS **Serves 4**

4 thin slices of white bread, crusts removed
125 g/4 oz chestnut mushrooms, wiped and sliced
125 g/4 oz oyster mushrooms, wiped
1 garlic clove, peeled and crushed
1 tsp Dijon mustard
300 ml/½ pint chicken stock
salt and freshly ground black pepper
1 tbsp freshly chopped parsley
1 tbsp freshly snipped chives, plus extra to garnish
mixed salad leaves, to serve

Preheat the oven to 180°C/350°F/Gas Mark 4. With a rolling pin, roll each piece of bread out as thinly as possible. Press each piece of bread into a 10 cm/4 inch tartlet tin. Push each piece firmly down, then bake in the preheated oven for 20 minutes.

Place the mushrooms in a frying pan with the garlic, mustard and chicken stock and stir-fry over a moderate heat until the mushrooms are tender and the liquid is reduced by half.

Carefully remove the mushrooms from the frying pan with a slotted spoon and transfer to a heat-resistant dish. Cover with tinfoil and place in the bottom of the oven to keep the mushrooms warm.

Boil the remaining pan juices until reduced to a thick sauce. Season with salt and pepper. Stir the parsley and the chives into the mushrooms.

Place one bread tartlet case on each plate and divide the mushroom mixture between them. Spoon over the pan juices, garnish with the chives and serve immediately with mixed salad leaves.

**ENTERTAINING ALTERNATIVE**
## Garlic Wild Mushroom Galettes

INGREDIENTS **Serves 4**

1 quantity quick flaky pastry (see French Onion Tart, page 234), chilled
1 onion, peeled
1 red chilli, deseeded
2 garlic cloves, peeled
275 g/10 oz mixed mushrooms, e.g. oysters, chestnuts, morels, ceps and chanterelles
25 g/1 oz butter
2 tbsp freshly chopped parsley
125 g/4 oz mozzarella cheese, sliced

**To serve:**
cherry tomatoes
mixed green salad leaves

Preheat the oven to 220°C/425°F/Gas Mark 7. On a lightly floured surface roll out the chilled pastry very thinly. Cut out 6 x 15 cm/6 inch circles and place on a lightly oiled baking sheet.

Thinly slice the onion, then divide into rings and reserve. Thinly slice the chilli and slice the garlic into wafer-thin slivers. Add to the onions and reserve.

Wipe or lightly rinse the mushrooms. Half or quarter any large mushrooms and keep the small ones whole. Heat the butter in a frying pan and sauté the onion, chilli and garlic gently for about 3 minutes. Add the mushrooms and cook for about 5 minutes, or until beginning to soften.

Stir the parsley into the mushroom mixture and drain off any excess liquid. Pile the mushroom mixture on to the pastry circles within 5 mm/¼ inch of the edges. Arrange the sliced mozzarella cheese on top. Bake in the preheated oven for 12–15 minutes or until golden brown and serve with the tomatoes and salad.

# Wild Garlic Mushrooms with Pizza Breadsticks

INGREDIENTS **Serves 6**

**For the breadsticks:**

7 g/¼ oz dried yeast

250 ml/8 fl oz warm water

400 g/14 oz strong, plain flour

2 tbsp olive oil

1 tsp salt

**For the mushrooms:**

9 tbsp olive oil

4 garlic cloves, peeled and crushed

450 g/1 lb mixed wild mushrooms, wiped and dried

salt and freshly ground black pepper

1 tbsp freshly chopped parsley

1 tbsp freshly chopped basil

1 tsp fresh oregano leaves

juice of 1 lemon

Preheat the oven to 240°C/475°F/Gas Mark 9, 15 minutes before baking. Place the dried yeast in the warm water for 10 minutes. Place the flour in a large bowl and gradually blend in the olive oil, salt and the dissolved yeast.

Knead on a lightly floured surface to form a smooth and pliable dough. Cover with clingfilm and leave in a warm place for 15 minutes to allow the dough to rise, then roll out again and cut into sticks of equal length. Cover and leave to rise again for 10 minutes. Brush with the olive oil, sprinkle with salt and bake in the preheated oven for 10 minutes.

Pour 3 tablespoons of the oil into a frying pan and add the crushed garlic. Cook over a very low heat, stirring well for 3–4 minutes to flavour the oil.

Cut the wild mushrooms into bite-sized slices if very large, then add to the pan. Season well with salt and pepper and cook very gently for 6–8 minutes, or until tender.

Whisk the fresh herbs, the remaining olive oil and lemon juice together. Pour over the mushrooms and heat through. Season to taste and place on individual serving dishes. Serve with the pizza breadsticks.

HEALTH RATING 

**LOW FAT ALTERNATIVE**

Hot Herby Mushrooms

**ENTERTAINING ALTERNATIVE**

Garlic Wild Mushroom Galettes

# Mushroom & Red Wine Pâté

INGREDIENTS **Serves 4**

3 large slices of white bread, crusts removed
2 tsp oil
1 small onion, peeled and finely chopped
1 garlic clove, peeled and crushed
350 g/12 oz button mushrooms, wiped and finely chopped
150 ml/¼ pint red wine
½ tsp dried mixed herbs
1 tbsp freshly chopped parsley
salt and freshly ground black pepper
2 tbsp low-fat cream cheese

**To serve:**
finely chopped cucumber
finely chopped tomato

Preheat the oven to 180°C/350°F/Gas Mark 4. Cut the bread in half diagonally. Place the bread triangles on a baking tray and cook for 10 minutes.

Remove from the oven and split each bread triangle in half to make 12 triangles and return to the oven until golden and crisp. Leave to cool on a wire rack.

Heat the oil in a saucepan and gently cook the onion and garlic until transparent.

Add the mushrooms and cook, stirring for 3–4 minutes or until the mushroom juices start to run.

Stir the wine and herbs into the mushroom mixture and bring to the boil. Reduce the heat and simmer uncovered until all the liquid is absorbed. Remove from the heat and season to taste with salt and pepper. Leave to cool.

When cold, beat in the soft cream cheese and adjust the seasoning. Place in a small clean bowl and chill until required. Serve the toast triangles with the cucumber and tomato.

HEALTH RATING 🍎🍎🍎🍎

**LOW FAT ALTERNATIVE**
Aubergine Dip with Pitta Strips

**CHILDREN'S ALTERNATIVE**
Potato Skins

## LOW FAT ALTERNATIVE
## Aubergine Dip with Pitta Strips

Preheat the oven to 180°C/350°F/Gas Mark 4. On a chopping board cut the pitta breads into strips. Spread the bread in a single layer on to a large baking tray. Cook in the preheated oven for 15 minutes until golden and crisp. Leave to cool on a wire cooling rack.

Trim the aubergines, rinse lightly and reserve. Heat a griddle pan until almost smoking. Cook the aubergines and garlic for about 15 minutes. Turn the aubergines frequently, until very tender with wrinkled and charred skins. Remove from heat and leave to cool.

When the aubergines are cool enough to handle, cut in half and scoop out the cooked flesh and place in a food processor. Squeeze the softened garlic flesh from the papery skin and add to the aubergine.

Blend the aubergine and garlic until smooth, then add the sesame oil, lemon juice and cumin and blend again to mix. Season to taste with salt and pepper, stir in the parsley and serve with the pitta strips and mixed salad leaves.

INGREDIENTS **Serves 4**

4 pitta breads
2 large aubergines
1 garlic clove, peeled
¼ tsp sesame oil
1 tbsp lemon juice
½ tsp ground cumin
salt and freshly ground black pepper
2 tbsp freshly chopped parsley
fresh salad leaves, to serve

## CHILDREN'S ALTERNATIVE
## Potato Skins

Preheat the oven to 200°C/400°F/Gas Mark 6. Scrub the potatoes, then prick a few times with a fork or skewer and place directly on the top shelf of the oven. Bake in the preheated oven for at least 1 hour, or until tender. The potatoes are cooked when they yield gently to the pressure of your hand.

Set the potatoes aside until cool enough to handle, then cut in half and scoop the flesh into a bowl and reserve. Preheat the grill and line the grill rack with tinfoil.

Mix together the oil and the paprika and use half to brush the outside of the potato skins. Place on the grill rack under the preheated hot grill and cook for 5 minutes or until crisp, turning as necessary.

Heat the remaining paprika-flavoured oil and gently fry the pancetta until crisp. Add to the potato flesh along with the cream, Gorgonzola cheese and parsley. Halve the potato skins and fill with the Gorgonzola filling. Return to the oven for a further 15 minutes to heat through. Sprinkle with a little more paprika and serve immediately with mayonnaise, sweet chilli sauce and a green salad.

INGREDIENTS **Serves 4**

4 large baking potatoes
2 tbsp olive oil
2 tsp paprika
125 g/4 oz pancetta, roughly chopped
6 tbsp double cream
125 g/4 oz Gorgonzola cheese
1 tbsp freshly chopped parsley

**To serve:**
mayonnaise
sweet chilli dipping sauce
tossed green salad

# Thai Fish Cakes

INGREDIENTS **Serves 4**

1 red chilli, deseeded and roughly chopped
4 tbsp roughly chopped fresh coriander
1 garlic clove, peeled and crushed
2 spring onions, trimmed and roughly chopped
1 lemon grass, outer leaves discarded and roughly chopped
75 g/3 oz prawns, thawed if frozen
275 g/10 oz cod fillet, skinned, pin bones removed and cubed
salt and freshly ground black pepper
sweet chilli dipping sauce, to serve

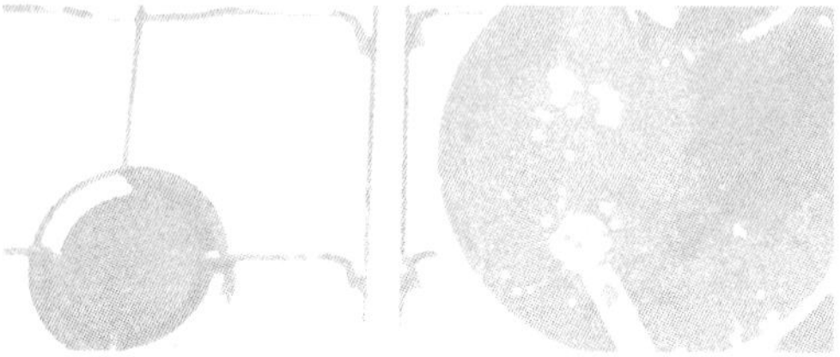

Preheat the oven to 190°C/375°F/Gas Mark 5. Place the chilli, coriander, garlic, spring onions and lemon grass in a food processor and blend together.

Pat the prawns and cod dry with kitchen paper.

Add to the food processor and blend until the mixture is roughly chopped.

Season to taste with salt and pepper and blend to mix.

Dampen your hands, then shape heaped tablespoons of the mixture into 12 small patties.

Place the patties on a lightly oiled baking sheet and cook in the preheated oven for 12–15 minutes or until piping hot and cooked through. Turn the patties over halfway through the cooking time.

Serve the fish cakes immediately with the sweet chilli sauce for dipping.

HEALTH RATING ●●●●●

**MILD ALTERNATIVE**
Sesame Prawn Toasts

**ENTERTAINING ALTERNATIVE**
Smoked Mackerel Vol-au-Vents

## MILD ALTERNATIVE
## Sesame Prawn Toasts

INGREDIENTS **Serves 4**

125 g/4 oz peeled cooked prawns
1 tbsp cornflour
2 spring onions, peeled and roughly chopped
2 tsp freshly grated root ginger
2 tsp dark soy sauce
pinch of Chinese five spice powder
1 small egg, beaten
salt and freshly ground black pepper
6 thin slices day-old white bread
40 g/1½ oz sesame seeds
vegetable oil for deep-frying
chilli sauce, to serve (optional)

Place the prawns in a food processor or blender with the cornflour, spring onions, ginger, soy sauce and Chinese five spice powder, if using. Blend to a fairly smooth paste. Spoon into a bowl and stir in the beaten egg. Season to taste with salt and pepper.

Cut the crusts off the bread. Spread the prawn paste in an even layer on one side of each slice. Sprinkle over the sesame seeds and press down lightly. Cut each slice diagonally into 4 triangles, then place on a board and chill in the refrigerator for 30 minutes.

Pour sufficient oil into a heavy-based saucepan or deep-fat fryer so that it is one-third full. Heat until it reaches a temperature of 180°C/350°F. Cook the toasts in batches of 5 or 6, carefully lowering them seeded-side down into the oil. Deep-fry for 2–3 minutes, or until lightly browned, then turn over and cook for 1 minute more. Using a slotted spoon, lift out the toasts and drain on absorbent kitchen paper. Keep warm while frying the remaining toasts. Arrange on a warmed platter and serve immediately with some chilli sauce for dipping.

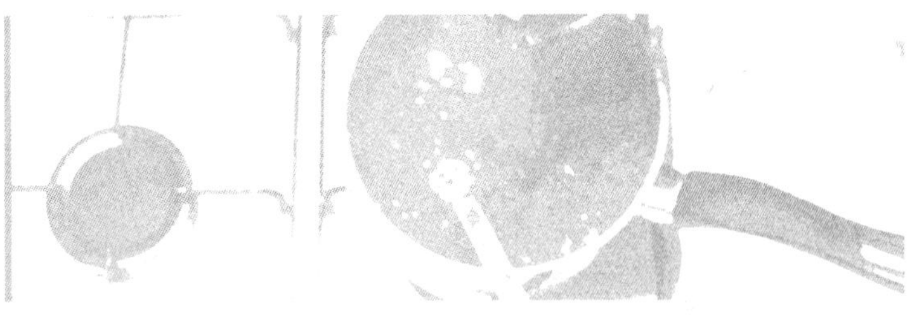

## ENTERTAINING ALTERNATIVE
## Smoked Mackerel Vol-au-Vents

INGREDIENTS **Serves 1–2**

350 g/12 oz prepared puff pastry
1 small egg, beaten
2 tsp sesame seeds
225 g/8 oz peppered smoked mackerel, skinned and chopped
5 cm/2 inch piece cucumber
4 tbsp soft cream cheese
2 tbsp cranberry sauce
1 tbsp freshly chopped dill
1 tbsp finely grated lemon rind
dill sprigs, to garnish
mixed salad leaves, to serve

Preheat the oven to 230°C/450°F/Gas Mark 8. Roll the pastry out on a lightly floured surface and using a 9 cm/3½ inch fluted cutter cut out 12 rounds.

Using a 1 cm/½ inch cutter mark a lid in the centre of each round. Place on a damp baking sheet and brush the rounds with a little beaten egg. Sprinkle the pastry with the sesame seeds and bake in the preheated oven for 10–12 minutes, or until golden brown and well risen.

Transfer the vol-au-vents to a chopping board and, when cool enough to touch, carefully remove the lids with a small sharp knife. Scoop out any uncooked pastry from the inside of each vol-au-vent, then return to the oven for 5–8 minutes to dry out. Remove and allow to cool.

Flake the mackerel into small pieces and reserve. Peel the cucumber if desired, cut into very small cubes and add to the mackerel. Beat the soft cream cheese with the cranberry sauce, dill and lemon rind. Stir in the mackerel and cucumber and use to fill the vol-au-vents. Place the lids on top, garnish with dill sprigs and serve with mixed salad leaves.

# Fish & Shellfish

The beauty of cooking with fish is that very little needs to be done to it to create a simple, healthy, delicious meal. Even the fussiest eater will love these recipes, which include everything from a basic fish casserole and fish cakes to meals for more sophisticated tastes. You can cater for everyone with these mouthwatering, yet straightforward, recipes.

3.07
2.35
2.20
1.82
2.10
Marina

# Smoked Haddock Kedgeree

INGREDIENTS **Serves 4**

450 g/1 lb smoked haddock fillets
50 g/2 oz butter
1 onion, peeled and finely chopped
2 tsp mild curry powder
175 g/6 oz long-grain rice
450 ml/¾ pint fish or vegetable stock, heated
2 large eggs, hard-boiled and shelled
2 tbsp freshly chopped parsley
2 tbsp whipping cream (optional)
salt and freshly ground black pepper
pinch of cayenne pepper

Place the haddock in a shallow frying pan and cover with 300 ml/½ pint water. Simmer gently for 8–10 minutes, or until the fish is cooked. Drain, then remove all the skin and bones from the fish and flake into a dish. Keep warm.

Melt the butter in a saucepan and add the chopped onion and curry powder. Cook, stirring, for 3–4 minutes or until the onion is soft, then stir in the rice. Cook for a further minute, stirring continuously, then stir in the hot stock.

Cover and simmer gently for 15 minutes, or until the rice has absorbed all the liquid. Cut the eggs into quarters or eighths and add half to the mixture with half the parsley.

Carefully fold in the cooked fish to the mixture and add the cream, if using. Season to taste with salt and pepper. Heat the kedgeree through briefly until piping hot.

Transfer the mixture to a large dish and garnish with the remaining quartered eggs and parsley and serve with a pinch of cayenne pepper. Serve immediately.

HEALTH RATING

**LOW FAT ALTERNATIVE**
Smoked Haddock Rosti

**SUGGESTED ACCOMPANIMENT**
Mixed Salad with Anchovy Dressing & Ciabatta Croûtons

**LOW FAT ALTERNATIVE**

## Smoked Haddock Rosti

Dry the grated potatoes in a clean tea towel. Rinse the grated onion thoroughly in cold water, dry in a clean tea towel and place in a bowl with the potatoes. Add the garlic and stir. Skin the smoked haddock and remove as many of the tiny pin bones as possible. Cut into thin slices and reserve.

Heat the oil in a non-stick frying pan. Add half the potatoes and press down firmly in the frying pan. Season to taste with salt and pepper.

Add a layer of fish and a sprinkling of lemon rind, parsley and a little black pepper. Top with the remaining potatoes and press down firmly. Cover with a sheet of tinfoil and cook on the lowest heat for 25–30 minutes.

Preheat the grill 2–3 minutes before the end of the cooking time. Remove the tinfoil and place the rosti under the grill to brown. Turn out on to a warmed serving dish, and serve immediately with spoonfuls of crème fraîche, lemon wedges and mixed salad leaves.

INGREDIENTS **Serves 4**

450 g/1 lb potatoes, peeled and coarsely grated

1 large onion, peeled and coarsely grated

2–3 garlic cloves, peeled and crushed

450 g/1 lb smoked haddock

1 tbsp olive oil

salt and freshly ground black pepper

finely grated rind of ½ lemon

1 tbsp freshly chopped parsley

2 tbsp half-fat crème fraîche

mixed salad leaves, to garnish

lemon wedges, to serve

**SUGGESTED ACCOMPANIMENT**

## Mixed Salad with Anchovy Dressing & Ciabatta Croûtons

Divide the endive and chicory into leaves and reserve some of the larger ones. Arrange the smaller leaves in a wide salad bowl.

Cut the fennel bulb in half from the stalk to the root end, then cut across in fine slices. Quarter the artichokes, then quarter and slice the cucumber and halve the tomatoes. Add to the salad bowl with the olives.

To make the dressing, drain the anchovies and put in a blender with the mustard, garlic, olive oil, lemon juice, 2 tablespoons of hot water and black pepper. Whizz together until smooth and thickened.

To make the croûtons, cut the bread into 1 cm/½ inch cubes. Heat the oil in a frying pan, add the bread cubes and fry for 3 minutes, turning frequently until golden. Remove and drain on absorbent kitchen paper.

Drizzle half the anchovy dressing over the prepared salad and toss to coat. Arrange the reserved endive and chicory leaves around the edge, then drizzle over the remaining dressing. Scatter over the croûtons and serve immediately.

INGREDIENTS **Serves 4**

1 small head endive

1 small head chicory

1 fennel bulb

400 g can artichokes, drained and rinsed

½ cucumber

125 g/4 oz cherry tomatoes

75 g/3 oz black olives

**For the anchovy dressing:**

50 g can anchovy fillets

1 tsp Dijon mustard

1 small garlic clove, peeled and crushed

4 tbsp olive oil

1 tbsp lemon juice

freshly ground black pepper

**For the ciabatta croûtons:**

2 thick slices ciabatta bread

2 tbsp olive oil

**BUDGET ALTERNATIVE**
## Gingered Cod Steaks

INGREDIENTS **Serves 4**

2.5 cm /1 inch piece fresh root ginger, peeled

4 spring onions

2 tsp freshly chopped parsley

1 tbsp soft brown sugar

4 x 175 g /6 oz thick cod steaks

salt and freshly ground black pepper

25 g/1 oz butter

freshly cooked vegetables, to serve

Preheat the grill and line the grill rack with a layer of tinfoil. Coarsely grate the piece of ginger. Trim the spring onions and cut into thin strips. Mix the spring onions, ginger, chopped parsley and sugar. Add 1 tablespoon of water.

Wipe the fish steaks. Season to taste with salt and pepper. Place onto four separate 20.5 x 20.5 cm/ 8 x 8 inch tinfoil squares. Carefully spoon the spring onions and ginger mixture over the fish.

Cut the butter into small cubes and place over the fish. Loosely fold the foil over the steaks to enclose the fish and to make a parcel. Place under the preheated grill and cook for 10–12 minutes or until the fish is cooked and the flesh has turned opaque.

Place the fish parcels on individual serving plates. Serve immediately with the freshly cooked vegetables.

**SUGGESTED ACCOMPANIMENT**
## Royal Fried Rice

INGREDIENTS **Serves 4**

450 g/1 lb Thai fragrant rice

2 large eggs

2 tsp sesame oil

salt and freshly ground black pepper

3 tbsp vegetable oil

1 red pepper, deseeded and finely diced

1 yellow pepper, deseeded and finely diced

1 green pepper, deseeded and finely diced

2 red onions, peeled and diced

125 g/4 oz sweetcorn kernels

125 g/4 oz cooked peeled prawns, thawed if frozen

125 g/4 oz white crabmeat, drained if canned

¼ tsp sugar

2 tsp light soy sauce

**To garnish:**

radish roses

freshly snipped and whole chives

Place the rice in a sieve, rinse with cold water, then drain. Place in a saucepan and add twice the volume of water, stirring briefly. Bring to the boil, cover and simmer gently for 15 minutes without further stirring. If the rice has fully absorbed the water while covered, add a little more water. Continue to simmer, uncovered, for another 5 minutes, or until the rice is fully cooked and the water has evaporated. Leave to cool.

Place the eggs, sesame oil and a pinch of salt in a small bowl. Using a fork, mix just to break the egg. Reserve.

Heat a wok and add 1 tablespoon of the vegetable oil. When very hot, stir-fry the peppers, onion and sweetcorn for 2 minutes or until the onion is soft. Remove the vegetables and reserve.

Clean the wok and add the remaining oil. When very hot, add the cold cooked rice and stir-fry for 3 minutes, or until it is heated through. Drizzle in the egg mixture and continue to stir-fry for 2–3 minutes or until the eggs have set.

Add the prawns and crabmeat to the rice. Stir-fry for 1 minute. Season to taste with salt and pepper and add the sugar with the soy sauce. Stir to mix and spoon into a warmed serving dish. Garnish with a radish flower and sprinkle with freshly snipped and whole chives. Serve immediately.

# Steamed Whole Trout with Ginger & Spring Onion

INGREDIENTS **Serves 4**

2 x 700 g/1½ lb whole trout, gutted with heads removed
coarse sea salt
2 tbsp groundnut oil
½ tbsp soy sauce
1 tbsp sesame oil
2 garlic cloves, peeled and thinly sliced
2.5 cm/1 inch piece fresh root ginger, peeled and thinly slivered
2 spring onions, trimmed and thinly sliced diagonally

**To garnish:**
fresh chives
lemon slices

**To serve:**
freshly cooked rice
Oriental salad

Wipe the fish inside and out with absorbent kitchen paper then rub with salt inside and out and leave for about 20 minutes. Pat dry with absorbent kitchen paper.

Set a steamer rack or inverted ramekin in a large wok and pour in enough water to come about 5 cm/2 inches up the side of the wok. Bring to the boil.

Brush a heatproof dinner plate with a little of the groundnut oil and place the fish on the plate with the tails pointing in opposite directions. Place the plate on the rack, cover tightly and simmer over a medium heat for 10–12 minutes, or until tender and the flesh is opaque near the bone. Carefully transfer the plate to a heatproof surface and divide the fish into four servings. Sprinkle with the soy sauce and keep warm.

Pour the water out of the wok and return to the heat. Add the remaining groundnut and sesame oils and when hot, add the garlic, ginger and spring onion and stir-fry for 2 minutes, or until golden. Pour over the fish, garnish with chive leaves and lemon slices and serve immediately with rice and an Oriental salad.

HEALTH RATING

**BUDGET ALTERNATIVE**
Gingered Cod Steaks

**SUGGESTED ACCOMPANIMENT**
Royal Fried Rice

# Trout with Cream Sauce

INGREDIENTS **Serves 4**

550 g/1¼ lb rainbow trout fillets, cut into pieces
salt and freshly ground black pepper
2 tbsp plain white flour
1 tbsp finely chopped dill
groundnut oil for frying

**For the cream sauce:**
50 g/2 oz butter
2 bunches spring onions, trimmed and thickly sliced
1 garlic clove, peeled and finely chopped
300 ml/½ pint dry white wine
150 ml/¼ pint double cream
3 tomatoes, skinned, deseeded and cut into wedges
3 tbsp freshly chopped basil
freshly snipped basil, to garnish
freshly cooked herby mashed potatoes, to serve

Remove as many of the tiny pin bones as possible from the trout fillets, rinse lightly and pat dry on absorbent kitchen paper. Season the flour and stir in the chopped dill, then use to coat the trout fillets.

Pour sufficient oil into a large wok to a depth of 2.5 cm/1 inch deep. Heat until hot and cook the trout in batches for about 3–4 minutes, turning occasionally, or until cooked. Using a slotted spoon, remove and drain on absorbent kitchen paper and keep warm. You may need to cook the trout in batches. Drain the wok and wipe clean.

Melt 25 g/1 oz of the butter in the wok, then stir-fry the spring onions and garlic for 2 minutes. Add the wine, bring to the boil and boil rapidly until reduced by half. Stir in the cream, with the tomatoes and basil, and bring to the boil. Simmer for 1 minute, then add seasoning to taste.

Add the trout to the sauce and heat through until piping hot. Garnish with freshly snipped basil and serve immediately on a bed of herby mashed potatoes.

HEALTH RATING

**LOW FAT ALTERNATIVE**
Haddock with an Olive Crust

**SUGGESTED ACCOMPANIMENT**
Baby Roast Potato Salad

## LOW FAT ALTERNATIVE
# Haddock with an Olive Crust

INGREDIENTS **Serves 4**

- 12 pitted black olives, finely chopped
- 75 g/3 oz fresh white breadcrumbs
- 1 tbsp freshly chopped tarragon
- 1 garlic clove, peeled and crushed
- 3 spring onions, trimmed and finely chopped
- 1 tbsp olive oil
- 4 x 175 g/6 oz thick skinless haddock fillets

**To serve:**

- freshly cooked carrots
- freshly cooked beans

Preheat the oven to 190°C/375°F/Gas Mark 5. Place the black olives in a small bowl with the breadcrumbs and add the chopped tarragon.

Add the garlic to the olives with the chopped spring onions and the olive oil. Mix together lightly.

Wipe the fillets with either a clean damp cloth or damp kitchen paper, then place on a lightly oiled baking sheet.

Place spoonfuls of the olive and breadcrumb mixture on top of each fillet and press the mixture down lightly and evenly over the top of the fish.

Bake the fish in the preheated oven for 20–25 minutes or until the fish is cooked thoroughly and the topping is golden brown. Serve immediately with the freshly cooked carrots and beans.

## SUGGESTED ACCOMPANIMENT
# Baby Roast Potato Salad

INGREDIENTS **Serves 4**

- 350 g/12 oz small shallots
- sea salt and freshly ground black pepper
- 900 g/2 lb small even-sized new potatoes
- 2 tbsp olive oil
- 2 medium courgettes
- 2 sprigs of fresh rosemary
- 175 g/6 oz cherry tomatoes
- 150 ml/¼ pint soured cream
- 2 tbsp freshly snipped chives
- ¼ tsp paprika

Preheat the oven to 200°C/400°F/Gas Mark 6. Trim the shallots, but leave the skins on. Put in a saucepan of lightly salted boiling water with the potatoes and cook for 5 minutes, then drain. Separate the shallots and plunge them into cold water for 1 minute.

Put the oil in a baking sheet lined with tinfoil or a roasting tin and heat for a few minutes. Peel the skins off the shallots – they should now come away easily. Add to the baking sheet or roasting tin with the potatoes and toss in the oil to coat. Sprinkle with a little sea salt. Roast the potatoes and shallots in the preheated oven for 10 minutes.

Meanwhile, trim the courgettes, halve lengthways and cut into 5 cm/2 inch chunks. Add to the baking sheet or roasting tin, toss to mix and cook for 5 minutes.

Pierce the tomato skins with a sharp knife. Add to the sheet or roasting tin with the rosemary and cook for a further 5 minutes, or until all the vegetables are tender. Remove the rosemary and discard. Grind a little black pepper over the vegetables.

Spoon into a wide serving bowl. Mix together the soured cream and chives and drizzle over the vegetables just before serving.

# Roasted Monkfish with Parma Ham

INGREDIENTS **Serves 4**

700 g/1½ lb monkfish tail
sea salt and freshly ground black pepper
4 bay leaves
4 slices fontina cheese, rind removed
8 slices Parma ham
225 g/8 oz angel hair pasta
50 g/2 oz butter
the zest and juice of 1 lemon
sprigs of fresh coriander, to garnish

**To serve:**
chargrilled courgettes
chargrilled tomatoes

Preheat the oven to 200°C/400°F/Gas Mark 6, 15 minutes before cooking. Discard any skin from the monkfish tail and cut away and discard the central bone. Cut the fish into 4 equal-sized pieces and season to taste with salt and pepper. Lay a bay leaf on each fillet, along with a slice of cheese.

Wrap each fillet with 2 slices of the Parma ham, so that the fish is covered completely. Tuck the ends of the Parma ham in and secure with a cocktail stick.

Lightly oil a baking sheet and place in the preheated oven for a few minutes. Place the fish on the preheated baking sheet, then place in the oven and cook for 12–15 minutes.

Bring a large saucepan of lightly salted water to the boil, then slowly add the pasta and cook for 5 minutes until 'al dente', or according to packet directions. Drain, reserving 2 tablespoons of the pasta-cooking water. Return the pasta to the saucepan and add the reserved pasta water, butter, lemon zest and juice. Toss until the pasta is well coated and glistening.

Twirl the pasta into small nests on four warmed serving plates and top with the monkfish parcels. Garnish with sprigs of coriander and serve with chargrilled courgettes and tomatoes.

HEALTH RATING 🍎🍎🍎

**ALTERNATIVE ACCOMPANIMENT**
Mediterranean Rice Salad

**PUDDING SUGGESTION**
Bomba Siciliana

**ALTERNATIVE ACCOMPANIMENT**
## Mediterranean Rice Salad

INGREDIENTS **Serves 4**

250 g/9 oz Camargue red rice
2 sun-dried tomatoes, finely chopped
2 garlic cloves, peeled and finely chopped
4 tbsp oil from a jar of sun-dried tomatoes
2 tsp balsamic vinegar
2 tsp red wine vinegar
salt and freshly ground black pepper
1 red onion, peeled and thinly sliced
1 yellow pepper, quartered and deseeded
1 red pepper, quartered and deseeded
½ cucumber, peeled and diced
6 ripe plum tomatoes, cut into wedges
1 fennel bulb, halved and thinly sliced
fresh basil leaves, to garnish

Cook the rice in a saucepan of lightly salted boiling water for 35–40 minutes, or until tender. Drain well and reserve.

Whisk the sun-dried tomatoes, garlic, oil and vinegars together in a small bowl or jug. Season to taste with salt and pepper. Put the sliced red onion in a large bowl, pour over the dressing and leave to allow the flavours to develop.

Put the peppers, skin-side up on a grill rack and cook under a preheated hot grill for 5–6 minutes, or until blackened and charred. Remove and place in a plastic bag (the moisture will help loosen the skins). When cool enough to handle, peel off the skins and slice the peppers.

Add the peppers, cucumber, tomatoes, fennel and rice to the onions. Mix gently together to coat in the dressing. Cover and chill in the refrigerator for 30 minutes to allow the flavours to mingle.

Remove the salad from the refrigerator and leave to stand at room temperature for 20 minutes. Garnish with fresh basil leaves and serve.

**PUDDING SUGGESTION**
## Bomba Siciliana

INGREDIENTS **Serves 6–8**

100 g/3½ oz plain chocolate, broken into pieces
200 g/7 oz fresh chilled custard
150 ml/¼ pint whipping cream
25 g/1 oz candied peel, finely chopped
25 g/1 oz glacé cherries, chopped
25 g/1 oz sultanas
3 tbsp rum
225 g/8 oz good quality vanilla ice cream
200 ml/⅓ pint double cream
3 tbsp caster sugar

Melt the plain chocolate in a bowl set over a saucepan of simmering water until smooth, then allow to cool. Whisk together the custard with the whipping cream and slightly cooled chocolate. Spoon the mixture into a shallow, lidded freezer box and freeze. Every 2 hours, remove from the freezer and whisk thoroughly using an electric or balloon whisk. Repeat three times, then leave until frozen solid. Soak the candied peel, cherries and sultanas in the rum and leave until needed.

Chill a bombe or 1 litre/1¾ pint pudding mould in the freezer for about 30 minutes. Remove the chocolate ice cream from the freezer to soften, then spoon the ice cream into the mould and press down well, smoothing around the edges and leaving a hollow in the centre. Return the ice cream to the freezer for about 1 hour, or until frozen hard.

Remove the vanilla ice cream from the freezer to soften. Spoon the softened vanilla ice cream into the hollow, making sure to leave another hollow for the cream. Return to the freezer again and freeze until hard.

Whip the cream and sugar until it is just holding its shape, then fold in the soaked fruit. Remove the mould from the freezer and spoon in the cream mixture. Return to the freezer for at least another hour.

When ready to serve, remove the mould from the freezer and dip into hot water for a few seconds, then turn on to a large serving plate. Dip a knife into hot water and cut into wedges to serve.

# Roasted Cod with Saffron Aïoli

INGREDIENTS **Serves 4**

**For the saffron aïoli:**

2 garlic cloves, peeled
¼ tsp saffron strands
sea salt, to taste
1 medium egg yolk
200 ml/7 fl oz extra virgin olive oil
2 tbsp lemon juice

**For the marinade:**

2 tbsp olive oil
4 garlic cloves, peeled and finely chopped
1 red onion, peeled and finely chopped
1 tbsp freshly chopped rosemary
2 tbsp freshly chopped thyme
4–6 sprigs of fresh rosemary
1 lemon, sliced
4 x 175 g/6 oz thick cod fillets with skin
freshly cooked vegtables, to serve

Preheat the oven to 180°C/350°F/Gas Mark 4, 10 minutes before cooking. Crush the garlic, saffron and a pinch of salt in a pestle and mortar to form a paste. Place in a blender with the egg yolk and blend for 30 seconds. With the motor running, slowly add the olive oil in a thin, steady stream until the mayonnaise is smooth and thick. Spoon into a small bowl and stir in the lemon juice. Cover and leave in the refrigerator until required.

Combine the olive oil, garlic, red onion, rosemary and thyme for the marinade and leave to infuse for about 10 minutes.

Place the sprigs of rosemary and slices of lemon in the bottom of a lightly oiled roasting tin. Add the cod, skin-side up. Pour over the prepared marinade and leave to marinate in the refrigerator for 15–20 minutes. Bake in the preheated oven for 15–20 minutes, or until the cod is cooked and the flesh flakes easily with a fork. Leave the cod to rest for 1 minute before serving with the saffron aïoli and vegetables.

HEALTH RATING ●●●

**ENTERTAINING ALTERNATIVE**
Plaice with Parmesan & Anchovies

**SUGGESTED ACCOMPANIMENT**
Potato Gnocchi with Pesto Sauce

INGREDIENTS **Serves 4**

4 plaice fillets
4 anchovy fillets, finely chopped
450 g/1 lb spinach, rinsed
3 firm tomatoes, sliced
200 ml/7 fl oz double cream
5 slices of olive ciabatta bread
50 g/2 oz wild rocket
8 tbsp Parmesan cheese, grated
freshly cooked pasta, to serve

**ENTERTAINING ALTERNATIVE**

## Plaice with Parmesan & Anchovies

Preheat the oven to 220°C/425°F/Gas Mark 7, 15 minutes before cooking. Put the plaice on a chopping board and holding the tail, strip off the skin from both sides. With a filleting knife, fillet the fish, then wipe with a clean, damp cloth or dampened kitchen paper.

Place the fillets on a large chopping board, skinned-side up and halve lengthways along the centre. Dot each one with some of the chopped anchovies, then roll up from the thickest end and reserve.

Pour boiling water over the spinach, leave for 2 minutes then drain, squeezing out as much moisture as possible. Place in the base of an ovenproof dish, and arrange the tomatoes on top of the spinach. Arrange the rolled-up fillets standing up in the dish and pour over the cream.

Place the ciabatta and rocket in a food processor and blend until finely chopped, then stir in the grated Parmesan cheese.

Sprinkle the topping over the fish and bake in the preheated oven for 8–10 minutes or until the fish is cooked and has lost its translucency and the topping is golden brown. Serve with freshly cooked pasta.

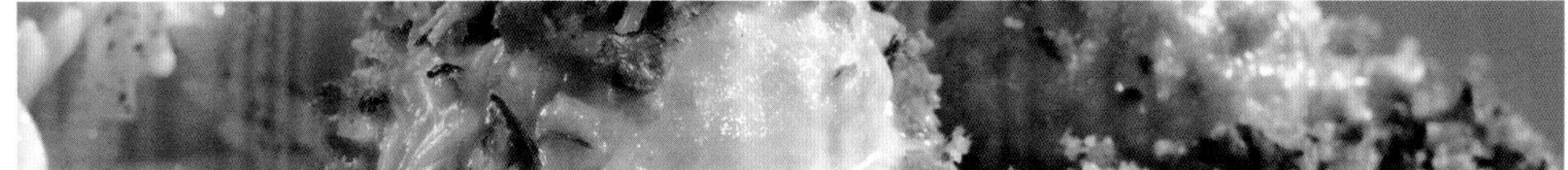

INGREDIENTS **Serves 6**

900 g/2 lb floury potatoes
40 g/1½ oz butter
1 medium egg, beaten
225 g/8 oz plain flour
1 tsp salt
freshly ground black pepper
25 g/1 oz Parmesan cheese, shaved
rocket salad, to serve

**For the pesto sauce:**

50 g/2 oz fresh basil leaves
1 large garlic clove, peeled
2 tbsp pine nuts
125 ml/4 fl oz olive oil
40 g/1½ oz Parmesan cheese, grated

**SUGGESTED ACCOMPANIMENT**

## Potato Gnocchi with Pesto Sauce

Cook the potatoes in their skins in boiling water for 20 minutes, or until tender. Drain and peel. While still warm, push the potatoes through a fine sieve into a bowl. Stir in the butter, egg, 175 g/6 oz of the flour, the salt and pepper.

Sift the remaining flour onto a board or work surface and add the potato mixture. Gently knead in enough flour until a soft, slightly sticky dough is formed.

With floured hands, break off portions of the dough and roll into 2.5 cm/1 inch thick ropes. Cut into 2 cm/¾ inch lengths. Lightly press each piece against the inner prongs of a fork. Put on a tray covered with a floured tea towel and chill in the refrigerator for about 30 minutes.

To make the pesto sauce, put the basil, garlic, pine nuts and oil in a processor and blend until smooth and creamy. Turn into a bowl and stir in the Parmesan cheese. Season to taste.

Cooking in several batches, drop the gnocchi into a saucepan of barely simmering salted water. Cook for 3–4 minutes, or until they float to the surface. Remove with a slotted spoon and keep warm in a covered oiled baking dish in a low oven.

Add the gnocchi to the pesto sauce and toss gently to coat. Serve immediately, scattered with the Parmesan cheese and accompanied by a rocket salad.

**LOW FAT ALTERNATIVE**
## Citrus-grilled Plaice

INGREDIENTS **Serves 4**

1 tsp sunflower oil
1 onion, peeled and chopped
1 orange pepper, deseeded and chopped
175 g/6 oz long-grain rice
150 ml/¼ pint orange juice
2 tbsp lemon juice
225 ml/8 fl oz vegetable stock
spray of oil
4 x 175 g/6 oz plaice fillets, skinned
1 orange
1 lemon
25 g/1 oz half-fat butter or low fat margerine
2 tbsp freshly chopped tarragon
salt and freshly ground black pepper
lemon wedges, to garnish

Heat the oil in a large frying pan, then sauté the onion, pepper and rice for 2 minutes. Add the orange and lemon juice and bring to the boil. Reduce the heat, add half the stock and simmer for 15–20 minutes, or until the rice is tender, adding the remaining stock as necessary.

Preheat the grill. Finely spray the base of the grill pan with oil. Put the plaice fillets in the base and reserve. Finely grate the orange and lemon rind. Squeeze the juice from half of each fruit.

Melt the butter or margerine in a small saucepan. Add the grated rind, juice and half of the tarragon and use to baste the plaice fillets.

Cook one side only of the fish under the preheated grill at a medium heat for 4–6 minutes, basting continuously. Once the rice is cooked, stir in the remaining tarragon and season to taste with salt and pepper. Garnish the fish with the lemon wedges and serve immediately with the rice.

**STARTER SUGGESTION**
## Rich Tomato Soup with Roasted Red Peppers

INGREDIENTS **Serves 4**

2 tsp light olive oil
700 g/1½ lb red peppers, halved and deseeded
450 g/1 lb ripe plum tomatoes, halved
2 onions, unpeeled and quartered
4 garlic cloves, unpeeled
600 ml/1 pint chicken stock
salt and freshly ground black pepper
4 tbsp soured cream
1 tbsp freshly shredded basil

Preheat the oven to 200°C/400°F/Gas Mark 6. Lightly oil a roasting tin with 1 teaspoon of the olive oil. Place the peppers and tomatoes cut side down in the roasting tin with the onion quarters and the garlic cloves. Spoon over the remaining oil.

Bake in the preheated oven for 30 minutes, or until the skins on the peppers have started to blacken and blister. Allow the vegetables to cool for about 10 minutes, then remove the skins, stalks and seeds from the peppers. Peel away the skins from the tomatoes and onions and squeeze out the garlic.

Place the cooked vegetables into a blender or food processor and blend until smooth. Add the stock and blend again to form a smooth purée. Pour the puréed soup through a sieve, if a smooth soup is preferred, then pour into a saucepan. Bring to the boil, simmer gently for 2–3 minutes, and season to taste with salt and pepper. Serve hot with a swirl of soured cream and a sprinkling of shredded basil on the top.

# Zesty Whole-baked Fish

INGREDIENTS **Serves 8**

1.8 kg/4 lb whole salmon, cleaned
sea salt and freshly ground black pepper
50 g/2 oz butter
1 garlic clove, peeled and finely sliced
zest and juice of 1 lemon
zest of 1 orange
1 tsp freshly grated nutmeg
3 tbsp Dijon mustard
2 tbsp fresh white breadcrumbs
2 bunches fresh dill
1 bunch fresh tarragon
1 lime sliced
150 ml/¼ pint crème fraîche
450 ml/¾ pint fromage frais
dill sprigs, to garnish

Preheat the oven to 220°C/425°F/Gas Mark 7. Lightly rinse the fish and pat dry with absorbent kitchen paper. Season the cavity with a little salt and pepper. Make several diagonal cuts across the flesh of the fish and season.

Mix together the butter, garlic, lemon and orange zest and lemon juice, nutmeg, mustard and fresh breadcrumbs. Mix together well. Spoon the breadcrumb mixture into the slits with a small sprig of dill. Place the remaining herbs inside the fish cavity. Weigh the fish and calculate the cooking time. Allow 10 minutes per 450 g/1 lb.

Lay the fish on a double thickness of tinfoil. If liked, smear the fish with a little butter. Top with the lime slices and fold the foil into a parcel. Chill in the refrigerator for about 15 minutes.

Place in a roasting tin and cook in the preheated oven for the calculated cooking time. Fifteen minutes before the end of cooking, open the foil and return to the oven until the skin begins to crisp. Remove the fish from the oven and stand for 10 minutes.

Pour the juices from the roasting tin into a saucepan. Bring to the boil and stir in the crème fraîche and fromage frais. Simmer for 3 minutes or until hot. Garnish with dill sprigs and serve immediately alongside the fish.

HEALTH RATING

**LOW FAT ALTERNATIVE**

Citrus-grilled Plaice

**STARTER SUGGESTION**

Rich Tomato Soup with Roasted Red Peppers

# Grilled Snapper with Roasted Pepper

INGREDIENTS **Serves 4**

1 medium red pepper

1 medium green pepper

4–8 snapper fillets, depending on size, about 450 g/1 lb

sea salt and freshly ground black pepper

1 tbsp olive oil

5 tbsp double cream

125 ml/4 fl oz white wine

1 tbsp freshly chopped dill

sprigs of fresh dill, to garnish

freshly cooked tagliatelle, to serve

Preheat the grill to a high heat and line the grill rack with tinfoil. Cut the tops off the peppers and divide into quarters. Remove the seeds and the membrane, then place on the foil-lined grill rack and cook for 8–10 minutes, turning frequently, until the skins have become charred and blackened. Remove from the grill rack, place in a polythene bag and leave until cool. When the peppers are cool, strip off the skin, slice thinly and reserve.

Cover the grill rack with another piece of tinfoil, then place the snapper fillets skin-side up on the grill rack. Season to taste with salt and pepper and brush with a little of the olive oil. Cook for 10-12 minutes, turning over once and brushing again with a little olive oil.

Pour the cream and wine into a small saucepan, bring to the boil and simmer for about 5 minutes until the sauce has thickened slightly. Add the dill, season to taste and stir in the sliced peppers. Arrange the cooked snapper fillets on warm serving plates and pour over the cream and pepper sauce. Garnish with sprigs of dill and serve immediately with freshly cooked tagliatelle.

## HEALTH RATING

**ENTERTAINING ALTERNATIVE**

Sea Bass in Creamy Watercress & Prosciutto Sauce

**STARTER SUGGESTION**

Pesto Pasta with Cheese & Herb Bread

**ENTERTAINING ALTERNATIVE**
## Sea Bass in Creamy Watercress & Prosciutto Sauce

INGREDIENTS **Serves 4**

75 g/3 oz watercress
450 ml/¾ pint fish or chicken stock
150 ml/¼ pint dry white wine
225 g/8 oz tagliatelle pasta
40 g/1½ oz butter
75 g/3 oz prosciutto ham
2 tbsp plain flour
300 ml/½ pint single cream
salt and freshly ground black pepper
olive oil, for spraying
4 x 175 g/6 oz sea bass fillets
fresh watercress, to garnish

Remove the leaves from the watercress stalks and reserve. Chop the stalks roughly and put in a large pan with the stock. Bring to the boil slowly, cover, and simmer for 20 minutes. Strain, and discard the stalks. Make the stock up to 300 ml/½ pint with the wine. Bring a large saucepan of lightly salted water to the boil and cook the pasta for 8–10 minutes or until 'al dente'. Drain and reserve.

Melt the butter in a saucepan and cook the prosciutto gently for 3 minutes. Remove with a slotted spoon. Stir the flour into the saucepan and cook on a medium heat for 2 minutes. Remove from the heat and gradually pour in the hot watercress stock, stirring continuously. Return to the heat and bring to the boil, stirring throughout. Simmer for 3 minutes, or until the sauce has thickened and is smooth.

Purée the watercress leaves and cream in a food processor, then add to the sauce with the prosciutto. Season to taste with salt and pepper, add the pasta, toss lightly and keep warm.

Meanwhile, spray a griddle pan lightly with olive oil, then heat until hot. When hot, cook the fillets for 3–4 minutes on each side, or until cooked. Arrange the sea bass on a bed of pasta and drizzle with a little sauce. Garnish with watercress and serve immediately.

**STARTER SUGGESTION**
## Pesto Pasta with Cheese & Herb Bread

INGREDIENTS **Serves 4**

1 small onion, peeled and grated
2 tsp freshly chopped oregano
1 tbsp freshly chopped parsley
75 g/3 oz butter
125 g/4 oz pecorino cheese, grated
8 slices of Italian flat bread
275 g/10 oz dried spaghettini
4 tbsp olive oil
1 large bunch of basil, approximately 30 g/1 oz
75 g/3 oz pine nuts
1 garlic clove, peeled and crushed
75 g/3 oz Parmesan cheese, grated
finely grated rind and juice of 2 lemons
salt and freshly ground black pepper
4 tsp butter

Preheat the oven to 200°C/400°F/Gas Mark 6, 15 minutes before baking. Mix together the onion, oregano, parsley, butter and cheese. Spread the bread with the cheese mixture, place on a lightly oiled baking tray and cover with tinfoil. Bake in the preheated oven for 10–15 minutes, then keep warm.

Add the spaghettini with 1 tablespoon of olive oil to a large saucepan of fast-boiling, lightly salted water and cook for 3–4 minutes, or until 'al dente'. Drain, reserving 2 tablespoons of the cooking water.

Blend the basil, pine nuts, garlic, Parmesan cheese, lemon rind and juice and remaining olive oil in a food processor or blender until a purée is formed. Season to taste with salt and pepper, then place in a saucepan.

Heat the lemon pesto very gently until piping hot, then stir in the pasta together with the reserved cooking water. Add the butter and mix well together. Add plenty of black pepper to the pasta and serve immediately with the warm cheese and herb bread.

# Marinated Mackerel with Tomato & Basil Salad

INGREDIENTS **Serves 3**

3 mackerel, filleted
3 beefsteak tomatoes, sliced
50 g/2 oz watercress
2 oranges, peeled and segmented
75 g/3 oz mozzarella cheese, sliced
2 tbsp basil leaves, shredded
sprig of fresh basil, to garnish

**For the marinade:**

juice of 2 lemons
4 tbsp olive oil
4 tbsp basil leaves

**For the dressing:**

1 tbsp lemon juice
1 tsp Dijon mustard
1 tsp caster sugar
salt and freshly ground black pepper
5 tbsp olive oil

Remove as many of the fine pin bones as possible from the mackerel fillets, lightly rinse and pat dry with absorbent kitchen paper and place in a shallow dish.

Blend the marinade ingredients together and pour over the mackerel fillets. Make sure the marinade has covered the fish completely. Cover and leave in a cool place for at least 8 hours, but preferably overnight. As the fillets marinate, they will loose their translucency and look as if they are cooked.

Place the tomatoes, watercress, oranges and mozzarella cheese in a large bowl and toss.

To make the dressing, whisk the lemon juice with the mustard, sugar and seasoning in a bowl. Pour over half the dressing, toss again and then arrange on a serving platter. Remove the mackerel from the marinade, cut into bite-sized pieces and sprinkle with the shredded basil. Arrange on top of the salad, drizzle over the remaining dressing, scatter with basil leaves and garnish with a basil sprig. Serve.

HEALTH RATING 🍎🍎🍎🍎

**SUGGESTED ACCOMPANIMENT**

Spinach Dumplings with Rich Tomato Sauce

**PUDDING SUGGESTION**

Ricotta Cheesecake with Strawberry Coulis

**SUGGESTED ACCOMPANIMENT**

## Spinach Dumplings with Rich Tomato Sauce

INGREDIENTS **Serves 4**

**For the sauce:**

2 tbsp olive oil
1 onion, peeled and chopped
1 garlic clove, peeled and crushed
1 red chilli, deseeded and chopped
150 ml/¼ pint dry white wine
400 g can chopped tomatoes
pared strip of lemon rind

**For the dumplings:**

450 g/1 lb fresh spinach
50 g/2 oz ricotta cheese
25 g/1 oz fresh white breadcrumbs
25 g/1 oz Parmesan cheese, grated
1 medium egg yolk
¼ tsp freshly grated nutmeg
salt and freshly ground black pepper
5 tbsp plain flour
2 tbsp olive oil, for frying
fresh basil leaves, to garnish
freshly cooked tagliatelle, to serve

To make the tomato sauce, heat the olive oil in a large saucepan and fry the onion gently for 5 minutes. Add the garlic and chilli and cook for a further 5 minutes, until softened.

Stir in the wine, chopped tomatoes and lemon rind. Bring to the boil, cover and simmer for 20 minutes, then uncover and simmer for 15 minutes or until the sauce has thickened. Remove the lemon rind and season to taste with salt and pepper.

To make the spinach dumplings, wash the spinach thoroughly and remove any tough stalks. Cover and cook in a large saucepan over a low heat with just the water clinging to the leaves. Drain, then squeeze out all the excess water. Finely chop and put in a large bowl.

Add the ricotta, breadcrumbs, Parmesan cheese and egg yolk to the spinach. Season with nutmeg and salt and pepper. Mix together and shape into 20 walnut-sized balls.

Toss the spinach balls in the flour. Heat the olive oil in a large non-stick frying pan and fry the balls gently for 5–6 minutes, carefully turning occasionally. Garnish with fresh basil leaves and serve immediately with the tomato sauce and tagliatelle.

**PUDDING SUGGESTION**

## Ricotta Cheesecake with Strawberry Coulis

INGREDIENTS **Serves 6–8**

125 g/4 oz digestive biscuits
100 g/3½ oz candied peel, chopped
65 g/2½ oz butter, melted
150 ml/¼ pint crème fraîche
375 g/13 oz ricotta cheese
100 g/3½ oz caster sugar
1 vanilla pod, seeds only
2 large eggs
225 g/8 oz strawberries
25–50 g/1–2 oz caster sugar, to taste
zest and juice of 1 orange

Preheat the oven to 170°C/325°F/Gas Mark 3. Line a 20.5 cm/8 inch springform tin with baking parchment. Place the biscuits into a food processor together with the peel. Blend until the biscuits are crushed and the peel is chopped. Add 50 g/2 oz of the melted butter and process until mixed. Tip into the tin and spread evenly over the bottom. Press firmly into place and reserve.

Blend together the crème fraîche, ricotta cheese, sugar, vanilla seeds and eggs in a food processor. With the motor running, add the remaining melted butter and blend for a few seconds. Pour the mixture on to the base. Transfer to the preheated oven and cook for about 1 hour, until set and risen round the edges, but slightly wobbly in the centre. Switch off the oven and allow to cool there. Chill in the refrigerator for at least 8 hours, or preferably overnight.

Wash and drain the strawberries. Hull the fruit and remove any soft spots. Put into the food processor along with 25 g/1 oz of the sugar and orange juice and zest. Blend until smooth. Add the remaining sugar to taste. Pass through a sieve to remove seeds and chill in the refrigerator until needed. Cut the cheesecake into wedges, spoon over some of the strawberry coulis and serve.

# Pan-fried Salmon with Herb Risotto

INGREDIENTS **Serves 4**

4 x 175 g/6 oz salmon fillets
3–4 tbsp plain flour
1 tsp dried mustard powder
salt and freshly ground black pepper
2 tbsp olive oil
3 shallots, peeled and chopped
225 g/8 oz Arborio rice
150 ml/¼ pint dry white wine
1.4 litres/2½ pints vegetable or fish stock
50 g/2 oz butter
2 tbsp freshly snipped chives
2 tbsp freshly chopped dill
2 tbsp freshly chopped flat-leaf parsley
knob of butter

**To garnish:**
slices of lemon
sprigs of fresh dill
tomato salad, to serve

Wipe the salmon fillets with a clean, damp cloth. Mix together the flour, mustard powder and seasoning on a large plate and use to coat the salmon fillets and reserve.

Heat half the olive oil in a large frying pan and fry the shallots for 5 minutes until softened, but not coloured. Add the rice and stir for 1 minute, then slowly add the wine, bring to the boil and boil rapidly until reduced by half.

Bring the stock to a gentle simmer then add to the rice, a ladleful at a time. Cook, stirring frequently, until all the stock has been added and the rice is cooked but still retains a bite. Stir in the butter and freshly chopped herbs and season to taste with salt and pepper.

Heat the remaining olive oil and the knob of butter in a large griddle pan, add the salmon fillets and cook for 2–3 minutes on each side, or until cooked. Arrange the herb risotto on warm serving plates and top with the salmon. Garnish with slices of lemon and sprigs of dill and serve immediately with a tomato salad.

HEALTH RATING

**ENTERTAINING ALTERNATIVE**
Seared Tuna with Italian Salsa

**PUDDING SUGGESTION**
Baked Stuffed Amaretti Peaches

**ENTERTAINING ALTERNATIVE**
## Seared Tuna with Italian Salsa

INGREDIENTS **Serves 4**

4 x 175 g/6 oz tuna or swordfish steaks
salt and freshly ground black pepper
3 tbsp Pernod
2 tbsp olive oil
zest and juice of 1 lemon
2 tsp fresh thyme leaves
2 tsp fennel seeds, lightly roasted
4 sun-dried tomatoes, chopped
1 tsp dried chilli flakes
assorted salad leaves, to serve

**For the salsa:**
1 white onion, peeled and finely chopped
2 tomatoes, deseeded and sliced
2 tbsp freshly shredded basil leaves
1 red chilli, deseeded and finely sliced
3 tbsp extra virgin olive oil
2 tsp balsamic vinegar
1 tsp caster sugar

Wipe the fish and season lightly with salt and pepper, then place in a shallow dish. Mix together the Pernod, olive oil, lemon zest and juice, thyme, fennel seeds, sun-dried tomatoes and chilli flakes and pour over the fish. Cover lightly and leave to marinate in a cool place for 1–2 hours, occasionally spooning the marinade over the fish.

Meanwhile, mix all the ingredients for the salsa together in a small bowl. Season to taste with salt and pepper, then cover and leave for about 30 minutes to allow all the flavours to develop.

Lightly oil a griddle pan and heat until hot. When the pan is very hot, drain the fish, reserving the marinade. Cook the fish for 3–4 minutes on each side, taking care not to overcook them – the tuna steaks should be a little pink inside. Pour any remaining marinade into a small saucepan, bring to the boil and boil for 1 minute. Serve the steaks hot with the marinade, chilled salsa and a few assorted salad leaves.

**PUDDING SUGGESTION**
## Baked Stuffed Amaretti Peaches

INGREDIENTS **Serves 4**

4 ripe peaches
grated zest and juice of 1 lemon
75 g/3 oz Amaretti biscuits
50 g/2 oz chopped blanched almonds, toasted
50 g/2 oz pine nuts, toasted
40 g/1½ oz light muscovado sugar
50 g/2 oz butter
1 medium egg yolk
2 tsp clear honey
crème fraîche or Greek yogurt, to serve

Preheat the oven to 180°C/350°F/Gas Mark 4. Halve the peaches and remove the stones. Take a very thin slice from the bottom of each peach half so that it will sit flat on the baking sheet. Dip the peach halves in lemon juice and arrange on a baking sheet.

Crush the Amaretti biscuits lightly and put into a large bowl. Add the almonds, pine nuts, sugar, lemon zest and butter. Work with the fingertips until the mixture resembles coarse breadcrumbs. Add the egg yolk and mix well until the mixture is just binding.

Divide the Amaretti and nut mixture between the peach halves, pressing down lightly. Bake in the preheated oven for 15 minutes, or until the peaches are tender and the filling is golden. Remove from the oven and drizzle with the honey.

Place two peach halves on each serving plate and spoon over a little crème fraîche or Greek yogurt, then serve.

# Salmon Fish Cakes

INGREDIENTS **Serves 4**

450 g/1 lb salmon fillet, skinned
salt and freshly ground black pepper
450 g/1 lb potatoes, peeled and cut into chunks
25 g/1 oz butter
1 tbsp milk
2 medium tomatoes, skinned, deseeded and chopped
2 tbsp freshly chopped parsley
75 g/3 oz wholemeal breadcrumbs
25 g/1 oz Cheddar cheese, grated
2 tbsp plain flour
2 medium eggs, beaten
3–4 tbsp vegetable oil

**To serve:**
ready-made raita
sprigs of fresh mint

Place the salmon in a shallow frying pan and cover with water. Season to taste with salt and pepper and simmer for 8–10 minutes until the fish is cooked. Drain and flake into a bowl.

Boil the potatoes in lightly salted water until soft, then drain. Mash with the butter and milk until smooth. Add the potato to the bowl of fish and stir in the tomatoes and half the parsley. Adjust the seasoning to taste. Chill the mixture in the refrigerator for at least 2 hours to firm up.

Mix the breadcrumbs with the grated cheese and the remaining parsley. When the fish mixture is firm, form into eight flat cakes. First, lightly coat the fish cakes in the flour, then dip into the beaten egg, allowing any excess to drip back into the bowl. Finally, press into the breadcrumb mixture until well coated.

Heat a little of the oil in a frying pan and fry the fish cakes in batches for 2–3 minutes on each side until golden and crisp, adding more oil if necessary. Serve with raita garnished with sprigs of mint.

HEALTH RATING 🍎🍎🍎

**BUDGET ALTERNATIVE**
Tuna Fish Burgers

**SUGGESTED ACCOMPANIMENT**
Venetian-style Vegetables & Beans

## BUDGET ALTERNATIVE
## Tuna Fish Burgers

INGREDIENTS **Serves 4**

- 450 g/1 lb potatoes, peeled and cut into chunks
- 50 g/2 oz butter
- 2 tbsp milk
- 400 g can tuna in oil
- 1 spring onion, trimmed and finely chopped
- 1 tbsp freshly chopped parsley
- salt and freshly ground black pepper
- 2 medium eggs, beaten
- 2 tbsp seasoned plain flour
- 125 g/4 oz fresh white breadcrumbs
- 4 tbsp vegetable oil
- 4 sesame seed baps (optional)

**To serve:**

- fat chips
- mixed salad
- tomato chutney

Place the potatoes in a large saucepan, cover with boiling water and simmer until soft. Drain, then mash with 40 g/1½ oz of the butter and the milk. Turn into a large bowl. Drain the tuna, discarding the oil and flake into the bowl of potato. Stir well to mix.

Add the spring onions and parsley to the mixture and season to taste with salt and pepper. Add 1 tablespoon of the beaten egg to bind the mixture together. Chill in the refrigerator for at least 1 hour.

Shape the chilled mixture with your hands into four large burgers. First, coat the burgers with seasoned flour, then brush them with the remaining beaten egg, allowing any excess to drip back into the bowl. Finally, coat them evenly in the breadcrumbs, pressing the crumbs on with your hands, if necessary.

Heat a little of the oil in a frying pan and fry the burgers for 2–3 minutes on each side until golden, adding more oil if necessary. Drain on absorbent kitchen paper and serve hot in baps, if using, with chips, mixed salad and chutney.

## SUGGESTED ACCOMPANIMENT
## Venetian-style Vegetables & Beans

INGREDIENTS **Serves 4**

- 250 g/9 oz dried pinto beans
- 3 sprigs of fresh parsley
- 1 sprig of fresh rosemary
- 2 tbsp olive oil
- 200 g can chopped tomatoes
- 2 shallots, peeled

**For the vegetable mixture:**

- 1 large red onion, peeled
- 1 large white onion, peeled
- 1 medium carrot, peeled
- 2 sticks celery, trimmed
- 3 tbsp olive oil
- 3 bay leaves
- 1 tsp caster sugar
- 3 tbsp red wine vinegar
- salt and freshly ground black pepper

Put the beans in a bowl, cover with plenty of cold water and leave to soak for at least 8 hours, or overnight.

Drain and rinse the beans. Put in a large saucepan with 1.1 litres/ 2 pints cold water. Tie the parsley and rosemary in muslin and add to the beans with the olive oil. Boil rapidly for 10 minutes, then lower the heat and simmer for 20 minutes with the saucepan half covered. Stir in the tomatoes and shallots and simmer for a further 10–15 minutes, or until the beans are cooked.

Meanwhile, slice the red and white onion into rings and then finely dice the carrot and celery. Heat the olive oil in a saucepan and cook the onions over a very low heat for about 10 minutes. Add the carrot, celery and bay leaves to the saucepan and cook for a further 10 minutes, stirring frequently, until the vegetables are tender. Sprinkle with sugar, stir and cook for 1 minute.

Stir in the vinegar. Cook for 1 minute, then remove the saucepan from the heat. Drain the beans through a fine sieve, discarding all the herbs, then add the beans to the onion mixture and season well with salt and pepper. Mix gently, then tip the beans into a large serving bowl. Leave to cool, then serve at room temperature.

# Russian Fish Pie

INGREDIENTS **Serves 4–6**

450 g/1 lb orange roughy or haddock fillet
150 ml/¼ pint dry white wine
salt and freshly ground black pepper
75 g/3 oz butter or margarine
1 large onion, peeled and finely chopped
75 g/3 oz long-grain rice
1 tbsp freshly chopped dill
125 g/4 oz baby button mushrooms, quartered
125 g/4 oz peeled prawns, thawed if frozen
3 medium eggs, hard-boiled and chopped
550 g/1¼ lb ready-prepared puff pastry, thawed if frozen
1 small egg, beaten with a pinch of salt
assorted bitter salad leaves, to serve

Preheat the oven to 200°C/400°F/Gas Mark 6, 15 minutes before cooking. Place the fish in a shallow frying pan with the wine, 150 ml/ ¼ pint water and salt and pepper. Simmer for 8–10 minutes. Strain the fish, reserving the liquid, and when cool enough to handle, flake into a bowl.

Melt the butter or margarine in a saucepan and cook the onions for 2–3 minutes, then add the rice, reserved fish liquid and dill. Season lightly. Cover and simmer for 10 minutes, then stir in the mushrooms and cook for a further 10 minutes, or until all the liquid is absorbed. Mix the rice with the cooked fish, prawns and eggs. Leave to cool.

Roll half the pastry out on a lightly floured surface into a 23 x 30.5 cm/9 x 12 inch rectangle. Place on a dampened baking sheet and arrange the fish mixture on top, leaving a 1 cm/½ inch border. Brush the border with a little water.

Roll out the remaining pastry to a rectangle and use to cover the fish. Brush the edges lightly with a little of the beaten egg and press to seal. Roll out the pastry trimmings and use to decorate the top. Chill in the refrigerator for 30 minutes. Brush with the beaten egg and bake for 30 minutes, or until golden. Serve immediately with salad leaves.

HEALTH RATING 🍎🍎

**SPEEDY ALTERNATIVE**
Traditional Fish Pie

**PUDDING SUGGESTION**
Fruit Salad

**SPEEDY ALTERNATIVE**
## Traditional Fish Pie

Preheat the oven to 200°C/400°F/Gas Mark 6, about 15 minutes before cooking. Place the fish in a shallow frying pan, pour over 300 ml/½ pint of the milk and add the onion. Season to taste with salt and pepper. Bring to the boil and simmer for 8–10 minutes until the fish is cooked.

Remove the fish with a slotted spoon and place in a 1.4 litre/2½ pint baking dish. Strain the cooking liquid and reserve.

Boil the potatoes until soft, then mash with 40 g/1½ oz of the butter and 2–3 tablespoons of the remaining milk. Reserve.

Arrange the prawns and sliced eggs on top of the fish, then scatter over the sweetcorn and sprinkle with the parsley.

Melt the remaining butter in a saucepan, stir in the flour and cook gently for 1 minute, stirring. Whisk in the reserved cooking liquid and remaining milk. Cook for 2 minutes, or until thickened, then pour over the fish mixture and cool slightly.

Spread the mashed potato over the top of the pie and sprinkle over the grated cheese. Bake in the preheated over for 30 minutes until golden. Serve immediately.

INGREDIENTS **Serves 4**

450 g/1 lb cod or coley fillets, skinned
450 ml/¾ pint milk
1 small onion, peeled and quartered
salt and freshly ground black pepper
900 g/2 lb potatoes, peeled and cut into chunks
100 g/3½ oz butter
125 g/4 oz large prawns
2 large eggs, hard-boiled and quartered
198 g can of sweetcorn, drained
2 tbsp freshly chopped parsley
3 tbsp plain flour
50 g/2 oz Cheddar cheese, grated

**PUDDING SUGGESTION**
## Fruit Salad

Place the sugar and 300 ml/½ pint of water in a small pan and heat, gently stirring until the sugar has dissolved. Bring to the boil and simmer for 2 minutes. Once a syrup has formed, remove from the heat and allow to cool.

Using a sharp knife, cut away the skin from the oranges, then slice thickly. Cut each slice in half and place in a serving dish with the syrup and lychees.

Peel the mango, then cut into thick slices around each side of the stone. Discard the stone, cut the slices into bite-sized pieces and add to the syrup.

Using a sharp knife again, carefully cut away the skin from the pineapple.

Remove the central core using the knife or an apple corer, then cut the pineapple into segments and add to the syrup.

Peel the papaya, then cut in half and remove the seeds. Cut the flesh into chunks, slice the ginger into matchsticks and add with the ginger syrup to the fruit in the syrup.

Prepare the Cape gooseberries by removing the thin, papery skins and rinsing lightly.

Halve the strawberries, add to the fruit with the almond essence and chill for 30 minutes. Scatter with mint leaves and lime zest to decorate and serve.

INGREDIENTS **Serves 4**

125 g/4 oz caster sugar
3 oranges
700 g/1½ lb lychees, peeled and stoned
1 small mango
1 small pineapple
1 papaya
4 pieces stem ginger in syrup
4 tbsp stem ginger syrup
125 g/4 oz Cape gooseberries
125 g/4 oz strawberries, hulled
½ tsp almond essence

**To decorate:**
lime zest
mint leaves

**CHILDREN'S ALTERNATIVE**

## Cheesy Vegetable & Prawn Bake

INGREDIENTS **Serves 4**

175 g/6 oz long-grain rice
salt and freshly ground black pepper
1 garlic clove, peeled and crushed
1 large egg, beaten
3 tbsp freshly shredded basil
4 tbsp Parmesan cheese, grated
125 g/4 oz baby asparagus spears, trimmed
150 g/5 oz baby carrots, trimmed
150 g/5 oz fine green beans, trimmed
150 g/5 oz cherry tomatoes
175 g/6 oz peeled prawns, thawed if frozen
125 g/4 oz mozzarella cheese, thinly sliced

Preheat the oven to 200°C/400°F/Gas Mark 6, about 10 minutes before required. Cook the rice in lightly salted boiling water for 12–15 minutes, or until tender, and drain. Stir in the garlic, beaten egg, shredded basil, 2 tablespoons of the Parmesan cheese and season to taste with salt and pepper. Press this mixture into a greased 23 cm/9 inch square ovenproof dish and reserve.

Bring a large saucepan of water to the boil, then drop in the asparagus, carrots and green beans. Return to the boil and cook for 3–4 minutes. Drain and leave to cool.

Quarter or halve the cherry tomatoes and mix them into the cooled vegetables. Spread the prepared vegetables over the rice and top with the prawns. Season to taste with salt and pepper.

Cover the prawns with the mozzarella and sprinkle over the remaining Parmesan cheese. Bake in the preheated oven for 20–25 minutes until piping hot and golden brown in places. Serve immediately.

**SUGGESTED ACCOMPANIMENT**

## Chinese Leaves with Sweet-&-Sour Sauce

Discard any tough outer leaves and stalks from the Chinese leaves and pak choi and wash well. Drain thoroughly and pat dry with absorbent kitchen paper. Shred the Chinese leaves and pak choi lengthways and reserve.

In a small bowl, blend the cornflour with 4 tablespoons of water. Add the soy sauce, sugar, vinegar, orange juice and tomato purée and stir until blended thoroughly.

Pour the sauce into a small saucepan and bring to the boil. Simmer gently for 2–3 minutes, or until the sauce is thickened and smooth.

Meanwhile, heat a wok or large frying pan and add the sunflower oil and butter. When melted, add the prepared Chinese leaves and pak choi, sprinkle with the salt and stir-fry for 2 minutes. Reduce the heat and cook gently for a further 1–2 minutes or until tender.

Transfer the Chinese leaves and pak choi to a warmed serving platter and drizzle over the warm sauce. Sprinkle with the toasted sesame seeds and serve immediately.

INGREDIENTS **Serves 4**

1 head Chinese leaves
200 g pack pak choi
1 tbsp cornflour
1 tbsp soy sauce
2 tbsp brown sugar
3 tbsp red wine vinegar
3 tbsp orange juice
2 tbsp tomato purée
3 tbsp sunflower oil
15 g/½ oz butter
1 tsp salt
2 tbsp toasted sesame seeds

# Chunky Halibut Casserole

INGREDIENTS **Serves 6**

50 g/2 oz butter or margarine
2 large onions, peeled and sliced into rings
1 red pepper, deseeded and roughly chopped
450 g/1 lb potatoes, peeled
450 g/1 lb courgettes, trimmed and thickly sliced
2 tbsp plain flour
1 tbsp paprika
2 tsp vegetable oil
300 ml/½ pint white wine
150 ml/¼ pint fish stock
400 g can chopped tomatoes
2 tbsp freshly chopped basil
salt and freshly ground black pepper
450 g/1 lb halibut fillet, skinned and cut into 2.5 cm/1 inch cubes
sprigs of fresh basil, to garnish
freshly cooked rice, to serve

Melt the butter or margarine in a large saucepan, add the onions and pepper and cook for 5 minutes, or until softened.

Cut the peeled potatoes into 2.5 cm/1 inch cubes, rinse lightly and shake dry, then add them to the onions and pepper in the saucepan. Add the courgettes and cook, stirring frequently, for a further 2–3 minutes.

Sprinkle the flour, paprika and vegetable oil into the saucepan and cook, stirring continuously, for 1 minute. Pour in 150 ml/¼ pint of the wine, with all the stock and the chopped tomatoes, and bring to the boil.

Add the basil to the casserole, season to taste with salt and pepper and cover. Simmer for 15 minutes, then add the halibut and the remaining wine and simmer very gently for a further 5–7 minutes, or until the fish and vegetables are just tender. Garnish with basil sprigs and serve immediately with freshly cooked rice.

HEALTH RATING 🍏🍏🍏🍏

**CHILDREN'S ALTERNATIVE**

Cheesy Vegetable & Prawn Bake

**SUGGESTED ACCOMPANIMENT**

Chinese Leaves with Sweet-&-Sour Sauce

# Fish Crumble

Preheat the oven to 200°C/400°F/Gas Mark 6, 15 minutes before cooking. Oil a 1.4 litre/ 2½ pint pie dish. Place the fish in a saucepan with the milk, salt and pepper. Bring to the boil, cover and simmer for 8–10 minutes until the fish is cooked. Remove with a slotted spoon, reserving the cooking liquid. Flake the fish into the prepared dish.

Heat the oil and 1 tablespoon of the butter or margarine in a small frying pan and gently fry the onion, leeks, carrot and potatoes for 1–2 minutes. Cover tightly and cook over a gentle heat for a further 10 minutes until softened. Spoon the vegetables over the fish.

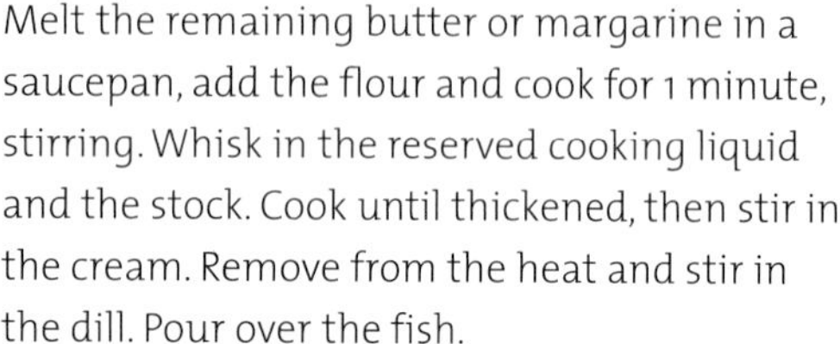

Melt the remaining butter or margarine in a saucepan, add the flour and cook for 1 minute, stirring. Whisk in the reserved cooking liquid and the stock. Cook until thickened, then stir in the cream. Remove from the heat and stir in the dill. Pour over the fish.

To make the crumble, rub the butter or margarine into the flour until it resembles bread-crumbs, then stir in the cheese and cayenne pepper. Sprinkle over the dish, and bake in the preheated oven for 20 minutes until piping hot. Serve with runner beans.

HEALTH RATING

**MEDITERRANEAN ALTERNATIVE**

Mediterranean Fish Stew

**STARTER SUGGESTION**

Potato Pancakes

INGREDIENTS **Serves 6**

450 g/1 lb whiting or halibut fillets
300 ml/½ pint milk
salt and freshly ground black pepper
1 tbsp sunflower oil
75 g/3 oz butter or margarine
1 medium onion, peeled and finely chopped
2 leeks, trimmed and sliced
1 medium carrot, peeled and cut into small cubes
2 medium potatoes, peeled and cut into small pieces
175 g/6 oz plain flour
300 ml/½ pint fish or vegetable stock
2 tbsp whipping cream
1 tsp freshly chopped dill
runner beans, to serve

**For the crumble topping:**

75 g/3 oz butter or margarine
175 g/6 oz plain flour
75 g/3 oz Parmesan cheese, grated
¾ tsp cayenne pepper

**MEDITERRANEAN ALTERNATIVE**
## Mediterranean Fish Stew

Heat the olive oil in a large saucepan. Add the onion, garlic, fennel and celery and cook over a low heat for 15 minutes, stirring frequently until the vegetables are soft and just beginning to turn brown.

Add the canned tomatoes with their juice, oregano, bay leaf, orange zest and juice and the saffron strands. Bring to the boil, then reduce the heat and simmer for 5 minutes. Add the fish stock, vermouth and season to taste with salt and pepper. Bring to the boil. Reduce the heat and simmer for 20 minutes.

Wipe or rinse the haddock and bass fillets and remove as many of the bones as possible. Place on a chopping board and cut into 5 cm/2 inch cubes. Add to the saucepan and cook for 3 minutes. Add the prawns and cook for a further 5 minutes. Adjust the seasoning to taste and serve with crusty bread.

INGREDIENTS **Serves 4–6**

4 tbsp olive oil
1 onion, peeled and finely sliced
5 garlic cloves, peeled and finely sliced
1 fennel bulb, trimmed and finely chopped
3 celery sticks, trimmed and finely chopped
400 g can chopped tomatoes with Italian herbs
1 tbsp freshly chopped oregano
1 bay leaf
zest and juice of 1 orange
1 tsp saffron strands
750 ml/1¼ pints fish stock
3 tbsp dry vermouth
salt and freshly ground black pepper
225 g/8 oz thick haddock fillets
225 g/8 oz sea bass or bream fillets
225 g/8 oz raw tiger prawns, peeled
crusty bread, to serve

**STARTER SUGGESTION**
## Potato Pancakes

To make the sauce, mix together the crème fraîche, horseradish, lime rind and juice and chives. Cover and reserve.

Place the potatoes in a large saucepan and cover with lightly salted boiling water. Bring back to the boil, cover and simmer for 15 minutes, or until the potatoes are tender. Drain and mash until smooth. Cool for 5 minutes, then whisk in the egg white, milk, flour, thyme and salt to form a thick smooth batter. Leave to stand for 30 minutes, then stir before using.

Heat a little oil in a heavy-based frying pan. Add 2–3 large spoonfuls of batter to make a small pancake and cook for 1–2 minutes until golden. Flip the pancake and cook for a further minute, or until golden. Repeat with the remaining batter to make eight pancakes.

Arrange the pancakes on a plate and top with the smoked mackerel. Garnish with herbs and serve immediately with spoonfuls of the reserved horseradish sauce.

INGREDIENTS **Serves 6**

**For the sauce:**
4 tbsp crème fraîche
1 tbsp horseradish sauce
grated rind and juice of 1 lime
1 tbsp freshly snipped chives

225 g/8 oz floury potatoes, peeled and cut into chunks
1 small egg white
2 tbsp milk
2 tsp self-raising flour
1 tbsp freshly chopped thyme
large pinch of salt
a little vegetable oil, for frying
225 g/8 oz smoked mackerel fillets, skinned and roughly chopped
fresh herbs, to garnish

**MILD ALTERNATIVE**
## Coconut Seafood

Heat a large wok, add the oil and heat until it is almost smoking, swirling the oil around the wok to coat the sides. Add the prawns and stir-fry over a high heat for 4-5 minutes, or until browned on all sides. Using a slotted spoon, transfer the prawns to a plate and keep warm in a low oven.

Add the spring onions, garlic and ginger to the wok and stir-fry for 1 minute. Add the mushrooms and stir-fry for a further 3 minutes. Using a slotted spoon, transfer the mushroom mixture to a plate and keep warm in a low oven.

Add the wine and coconut cream to the wok, bring to the boil and boil rapidly for 4 minutes, until reduced slightly. Return the mushroom mixture and prawns to the wok, bring back to the boil, then simmer for 1 minute, stirring occasionally, until piping hot. Stir in the freshly chopped coriander and season to taste with salt and pepper. Serve immediately with the freshly cooked fragrant Thai rice.

INGREDIENTS **Serves 4**

- 2 tbsp groundnut oil
- 450 g/1 lb raw king prawns, peeled
- 2 bunches spring onions, trimmed and thickly sliced
- 1 garlic clove, peeled and chopped
- 2.5 cm/1 inch piece fresh root ginger, peeled and cut into matchsticks
- 125 g/4 oz fresh shiitake mushrooms, rinsed and halved
- 150 ml/¼ pint dry white wine
- 200 ml/7 fl oz carton coconut cream
- 4 tbsp freshly chopped coriander
- salt and freshly ground black pepper
- freshly cooked fragrant Thai rice

**ENTERTAINING ALTERNATIVE**
## Thai Coconut Crab Curry

Peel the onion and chop finely. Peel the garlic cloves, then either crush or finely chop. Peel the ginger and either grate coarsely or cut into very thin shreds. Reserve.

Heat a wok or large frying pan, add the oil and when hot, add the onion, garlic and ginger and stir-fry for 2 minutes, or until the onion is beginning to soften. Stir in the curry paste and stir-fry for 1 minute.

Stir the coconut milk into the vegetable mixture with the dark crabmeat. Add the lemon grass, then bring the mixture slowly to the boil, stirring frequently.

Add the spring onions and simmer gently for 15 minutes or until the sauce has thickened. Remove and discard the lemon grass stalks.

Add the white crabmeat and the shredded basil or mint and stir very gently for 1–2 minutes or until heated through and piping hot. Try to prevent the crabmeat from breaking up. Spoon the curry over boiled rice on warmed individual plates, sprinkle with basil or mint leaves and serve immediately.

INGREDIENTS **Serves 4–6**

- 1 onion
- 4 garlic cloves
- 5 cm/2 inch piece fresh root ginger
- 2 tbsp vegetable oil
- 2–3 tsp hot curry paste
- 400 ml can of coconut milk
- 2 large dressed crabs, white and dark meat separated
- 2 lemon grass stalks, peeled and bruised
- 6 spring onions, trimmed and chopped
- 2 tbsp freshly shredded Thai basil or mint, plus extra to garnish
- freshly boiled rice, to serve

# Coconut Fish Curry

INGREDIENTS **Serves 4**

- 2 tbsp sunflower oil
- 1 medium onion, peeled and very finely chopped
- 1 yellow pepper, deseeded and finely chopped
- 1 garlic clove, peeled and crushed
- 1 tbsp mild curry paste
- 2.5 cm/1 inch piece of root ginger, peeled and grated
- 1 red chilli, deseeded and finely chopped
- 400 ml can coconut milk
- 700 g/1½ lb firm white fish, e.g. monkfish fillets, skinned and cut into chunks
- 225 g/8 oz basmati rice
- 1 tbsp freshly chopped coriander
- 1 tbsp mango chutney
- salt and freshly ground black pepper

**To garnish:**

- lime wedges
- fresh coriander sprigs

**To serve:**

- Greek yogurt
- warm naan bread

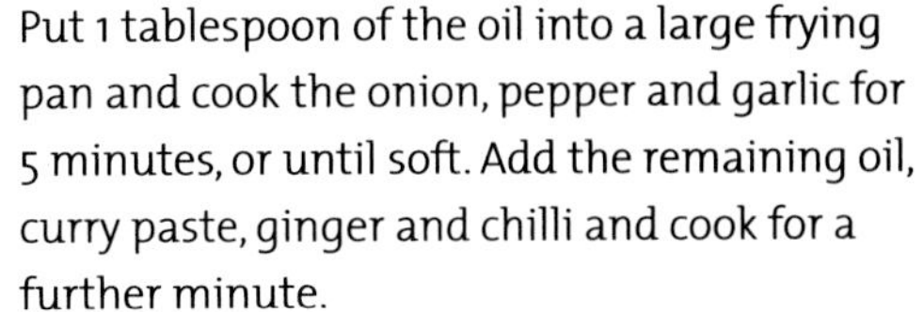

Put 1 tablespoon of the oil into a large frying pan and cook the onion, pepper and garlic for 5 minutes, or until soft. Add the remaining oil, curry paste, ginger and chilli and cook for a further minute.

Pour in the coconut milk and bring to the boil, reduce the heat and simmer gently for 5 minutes, stirring occasionally. Add the monkfish to the pan and continue to simmer gently for 5–10 minutes, or until the fish is tender, but not overcooked.

Meanwhile, cook the rice in a saucepan of boiling salted water for 15 minutes, or until tender. Drain the rice thoroughly and turn out into a serving dish.

Stir the chopped coriander and chutney gently into the fish curry and season to taste with salt and pepper. Spoon the fish curry over the cooked rice, garnish with lime wedges and coriander sprigs and serve immediately with spoonfuls of Greek yogurt and warm naan bread.

HEALTH RATING

**MILD ALTERNATIVE**

Coconut Seafood

**ENTERTAINING ALTERNATIVE**

Thai Coconut Crab Curry

# Smoked Salmon Quiche

INGREDIENTS **Serves 6**

225 g/8 oz plain flour
50 g/2 oz butter
50 g/2 oz white vegetable fat or lard
2 tsp sunflower oil
225 g/8 oz potato, peeled and diced
125 g/4 oz Gruyère cheese, grated
75 g/3 oz smoked salmon trimmings
5 medium eggs, beaten
300 ml/½ pint single cream
salt and freshly ground black pepper
1 tbsp freshly chopped flat-leaf parsley

**To serve:**
mixed salad
baby new potatoes

Preheat the oven to 200°C/400°F/Gas Mark 6. Blend the flour, butter and white vegetable fat or lard together until it resembles fine breadcrumbs. Blend again, adding sufficient water to make a firm but pliable dough. Use the dough to line a 23 cm/9 inch flan dish or tin, then chill the pastry case in the refrigerator for 30 minutes. Bake blind with baking beans for 10 minutes.

Heat the oil in a small frying pan, add the diced potato and cook for 3–4 minutes until lightly browned. Reduce the heat and cook for 2–3 minutes, or until tender. Leave to cool.

Scatter the grated cheese evenly over the base of the pastry case, then arrange the cooled potato on top. Add the smoked salmon in an even layer.

Beat the eggs with the cream and season to taste with salt and pepper. Whisk in the parsley and pour the mixture carefully into the dish.

Reduce the oven to 180°C/350°F/Gas Mark 4 and bake for about 30–40 minutes, or until the filling is set and golden. Serve hot or cold with a mixed salad and baby new potatoes.

HEALTH RATING 

**SPEEDY ALTERNATIVE**
Spanish Omelette with Smoked Cod

**SUGGESTED ACCOMPANIMENT**
Fusilli Pasta with Spicy Tomato Salsa

## SPEEDY ALTERNATIVE
# Spanish Omelette with Smoked Cod

INGREDIENTS **Serves 3–4**

3 tbsp sunflower oil
350 g/12 oz potatoes, peeled and cut into 1 cm/½ inch cubes
2 medium onions, peeled and cut into wedges
2–4 large garlic cloves, peeled and thinly sliced
1 large red pepper, deseeded, quartered and thinly sliced
125 g/4 oz smoked cod
salt and freshly ground black pepper
25 g/1 oz butter, melted
1 tbsp double cream
6 medium eggs, beaten
2 tbsp freshly chopped flat-leaf parsley
50 g/2 oz mature Cheddar cheese, grated

**To serve:**
crusty bread
tossed green salad

Heat the oil in a large, non-stick heavy-based frying pan, add the potatoes, onions and garlic and cook gently for 10–15 minutes until golden brown, then add the red pepper and cook for 3 minutes.

Meanwhile, place the fish in a shallow frying pan and cover with water. Season to taste with salt and pepper and poach gently for 10 minutes. Drain and flake the fish into a bowl, toss in the melted butter and cream, adjust the seasoning and reserve.

When the vegetables are cooked, drain off any excess oil and stir in the beaten egg with the chopped parsley. Pour the fish mixture over the top and cook gently for 5 minutes, or until the eggs become firm.

Sprinkle the grated cheese over the top and place the pan under a preheated hot grill. Cook for 2–3 minutes until the cheese is golden and bubbling. Carefully slide the omelette onto a large plate and serve immediately with plenty of bread and salad.

## SUGGESTED ACCOMPANIMENT
# Fusilli Pasta with Spicy Tomato Salsa

INGREDIENTS **Serves 4**

6 large ripe tomatoes
2 tbsp lemon juice
2 tbsp lime juice
grated rind of 1 lime
2 shallots, peeled and finely chopped
2 garlic cloves, peeled and finely chopped
1–2 red chillies
1–2 green chillies
450 g/1 lb fresh fusilli pasta
4 tbsp crème fraîche
2 tbsp freshly chopped basil
sprig of oregano, to garnish

Place the tomatoes in a bowl and cover with boiling water. Allow to stand until the skins start to peel away.

Remove the skins from the tomatoes, divide each tomato in four and remove all the seeds. Chop the flesh into small cubes and put in a small pan. Add the lemon and lime juice and the grated lime rind and stir well.

Add the chopped shallots and garlic. Carefully remove and discard the seeds from the chillies, then chop finely and add to the pan. Bring to the boil and simmer gently for 5–10 minutes until the salsa has thickened slightly. Reserve the salsa to allow the flavours to develop while the pasta is cooking.

Bring a large pan of water to the boil and add the pasta. Simmer gently for 3–4 minutes or until the pasta is just tender. Drain the pasta and rinse in boiling water. Top with a large spoonful of salsa and a small spoonful of crème fraîche. Garnish with the chopped basil and oregano and serve immediately.

# Goujons of Plaice with Tartare Sauce

INGREDIENTS **Serves 4**

75 g/3 oz fresh white breadcrumbs
3 tbsp freshly grated Parmesan cheese
salt and freshly ground black pepper
1 tbsp dried oregano
1 medium egg
450 g/1 lb plaice fillets
300 ml/½ pint vegetable oil for deep frying
fat chips, to serve

**For the tartare sauce:**

200 ml/7 fl oz prepared mayonnaise
50 g/2 oz gherkins, finely chopped
2 tbsp freshly snipped chives
1 garlic clove, peeled and crushed
2–3 tbsp capers, drained and chopped
pinch of cayenne pepper

Mix together the breadcrumbs, Parmesan cheese, seasoning and oregano on a large plate. Lightly beat the egg in a shallow dish. Then, using a sharp knife, cut the plaice fillets into thick strips. Coat the plaice strips in the beaten egg, allowing any excess to drip back into the dish, then dip the strips into the breadcrumbs until well coated. Place the goujons on a baking sheet, cover and chill in the refrigerator for 30 minutes.

Meanwhile, to make the tartare sauce, mix together the mayonnaise, gherkins, chives, garlic, capers and cayenne pepper. Stir, then season to taste with salt and pepper. Place in a bowl, cover loosely and store in the refrigerator until required.

Pour the oil into a large wok. Heat to 190°C/375°F, or until a small cube of bread turns golden and crisp in about 30 seconds. Cook the plaice goujons in batches for about 4 minutes, turning occasionally until golden. Using a slotted spoon, remove and drain on absorbent kitchen paper. Serve immediately with the tartare sauce and chips.

HEALTH RATING 

**ENTERTAINING ALTERNATIVE**
Teriyaki Salmon

**CHILDREN'S ALTERNATIVE**
Battered Cod & Chunky Chips

**ENTERTAINING ALTERNATIVE**
## Teriyaki Salmon

Using a sharp knife, cut the salmon into thick slices and place in a shallow dish. Mix together the teriyaki sauce, rice wine vinegar, tomato paste, Tabasco sauce, lemon zest and seasoning.

Spoon the marinade over the salmon, then cover loosely and leave to marinate in the refrigerator for 30 minutes, turning the salmon or spooning the marinade occasionally over the salmon.

Heat a large wok, then add 2 tablespoons of the oil until almost smoking. Stir-fry the carrot for 2 minutes, then add the mangetout peas and stir-fry for a further 2 minutes. Add the oyster mushrooms and stir-fry for 4 minutes, until softened. Using a slotted spoon, transfer the vegetables to 4 warmed serving plates and keep warm.

Remove the salmon from the marinade, reserving both the salmon and marinade. Add the remaining oil to the wok, heat until almost smoking, then cook the salmon for 4–5 minutes, turning once during cooking, or until the fish is just flaking. Add the marinade and heat through for 1 minute.

Serve immediately, with the salmon arranged on top of the vegetables and the marinade drizzled over.

INGREDIENTS **Serves 4**

450 g/1 lb salmon fillet, skinned
6 tbsp Japanese teriyaki sauce
1 tbsp rice wine vinegar
1 tbsp tomato paste
dash of tabasco sauce
grated zest of ½ lemon
salt and freshly ground black pepper
4 tbsp groundnut oil
1 carrot, peeled and cut into matchsticks
125 g/4 oz mangetout peas
125 g/4 oz oyster mushrooms, wiped

**CHILDREN'S ALTERNATIVE**
## Battered Cod & Chunky Chips

Dissolve the yeast with a little of the beer in a jug and mix to a paste. Pour in the remaining beer, whisking all the time until smooth. Place the flour and salt in a bowl, and gradually pour in the beer mixture, whisking continuously to make a thick smooth batter. Cover the bowl and allow the batter to stand at room temperature for 1 hour.

Peel the potatoes and cut into thick slices. Cut each slice lengthways to make chunky chips. Place them in a non-stick frying pan and heat, shaking the pan until all the moisture has evaporated. Turn them onto absorbent kitchen paper to dry off.

Heat the oil to 180°C/350°F, then fry the chips a few at a time for 4–5 minutes until crisp and golden. Drain on absorbent kitchen paper and keep warm.

Pat the cod fillets dry, then coat in the flour. Dip the floured fillets into the reserved batter. Fry for 2–3 minutes until cooked and crisp, then drain. Garnish with lemon wedges and parsley and serve immediately with the chips, tomato ketchup and vinegar.

INGREDIENTS **Serves 4**

15 g/½ oz fresh yeast
300 ml/½ pint beer
225 g/8 oz plain flour
1 tsp salt
700 g/1½ lb potatoes
450 ml/¾ pint groundnut oil
4 cod fillets, about 225 g/8 oz each, skinned and boned
2 tbsp seasoned plain flour

**To garnish:**
lemon wedges
sprigs of flat-leaf parsley

**To serve:**
tomato ketchup
vinegar

# Barbecued Fish Kebabs

INGREDIENTS **Serves 4**

450 g/1 lb herring or mackerel fillets, cut into chunks
2 small red onions, peeled and quartered
16 cherry tomatoes
salt and freshly ground black pepper

**For the sauce:**

150 ml/¼ pint fish stock
5 tbsp tomato ketchup
2 tbsp Worcestershire sauce
2 tbsp wine vinegar
2 tbsp brown sugar
2 drops tabasco sauce
2 tbsp tomato purée

Line a grill rack with a single layer of tinfoil and preheat the grill at a high temperature 2 minutes before use.

If using wooden skewers, soak in cold water for 30 minutes to prevent them from catching alight during cooking.

Meanwhile, prepare the sauce. Add the fish stock, tomato ketchup, Worcestershire sauce, vinegar, sugar, tabasco and tomato purée to a small saucepan. Stir well and leave to simmer for 5 minutes.

When ready to cook, drain the skewers, if necessary, then thread the fish chunks, the quartered red onions and the cherry tomatoes alternately on to the skewers.

Season the kebabs to taste with salt and pepper and brush with the sauce. Cook under the preheated grill for 8–10 minutes, basting with the sauce occasionally during cooking. Turn the kebabs often to ensure that they are cooked thoroughly and evenly on all sides. Serve immediately with couscous.

HEALTH RATING

**ENTERTAINING ALTERNATIVE**
Citrus Monkfish Kebabs

**VEGETARIAN ALTERNATIVE**
Marinated Vegetable Kebabs

## ENTERTAINING ALTERNATIVE
# Citrus Monkfish Kebabs

INGREDIENTS **Serves 4**

**For the marinade:**

1 tbsp sunflower oil

finely grated rind and juice of 1 lime

1 tbsp lemon juice

1 sprig of freshly chopped rosemary

1 tbsp whole grain mustard

1 garlic clove, peeled and crushed

salt and freshly ground black pepper

**For the kebabs:**

450 g/1 lb monkfish tail

8 raw tiger prawns

1 small green courgette, trimmed and sliced

4 tbsp crème fraîche

Preheat the grill and line the grill rack with tinfoil. Mix all the marinade ingredients together in a small bowl and reserve.

Using a sharp knife, cut down both sides of the monkfish tail. Remove the bone and discard. Cut away and discard any skin, then cut the monkfish into bite-sized cubes.

Peel the prawns, leaving the tails intact and remove the thin black vein that runs down the back of each prawn. Place the fish and prawns in a shallow dish.

Pour the marinade over the fish and prawns. Cover lightly and leave to marinate in the refrigerator for 30 minutes. Spoon the marinade over the fish and prawns occasionally during this time. If using wooden skewers, soak them in cold water for 30 minutes, then drain.

Thread the cubes of fish, prawns and courgettes on to the skewers. Arrange on the grill rack then place under the preheated grill and cook for 5–7 minutes, or until cooked thoroughly and the prawns have turned pink. Occasionally brush with the remaining marinade and turn the kebabs during cooking. Mix 2 tablespoons of the marinade with the crème fraîche and serve as a dip with the kebabs.

## VEGETARIAN ALTERNATIVE
# Marinated Vegetable Kebabs

INGREDIENTS **Serves 4**

2 small courgettes, cut into 2 cm/¾ inch pieces

½ green pepper, deseeded and cut into 2.5 cm/1 inch pieces

½ red pepper, deseeded and cut into 2.5 cm /1 inch pieces

½ yellow pepper, deseeded and cut into 2.5 cm/1 inch pieces

8 baby onions, peeled

8 button mushrooms

8 cherry tomatoes

freshly chopped parsley, to garnish

freshly cooked couscous, to serve

**For the marinade:**

1 tbsp light olive oil

4 tbsp dry sherry

2 tbsp light soy sauce

1 red chilli, deseeded and finely chopped

2 garlic cloves, peeled and crushed

2.5 cm/1 inch piece root ginger, peeled and finely grated

Place the courgettes, peppers and baby onions in a pan of just boiled water. Bring back to the boil and simmer for about 30 seconds.

Drain and rinse the cooked vegetables in cold water and dry on absorbent kitchen paper.

Thread the cooked vegetables and the mushrooms and tomatoes alternately on to skewers and place in a large shallow dish.

Make the marinade by whisking all the ingredients together until thoroughly blended. Pour the marinade evenly over the kebabs, then chill in the refrigerator for at least 1 hour. Spoon the marinade over the kebabs occasionally during this time.

Place the kebabs in a hot griddle pan or on a hot barbecue and cook gently for 10–12 minutes. Turn the kebabs frequently and brush with the marinade when needed. When the vegetables are tender, sprinkle over the chopped parsley and serve immediately with couscous.

**ENTERTAINING ALTERNATIVE**
## Sweet-&-Sour Prawns with Noodles

INGREDIENTS **Serves 4**

425 g can pineapple pieces in natural juice
1 green pepper, deseeded and cut into quarters
1 tbsp groundnut oil
1 onion, cut into thin wedges
3 tbsp soft brown sugar
150 ml/¼ pint chicken stock
4 tbsp wine vinegar
1 tbsp tomato purée
1 tbsp light soy sauce
1 tbsp cornflour
350 g/12 oz raw tiger prawns, peeled
225 g/8 oz pak choi, shredded
350 g/12 oz medium egg noodles
coriander leaves, to garnish

Make the sauce by draining the pineapple and reserving 2 tablespoons of the juice.

Remove the membrane from the quartered peppers and cut into thin strips.

Heat the oil in a saucepan. Add the onion and pepper and cook for about 4 minutes or until the onion has softened. Add the pineapple, the sugar, stock, vinegar, tomato purée and the soy sauce.

Bring the sauce to the boil and simmer for about 4 minutes. Blend the cornflour with the reserved pineapple juice and stir into the pan, stirring until thickened.

Clean the prawns if needed. Wash the pak choi thoroughly, then shred. Add the prawns and pak choi to the sauce. Simmer gently for 3 minutes or until the prawns are cooked and have turned pink.

Cook the noodles in boiling water for 4–5 minutes until just tender. Drain and arrange the noodles on a warmed plate and pour over the sweet-and-sour prawns. Garnish with coriander leaves and serve immediately.

**STARTER SUGGESTION**
## Chinese Chicken Soup

Remove any skin from the chicken. Place on a chopping board and use two forks to tear the chicken into fine shreds.

Heat the oil in a large saucepan and fry the spring onions and chilli for 1 minute. Add the garlic and ginger and cook for another minute. Stir in the chicken stock and gradually bring the mixture to the boil.

Break up the noodles a little and add to the boiling stock with the carrot. Stir to mix, then reduce the heat to a simmer and cook for 3–4 minutes. Add the shredded chicken, beansprouts, soy sauce and fish sauce and stir. Cook for a further 2–3 minutes until piping hot. Ladle the soup into bowls and sprinkle with the coriander leaves. Serve immediately.

INGREDIENTS **Serves 4**

225 g/8 oz cooked chicken
1 tsp oil
6 spring onions, trimmed and diagonally sliced
1 red chilli, deseeded and finely chopped
1 garlic clove, peeled and crushed
2.5 cm/1 inch piece root ginger, peeled and finely grated
1 litre/1¾ pint chicken stock
150 g/5 oz medium egg noodles
1 carrot, peeled and cut into matchsticks
125 g/4 oz beansprouts
2 tbsp soy sauce
1 tbsp fish sauce
fresh coriander leaves, to garnish

# Crispy Prawn Stir Fry

INGREDIENTS **Serves 4**

3 tbsp soy sauce
1 tsp cornflour
pinch of sugar
6 tbsp groundnut oil
450 g/1 lb raw shelled tiger prawns, halved lengthways
125 g/4 oz carrots, peeled and cut into matchsticks
2.5 cm/1 inch piece fresh root ginger, peeled and cut into matchsticks
125 g/4 oz mangetout peas, trimmed and shredded
125 g/4 oz asparagus spears, cut into short lengths
125 g/4 oz beansprouts
¼ head Chinese leaves, shredded
2 tsp sesame oil

Mix together the soy sauce, cornflour and sugar in a small bowl and reserve.

Heat a large wok, then add 3 tablespoons of the oil and heat until almost smoking. Add the prawns and stir-fry for 4 minutes, or until pink all over. Using a slotted spoon, transfer the prawns to a plate and keep warm in a low oven.

Add the remaining oil to the wok and when just smoking, add the carrots and ginger and stir-fry for 1 minute, or until slightly softened, then add the mangetout peas and stir-fry for a further 1 minute. Add the asparagus and stir-fry for 4 minutes, or until softened.

Add the beansprouts and Chinese leaves and stir-fry for 2 minutes, or until the leaves are slightly wilted. Pour in the soy sauce mixture and return the prawns to the wok. Stir-fry over a medium heat until piping hot, then add the sesame oil, give a final stir and serve immediately.

## HEALTH RATING

**ENTERTAINING ALTERNATIVE**

Sweet-&-Sour Prawns with Noodles

**STARTER SUGGESTION**

Chinese Chicken Soup

# Meat

From updated classics such as Spaghetti Bolognese and Lasagne to delicious dishes from India and the Far East, the mouth-watering recipes in this section will inspire you to try new things with beef, pork and lamb. And if you're not a meat-lover, vegetarian alternatives and suggested accompaniments, starters and puddings mean that there's something for everyone.

# Spaghetti Bolognese

INGREDIENTS **Serves 4**

3 tbsp olive oil
50 g/2 oz unsmoked streaky bacon, rind removed and chopped
1 small onion, peeled and finely chopped
1 carrot, peeled and finely chopped
1 celery, trimmed and finely chopped
2 garlic cloves, peeled and crushed
1 bay leaf
500 g/1 lb 2 oz minced beef steak
400 g can chopped tomatoes
2 tbsp tomato paste
150 ml/¼ pint red wine
150 ml/¼ pint beef stock
salt and freshly ground black pepper
450 g/1 lb spaghetti
freshly grated Parmesan cheese, to serve

Heat the olive oil in a large heavy-based pan, add the bacon and cook for 5 minutes or until slightly coloured. Add the onion, carrot, celery, garlic and bay leaf and cook, stirring, for 8 minutes, or until the vegetables are soft.

Add the minced beef to the pan and cook, stirring with a wooden spoon to break up any lumps in the meat, for 5–8 minutes or until browned.

Stir the tomatoes and tomato paste into the mince and pour in the wine and stock. Bring to the boil, lower the heat and simmer for a least 40 minutes, stirring occasionally. The longer you leave the sauce to cook, the more intense the flavour. Season to taste with salt and pepper and remove the bay leaf.

Meanwhile, bring a large pan of lightly salted water to a rolling boil, add the spaghetti and cook for about 8 minutes or until 'al dente'. Drain and arrange on warmed serving plates. Top with the prepared Bolognese sauce and serve immediately sprinkled with grated Parmesan cheese.

HEALTH RATING

**VEGETARIAN ALTERNATIVE**
Vegetarian Spaghetti Bolognese

**SUGGESTED ACCOMPANIMENT**
Warm Leek & Tomato Salad

## VEGETARIAN ALTERNATIVE
# Vegetarian Spaghetti Bolognese

INGREDIENTS **Serves 4**

2 tbsp olive oil
1 onion, peeled and finely chopped
1 carrot, peeled and finely chopped
1 celery stick, trimmed and finely chopped
225 g/8 oz Quorn™ mince
150 ml/¼ pint red wine
300 ml/½ pint vegetable stock
1 tsp mushroom ketchup
4 tbsp tomato purée
350 g/12 oz dried spaghetti
4 tbsp crème fraîche
salt and freshly ground black pepper
1 tbsp freshly chopped parsley

Heat the oil in a large saucepan and add the onion, carrot and celery. Cook gently for 10 minutes, adding a little water if necessary, until softened and starting to brown.

Add the Quorn™ mince and cook for a further 2–3 minutes before adding the red wine. Increase the heat and simmer gently until nearly all the wine has evaporated.

Mix together the vegetable stock and mushroom ketchup and add about half to the Quorn™ mixture along with the tomato purée. Cover and simmer gently for about 45 minutes, adding the remaining stock as necessary.

Meanwhile, bring a large pan of salted water to the boil and add the spaghetti. Cook until 'al dente' or according to the packet instructions. Drain well. Remove the sauce from the heat, add the crème fraîche and season to taste with salt and pepper. Stir in the parsley and serve immediately with the pasta.

## SUGGESTED ACCOMPANIMENT
# Warm Leek & Tomato Salad

INGREDIENTS **Serves 4**

450 g/1 lb trimmed baby leeks
225 g/8 oz ripe, but firm tomatoes
2 shallots, peeled and cut into thin wedges

**Honey and lime dressing:**

2 tbsp clear honey
grated rind of 1 lime
4 tbsp lime juice
1 tbsp light olive oil
1 tsp Dijon mustard
salt and freshly ground black pepper

**To garnish:**

freshly chopped tarragon
freshly chopped basil

Trim the leeks so that they are all the same length. Place in a steamer over a pan of boiling water and steam for 8 minutes or until just tender.

Drain the leeks thoroughly and arrange in a shallow serving dish.

Make a cross in the top of the tomatoes, place in a bowl and cover them with boiling water until the skins start to peel away. Remove from the bowl and carefully remove the skins.

Cut the tomatoes into quarters and remove the seeds, then chop into small dice. Spoon over the top of the leeks together with the shallots.

In a small bowl make the dressing by whisking the honey, lime rind, lime juice, olive oil, mustard and salt and pepper. Pour 3 tablespoons of the dressing over the leeks and tomatoes and garnish with the tarragon and basil. Serve while the leeks are still warm, with the remaining dressing served separately.

# Lasagne

INGREDIENTS **Serves 4**

**For the white sauce:**

75 g/3 oz butter
4 tbsp plain flour
750 ml/1¼ pints milk
1 tsp wholegrain mustard
salt and freshly ground black pepper
¼ tsp freshly grated nutmeg

9 sheets lasagne
1 quantity of prepared Bolognese sauce (see page 124)
75g/3oz freshly grated Parmesan cheese
freshly chopped parsley, to garnish
garlic bread, to serve

Preheat the oven to 200°C/400°F/Gas Mark 6, 15 minutes before cooking. Melt the butter in a small heavy-based pan, add the flour and cook gently, stirring, for 2 minutes. Remove from the heat and gradually stir in the milk. Return to the heat and cook, stirring, for 2 minutes, or until the sauce thickens. Bring to the boil, remove from the heat and stir in the mustard. Season to taste with salt, pepper and nutmeg.

Butter a rectangular ovenproof dish and spread a thin layer of the white sauce over the base. Cover completely with 3 sheets of lasagne. Spoon a quarter of the prepared Bolognese sauce over the lasagne. Spoon over a quarter of the remaining white sauce, then sprinkle with a quarter of the grated Parmesan cheese. Repeat the layers, finishing with Parmesan cheese. Bake in the preheated oven for 30 minutes, or until golden brown. Garnish with chopped parsley and serve immediately with warm garlic bread.

## HEALTH RATING 

**SEAFOOD ALTERNATIVE**
Fish Lasagne

**VEGETARIAN ALTERNATIVE**
Courgette Lasagne

**SEAFOOD ALTERNATIVE**
## Fish Lasagne

INGREDIENTS **Serves 4**

75 g/3 oz mushrooms
1 tsp sunflower oil
1 small onion, peeled and finely chopped
1 tbsp freshly chopped oregano
400 g can chopped tomatoes
1 tbsp tomato purée
salt and freshly ground black pepper
450 g/1 lb cod or haddock fillets, skinned
9–12 sheets pre-cooked lasagne verde

**For the topping:**

1 medium egg, beaten
125 g/4 oz cottage cheese
150 ml/¼ pint natural yogurt
50 g/2 oz Cheddar cheese, grated

**To serve:**

mixed salad leaves
cherry tomatoes

Preheat the oven to 190°C/375°F/Gas Mark 5. Wipe the mushrooms, trim the stalks and chop. Heat the oil in a large heavy-based pan, add the onion and gently cook for 3–5 minutes or until soft. Stir in the mushrooms, the oregano and the chopped tomatoes with their juice.

Blend the tomato purée with 1 tablespoon of water. Stir into the pan and season to taste with salt and pepper.

Bring the sauce to the boil, then simmer uncovered for 5–10 minutes.

Remove as many of the tiny pin bones as possible from the fish and cut into cubes and add to the tomato sauce mixture. Stir gently and remove the pan from the heat.

Cover the base of an ovenproof dish with 2–3 sheets of the lasagne verde. Top with half of the fish mixture. Repeat the layers finishing with the lasagne sheets.

To make the topping, mix together the beaten egg, cottage cheese and yogurt. Pour over the lasagne and sprinkle with the cheese.

Cook the lasagne in the preheated oven for 35–40 minutes or until the topping is golden brown and bubbling. Serve the lasagne immediately with the mixed salad leaves and cherry tomatoes.

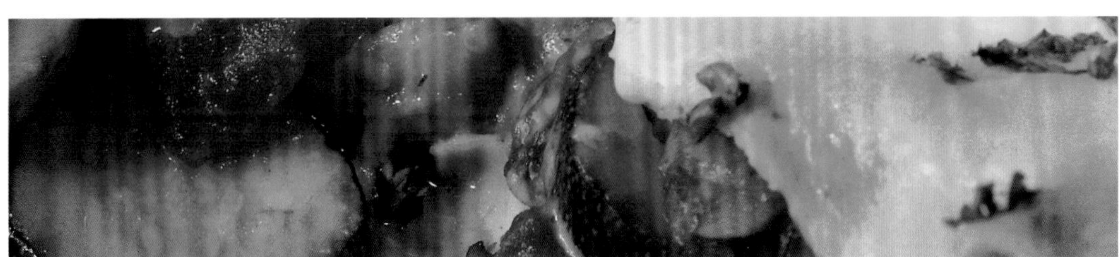

**VEGETARIAN ALTERNATIVE**
## Courgette Lasagne

INGREDIENTS **Serves 4**

2 tbsp olive oil
1 medium onion, peeled and finely chopped
225 g/8 oz mushrooms, wiped and thinly sliced
3–4 courgettes, trimmed and thinly sliced
2 garlic cloves, peeled and finely chopped
½ tsp dried thyme
1–2 tbsp freshly chopped basil or flat leaf parsley
salt and freshly ground black pepper
1 quantity prepared white sauce (see page 126)
350 g/12 oz lasagne sheets, cooked
225 g/8 oz mozzarella cheese, grated
50 g/2 oz Parmesan cheese, grated
400 g can chopped tomatoes, drained

Preheat the oven to 200°C/400°F/Gas Mark 6, 15 minutes before cooking. Heat the oil in a large frying pan, add the onion and cook for 3–5 minutes. Add the mushrooms, cook for 2 minutes then add the courgettes and cook for a further 3–4 minutes, or until tender. Stir in the garlic, thyme and basil or parsley and season to taste with salt and pepper. Remove from the heat and reserve.

Spoon a third of the white sauce on to the base of a lightly-oiled large baking dish. Arrange a layer of lasagne over the sauce. Spread half the courgette mixture over the pasta, then sprinkle with some of the mozzarella and some of the Parmesan cheese. Repeat with more white sauce and another layer of lasagne, then cover with half the drained tomatoes.

Cover the tomatoes with lasagne, the remaining courgette mixture, and some mozzarella and Parmesan cheese. Repeat the layers ending with a layer of lasagne sheets, white sauce and the remaining Parmesan cheese. Bake in the preheated oven for 35 minutes or until golden. Serve immediately.

# Pan-fried Beef with Creamy Mushrooms

INGREDIENTS **Serves 4**

225 g/8 oz shallots, peeled
2 garlic cloves, peeled
2 tbsp olive oil
4 medallions of beef
4 plum tomatoes
125 g/4 oz flat mushrooms
3 tbsp brandy
150 ml/¼ pint red wine
salt and freshly ground black pepper
4 tbsp double cream

**To serve:**

baby new potatoes
freshly cooked green beans

Cut the shallots in half if large, then chop the garlic. Heat the oil in a large frying pan and cook the shallots for about 8 minutes, stirring occasionally, until almost softened. Add the garlic and beef and cook for 8–10 minutes, turning once during cooking until the meat is browned all over. Using a slotted spoon, transfer the beef to a plate and keep warm.

Rinse the tomatoes and cut into eighths, then wipe the mushrooms and slice. Add to the pan and cook for 5 minutes, stirring frequently until the mushrooms have softened.

Pour in the brandy and heat through. Draw the pan off the heat and carefully ignite. Allow the flames to subside. Pour in the wine, return to the heat and bring to the boil. Boil until reduced by one-third. Draw the pan off the heat, season to taste with salt and pepper, add the cream and stir.

Arrange the beef on serving plates and spoon over the sauce. Serve with baby new potatoes and a few green beans.

HEALTH RATING

**MEDITERRANEAN ALTERNATIVE**

Fillet Steaks with Tomato & Garlic Sauce

**SUGGESTED ACCOMPANIMENT**

Hot & Spicy Red Cabbage with Apples

**MEDITERRANEAN ALTERNATIVE**
## Fillet Steaks with Tomato & Garlic Sauce

INGREDIENTS **Serves 4**

- 700 g/1½ lb ripe tomatoes
- 2 garlic cloves
- 2 tbsp olive oil
- 2 tbsp freshly chopped basil
- 2 tbsp freshly chopped oregano
- 2 tbsp red wine
- salt and freshly ground black pepper
- 75 g/3 oz pitted black olives, chopped
- 4 fillet steaks, about 175 g/6 oz each in weight
- freshly cooked vegetables, to serve

Make a small cross on the top of each tomato and place in a large bowl. Cover with boiling water and leave for 2 minutes. Using a slotted spoon, remove the tomatoes and skin carefully. Repeat until all the tomatoes are skinned. Place on a chopping board, cut into quarters, remove the seeds and roughly chop, then reserve.

Peel and chop the garlic. Heat half the olive oil in a saucepan and cook the garlic for 30 seconds. Add the chopped tomatoes with the basil, oregano, red wine and season to taste with salt and pepper. Bring to the boil then reduce the heat, cover and simmer for 15 minutes, stirring occasionally, or until the sauce is reduced and thickened. Stir the olives into the sauce and keep warm while cooking the steaks.

Lightly oil a griddle pan or heavy-based frying pan with the remaining olive oil and cook the steaks for 2 minutes on each side to seal. Continue to cook the steaks for a further 2–4 minutes, depending on personal preference. Serve the steaks immediately with the garlic sauce and freshly cooked vegetables.

**SUGGESTED ACCOMPANIMENT**
## Hot & Spicy Red Cabbage with Apples

Preheat the oven to 150°C/300°F/Gas Mark 2. Put just enough cabbage in a large casserole dish to cover the base evenly.

Place a layer of the onions and apples on top of the cabbage. Sprinkle a little of the mixed spice, cinnamon and sugar over the top. Season with salt and pepper.

Spoon over a small portion of the orange rind, orange juice and the cider.

Continue to layer the casserole dish with the ingredients in the same order until used up.

Pour the vinegar as evenly as possible over the top layer of the ingredients.

Cover the casserole dish with a close-fitting lid and bake in the preheated oven, stirring occasionally, for 2 hours until the cabbage is moist and tender. Serve immediately with the crème fraîche and black pepper.

INGREDIENTS **Serves 4**

- 900 g/2 lb red cabbage, cored and shredded
- 450 g/1 lb onions, peeled and finely sliced
- 450 g/1 lb cooking apples, peeled, cored and finely sliced
- ½ tsp mixed spice
- 1 tsp ground cinnamon
- 2 tbsp soft light brown sugar
- salt and freshly ground black pepper
- grated rind of 1 large orange
- 1 tbsp fresh orange juice
- 50 ml/2 fl oz medium sweet cider (or apple juice)
- 2 tbsp wine vinegar

**To serve:**

- crème fraîche
- freshly ground black pepper

**SUGGESTED ACCOMPANIMENT**
## Sicilian Baked Aubergine

INGREDIENTS **Serves 4**

- 1 large aubergine, trimmed
- 2 celery stalks, trimmed
- 4 large ripe tomatoes
- 1 tsp sunflower oil
- 2 shallots, peeled and finely chopped
- 1½ tsp tomato purée
- 25 g/1 oz green pitted olives
- 25 g/1 oz black pitted olives
- salt and freshly ground black pepper
- 1 tbsp white wine vinegar
- 2 tsp caster sugar
- 1 tbsp freshly chopped basil, to garnish
- mixed salad leaves, to serve

Preheat the oven to 200°C/400°F/Gas Mark 6. Cut the aubergine into small cubes and place on an oiled baking tray. Cover the tray with tinfoil and bake in the preheated oven for 15–20 minutes until soft. Reserve, to allow the aubergine to cool.

Place the celery and tomatoes in a large bowl and cover with boiling water. Remove the tomatoes from the bowl when their skins begin to peel away. Remove the skins, then deseed and chop the flesh into small pieces. Remove the celery from the bowl of water, finely chop and reserve.

Pour the vegetable oil into a non-stick saucepan, add the chopped shallots and fry gently for 2–3 minutes until soft. Add the celery, tomatoes, tomato purée and olives. Season to taste with salt and pepper.

Simmer gently for 3–4 minutes. Add the vinegar, sugar and cooled aubergine to the pan and heat gently for 2–3 minutes until all the ingredients are well blended. Reserve to allow the aubergine mixture to cool. When cool, garnish with the chopped basil and serve cold with salad leaves.

**STARTER SUGGESTION**
## Stilton, Tomato & Courgette Quiche

INGREDIENTS **Serves 4**

- 1 quantity shortcrust pastry (see page 10)
- 25 g/1 oz butter
- 1 onion, peeled and finely chopped
- 1 courgette, trimmed and sliced
- 125 g/4 oz Stilton cheese, crumbled
- 6 cherry tomatoes, halved
- 2 large eggs, beaten
- 200 ml tub crème fraîche
- salt and freshly ground black pepper

Preheat the oven to 190°C/375°F/Gas Mark 5. On a lightly floured surface, roll out the pastry and use to line an 18 cm/7 inch lightly oiled quiche or flan tin, trimming any excess pastry with a knife.

Prick the base all over with a fork and bake blind in the preheated oven for 15 minutes. Remove the pastry from the oven and brush with a little of the beaten egg. Return to the oven for a further 5 minutes.

Heat the butter in a frying pan and gently fry the onion and courgette for about 4 minutes until soft and starting to brown. Transfer into the pastry case.

Sprinkle the Stilton over evenly and top with the halved cherry tomatoes. Beat together the eggs and crème fraîche and season to taste with salt and pepper.

Pour the filling into the pastry case and bake in the oven for 35–40 minutes, or until the filling is golden brown and set in the centre. Serve the quiche hot or cold.

# Grilled Steaks with Saffron Potatoes & Roast Tomatoes

INGREDIENTS **Serves 4**

700 g/1½ lb new potatoes, halved
few strands of saffron
300 ml/½ pint vegetable or beef stock
1 small onion, peeled and finely chopped
75 g/3 oz butter
salt and freshly ground black pepper
2 tsp balsamic vinegar
2 tbsp olive oil
1 tsp caster sugar
8 plum tomatoes, halved
4 boneless sirloin steaks, each weighing 225 g/8 oz
2 tbsp freshly chopped parsley

Cook the potatoes in boiling salted water for 8 minutes and drain well. Return the potatoes to the saucepan along with the saffron, stock, onion and 25 g/1 oz of the butter. Season to taste with salt and pepper and simmer, uncovered for 10 minutes until the potatoes are tender.

Meanwhile, preheat the grill to medium. Mix together the vinegar, olive oil, sugar and seasoning. Arrange the tomatoes cut-side up in a foil-lined grill pan and drizzle over the dressing. Grill for 12–15 minutes, basting occasionally, until tender.

Melt the remaining butter in a frying pan. Add the steaks and cook for 4–8 minutes to taste and depending on thickness.

Arrange the potatoes and tomatoes in the centre of four serving plates. Top with the steaks along with any pan juices. Sprinkle over the parsley and serve immediately.

## HEALTH RATING

**SUGGESTED ACCOMPANIMENT**
Sicilian Baked Aubergine

**STARTER SUGGESTION**
Stilton, Tomato & Courgette Quiche

# Thai Beef Curry with Lemon & Arborio Rice

INGREDIENTS **Serves 4**

450 g/1 lb beef fillet
1 tbsp olive oil
2 tbsp Thai green curry paste
1 green pepper, deseeded and cut into strips
1 red pepper, deseeded and cut into strips
1 celery stick, trimmed and sliced
juice of 1 fresh lemon
2 tsp Thai fish sauce
2 tsp demerara sugar
225 g/8 oz Arborio rice
15 g/½ oz butter
2 tbsp freshly chopped coriander
4 tbsp crème fraîche

Trim the beef fillet, discarding any fat, then cut across the grain into thin slices. Heat a wok, add the oil and when hot, add the green curry paste and cook for 30 seconds. Add the beef strips and stir-fry for 3–4 minutes.

Add the sliced peppers and the celery and continue to stir-fry for 2 minutes. Add the lemon juice, Thai fish sauce and sugar and cook for a further 3–4 minutes, or until the beef is tender and cooked to personal preference.

Meanwhile, cook the Arborio rice in a saucepan of lightly salted boiling water for 15–20 minutes, or until tender. Drain, rinse with boiling water and drain again. Return to the saucepan and add the butter. Cover and allow the butter to melt before turning it out onto a large serving dish. Sprinkle the cooked curry with the chopped coriander and serve immediately with the rice and crème fraîche.

## HEALTH RATING ❛❛❛

**SUGGESTED ACCOMPANIMENT**

Spicy Filled Naan Bread

**PUDDING SUGGESTION**

Lemony Coconut Cake

**SUGGESTED ACCOMPANIMENT**
## Spicy Filled Naan Bread

INGREDIENTS **Makes 6**

- 400 g/14 oz strong white flour
- 1 tsp salt
- 1 tsp easy-blend dried yeast
- 15 g/½ oz ghee or unsalted butter, melted
- 1 tsp clear honey
- 200 ml/7 fl oz warm water

**For the filling:**

- 25 g/1 oz ghee or unsalted butter
- 1 small onion, peeled and finely chopped
- 1 garlic clove, peeled and crushed
- 1 tsp ground coriander
- 1 tsp ground cumin
- 2 tsp grated fresh root ginger
- pinch of chilli powder
- pinch of ground cinnamon
- salt and freshly ground black pepper

Preheat the oven to 220°C/450°F/Gas Mark 8, 15 minutes before baking and place a large baking sheet in to heat up. Sift the flour and salt into a large bowl. Stir in the yeast and make a well in the centre. Add the ghee or melted butter, honey and warm water. Mix to a soft dough.

Knead the dough on a lightly floured surface until smooth and elastic. Put in a lightly oiled bowl, cover with clingfilm and leave to rise for 1 hour, or until doubled in size.

For the filling, melt the ghee or butter in a frying pan and gently cook the onion for about 5 minutes. Stir in the garlic and spices and season to taste with salt and pepper. Cook for a further 6–7 minutes, until soft. Remove from the heat, stir in 1 tablespoon of water and leave to cool.

Briefly knead the dough, then divide into six pieces. Roll out each piece of dough to 12.5 cm/5 inch rounds. Spoon the filling on to one half of each round. Fold over and press the edges together to seal. Re-roll to shape into flat ovals, about 16 cm/6½ inches long. Cover with oiled clingfilm and leave to rise for about 15 minutes.

Transfer the breads to the hot baking sheet and cook in the preheated oven for 10–12 minutes, until puffed up and lightly browned. Serve hot.

**PUDDING SUGGESTION**
## Lemony Coconut Cake

INGREDIENTS **Cuts into 10–12 slices**

- 275 g/10 oz plain flour
- 2 tbsp cornflour
- 1 tbsp baking powder
- 1 tsp salt
- 150 g/5 oz white vegetable fat or soft margarine
- 275 g/10 oz caster sugar
- grated zest of 2 lemons
- 1 tsp vanilla essence
- 3 large eggs
- 150 ml/¼ pint milk
- 4 tbsp Malibu or rum
- 450 g/1 lb jar lemon curd
- lime zest, to decorate

**For the frosting:**

- 275 g/10 oz caster sugar
- 125 ml/4 fl oz water
- 1 tbsp glucose
- ¼ tsp salt
- 1 tsp vanilla essence
- 3 large egg whites
- 75 g/3 oz shredded coconut

Preheat the oven to 180°C/350°F/Gas Mark 4, 10 minutes before baking. Lightly oil and flour two 20.5 cm/8 inch non-stick cake tins.

Sift the flour, cornflour, baking powder and salt into a large bowl and add the white vegetable fat or margarine, sugar, lemon zest, vanilla essence, eggs and milk. With an electric whisk on a low speed, beat until blended, adding a little extra milk if the mixture is very stiff. Increase the speed to medium and beat for about 2 minutes.

Divide the mixture between the tins and smooth the tops evenly. Bake in the preheated oven for 20–25 minutes, or until the cakes feel firm and are cooked. Remove from the oven and cool before removing from the tins.

Put all the ingredients for the frosting, except the coconut, into a heatproof bowl placed over a saucepan of simmering water. (Do not allow the base of the bowl to touch the water.) Using an electric whisk, blend the frosting ingredients on a low speed. Increase the speed to high and beat for 7 minutes, until the whites are stiff and glossy. Remove the bowl from the heat and continue beating until cool. Cover with clingfilm.

Using a serrated knife, split the cake layers horizontally in half and sprinkle each cut surface with the Malibu or rum. Sandwich the cakes together with the lemon curd and press lightly.

Spread the top and sides generously with the frosting, swirling and peaking the top. Sprinkle the coconut over the top of the cake and gently press on to the sides to cover. Decorate the coconut cake with the lime zest and serve.

# Beef & Red Wine Pie

INGREDIENTS **Serves 4**

- 1 quantity quick flaky pastry (see French Onion Tart, page 234), chilled
- 700 g/1½ lb stewing beef, cubed
- 4 tbsp seasoned plain flour
- 2 tbsp sunflower oil
- 2 onions, peeled and chopped
- 2 garlic cloves, peeled and crushed
- 1 tbsp fresh thyme
- 300 ml/½ pint red wine
- 150 ml/¼ pint beef stock
- 1–2 tsp Worcestershire sauce
- 2 tbsp tomato ketchup
- 2 bay leaves
- a knob of butter
- 225 g/8 oz button mushrooms
- beaten egg or milk, to glaze
- sprig of parsley, to garnish

Preheat the oven to 200°C/400°F/Gas Mark 6. Toss the beef cubes in the seasoned flour.

Heat the oil in a large, heavy-based frying pan. Fry the beef in batches for about 5 minutes until golden brown.

Return all of the beef to the pan and add the onions, garlic and thyme. Fry for about 10 minutes, stirring occasionally. If the beef begins to stick, add a little water.

Add the red wine and stock and bring to the boil. Stir in the Worcestershire sauce, tomato ketchup and bay leaves.

Cover and simmer on a very low heat for about 1 hour or until the beef is tender.

Heat the butter and gently sauté the mushrooms until golden brown. Add to the stew. Simmer uncovered for a further 15 minutes. Remove the bay leaves, spoon the beef into a 1.1 litre/2 pint pie dish and reserve.

Roll out the pastry on a lightly floured surface. Cut out the lid to 5 mm/¼ inch wider than the dish. Brush the rim with the beaten egg and lay the pastry lid on top. Press to seal, then knock the edges with the back of the knife.

Cut a slit in the lid and brush with the beaten egg or milk to glaze. Bake in the preheated oven for 30 minutes, or until golden brown. Garnish with the sprig of parsley and serve immediately.

HEALTH RATING

**MEDITERRANEAN ALTERNATIVE**

Italian Beef Pot Roast

**PUDDING SUGGESTION**

Egg Custard Tart

**MEDITERRANEAN ALTERNATIVE**
## Italian Beef Pot Roast

INGREDIENTS **Serves 6**

1.8 kg/4 lb brisket of beef
225 g/8 oz small onions, peeled
3 garlic cloves, peeled and chopped
2 celery sticks, trimmed and chopped
2 carrots, peeled and sliced
450 g/1 lb ripe tomatoes
300 ml/½ pint Italian red wine
2 tbsp olive oil
300 ml/½ pint beef stock
1 tbsp tomato purée
2 tsp freeze-dried mixed herbs
salt and freshly ground black pepper
25 g/1 oz butter
25 g/1 oz plain flour
freshly cooked vegetables, to serve

Preheat the oven to 150°C/300°F/Gas Mark 2, 10 minutes before cooking. Place the beef in a bowl. Add the onions, garlic, celery and carrots. Place the tomatoes in a bowl and cover with boiling water. Allow to stand for 2 minutes and drain. Peel away the skins, discard the seeds and chop, then add to the bowl with the red wine. Cover tightly and marinate in the refrigerator overnight.

Lift the marinated beef from the bowl and pat dry with absorbent kitchen paper. Heat the olive oil in a large casserole dish and cook the beef until it is browned all over, then remove from the dish. Drain the vegetables from the marinade, reserving the marinade. Add the vegetables to the casserole dish and fry gently for 5 minutes, stirring occasionally, until all the vegetables are browned.

Return the beef to the casserole dish with the marinade, beef stock, tomato purée, mixed herbs and season with salt and pepper. Bring to the boil, then cover and cook in the preheated oven for 3 hours.

Using a slotted spoon transfer the beef and any large vegetables to a plate and leave in a warm place. Blend the butter and flour to form a paste. Bring the casserole juices to the boil and then gradually stir in small spoonfuls of the paste. Cook until thickened. Serve with the sauce and a selection of vegetables.

**PUDDING SUGGESTION**
## Egg Custard Tart

INGREDIENTS **Serves 6**

**Sweet pastry:**
50 g/2 oz butter
50 g/2 oz white vegetable fat
175 g/6 oz plain flour
1 medium egg yolk, beaten
2 tsp caster sugar

**For the filling:**
300 ml/½ pint milk
2 medium eggs, plus 1 medium egg yolk
25 g/1 oz caster sugar
½ tsp freshly grated nutmeg

Preheat the oven to 200°C/400°F/Gas Mark 6. Oil a 20.5 cm/8 inch flan tin or dish.

Make the pastry by cutting the butter and vegetable fat into small cubes. Add to the flour in a large bowl and rub in, until the mixture resembles fine breadcrumbs.

Add the egg, sugar and enough water to form a soft and pliable dough. Turn on to a lightly floured board and knead. Wrap and chill in the refrigerator for 30 minutes.

Roll the pastry out on to a lightly floured surface or pastry board and use to line the oiled flan tin. Place in the refrigerator to chill.

Warm the milk in a small saucepan. Briskly whisk together the eggs, egg yolk and caster sugar.

Pour the milk into the egg mixture and whisk until blended.

Strain through a sieve into the pastry case. Place the flan tin on a baking sheet.

Sprinkle the top of the tart with nutmeg and bake in the preheated oven for about 15 minutes.

Turn the oven down to 170°C/325°F/Gas Mark 3 and bake for a further 30 minutes, or until the custard has set. Serve hot or cold.

**MILD ALTERNATIVE**
## Beef with Paprika

INGREDIENTS **Serves 4**

700 g/1½ lb rump steak
3 tbsp plain flour
salt and freshly ground black pepper
1 tbsp paprika
350 g/12 oz long-grain rice
75 g/3 oz butter
1 tsp oil
1 onion, peeled and thinly sliced into rings
225 g/8 oz button mushrooms, wiped and sliced
2 tsp dry sherry
150 ml/¼ pint soured cream
2 tbsp freshly snipped chives
bundle of chives, to garnish

Beat the steak until very thin, then trim off and discard the fat and cut into thin strips. Season the flour with the salt, pepper and paprika, then toss the steak in the flour until coated.

Meanwhile, place the rice in a saucepan of boiling salted water and simmer for 15 minutes until tender, or according to packet directions. Drain the rice, then return to the saucepan, add 25 g/1 oz of the butter, cover and keep warm.

Heat the wok, then add the oil and 25 g/1 oz of the butter. When hot, stir-fry the meat for 3–5 minutes until sealed. Remove from the wok with a slotted spoon and reserve. Add the remaining butter to the wok and stir-fry the onion rings and button mushrooms for 3–4 minutes.

Add the sherry while the wok is very hot, then turn down the heat. Return the steak to the wok with the soured cream and seasoning to taste. Heat through until piping hot, then sprinkle with the snipped chives. Garnish with bundles of chives and serve immediately with the cooked rice.

**SUGGESTED ACCOMPANIMENT**
## Oriental Noodle & Peanut Salad with Coriander

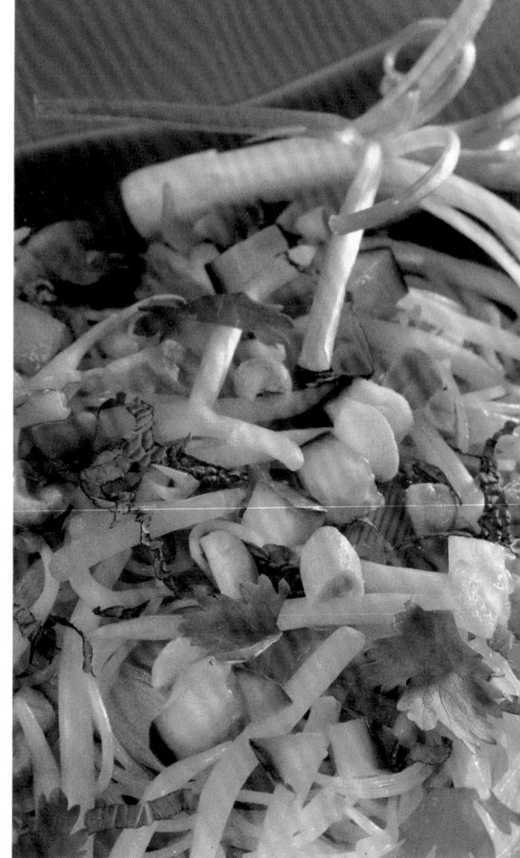

Put the noodles into a large bowl. Bring the stock to the boil and immediately pour over the noodles. Leave to soak for 4 minutes, or according to the packet directions. Drain well, discarding the stock or saving it for another use. Mix together the sesame oil and soy sauce and pour over the hot noodles. Toss well to coat and leave until cold.

Trim and thinly slice four of the spring onions. Heat the oil in a wok over a low heat. Add the spring onions and, as soon as they sizzle, remove from the heat and leave to cool. When cold, toss with the noodles.

Cut the remaining spring onions lengthways 4–6 times and leave in a bowl of cold water until tassels form. Serve the noodles in individual bowls, each dressed with a little chilli, coriander, mint, cucumber, beansprouts and peanuts. Garnish with the spring onion tassels and serve.

INGREDIENTS **Serves 4**

350 g/12 oz rice vermicelli
1 litre/1¾ pints light chicken stock
2 tsp sesame oil
2 tbsp light soy sauce
8 spring onions
3 tbsp groundnut oil
2 hot green chillis, deseeded and thinly sliced
25 g/1 oz roughly chopped coriander
2 tbsp freshly chopped mint
125 g/4 oz cucumber, finely chopped
40 g/1½ oz beansprouts
40 g/1½ oz roasted peanuts, roughly chopped

# Shredded Chilli Beef

INGREDIENTS **Serves 4**

450 g/1 lb lean beef steak, cut into very thin strips
1 tbsp Chinese rice wine
1 tbsp light soy sauce
2 tsp sesame oil
2 tsp cornflour
8 red chillies, deseeded
8 garlic cloves, peeled
225 g/8 oz onion, peeled and sliced
1 tsp Thai red curry paste
6 tbsp groundnut oil
2 red peppers, deseeded and sliced
2 celery stalks, trimmed and sliced
2 tbsp Thai fish sauce
1 tbsp dark soy sauce
shredded basil leaves and a sprig of fresh basil, to garnish
freshly cooked noodles, to serve

Place the beef in a bowl with the Chinese rice wine, light soy sauce, sesame oil and cornflour and mix well. Cover with clingfilm and leave to marinate in the refrigerator for 20 minutes, turning the beef over at least once.

Place the chillies, garlic, onion and red curry paste in a food processor and blend to form a smooth paste.

Drain the beef, shaking off any excess marinade. Heat a wok and add 3 tablespoons of the groundnut oil. When almost smoking, add the beef and stir-fry for 1 minute. Using a slotted spoon, remove the beef and reserve.

Wipe the wok clean, reheat and add the remaining oil. When hot add the chilli paste and stir-fry for 30 seconds. Add the peppers and celery with the fish sauce and dark soy sauce. Stir-fry for 2 minutes. Return the beef to the wok and stir-fry for a further 2 minutes or until the beef is cooked. Place into a warmed serving dish, sprinkle with shredded basil and a basil sprig and serve immediately with noodles.

HEALTH RATING

**MILD ALTERNATIVE**
Beef with Paprika

**SUGGESTED ACCOMPANIMENT**
Oriental Noodle & Peanut Salad with Coriander

# Coconut Beef

INGREDIENTS **Serves 4**

450 g/1 lb beef rump or sirloin steak
4 tbsp groundnut oil
2 bunches spring onions, trimmed and thickly sliced
1 red chilli, deseeded and chopped
1 garlic clove, peeled and chopped
2 cm/1 inch piece fresh root ginger, peeled and cut into matchsticks
125 g/4 oz Chinese (shiitake) mushrooms
200 ml/7 fl oz coconut milk
150 ml/¼ pint chicken stock
4 tbsp freshly chopped coriander
salt and freshly ground black pepper
freshly cooked rice, to serve

Trim off any fat or gristle from the beef and cut into thin strips. Heat a wok or large frying pan, add 2 tablespoons of the oil and heat until just smoking.

Add the beef and cook for 5–8 minutes, turning occasionally, until browned on all sides. Using a slotted spoon, transfer the beef to a plate and keep warm.

Add the remaining oil to the wok and heat until almost smoking. Add the spring onions, chilli, garlic and ginger and cook for 1 minute, stirring occasionally.

Add the mushrooms and stir-fry for 3 minutes. Using a slotted spoon, transfer the mushroom mixture to a plate and keep warm.

Return the beef to the wok, pour in the coconut cream and stock. Bring to the boil and simmer for 3–4 minutes, or until the juices are slightly reduced and the beef is just tender.

Return the mushroom mixture to the wok and heat through. Stir in the chopped coriander and season to taste with salt and pepper. Serve immediately with freshly cooked rice.

HEALTH RATING

**STARTER SUGGESTION**

Crispy Prawns with Chinese Dipping Sauce

**PUDDING SUGGESTION**

Chocolate & Lemon Grass Mousse

**STARTER SUGGESTION**
## Crispy Prawns with Chinese Dipping Sauce

INGREDIENTS **Serves 4**

450 g/1 lb medium-sized raw prawns, peeled
¼ tsp salt
6 tbsp groundnut oil
2 garlic cloves, peeled and finely chopped
2.5 cm/1 inch piece fresh root ginger, peeled and finely chopped
1 green chilli, deseeded and finely chopped
4 stems fresh coriander, leaves and stems roughly chopped

**For the Chinese dipping sauce:**
3 tbsp dark soy sauce
3 tbsp rice wine vinegar
1 tbsp caster sugar
2 tbsp chilli oil
2 spring onions, finely shredded

Using a sharp knife, remove the black vein along the back of the prawns. Sprinkle the prawns with the salt and leave to stand for 15 minutes. Pat dry on absorbent kitchen paper.

Heat a wok or large frying pan, add the groundnut oil and when hot, add the prawns and stir-fry in 2 batches for about 1 minute, or until they turn pink and are almost cooked. Using a slotted spoon, remove the prawns and keep warm in a low oven.

Drain the oil from the wok, leaving 1 tablespoon. Add the garlic, ginger and chilli and cook for about 30 seconds. Add the coriander, return the prawns and stir-fry for 1–2 minutes, or until the prawns are cooked through and the garlic is golden. Turn into a warmed serving dish.

For the dipping sauce, using a fork, beat together the soy sauce, rice wine vinegar, caster sugar and chilli oil in a small bowl. Stir in the spring onions and serve immediately with the hot prawns.

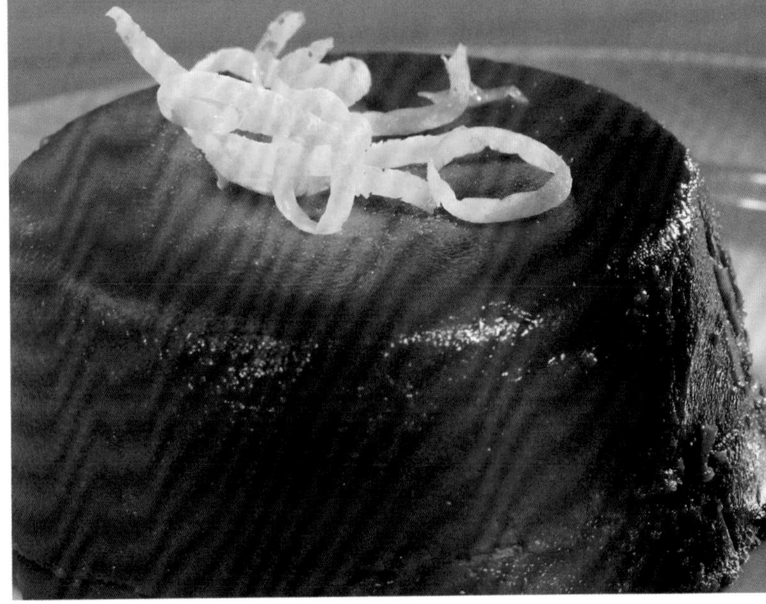

**PUDDING SUGGESTION**
## Chocolate & Lemon Grass Mousse

INGREDIENTS **Serves 4**

3 lemon grass stalks, outer leaves removed
200 ml/7 fl oz milk
2 sheets gelatine
150 g/5 oz milk chocolate, broken into small pieces
2 medium egg yolks
50 g/2 oz caster sugar
150 ml/¼ pint double cream
juice of 2 lemons
1 tbsp caster sugar
lemon zest, to decorate

Use a wooden spoon to bruise the lemon grass, then cut in half. Pour the milk into a large, heavy-based saucepan, add the lemon grass and bring to the boil. Remove from the heat, leave to infuse for 1 hour, then strain. Place the gelatine in a shallow dish, pour over cold water to cover and leave for 15 minutes. Squeeze out excess moisture before use.

Place the chocolate in a small bowl set over a saucepan of gently simmering water and leave until melted. Make sure the water does not touch the bowl. Whisk the egg yolks and sugar together until thick, then whisk in the flavoured milk. Pour into a clean saucepan and cook gently, stirring continuously, until the mixture starts to thicken. Remove from the heat, stir in the melted chocolate and gelatine and leave to cool for a few minutes. Whisk the double cream until soft peaks form, then stir into the cooled milk mixture to form a mousse. Spoon into individual ramekins or moulds and leave in the refrigerator for 2 hours or until set.

Just before serving, pour the lemon juice into a small saucepan, bring to the boil, then simmer for 3 minutes or until reduced. Add the sugar and heat until dissolved, stirring continuously. Serve the mousse drizzled with the lemon sauce and decorated with lemon zest.

# Chilli Con Carne with Crispy-skinned Potatoes

INGREDIENTS **Serves 4**

2 tbsp vegetable oil, plus extra for brushing
1 large onion, peeled and finely chopped
1 garlic clove, peeled and finely chopped
1 red chilli, deseeded and finely chopped
450 g/1 lb chuck steak, finely chopped, or lean beef mince
1 tbsp chilli powder
400 g can chopped tomatoes
2 tbsp tomato purée
400 g can red kidney beans, drained and rinsed
4 large baking potatoes
coarse salt and freshly ground black pepper

**To serve:**
ready-made guacamole
soured cream

Preheat the oven to 150°C/300°F/Gas Mark 2. Heat the oil in a large flameproof casserole dish and add the onion. Cook gently for 10 minutes until soft and lightly browned.

Add the garlic and chilli and cook briefly. Increase the heat, add the chuck steak or lean mince and cook for a further 10 minutes, stirring occasionally, until browned.

Add the chilli powder and stir well. Cook for about 2 minutes, then add the chopped tomatoes and tomato purée. Bring slowly to the boil. Cover and cook in the preheated oven for 1½ hours. Remove from the oven and stir in the kidney beans. Return to the oven for a further 15 minutes.

Meanwhile, brush a little vegetable oil all over the potatoes and rub on some coarse salt. Put the potatoes in the oven alongside the chilli.

Remove the chilli and potatoes from the oven. Cut a cross in each potato, then squeeze to open slightly and season to taste with salt and pepper. Serve with the chilli, guacamole and soured cream.

HEALTH RATING ●●●

**STARTER SUGGESTION**
Pumpkin & Smoked Haddock Soup

**PUDDING SUGGESTION**
Orange Curd & Plum Puddings

## STARTER SUGGESTION
# Pumpkin & Smoked Haddock Soup

INGREDIENTS **Serves 4–6**

2 tbsp olive oil
1 medium onion, peeled and chopped
2 garlic cloves, peeled and chopped
3 celery stalks, trimmed and chopped
700 g/1½ lb pumpkin, peeled, deseeded and cut into chunks
450 g/1 lb potatoes, peeled and cut into chunks
750 ml/1¼ pints chicken stock, heated
125 ml/4 fl oz dry sherry
200 g/7 oz smoked haddock fillet
150 ml/¼ pint milk
freshly ground black pepper
2 tbsp freshly chopped parsley

Heat the oil in a large, heavy-based saucepan and gently cook the onion, garlic, and celery for about 10 minutes. This will release the sweetness but not colour the vegetables. Add the pumpkin and potatoes to the saucepan and stir to coat the vegetables with the oil.

Gradually pour in the stock and bring to the boil. Cover, then reduce the heat and simmer for 25 minutes, stirring occasionally. Stir in the dry sherry, then remove the saucepan from the heat and leave to cool for 5–10 minutes. Blend the mixture in a food processor or blender to form a chunky purée and return to the cleaned saucepan.

Meanwhile, place the fish in a shallow frying pan. Pour in the milk with 3 tablespoons of water and bring to almost boiling point. Reduce the heat, cover and simmer for 6 minutes, or until the fish is cooked and flakes easily. Remove from the heat and, using a slotted spoon, remove the fish from the liquid, reserving both liquid and fish.

Discard the skin and any bones from the fish and flake into pieces. Stir the fish liquid into the soup, together with the flaked fish. Season with freshly ground black pepper, stir in the parsley and serve immediately.

## PUDDING SUGGESTION
# Orange Curd & Plum Puddings

INGREDIENTS **Serves 4**

700 g/1½ lb plums, stoned and quartered
2 tbsp light brown sugar
grated rind of ½ lemon
25 g/1 oz butter, melted
1 tbsp olive oil
6 sheets filo pastry plus 1 sheet for decoration
½ x 411 g jar luxury orange curd
50 g/2 oz sultanas
icing sugar, to decorate
thick set Greek yogurt, to serve

Preheat the oven to 200°C/400°F/Gas Mark 6. Lightly oil a 20.5 cm/8 inch round cake tin. Cook the plums with 2 tablespoons of the light brown sugar for 8–10 minutes to soften them. Remove from the heat and reserve.

Mix together the lemon rind, butter and oil. Lay a sheet of pastry in the prepared cake tin and brush with the lemon rind mixture.

Cut the sheets of filo pastry in half and then place one half sheet in the cake tin and brush again. Top with the remaining halved sheets of pastry brushing each time with the lemon rind mixture. Fold each sheet in half lengthwise to line the sides of the tin to make a filo case.

Mix together the plums, orange curd and sultanas and spoon into the pastry case. Draw the pastry edges up over the filling to enclose. Brush the extra remaining sheet of filo pastry with the lemon rind mixture and cut into thick strips.

Scrunch each strip of pastry and arrange on top of the pie. Bake in the preheated oven for 25 minutes, until golden. Sprinkle with icing sugar and serve with the Greek yogurt.

# Pork with Spring Vegetables & Sweet Chilli Sauce

INGREDIENTS **Serves 4**

450 g/1 lb pork fillet
2 tbsp sunflower oil
2 garlic cloves, peeled and crushed
2.5 cm/1 inch piece fresh root ginger, peeled and grated
125 g/4 oz carrots, peeled and cut into matchsticks
4 spring onions, trimmed
125 g/4 oz sugar snap peas
125 g/4 oz baby sweetcorn
2 tbsp sweet chilli sauce
2 tbsp light soy sauce
1 tbsp vinegar
½ tsp sugar, or to taste
125 g/4 oz beansprouts
grated zest of 1 orange
freshly cooked rice, to serve

Trim, then cut the pork fillet into thin strips and reserve. Heat a wok and pour in the oil. When hot, add the garlic and ginger and stir-fry for 30 seconds. Add the carrots to the wok and continue to stir-fry for 1–2 minutes, or until they start to soften.

Slice the spring onions lengthways, then cut into three lengths. Trim the sugar snap peas and the sweetcorn. Add the spring onions, sugar snap peas and sweetcorn to the wok and stir-fry for 30 seconds.

Add the pork to the wok and continue to stir-fry for 2–3 minutes, or until the meat is sealed and browned all over. Blend the sweet chilli sauce, soy sauce, vinegar and sugar together, then stir into the wok with the beansprouts.

Continue to stir-fry until the meat is cooked and the vegetables are tender but still crisp. Sprinkle with the orange zest and serve immediately with the freshly cooked rice.

HEALTH RATING

**MILD ALTERNATIVE**
Spanish-style Pork Stew with Saffron Rice

**STARTER SUGGESTION**
Chicken Noodle Soup

INGREDIENTS **Serves 4**

2 tbsp olive oil
900 g/2 lb boneless pork shoulder, diced
1 large onion, peeled and sliced
2 garlic cloves, peeled and finely chopped
1 tbsp plain flour
450 g/1 lb plum tomatoes, peeled and chopped
175 ml/6 fl oz red wine
1 tbsp freshly chopped basil
1 green pepper, deseeded and sliced
50 g/2 oz pimento-stuffed olives, cut in half crossways
salt and freshly ground black pepper
fresh basil leaves, to garnish

**For the saffron rice:**

1 tbsp olive oil
25 g/1 oz butter
1 small onion, peeled and finely chopped
few strands of saffron, crushed
250 g/9 oz long-grain white rice
600 ml/1 pint chicken stock

**MILD ALTERNATIVE**

## Spanish-style Pork Stew with Saffron Rice

Preheat the oven to 150°C/300°F/Gas Mark 2. Heat the oil in a large flameproof casserole and add the pork in batches. Fry over a high heat until browned. Transfer to a plate until all the pork is browned.

Lower the heat and add the onion to the casserole. Cook for a further 5 minutes until soft and starting to brown. Add the garlic and stir briefly before returning the pork to the casserole. Add the flour and stir.

Add the tomatoes. Gradually stir in the red wine and add the basil. Bring to simmering point and cover. Transfer the casserole to the lower part of the preheated oven and cook for 1½ hours. Stir in the green pepper and olives and cook for 30 minutes. Season to taste with salt and pepper.

Meanwhile, to make the saffron rice, heat the oil with the butter in a saucepan. Add the onion and cook for 5 minutes over a medium heat until softened. Add the saffron and rice and stir well. Add the stock, bring to the boil, cover and reduce the heat as low as possible. Cook for 15 minutes, covered, until the rice is tender and the stock is absorbed. Adjust the seasoning and serve with the stew, garnished with fresh basil.

**STARTER SUGGESTION**

## Chicken Noodle Soup

Break the chicken carcass into smaller pieces and place in a wok with the carrot, onion, leek, bay leaves, peppercorns and water. Bring slowly to the boil. Skim away any fat or scum that rises for the first 15 minutes. Simmer very gently for 1–1½ hours. If the liquid reduces by more than one third, add a little more water.

Remove from the heat and leave until cold. Strain into a large bowl and chill in the refrigerator until any fat in the stock rises and sets on the surface. Remove the fat and discard. Draw a sheet of absorbent kitchen paper across the surface of the stock to absorb any remaining fat.

Return the stock to the wok and bring to a simmer. Add the Chinese cabbage, mushrooms and chicken and simmer gently for 7–8 minutes until the vegetables are tender.

Meanwhile, cook the noodles until tender and drain well. Transfer a portion of noodles to each serving bowl before pouring in some soup and vegetables. Serve immediately.

INGREDIENTS **Serves 4**

carcass of a medium-sized cooked chicken
1 large carrot, peeled and roughly chopped
1 medium onion, peeled and quartered
1 leek, trimmed and roughly chopped
2–3 bay leaves
a few black peppercorns
2 litres/3½ pints water
225 g/8 oz Chinese cabbage, trimmed
50 g/2 oz chestnut mushrooms, wiped and sliced
125 g/4 oz cooked chicken, sliced or chopped
50 g/2 oz medium or fine egg thread noodles

**MILD ALTERNATIVE**

## Speedy Pork with Yellow Bean Sauce

INGREDIENTS **Serves 4**

- 450 g/1 lb pork fillet
- 2 tbsp light soy sauce
- 2 tbsp orange juice
- 2 tsp cornflour
- 3 tbsp groundnut oil
- 2 garlic cloves, peeled and crushed
- 175 g/6 oz carrots, peeled and cut into matchsticks
- 125 g/4 oz fine green beans, trimmed and halved
- 2 spring onions, trimmed and cut into strips
- 4 tbsp yellow bean sauce
- 1 tbsp freshly chopped flat leaf parsley, to garnish
- freshly cooked egg noodles, to serve

Remove any fat or sinew from the pork fillet and cut into thin strips. Blend the soy sauce, orange juice and cornflour in a bowl and mix thoroughly. Place the meat in a shallow dish, pour over the soy sauce mixture, cover and leave to marinate in the refrigerator for 1 hour. Drain with a slotted spoon, reserving the marinade.

Heat the wok, then add 2 tablespoons of the oil and stir-fry the pork with the garlic for 2 minutes, or until the meat is sealed. Remove with a slotted spoon and reserve.

Add the remaining oil to the wok and cook the carrots, beans and spring onions for about 3 minutes, until tender but still crisp. Return the pork to the wok with the reserved marinade, then pour over the yellow bean sauce. Stir-fry for a further 1–2 minutes, or until the pork is tender. Sprinkle with the chopped parsley and serve immediately with freshly cooked egg noodles.

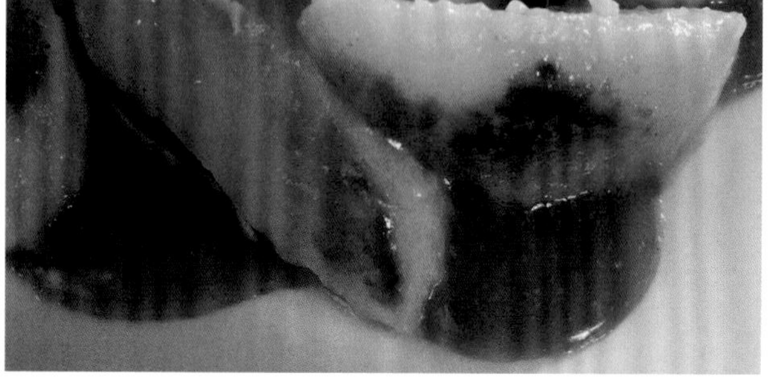

**PUDDING SUGGESTION**

## Stir-fried Bananas & Peaches with Rum Butterscotch Sauce

INGREDIENTS **Serves 4**

- 2 medium-firm bananas
- 1 tbsp caster sugar
- 2 tsp lime juice
- 4 firm, ripe peaches or nectarines
- 1 tbsp sunflower oil

**For the rum butterscotch sauce:**

- 50 g/2 oz unsalted butter
- 50 g/2 oz soft light brown sugar
- 125 g/4 oz demerara sugar
- 300 ml/½ pint double cream
- 2 tbsp dark rum

Peel the bananas and cut into 2.5 cm/1 inch diagonal slices. Place in a bowl and sprinkle with the caster sugar and lime juice and stir until lightly coated. Reserve.

Place the peaches or nectarines in a large bowl and pour over boiling water to cover. Leave for 30 seconds, then plunge them into cold water and peel off their skins. Cut each one into eight thick slices, discarding the stone.

Heat a wok, add the oil and swirl it round the wok to coat the sides. Add the fruit and cook for 3–4 minutes, shaking the wok and gently turning the fruit until lightly browned. Spoon the fruit into a warmed serving bowl and clean the wok with absorbent kitchen paper.

Add the butter and sugars to the wok and stir continuously over a very low heat until the sugar has dissolved. Remove from the heat and leave to cool for 2–3 minutes.

Stir the cream and rum into the sugar syrup and return to the heat. Bring to the boil and simmer for 2 minutes, stirring continuously until smooth. Leave for 2–3 minutes to cool slightly, then serve warm with the stir-fried peaches and bananas.

# Honey Pork with Rice Noodles & Cashews

INGREDIENTS **Serves 4**

125 g/4 oz rice noodles
450 g/1 lb pork fillet
2 tbsp groundnut oil
1 tbsp softened butter
1 onion, peeled and finely sliced into rings
2 garlic cloves, peeled and crushed
125 g/4 oz baby button mushrooms, halved
3 tbsp light soy sauce
3 tbsp clear honey
50 g/2 oz unsalted cashew nuts
1 red chilli, deseeded and finely chopped
4 spring onions, trimmed and finely chopped
freshly stir-fried vegetables, to serve

Soak the rice noodles in boiling water for 4 minutes or according to packet instructions, then drain and reserve.

Trim and slice the pork fillet into thin strips. Heat the wok, pour in the oil and butter, and stir-fry the pork for 4–5 minutes, until cooked. Remove with a slotted spoon and keep warm.

Add the onion to the wok and stir-fry gently for 2 minutes. Stir in the garlic and mushrooms and cook for a further 2 minutes, or until juices start to run from the mushrooms.

Blend the soy sauce with the honey then return the pork to the wok with this mixture. Add the cashew nuts and cook for 1–2 minutes, then add the rice noodles a little at a time. Stir-fry until everything is piping hot. Sprinkle with chopped chilli and spring onions. Serve immediately with freshly stir-fried vegetables.

HEALTH RATING ♥♥♥

**MILD ALTERNATIVE**

Speedy Pork with Yellow Bean Sauce

**PUDDING SUGGESTION**

Stir-fried Bananas & Peaches with Rum Butterscotch Sauce

# Pork Meatballs with Vegetables

INGREDIENTS **Serves 4**

450 g/1 lb pork mince
2 tbsp freshly chopped coriander
2 garlic cloves, peeled and chopped
1 tbsp light soy sauce
salt and freshly ground black pepper
2 tbsp groundnut oil
2 cm/1 inch piece fresh root ginger, peeled and cut into matchsticks
1 red pepper, deseeded and cut into chunks
1 green pepper, deseeded and cut into chunks
2 courgettes, trimmed and cut into sticks
125 g/4 oz baby sweetcorn, halved lengthways
3 tbsp light soy sauce
1 tsp sesame oil
fresh coriander leaves, to garnish
freshly cooked noodles, to serve

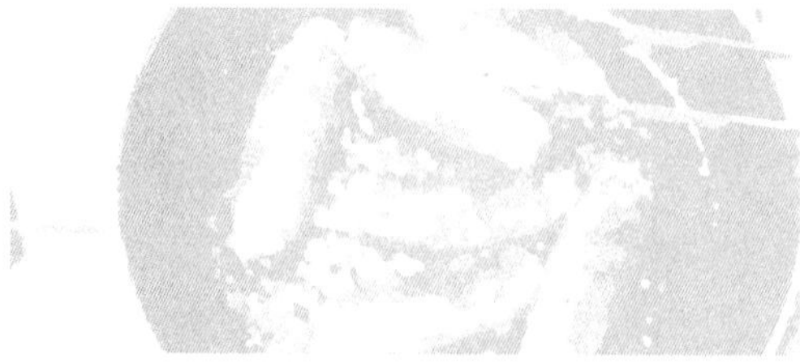

Mix together the pork mince, the chopped coriander, half the garlic and the soy sauce, then season to taste with salt and pepper. Divide into 20 portions and roll into balls. Place on a baking sheet, cover with clingfilm and chill in the refrigerator for at least 30 minutes.

Heat a wok or large frying pan, add the groundnut oil and when hot, add the meatballs and cook for 8–10 minutes, or until the pork balls are browned all over, turning occasionally. Using a slotted spoon, transfer the balls to a plate and keep warm.

Add the ginger and remaining garlic to the wok and stir-fry for 30 seconds. Add the red and green peppers and stir-fry for 5 minutes. Add the courgettes and sweetcorn and stir-fry for 3 minutes.

Return the pork balls to the wok, add the soy sauce and sesame oil and stir-fry for 1 minute, until heated through. Garnish with coriander leaves and serve immediately on a bed of noodles.

HEALTH RATING

**CHILDREN'S ALTERNATIVE**
Italian Meatballs in Tomato Sauce

**SUGGESTED ACCOMPANIMENT**
Panzanella

## CHILDREN'S ALTERNATIVE
# Italian Meatballs in Tomato Sauce

INGREDIENTS **Serves 4**

**For the tomato sauce:**

4 tbsp olive oil
1 large onion, peeled and finely chopped
2 garlic cloves, peeled and chopped
400 g can chopped tomatoes
1 tbsp sun-dried tomato paste
1 tbsp dried mixed herbs
150 ml/¼ pint water
salt and freshly ground black pepper

**For the meatballs:**

450 g/1 lb fresh pork mince
50 g/2 oz fresh breadcrumbs
1 medium egg yolk
75 g/3 oz Parmesan cheese, grated
20 small stuffed green olives
freshly snipped chives, to garnish
freshly cooked pasta, to serve

To make the tomato sauce, heat half the olive oil in a saucepan and cook half the chopped onion for 5 minutes, until softened. Add the garlic, chopped tomatoes, tomato paste, mixed herbs and water to the pan and season to taste with salt and pepper. Stir well until blended. Bring to the boil, then cover and simmer for 15 minutes.

To make the meatballs, place the pork, breadcrumbs, remaining onion, egg yolk and half the Parmesan in a large bowl. Season well and mix together with your hands. Divide the mixture into 20 balls.

Flatten 1 ball out in the palm of your hands, place an olive in the centre, then squeeze the meat around the olive to enclose completely. Repeat with remaining mixture and olives. Place the meatballs on a baking sheet and cover with clingfilm and chill in the refrigerator for 30 minutes.

Heat the remaining oil in a large frying pan and cook the meatballs for 8–10 minutes, turning occasionally, until golden brown. Pour in the sauce and heat through. Sprinkle with chives and the remaining Parmesan. Serve immediately with the freshly cooked pasta.

## SUGGESTED ACCOMPANIMENT
# Panzanella

INGREDIENTS **Serves 4**

250 g/9 oz day-old Italian-style bread
1 tbsp red wine vinegar
4 tbsp olive oil
1 tsp lemon juice
1 small garlic clove, peeled and finely chopped
1 red onion, peeled and finely sliced
1 cucumber, peeled if preferred
225 g/8 oz ripe tomatoes, deseeded
150 g/5 oz pitted black olives
about 20 basil leaves, coarsely torn or left whole if small
sea salt and freshly ground black pepper

Cut the bread into thick slices, leaving the crusts on. Add 1 teaspoon of the red wine vinegar to a jug of iced water, put the slices of bread in a bowl and pour over the water. Make sure the bread is covered completely. Leave to soak for 3–4 minutes until just soft.

Remove the soaked bread from the water and squeeze it gently, first with your hands and then in a clean tea towel to remove any excess water. Put the bread on a plate, cover with clingfilm and chill in the refrigerator for about 1 hour.

Meanwhile, whisk together the olive oil, the remaining red wine vinegar and lemon juice in a large serving bowl. Add the garlic and onion and stir to coat well.

Halve the cucumber and remove the seeds. Chop both the cucumber and tomatoes into 1 cm/½ inch dice. Add to the garlic and onions with the olives. Tear the bread into bite-sized chunks and add to the bowl with the fresh basil leaves. Toss together to mix and serve immediately, with a grinding of sea salt and black pepper.

# Pork Sausages with Onion Gravy & Best-ever Mash

INGREDIENTS **Serves 4**

50 g/2 oz butter
1 tbsp olive oil
2 large onions, peeled and thinly sliced
pinch of sugar
1 tbsp freshly chopped thyme
1 tbsp plain flour
100 ml/3½ fl oz Madeira
200 ml/7 fl oz vegetable stock
8–12 good-quality butchers pork sausages, depending on size

**For the mash:**

900 g/2 lb floury potatoes, peeled
75 g/3 oz butter
4 tbsp crème fraîche or sour cream
salt and freshly ground black pepper

Melt the butter with the oil and add the onions. Cover and cook gently for about 20 minutes until the onions have collapsed. Add the sugar and stir well. Uncover and continue to cook, stirring often, until the onions are very soft and golden. Add the thyme, stir well, then add the flour, stirring. Gradually add the Madeira and the stock. Bring to the boil and simmer gently for 10 minutes.

Meanwhile, put the sausages in a large frying pan and cook over a medium heat for about 15–20 minutes, turning often, until golden brown and slightly sticky all over.

For the mash, boil the potatoes in plenty of lightly salted water for 15–18 minutes until tender. Drain well and return to the saucepan. Put the saucepan over a low heat to allow the potatoes to dry thoroughly. Remove from the heat and add the butter, crème fraîche or sour cream and salt and pepper. Mash thoroughly. Serve the potato mash topped with the sausages and onion gravy.

HEALTH RATING

**LOW FAT ALTERNATIVE**

Seared Calves' Liver with Onions & Mustard Mash

**PUDDING SUGGESTION**

Apple and Cinnamon Brown Betty

**LOW FAT ALTERNATIVE**

## Seared Calves' Liver with Onions & Mustard Mash

INGREDIENTS **Serves 2**

- 2 tbsp olive oil
- 100 g/3½ oz butter
- 3 large onions, peeled and finely sliced
- pinch of sugar
- salt and freshly ground black pepper
- 1 tbsp sprigs of fresh thyme
- 1 tbsp balsamic vinegar
- 700 g/1½ lb potatoes, peeled and cut into chunks
- 6–8 tbsp milk
- 1 tbsp wholegrain mustard
- 3–4 fresh sage leaves
- 550 g/1¼ lb thinly sliced calves' liver
- 1 tsp lemon juice

Preheat the oven to 150°C/300°F/Gas Mark 2. Heat half the oil and 25 g/1 oz of the butter in a flameproof casserole. When foaming, add the onions. Cover and cook over a low heat for 20 minutes until softened and beginning to collapse. Add the sugar and season with salt and pepper. Stir in the thyme. Cover the casserole and transfer to the preheated oven. Cook for a further 30–45 minutes until softened completely, but not browned. Remove from the oven and stir in the balsamic vinegar.

Meanwhile, boil the potatoes in boiling salted water for 15–18 minutes until tender. Drain well, then return to the pan. Place over a low heat to dry completely, remove from the heat and stir in 50 g/2 oz of the butter, the milk, mustard and salt and pepper to taste. Mash thoroughly until creamy and keep warm.

Heat a large frying pan and add the remaining butter and oil. When it is foaming, add the sage leaves and stir for a few seconds, then add the liver. Cook over a high heat for 1–2 minutes on each side. It should remain slightly pink – do not overcook. Remove the liver from the pan. Add the lemon juice to the pan and swirl around to deglaze.

To serve, place a large spoonful of the mashed potato on each plate. Top with some of the melting onions, the liver and finally the pan juices.

**PUDDING SUGGESTION**

## Apple & Cinnamon Brown Betty

INGREDIENTS **Serves 2**

- 450 g/1 lb cooking apples
- 50 g/2 oz caster sugar
- finely grated rind of 1 lemon
- 125 g/4 oz fresh white breadcrumbs
- 125 g/4 oz demerara sugar
- ½ tsp ground cinnamon
- 25 g/1 oz butter

**For the custard:**

- 3 medium egg yolks
- 1 tbsp caster sugar
- 500 ml/1 pint milk
- 1 tbsp cornflour
- few drops of vanilla essence

Preheat the oven to 180°C/350°F/Gas Mark 4. Lightly oil a 900 ml/1½ pint ovenproof dish. Peel, core and slice the apples and place in a saucepan with the caster sugar, lemon rind and 2 tablespoons of water. Simmer for 10–15 minutes or until tender.

Mix the breadcrumbs with the sugar and the cinnamon. Place half the sweetened apples in the base of the prepared dish and spoon over half of the crumb mixture. Place the remaining apples on top and cover with the rest of the crumb mixture.

Melt the butter and pour over the surface of the pudding. Cover the dish with non-stick baking paper and bake in the preheated oven for 20 minutes. Remove the paper and bake for a further 10–15 minutes, or until golden.

Meanwhile, make the custard by whisking the egg yolks and sugar together until creamy. Mix 1 tablespoon of the milk with the cornflour until a paste forms and reserve. Warm the rest of the milk until nearly boiling and pour over the egg mixture with the paste and vanilla essence.

Place the bowl over a sauce pan of gently simmering water. Stir over the heat until thickened and can coat the back of a spoon. Strain into a jug and serve hot over the pudding.

# Hoisin Pork

INGREDIENTS **Serves 4**

1.4 kg/3 lb piece lean belly pork, boned

sea salt

2 tsp Chinese five spice powder

2 garlic cloves, peeled and chopped

1 tsp sesame oil

4 tbsp hoisin sauce

1 tbsp clear honey

assorted salad leaves, to garnish

Preheat the oven to 200°C/400°F/Gas Mark 6, 15 minutes before cooking. Using a sharp knife, cut the pork skin in a criss-cross pattern, making sure not to cut all the way through into the flesh. Rub the salt evenly over the skin and leave to stand for 30 minutes.

Meanwhile, mix together the five spice powder, garlic, sesame oil, hoisin sauce and honey until smooth. Rub the mixture evenly over the pork skin. Place the pork on a plate and chill in the refrigerator to marinate for up to 6 hours.

Place the pork on a wire rack set inside a roasting tin and roast the pork in the preheated oven for 1–1¼ hours, or until the pork is very crisp and the juices run clear when pierced with a skewer.

Remove the pork from the heat, leave to rest for 15 minutes, then cut into strips. Arrange on a warmed serving platter. Garnish with salad leaves and serve immediately.

HEALTH RATING ⚫⚫⚫⚫

**SPEEDY ALTERNATIVE**

Pork Fried Noodles

**SUGGESTED ACCOMPANIMENT**

Stir-fried Greens

**SPEEDY ALTERNATIVE**

## Pork Fried Noodles

Place the noodles in a bowl and cover with boiling water. Leave to stand for 20 minutes, stirring occasionally, or until tender. Drain and reserve. Meanwhile, blanch the broccoli in a saucepan of lightly salted boiling water for 2 minutes. Drain, refresh under cold running water and reserve.

Heat a large wok or frying pan, add the groundnut oil and heat until just smoking. Add the pork and stir-fry for 5 minutes, or until browned. Using a slotted spoon, remove the pork slices and reserve.

Mix together the soy sauce, lemon juice, sugar, chilli sauce and sesame oil and reserve.

Add the ginger to the wok and stir-fry for 30 seconds. Add the garlic and chilli and stir-fry for 30 seconds. Add the reserved broccoli and stir-fry for 3 minutes. Stir in the mangetout, pork and reserved noodles with the beaten eggs and water chestnuts and stir-fry for 5 minutes or until heated through. Pour over the reserved chilli sauce, toss well and turn into a warmed serving dish. Garnish and serve immediately.

INGREDIENTS **Serves 4**

125 g/4 oz dried thread egg noodles
125 g/4 oz broccoli florets
4 tbsp groundnut oil
350 g/12 oz pork tenderloin, cut into slices
3 tbsp soy sauce
1 tbsp lemon juice
pinch of sugar
1 tsp chilli sauce
1 tbsp sesame oil
2.5 cm/1 inch piece fresh root ginger, peeled and cut into sticks
1 garlic clove, peeled and chopped
1 green chilli, deseeded and sliced
125 g/4 oz mangetout, halved
2 medium eggs, lightly beaten
227 g can water chestnuts, drained and sliced

**To garnish:**
radish rose
spring onion tassels

**SUGGESTED ACCOMPANIMENT**

## Stir-fried Greens

Separate the Chinese leaves and pak choi and wash well. Cut into 2.5 cm/1 inch strips. Separate the broccoli into small florets. Heat a wok or large frying pan, add the sesame seeds and stir-fry for 30 seconds or until browned.

Add the oil to the wok and when hot, add the ginger, garlic and chillies and stir-fry for 30 seconds. Add the broccoli and stir-fry for 1 minute. Add the Chinese leaves and pak choi and stir-fry for a further 1 minute.

Pour the chicken stock and Chinese rice wine into the wok with the soy and black bean sauces. Season to taste with pepper and add the sugar. Reduce the heat and simmer for 6–8 minutes, or until the vegetables are tender but still firm to the bite. Tip into a warmed serving dish, removing the chillies if preferred. Drizzle with the sesame oil and serve immediately.

INGREDIENTS **Serves 4**

450 g/1 lb Chinese leaves
225 g/8 oz pak choi
225 g/8 oz broccoli florets
1 tbsp sesame seeds
1 tbsp groundnut oil
1 tbsp fresh root ginger, peeled and finely chopped
3 garlic cloves, peeled and finely chopped
2 red chillies, deseeded and split in half
50 ml/2 fl oz chicken stock
2 tbsp Chinese rice wine
1 tbsp dark soy sauce
1 tsp light soy sauce
2 tsp black bean sauce
freshly ground black pepper
2 tsp sugar
1 tsp sesame oil

**SPICY ALTERNATIVE**
## Chicken Satay Salad

Place the peanut butter, chilli sauce, garlic, cider vinegar, soy sauces, sugar, salt and ground peppercorns in a food processor and blend to form a smooth paste. Scrape into a bowl, cover and chill in the refrigerator until required. Bring a large saucepan of lightly salted water to the boil. Add the noodles and cook for 3–5 minutes. Drain and plunge into cold water. Drain again and toss in the sesame oil. Leave to cool.

Heat the wok until very hot, add the oil and when hot, add the chicken cubes. Stir-fry for 5–6 minutes until the chicken is golden brown and cooked through. Remove the chicken from the wok using a slotted spoon and add to the noodles, together with the peanut sauce. Mix lightly together, then sprinkle with the shredded celery leaves and either serve immediately or leave until cold, then serve with cos lettuce.

INGREDIENTS **Serves 4**

4 tbsp crunchy peanut butter
1 tbsp chilli sauce
1 garlic clove, peeled and crushed
2 tbsp cider vinegar
2 tbsp light soy sauce
2 tbsp dark soy sauce
2 tsp soft brown sugar
pinch of salt
2 tsp freshly ground Sichuan peppercorns
450 g/1 lb dried egg noodles
2 tbsp sesame oil
1 tbsp groundnut oil
450 g/1 lb skinless, boneless chicken breast fillets, cut into cubes
shredded celery leaves, to garnish
cos lettuce, to serve

**ENTERTAINING ALTERNATIVE**
## Chicken & Cashew Nuts

Place the cubes of chicken in a large bowl. Add the beaten egg white, salt, sesame oil and cornflour. Mix well to ensure the chicken is coated thoroughly. Chill in the refrigerator for 20 minutes.

Heat the wok until very hot, add the groundnut oil and when hot, remove the wok from the heat and add the chicken. Stir continuously to prevent the chicken from sticking to the wok. When the chicken turns white, after about 2 minutes, remove it using a slotted spoon and reserve. Discard the oil.

Wipe the wok clean with absorbent kitchen paper and heat it again until very hot. Add the sunflower oil and heat. When hot, add the cashew nuts, spring onions and mangetout and stir-fry for 1 minute. Add the rice wine and soy sauce. Return the chicken to the wok and stir-fry for 2 minutes. Garnish with shredded spring onions and serve immediately with freshly steamed rice sprinkled with fresh coriander.

INGREDIENTS **Serves 4**

450 g/1 lb skinless, boneless chicken breast fillets, cut into 1 cm/½ inch cubes
1 medium egg white, beaten
1 tsp salt
1 tsp sesame oil
2 tsp cornflour
300 ml/½ pint groundnut oil for deep frying
2 tsp sunflower oil
50 g/2 oz unsalted cashews
4 spring onions, shredded
50 g/2 oz mangetout, diagonally sliced
1 tbsp Chinese rice wine
1 tbsp light soy sauce
shredded spring onions, to garnish
freshly steamed white rice with fresh coriander leaves, to serve

# Pork in Peanut Sauce

INGREDIENTS **Serves 4**

450 g/1 lb pork fillet
2 tbsp light soy sauce
1 tbsp vinegar
1 tsp sugar
1 tsp Chinese five spice powder
2–4 garlic cloves, peeled and crushed
2 tbsp groundnut oil
1 large onion, peeled and finely sliced
125 g/4 oz carrots, peeled and cut into matchsticks
2 celery sticks, trimmed and sliced
125 g/4 oz French beans, trimmed and halved
3 tbsp smooth peanut butter
1 tbsp freshly chopped flat leaf parsley

**To serve:**
freshly cooked basmati and wild rice
green salad

Remove any fat or sinew from the pork fillet, cut into thin strips and reserve. Blend the soy sauce, vinegar, sugar, Chinese five spice powder and garlic in a bowl and add the pork. Cover and leave to marinate in the refrigerator for at least 30 minutes.

Drain the pork, reserving any marinade. Heat the wok, then add the oil and, when hot, stir-fry the pork for 3–4 minutes, or until sealed.

Add the onion, carrots, celery and beans to the wok and stir-fry for 4–5 minutes, or until the meat is tender and the vegetables are softened.

Blend the reserved marinade, the peanut butter and 2 tablespoons of hot water together. When smooth, stir into the wok and cook for several minutes more until the sauce is thick and the pork is piping hot. Sprinkle with the chopped parsley and serve immediately with the basmati and wild rice and a green salad.

HEALTH RATING

**SPICY ALTERNATIVE**
Chicken Satay Salad

**ENTERTAINING ALTERNATIVE**
Chicken & Cashew Nuts

# Caribbean Pork

INGREDIENTS **Serves 4**

450 g/1 lb pork fillet

2.5 cm/1 inch piece fresh root ginger, peeled and grated

2 garlic cloves, peeled and crushed

2 tbsp freshly chopped parsley

150 ml/¼ pint orange juice

2 tbsp dark soy sauce

2 tbsp groundnut oil

1 large onion, peeled and sliced into wedges

1 large courgette (about 225 g/8 oz), trimmed and cut into strips

1 orange pepper, deseeded and cut into strips

1 ripe but firm mango, peeled and pitted

freshly cooked rice to serve

Cut the pork fillet into thin strips and place in a shallow dish. Sprinkle with the ginger, garlic and 1 tablespoon of the parsley. Blend together the orange juice, soy sauce and 1 tablespoon of the oil, then pour over the pork. Cover and chill in the refrigerator for 30 minutes, stirring occasionally. Remove the pork strips with a slotted spoon and reserve the marinade.

Heat the wok, pour in the remaining oil and stir-fry the pork for 3–4 minutes. Add the onion rings and the courgette and pepper strips and cook for 2 minutes. Add the reserved marinade to the wok and stir-fry for a further 2 minutes.

Remove the stone from the mango, cut the flesh into strips, then stir it into the pork mixture. Continue to stir-fry until everything is piping hot. Garnish with the remaining parsley and serve immediately with plenty of freshly cooked rice.

HEALTH RATING

**SPICY ALTERNATIVE**

Jamaican Jerk Pork with Rice & Peas

**SUGGESTED ACCOMPANIMENT**

Special Rosti

**SPICY ALTERNATIVE**
## Jamaican Jerk Pork with Rice & Peas

INGREDIENTS **Serves 4**

175 g/6 oz dried red kidney beans, soaked overnight
2 onions, peeled and chopped
2 garlic cloves, peeled and crushed
4 tbsp lime juice
2 tbsp each dark molasses, soy sauce and chopped fresh root ginger
2 jalapeño chillies, deseeded and chopped
½ tsp ground cinnamon
¼ tsp each ground allspice and ground nutmeg
4 pork loin chops, on the bone

**For the rice:**

1 tbsp vegetable oil
1 onion, peeled and finely chopped
1 celery stalk, trimmed and finely sliced
3 garlic cloves, peeled and crushed
2 bay leaves
225 g/8 oz long-grain white rice
475 ml/18 fl oz chicken or ham stock
sprigs of fresh flat leaf parsley, to garnish

To make the jerk pork marinade, purée the onions, garlic, lime juice, molasses, soy sauce, ginger, chillies, cinnamon, allspice and nutmeg together in a food processor until smooth. Put the pork chops into a glass dish and pour over the marinade, turning the chops to coat. Marinate in the refrigerator for at least 1 hour or overnight.

Drain the beans and place in a large saucepan with about 2 litres/3½ pints cold water. Bring to the boil and boil rapidly for 10 minutes. Reduce the heat, cover and simmer gently, for 1 hour until tender, adding more water if necessary. When cooked, drain well and mash roughly.

Heat the oil for the rice in a saucepan with a tight fitting lid and add the onion, celery and garlic. Cook gently for 5 minutes until softened. Add the bay leaves, rice and stock and stir. Bring to the boil, cover and cook very gently for 10 minutes. Add the beans and stir well again. Cook for a further 5 minutes, then remove from the heat.

Heat a griddle pan until almost smoking. Remove the pork chops from the marinade, scraping off any surplus and add to the hot pan. Cook for 5–8 minutes on each side, or until cooked. Garnish with the parsley and serve immediately with the rice.

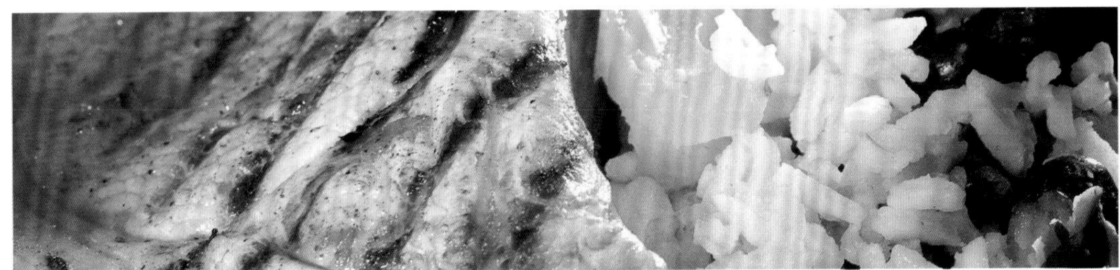

**SUGGESTED ACCOMPANIMENT**
## Special Rosti

INGREDIENTS **Serves 4**

700 g/1½ lb potatoes, scrubbed but not peeled
salt and freshly ground black pepper
75 g/3 oz butter
1 large onion, peeled and finely chopped
1 garlic clove, peeled and crushed
2 tbsp freshly chopped parsley
1 tbsp olive oil
75 g/3 oz Parma ham, thinly sliced
50 g/2 oz sun-dried tomatoes, chopped
175 g/6 oz Emmenthal cheese, grated
mixed green salad, to serve

Cook the potatoes in a large saucepan of salted boiling water for about 10 minutes, until just tender. Drain in a colander, then rinse in cold water. Drain again. Leave until cool enough to handle, then peel off the skins.

Melt the butter in a large frying pan and gently fry the onion and garlic for about 3 minutes until softened and beginning to colour. Remove from the heat. Coarsely grate the potatoes into a large bowl, then stir in the onion and garlic mixture. Sprinkle over the parsley and stir well to mix. Season to taste with salt and pepper.

Heat the oil in the frying pan and cover the base of the pan with half the potato mixture. Lay the slices of Parma ham on top. Sprinkle with the chopped sun-dried tomatoes, then scatter the grated Emmenthal over the top.

Finally, top with the remaining potato mixture. Cook over a low heat, pressing down with a palette knife from time to time, for 10–15 minutes, or until the bottom is golden brown. Carefully invert the rosti onto a large plate, then carefully slide back into the pan and cook the other side until golden. Serve cut into wedges with a mixed green salad.

# Gammon with Red Wine Sauce & Pasta

INGREDIENTS **Serves 2**

25 g/1 oz butter
150 ml/¼ pint red wine
4 red onions, peeled and sliced
4 tbsp orange juice
1 tsp soft brown sugar
225 g/8 oz gammon steak, trimmed
freshly ground black pepper
175 g/6 oz fusilli
3 tbsp wholegrain mustard
2 tbsp freshly chopped flat leaf parsley, plus sprigs to garnish

Preheat the grill to a medium heat before cooking. Heat the butter with the red wine in a large heavy-based pan. Add the onions, cover with a tight fitting lid and cook over a very low heat for 30 minutes, or until softened and transparent. Remove the lid from the pan, stir in the orange juice and sugar, then increase the heat and cook for about 10 minutes, until the onions are golden.

Meanwhile cook the gammon steak under the preheated grill, turning at least once, for 4–6 minutes, or until tender. Cut the cooked gammon into bite-sized pieces. Reserve and keep warm.

Meanwhile, bring a large pan of very lightly salted water to a rolling boil. Add the pasta and cook according to the packet instructions, or until 'al dente'. Drain the pasta thoroughly, return to the pan, season with a little pepper and keep warm.

Stir the wholegrain mustard and chopped parsley into the onion sauce then pour over the pasta. Add the gammon pieces to the pan and toss lightly to thoroughly coat the pasta with the sauce. Pile the pasta mixture on to two warmed serving plates. Garnish with sprigs of flat leaf parsley and serve immediately.

HEALTH RATING

**SUGGESTED ACCOMPANIMENT**

Vegetables Braised in Olive Oil & Lemon

**STARTER SUGGESTION**

Courgette & Tarragon Tortilla

**SUGGESTED ACCOMPANIMENT**
## Vegetables Braised in Olive Oil & Lemon

INGREDIENTS **Serves 4**

pared rind and juice of ½ lemon
4 tbsp olive oil
1 bay leaf
large sprig of thyme
150 ml/¼ pint water
4 spring onions, trimmed and finely chopped
175 g/6 oz baby button mushrooms
175 g/6 oz broccoli, cut into small florets
175 g/6 oz cauliflower, cut into small florets
1 medium courgette, sliced on the diagonal
2 tbsp freshly snipped chives
salt and freshly ground black pepper
lemon zest, to garnish

Put the pared lemon rind and juice into a large saucepan. Add the olive oil, bay leaf, thyme and the water. Bring to the boil. Add the spring onions and mushrooms. Top with the broccoli and cauliflower, adding them so that the stalks are submerged in the water and the tops are just above it. Cover and simmer for 3 minutes.

Scatter the courgettes on top, so that they are steamed rather than boiled. Cook, covered, for a further 3–4 minutes, until all the vegetables are tender.

Using a slotted spoon, transfer the vegetables from the liquid into a warmed serving dish. Increase the heat and boil rapidly for 3–4 minutes, or until the liquid is reduced to about 8 tablespoons. Remove the lemon rind, bay leaf and thyme sprig and discard.

Stir the chives into the reduced liquid, season to taste with salt and pepper and pour over the vegetables. Sprinkle with lemon zest and serve immediately.

**STARTER SUGGESTION**
## Courgette & Tarragon Tortilla

INGREDIENTS **Serves 6**

700 g/1½ lb potatoes
3 tbsp olive oil
1 onion, peeled and thinly sliced
salt and freshly ground black pepper
1 courgette, trimmed and thinly sliced
6 medium eggs
2 tbsp freshly chopped tarragon
tomato wedges, to serve

Peel the potatoes and thinly slice. Dry the slices in a clean tea towel to get them as dry as possible. Heat the oil in a large heavy-based pan, add the onion and cook for 3 minutes. Add the potatoes with a little salt and pepper, then stir the potatoes and onion lightly to coat in the oil.

Reduce the heat to the lowest possible setting, cover and cook gently for 5 minutes. Turn the potatoes and onion over and continue to cook for a further 5 minutes. Give the pan a shake every now and again to ensure that the potatoes do not stick to the base or burn. Add the courgette, then cover and cook for a further 10 minutes.

Beat the eggs and tarragon together and season to taste with salt and pepper. Pour the egg mixture over the vegetables and return to the heat. Cook on a low heat for up to 20–25 minutes, or until there is no liquid egg left on the surface of the tortilla.

Turn the tortilla over by inverting the tortilla onto a saucepan lid or a flat plate. Return the pan to the heat and cook for a final 3–5 minutes, or until the underside is golden brown. If preferred, place the tortilla under a preheated grill for 4 minutes, or until set and golden brown on top. Cut into small squares and serve hot or cold with tomato wedges.

# Shepherd's Pie

INGREDIENTS **Serves 4**

2 tbsp vegetable or olive oil
1 onion, peeled and finely chopped
1 carrot, peeled and finely chopped
1 celery stalk, trimmed and finely chopped
1 tbsp sprigs of fresh thyme
450 g/1 lb leftover roast lamb, finely chopped
150 ml/¼ pint red wine
150 ml/¼ pint lamb or vegetable stock or leftover gravy
2 tbsp tomato purée
salt and freshly ground black pepper
700 g/1½ lb potatoes, peeled and cut into chunks
25 g/1 oz butter
6 tbsp milk
1 tbsp freshly chopped parsley
fresh herbs, to garnish

Preheat the oven to 200°C/400°F/Gas Mark 6, about 15 minutes before cooking. Heat the oil in a large saucepan and add the onion, carrot and celery. Cook over a medium heat for 8–10 minutes until softened and starting to brown.

Add the thyme and cook briefly, then add the cooked lamb, wine, stock and tomato purée. Season to taste with salt and pepper and simmer gently for 25–30 minutes until reduced and thickened. Remove from the heat to cool slightly and season again.

Meanwhile, boil the potatoes in plenty of salted water for 12–15 minutes until tender. Drain and return to the saucepan over a low heat to dry out. Remove from the heat and add the butter, milk and parsley. Mash until creamy, adding a little more milk, if necessary. Adjust the seasoning.

Transfer the lamb mixture to a shallow ovenproof dish. Spoon the mash over the filling and spread evenly to cover completely. Fork the surface, place on a baking sheet, then cook in the preheated oven for 25–30 minutes until the potato topping is browned and the filling is piping hot. Garnish and serve.

HEALTH RATING 🍏🍏🍏

**MEDITERRANEAN ALTERNATIVE**
Lamb & Potato Moussaka

**STARTER SUGGESTION**
Curried Parsnip Soup

## MEDITERRANEAN ALTERNATIVE
## Lamb & Potato Moussaka

Preheat the oven to 200°C/400°F/Gas Mark 6, about 15 minutes before required. Trim the lamb, discarding any fat, then cut into small cubes and reserve. Thinly slice the potatoes and rinse thoroughly in cold water, then pat dry with a clean tea towel.

Melt 50 g/2 oz of the butter in a frying pan and fry the potatoes, in batches, until crisp and golden. Using a slotted spoon, remove from the pan and reserve. Use a third of the potatoes to line the base of an ovenproof dish.

Add the onion and garlic to the butter remaining in the pan and cook for 5 minutes. Add the lamb and fry for 1 minute. Blend the tomato purée with 3 tablespoons of water and stir into the pan with the parsley and salt and pepper. Spoon over the layer of potatoes, then top with the remaining potato slices.

Heat the oil and the remaining butter in the pan and brown the aubergine slices for 5–6 minutes. Arrange the tomatoes on top of the potatoes, then the aubergines on top of the tomatoes. Beat the eggs with the yogurt and Parmesan cheese and pour over the aubergine and tomatoes. Bake in the preheated oven for 25 minutes or until golden and piping hot. Serve.

INGREDIENTS **Serves 4**

700 g/1½ lb cooked roast lamb
700 g/1½ lb potatoes, peeled
125 g/4 oz butter
1 large onion, peeled and chopped
2–4 garlic cloves, peeled and crushed
3 tbsp tomato purée
1 tbsp freshly chopped parsley
salt and freshly ground black pepper
3–4 tbsp olive oil
2 medium aubergines, trimmed and sliced
4 medium tomatoes, sliced
2 medium eggs
300 ml/½ pint Greek yogurt
2–3 tbsp Parmesan cheese, grated

## STARTER SUGGESTION
## Curried Parsnip Soup

In a small frying pan, dry-fry the cumin and coriander seeds over a moderately high heat for 1–2 minutes. Shake the pan during cooking until the seeds are lightly toasted.

Reserve until cooled. Grind the toasted seeds in a pestle and mortar.

Heat the oil in a saucepan. Cook the onion until softened and starting to turn golden.

Add the garlic, turmeric, chilli powder and cinnamon stick to the pan. Continue to cook for a further minute. Add the parsnips and stir well. Pour in the stock and bring to the boil. Cover and simmer for 15 minutes or until the parsnips are cooked.

Allow the soup to cool. Once cooled, remove the cinnamon stick and discard.

Blend the soup in a food processor until very smooth. Transfer to a saucepan and reheat gently. Season to taste with salt and pepper. Garnish with fresh coriander and serve immediately with the yogurt.

INGREDIENTS **Serves 4**

1 tsp cumin seeds
2 tsp coriander seeds
1 tsp oil
1 onion, peeled and chopped
1 garlic clove, peeled and crushed
½ tsp turmeric
¼ tsp chilli powder
1 cinnamon stick
450 g/1 lb parsnips, peeled and chopped
1 litre/1¾ pint vegetable stock
salt and freshly ground black pepper
2–3 tbsp natural yogurt, to serve
fresh coriander leaves, to garnish

**STARTER SUGGESTION**
## Tortellini, Cherry Tomato & Mozzarella Skewers

Preheat the grill and line a grill pan with tinfoil, just before cooking. Bring a large pan of lightly salted water to a rolling boil. Add the tortellini and cook according to the packet instructions, or until 'al dente'. Drain, rinse under cold running water, drain again and toss with 2 tablespoons of the olive oil and reserve.

Pour the remaining olive oil into a small bowl. Add the crushed garlic and thyme or basil, then blend well. Season to taste with salt and black pepper and reserve.

To assemble the skewers, thread the tortellini alternately with the cherry tomatoes and cubes of mozzarella. Arrange the skewers on the grill pan and brush generously on all sides with the olive oil mixture.

Cook the skewers under the preheated grill for about 5 minutes, or until they begin to turn golden, turning them halfway through cooking. Arrange 2 skewers on each plate and garnish with a few basil leaves. Serve immediately with dressed salad leaves.

INGREDIENTS **Serves 6**

250 g/9 oz mixed green and plain cheese or vegetable-filled fresh tortellini
150 ml/¼ pint extra virgin olive oil
2 garlic cloves, peeled and crushed
pinch dried thyme or basil
salt and freshly ground black pepper
225 g/8 oz cherry tomatoes
450 g/1 lb mozzarella, cut into 2.5 cm/1 inch cubes
basil leaves, to garnish
dressed salad leaves, to serve

**PUDDING SUGGESTION**
## Marzipan Cake

INGREDIENTS **Serves 12–14**

450 g/1 lb blanched almonds
300 g/11 oz icing sugar (includes sugar for dusting and rolling)
4 medium egg whites
125 g/4 oz Madeira cake
2 tbsp Marsala wine
225 g/8 oz ricotta cheese
50 g/2 oz caster sugar
grated zest of 1 lemon
50 g/2 oz candied peel, finely chopped
25 g/1 oz glacé cherries, finely chopped
425 g can peach halves, drained
200 ml/⅓ pint double cream

Grind the blanched almonds in a food processor until fairly fine. Mix with 200 g/7 oz of the icing sugar. Beat the egg whites until stiff then fold into the almond mixture using a metal spoon or rubber spatula to form a stiffish dough. It will still be quite sticky but will firm up as it rests. Leave for 30 minutes.

Dust a work surface very generously with some of the remaining icing sugar so that the marzipan does not stick. Roll out two-thirds of the marzipan into a large sheet to a thickness of about 5 mm/¼ inch. Use to line a sloping-sided baking dish with a base measuring 25.5 cm x 20.5 cm/10 x 8 inches. Trim the edges and put any trimmings with the remainder of the marzipan.

Cut the Madeira cake into thin slices and make a layer of sponge to cover the bottom of the marzipan. Sprinkle with the Marsala wine. Beat the ricotta with the sugar and add the lemon zest, candied peel and cherries. Spread this over the sponge. Slice the peaches and put them on top of the ricotta. Whip the cream and spread it over the peaches. Roll out the remaining marzipan and lay it over the cream to seal the whole cake, pressing down gently to remove any air. Press the edges of the marzipan together. Chill in the refrigerator for 2 hours.

Turn the cake out on to a serving plate and dust generously with icing sugar. Slice thickly and serve immediately.

# Roasted Lamb with Rosemary & Garlic

INGREDIENTS **Serves 4**

1.6 kg/3½ lb leg of lamb
8 garlic cloves, peeled
few sprigs of fresh rosemary
salt and freshly ground black pepper
4 slices pancetta
4 tbsp olive oil
4 tbsp red wine vinegar
900 g/2 lb potatoes
1 large onion
sprigs of fresh rosemary, to garnish
freshly cooked ratatouille, to serve

Preheat oven to 200°C/400°F/Gas Mark 6, 15 minutes before roasting. Wipe the leg of lamb with a clean damp cloth, then place the lamb in a large roasting tin. With a sharp knife, make small, deep incisions into the meat. Cut 2–3 garlic cloves into small slivers, then insert with a few small sprigs of rosemary into the lamb. Season to taste with salt and pepper and cover the lamb with the slices of pancetta.

Drizzle over 1 tablespoon of the olive oil and lay a few more rosemary sprigs across the lamb. Roast in the preheated oven for 30 minutes, then pour over the vinegar.

Peel the potatoes and cut into large dice. Peel the onion and cut into thick wedges then thickly slice the remaining garlic. Arrange around the lamb. Pour the remaining olive oil over the potatoes, then reduce the oven temperature to 180°C/350°F/Gas Mark 4 and roast for a further 1 hour, or until the lamb is tender. Garnish with fresh sprigs of rosemary and serve immediately with the roast potatoes and ratatouille.

## HEALTH RATING 🍎🍎

**STARTER SUGGESTION**

Tortellini, Cherry Tomato & Mozzarella Skewers

**PUDDING SUGGESTION**

Marzipan Cake

# Roast Leg of Lamb & Boulangere Potatoes

INGREDIENTS **Serves 6**

1.1 kg/2½ lb potatoes, peeled
1 large onion, peeled and finely sliced
salt and freshly ground black pepper
2 tbsp olive oil
50 g/2 oz butter
200 ml/7 fl oz lamb stock
100 ml/3½ fl oz milk
2 kg/4½ lb leg of lamb
2–3 sprigs of fresh rosemary
6 large garlic cloves, peeled and finely sliced
6 anchovy fillets, drained
extra sprigs of fresh rosemary, to garnish

Preheat the oven to 230°C/450°F/Gas Mark 8. Finely slice the potatoes – a mandolin is the best tool for this. Layer the potatoes with the onion in a large roasting tin, seasoning each layer with salt and pepper. Drizzle about 1 tablespoon of the olive oil over the potatoes and add the butter in small pieces. Pour in the lamb stock and milk. Set aside.

Make small incisions all over the lamb with the point of a small, sharp knife. Into each incision insert a small piece of rosemary, a sliver of garlic and a piece of anchovy fillet.

Drizzle the leg of lamb and its flavourings with the rest of the olive oil and season well. Place the meat directly onto a shelf in the preheated oven. Position the roasting tin of potatoes directly underneath to catch the juices during cooking. Roast for 20 minutes per 450 g/1 lb 2 oz (about 1 hour, 40 minutes for a joint this size), reducing the oven temperature after 20 minutes to 200°C/400°F/Gas Mark 6.

When the lamb is cooked, remove from the oven and allow to rest for 10 minutes before carving. Meanwhile, increase the oven heat and cook the potatoes for a further 10–15 minutes to crisp up. Garnish with fresh rosemary sprigs and serve immediately with the lamb.

HEALTH RATING 🍎🍎

**ENTERTAINING ALTERNATIVE**

Leg of Lamb with Minted Rice

**SPEEDY ALTERNATIVE**

Marinated Lamb Chops with Garlic Fried Potatoes

## ENTERTAINING ALTERNATIVE
# Leg of Lamb with Minted Rice

INGREDIENTS **Serves 4**

1 tbsp olive oil
1 medium onion, peeled and finely chopped
1 garlic clove, peeled and crushed
1 celery stalk, trimmed and chopped
1 large mild red chilli, deseeded and chopped
75 g/3 oz long-grain rice
150 ml/¼ pint lamb or chicken stock
2 tbsp freshly chopped mint
salt and freshly ground black pepper
1.4 kg/3 lb boned leg of lamb
freshly cooked vegetables, to serve

Preheat the oven to 190°C/375°F/Gas Mark 5, 10 minutes before roasting. Heat the oil in a frying pan and gently cook the onion for 5 minutes. Stir in the garlic, celery and chilli and continue to cook for 3–4 minutes.

Place the rice and the stock in a large saucepan and cook, covered, for 10–12 minutes or until the rice is tender and all the liquid is absorbed. Stir in the onion and celery mixture, then leave to cool. Once the rice mixture is cold, stir in the chopped mint and season to taste with salt and pepper.

Place the boned lamb skin-side down and spoon the rice mixture along the centre of the meat. Roll up the meat to enclose the stuffing and tie securely with string. Place in a roasting tin and roast in the preheated oven for 1 hour 20 minutes, or until cooked to personal preference. Remove from the oven and leave to rest in a warm place for 20 minutes before carving. Serve with a selection of cooked vegetables.

## SPEEDY ALTERNATIVE
# Marinated Lamb Chops with Garlic Fried Potatoes

INGREDIENTS **Serves 6**

4 thick lamb chump chops
3 tbsp olive oil
550 g/1¼ lb potatoes, peeled and cut into 1 cm/½ inch dice
6 unpeeled garlic cloves
mixed salad or freshly cooked vegetables, to serve

**For the marinade:**

1 small bunch of fresh thyme, leaves removed
1 tbsp freshly chopped rosemary
1 tsp salt
2 garlic cloves, peeled and crushed
rind and juice of 1 lemon
2 tbsp olive oil

Trim the chops of any excess fat, wipe with a clean damp cloth and reserve. To make the marinade, using a pestle and mortar, pound the thyme leaves and rosemary with the salt until pulpy. Add the garlic and continue pounding until crushed. Stir in the lemon rind and juice and the olive oil.

Pour the marinade over the lamb chops, turning them until they are well coated. Cover lightly and leave to marinate in the refrigerator for about 1 hour.

Meanwhile, heat the oil in a large, non-stick frying pan. Add the potatoes and garlic and cook over a low heat for about 20 minutes, stirring occasionally. Increase the heat and cook for a further 10–15 minutes until golden. Drain on absorbent kitchen paper and add salt to taste. Keep warm.

Heat a griddle pan until almost smoking. Add the lamb chops and cook for 3–4 minutes on each side until golden, but still pink in the middle. Serve with the potatoes, and either a mixed salad or freshly cooked vegetables.

# Lamb Arrabbiata

INGREDIENTS **Serves 4**

4 tbsp olive oil
450 g/1 lb lamb fillets, cubed
1 large onion, peeled and sliced
4 garlic cloves, peeled and finely chopped
1 red chilli, deseeded and finely chopped
400 g can chopped tomatoes
175 g/6 oz pitted black olives, halved
150 ml/¼ pint white wine
salt and freshly ground black pepper
280 g/10 oz farfalle pasta
1 tsp butter
4 tbsp freshly chopped parsley, plus 1 tbsp to garnish

Heat 2 tablespoons of the olive oil in a large frying pan and cook the lamb for 5–7 minutes, or until sealed. Remove from the pan using a slotted spoon and reserve.

Heat the remaining oil in the pan, add the onion, garlic and chilli and cook until softened. Add the tomatoes, bring to the boil, then simmer for 10 minutes.

Return the browned lamb to the pan with the olives and pour in the wine. Bring the sauce back to the boil, reduce the heat then simmer, uncovered, for 15 minutes until the lamb is tender. Season to taste with salt and pepper.

Meanwhile, bring a large pan of lightly salted water to a rolling boil. Add the pasta and cook according to the packet instructions, or until 'al dente'.

Drain the pasta, toss in the butter, then add to the sauce and mix lightly. Stir in 4 tablespoons of the chopped parsley, then tip into a warmed serving dish. Sprinkle with the remaining parsley and serve immediately.

HEALTH RATING

**SPEEDY ALTERNATIVE**
Creamed Lamb & Wild Mushroom Pasta

**STARTER SUGGESTION**
Sweetcorn Fritters

INGREDIENTS **Serves 4**

25 g/1 oz dried porcini
450 g/1 lb pasta shapes
25g/1 oz butter
1 tbsp olive oil
350 g/12 oz lamb neck fillet, thinly sliced
1 garlic clove, peeled and crushed
225 g/8 oz chestnut mushrooms, wiped and sliced
4 tbsp white wine
125 ml/4 fl oz double cream
salt and freshly ground black pepper
1 tbsp freshly chopped parsley, to garnish
freshly grated Parmesan cheese, to serve

**SPEEDY ALTERNATIVE**

## Creamed Lamb & Wild Mushroom Pasta

Place the porcini in a small bowl and cover with almost boiling water. Leave to soak for 30 minutes. Drain the porcini, reserving the soaking liquid. Chop the porcini finely. Bring a large pan of lightly salted water to a rolling boil. Add the pasta and cook according to the packet instructions, or until 'al dente'.

Meanwhile, melt the butter with the olive oil in a large frying pan and fry the lamb to seal. Add the garlic, mushrooms and prepared porcini and cook for 5 minutes, or until just soft. Add the wine and the reserved porcini soaking liquid, then simmer for 2 minutes. Stir in the cream with the seasoning and simmer for 1–2 minutes, or until just thickened.

Drain the pasta thoroughly, reserving about 4 tablespoons of the cooking water. Return the pasta to the pan. Pour over the mushroom sauce and toss lightly together, adding the pasta water if the sauce is too thick. Tip into a warmed serving dish or spoon on to individual plates. Garnish with the chopped parsley and serve immediately with grated Parmesan cheese.

**STARTER SUGGESTION**

## Sweetcorn Fritters

Heat 1 tablespoon of the groundnut oil in a frying pan, add the onion and cook gently for 7–8 minutes or until beginning to soften. Add the chilli, garlic and ground coriander and cook for 1 minute, stirring continuously. Remove from the heat.

Drain the sweetcorn and tip into a mixing bowl. Lightly mash with a potato masher to break down the corn a little. Add the cooked onion mixture to the bowl with the spring onions and beaten egg. Season to taste with salt and pepper, then stir to mix together. Sift the flour and baking powder over the mixture and stir in.

Heat 2 tablespoons of the groundnut oil in a large frying pan. Drop 4 or 5 heaped teaspoonfuls of the sweetcorn mixture into the pan, and using a fish slice or spatula, flatten each to make a 1 cm/½ inch thick fritter.

Fry the fritters for 3 minutes, or until golden brown on the underside, turn over and fry for a further 3 minutes, or until cooked through and crisp.

Remove the fritters from the pan and drain on absorbent kitchen paper. Keep warm while cooking the remaining fritters, adding a little more oil if needed. Garnish with spring onion curls and serve immediately with a Thai-style chutney.

INGREDIENTS **Serves 4**

4 tbsp groundnut oil
1 small onion, peeled and finely chopped
1 red chilli, deseeded and finely chopped
1 garlic clove, peeled and crushed
1 tsp ground coriander
325 g can sweetcorn
6 spring onions, trimmed and finely sliced
1 medium egg, lightly beaten
salt and freshly ground black pepper
3 tbsp plain flour
1 tsp baking powder
spring onion curls, to garnish
Thai-style chutney, to serve

# Lancashire Hotpot

INGREDIENTS **Serves 4**

1 kg/2¼ lb middle end neck of lamb, divided into cutlets
2 tbsp vegetable oil
2 large onions, peeled and sliced
2 tsp plain flour
150 ml/¼ pint vegetable or lamb stock
700 g/1½ lb waxy potatoes, peeled and thickly sliced
salt and freshly ground black pepper
1 bay leaf
2 sprigs of fresh thyme
1 tbsp melted butter
2 tbsp freshly chopped herbs, to garnish
freshly cooked green beans, to serve

Preheat the oven to 170°C/325°F/Gas Mark 3. Trim any excess fat from the lamb cutlets. Heat the oil in a frying pan and brown the cutlets in batches for 3–4 minutes. Remove with a slotted spoon and reserve. Add the onions to the frying pan and cook for 6–8 minutes until softened and just beginning to colour, then remove and reserve.

Stir in the flour and cook for a few seconds, then gradually pour in the stock, stirring well, and bring to the boil. Remove from the heat.

Spread the base of a large casserole dish with half the potato slices. Top with half the onions and season well with salt and pepper. Arrange the browned meat in a layer. Season again and add the remaining onions, bay leaf and thyme. Pour in the remaining liquid from the onions and top with remaining potatoes so that they overlap in a single layer. Brush the potatoes with the melted butter and season again.

Cover the saucepan and cook in the preheated oven for 2 hours, uncovering for the last 30 minutes to allow the potatoes to brown. Garnish with chopped herbs and serve immediately with green beans.

HEALTH RATING ✓✓

**ENTERTAINING ALTERNATIVE**
Pork Chop Hotpot

**STARTER SUGGESTION**
Fried Whitebait with Rocket Salad

**ENTERTAINING ALTERNATIVE**
## Pork Chop Hotpot

INGREDIENTS **Serves 4**

4 pork chops
flour for dusting
225 g/8 oz shallots, peeled
2 garlic cloves, peeled
50 g/2 oz sun-dried tomatoes
2 tbsp olive oil
400 g can plum tomatoes
150 ml/¼ pint red wine
150 ml/¼ pint chicken stock
3 tbsp tomato purée
2 tbsp freshly chopped oregano
salt and freshly ground black pepper
fresh oregano leaves, to garnish

**To serve:**
freshly cooked new potatoes
French beans

Preheat the oven to 190°C/375°F/Gas Mark 5, 10 minutes before cooking. Trim the pork chops, removing any excess fat, wipe with a clean, damp cloth, then dust with a little flour and reserve. Cut the shallots in half if large. Chop the garlic and slice the sun-dried tomatoes.

Heat the olive oil in a large casserole dish and cook the pork chops for about 5 minutes, turning occasionally during cooking until browned all over. Using a slotted spoon, carefully lift out of the dish and reserve. Add the shallots and cook for 5 minutes, stirring occasionally.

Return the pork chops to the casserole dish and scatter with the garlic and sun-dried tomatoes, then pour over the can of tomatoes with their juice.

Blend the red wine, stock and tomato purée together and add the chopped oregano. Season to taste with salt and pepper, then pour over the pork chops and bring to a gentle boil. Cover with a close fitting lid and cook in the preheated oven for 1 hour, or until the pork chops are tender. Adjust the seasoning to taste, then scatter with a few oregano leaves and serve immediately with freshly cooked potatoes and French beans.

**STARTER SUGGESTION**
## Fried Whitebait with Rocket Salad

INGREDIENTS **Serves 4**

450 g/1 lb whitebait, fresh or frozen
oil, for frying
85 g/3 oz plain flour
½ tsp of cayenne pepper
salt and freshly ground black pepper

**For the salad:**
125 g/4 oz rocket leaves
125 g/4 oz cherry tomatoes, halved
75 g/3 oz cucumber, cut into cubes
3 tbsp olive oil
1 tbsp fresh lemon juice
½ tsp Dijon mustard
½ tsp caster sugar

If the whitebait are frozen, thaw completely then wipe dry with absorbent kitchen paper.

Start to heat the oil in a deep-fat fryer. Arrange the fish in a large, shallow dish and toss well in the flour, cayenne pepper and salt and pepper.

Deep fry the fish in batches for 2–3 minutes, or until crisp and golden. Keep the cooked fish warm while deep frying the remaining fish.

Meanwhile, to make the salad, arrange the rocket leaves, cherry tomatoes and cucumber on individual serving dishes. Whisk the olive oil and the remaining ingredients together and season lightly. Drizzle the dressing over the salad and serve with the whitebait.

# Spicy Lamb in Yogurt Sauce

INGREDIENTS **Serves 4**

1 tsp hot chilli powder
1 tsp ground cinnamon
1 tsp medium hot curry powder
1 tsp ground cumin
salt and freshly ground black pepper
2 tbsp groundnut oil
450 g/1 lb lamb fillet, trimmed
4 cardamom pods, bruised
4 whole cloves
1 onion, peeled and finely sliced
2 garlic cloves, peeled and crushed
2.5 cm/1 inch piece fresh root ginger, peeled and grated
150 ml/¼ pint Greek style yogurt
1 tbsp freshly chopped coriander
2 spring onions, trimmed and finely sliced

**To serve:**
freshly cooked rice
naan bread

Blend the chilli powder, cinnamon, curry powder, cumin and seasoning with 2 tablespoons of the oil in a bowl and reserve. Cut the lamb fillet into thin strips, add to the spice and oil mixture and stir until coated thoroughly. Cover and leave to marinate in the refrigerator for at least 30 minutes.

Heat the wok, then pour in the remaining oil. When hot, add the cardamom pods and cloves and stir-fry for 10 seconds. Add the onion, garlic and ginger to the wok and stir fry for 3–4 minutes until softened.

Add the lamb along with the marinading ingredients and stir-fry for a further 3 minutes until cooked. Pour in the yogurt, stir thoroughly and heat until piping hot. Sprinkle with the chopped coriander and sliced spring onions then serve immediately with freshly cooked rice and naan bread.

HEALTH RATING 🍎🍎🍎

**MILD ALTERNATIVE**
Sweet-&-Sour Pork

**SUGGESTED ACCOMPANIMENT**
Beetroot & Potato Medley

**MILD ALTERNATIVE**
## Sweet-&-Sour Pork

INGREDIENTS **Serves 4**

- 450 g/1 lb pork fillet
- 1 medium egg white
- 4 tsp cornflour
- salt and freshly ground black pepper
- 300 ml/½ pint groundnut oil
- 1 small onion, peeled and finely sliced
- 125 g/4 oz carrots, peeled and cut into matchsticks
- 2.5 cm/1 inch piece fresh root ginger, peeled and cut into thin strips
- 150 ml/¼ pint orange juice
- 150 ml/¼ pint chicken stock
- 1 tbsp light soy sauce
- 220 g can pineapple pieces, drained with juice reserved
- 1 tbsp white wine vinegar
- 1 tbsp freshly chopped parsley
- freshly cooked rice, to serve

Trim, then cut the pork fillet into small cubes. In a bowl, whisk the egg white and cornflour with a little seasoning, then add the pork to the egg white mixture and stir until the cubes are well coated.

Heat the wok, then add the oil and heat until very hot before adding the pork and stir-frying for 30 seconds. Turn off the heat and continue to stir for 3 minutes. The meat should be white and sealed. Drain off the oil, reserve the pork and wipe the wok clean.

Pour 2 teaspoons of the drained groundnut oil back into the wok and cook the onion, carrots and ginger for 2–3 minutes. Blend the orange juice with the chicken stock and soy sauce and make up to 300 ml/½ pint with the reserved pineapple juice.

Return the pork to the wok with the juice mixture and simmer for 3–4 minutes. Then stir in the pineapple pieces and vinegar. Heat through, then sprinkle with the chopped parsley and serve immediately with freshly cooked rice.

**SUGGESTED ACCOMPANIMENT**
## Beetroot & Potato Medley

INGREDIENTS **Serves 4**

- 350 g/12 oz raw baby beetroot
- ½ tsp sunflower oil
- 225 g/8 oz new potatoes
- ½ cucumber, peeled
- 3 tbsp white wine vinegar
- 150 ml/¼ pint natural yogurt
- salt and freshly ground black pepper
- fresh salad leaves
- 1 tbsp freshly snipped chives, to garnish

Preheat the oven to 180°C/350°F/Gas Mark 4. Scrub the beetroot thoroughly and place on a baking tray.

Brush the beetroot with a little oil and cook for 1½ hours or until a skewer is easily insertable into the beetroot. Allow to cool a little, then remove the skins.

Cook the potatoes in boiling water for about 10 minutes. Rinse in cold water and drain. Reserve the potatoes until cool. Dice evenly.

Cut the cucumber into cubes and place in a mixing bowl. Chop the beetroot into small cubes and add to the bowl with the reserved potatoes. Gently mix the vegetables together.

Mix together the vinegar and yogurt and season to taste with a little salt and pepper. Pour over the vegetables and combine gently.

Arrange on a bed of salad leaves garnished with the snipped chives and serve.

# Lamb with Stir-fried Vegetables

INGREDIENTS **Serves 4**

550 g/1¼ lb lamb fillet, cut into strips
2.5 cm/1 inch piece fresh root ginger, peeled and cut into matchsticks
2 garlic cloves, peeled and chopped
4 tbsp soy sauce
2 tbsp dry sherry
2 tsp cornflour
4 tbsp groundnut oil
75 g/3 oz French beans, trimmed and cut in half
2 medium carrots, peeled and cut into matchsticks
1 red pepper, deseeded and cut into chunks
1 yellow pepper, deseeded and cut into chunks
225 g can water chestnuts, drained and halved
3 tomatoes, chopped
freshly cooked sticky rice in banana leaves, to serve (optional)

Place the lamb strips in a shallow dish. Mix together the ginger and half the garlic in a small bowl. Pour over the soy sauce and sherry and stir well. Pour over the lamb and stir until coated lightly. Cover with clingfilm and leave to marinate for at least 30 minutes, occasionally spooning the marinade over the lamb.

Using a slotted spoon, lift the lamb from the marinade and place on a plate. Blend the cornflour and the marinade together until smooth and reserve.

Heat a wok or large frying pan, add 2 tablespoons of the oil and when hot, add the remaining garlic, French beans, carrots and peppers and stir-fry for 5 minutes. Using a slotted spoon, transfer the vegetables to a plate and keep warm.

Heat the remaining oil in the wok, add the lamb and stir-fry for 2 minutes or until tender. Return the vegetables to the wok with the water chestnuts, tomatoes and reserved marinade mixture. Bring to the boil then simmer for 1 minute. Serve immediately with freshly cooked sticky rice in banana leaves, if liked.

HEALTH RATING

**SPICY ALTERNATIVE**

Spicy Lamb & Peppers

**CHILDREN'S ALTERNATIVE**

Lamb Meatballs with Savoy Cabbage

## SPICY ALTERNATIVE
# Spicy Lamb & Peppers

INGREDIENTS **Serves 4**

550 g/1¼ lb lamb fillet
4 tbsp soy sauce
1 tbsp dry sherry
1 tbsp cornflour
3 tbsp vegetable oil
1 bunch spring onions, shredded
225 g/8 oz broccoli florets
2 garlic cloves, peeled and chopped
2.5 cm/1 inch piece fresh root ginger, peeled and cut into matchsticks
1 red pepper, deseeded and cut into chunks
1 green pepper, deseeded and cut into chunks
2 tsp Chinese five spice powder
1–2 tsp dried crushed chillies, or to taste
1 tbsp tomato purée
1 tbsp rice wine vinegar
1 tbsp soft brown sugar
freshly cooked noodles, to serve

Cut the lamb into 2 cm/¾ inch slices, then place in a shallow dish. Blend the soy sauce, sherry and cornflour together in a small bowl and pour over the lamb. Turn the lamb until coated lightly with the marinade. Cover with clingfilm and leave to marinate in the refrigerator for at least 30 minutes, turning occasionally.

Heat a wok or large frying pan, add the oil and when hot, stir-fry the spring onions and broccoli for 2 minutes. Add the garlic, ginger and peppers and stir-fry for a further 2 minutes. Using a slotted spoon, transfer the vegetables to a plate and keep warm.

Using a slotted spoon, lift the lamb from the marinade, shaking off any excess marinade. Add to the wok and stir-fry for 5 minutes, or until browned all over. Reserve the marinade.

Return the vegetables to the wok and stir in the Chinese five spice powder, chillies, tomato purée, reserved marinade, vinegar and sugar. Bring to the boil, stirring constantly, until thickened. Simmer for 2 minutes or until heated through thoroughly. Serve immediately with noodles.

## CHILDREN'S ALTERNATIVE
# Lamb Meatballs with Savoy Cabbage

INGREDIENTS **Serves 4**

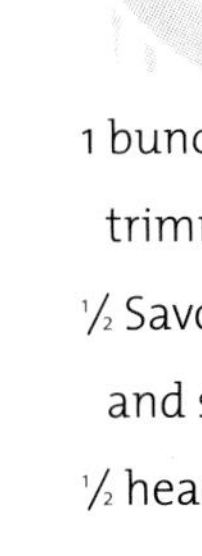

450 g/1 lb fresh lamb mince
1 tbsp freshly chopped parsley
1 tbsp freshly grated root ginger
1 tbsp light soy sauce
1 medium egg yolk
4 tbsp dark soy sauce
2 tbsp dry sherry
1 tbsp cornflour
3 tbsp vegetable oil
2 garlic cloves, peeled and chopped
1 bunch spring onions, trimmed and shredded
½ Savoy cabbage, trimmed and shredded
½ head Chinese leaves, trimmed and shredded
freshly chopped red chilli to garnish, if liked

Place the lamb mince in a large bowl with the parsley, ginger, light soy sauce and egg yolk and mix together. Divide the mixture into walnut-sized pieces and using your hands roll into balls. Place on a baking sheet, cover with clingfilm and chill in the refrigerator for at least 30 minutes.

Meanwhile, blend together the dark soy sauce, sherry and cornflour with 2 tablespoons of water in a small bowl until smooth. Reserve.

Heat a wok, add the oil and when hot, add the meatballs and cook for 5–8 minutes, or until browned all over, turning occasionally. Using a slotted spoon, transfer the meatballs to a large plate and keep warm.

Add the garlic, spring onions, Savoy cabbage and the Chinese leaves to the wok and stir-fry for 3 minutes. Pour over the reserved soy sauce mixture, bring to the boil, then simmer for 30 seconds or until thickened. Return the meatballs to the wok and mix in. Garnish with chopped red chilli, if liked, and serve immediately.

# Poultry & Game

Whatever you need inspiration for, whether it's a traditional Sunday roast or something that little bit different for a dinner party, you'll find it amongst these delicious, easy-to-follow recipes. Tackling everything from chicken and turkey to duck, pheasant and even rabbit, these recipes give old favourites a fresh twist and introduce some new ideas that the whole family will love.

**ENTERTAINING ALTERNATIVE**
## Red Chicken Curry

INGREDIENTS **Serves 4**

225 ml/8 fl oz coconut cream
2 tbsp vegetable oil
2 garlic clove, peeled and finely chopped
2 tbsp Thai red curry paste
2 tbsp Thai fish sauce
2 tsp sugar
350 g/12 oz boneless, skinless chicken breast, finely sliced
450 ml/¾ pint chicken stock
2 lime leaves, shredded
chopped red chilli, to garnish
freshly boiled rice or steamed Thai fragrant rice, to serve

Pour the coconut cream into a small saucepan and heat gently. Meanwhile, heat a wok or large frying pan and add the oil. When the oil is very hot, swirl the oil around the wok until it is lightly coated, then add the garlic and stir-fry for about 10–20 seconds, or until the garlic begins to brown. Add the curry paste and stir-fry for a few more seconds, then pour in the warmed coconut cream.

Cook the coconut cream mixture for 5 minutes, or until the cream has curdled and thickened. Stir in the fish sauce and sugar. Add the finely sliced chicken breast and cook for 3–4 minutes, or until the chicken has turned white.

Pour the stock into the wok, bring to the boil, then simmer for 1–2 minutes, or until the chicken is cooked through. Stir in the shredded lime leaves. Turn into a warmed serving dish, garnish with chopped red chilli and serve immediately with rice.

**VEGETARIAN ALTERNATIVE**
## Thai-style Cauliflower & Potato Curry

INGREDIENTS **Serves 4**

450 g/1 lb new potatoes, peeled and halved or quartered
350 g/12 oz cauliflower florets
3 garlic cloves, peeled and crushed
1 onion, peeled and finely chopped
40 g/1½ oz ground almonds
1 tsp ground coriander
½ tsp ground cumin
½ tsp turmeric
3 tbsp groundnut oil
salt and freshly ground black pepper
50 g/2 oz creamed coconut, broken into small pieces
200 ml/7 fl oz vegetable stock
1 tbsp mango chutney
sprigs of fresh coriander, to garnish
freshly cooked long-grain rice, to serve

Bring a saucepan of lightly salted water to the boil, add the potatoes and cook for 15 minutes or until just tender. Drain and leave to cool. Boil the cauliflower for 2 minutes, then drain and refresh under cold running water. Drain again and reserve.

Meanwhile, blend the garlic, onion, ground almonds and spices with 2 tablespoons of the oil and salt and pepper to taste in a food processor until a smooth paste is formed. Heat a wok, add the remaining oil and when hot, add the spice paste and cook for 3–4 minutes, stirring continuously.

Dissolve the creamed coconut in 6 tablespoons of boiling water and add to the wok. Pour in the stock, cook for 2–3 minutes, then stir in the cooked potatoes and cauliflower.

Stir in the mango chutney and heat through for 3–4 minutes or until piping hot. Tip into a warmed serving dish, garnish with sprigs of fresh coriander and serve immediately with freshly cooked rice.

# Green Chicken Curry

INGREDIENTS **Serves 4**

1 onion, peeled and chopped
3 lemon grass stalks, outer leaves discarded and finely sliced
2 garlic cloves, peeled and finely chopped
1 tbsp freshly grated root ginger
3 green chillies
zest and juice of 1 lime
2 tbsp groundnut oil
2 tbsp Thai fish sauce
6 tbsp freshly chopped coriander
6 tbsp freshly chopped basil
450 g/1 lb skinless, boneless chicken breasts, cut into strips
125 g /4 oz fine green beans, trimmed
400 ml can coconut milk
fresh basil leaves, to garnish
freshly cooked rice, to serve

Place the onion, lemon grass, garlic, ginger, chillies, lime zest and juice, 1 tablespoon of groundnut oil, the fish sauce, coriander and basil in a food processor. Blend to a form a smooth paste, which should be of a spoonable consistency. If the sauce looks thick, add a little water. Remove and reserve.

Heat the wok, add the remaining 1 tablespoon of oil and when hot add the chicken. Stir-fry for 2–3 minutes, until the chicken starts to colour, then add the green beans and stir-fry for a further minute. Remove the chicken and beans from the wok and reserve. Wipe the wok clean with absorbent kitchen paper.

Spoon the reserved green paste into the wok and heat for 1 minute. Add the coconut milk and whisk to blend. Return the chicken and beans to the wok and bring to the boil. Simmer for 5–7 minutes, or until the chicken is cooked. Sprinkle with basil leaves and serve immediately with freshly cooked rice.

HEALTH RATING

**ENTERTAINING ALTERNATIVE**
Red Chicken Curry

**VEGETARIAN ALTERNATIVE**
Thai-style Cauliflower & Potato Curry

# Steamed, Crispy, Citrus Chicken

INGREDIENTS **Serves 6**

200 ml/7 fl oz light soy sauce
1 tbsp brown sugar
4 star anise
2 slices fresh root ginger, peeled
5 spring onions, trimmed and sliced
1 small orange, cut into wedges
1 lime, cut into wedges
1.1 kg/2½ lb oven-ready chicken
2 garlic cloves, peeled and finely chopped
2 tbsp Chinese rice wine
2 tbsp dark soy sauce
300 ml/½ pint groundnut oil
orange slices, to garnish
freshly cooked steamed rice, to serve

Pour the light soy sauce and 200 ml/7 fl oz water into the wok and add the sugar and star anise. Bring to the boil over a gentle heat. Pour into a small bowl and leave to cool slightly. Wipe the wok clean with absorbent kitchen paper.

Put the ginger, 2 spring onions, orange and lime inside the cavity of the chicken. Place a rack in the wok and pour in boiling water to a depth of 5 cm/2 inches. Put a piece of tinfoil onto the rack and place the chicken in the centre, then pour over the soy sauce mixture.

Cover the wok and steam gently for 1 hour–1 hour 10 minutes, or until the chicken is cooked through, pouring off excess fat from time to time. Add more water if necessary. Leave the chicken to cool and dry for up to 3 hours, then cut the chicken into quarters.

Mix together the garlic, Chinese rice wine, dark soy sauce and remaining spring onions, then reserve. Dry the wok and heat again, then add the oil. When hot, shallow fry the chicken quarters for 4 minutes, or until golden and crisp. Do this 1 portion at a time, remove and drain on absorbent kitchen paper.

When cool enough to handle shred into bite-sized pieces and drizzle over the sauce. Garnish with slices of orange and serve with freshly steamed rice.

HEALTH RATING 🍎🍎🍎🍎

**SPEEDY ALTERNATIVE**
Stir-fried Lemon Chicken

**SUGGESTED ACCOMPANIMENT**
Mixed Vegetables Stir Fry

## SPEEDY ALTERNATIVE
# Stir-fried Lemon Chicken

INGREDIENTS **Serves 4**

350 g/12 oz boneless, skinless chicken breast
1 large egg white
5 tsp cornflour
3 tbsp vegetable or groundnut oil
150 ml/¼ pint chicken stock
2 tbsp fresh lemon juice
2 tbsp light soy sauce
1 tbsp Chinese rice wine or dry sherry
1 tbsp sugar
2 garlic cloves, peeled and finely chopped
¼ tsp dried chilli flakes, or to taste

**To garnish:**
lemon rind strips
red chilli slices

Using a sharp knife, trim the chicken, discarding any fat and cut into thin strips, about 5 cm/2 inch long and 1 cm/½ inch wide. Place in a shallow dish. Lightly whisk the egg white and 1 tablespoon of the cornflour together until smooth. Pour over the chicken strips and mix well until coated evenly. Leave to marinate in the refrigerator for at least 20 minutes.

When ready to cook, drain the chicken and reserve. Heat a wok or large frying pan, add the oil and when hot, add the chicken and stir-fry for 1–2 minutes, or until the chicken has turned white. Using a slotted spoon, remove from the wok and reserve.

Wipe the wok clean and return to the heat. Add the chicken stock, lemon juice, soy sauce, Chinese rice wine or sherry, sugar, garlic and chilli flakes and bring to the boil. Blend the remaining cornflour with 1 tablespoon of water and stir into the stock. Simmer for 1 minute.

Return the chicken to the wok and continue simmering for a further 2–3 minutes, or until the chicken is tender and the sauce has thickened. Garnish with lemon strips and red chilli slices. Serve immediately.

## SUGGESTED ACCOMPANIMENT
# Mixed Vegetables Stir Fry

Heat a wok, add the oil and when hot, add the garlic and ginger slices and stir-fry for 1 minute.

Add the broccoli florets to the wok, stir-fry for 1 minute, then add the mangetout, carrots and the green and red peppers and stir-fry for a further 3–4 minutes until tender but still crisp.

Blend the soy sauce, hoisin sauce and sugar in a small bowl. Stir well, season to taste with salt and pepper and pour into the wok. Transfer the vegetables to a warmed serving dish. Garnish with shredded spring onions and serve immediately as an accompaniment to Thai or Chinese dishes.

INGREDIENTS **Serves 4**

2 tbsp groundnut oil
4 garlic cloves, peeled and finely sliced
2.5 cm/1 inch piece fresh root ginger, peeled and finely sliced
75 g/3 oz broccoli florets
50 g/2 oz mangetout, trimmed
75 g/3 oz carrots, peeled and cut into matchsticks
1 green pepper, deseeded and cut into strips
1 red pepper, deseeded and cut into strips
1 tbsp soy sauce
1 tbsp hoisin sauce
1 tsp sugar
salt and freshly ground black pepper
4 spring onions, trimmed and shredded, to garnish

# Slow Roast Chicken with Potatoes & Oregano

INGREDIENTS **Serves 6**

1.4–1.8 kg/3–4 lb oven-ready chicken, preferably free range
1 lemon, halved
1 onion, peeled and quartered
50 g/2 oz butter, softened
salt and freshly ground black pepper
1 kg/2¼ lb potatoes, peeled and quartered
3–4 tbsp extra-virgin olive oil
1 tbsp dried oregano, crumbled
1 tsp fresh thyme leaves
2 tbsp freshly chopped thyme
fresh sage leaves, to garnish

Preheat the oven to 200°C/400°F/Gas Mark 6. Rinse the chicken and dry well, inside and out, with absorbent kitchen paper. Rub the chicken all over with the lemon halves, then squeeze the juice over it and into the cavity. Put the squeezed halves into the cavity with the quartered onion.

Rub the softened butter all over the chicken and season to taste with salt and pepper, then put it in a large roasting tin, breast-side down.

Toss the potatoes in the oil, season with salt and pepper to taste and add the dried oregano and fresh thyme. Arrange the potatoes with the oil around the chicken and carefully pour 150 ml/¼ pint water into one end of the pan (not over the oil).

Roast in the preheated oven for 25 minutes. Reduce the oven temperature to 190°C/375°F/Gas Mark 5 and turn the chicken breast-side up. Turn the potatoes, sprinkle over half the fresh herbs and baste the chicken and potatoes with the juices. Continue roasting for 1 hour, or until the chicken is cooked, basting occasionally. If the liquid evaporates completely, add a little more water. The chicken is done when the juices run clear when the thigh is pierced with a skewer.

Transfer the chicken to a carving board and rest for 5 minutes, covered with tinfoil. Return the potatoes to the oven while the chicken is resting.

Carve the chicken into serving pieces and arrange on a large heatproof serving dish. Arrange the potatoes around the chicken and drizzle over any remaining juices. Sprinkle with the remaining herbs and serve.

HEALTH RATING 🍎🍎🍎

**SUGGESTED ACCOMPANIMENT**
Stuffed Onions with Pine Nuts

**PUDDING SUGGESTION**
Baked Apple Dumplings

INGREDIENTS **Serves 4**

4 medium onions, peeled
2 garlic cloves, peeled and crushed
2 tbsp fresh brown breadcrumbs
2 tbsp white breadcrumbs
25 g/1 oz sultanas
25 g/1 oz pine nuts
50 g/2 oz low-fat hard cheese such as Edam, grated
2 tbsp freshly chopped parsley
1 medium egg, beaten
salt and freshly ground black pepper

**SUGGESTED ACCOMPANIMENT**
## Stuffed Onions with Pine Nuts

Preheat the oven to 200°C/400°F/Gas Mark 6. Bring a pan of water to the boil, add the onions and cook gently for about 15 minutes. Drain well, allow the onions to cool, then slice each one in half horizontally. Scoop out most of the onion flesh but leave a reasonably firm shell.

Chop up 4 tablespoons of the onion flesh and place in a bowl with the crushed garlic, breadcrumbs, sultanas, pine nuts, grated cheese and parsley.

Mix the breadcrumb mixture together thoroughly. Bind together with as much of the beaten egg as necessary to make a firm filling. Season to taste with salt and pepper.

Pile the mixture back into the onion shells and top with the grated cheese. Place on a oiled baking tray and cook in the preheated oven for 20–30 minutes or until golden brown. Serve immediately.

**PUDDING SUGGESTION**
## Baked Apple Dumplings

Preheat the oven to 200°C/400°F/Gas Mark 6. Lightly oil a baking tray. Place the flour and salt in a bowl and stir in the suet. Add just enough water to the mixture to mix to a soft but not sticky dough, using the fingertips.

Turn the dough on to a lightly floured board and knead lightly into a ball. Divide the dough into four pieces and roll out each piece into a thin square, large enough to encase the apples.

Peel and core the apples and place one apple in the centre of each square of pastry. Fill the centre of the apple with mincemeat, brush the edges of each pastry square with water and draw the corners up to meet over each apple.

Press the edges of the pastry firmly together and decorate with pastry leaves and shapes made from the extra pastry trimmings.

Place the apples on the prepared baking tray, brush with the egg white and sprinkle with the sugar. Bake in the preheated oven for 30 minutes or until golden and the pastry and apples are cooked. Serve the dumplings hot with the custard or vanilla sauce.

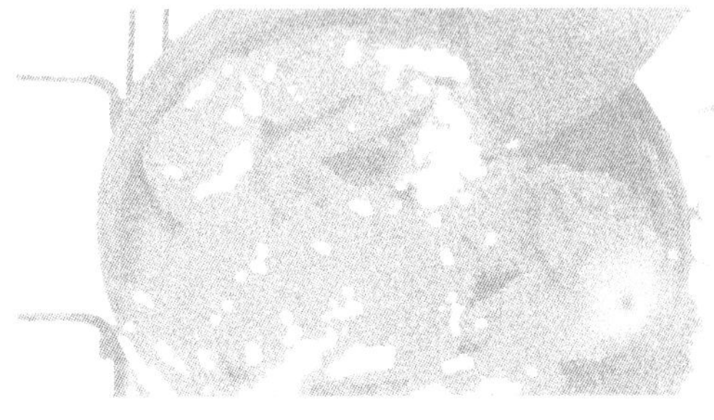

INGREDIENTS **Serves 4**

225 g/8 oz self-raising flour
¼ tsp salt
125 g/4 oz shredded suet
4 medium cooking apples
4–6 tsp luxury mincemeat
1 medium egg white, beaten
2 tsp caster sugar
custard or vanilla sauce, to serve

# Saffron Roast Chicken with Crispy Onions

INGREDIENTS **Serves 6**

1.6 kg/3½ lb oven-ready chicken, preferably free range
75 g/3 oz butter, softened
1 tsp saffron strands, lightly toasted
grated rind of 1 lemon
2 tbsp freshly chopped flat-leaf parsley
2 tbsp extra virgin olive oil
450 g/1 lb onions, peeled and cut into thin wedges
8–12 garlic cloves, peeled
1 tsp cumin seeds
½ tsp ground cinnamon
50 g/2 oz pine nuts
50 g/2 oz sultanas
salt and freshly ground black pepper
sprig of fresh flat leaf parsley, to garnish

Preheat the oven to 200°C/400°F/Gas Mark 6. Using your fingertips, gently loosen the skin from the chicken breast by sliding your hand between the skin and flesh. Cream together 50 g/2 oz of the butter with the saffron threads, the lemon rind and half the parsley, until smooth. Push the butter mixture under the skin. Spread over the breast and the top of the thighs with your fingers. Pull the neck skin to tighten the skin over the breast and tuck under the bird, then secure with a skewer or cocktail stick.

Heat the olive oil and remaining butter in a large heavy-based frying pan and cook the onions and garlic cloves for 5 minutes, or until the onions are soft. Stir in the cumin seeds, cinnamon, pine nuts and sultanas and cook for 2 minutes. Season to taste with salt and pepper and place in a roasting tin.

Place the chicken, breast-side down, on the base of the onions and roast in the preheated oven for 45 minutes. Reduce the oven temperature to 170°C/325°F/Gas Mark 3. Turn the chicken breast-side up and stir the onions. Continue roasting until the chicken is a deep golden yellow and the onions are crisp. Allow to rest for 10 minutes, then sprinkle with the remaining parsley. Before serving, garnish with a sprig of parsley and serve immediately with the onions and garlic.

HEALTH RATING

**SUGGESTED ACCOMPANIMENT**
Roast Butternut Squash Risotto

**PUDDING SUGGESTION**
Osborne Pudding

**SUGGESTED ACCOMPANIMENT**
## Roast Butternut Squash Risotto

INGREDIENTS **Serves 4**

1 medium butternut squash
2 tbsp olive oil
1 garlic bulb, cloves separated, but unpeeled
15 g/½ oz unsalted butter
280 g/10 oz Arborio rice
large pinch of saffron strands
150 ml/¼ pint dry white wine
1 litre/1¾ pints vegetable stock
1 tbsp freshly chopped parsley
1 tbsp freshly chopped oregano
50 g/2 oz Parmesan cheese, finely grated
salt and freshly ground black pepper
sprigs of fresh oregano, to garnish
extra Parmesan cheese, to serve

Preheat the oven to 190°C/375°F/Gas Mark 5. Cut the butternut squash in half, thickly peel, then scoop out the seeds and discard. Cut the flesh into 2 cm/¾ inch cubes.

Pour the oil into a large roasting tin and heat in the preheated oven for 5 minutes. Add the butternut squash and garlic cloves. Turn in the oil to coat, then roast in the oven for about 25–30 minutes, or until golden brown and very tender, turning the vegetables halfway through cooking time.

Melt the butter in a large saucepan. Add the rice and stir over a high heat for a few seconds. Add the saffron and the wine and bubble fiercely until almost totally reduced, stirring frequently. At the same time heat the stock in a separate saucepan and keep at a steady simmer.

Reduce the heat under the rice to low. Add a ladleful of stock to the saucepan and simmer, stirring, until absorbed. Continue adding the stock in this way until the rice is tender. This will take about 20 minutes and it may not be necessary to add all the stock.

Turn off the heat, stir in the herbs, Parmesan cheese and seasoning. Cover and leave to stand for 2–3 minutes. Quickly remove the skins from the roasted garlic. Add to the risotto with the butternut squash and mix gently. Garnish with sprigs of oregano and serve immediately with Parmesan cheese.

**PUDDING SUGGESTION**
## Osborne Pudding

Preheat the oven to 170°C/325°F/Gas Mark 3. Lightly oil a 1.1 litre/2 pint baking dish. Remove the crusts from the bread and spread thickly with butter and marmalade. Cut the bread into small triangles. Place half the bread in the base of the dish and sprinkle over the dried mixed fruit, 1 tablespoon of the orange juice and half the caster sugar.

Top with the remaining bread and marmalade, buttered side up and pour over the remaining orange juice. Sprinkle over the remaining caster sugar. Whisk the eggs with the milk and cream and pour over the pudding. Reserve for about 30 minutes to allow the bread to absorb the liquid.

Place in a roasting tin and pour in enough boiling water to come halfway up the sides of the dish. Bake in the preheated oven for 50–60 minutes, or until the pudding is set and the top is crisp and golden. Meanwhile, make the marmalade sauce. Heat the orange zest and juice with the marmalade and brandy if using. Mix 1 tablespoon of water with the cornflour and mix together well. Add to the saucepan and cook on a low heat, stirring until warmed through and thickened. Serve the pudding hot with the marmalade sauce.

INGREDIENTS **Serves 4**

8 slices of white bread
50 g/2 oz butter
2 tbsp marmalade
50 g/2 oz luxury mixed dried fruit
2 tbsp fresh orange juice
40 g/1½ oz caster sugar
2 large eggs
450 ml/¾ pint milk
150 ml/¼ pint whipping cream

**For the marmalade sauce:**
zest and juice of 1 orange
2 tbsp thick-cut orange marmalade
1 tbsp brandy (optional)
2 tsp cornflour

## ENTERTAINING ALTERNATIVE
## Poached Chicken with Salsa Verde Herb Sauce

INGREDIENTS **Serves 6**

6 boneless chicken breasts, each about 175 g/6 oz
600 ml/1 pint chicken stock, preferably homemade

**For the salsa verde:**

2 garlic cloves, peeled and chopped
4 tbsp freshly chopped parsley
3 tbsp freshly chopped mint
2 tsp capers
2 tbsp chopped gherkins (optional)
2–3 anchovy fillets in olive oil, drained and finely chopped (optional)
1 handful wild rocket leaves, chopped (optional)
2 tbsp lemon juice or red wine vinegar
125 ml/4 fl oz extra virgin olive oil
salt and freshly ground black pepper
sprigs of mint, to garnish
freshly cooked vegetables, to serve

Place the chicken breasts with the stock in a large frying pan and bring to the boil. Reduce the heat and simmer for 15–20 minutes or until cooked. Leave to cool in the stock.

To make the salsa verde, switch on the motor of a food processor, drop in the garlic cloves and chop finely. Add the parsley and mint and, using the pulse button, pulse 2–3 times.

Add the capers and, if using, add the gherkins, anchovies and rocket. Pulse 2–3 times until the sauce is evenly textured.

With the machine still running, pour in the lemon juice or red wine vinegar, then add the olive oil in a slow, steady stream until the sauce is smooth. Season to taste with salt and pepper, then transfer to a large serving bowl and reserve.

Carve each chicken breast into thick slices and arrange on serving plates, fanning out the slices slightly. Spoon over a little of the salsa verde on to each chicken breast, garnish with sprigs of mint and serve immediately with freshly cooked vegetables.

## PUDDING SUGGESTION
## Sticky Chocolate Surprise Pudding

Preheat the oven to 180°C/350°F/Gas Mark 4, 10 minutes before baking. Lightly oil a 1.4 litre/2½ pint ovenproof soufflé dish. Sift the flour and cocoa powder into a large bowl and stir in the caster sugar and the chopped mint-flavoured chocolate and make a well in the centre.

Whisk the milk, vanilla essence and the melted butter together, then beat in the egg. Pour into the well in the dry ingredients and gradually mix together, drawing the dry ingredients in from the sides of the bowl. Beat well until mixed thoroughly. Spoon into the prepared soufflé dish.

To make the sauce, blend the dark muscovado sugar and the cocoa powder together and spoon over the top of the pudding. Carefully pour the hot water over the top of the pudding, but do not mix.

Bake in the preheated oven for 35–40 minutes, or until firm to the touch and the mixture has formed a sauce underneath. Decorate with mint and serve immediately.

INGREDIENTS **Serves 6–8**

150 g/5 oz self-raising flour
25 g/1 oz cocoa powder
200 g/7 oz golden caster sugar
75 g/3 oz mint-flavoured chocolate, chopped
175 ml/6 fl oz full cream milk
2 tsp vanilla essence
50 g/2 oz unsalted butter, melted
1 medium egg
sprig of fresh mint, to decorate

**For the sauce:**

175 g/6 oz dark muscovado sugar
125 g/4 oz cocoa powder
600 ml/1 pint very hot water

# Chicken with Porcini Mushrooms

INGREDIENTS **Serves 4**

2 tbsp olive oil
4 boneless chicken breasts, preferably free range
2 garlic cloves, peeled and crushed
150 ml/¼ pint dry vermouth or dry white wine
salt and freshly ground black pepper
25 g/1 oz butter
450 g/1 lb porcini or wild mushrooms, thickly sliced
1 tbsp freshly chopped oregano
sprigs of fresh basil, to garnish (optional)
freshly cooked rice, to serve

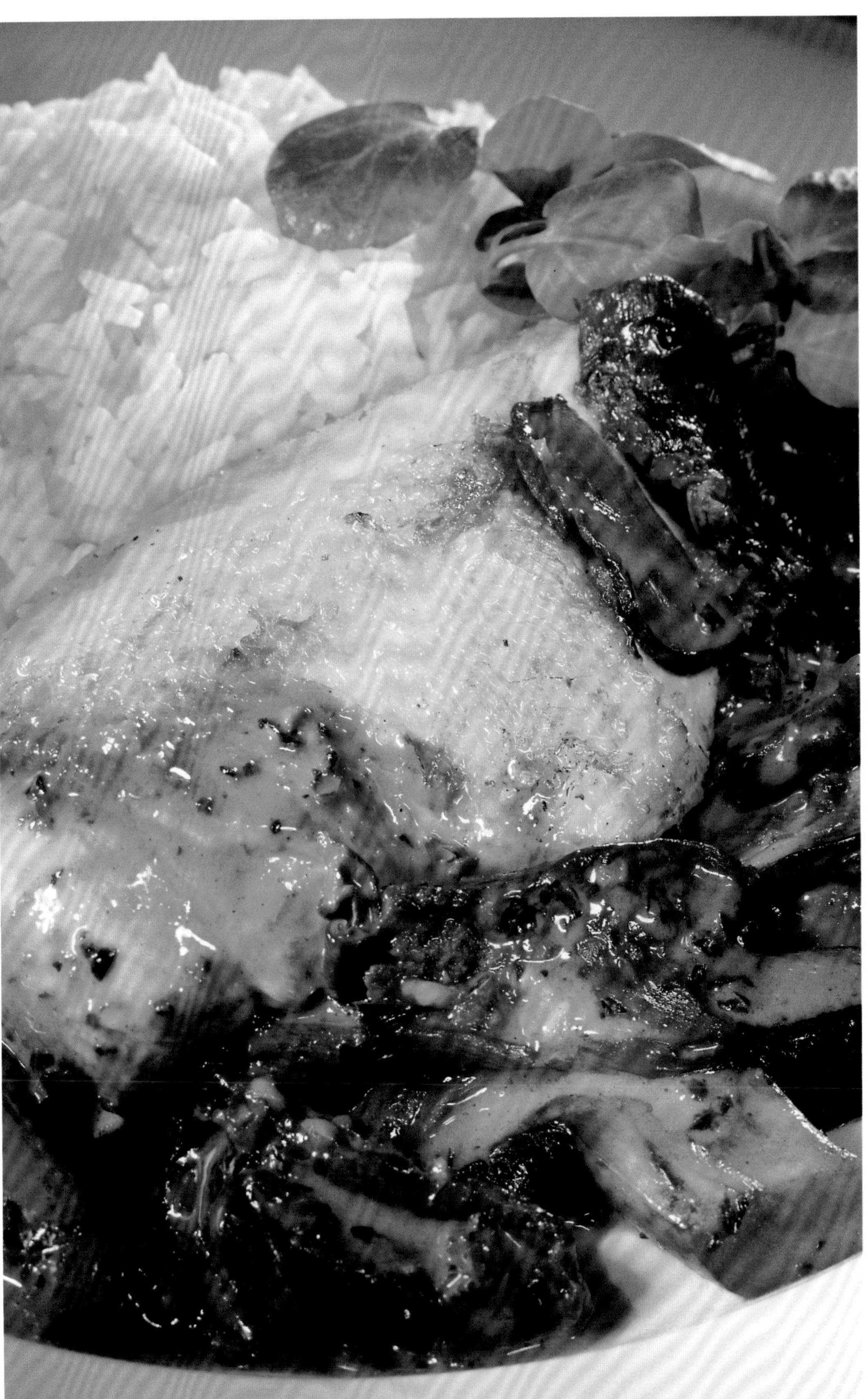

Heat the olive oil in a large, heavy-based frying pan, then add the chicken breasts, skin-side down and cook for about 10 minutes, or until they are well browned. Remove the chicken breasts and reserve. Add the garlic, stir into the juices and cook for 1 minute.

Pour the vermouth or white wine into the pan and season to taste with salt and pepper. Return the chicken to the pan. Bring to the boil, reduce the heat to low and simmer for about 20 minutes, or until tender.

In another large frying pan, heat the butter and add the sliced porcini or wild mushrooms. Stir-fry for about 5 minutes, or until the mushrooms are golden and tender.

Add the porcini or wild mushrooms and any juices to the chicken. Season to taste, then add the chopped oregano. Stir together gently and cook for 1 minute longer. Transfer to a large serving plate and garnish with sprigs of fresh basil, if desired. Serve immediately with rice.

HEALTH RATING 🍎🍎🍎

**ENTERTAINING ALTERNATIVE**

Poached Chicken with Salsa Verde Herb Sauce

**PUDDING SUGGESTION**

Sticky Chocolate Surprise Pudding

# Lemon Chicken with Basil & Linguine

INGREDIENTS **Serves 4**

grated rind and juice of 1 large lemon
2 garlic cloves, peeled and crushed
2 tbsp basil-flavoured extra virgin olive oil
4 tbsp freshly chopped basil
salt and freshly ground black pepper
450 g/1 lb skinless, boneless chicken breast, cut into bite-sized pieces
1 onion, peeled and finely chopped
3 celery stalks, trimmed and thinly sliced
175 g/6 oz mushrooms, wiped and halved
2 tbsp plain flour
150 ml/¼ pint white wine
150 ml/¼ pint chicken stock
350–450 g/12 oz–1 lb linguine

**To garnish:**
lemon zest
fresh basil leaves

Blend the lemon rind and juice, garlic, half the oil, half the basil and salt and pepper in a large bowl. Add the chicken pieces and toss well to coat. Allow to stand for about 1 hour, stirring occasionally.

Heat the remaining oil in a large non-stick frying pan, then add the sliced onion and cook for 3–4 minutes, or until slightly softened. Using a slotted spoon, drain the chicken pieces and add to the frying pan, reserving the marinade. Cook the chicken for 2–3 minutes, or until golden brown, then add the sliced celery and mushroom halves and cook for a further 2–3 minutes.

Sprinkle in the flour and stir until the chicken and vegetables are coated. Gradually stir the wine into the pan until a thick sauce forms, then stir in the stock and reserved marinade. Bring to the boil, stirring constantly. Cover and simmer for about 10 minutes, then stir in the remaining basil.

Meanwhile, bring a large saucepan of lightly salted water to the boil. Slowly add the linguine and simmer for 7–10 minutes, or until 'al dente'. Drain well and turn into a large serving bowl, pour over the sauce and garnish with the lemon zest and fresh basil leaves. Serve immediately.

HEALTH RATING ❦❦❦

**ENTERTAINING ALTERNATIVE**
Lemon Chicken with Potatoes, Rosemary & Olives

**PUDDING SUGGESTION**
White Chocolate Mousse & Strawberry Tart

**ENTERTAINING ALTERNATIVE**

## Lemon Chicken with Potatoes, Rosemary & Olives

INGREDIENTS **Serves 6**

12 skinless boneless chicken thighs
1 large lemon
125 ml/4 fl oz extra virgin olive oil
6 garlic cloves, peeled and sliced
2 onions, peeled and thinly sliced
bunch of fresh rosemary
1.1 kg/2½ lb potatoes, peeled and cut into 4 cm/1½ inch pieces
salt and freshly ground black pepper
18–24 black olives, pitted

**To serve:**

steamed carrots
courgettes

Preheat the oven to 200°C/400°F/Gas Mark 6, 15 minutes before cooking. Trim the chicken thighs and place in a shallow baking dish large enough to hold them in a single layer. Remove the rind from the lemon with a zester or if using a peeler cut into thin julienne strips. Reserve half and add the remainder to the chicken. Squeeze the lemon juice over the chicken, toss to coat well and leave to stand for 10 minutes.

Transfer the chicken to a roasting tin. Add the remaining lemon zest or julienne strips, olive oil, garlic, onions and half of the rosemary sprigs. Toss gently and leave for about 20 minutes.

Cover the potatoes with lightly salted water and bring to the boil. Cook for 2 minutes, then drain well and add to the chicken. Season to taste with salt and pepper.

Roast the chicken in the preheated oven for 50 minutes, turning frequently and basting, or until the chicken is cooked. Just before the end of cooking time, discard the rosemary, and add fresh sprigs of rosemary. Add the olives and stir. Serve immediately with steamed carrots and courgettes.

**PUDDING SUGGESTION**

## White Chocolate Mousse & Strawberry Tart

INGREDIENTS **Cuts into 10 slices**

1 quantity sweet shortcrust pastry (see page 10)
60 g/2½ oz strawberry jam
1–2 tbsp kirsch or framboise liqueur
450–700 g/1–1½ lb ripe strawberries, sliced lengthways

**For the white chocolate mousse:**

250 g/9 oz white chocolate, chopped
350 ml/12 oz double cream
3 tbsp kirsch or framboise liqueur
1–2 large egg whites (optional)

Preheat the oven to 200°C/400°F/Gas Mark 6, 15 minutes before baking. Roll the prepared pastry out on a lightly floured surface and use to line a 25.5 cm/10 inch flan tin.

Line with either tinfoil or non-stick baking parchment and baking beans then bake blind in the preheated oven for 15–20 minutes. Remove the tinfoil or baking parchment and return to the oven for a further 5 minutes.

To make the mousse, place the white chocolate with 2 tablespoons of water and 125 ml/4 fl oz of the cream in a saucepan and heat gently, stirring until the chocolate has melted and is smooth. Remove from the heat, stir in the kirsch or framboise liqueur and cool.

Whip the remaining cream until soft peaks form. Fold 1 spoonful of the cream into the cooled white chocolate mixture, then fold in the remaining cream. If using, whisk the egg whites until stiff and gently fold into the white chocolate cream mixture to make a softer, lighter mousse. Chill in the refrigerator for 15–20 minutes.

Heat the strawberry jam with the kirsch or framboise liqueur and brush or spread half the mixture on to the pastry base. Leave to cool.

Spread the chilled chocolate mousse over the jam and arrange the sliced strawberries in concentric circles over the mousse. If necessary, reheat the strawberry jam and glaze the strawberries lightly.

Chill the tart in the refrigerator for about 3–4 hours, or until the chocolate mousse has set. Cut into slices and serve.

# Herbed Hasselback Potatoes with Roast Chicken

INGREDIENTS **Serves 4**

8 medium, evenly-sized potatoes, peeled
3 large sprigs of fresh rosemary
1 tbsp oil
salt and freshly ground black pepper
350 g/12 oz baby parsnips, peeled
350 g/12 oz baby carrots, peeled
350 g/12 oz baby leeks, trimmed
75 g/3 oz butter
finely grated rind of 1 lemon, preferably unwaxed
1.6 kg/3½ lb chicken

Preheat the oven to 200°C/400°F/Gas Mark 6, about 15 minutes before cooking. Place a chopstick on either side of a potato and, with a sharp knife, cut down through the potato until you reach the chopsticks; take care not to cut right through the potato. Repeat these cuts every 5 mm/¼ inch along the length of the potato. Carefully ease 2–4 of the slices apart and slip in a few rosemary sprigs. Repeat with remaining potatoes. Brush with the oil and season well with salt and pepper.

Place the seasoned potatoes in a large roasting tin. Add the parsnips, carrots and leeks to the potatoes in the tin and cover with a wire rack or trivet.

Beat the butter and lemon rind together and season to taste. Smear the chicken with the lemon butter and place on the rack over the vegetables.

Roast in the preheated oven for 1 hour, 40 minutes, basting the chicken and vegetables occasionally until thoroughly cooked. The juices should run clear when the thigh is pierced with a skewer. Place the cooked chicken on a warmed serving platter, arrange the roast vegetables around it and serve immediately.

HEALTH RATING

**SPICY ALTERNATIVE**

Spiced Indian Roast Potatoes with Chicken

**PUDDING SUGGESTION**

Frozen Amaretti Soufflé with Strawberries

**SPICY ALTERNATIVE**
## Spiced Indian Roast Potatoes with Chicken

INGREDIENTS **Serves 4**

700 g/1½ lb waxy potatoes, peeled and cut into large chunks
salt and freshly ground black pepper
4 tbsp sunflower oil
1 large Spanish onion, peeled and roughly chopped
8 chicken drumsticks
3 shallots, peeled and roughly chopped
2 large garlic cloves, peeled and crushed
1 red chilli
2 tsp fresh root ginger, peeled and finely grated
2 tsp ground cumin
2 tsp ground coriander
pinch of cayenne pepper
4 cardamom pods, crushed
sprigs of fresh coriander, to garnish

Preheat the oven to 190°C/375°F/Gas Mark 5, about 10 minutes before cooking. Parboil the potatoes for 5 minutes in lightly salted boiling water, then drain thoroughly and reserve. Heat the oil in a large frying pan, add the chicken drumsticks and cook until sealed on all sides. Remove and reserve.

Add the onions and shallots to the pan and fry for 4–5 minutes, or until softened. Stir in the garlic, chilli and ginger and cook for 1 minute, stirring constantly. Stir in the ground cumin, coriander, cayenne pepper and crushed cardamom pods and continue to cook, stirring, for a further minute.

Add the potatoes to the pan, then add the chicken. Season to taste with salt and pepper. Stir gently until the potatoes and chicken pieces are coated in the onion and spice mixture. Spoon into a large roasting tin and roast in the preheated oven for 35 minutes, or until the chicken and potatoes are thoroughly cooked. Garnish with fresh coriander and serve immediately.

**PUDDING SUGGESTION**
## Frozen Amaretti Soufflé with Strawberries

INGREDIENTS **Serves 6–8**

125 g/4 oz Amaretti biscuits
9 tbsp Amaretto liqueur
grated zest and juice of 1 lemon
1 tbsp powdered gelatine
6 medium eggs, separated
175 g/6 oz soft brown sugar
600 ml/1 pint double cream
450 g/1 lb fresh strawberries, halved if large
1 vanilla pod, split and seeds scraped out
2 tbsp caster sugar
few finely crushed Amaretti biscuits, to decorate

Wrap a collar of greaseproof paper around a 900 ml/1½ pint soufflé dish or 6–8 individual ramekin dishes to extend at least 5 cm/2 inch above the rim and secure with string. Break the Amaretti biscuits into a bowl. Sprinkle over 6 tablespoons of the Amaretto liqueur and leave to soak.

Put the lemon zest and juice into a small heatproof bowl and sprinkle over the gelatine. Leave for 5 minutes to sponge, then put the bowl over a saucepan of simmering water, ensuring that the base of the bowl does not touch the water. Stir occasionally until the gelatine has dissolved completely.

In a clean bowl, whisk the egg yolks and sugar until pale and thick then stir in the gelatine and the soaked biscuits. In another bowl, lightly whip 450 ml/¾ pint of the cream and using a large metal spoon or rubber spatula fold into the mixture. In a third clean bowl, whisk the egg whites until stiff, then fold into the soufflé mixture. Transfer to the prepared dish, or individual ramekin dishes, and level the top. Freeze for at least 8 hours, or preferably overnight.

Put the strawberries into a bowl with the vanilla pod and seeds, sugar and remaining Amaretto liqueur. Leave overnight in the refrigerator, then allow to come to room temperature before serving. Place the soufflé in the refrigerator for about 1 hour. Whip the remaining cream and use to decorate the soufflé, then sprinkle a few finely crushed Amaretti biscuits on the top and serve with the strawberries.

# Chicken & Ham Pie

INGREDIENTS **Serves 6**

2 quantities shortcrust pastry (see page 10)
1 tbsp olive oil
1 leek, trimmed and sliced
175 g/6 oz piece of bacon, cut into small cubes
225 g/8 oz cooked boneless chicken meat
2 avocados, peeled, pitted and chopped
1 tbsp lemon juice
salt and freshly ground black pepper
2 large eggs, beaten
150 ml/¼ pint natural yogurt
4 tbsp chicken stock
1 tbsp poppy seeds

**To serve:**
sliced red onion
mixed salad leaves

Preheat the oven to 200°C/400°F/Gas Mark 6. Heat the oil in a frying pan and fry the leek and bacon for 4 minutes until soft but not coloured. Transfer to a bowl and reserve.

Cut the chicken into bite-sized pieces and add to the leek and bacon. Toss the avocado in the lemon juice, add to the chicken and season to taste with salt and pepper.

Roll out half the pastry on a lightly floured surface and use to line a 18 cm/7 inch loose-bottomed deep flan tin. Scoop the chicken mixture into the pastry case.

Mix together 1 egg, the yogurt and the chicken stock. Pour the yogurt mixture over the chicken. Roll out the remaining pastry on a lightly floured surface, and cut out the lid to 5 mm/¼ inch wider than the dish.

Brush the rim with the remaining beaten egg and lay the pastry lid on top, pressing to seal. Knock the edges with the back of a knife to seal further. Cut a slit in the lid and brush with the egg.

Sprinkle with the poppy seeds and bake in the preheated oven for about 30 minutes, or until the pastry is golden brown. Serve with the onion and mixed salad leaves.

HEALTH RATING

**STARTER SUGGESTION**
Tuna Chowder

**PUDDING SUGGESTION**
Apricot & Almond Slice

**STARTER SUGGESTION**
## Tuna Chowder

INGREDIENTS **Serves 4**

2 tsp oil
1 onion, peeled and finely chopped
2 sticks of celery, trimmed and finely sliced
1 tbsp plain flour
600 ml/1 pint skimmed milk
200 g can of tuna in water
320 g can of sweetcorn in water, drained
2 tsp freshly chopped thyme
salt and freshly ground black pepper
pinch cayenne pepper
2 tbsp freshly chopped parsley

Heat the oil in a large, heavy-based saucepan. Add the onion and celery and gently cook for about 5 minutes, stirring from time to time until the onion is softened.

Stir in the flour and cook for about 1 minute to thicken. Draw the pan off the heat and gradually pour in the milk, stirring throughout.

Add the tuna and its liquid, the drained sweetcorn and the thyme. Mix gently, then bring to the boil. Cover and simmer for 5 minutes.

Remove the pan from the heat and season to taste with salt and pepper. Sprinkle the chowder with the cayenne pepper and chopped parsley. Divide into soup bowls and serve immediately.

**PUDDING SUGGESTION**
## Apricot & Almond Slice

INGREDIENTS **Cuts into 10 slices**

2 tbsp demerara sugar
25 g/1 oz flaked almonds
400 g can apricot halves, drained
225 g/8 oz butter
225 g/8 oz caster sugar
4 medium eggs
200 g/7 oz self-raising flour
25 g/1 oz ground almonds
½ tsp almond essence
50 g/2 oz ready-to-eat dried apricots, chopped
3 tbsp clear honey
3 tbsp roughly chopped almonds, toasted

Preheat the oven to 180°C/350°F/Gas Mark 4. Oil a 20.5 cm/8 inch square tin and line with non-stick baking paper.

Sprinkle the sugar and the flaked almonds over the paper, then arrange the apricot halves cut-side down on top.

Cream the butter and sugar together in a large bowl until light and fluffy. Gradually beat the eggs into the butter mixture, adding a spoonful of flour after each addition of egg.

When all the eggs have been added, stir in the remaining flour and ground almonds and mix thoroughly. Add the almond essence and the apricots and stir well.

Spoon the mixture into the prepared tin, taking care not to dislodge the apricot halves. Bake in the preheated oven for 1 hour, or until golden and firm to touch.

Remove from the oven and allow to cool slightly for 15–20 minutes. Turn out carefully, discard the lining paper and transfer to a serving dish. Pour the honey over the top of the cake, sprinkle on the toasted almonds and serve.

**VEGETARIAN ALTERNATIVE**
## Aduki Bean & Rice Burgers

INGREDIENTS **Serves 4**

2½ tbsp sunflower oil
1 medium onion, peeled and very finely chopped
1 garlic clove, peeled and crushed
1 tsp curry paste
225 g/8 oz basmati rice
400 g can of aduki beans, drained and rinsed
225 ml/8 fl oz vegetable stock
125 g/4 oz firm tofu, crumbled
1 tsp garam masala
2 tbsp freshly chopped coriander
salt and freshly ground black pepper
wholemeal baps, to serve

**For the carrot raita:**

2 large carrots, peeled and grated
½ cucumber, cut into tiny cubes
150 ml/¼ pint Greek yogurt

Heat 1 tablespoon of the oil in a saucepan and gently cook the onion for 10 minutes until soft. Add the garlic and curry paste and cook for a few more seconds. Stir in the rice and beans.

Pour in the stock, bring to the boil and simmer for 12 minutes, or until all the stock has been absorbed – do not lift the lid for the first 10 minutes of cooking. Reserve.

Lightly mash the tofu. Add to the rice mixture with the garam masala, coriander, salt and pepper. Mix well. Divide the mixture into eight and shape into burgers. Chill in the refrigerator for 30 minutes.

Meanwhile, make the raita by mixing together the carrots, cucumber and Greek yogurt. Spoon into a small bowl and chill in the refrigerator until ready to serve.

Heat the remaining oil in a large frying pan. Fry the burgers, in batches if necessary, for 4–5 minutes on each side, or until lightly browned. Serve in in wholemeal baps with tomato slices and lettuce. Accompany with the raita.

**ENTERTAINING ALTERNATIVE**
## Aromatic Duck Burgers on Potato Pancakes

INGREDIENTS **Serves 4**

700 g/1½ lb boneless duck breasts
2 tbsp hoisin sauce
1 garlic clove, peeled and finely chopped
4 spring onions, trimmed and finely chopped
2 tbsp Japanese soy sauce
½ tsp Chinese five spice powder
salt and freshly ground black pepper
freshly chopped coriander, to garnish
extra hoisin sauce, to serve

**For the potato pancakes:**

450 g/1 lb floury potatoes
1 small onion, peeled and grated
1 small egg, beaten
1 heaped tbsp plain flour

Peel off the thick layer of fat from the duck breasts and cut into small pieces. Put the fat in a small dry saucepan and set over a low heat for 10–15 minutes, or until the fat runs clear and the crackling goes crisp; reserve.

Cut the duck meat into pieces and blend in a food processor until coarsely chopped. Spoon into a bowl and add the hoisin sauce, garlic, half the spring onions, soy sauce and Chinese five spice powder. Season to taste with salt and pepper and shape into four burgers. Cover and chill in the refrigerator for 1 hour.

To make the potato pancakes, grate the potatoes into a large bowl, squeeze out the water with your hands, then put on a clean tea towel and twist the ends to squeeze out any remaining water. Return the potato to the bowl, add the onion and egg and mix well. Add the flour and salt and pepper. Stir to blend.

Heat about 2 tablespoons of the clear duck fat in a large frying pan. Spoon the potato mixture into 2–4 pattie shapes and cook for 6 minutes, or until golden and crisp, turning once. Keep warm in the oven. Repeat with the remaining mixture, adding duck fat as needed.

Preheat the grill and line the grill rack with tinfoil. Brush the burgers with a little of the duck fat and grill for 6–8 minutes, or longer if wished, turning once. Arrange 1–2 potato pancakes on a plate and top with a burger. Spoon over a little hoisin sauce and garnish with the remaining spring onions and coriander.

# Cheesy Chicken Burgers

INGREDIENTS **Serves 6**

1 tbsp sunflower oil
1 small onion, peeled and finely chopped
1 garlic clove, peeled and crushed
½ red pepper, deseeded and finely chopped
450 g/1 lb fresh chicken mince
2 tbsp Greek yogurt
50 g/2 oz fresh brown breadcrumbs
1 tbsp freshly chopped herbs, such as parsley or tarragon
50 g/2 oz Cheshire cheese, crumbled
salt and freshly ground black pepper

**For the sweetcorn and carrot relish:**

200 g can of sweetcorn, drained
1 carrot, peeled, grated
½ green chilli, deseeded and finely chopped
2 tsp cider vinegar
2 tsp soft light brown sugar

**To serve:**

wholemeal or granary rolls
lettuce
sliced tomatoes
mixed salad leaves

Preheat the grill. Heat the oil in a frying pan and gently cook the onion and garlic for 5 minutes. Add the red pepper and cook for 5 minutes. Transfer into a mixing bowl.

Add the chicken, yogurt, breadcrumbs, herbs and cheese and season to taste with salt and pepper. Mix well. Divide the mixture equally into six and shape into burgers. Cover and chill in the refrigerator for at least 20 minutes.

To make the relish, put all the ingredients in a small saucepan with 1 tablespoon of water and heat gently, stirring occasionally until all the sugar has dissolved.

Cover and cook over a low heat for 2 minutes, then uncover and cook for a further minute, or until the relish is thick. Place the burgers on a lightly oiled grill pan and grill under a medium heat for 8–10 minutes on each side, or until browned and completely cooked through.

Warm the rolls if liked, then split in half and fill with the burgers, lettuce, sliced tomatoes and the prepared relish. Serve immediately with the salad leaves.

HEALTH RATING 🍎🍎🍎

**VEGETARIAN ALTERNATIVE**

Aduki Bean & Rice Burgers

**ENTERTAINING ALTERNATIVE**

Aromatic Duck Burgers on Potato Pancakes

# Stir-fried Chicken with Spinach, Tomatoes & Pine Nuts

INGREDIENTS **Serves 4**

50 g/2 oz pine nuts
2 tbsp sunflower oil
1 red onion, peeled and finely chopped
450 g/1 lb skinless, boneless chicken breast fillets, cut into strips
450 g/1 lb cherry tomatoes, halved
225 g/8 oz baby spinach, washed
salt and freshly ground black pepper
¼ tsp freshly grated nutmeg
2 tbsp balsamic vinegar
50 g/2 oz raisins
freshly cooked ribbon noodles tossed in butter, to serve

Heat the wok and add the pine nuts. Dry-fry for about 2 minutes, shaking often to ensure that they toast but do not burn. Remove and reserve. Wipe any dust from the wok.

Heat the wok again, add the oil and when hot, add the red onion and stir-fry for 2 minutes. Add the chicken and stir-fry for 2–3 minutes, or until golden brown. Reduce the heat, toss in the cherry tomatoes and stir-fry gently until the tomatoes start to disintegrate.

Add the baby spinach and stir-fry for 2–3 minutes, or until it starts to wilt. Season to taste with salt and pepper, then sprinkle in the grated nutmeg and drizzle in the balsamic vinegar. Finally, stir in the raisins and reserved toasted pine nuts. Serve immediately on a bed of buttered ribbon noodles.

## HEALTH RATING 🍎🍎🍎

**SPICY ALTERNATIVE**
Stir-fried Chicken with Basil

**PUDDING SUGGESTION**
Lemon & Apricot Pudding

NGREDIENTS **Serves 4**

tbsp sunflower oil

tbsp green curry paste

50 g/1 lb skinless, boneless chicken breast fillets, trimmed and cut into cubes

cherry tomatoes

00 ml/4 fl oz coconut cream

tbsp soft brown sugar

2 tbsp Thai fish sauce

red chilli, deseeded and thinly sliced

green chilli, deseeded and thinly sliced

75 g/3 oz fresh torn basil leaves

sprigs of fresh coriander, to garnish

freshly steamed white rice, to serve

**SPICY ALTERNATIVE**

## Stir-fried Chicken with Basil

Heat the wok, then add the oil and heat for 1 minute. Add the green curry paste and cook, stirring for 1 minute to release the flavour and cook the paste. Add the chicken and stir-fry over a high heat for 2 minutes, making sure the chicken is coated thoroughly with the green curry paste.

Reduce the heat under the wok, then add the cherry tomatoes and cook, stirring gently, for 2–3 minutes or until the tomatoes burst and begin to disintegrate into the green curry paste.

Add half the coconut cream and add to the wok with the brown sugar, Thai fish sauce and the red and green chillies. Stir-fry gently for 5 minutes, or until the sauce is amalgamated and the chicken is cooked thoroughly.

Just before serving, sprinkle the chicken with the torn basil leaves and add the remaining coconut cream, then serve immediately with freshly steamed white rice garnished with fresh coriander sprigs.

INGREDIENTS **Serves 4**

125 g/4 oz ready-to-eat dried apricots

3 tbsp orange juice, warmed

50 g/2 oz butter

125 g/4 oz caster sugar

juice and grated rind of 2 lemons

2 medium eggs

100 g/4 oz self-raising flour

300 ml/½ pint milk

custard or fresh cream, to serve

**PUDDING SUGGESTION**

## Lemon & Apricot Pudding

Preheat the oven to 180°C/350°F/Gas Mark 4. Oil a 1.1 litre/2 pint pie dish.

Soak the apricots in the orange juice for 10–15 minutes or until most of the juice has been absorbed, then place in the base of the pie dish. Cream the butter and sugar together with the lemon rind until light and fluffy. Separate the eggs. Beat the egg yolks into the creamed mixture with a spoonful of flour after each addition. Add the remaining flour and beat well until smooth.

Stir the milk and lemon juice into the creamed mixture. Whisk the egg whites in a grease-free mixing bowl until stiff and standing in peaks. Fold into the mixture using a metal spoon or rubber spatula. Pour into the prepared dish and place in a baking tray filled with enough cold water to come halfway up the sides of the dish.

Bake in the preheated oven for about 45 minutes, or until the sponge is firm and golden brown. Remove from the oven. Serve immediately with the custard or fresh cream.

# Chicken Marengo

INGREDIENTS **Serves 4**

2 tbsp plain flour
salt and freshly ground black pepper
4 boneless and skinless chicken breasts, cut into bite-sized pieces
4 tbsp olive oil
1 Spanish onion, peeled and chopped
1 garlic clove, peeled and chopped
400 g can chopped tomatoes
2 tbsp sun-dried tomato paste
3 tbsp freshly chopped basil
3 tbsp freshly chopped thyme
125 ml/4 fl oz dry white wine or chicken stock
350 g/12 oz rigatoni
3 tbsp freshly chopped flat leaf parsley

Season the flour with salt and pepper and toss the chicken in the flour to coat. Heat 2 tablespoons of the olive oil in a large frying pan and cook the chicken for 7 minutes, or until browned all over, turning occasionally. Remove from the pan using a slotted spoon and keep warm.

Add the remaining oil to the pan, add the onion and cook, stirring occasionally, for 5 minutes, or until softened and starting to brown. Add the garlic, tomatoes, tomato paste, basil and thyme. Pour in the wine or chicken stock and season well. Bring to the boil. Stir in the chicken pieces and simmer for 15 minutes, or until the chicken is tender and the sauce has thickened.

Meanwhile, bring a large pan of lightly salted water to a rolling boil. Add the rigatoni and cook according to the packet instructions, or until 'al dente'.

Drain the rigatoni thoroughly, return to the pan and stir in the chopped parsley. Tip the pasta into a large, warmed serving dish or spoon on to individual plates. Spoon over the chicken sauce and serve immediately.

HEALTH RATING 🍎🍎🍎

**ENTERTAINING ALTERNATIVE**
Spicy Chicken with Open Ravioli & Tomato Sauce

**SUGGESTED ACCOMPANIMENT**
Ginger & Garlic Potatoes

**ENTERTAINING ALTERNATIVE**

## Spicy Chicken with Open Ravioli & Tomato Sauce

INGREDIENTS **Serves 2–3**

2 tbsp olive oil
1 onion, peeled and finely chopped
1 tsp ground cumin
1 tsp hot paprika pepper
1 tsp ground cinnamon
175 g/6 oz boneless and skinless chicken breasts, chopped
salt and freshly ground black pepper
1 tbsp smooth peanut butter
50 g/2 oz butter
1 shallot, peeled and finely chopped
2 garlic cloves, peeled and crushed
400 g can chopped tomatoes
125 g/4 oz fresh egg lasagne
2 tbsp freshly chopped coriander

Heat the olive oil in a frying pan, add the onion and cook gently for 2–3 minutes then add the cumin, paprika pepper and cinnamon and cook for a further 1 minute. Add the chicken, season to taste with salt and pepper and cook for 3–4 minutes, or until tender. Add the peanut butter and stir until well mixed and reserve.

Melt the butter in the frying pan, add the shallot and cook for 2 minutes. Add the tomatoes and garlic and season to taste. Simmer gently for 20 minutes, or until thickened, then keep the sauce warm.

Cut each sheet of lasagne into six squares. Bring a large pan of lightly salted water to a rolling boil. Add the lasagne squares and cook according to the packet instructions, about 3–4 minutes, or until 'al dente'. Drain the lasagne pieces thoroughly, reserve and keep warm.

Layer the pasta squares with the spicy filling on individual warmed plates. Pour over a little of the hot tomato sauce and sprinkle with chopped coriander. Serve immediately.

**SUGGESTED ACCOMPANIMENT**

## Ginger & Garlic Potatoes

INGREDIENTS **Serves 4**

700 g/1½ lb potatoes
2.5 cm/1 inch piece of root ginger, peeled and coarsely chopped
3 garlic cloves, peeled and chopped
½ tsp turmeric
1 tsp salt
½ tsp cayenne pepper
5 tbsp vegetable oil
1 tsp whole fennel seeds
1 large eating apple, cored and diced
6 spring onions, trimmed and sliced diagonally
1 tbsp freshly chopped coriander

**To serve:**

assorted bitter salad leaves
curry-flavoured mayonnaise

Scrub the potatoes, then place, unpeeled, in a large saucepan and cover with boiling salted water. Bring to the boil and cook for 15 minutes, then drain and leave the potatoes to cool completely. Peel and cut into 2.5 cm/1 inch cubes.

Place the root ginger, garlic, turmeric, salt and cayenne pepper in a food processor and blend for 1 minute. With the motor still running, slowly add 3 tablespoons of water and blend into a paste. Alternatively, pound the ingredients to a paste with a pestle and mortar.

Heat the oil in a large heavy-based frying pan and when hot, but not smoking, add the fennel seeds and fry for a few minutes. Stir in the ginger paste and cook for 2 minutes, stirring frequently. Take care not to burn the mixture.

Reduce the heat, then add the potatoes and cook for 5–7 minutes, stirring frequently, until the potatoes have a golden brown crust. Add the diced apple and spring onions, then sprinkle with the freshly chopped coriander. Heat through for 2 minutes, then serve on assorted salad leaves with curry-flavoured mayonnaise.

# Chicken & Baby Vegetable Stir Fry

INGREDIENTS **Serves 4**

2 tbsp groundnut oil
1 small red chilli, deseeded and finely chopped
150 g/5 oz chicken breast or thigh meat, skinned and cut into cubes
2 baby leeks, trimmed and sliced
12 asparagus spears, halved
125 g/4 oz mangetout, trimmed
125 g/4 oz baby carrots, trimmed and halved lengthways
125 g/4 oz fine green beans, trimmed and diagonally sliced
125 g/4 oz baby sweetcorn, diagonally halved
50 ml/2 fl oz chicken stock
2 tsp light soy sauce
1 tbsp dry sherry
1 tsp sesame oil
toasted sesame seeds, to garnish

Heat the wok until very hot and add the oil. Add the chopped chilli and chicken and stir-fry for 4–5 minutes, or until the chicken is cooked and golden.

Increase the heat, add the leeks to the chicken and stir-fry for 2 minutes. Add the asparagus spears, mangetout, baby carrots, green beans, and baby sweetcorn. Stir-fry for 3–4 minutes, or until the vegetables soften slightly but still retain a slight crispness.

In a small bowl, mix together the chicken stock, soy sauce, dry sherry and sesame oil. Pour into the wok, stir and cook until heated through. Sprinkle with the toasted sesame seeds and serve immediately.

HEALTH RATING 🍎🍎🍎🍎

**STARTER SUGGESTION**
Honey & Ginger Prawns

**PUDDING SUGGESTION**
Grape & Almond Layer

**STARTER SUGGESTION**
## Honey & Ginger Prawns

INGREDIENTS **Serves 4**

1 carrot
50 g/2 oz bamboo shoots
4 spring onions
1 tbsp clear honey
1 tbsp tomato ketchup
1 tsp soy sauce
2.5 cm/1 inch piece fresh root ginger, peeled and finely grated
1 garlic clove, peeled and crushed
1 tbsp lime juice
175 g/6 oz peeled prawns, thawed if frozen
2 heads little gem lettuce leaves
2 tbsp freshly chopped coriander
salt and freshly ground black pepper

**To garnish:**
fresh coriander sprigs
lime slices

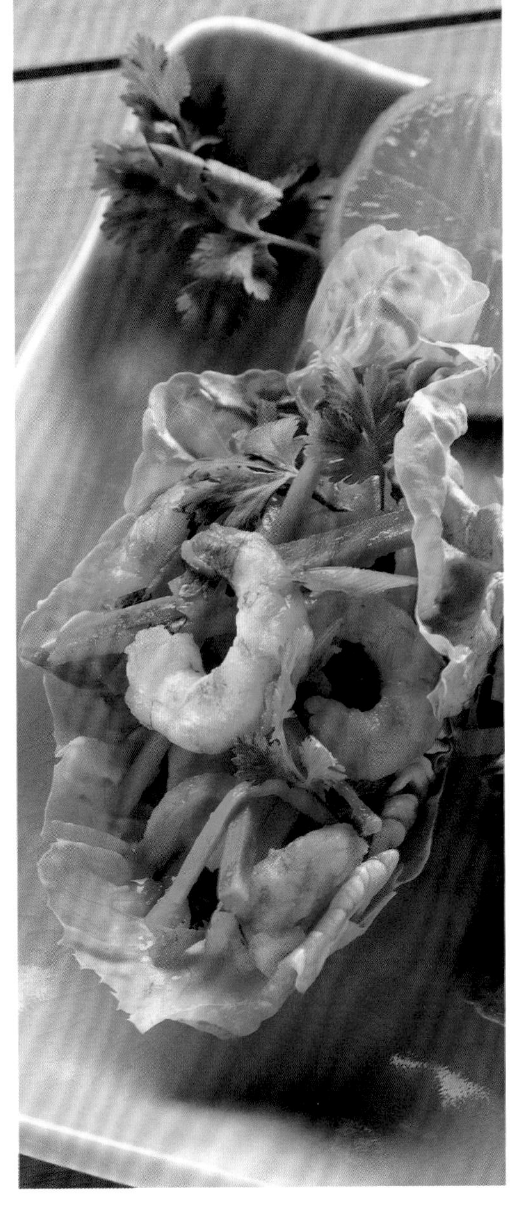

Cut the carrot into matchstick-size pieces, roughly chop the bamboo shoots and finely slice the spring onions. Combine the bamboo shoots with the carrot matchsticks and spring onions.

In a wok or large frying pan gently heat the honey, tomato ketchup, soy sauce, ginger, garlic and lime juice with 3 tablespoons of water. Bring to the boil.

Add the carrot mixture and stir-fry for 2–3 minutes until the vegetables are hot. Add the prawns and continue to stir-fry for 2 minutes. Remove the wok or frying pan from the heat and reserve until cooled slightly.

Divide the little gem lettuce into leaves and rinse lightly. Stir the chopped coriander into the prawn mixture and season to taste with salt and pepper. Spoon into the lettuce leaves and serve immediately garnished with sprigs of fresh coriander and lime slices.

**PUDDING SUGGESTION**
## Grape & Almond Layer

INGREDIENTS **Serves 4**

300 ml/½ pint fromage frais
300 ml/½ pint Greek-set yogurt
3 tbsp icing sugar, sifted
2 tbsp crème de cassis
450 g/1 lb red grapes
175 g/6 oz Amaretti biscuits
2 ripe passion fruit

**To decorate:**
icing sugar
extra grapes, optional

Mix together the fromage frais and yogurt in a bowl and lightly fold in the sifted icing sugar and crème de cassis with a large metal spoon or rubber spatula until lightly blended.

Using a small knife, remove the seeds from the grapes if necessary. Rinse lightly and pat dry on absorbent kitchen paper.

Place the deseeded grapes in a bowl and stir in any juice from the grapes from deseeding.

Place the Amaretti biscuits in a polythene bag and crush roughly with a rolling pin, or use a food processor.

Cut the passion fruit in half, scoop out the seeds with a teaspoon and reserve.

Divide the yogurt mixture between four tall glasses, then layer alternately with grapes, crushed biscuits and most of the passion fruit seeds. Top with the yogurt mixture and the remaining passion fruit seeds. Chill for 1 hour and decorate with extra grapes. Lightly dust with icing sugar and serve.

**ENTERTAINING ALTERNATIVE**
## Duck in Black Bean Sauce

INGREDIENTS **Serves 4**

450 g/1 lb duck breast, skinned
1 tbsp light soy sauce
1 tbsp Chinese rice wine or dry sherry
2.5 cm/1 inch piece fresh root ginger
3 garlic cloves
2 spring onions
2 tbsp Chinese preserved black beans
1 tbsp groundnut or vegetable oil
150 ml/¼ pint chicken stock
shredded spring onions, to garnish
freshly cooked noodles, to serve

Using a sharp knife, trim the duck breasts, removing any fat. Slice thickly and place in a shallow dish. Mix together the soy sauce and Chinese rice wine or sherry and pour over the duck. Leave to marinate for 1 hour in the refrigerator, then drain and discard the marinade.

Peel the ginger and chop finely. Peel the garlic cloves and either chop finely or crush. Trim the root from the spring onions, discard the outer leaves and chop. Finely chop the black beans.

Heat a wok or large frying pan, add the oil and when very hot, add the ginger, garlic, spring onions and black beans and stir-fry for 30 seconds. Add the drained duck and stir-fry for 3–5 minutes or until the duck is browned.

Add the chicken stock to the wok, bring to the boil, then reduce the heat and simmer for 5 minutes, or until the duck is cooked and the sauce is reduced and thickened. Remove from the heat. Tip on to a bed of freshly cooked noodles, garnish with spring onion shreds and serve immediately.

**PUDDING SUGGESTION**
## Hot Cherry Fritters

Place the butter, salt and sugar in a small saucepan with 225 ml/8 fl oz water. Heat gently until the butter has melted, then add the flour and ground cinnamon and beat over a low heat until the mixture leaves the sides of the pan.

Remove the saucepan from the heat and beat in the ground almonds. Gradually add the eggs, beating well after each addition. Finally stir in the cherries.

Pour 5 cm/2 inches depth of oil in a wok and heat until it reaches 180°C/350°F on a sugar thermometer. Drop in heaped teaspoons of the mixture, cooking 4 or 5 at a time for about 2 minutes, or until lightly browned and crisp. Remove the fritters from the pan with a slotted spoon and drain on absorbent kitchen paper. Keep warm in a low oven while cooking the remaining fritters. Arrange on a warmed serving plate and dust with the icing sugar and cocoa powder. Decorate with mint sprigs and serve hot.

INGREDIENTS **Serves 4**

50 g/2 oz butter
pinch of salt
2 tbsp caster sugar
125 g/4 oz plain flour, sifted
¼ tsp ground cinnamon
25 g/1 oz ground almonds
3 medium eggs, lightly beaten
175 g/6 oz cherries, stoned
sunflower oil for frying
2 tbsp icing sugar
1 tsp cocoa powder
sprigs of fresh mint, to decorate

# Chicken Chow Mein

INGREDIENTS **Serves 4**

225 g/8 oz egg noodles
5 tsp sesame oil
4 tsp light soy sauce
2 tbsp Chinese rice wine or dry sherry
salt and freshly ground black pepper
225 g/8 oz skinless chicken breast fillets, cut into strips
3 tbsp groundnut oil
2 garlic cloves, peeled and finely chopped
50 g/2 oz mangetout, finely sliced
50 g/2 oz cooked ham, cut into fine strips
2 tsp dark soy sauce
pinch of sugar

**To garnish:**
shredded spring onions
toasted sesame seeds

Bring a large saucepan of water to the boil and add the noodles. Cook for 3–5 minutes, drain and plunge into cold water. Drain again, add 1 tablespoon of the sesame oil and stir lightly.

Place 2 teaspoons of light soy sauce, 1 tablespoon of Chinese rice wine or sherry, and 1 teaspoon of the sesame oil, with seasoning to taste, in a bowl. Add the chicken and stir well. Cover lightly and leave to marinate in the refrigerator for about 15 minutes.

Heat the wok over a high heat, add 1 tablespoon of the groundnut oil and when very hot, add the chicken and its marinade and stir-fry for 2 minutes. Remove the chicken and juices and reserve. Wipe the wok clean with absorbent kitchen paper.

Reheat the wok and add the oil. Add the garlic and toss in the oil for 20 seconds. Add the mangetout and the ham and stir-fry for 1 minute. Add the noodles, remaining light soy sauce, Chinese rice wine or sherry, the dark soy sauce and sugar. Season to taste with salt and pepper and stir-fry for 2 minutes.

Add the chicken and juices to the wok and stir-fry for 4 minutes, or until the chicken is cooked. Drizzle over the remaining sesame oil. Garnish with spring onions and sesame seeds and serve.

HEALTH RATING 🍎🍎🍎

**ENTERTAINING ALTERNATIVE**
Duck in Black Bean Sauce

**PUDDING SUGGESTION**
Hot Cherry Fritters

# Grilled Spiced Chicken with Tomato & Shallot Chutney

INGREDIENTS **Serves 4**

3 tbsp sunflower oil
2 hot red chillies, deseeded and chopped
3 garlic cloves, peeled and chopped
1 tsp ground turmeric
1 tsp cumin seeds
1 tsp fennel seeds
1 tbsp freshly chopped basil
1 tbsp dark brown sugar
125 ml/4 fl oz rice or white wine vinegar
2 tsp sesame oil
4 large chicken breast quarters, wings attached
225 g/8 oz small shallots, peeled and halved
2 tbsp Chinese rice wine or dry sherry
50 g/2 oz caster sugar
175 g/6 oz cherry tomatoes, halved
2 tbsp light soy sauce

**To garnish:**
sprigs of fresh coriander
sprigs of fresh dill
lemon wedges

Preheat the grill to medium, 5 minutes before cooking. Heat a wok or large frying pan, add 1 tablespoon of the sunflower oil and when hot, add the chillies, garlic, turmeric, cumin, fennel seeds and basil. Fry for 5 minutes, add the sugar and 2 tablespoons of vinegar and stir until the sugar has dissolved. Remove, stir in the sesame oil and leave to cool.

Cut 3 or 4 deep slashes in the thickest part of the chicken breasts. Spread the spice paste over the chicken, place in a dish, cover and marinate in the refrigerator for at least 4 hours or overnight.

Heat the remaining sunflower oil in a saucepan, add the shallots and remaining garlic and cook gently for 15 minutes. Add the remaining vinegar, Chinese rice wine or sherry and caster sugar with 50 ml/2 fl oz water. Bring to the boil and simmer rapidly for 10 minutes, or until thickened. Add the tomatoes with the soy sauce. Simmer for 5–10 minutes, or until the liquid is reduced. Leave the chutney to cool.

Transfer the chicken pieces to a grill pan and cook under the preheated grill for 15–20 minutes on each side, or until the chicken is cooked through, basting frequently. Garnish with coriander sprigs and lemon wedges and serve immediately with the chutney.

HEALTH RATING 🍎🍎🍎

**MILD ALTERNATIVE**
Chinese Braised White Chicken with Three Sauces

**SUGGESTED ACCOMPANIMENT**
Spicy Cucumber Stir Fry

**MILD ALTERNATIVE**

## Chinese Braised White Chicken with Three Sauces

INGREDIENTS **Serves 4**

1.4 kg/3 lb oven-ready chicken
salt
6 spring onions, trimmed
5 cm/2 inch piece fresh root ginger, peeled and sliced
2 tsp Szechuan peppercorns, crushed
2½ tsp sea salt flakes or crushed coarse sea salt
2 tsp freshly grated root ginger
4 tbsp dark soy sauce
4 tbsp sunflower oil
1 tsp caster sugar
2 garlic cloves, finely chopped
3 tbsp light soy sauce
1 tbsp Chinese rice wine or dry sherry
1 tsp sesame oil
3 tbsp rice vinegar
1 small hot red chilli, deseeded and finely sliced
spring onion curls, to garnish
freshly steamed saffron-flavoured rice, to serve

Remove any fat from inside the chicken, rub inside and out with ½ teaspoon of salt and leave for 20 minutes. Place 3.4 litres/6 pints water with 2 spring onions and the ginger in a saucepan and bring to the boil. Add the chicken, breast-side down, return to the boil, cover and simmer for 50 minutes. Remove from the heat and leave for 1 hour. Remove the chicken and leave to cool.

Dry-fry the Szechuan peppercorns in a non-stick frying pan until they darken slightly and smell aromatic. Crush, mix with the sea salt and reserve.

Squeeze the juice from half of the grated ginger, mix with the dark soy sauce, 1 tablespoon of the sunflower oil and half the sugar. Reserve.

Finely chop the remaining spring onions and mix with the remaining ginger and garlic in a bowl. Heat the remaining oil to smoking and pour over the onion and ginger. When they stop sizzling, stir in the light soy sauce, Chinese rice wine or sherry and sesame oil. Reserve.

Mix together the rice vinegar, remaining sugar and chilli. Stir until the sugar dissolves. Reserve.

Remove the skin from the chicken, then remove the legs and cut them in two at the joint. Lift the breast meat away from the carcass in two pieces and slice thickly crossways. Sprinkle the pepper and salt mixture over the chicken, garnish with spring onion curls and serve with the dipping sauces, spring onion mixture and rice.

**SUGGESTED ACCOMPANIMENT**

## Spicy Cucumber Stir Fry

INGREDIENTS **Serves 4**

25 g/1 oz black soya beans, soaked in cold water overnight
1½ cucumbers
2 tsp salt
1 tbsp groundnut oil
½ tsp mild chilli powder
4 garlic cloves, peeled and crushed
5 tbsp chicken stock
1 tsp sesame oil
1 tbsp freshly chopped parsley, to garnish

Rinse the soaked beans thoroughly, then drain. Place in a saucepan, cover with cold water and bring to the boil, skimming off any scum that rises to the surface. Boil for 10 minutes, then reduce the heat and simmer for 1–1½ hours. Drain and reserve.

Peel the cucumbers, slice lengthways and remove the seeds. Cut into 2.5 cm/1 inch slices and place in a colander over a bowl. Sprinkle the salt over the cucumber and leave for 30 minutes. Rinse thoroughly in cold water, drain and pat dry with absorbent kitchen paper.

Heat a wok or large frying pan, add the oil and when hot, add the chilli powder, garlic and black beans and stir-fry for 30 seconds. Add the cucumber and stir-fry for 20 seconds.

Pour the stock into the wok and cook for 3–4 minutes, or until the cucumber is very tender. The liquid will have evaporated at this stage. Remove from the heat and stir in the sesame oil. Turn into a warmed serving dish, garnish with chopped parsley and serve immediately.

# Szechuan Sesame Chicken

INGREDIENTS **Serves 4**

1 medium egg white
pinch of salt
2 tsp cornflour
450 g/1 lb boneless, skinless chicken breast, cut into 7.5 cm/3 inch strips
300 ml/½ pint groundnut oil
1 tbsp sesame seeds
2 tsp dark soy sauce
2 tsp cider vinegar
2 tsp chilli bean sauce
2 tsp sesame oil
2 tsp sugar
1 tbsp Chinese rice wine
1 tsp whole Szechuan peppercorns, roasted
2 tbsp spring onion, trimmed and finely chopped
mixed salad, to serve

Beat the egg white with a pinch of salt and the cornflour, pour into a shallow dish and add the chicken strips. Turn to coat, cover with clingfilm and leave in the refrigerator for 20 minutes.

Heat a wok, add the groundnut oil and when hot, add the chicken pieces and stir-fry for 2 minutes or until the chicken turns white. Using a slotted spoon, remove the chicken and drain on absorbent kitchen paper. Pour off the oil, reserving 1 tablespoon of it. Wipe the wok clean.

Reheat the wok, add 1 tablespoon of the groundnut oil with the sesame seeds and stir-fry for 30 seconds, or until golden. Stir in the dark soy sauce, cider vinegar, chilli bean sauce, sesame oil, sugar, Chinese rice wine, Szechuan peppercorns and the spring onions. Bring to the boil.

Return the chicken to the wok and stir-fry for 2 minutes, making sure that the chicken is coated evenly with the sauce and sesame seeds. Turn into a warmed serving dish and serve immediately with a mixed salad.

HEALTH RATING 

**MILD ALTERNATIVE**
Szechuan Turkey Noodles

**SEAFOOD ALTERNATIVE**
Szechuan Chilli Prawns

## MILD ALTERNATIVE
## Szechuan Turkey Noodles

INGREDIENTS **Serves 4**

- 1 tbsp tomato paste
- 2 tsp black bean sauce
- 2 tsp cider vinegar
- salt and freshly ground black pepper
- ½ tsp Szechuan pepper
- 2 tsp sugar
- 4 tsp sesame oil
- 225 g/8 oz dried egg noodles
- 2 tbsp groundnut oil
- 2 tsp freshly grated root ginger
- 3 garlic cloves, peeled and roughly chopped
- 2 shallots, peeled and finely chopped
- 2 courgettes, trimmed and cut into fine matchsticks
- 450 g/1 lb turkey breast, skinned and cut into strips
- deep-fried onion rings, to garnish

Mix together the tomato paste, black bean sauce, cider vinegar, a pinch of salt and pepper, the sugar and half the sesame oil. Chill in the refrigerator for 30 minutes.

Bring a large saucepan of lightly salted water to the boil and add the noodles. Cook for 3–5 minutes, drain and plunge immediately into cold water. Toss with the remaining sesame oil and reserve.

Heat the wok until very hot, then add the oil and when hot, add the ginger, garlic and shallots. Stir-fry for 20 seconds, then add the courgettes and turkey strips. Stir-fry for 3–4 minutes, or until the turkey strips are sealed.

Add the prepared chilled black bean sauce and continue to stir-fry for another 4 minutes over a high heat. Add the drained noodles to the wok and stir until the noodles, turkey, vegetables and the sauce are well mixed together. Garnish with the deep-fried onion rings and serve immediately.

## SEAFOOD ALTERNATIVE
## Szechuan Chilli Prawns

Peel the prawns, leaving the tails attached if you like. Using a sharp knife, remove the black vein along the back of the prawns. Rinse and pat dry with absorbent kitchen paper.

Heat a wok or large frying pan, add the oil and when hot, add the onion, pepper and chilli and stir-fry for 4–5 minutes, or until the vegetables are tender but retain a bite. Stir in the garlic and cook for 30 seconds. Using a slotted spoon, transfer to a plate and reserve.

Add the prawns to the wok and stir-fry for 1–2 minutes, or until they turn pink and opaque. Blend all the chilli sauce ingredients together in a bowl or jug, then stir into the prawns. Add the reserved vegetables and bring to the boil, stirring constantly. Cook for 1–2 minutes, or until the sauce is thickened and the prawns and vegetables are well coated. Stir in the spring onions, tip on to a warmed platter and garnish with chilli flowers or coriander sprigs. Serve immediately with freshly cooked rice or noodles.

INGREDIENTS **Serves 4**

- 450 g/1 lb raw tiger prawns
- 2 tbsp groundnut oil
- 1 onion, peeled and sliced
- 1 red pepper, deseeded and cut into strips
- 1 small red chilli, deseeded and thinly sliced
- 2 garlic cloves, peeled and finely chopped
- 2–3 spring onions, trimmed and diagonally sliced
- freshly cooked rice or noodles, to serve
- sprigs of fresh coriander or chilli flowers, to garnish

**For the chilli sauce:**

- 1 tbsp cornflour
- 4 tbsp cold fish stock or water
- 2 tbsp soy sauce
- 2 tbsp sweet or hot chilli sauce, or to taste
- 2 tsp soft light brown sugar

# Thai Coconut Chicken

INGREDIENTS **Serves 4**

1 tsp cumin seeds
1 tsp mustard seeds
1 tsp coriander seeds
1 tsp turmeric
1 bird's-eye chilli, deseeded and finely chopped
1 tbsp freshly grated root ginger
2 garlic cloves, peeled and finely chopped
125 ml/4 fl oz double cream
8 skinless chicken thighs
2 tbsp groundnut oil
1 onion, peeled and finely sliced
200 ml/7 fl oz coconut milk
salt and freshly ground black pepper
4 tbsp freshly chopped coriander
2 spring onions, shredded, to garnish
freshly cooked Thai fragrant rice, to serve

Heat the wok and add the cumin seeds, mustard seeds and coriander seeds. Dry-fry over a low to medium heat for 2 minutes, or until the fragrance becomes stronger and the seeds start to pop. Add the turmeric and leave to cool slightly. Grind the spices in a pestle and mortar or blend to a fine powder in a food processor.

Mix the chilli, ginger, garlic and the cream together in a small bowl, add the ground spices and mix. Place the chicken thighs in a shallow dish and spread the spice paste over the thighs.

Heat the wok over a high heat, add the oil and when hot, add the onion and stir-fry until golden brown. Add the chicken and spice paste. Cook for 5–6 minutes, stirring occasionally, until evenly coloured. Add the coconut milk and season to taste with salt and pepper. Simmer the chicken for 15–20 minutes, or until the thighs are cooked through, taking care not to allow the mixture to boil. Stir in the chopped coriander and serve immediately with the freshly cooked rice sprinkled with shredded spring onions.

HEALTH RATING

**SPEEDY ALTERNATIVE**
Pan-cooked Chicken with Thai Spices

**MILD ALTERNATIVE**
Chicken in Black Bean Sauce

## SPEEDY ALTERNATIVE
## Pan-cooked Chicken with Thai Spices

Lightly bruise the kaffir lime leaves and put in a bowl with the chopped ginger. Pour over the chicken stock, cover and leave to infuse for 30 minutes.

Meanwhile, cut each chicken breast into two pieces. Heat the oil in a large, non-stick frying pan or flameproof casserole dish and brown the chicken pieces for 2–3 minutes on each side.

Strain the infused chicken stock into the pan. Half cover the pan with a lid and gently simmer for 10 minutes.

Stir in the coconut milk, fish sauce and chopped chillies. Simmer, uncovered for 5–6 minutes, or until the chicken is tender and cooked through and the sauce has reduced slightly.

Meanwhile, cook the rice in boiling salted water according to the packet instructions. Drain the rice thoroughly.

Stir the lime juice and chopped coriander into the sauce. Season to taste with salt and pepper. Serve the chicken and sauce on a bed of rice. Garnish with wedges of lime and freshly chopped coriander and serve immediately.

INGREDIENTS **Serves 4**

4 kaffir lime leaves
5 cm/2 inch piece of root ginger, peeled and chopped
300 ml/½ pint chicken stock, boiling
4 x 175 g/6 oz chicken breasts
2 tsp groundnut oil
5 tbsp coconut milk
1 tbsp fish sauce
2 red chillies, deseeded and finely chopped
225 g/8 oz Thai jasmine rice
1 tbsp lime juice
3 tbsp freshly chopped coriander
salt and freshly ground black pepper

**To garnish:**
wedges of lime
freshly chopped coriander

## MILD ALTERNATIVE
## Chicken in Black Bean Sauce

Place the chicken strips in a large bowl. Mix together the soy sauce, Chinese rice wine or sherry, a little salt, caster sugar, sesame oil and cornflour and pour over the chicken.

Heat the wok over a high heat. Add the oil and, when very hot, add the chicken strips and stir-fry for 2 minutes. Add the green peppers and stir-fry for a further 2 minutes. Then add the ginger, garlic, shallots, spring onions and black beans and continue to stir-fry for another 2 minutes.

Add 4 tablespoons of the stock, stir-fry for 1 minute, then pour in the remaining stock and bring to the boil. Reduce the heat and simmer the sauce for 3–4 minutes, or until the chicken is cooked and the sauce has thickened slightly. Garnish with the shredded spring onions and serve immediately with noodles.

INGREDIENTS **Serves 4**

450 g/1 lb skinless, boneless chicken breast fillets, cut into strips
1 tbsp light soy sauce
2 tbsp Chinese rice wine or dry sherry
salt
1 tsp caster sugar
1 tsp sesame oil
2 tsp cornflour
2 tbsp sunflower oil
2 green peppers, deseeded and diced
1 tbsp freshly grated root ginger
2 garlic cloves, peeled and roughly chopped
2 shallots, peeled and finely chopped
4 spring onions, trimmed and finely sliced
3 tbsp salted black beans, chopped
150 ml/¼ pint chicken stock
shredded spring onions, to garnish
freshly cooked egg noodles, to serve

## SUGGESTED ACCOMPANIMENT
# Bulghur Wheat Salad with Minty Lemon Dressing

INGREDIENTS **Serves 4**

125 g/4 oz bulghur wheat
10 cm/4 inch piece cucumber
2 shallots, peeled
125 g/4 oz baby sweetcorn
3 ripe but firm tomatoes

**For the dressing:**

grated rind of 1 lemon
3 tbsp lemon juice
3 tbsp freshly chopped mint
2 tbsp freshly chopped parsley
1–2 tsp clear honey
2 tbsp sunflower oil
salt and freshly ground black pepper

Place the bulghur wheat in a saucepan and cover with boiling water. Simmer for about 10 minutes, then drain thoroughly and turn into a serving bowl.

Cut the cucumber into small cubes, chop the shallots finely and reserve. Steam the sweetcorn over a pan of boiling water for 10 minutes or until tender. Drain and slice into thick chunks.

Cut a cross on the top of each tomato and place in boiling water until their skins start to peel away. Remove the skins and the seeds and cut the tomatoes into small cubes.

Make the dressing by briskly whisking all the ingredients in a small bowl until well mixed. When the bulghur wheat has cooled a little, add all the prepared vegetables and stir in the dressing. Season to taste with salt and pepper and serve.

## PUDDING SUGGESTION
# Orange Chocolate Cheesecake

INGREDIENTS **Serves 8**

225 g/8 oz plain chocolate-coated digestive biscuits
50 g/2 oz butter
450 g/1 lb mixed fruits, such as blueberries and raspberries
1 tbsp icing sugar, sifted
few sprigs of fresh mint, to decorate

**For the filling:**

450 g/1 lb soft cream cheese
1 tbsp gelatine
350 g/12 oz orange chocolate, broken into segments
600 ml/1 pint double cream

Lightly oil and line a 20.5 cm/8 inch round loose-based cake tin with non-stick baking parchment. Place the biscuits in a polythene bag and crush using a rolling pin. Alternatively, use a food processor. Melt the butter in a medium-sized heavy-based saucepan, add the crushed biscuits and mix well. Press the biscuit mixture into the base of the lined tin, then chill in the refrigerator for 20 minutes.

For the filling, remove the cream cheese from the refrigerator at least 20 minutes before using, to allow the cheese to come to room temperature. Place the cream cheese in a bowl and beat until smooth, then reserve.

Pour 4 tablespoons of water into a small bowl and sprinkle over the gelatine. Leave to stand for 5 minutes until spongy. Place the bowl over a saucepan of simmering water and allow to dissolve, stirring occasionally. Leave to cool slightly.

Melt the orange chocolate in a heatproof bowl set over a saucepan of simmering water, then leave to cool slightly.

Whip the cream until soft peaks form. Beat the gelatine and chocolate into the cream cheese. Fold in the cream. Spoon into the tin and level the surface. Chill in the refrigerator for 4 hours until set.

Remove the cheesecake from the tin and place on a serving plate. Top with the fruits, dust with icing sugar and decorate with sprigs of mint.

# Sauvignon Chicken & Mushroom Filo Pie

INGREDIENTS **Serves 4**

1 onion, peeled and chopped
1 leek, trimmed and chopped
225 ml/8 fl oz chicken stock
3 x 175 g/ 6 oz chicken breasts
150 ml/¼ pint dry white wine
1 bay leaf
175 g/6 oz baby button mushrooms
2 tbsp plain flour
1 tbsp freshly chopped tarragon
salt and freshly ground black pepper
sprig of fresh parsley, to garnish
seasonal vegetables, to serve

**For the topping:**

75 g/3 oz (about 5 sheets) filo pastry
1 tbsp sunflower oil
1 tsp sesame seeds

Preheat the oven to 190°C/375°F/Gas Mark 5. Put the onion and leek in a heavy-based saucepan with 125 ml/4 fl oz of the stock.

Bring to the boil, cover and simmer for 5 minutes, then uncover and cook until all the stock has evaporated and the vegetables are tender.

Cut the chicken into bite-sized cubes. Add to the pan with the remaining stock, wine and bay leaf. Cover and gently simmer for 5 minutes. Add the mushrooms and simmer for a further 5 minutes.

Blend the flour with 3 tablespoons of cold water. Stir into the pan and cook, stirring all the time until the sauce has thickened. Stir the tarragon into the sauce and season with salt and pepper. Spoon the mixture into a 1.2 litre/2 pint pie dish, discarding the bay leaf.

Lightly brush a sheet of filo pastry with a little of the oil. Crumple the pastry slightly. Arrange on top of the filling. Repeat with the remaining filo sheets and oil, then sprinkle the top of the pie with the sesame seeds.

Bake the pie on the middle shelf of the preheated oven for 20 minutes until the filo pastry topping is golden and crisp. Garnish with a sprig of parsley. Serve the pie immediately with the seasonal vegetables.

HEALTH RATING ★★★

**SUGGESTED ACCOMPANIMENT**

Bulghur Wheat Salad with Minty Lemon Dressing

**PUDDING SUGGESTION**

Orange Chocolate Cheesecake

# Turkey Hash with Potato & Beetroot

INGREDIENTS **Serves 4–6**

2 tbsp vegetable oil
50 g/2 oz butter
4 slices streaky bacon, diced or sliced
1 medium onion, peeled and finely chopped
450 g/1 lb cooked turkey, diced
450 g/1 lb finely chopped cooked potatoes
2–3 tbsp freshly chopped parsley
2 tbsp plain flour
250 g/9 oz cooked medium beetroot, diced
green salad, to serve

In a large, heavy-based frying pan, heat the oil and half the butter over a medium heat until sizzling. Add the bacon and cook for 4 minutes, or until crisp and golden, stirring occasionally. Using a slotted spoon, transfer to a large bowl. Add the onion to the pan and cook for 3–4 minutes, or until soft and golden, stirring frequently.

Meanwhile, add the turkey, potatoes, parsley and flour to the cooked bacon in the bowl. Stir and toss gently, then fold in the diced beetroot.

Add half the remaining butter to the frying pan and then add the turkey vegetable mixture. Stir, then spread the mixture to evenly cover the bottom of the frying pan. Cook for 15 minutes or until the underside is crisp and brown, pressing the hash firmly into a cake with a spatula. Remove from the heat.

Invert a large plate over the frying pan and, holding the plate and frying pan together with an oven glove, turn the hash out onto the plate. Heat the remaining butter in the pan, slide the hash back into the pan and cook for 4 minutes, or until crisp and brown on the other side. Invert onto the plate again and serve immediately with a green salad.

HEALTH RATING 🍎🍎

**LOW FAT ALTERNATIVE**
Turkey & Tomato Tagine

**PUDDING SUGGESTION**
Chocolate Brioche Bake

**LOW FAT ALTERNATIVE**
## Turkey & Tomato Tagine

Preheat the oven to 190°C/375°F/Gas Mark 5. Put all the ingredients for the meatballs except the oil into a bowl and mix well. Season to taste with salt and pepper. Shape into 20 balls, about the size of walnuts.

Put on a tray, cover lightly and chill in the refrigerator while making the sauce.

Put the onion and garlic in a pan with 125 ml/4 fl oz of the stock. Cook over a low heat until all the stock has evaporated. Continue cooking for 1 minute, or until the onions begin to colour.

Add the remaining stock to the pan with the tomatoes, cumin, cinnamon and cayenne pepper. Simmer for 10 minutes, until slightly thickened and reduced. Stir in the parsley and season to taste.

Heat the oil in a large non-stick frying pan and cook the meatballs in two batches until lightly browned all over.

Lift the meatballs out with a slotted spoon and drain on kitchen paper.

Pour the sauce into a tagine or ovenproof casserole dish. Top with the meatballs, cover and cook in the preheated oven for 25–30 minutes, or until the meatballs are cooked through and the sauce is bubbling. Garnish with freshly chopped herbs and serve immediately on a bed of couscous or plain boiled rice.

INGREDIENTS **Serves 4**

**For the meatballs:**

450 g/1 lb fresh turkey mince
1 small onion, peeled and very finely chopped
1 garlic clove, peeled and crushed
1 tbsp freshly chopped coriander
1 tsp ground cumin
1 tbsp olive oil
salt and freshly ground black pepper

**For the sauce:**

1 onion, peeled and finely chopped
1 garlic clove, peeled and crushed
150 ml/¼ pint turkey stock
400 g can chopped tomatoes
½ tsp ground cumin
½ tsp ground cinnamon
pinch of cayenne pepper
freshly chopped parsley
freshly chopped herbs, to garnish
freshly cooked couscous or rice, to serve

**PUDDING SUGGESTION**
## Chocolate Brioche Bake

INGREDIENTS **Serves 6**

200 g/7 oz plain dark chocolate, broken into pieces
75 g/3 oz unsalted butter
225 g/8 oz brioche, sliced
1 tsp pure orange oil or 1 tbsp grated orange rind
½ tsp freshly grated nutmeg
3 medium eggs, beaten
25 g/1 oz golden caster sugar
600 ml/1 pint milk
cocoa powder and icing sugar for dusting

Preheat the oven to 180°C/350°F/Gas Mark 4, 10 minutes before baking. Lightly oil or butter a 1.7 litre/3 pint ovenproof dish. Melt the chocolate with 25 g/1 oz of the butter in a heatproof bowl set over a saucepan of simmering water. Stir until smooth.

Arrange half of the sliced brioche in the ovenproof dish, overlapping the slices slightly, then pour over half of the melted chocolate. Repeat the layers, finishing with a layer of chocolate.

Melt the remaining butter in a saucepan. Remove from the heat and stir in the orange oil or rind, the nutmeg and the beaten eggs. Continuing to stir, add the sugar and finally the milk. Beat thoroughly and pour over the brioche. Leave to stand for 30 minutes before baking.

Bake on the centre shelf in the preheated oven for 45 minutes, or until the custard is set and the topping is golden brown. Leave to stand for 5 minutes, then dust with cocoa powder and icing sugar. Serve warm.

# Sweet-&-Sour Turkey

INGREDIENTS **Serves 4**

2 tbsp groundnut oil
2 garlic cloves, peeled and chopped
1 tbsp freshly grated root ginger
4 spring onions, trimmed and cut into 4 cm/1½ inch lengths
450 g/1 lb turkey breast, skinned and cut into strips
1 red pepper, deseeded and cut into 2.5 cm/1 inch squares
225 g/8 oz canned water chestnuts, drained
150 ml/¼ pint chicken stock
2 tbsp Chinese rice wine
3 tbsp light soy sauce
2 tsp dark soy sauce
2 tbsp tomato paste
2 tbsp white wine vinegar
1 tbsp sugar
1 tbsp cornflour
egg-fried rice, to serve

Heat the wok over a high heat, add the oil and when hot, add the garlic, ginger and spring onions. Stir-fry for 20 seconds.

Add the turkey to the wok and stir-fry for 2 minutes, or until beginning to colour. Add the peppers and water chestnuts and stir-fry for a further 2 minutes.

Mix the chicken stock, Chinese rice wine, light and dark soy sauce, tomato paste, white wine vinegar and the sugar together in a small jug or bowl. Add the mixture to the wok, stir and bring the sauce to the boil.

Mix together the cornflour with 2 tablespoons of water and add to the wok. Reduce the heat and simmer for 3 minutes, or until the turkey is cooked thoroughly and the sauce slightly thickened and glossy. Serve immediately with egg-fried rice.

HEALTH RATING

**SUGGESTED ACCOMPANIMENT**

Warm Noodle Salad with Sesame & Peanut Dressing

**STARTER SUGGESTION**

Thai Marinated Prawns

## SUGGESTED ACCOMPANIMENT
## Warm Noodle Salad with Sesame & Peanut Dressing

Place the peanut butter, 4 tablespoons of the sesame oil, the soy sauce, vinegar and ginger in a food processor. Blend until smooth, then stir in 75 ml/3 fl oz hot water and blend again. Pour in the cream, blend briefly until smooth. Pour the dressing into a jug and reserve.

Bring a saucepan of lightly salted water to the boil, add the noodles and beansprouts and cook for 4 minutes or according to the packet instructions. Drain, rinse under cold running water and drain again. Stir in the remaining sesame oil and keep warm.

Bring a saucepan of lightly salted water to the boil and add the baby sweetcorn, carrots and mangetout and cook for 3–4 minutes, or until just tender but still crisp. Drain and cut the mangetout in half. Slice the baby sweetcorn (if very large) into 2–3 pieces and arrange on a warmed serving dish with the noodles. Add the cucumber strips and spring onions. Spoon over a little of the dressing and serve immediately with the remaining dressing.

INGREDIENTS **Serves 4–6**

125 g/4 oz smooth peanut butter
6 tbsp sesame oil
3 tbsp light soy sauce
2 tbsp red wine vinegar
1 tbsp freshly grated root ginger
2 tbsp double cream
250 g pack Chinese fine egg noodles
125 g/4 oz beansprouts
225 g/8 oz baby sweetcorn
125 g/4 oz carrots, peeled and cut into matchsticks
125 g/4 oz mangetout
125 g/4 oz cucumber, cut into thin strips
3 spring onions, trimmed and finely shredded

## STARTER SUGGESTION
## Thai Marinated Prawns

INGREDIENTS **Serves 4**

700 g/1½ lb large raw prawns, peeled with tails left on
2 large eggs
salt
50 g/2 oz cornflour
vegetable oil for deep-frying
lime wedges, to garnish

**For the marinade:**

2 lemon grass stalks, outer leaves discarded and bruised
2 garlic cloves, peeled and finely chopped
2 shallots, peeled and finely chopped
1 red chilli, deseeded and chopped
grated zest and juice of 1 small lime
400 ml can of coconut milk

Mix all the marinade ingredients together in a bowl, pressing on the solid ingredients to release their flavours. Season to taste with salt and reserve.

Using a sharp knife, remove the black vein along the back of the prawns and pat dry with absorbent kitchen paper. Add the prawns to the marinade and stir gently until coated evenly. Leave in the marinade for at least 1 hour, stirring occasionally.

Beat the eggs in a deep bowl with a little salt. Place the cornflour in a shallow bowl. Using a slotted spoon or spatula, transfer the prawns from the marinade to the cornflour. Stir gently until the prawns are coated on all sides and shake off any excess.

Holding each prawn by its tail, dip it into the beaten egg, then into the cornflour again, shaking off any excess.

Pour enough oil into a large wok to come 5 cm/2 inches up the sides and place over a high heat. Working in batches of 5 or 6, deep-fry the prawns for 2 minutes or until pink and crisp, turning once. Using a slotted spoon, remove and drain on absorbent kitchen paper and keep warm. Arrange on a warmed serving plate and garnish with lime wedges. Serve immediately.

# Teriyaki Turkey with Oriental Vegetables

INGREDIENTS **Serves 4**

1 red chilli

1 garlic clove, peeled and crushed

2.5 cm/1 inch piece root ginger, peeled and grated

3 tbsp dark soy sauce

1 tsp sunflower oil

350 g/12 oz skinless, boneless turkey breast

1 tbsp sesame oil

1 tbsp sesame seeds

2 carrots, peeled and cut into matchstick strips

1 leek, trimmed and shredded

125 g/4 oz broccoli, cut into small florets

1 tsp cornflour

3 tbsp dry sherry

125 g/4 oz mangetout, cut into thin strips

**To serve:**

freshly cooked egg noodles

sprinkling of sesame seeds

Halve, deseed and thinly slice the chilli. Put into a small bowl with the garlic, ginger, soy sauce and sunflower oil.

Cut the turkey into thin strips. Add to the mixture and mix until well coated. Cover with clingfilm and marinate in the refrigerator for at least 30 minutes.

Heat a wok or large frying pan. Add 2 teaspoons of the sesame oil. When hot, remove the turkey from the marinade. Stir-fry for 2–3 minutes until browned and cooked. Remove from the pan and reserve.

Heat the remaining 1 teaspoon of oil in the wok. Add the sesame seeds and stir-fry for a few seconds until they start to change colour. Add the carrots, leek and broccoli and continue stir-frying for 2–3 minutes.

Blend the cornflour with 1 tablespoon of cold water to make a smooth paste. Stir in the sherry and marinade. Add to the wok with the mangetout and cook for 1 minute, stirring all the time until thickened.

Return the turkey to the pan and continue cooking for 1–2 minutes or until the turkey is hot, the vegetables are tender and the sauce is bubbling. Serve the turkey and vegetables immediately with the egg noodles. Sprinkle with the sesame seeds.

HEALTH RATING 🍎🍎🍎🍎

**SUGGESTED ACCOMPANIMENT**

Chinese Salad with Soy & Ginger Dressing

**PUDDING SUGGESTION**

Autumn Fruit Layer

INGREDIENTS **Serves 4**

1 head of Chinese cabbage
200 g can of water chestnuts, drained
6 spring onions, trimmed
4 ripe but firm cherry tomatoes
125 g/4 oz mangetout
125 g/4 oz beansprouts
2 tbsp freshly chopped coriander

**For the soy and ginger dressing:**

2 tbsp sunflower oil
4 tbsp light soy sauce
2.5 cm/1 inch piece root ginger, peeled and finely grated
zest and juice of 1 lemon
salt and freshly ground black pepper

**SUGGESTED ACCOMPANIMENT**

## Chinese Salad with Soy & Ginger Dressing

Rinse and finely shred the Chinese cabbage and place in a serving dish.

Slice the water chestnuts into small slivers and cut the spring onions diagonally into 2.5 cm/1 inch lengths, then split lengthwise into thin strips.

Cut the tomatoes in half and then slice each half into three wedges and reserve.

Simmer the mangetout in boiling water for 2 minutes until beginning to soften, drain and cut in half diagonally.

Arrange the water chestnuts, spring onions, mangetout, tomatoes and beansprouts on top of the shredded Chinese cabbage. Garnish with the freshly chopped coriander.

Make the dressing by whisking all the ingredients together in a small bowl until mixed thoroughly. Serve with crusty white bread and the salad.

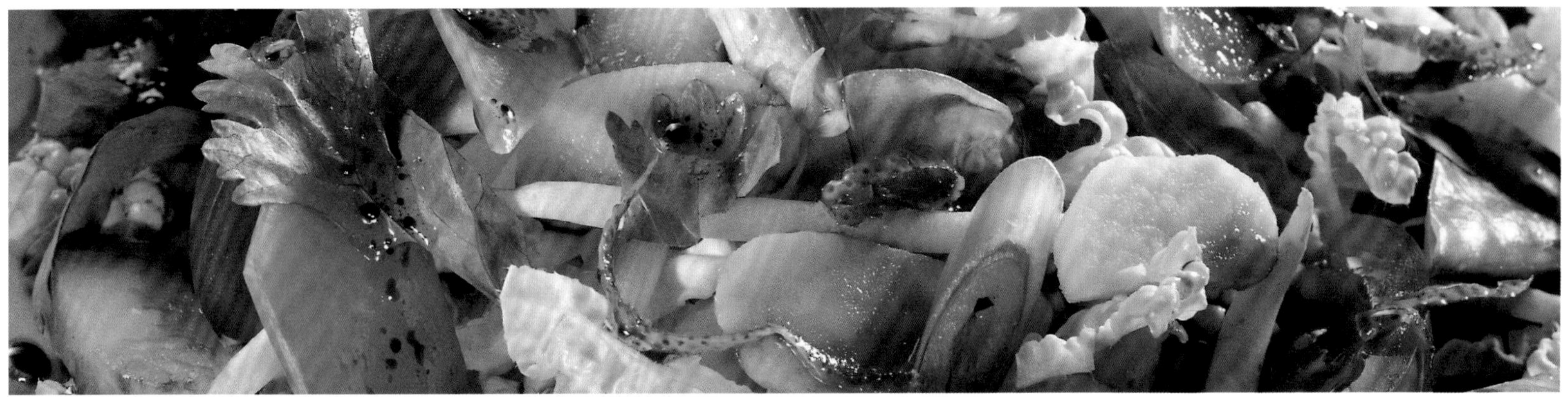

**PUDDING SUGGESTION**

## Autumn Fruit Layer

INGREDIENTS **Serves 4**

450 g/1 lb Bramley cooking apples
225 g/8 oz blackberries
50 g/2 oz soft brown sugar
juice of 1 lemon
50 g/2 oz butter or margerine
200 g/7 oz breadcrumbs
225 g/8 oz honey-coated nut mix, chopped
redcurrants and mint leaves, to decorate
whipped cream or ice cream, to serve

Peel, core and slice the cooking apples and place in a saucepan with the blackberries, sugar and lemon juice.

Cover the fruit mixture and simmer, stirring occasionally, for about 15 minutes or until the apples and blackberries have formed into a thick purée. Remove the pan from the heat and allow to cool.

Melt the butter or margerine in a frying pan and cook the breadcrumbs for 5–10 minutes, stirring occasionally until golden and crisp. Remove the pan from the heat and stir in the nuts. Allow to cool.

Alternately layer the fruit purée and breadcrumbs into four tall glasses. Store the desserts in the refrigerator to chill and remove when ready to serve.

Decorate with redcurrants and mint leaves and serve with whipped cream or vanilla or raspberry ice cream.

**MILD ALTERNATIVE**
## Noodles with Turkey & Mushrooms

Bring a large saucepan of lightly salted water to the boil and add the noodles. Cook for 3–5 minutes, then drain and plunge immediately into cold water. When cool, drain again and reserve.

Heat the wok, add the oil and when hot, add the onion and stir-fry for 3 minutes until it starts to soften. Add the ginger and garlic and stir-fry for a further 3 minutes, then add the turkey strips and stir-fry for 4–5 minutes until sealed and golden.

Wipe and slice the chestnut mushrooms into similar sized pieces and add to the wok with the whole button mushrooms. Stir-fry for 3–4 minutes, or until tender. When all the vegetables are tender and the turkey is cooked, add the soy sauce, hoisin sauce, sherry and vegetable stock.

Mix the cornflour with 2 tablespoons of water and add to the wok, then cook, stirring, until the sauce thickens. Add the drained noodles to the wok, then toss the mixture together and serve immediately.

INGREDIENTS **Serves 4**

- 225 g/8 oz dried egg noodles
- 1 tbsp groundnut oil
- 1 red onion, peeled and sliced
- 2 tbsp freshly grated root ginger
- 3 garlic cloves, peeled and finely chopped
- 350 g/12 oz turkey breast, skinned and cut into strips
- 125 g/4 oz baby button mushrooms
- 150 g/5 oz chestnut mushrooms
- 2 tbsp dark soy sauce
- 2 tbsp hoisin sauce
- 2 tbsp dry sherry
- 4 tbsp vegetable stock
- 2 tsp cornflour

**STARTER SUGGESTION**
## Sweetcorn Cakes

Place the flour in a bowl, make a well in the centre, then add the curry paste, soy sauce and the sugar together with the shredded kaffir lime leaves, French beans and sweetcorn. Season to taste with salt and pepper, then beat 1 of the eggs and add to the mixture. Stir in with a fork adding 1–2 tablespoons of cold water to form a stiff dough. Knead lightly on a floured surface and form into a ball.

Divide the mixture into 16 pieces and shape into small balls, then flatten to form cakes about 1 cm/½ inch thick and 7.5 cm/3 inches in diameter. Beat the remaining egg and pour into a shallow dish. Dip the cakes first in a little beaten egg, then in the breadcrumbs until lightly coated.

Heat the oil in either a wok or deep-fat fryer to 180°C/350°F and deep-fry the cakes for 2–3 minutes or until golden brown in colour. Using a slotted spoon, remove and drain on absorbent kitchen paper.

Meanwhile, blend the hoisin sauce, sugar, 1 tablespoon of water and the sesame oil together until smooth and pour into a small bowl. Serve immediately with the sweetcorn cakes, cucumber and spring onions.

INGREDIENTS **Serves 6–8**

- 250 g/9 oz self-raising flour
- 3 tbsp Thai red curry paste
- 2 tbsp light soy sauce
- 2 tsp sugar
- 2 kaffir lime leaves, finely shredded
- 12 fine French beans, trimmed, finely chopped and blanched
- 340 g can sweetcorn, drained
- salt and freshly ground black pepper
- 2 medium eggs
- 50 g/2 oz fresh white breadcrumbs
- vegetable oil for deep-frying

**For the dipping sauce:**

- 2 tbsp hoisin sauce
- 1 tbsp soft light brown sugar
- 1 tbsp sesame oil

**To serve:**

- halved cucumber slices
- spring onions, sliced diagonally

# Turkey with Oriental Mushrooms

INGREDIENTS **Serves 4**

15 g/½ oz dried Chinese mushrooms
450 g/1 lb turkey breast steaks
150 ml/¼ pint turkey or chicken stock
2 tbsp groundnut oil
1 red pepper, deseeded and sliced
225 g/8 oz sugar snap peas, trimmed
125 g/4 oz shiitake mushrooms, wiped and halved
125 g/4 oz oyster mushrooms, wiped and halved
2 tbsp yellow bean sauce
2 tbsp soy sauce
1 tbsp hot chilli sauce
freshly cooked noodles, to serve

Place the dried mushrooms in a small bowl, cover with almost boiling water and leave for 20–30 minutes. Drain and discard any woody stems from the mushrooms. Cut the turkey into thin strips.

Pour the turkey or chicken stock into a wok or large frying pan and bring to the boil. Add the turkey and cook gently for 3 minutes, or until the turkey is sealed completely, then using a slotted spoon, remove from the wok and reserve. Discard any stock.

Wipe the wok clean and reheat, then add the oil. When the oil is almost smoking, add the drained turkey and stir-fry for 2 minutes.

Add the drained mushrooms to the wok with the red pepper, the sugar snap peas and the shiitake and oyster mushrooms. Stir-fry for 2 minutes, then add the yellow bean, soy and hot chilli sauces.

Stir-fry the mixture for 1–2 minutes more, or until the turkey is cooked thoroughly and the vegetables are cooked but still retain a bite. Turn into a warmed serving dish and serve immediately with freshly cooked noodles.

HEALTH RATING 🍎🍎🍎🍎

**MILD ALTERNATIVE**

Noodles with Turkey & Mushrooms

**STARTER SUGGESTION**

Sweetcorn Cakes

# Turkey & Vegetable Stir Fry

INGREDIENTS **Serves 4**

- 350 g/12 oz mixed vegetables, such as baby sweetcorn, 1 small red pepper, pak choi, mushrooms, broccoli florets and baby carrots
- 2 tbsp groundnut oil
- 350 g/12 oz skinless, boneless turkey breast, sliced into fine strips across the grain
- 2 garlic cloves, peeled and finely chopped
- 2.5 cm/1 inch piece fresh root ginger, peeled and finely grated
- 3 spring onions, trimmed and finely sliced
- 2 tbsp light soy sauce
- 1 tbsp Chinese rice wine or dry sherry
- 2 tbsp chicken stock or water
- 1 tsp cornflour
- 1 tsp sesame oil
- freshly cooked noodles or rice, to serve

**To garnish:**

- 50 g/2 oz toasted cashew nuts
- 2 spring onions, finely shredded
- 25 g/1 oz beansprouts

Slice or chop the vegetables into small pieces, depending on which you use. Halve the baby sweetcorn lengthways, deseed and thinly slice the red pepper, tear or shred the pak choi, slice the mushrooms, break the broccoli into small florets and cut the carrots into matchsticks.

Heat a wok or large frying pan, add the oil and when hot, add the turkey strips and stir-fry for 1 minute or until they turn white. Add the garlic, ginger and spring onions and cook for a few seconds.

Add the prepared carrot, pepper, broccoli and mushrooms and stir-fry for 1 minute. Add the baby sweetcorn and pak choi and stir-fry for 1 minute.

Blend the soy sauce, Chinese rice wine or sherry and stock or water and pour over the vegetables. Blend the cornflour with 1 teaspoon of water and stir into the vegetables, mixing well. Bring to the boil, reduce the heat, then simmer for 1 minute. Stir in the sesame oil. Tip into a warmed serving dish, sprinkle with cashew nuts, shredded spring onions and beansprouts. Serve immediately with noodles or rice.

HEALTH RATING 🍎🍎🍎🍎

**SPICY ALTERNATIVE**

Lime & Sesame Turkey

**STARTER SUGGESTION**

Prawn Toasts

**SPICY ALTERNATIVE**
## Lime & Sesame Turkey

INGREDIENTS **Serves 4**

450 g/1 lb turkey breast, skinned and cut into strips
2 lemon grass stalks, outer leaves discarded and finely sliced
grated zest of 1 lime
4 garlic cloves, peeled and crushed
6 shallots, peeled and finely sliced
2 tbsp Thai fish sauce
2 tsp soft brown sugar
1 small red chilli, deseeded and finely sliced
3 tbsp sunflower oil
1 tbsp sesame oil
225 g/8 oz stir-fry rice noodles
1 tbsp sesame seeds
shredded spring onions, to garnish
freshly stir-fried vegetables, to serve

Place the turkey strips in a shallow dish. Mix together the lemon grass stalks, lime zest, garlic, shallots, Thai fish sauce, sugar and chilli with 2 tablespoons of the sunflower oil and the sesame oil. Pour over the turkey. Cover and leave to marinate in the refrigerator for 2–3 hours, spooning the marinade over the turkey occasionally.

Soak the noodles in warm water for 5 minutes. Drain through a sieve or colander, then plunge immediately into cold water. Drain again and reserve until ready to use.

Heat the wok until very hot and add the sesame seeds. Dry-fry for 1–2 minutes, or until toasted in colour. Remove from the wok and reserve. Wipe the wok to remove any dust left from the seeds.

Heat the wok again and add the remaining sunflower oil. When hot, drain the turkey from the marinade and stir-fry for 3–4 minutes, or until golden brown and cooked through (you may need to do this in two batches). When all the turkey has been cooked, add the noodles to the wok and cook, stirring, for 1–2 minutes or until heated through thoroughly. Garnish with the shredded spring onions and toasted sesame seeds and serve immediately with freshly stir-fried vegetables of your choice.

**STARTER SUGGESTION**
## Prawn Toasts

INGREDIENTS **Serves 8–10**

225 g/8 oz cooked peeled prawns, thawed if frozen, well drained and dried
1 medium egg white
2 spring onions, trimmed and chopped
1 cm/½ inch piece fresh root ginger, peeled and chopped
1 garlic clove, peeled and chopped
1 tsp cornflour
2–3 dashes hot pepper sauce
½ tsp sugar
salt and freshly ground black pepper
8 slices firm-textured white bread
4–5 tbsp sesame seeds
300 ml/½ pint vegetable oil for deep frying
sprigs of fresh coriander, to garnish

Put the prawns, egg white, spring onions, ginger, garlic, cornflour, hot pepper sauce and sugar into a food processor. Season to taste with about ½ teaspoon of salt and black pepper. Process until the mixture forms a smooth paste, scraping down the side of the bowl once or twice.

Using a metal palette knife, spread an even layer of the paste evenly over the bread slices. Sprinkle each slice generously with sesame seeds, pressing gently to bury them in the paste.

Trim the crusts off each slice, then cut each slice diagonally into four triangles. Cut each triangle in half again to make eight pieces from each slice.

Heat the vegetable oil in a large wok to 190°C/375°F, or until a small cube of bread browns in about 30 seconds. Working in batches, fry the prawn triangles for 30–60 seconds, or until they are golden, turning once.

Remove with a slotted spoon and drain on absorbent kitchen paper. Keep the toasts warm. Arrange them on a large serving plate and garnish with sprigs of fresh coriander. Serve immediately.

# Turkey Tetrazzini

INGREDIENTS **Serves 4**

280 g/10 oz green and white tagliatelle
50 g/2 oz butter
4 slices streaky bacon, diced
1 onion, peeled and finely chopped
175 g/6 oz mushrooms, thinly sliced
40 g/1½ oz plain flour
450 ml/¾ pint chicken stock
150 ml/¼ pint double cream
2 tbsp sherry
450 g/1 lb cooked turkey meat, cut into bite-sized pieces
1 tbsp freshly chopped parsley
freshly grated nutmeg
salt and freshly ground black pepper
25 g/1 oz Parmesan cheese, grated

**To garnish:**
freshly chopped parsley
Parmesan cheese, grated

Preheat the oven to 180°C/350°F/Gas Mark 4. Lightly oil a large ovenproof dish. Bring a large saucepan of lightly salted water to the boil. Add the tagliatelle and cook for 7–9 minutes or until 'al dente'. Drain well and reserve.

In a heavy-based saucepan, heat the butter and add the bacon. Cook for 2–3 minutes, or until crisp and golden. Add the onion and mushrooms and cook for 3–4 minutes, or until the vegetables are tender.

Stir in the flour and cook for 2 minutes. Remove from the heat and slowly stir in the stock. Return to the heat and cook, stirring until a smooth, thick sauce has formed. Add the tagliatelle, then pour in the cream and sherry. Add the turkey and parsley. Season to taste with the nutmeg and salt and pepper. Toss well to coat.

Turn the mixture into the prepared dish, spreading evenly. Sprinkle the top with the Parmesan cheese and bake in the preheated oven for 30–35 minutes, or until crisp, golden and bubbling. Garnish with chopped parsley and Parmesan cheese and serve straight from the dish.

HEALTH RATING 🍎🍎

**SUGGESTED ACCOMPANIMENT**
Mediterranean Feast

**PUDDING SUGGESTION**
Chocolate Fudge Sundae

**SUGGESTED ACCOMPANIMENT**
## Mediterranean Feast

Cut the lettuce into four and remove the hard core. Tear into bite-sized pieces and arrange on a large serving platter or four individual plates.

Cook the French beans in boiling salted water for 8 minutes and the potatoes for 10 minutes or until tender. Drain and rinse in cold water until cool, then cut both the beans and potatoes in half with a sharp knife.

Boil the eggs for 10 minutes, then rinse thoroughly under a cold running tap until cool. Remove the shells under water and cut each egg into four. Remove the seeds from the pepper and cut into thin strips and finely chop the onion.

Arrange the beans, potatoes, eggs, peppers and onion on top of the lettuce. Add the tuna, cheese and tomatoes. Sprinkle over the olives and garnish with the basil.

To make the vinaigrette, place all the ingredients in a screw-topped jar and shake vigorously until everything is thoroughly mixed. Spoon 4 tablespoons over the top of the prepared salad and serve the remainder separately.

INGREDIENTS **Serves 4**

- 1 small iceberg lettuce
- 225 g/8 oz French beans
- 225 g/8 oz baby new potatoes, scrubbed
- 4 medium eggs
- 1 green pepper
- 1 medium onion, peeled
- 200 g can tuna in brine, drained and flaked into small pieces
- 50 g/2 oz low-fat hard cheese, such as Edam, cut into small cubes
- 8 ripe but firm cherry tomatoes, quartered
- 50 g/2 oz black pitted olives, halved
- freshly chopped basil, to garnish

**For the lime vinaigrette:**

- 3 tbsp light olive oil
- 2 tbsp white wine vinegar
- 4 tbsp lime juice
- grated rind of 1 lime
- 1 tsp Dijon mustard
- 1-2 tsp caster sugar
- salt and freshly ground black pepper

**PUDDING SUGGESTION**
## Chocolate Fudge Sundae

To make the chocolate fudge sauce, place the chocolate and cream in a heavy-based saucepan and heat gently until the chocolate has melted into the cream. Stir until smooth. Mix the sugar with the flour and salt, then stir in sufficient chocolate mixture to make a smooth paste.

Gradually blend the remaining melted chocolate mixture into the paste, then pour into a clean saucepan. Cook over a low heat, stirring frequently until smooth and thick. Remove from the heat and add the butter and vanilla essence. Stir until smooth, then cool slightly.

To make the sundae, crush the raspberries lightly with a fork and reserve. Spoon a little of the chocolate sauce into the bottom of two sundae glasses. Add a layer of crushed raspberries, then a scoop each of vanilla and chocolate ice cream. Top each one with a scoop of the vanilla ice cream. Pour over the sauce, sprinkle over the almonds and serve with a wafer.

INGREDIENTS **Serves 2**

**For the chocolate fudge sauce:**

- 75 g/3 oz plain dark chocolate, broken into pieces
- 450ml/¾ pint double cream
- 175g/6 oz golden caster sugar
- 25 g/1 oz plain flour
- pinch of salt
- 15 g/½ oz unsalted butter
- 1 tsp vanilla essence

**For the sundae:**

- 125 g/4 oz raspberries, fresh or thawed if frozen
- 3 scoops vanilla ice cream
- 3 scoops chocolate ice cream
- 2 tbsp toasted flaked almonds
- a few wafers, to serve

**ORIENTAL ALTERNATIVE**

## Crispy Aromatic Duck

Mix together the Chinese five spice powder, Szechuan and black peppercorns, cumin seeds and salt. Rub the duck inside and out with the spice mixture. Wrap the duck with clingfilm and place in the refrigerator for 24 hours. Brush any loose spices from the duck. Place the ginger and spring onions into the duck cavity and put the duck on a heatproof plate.

Place a wire rack in a wok and pour in boiling water to a depth of 5 cm/2 inches. Lower the duck and plate on to the rack and cover. Steam gently for 2 hours or until the duck is cooked through, pouring off excess fat from time to time and adding more water, if necessary. Remove the duck, pour off all the liquid and discard the ginger and spring onions. Leave the duck in a cool place for 2 hours, or until it has dried and cooled.

Cut the duck into quarters and dust lightly with cornflour. Heat the oil in a wok or deep-fat fryer to 190°C/375°F, then deep-fry the duck quarters two at a time. Cook the breast for 8–10 minutes and the thighs and legs for 12–14 minutes, or until each piece is heated through. Drain on absorbent kitchen paper, then shred with a fork. Serve immediately with warm Chinese pancakes, spring onion shreds, cucumber slices and hoisin sauce.

INGREDIENTS **Serves 4–6**

- 2 tbsp Chinese five spice powder
- 75 g/3 oz Szechuan peppercorns, lightly crushed
- 25 g/1 oz whole black peppercorns, lightly crushed
- 3 tbsp cumin seeds, lightly crushed
- 200 g/7 oz rock salt
- 2.7 kg/6 lb oven-ready duck
- 7.5 cm/3 inch piece fresh root ginger, peeled and cut into 6 slices
- 6 spring onions, trimmed and cut into 7.5 cm/3 inch lengths
- cornflour for dusting
- 1.1 litres/2 pints groundnut oil

**To serve:**

- warm Chinese pancakes
- spring onion, cut into shreds
- cucumber, cut into slices lengthways
- hoisin sauce

**SUGGESTED ACCOMPANIMENT**

## Layered Cheese & Herb Potato Cake

Preheat the oven to 180°C/350°F/Gas Mark 4. Lightly oil and line the base of a 20.5 cm/8 inch round cake tin with lightly oiled greaseproof or baking parchment paper. Peel and thinly slice the potatoes and reserve. Stir the chives, parsley, cheese and egg yolks together in a small bowl and reserve. Mix the paprika into the breadcrumbs.

Sprinkle the almonds over the base of the lined tin. Cover with half the potatoes, arranging them in layers, then sprinkle with the paprika breadcrumb mixture and season to taste with salt and pepper.

Spoon the cheese and herb mixture over the breadcrumbs with a little more seasoning, then arrange the remaining potatoes on top. Drizzle over the melted butter and press the surface down firmly.

Bake in the preheated oven for 1¼ hours, or until golden and cooked through. Let the tin stand for 10 minutes before carefully turning out and serving in thick wedges. Serve immediately with salad or freshly cooked vegetables.

INGREDIENTS **Serves 4**

- 900 g/2 lb waxy potatoes
- 3 tbsp freshly snipped chives
- 2 tbsp freshly chopped parsley
- 225 g/8 oz mature Cheddar cheese
- 2 large egg yolks
- 1 tsp paprika
- 125 g/4 oz fresh white breadcrumbs
- 50 g/2 oz almonds, toasted and roughly chopped
- 50 g/2 oz butter, melted
- salt and freshly ground black pepper
- mixed salad or steamed vegetables, to serve

# Duck with Berry Sauce

INGREDIENTS **Serves 4**

4 x 175 g/6 oz boneless duck breasts
salt and freshly ground black pepper
tsp sunflower oil

**For the sauce:**

uice of 1 orange
1 bay leaf
3 tbsp redcurrant jelly
150 g/5 oz fresh or frozen mixed berries
2 tbsp dried cranberries or cherries
½ tsp soft light brown sugar
1 tbsp balsamic vinegar
1 tsp freshly chopped mint
sprigs of fresh mint, to garnish

**To serve:**

freshly cooked potatoes
freshly cooked green beans

Remove the skins from the duck breasts and season with a little salt and pepper. Brush a griddle pan with the oil, then heat on the stove until smoking hot.

Place the duck, skinned-side down, in the pan. Cook over a medium high heat for 5 minutes, or until well browned. Turn the duck and cook for 2 minutes. Lower the heat and cook for a further 5–8 minutes, or until cooked, but still slightly pink in the centre. Remove from the pan and keep warm.

While the duck is cooking, make the sauce. Put the orange juice, bay leaf, redcurrant jelly, fresh or frozen and dried berries and sugar in a small griddle pan. Add any juices left in the duck griddle pan to the small pan. Slowly bring to the boil, lower the heat and simmer uncovered for 4–5 minutes until the fruit is soft.

Remove the bay leaf. Stir in the vinegar and chopped mint and season to taste with salt and pepper.

Slice the duck breasts on the diagonal and arrange on serving plates. Spoon over the berry sauce and garnish with sprigs of fresh mint. Serve immediately with the potatoes and green beans.

HEALTH RATING

**ORIENTAL ALTERNATIVE**

Crispy Aromatic Duck

**SUGGESTED ACCOMPANIMENT**

Layered Cheese & Herb Potato Cake

# Hoisin Duck & Greens Stir Fry

INGREDIENTS **Serves 4**

350 g/12 oz duck breasts, skinned and cut into strips
1 medium egg white, beaten
½ tsp salt
1 tsp sesame oil
2 tsp cornflour
2 tbsp groundnut oil
2 tbsp freshly grated root ginger
50 g/2 oz bamboo shoots
50 g/2 oz fine green beans, trimmed
50 g/2 oz pak choi, trimmed
2 tbsp hoisin sauce
1 tsp Chinese rice wine or dry sherry
zest and juice of ½ orange
strips of orange zest, to garnish
freshly steamed egg noodles, to serve

Place the duck strips in a shallow dish, then add the egg white, salt, sesame oil and cornflour. Stir lightly until the duck is coated in the mixture. Cover and chill in the refrigerator for 20 minutes.

Heat the wok until very hot and add the oil. Remove the wok from the heat and add the duck, stirring continuously to prevent the duck from sticking to the wok. Add the ginger and stir-fry for 2 minutes. Add the bamboo shoots, the green beans and the pak choi, and stir-fry for 1–2 minutes until wilted.

Mix together the hoisin sauce, the Chinese rice wine or sherry and the orange zest and juice. Pour into the wok and stir to coat the duck and vegetables. Stir-fry for 1–2 minutes, or until the duck and vegetables are tender. Garnish with the strips of orange zest and serve immediately with freshly steamed egg noodles.

## HEALTH RATING 🍎🍎🍎

**ENTERTAINING ALTERNATIVE**
Duck & Exotic Fruit Stir Fry

**ENTERTAINING ALTERNATIVE**
Teriyaki Duck with Plum Chutney

**ENTERTAINING ALTERNATIVE**
## Duck & Exotic Fruit Stir Fry

INGREDIENTS **Serves 4**

4 duck breast fillets, skin removed and cut into strips
½ tsp Chinese five spice powder
2 tbsp soy sauce
1 tbsp sesame oil
1 tbsp groundnut oil
2 celery stalks, trimmed and diced
225 g can of pineapple chunks, drained
1 mango, peeled, stoned and cut into chunks
125 g/4 oz lychees, peeled if fresh, stoned and halved
125 ml/4 fl oz chicken stock
2 tbsp tomato paste
2 tbsp plum sauce
2 tsp wine vinegar
pinch of soft brown sugar
toasted nuts, to garnish
steamed rice, to serve

Place the duck strips in a shallow bowl. Mix together the Chinese five spice powder, soy sauce and sesame oil, pour over the duck and marinate for 2 hours in the refrigerator. Stir occasionally during that time. Remove the duck from the marinade and reserve.

Heat the wok, add the oil and when hot, stir-fry the marinated duck strips for 4 minutes. Remove from the wok and reserve.

Add the celery to the wok and stir-fry for 2 minutes, then add the pineapple, mango and lychees and stir-fry for a further 3 minutes. Return the duck to the wok.

Mix together the chicken stock, tomato paste, plum sauce, wine vinegar and a pinch of brown sugar. Add to the wok, bring to the boil and simmer, stirring, for 2 minutes. Sprinkle with the nuts and serve immediately with the freshly steamed rice.

**ENTERTAINING ALTERNATIVE**
## Teriyaki Duck with Plum Chutney

INGREDIENTS **Serves 4**

4 tbsp Japanese soy sauce
4 tbsp dry sherry
2 garlic cloves, peeled and finely chopped
2.5 cm/1 inch piece fresh root ginger, peeled and finely chopped
350 g/12 oz skinless duck breast fillets, cut into chunks
2 tbsp groundnut oil
225 g/8 oz carrots, peeled and cut into fine strips
½ cucumber, cut into strips
5 spring onions, trimmed and shredded
toasted almonds, to garnish
freshly cooked egg noodles, to serve

**For the plum chutney:**
25 g/1 oz butter
1 red onion, peeled and finely chopped
2 tsp soft brown sugar
4 plums, stoned and halved
zest and juice of ½ orange
50 g/2 oz raisins

Mix together the soy sauce, sherry, garlic and ginger and pour into a shallow dish. Add the duck chunks and stir until coated in the marinade. Cover and leave in the refrigerator for 30 minutes.

Meanwhile make the plum chutney. Melt the butter in a wok, add the onion and sugar and cook gently over a low heat for 20 minutes. Add the plums, orange zest and juice and simmer for 10 minutes, then stir in the raisins. Spoon into a small bowl and wipe the wok clean. Drain the duck, reserving the marinade.

Heat the wok, add the oil and when hot, add the carrots, cucumber and spring onions. Stir-fry for 2 minutes, or until tender. Remove and reserve.

Add the drained duck to the wok and stir-fry over a high heat for 2 minutes. Return the vegetables to the wok and add the reserved marinade. Stir-fry briefly, until heated through.

Garnish the duck with the toasted almonds and serve immediately with freshly cooked noodles and the plum chutney.

# Duck Lasagna with Porcini & Basil

INGREDIENTS **Serves 6**

- 1.4–1.8 kg/3–4 lb duck, quartered
- 1 onion, unpeeled and quartered
- 2 carrots, peeled and cut into pieces
- 1 celery stalk, cut into pieces
- 1 leek, trimmed and cut into pieces
- 2 garlic cloves, unpeeled and smashed
- 1 tbsp black peppercorns
- 2 bay leaves
- 6–8 sprigs of fresh thyme
- 50 g/2 oz dried porcini mushrooms
- 125 ml/4 oz dry sherry
- 75 g/3 oz butter, diced
- 1 bunch of fresh basil leaves, stripped from stems
- 24 precooked lasagna sheets
- 75 g/3 oz Parmesan cheese, grated
- sprig of parsley, to garnish
- mixed salad, to serve

Preheat the oven to 180°C/350°F/Gas Mark 4, 10 minutes before cooking. Put the duck with the vegetables, garlic, peppercorns, bay leaves and thyme into a large stock pot and cover with cold water. Bring to the boil, skimming off any fat, then reduce the heat and simmer for 1 hour. Transfer the duck to a bowl and cool slightly.

When cool enough to handle, remove the meat from the duck and dice. Return all the bones and trimmings to the simmering stock and continue to simmer for 1 hour. Strain the stock into a large bowl and leave until cold. Remove and discard the fat that has risen to the top of the stock.

Put the porcini in a colander and rinse under cold running water. Leave for 1 minute to dry off, then turn out on to a chopping board and chop finely. Place in a small bowl, then pour over the sherry and leave for about 1 hour, or until the porcini are plump and all the sherry is absorbed.

Heat 25 g/1 oz of the butter in a frying pan. Shred the basil leaves and add to the hot butter, stirring until wilted. Add the soaked porcini and any liquid, mix well and reserve.

Oil a 30.5 x 23 cm/12 x 9 inch-deep baking dish and pour a little stock into the base. Cover with 6–8 lasagna sheets, making sure that the sheets overlap slightly. Continue to layer the pasta with a little stock, duck meat, the mushroom-basil mixture and Parmesan. Add a little butter every other layer.

Cover with tinfoil and bake in the preheated oven for 40–45 minutes, or until cooked. Stand for 10 minutes before serving. Garnish with a sprig of parsley and serve with salad.

HEALTH RATING 🍎🍎

**SUGGESTED ACCOMPANIMENT**

Red Lentil Kedgeree with Avocado & Tomatoes

**PUDDING SUGGESTION**

Chestnut Cake

INGREDIENTS **Serves 4**

- 50 g/5 oz basmati rice
- 50 g/5 oz red lentils
- 5 g/½ oz butter
- tbsp sunflower oil
- medium onion, peeled and chopped
- tsp ground cumin
- 4 cardamom pods, bruised
- bay leaf
- 450 ml/¾ pint vegetable stock
- 1 ripe avocado, peeled, stoned and diced
- 1 tbsp lemon juice
- 4 plum tomatoes, peeled and diced
- 2 tbsp freshly chopped coriander
- salt and freshly ground black pepper
- lemon or lime slices, to garnish

**SUGGESTED ACCOMPANIMENT**

## Red Lentil Kedgeree with Avocado & Tomatoes

Put the rice and lentils in a sieve and rinse under cold running water. Tip into a bowl, then pour over enough cold water to cover and leave to soak for 10 minutes.

Heat the butter and oil in a saucepan. Add the sliced onion and cook gently, stirring occasionally, for 10 minutes until softened. Stir in the cumin, cardamon pods and bay leaf and cook for a further minute, stirring all the time.

Drain the rice and lentils, rinse again and add to the onions in the saucepan. Stir in the vegetable stock and bring to the boil. Reduce the heat, cover the saucepan and simmer for 14–15 minutes, or until the rice and lentils are tender.

Place the diced avocado in a bowl and toss with the lemon juice. Stir in the tomatoes and chopped coriander. Season to taste with salt and pepper.

Fluff up the rice with a fork, spoon into a warmed serving dish and spoon the avocado mixture on top. Garnish with lemon or lime slices and serve.

**PUDDING SUGGESTION**

## Chestnut Cake

Preheat the oven to 150°C/300°F/Gas Mark 2. Oil and line a 23 cm/9 inch springform tin. Beat together the butter and sugar until light and fluffy. Add the chestnut purée and beat. Gradually add the eggs, beating after each addition. Sift in the flour with the baking powder and cloves. Add the fennel seeds and beat. The mixture should drop easily from a wooden spoon when tapped against the side of the bowl. If not, add a little milk.

Beat in the raisins and pine nuts. Spoon the mixture into the prepared tin and smooth the top. Transfer to the centre of the oven and bake in the preheated oven for 55–60 minutes, or until a skewer inserted in the centre of the cake comes out clean. Remove from the oven and leave in the tin.

Meanwhile, mix together the icing sugar and lemon juice in a small saucepan until smooth. Heat gently until hot, but not boiling. Using a cocktail stick or skewer, poke holes into the cake all over. Pour the hot syrup evenly over the cake and leave to soak into the cake. Decorate with pared strips of lemon and serve.

INGREDIENTS **Serves 8–10**

- 175 g/6 oz butter, softened
- 175 g/6 oz caster sugar
- 250 g can sweetened chestnut purée
- 3 medium eggs, lightly beaten
- 175 g/6 oz plain flour
- 1 tsp baking powder
- pinch of ground cloves
- 1 tsp fennel seeds, crushed
- 75 g/3 oz raisins
- 50 g/2 oz pine nuts, toasted
- 125 g/4 oz icing sugar
- 5 tbsp lemons juice
- pared strips of lemon rind, to decorate

**SUGGESTED ACCOMPANIMENT**
## Cabbage Timbale

INGREDIENTS **Serves 4–6**

1 small Savoy cabbage, weighing about 350 g/12 oz
salt and freshly ground black pepper
2 tbsp olive oil
1 leek, trimmed and chopped
1 garlic clove, peeled and crushed
75 g/3 oz long-grain rice
200 g can chopped tomatoes
300 ml/½ pint vegetable stock
400 g can flageolet beans, drained and rinsed
75 g/3 oz Cheddar cheese, grated
1 tbsp freshly chopped oregano

**To garnish:**
Greek yogurt with paprika
tomato wedges

Preheat the oven to 180°C/350°F/Gas Mark 4, 10 minutes before required. Remove six of the outer leaves of the cabbage. Cut off the thickest part of the stalk and blanch the leaves in lightly salted boiling water for 2 minutes. Lift out with a slotted spoon and briefly rinse under cold water and reserve.

Remove the stalks from the rest of the cabbage leaves. Shred the leaves and blanch in the boiling water for 1 minute. Drain, rinse under cold water and pat dry on absorbent kitchen paper.

Heat the oil in a frying pan and cook the leek and garlic for 5 minutes. Stir in the rice, chopped tomatoes with their juice and stock. Bring to the boil, cover and simmer for 15 minutes. Remove the lid and simmer for a further 4–5 minutes, stirring frequently, until the liquid is absorbed and the rice is tender. Stir in the flageolet beans, cheese and oregano. Season to taste with salt and pepper.

Line an oiled 1.1 litre/2 pint pudding basin with some of the large cabbage leaves, overlapping them slightly. Fill the basin with alternate layers of rice mixture and shredded leaves, pressing down well. Cover the top with the remaining leaves. Cover with oiled tinfoil and bake in the preheated for 30 minutes. Leave to stand for 10 minutes, then turn out, cut into wedges and serve with yogurt sprinkled with paprika and tomato wedges.

**STARTER SUGGESTION**
## Oriental Minced Chicken on Rocket & Tomato

INGREDIENTS **Serves 4**

2 shallots, peeled
1 garlic clove, peeled
1 carrot, peeled
50 g/2 oz water chestnuts
1 tsp oil
350 g/12 oz fresh chicken mince
1 tsp Chinese five spice powder
pinch chilli powder
1 tsp soy sauce
1 tbsp fish sauce
8 cherry tomatoes
50 g/2 oz rocket

Finely chop the shallots and garlic. Cut the carrot into matchsticks, thinly slice the water chestnuts and reserve. Heat the oil in a wok or heavy-based frying pan and add the chicken. Stir-fry for 3–4 minutes over a moderately high heat, breaking up any large pieces of chicken.

Add the garlic and shallots and cook for 2–3 minutes until softened. Sprinkle over the Chinese five spice powder and the chilli powder and continue to cook for about 1 minute.

Add the carrot, water chestnuts, soy and fish sauce and 2 tablespoons of water. Stir-fry for a further 2 minutes. Remove from the heat and reserve to cool slightly.

Deseed the tomatoes and cut into thin wedges. Toss with the rocket and divide between four serving plates. Spoon the warm chicken mixture over the rocket and tomato wedges and serve immediately to prevent the rocket from wilting.

# Marinated Pheasant with Grilled Polenta

INGREDIENTS **Serves 4**

3 tbsp extra virgin olive oil
1 tbsp freshly chopped rosemary or sage leaves
½ tsp ground cinnamon
grated zest of 1 orange
salt and freshly ground black pepper
8 pheasant or wood pigeon breasts
600 ml/1 pint water
125 g/4 oz quick-cook polenta
2 tbsp butter, diced
40 g/1½ oz Parmesan cheese, grated
1–2 tbsp freshly chopped parsley
assorted salad leaves, to serve

Preheat grill just before cooking. Blend 2 tablespoons of the olive oil with the chopped rosemary or sage, cinnamon and orange zest and season to taste with salt and pepper.

Place the pheasant breasts in a large, shallow dish, pour over the oil and marinate until required, turning occasionally.

Bring the water and 1 teaspoon of salt to the boil in a large, heavy-based saucepan. Slowly whisk in the polenta in a thin, steady stream. Reduce the heat and simmer for 5–10 minutes, or until very thick, stirring constantly.

Stir the butter and cheese into the polenta, the parsley and a little black pepper.

Turn the polenta out on to a lightly oiled, non-stick baking tray and spread into an even layer about 2 cm/¾ inch thick. Leave to cool, then chill in the refrigerator for about 1 hour, or until the polenta is chilled.

Turn the cold polenta on to a work surface. Cut into 10 cm/4 inch squares. Brush with olive oil and arrange on a grill rack. Grill for 2–3 minutes on each side until crisp and golden, then cut each square into triangles and keep warm.

Transfer the marinated pheasant breasts to the grill rack and grill for 5 minutes, or until crisp and beginning to colour, turning once. Serve the pheasants immediately with the polenta triangles and salad leaves.

HEALTH RATING 🍎🍎

**SUGGESTED ACCOMPANIMENT**
Cabbage Timbale

**STARTER SUGGESTION**
Oriental Minced Chicken on Rocket & Tomato

# Rabbit Italian

INGREDIENTS **Serves 4**

450 g/1 lb diced rabbit, thawed if frozen
6 rashers streaky bacon
1 garlic clove, peeled
1 onion, peeled
1 carrot, peeled
1 celery stalk
25 g/1 oz butter
2 tbsp olive oil
400 g can chopped tomatoes
150 ml/¼ pint red wine
salt and freshly ground black pepper
125 g/4 oz mushrooms

**To serve:**
freshly cooked pasta
green salad

Trim the rabbit if necessary. Chop the bacon and reserve. Chop the garlic and onion and slice the carrot thinly, then trim the celery and chop.

Heat the butter and 1 tablespoon of the oil in a large saucepan and brown the rabbit for 5 minutes, stirring frequently, until sealed all over. Transfer the rabbit to a plate and reserve.

Add the garlic, bacon, celery, carrot and onion to the saucepan and cook for a further 5 minutes, stirring occasionally, until softened, then return the rabbit to the saucepan and pour over the tomatoes with their juice and the wine. Season to taste with salt and pepper. Bring to the boil, cover, reduce the heat and simmer for 45 minutes.

Meanwhile, wipe the mushrooms and if large, cut in half. Heat the remaining oil in a small frying pan and sauté the mushrooms for 2 minutes. Drain, then add to the rabbit and cook for 15 minutes, or until the rabbit is tender. Season to taste and serve immediately with freshly cooked pasta and a green salad.

HEALTH RATING 🍎🍎🍎

**ENTERTAINING ALTERNATIVE**
Braised Rabbit with Red Peppers

**SUGGESTED ACCOMPANIMENT**
Rice with Squash & Sage

**ENTERTAINING ALTERNATIVE**
## Braised Rabbit with Red Peppers

INGREDIENTS **Serves 4**

1.1 kg/2½ lb rabbit pieces
125 ml/4 fl oz olive oil
grated zest and juice of 1 lemon
2–3 tbsp freshly chopped thyme
salt and freshly ground black pepper
1 onion, peeled and thinly sliced
4 red peppers, deseeded and cut into 2.5 cm/1 inch pieces
2 garlic cloves, peeled and crushed
400 g can strained, crushed tomatoes
1 tsp brown sugar
freshly cooked polenta or creamy mashed potatoes, to serve

Place the rabbit pieces in a shallow dish with half the olive oil, the lemon zest and juice, thyme, and some black pepper. Turn until well coated, then cover and leave to marinate for about 1 hour.

Heat half the remaining oil in a large, heavy-based casserole dish, add the onion and cook for 5 minutes, then add the peppers and cook for a further 12–15 minutes, or until softened, stirring occasionally. Stir in the garlic, crushed tomatoes and brown sugar and cook, covered, until soft, stirring occasionally.

Heat the remaining oil in a large frying pan, drain the rabbit, reserving the marinade, and pat the rabbit dry with absorbent kitchen paper. Add the rabbit to the pan and cook on all sides until golden. Transfer the rabbit to the casserole dish and mix to cover with the tomato sauce.

Add the reserved marinade to the frying pan and cook, stirring to loosen any browned bits from the pan. Add the marinade to the rabbit and stir gently.

Cover the dish and simmer for 30 minutes or until the rabbit is tender. Serve the rabbit and the vegetable mixture on a bed of polenta or creamy mashed potatoes.

**SUGGESTED ACCOMPANIMENT**
## Rice with Squash & Sage

INGREDIENTS **Serves 4–6**

450 g/1 lb butternut squash
75 g/3 oz unsalted butter
1 small onion, peeled and finely chopped
3 garlic cloves, peeled and crushed
2 tbsp freshly chopped sage
1 litre/1¾ pints vegetable or chicken stock
450 g/1 lb Arborio rice
50 g/2 oz pine nuts, toasted
25 g/1 oz freshly grated Parmesan cheese
freshly snipped chives, to garnish
salt and freshly ground black pepper

Peel the squash, cut in half lengthways and remove seeds and stringy flesh. Cut remaining flesh into small cubes and reserve.

Heat the wok, add the butter and heat until foaming, then add the onion, garlic and sage and stir-fry for 1 minute. Add the squash to the wok and stir-fry for a further 10–12 minutes, or until the squash is tender. Remove from the heat.

Meanwhile, bring the vegetable or chicken stock to the boil and add the rice. Cook for 8–10 minutes, or until the rice is just tender but still quite wet.

Add the cooked rice to the squash mixture. Stir in the pine nuts and Parmesan, season to taste with salt and pepper. Garnish with snipped chives and serve immediately.

# Vegetables & Salads

You don't have to be vegetarian to appreciate these mouthwatering recipes, but if you are, you're in for a real treat. With lots of delicious main meals as well as lots of accompaniments and starters, these endlessly adaptable recipes will suit any occasion. From summer salads to winter warmers, even the meat-lovers in your family won't be able to resist.

# Red Pepper & Basil Tart

INGREDIENTS **Serves 4–6**

**For the olive pastry:**

225 g/8 oz plain flour
pinch of salt
50 g/2 oz pitted black olives, finely chopped
1 medium egg, lightly beaten, plus 1 egg yolk
3 tbsp olive oil

**For the filling:**

2 large red peppers, quartered and deseeded
175 g/6 oz mascarpone cheese
4 tbsp milk
2 medium eggs
3 tbsp freshly chopped basil
salt and freshly ground black pepper
sprig of fresh basil, to garnish
mixed salad, to serve

Preheat the oven to 200°C/400°F/Gas Mark 6, 15 minutes before cooking. Sift the flour and salt into a bowl and make a well in the centre. Stir together the egg, oil and 1 tablespoon of tepid water. Add to the dry ingredients, drop in the olives and mix to a dough. Knead on a lightly floured surface for a few seconds until smooth, then wrap in clingfilm and chill in the refrigerator for 30 minutes.

Roll out the pastry and use to line a 23 cm/ 9 inch loose-bottomed fluted flan tin. Lightly prick the base with a fork. Cover and chill in the refrigerator for 20 minutes.

Cook the peppers under a hot grill for 10 minutes, or until the skins are blackened and blistered. Put the peppers in a plastic bag, cool for 10 minutes, then remove the skin and slice.

Line the pastry case with tinfoil or greaseproof paper weighed down with baking beans and bake in the preheated oven for 10 minutes. Remove the tinfoil and beans and bake for a further 5 minutes. Reduce the oven temperature to 180°C/350°F/Gas Mark 4.

Beat the mascarpone cheese until smooth. Gradually add the milk and eggs. Stir in the peppers, basil and season to taste with salt and pepper. Spoon into the flan case and bake for 25–30 minutes, or until lightly set. Garnish with a sprig of fresh basil and serve immediately with a mixed salad.

HEALTH RATING

**SPEEDY ALTERNATIVE**

Tomato & Courgette Herb Tart

**SUGGESTED ACCOMPANIMENT**

Tortellini & Summer Vegetable Salad

INGREDIENTS **Serves 4**

- 4 tbsp olive oil
- 1 onion, peeled and finely chopped
- 3 garlic cloves, peeled and crushed
- 400 g/14 oz prepared puff pastry, thawed if frozen
- 1 small egg, beaten
- 2 tbsp freshly chopped rosemary
- 2 tbsp freshly chopped parsley
- 175 g/6 oz rindless fresh soft goats' cheese
- 4 ripe plum tomatoes, sliced
- 1 medium courgette, trimmed and sliced
- thyme sprigs, to garnish

## SPEEDY ALTERNATIVE
## Tomato & Courgette Herb Tart

Preheat the oven to 230°C/450°F/Gas Mark 8. Heat 2 tablespoons of the oil in a large frying pan. Fry the onion and garlic for about 4 minutes until softened and reserve.

Roll out the pastry on a lightly floured surface, and cut out a 30.5 cm/12 inch circle. Brush the pastry with a little beaten egg, then prick all over with a fork. Transfer on to a dampened baking sheet and bake in the preheated oven for 10 minutes.

Turn the pastry over and brush with a little more egg. Bake for 5 more minutes, then remove from the oven. Mix together the onion, garlic and herbs with the goats' cheese and spread over the pastry.

Arrange the tomatoes and courgettes over the goats' cheese and drizzle with the remaining oil. Bake for 20–25 minutes, or until the pastry is golden brown and the topping is bubbling. Garnish with the thyme sprigs and serve immediately.

## SUGGESTED ACCOMPANIMENT
## Tortellini & Summer Vegetable Salad

INGREDIENTS **Serves 6**

- 350 g/12 oz mixed green and plain cheese-filled fresh tortellini
- 150 ml/¼ pint extra virgin olive oil
- 225 g/8 oz fine green beans, trimmed
- 175 g/6 oz broccoli florets
- 1 yellow or red pepper, deseeded and thinly sliced
- 1 red onion, peeled and sliced
- 175 g jar marinated artichoke hearts, drained and halved
- 2 tbsp capers
- 75 g/3 oz dry-cured pitted black olives
- 3 tbsp raspberry or balsamic vinegar
- 1 tbsp Dijon mustard
- 1 tsp soft brown sugar
- salt and freshly ground black pepper
- 2 tbsp freshly chopped basil or flat leaf parsley
- 2 quartered hard-boiled eggs, to garnish

Bring a large pan of lightly salted water to a rolling boil. Add the tortellini and cook according to the packet instructions, or until 'al dente'.

Using a large slotted spoon, transfer the tortellini to a colander to drain. Rinse under cold running water and drain again. Transfer to a large bowl and toss with 2 tablespoons of the olive oil.

Return the pasta water to the boil and drop in the green beans and broccoli florets. Blanch them for 2 minutes, or until just beginning to soften. Drain, rinse under cold running water and drain again thoroughly. Add the vegetables to the reserved tortellini. Add the pepper, onion, artichoke hearts, capers and olives to the bowl and stir lightly.

Whisk together the vinegar, mustard and brown sugar in a bowl and season to taste with salt and pepper. Slowly whisk in the remaining olive oil to form a thick, creamy dressing. Pour over the tortellini and vegetables, add the chopped basil or parsley and stir until lightly coated. Transfer to a shallow serving dish or salad bowl. Garnish with the hard-boiled egg quarters and serve.

**ENTERTAINING ALTERNATIVE**
## French Onion Tart

INGREDIENTS **Serves 4**

**Quick flaky pastry:**

125 g/4 oz butter
175 g/6 oz plain flour
pinch of salt

**For the filling:**

2 tbsp olive oil
4 large onions, peeled and thinly sliced
3 tbsp white wine vinegar
2 tbsp muscovado sugar
a little beaten egg or milk
175 g/6 oz Cheddar cheese, grated
salt and freshly ground black pepper

Preheat the oven to 200°C/400°F/Gas Mark 6. Place the butter in the freezer for 30 minutes. Sift the flour and salt into a large bowl. Remove the butter from the freezer and grate using the coarse side of a grater, dipping the butter in the flour every now and again to make it easier to grate.

Mix the butter into the flour, using a knife, making sure all the butter is thoroughly coated with flour. Add 2 tablespoons of cold water and continue to mix, bringing the mixture together. Use your hands to complete the mixing. Add a little more water if needed to leave a clean bowl. Place the pastry in a polythene bag and chill in the refrigerator for 30 minutes.

Heat the oil in a large frying pan, then fry the onions for 10 minutes, stirring occasionally until softened. Stir in the white wine vinegar and sugar. Increase the heat and stir frequently for another 4–5 minutes until the onions turn a deep caramel colour. Cook for another 5 minutes, then reserve to cool.

On a lightly floured surface, roll out the pastry to a 35.5 cm/14 inch circle. Wrap over a rolling pin and move the circle on to a baking sheet.

Sprinkle half the cheese over the pastry, leaving a 5 cm/2 inch border around the edge, then spoon the caramelised onions over the cheese.

Fold the uncovered pastry edges over the edge of the filling to form a rim and brush the rim with beaten egg or milk.

Season to taste with salt and pepper. Sprinkle over the remaining Cheddar and bake for 20–25 minutes. Transfer to a large plate and serve immediately.

**SUGGESTED ACCOMPANIMENT**
## Roasted Mixed Vegetables with Garlic & Herb Sauce

INGREDIENTS **Serves 4**

1 large garlic bulb
1 large onion, peeled and cut into wedges
4 small carrots, peeled and quartered
4 small parsnips, peeled
6 small potatoes, scrubbed and halved
1 fennel bulb, thickly sliced
4 sprigs of fresh rosemary
4 sprigs of fresh thyme
2 tbsp olive oil
salt and freshly ground black pepper
200 g/7 oz low-fat soft cheese with herbs and garlic
4 tbsp milk
zest of ½ lemon
sprigs of thyme, to garnish

Preheat the oven to 220°C/425°F/Gas Mark 7. Cut the garlic in half horizontally. Put into a large roasting tin with all the vegetables and herbs.

Add the oil, season well with salt and pepper and toss together to coat lightly in the oil.

Cover with tinfoil and roast in the preheated oven for 50 minutes. Remove the tinfoil and cook for a further 30 minutes until all the vegetables are tender and slightly charred.

Remove the tin from the oven and allow to cool.

In a small saucepan, melt the low-fat soft cheese together with the milk and lemon zest.

Remove the garlic from the roasting tin and squeeze the flesh into a bowl. Mash thoroughly then add to the sauce. Heat through gently. Season the vegetables to taste. Pour some sauce into small ramekins and garnish with 4 sprigs of thyme. Serve immediately with the roasted vegetables and the sauce to dip.

# Leek & Potato Tart

INGREDIENTS **Serves 6**

225 g/8 oz plain flour
pinch of salt
150 g/5 oz butter, cubed
50 g/2 oz walnuts, very finely chopped
1 large egg yolk

**For the filling:**

450 g/1 lb leeks, trimmed and thinly sliced
40 g/1½ oz butter
450 g/1 lb large new potatoes, scrubbed
300 ml/½ pint soured cream
3 medium eggs, lightly beaten
175 g/6 oz Gruyère cheese, grated
freshly grated nutmeg
salt and freshly ground black pepper
fresh chives, to garnish

Preheat the oven to 200°C/400°F/Gas Mark 6, about 15 minutes before baking. Sift the flour and salt into a bowl. Rub in the butter until the mixture resembles breadcrumbs. Stir in the nuts. Mix together the egg yolk and 3 tablespoons of cold water. Sprinkle over the dry ingredients and mix to form a dough.

Knead on a lightly floured surface for a few seconds, then wrap in clingfilm and chill in the refrigerator for 20 minutes. Roll out and use to line a 20.5 cm/8 inch spring-form tin or a very deep flan tin. Chill for a further 30 minutes.

Cook the leeks in the butter over a high heat for 2–3 minutes, stirring constantly. Lower the heat, cover and cook for 25 minutes until soft, stirring occasionally. Remove the leeks from the heat.

Cook the potatoes in boiling salted water for 15 minutes, or until almost tender. Drain and thickly slice and add to the leeks. Stir the soured cream into the leeks and potatoes, followed by the eggs, cheese, nutmeg and salt and pepper. Pour into the pastry case and bake on the middle shelf in the preheated oven for 20 minutes.

Reduce the oven temperature to 190°C/375°F/Gas Mark 5 and cook for a further 30–35 minutes or until the filling is set. Garnish with chives and serve immediately.

HEALTH RATING 

**ENTERTAINING ALTERNATIVE**

French Onion Tart

**SUGGESTED ACCOMPANIMENT**

Roasted Mixed Vegetables with Garlic & Herb Sauce

# Potato & Goats' Cheese Tart

INGREDIENTS **Serves 6**

275 g/10 oz prepared shortcrust pastry, thawed if frozen
550 g/1¼ lb small waxy potatoes
salt and freshly ground black pepper
beaten egg, for brushing
2 tbsp sun-dried tomato paste
¼ tsp chilli powder, or to taste
1 large egg
150 ml/¼ pint soured cream
150 ml/¼ pint milk
2 tbsp freshly snipped chives
300 g/11 oz goats' cheese, sliced
salad and warm crusty bread, to serve

Preheat the oven to 190°C/375°F/Gas Mark 5, about 10 minutes before cooking. Roll the pastry out on a lightly floured surface and use to line a 23 cm/9 inch fluted flan tin. Chill in the refrigerator for 30 minutes.

Scrub the potatoes, place in a large saucepan of lightly salted water and bring to the boil. Simmer for 10–15 minutes, or until the potatoes are tender. Drain and reserve until cool enough to handle.

Line the pastry case with greaseproof paper and baking beans or crumpled tinfoil and bake blind in the preheated oven for 15 minutes. Remove from the oven and discard the paper and beans or tinfoil. Brush the base with a little beaten egg, then return to the oven and cook for a further 5 minutes. Remove from the oven.

Cut the potatoes into 1 cm/½ inch thick slices and reserve. Spread the sun-dried tomato paste over the base of the pastry case, sprinkle with the chilli powder, then arrange the potato slices on top in a decorative pattern.

Beat together the egg, soured cream, milk and chives, then season to taste with salt and pepper. Pour over the potatoes. Arrange the goats' cheese on top of the potatoes. Bake in the preheated oven for 30 minutes until golden brown and set. Serve immediately with salad and warm bread.

HEALTH RATING 🍎

**SUGGESTED ACCOMPANIMENT**
Stuffed Tomatoes with Grilled Polenta

**PUDDING SUGGESTION**
Chocolate Lemon Tartlets

**SUGGESTED ACCOMPANIMENT**

## Stuffed Tomatoes with Grilled Polenta

INGREDIENTS **Serves 4**

**For the polenta:**

300 ml/½ pint vegetable stock
salt and freshly ground black pepper
50 g/2 oz quick-cook polenta
15 g/½ oz butter

**For the stuffed tomatoes:**

4 large tomatoes
1 tbsp olive oil
1 garlic clove, peeled and crushed
1 bunch spring onions, trimmed and finely chopped
2 tbsp freshly chopped parsley
2 tbsp freshly chopped basil
2 slices Parma ham, cut into thin slivers
50 g/2 oz fresh white breadcrumbs
snipped chives, to garnish

Preheat the grill just before cooking. To make the polenta, pour the stock into a saucepan. Add a pinch of salt and bring to the boil. Pour in the polenta in a fine stream, stirring all the time. Simmer for about 15 minutes, or until very thick. Stir in the butter and add a little black pepper. Turn the polenta out on to a chopping board and spread to a thickness of just over 1 cm/½ inch. Cool, cover with clingfilm and chill in the refrigerator for 30 minutes.

To make the stuffed tomatoes, cut the tomatoes in half then scoop out the seeds and press through a fine sieve to extract the juices. Season the insides of the tomatoes with salt and pepper and reserve. Heat the olive oil in a saucepan and gently fry the garlic and spring onions for 3 minutes. Add the tomatoes' juices and bubble for 3–4 minutes until most of the liquid has evaporated. Stir in the herbs, Parma ham and a little black pepper with half the breadcrumbs. Spoon into the hollowed out tomatoes and reserve.

Cut the polenta into 5 cm/2 inch squares, then cut each in half diagonally to make triangles. Put the triangles on a piece of tinfoil on the grill rack and grill for 4–5 minutes on each side, until golden. Cover and keep warm. Grill the tomatoes under a medium-hot grill for about 4 minutes – any exposed Parma ham will become crisp. Sprinkle with the remaining breadcrumbs and grill for 1–2 minutes, or until the breadcrumbs are golden brown. Garnish with snipped chives and serve immediately with the grilled polenta.

**PUDDING SUGGESTION**

## Chocolate Lemon Tartlets

INGREDIENTS **Makes 10**

1 quantity sweet shortcrust pastry (see page 10)
175 ml/6 fl oz double cream
175 g/6 oz plain dark chocolate, chopped
2 tbsp butter, diced
1 tsp vanilla essence
350 g/12 oz lemon curd
225 ml/8 fl oz prepared custard sauce
225 ml/8 fl oz single cream
½–1 tsp almond essence

**To decorate:**

grated chocolate
toasted flaked almonds

Preheat the oven to 200°C/400°F/Gas Mark 6, 15 minutes before baking. Roll the prepared pastry out on a lightly floured surface and use to line 10 x 7.5 cm/3 inch tartlet tins. Place a small piece of crumpled tinfoil in each and bake blind in the preheated oven for 12 minutes. Remove from the oven and leave to cool.

Bring the cream to the boil, then remove from the heat and add the chocolate all at once. Stir until smooth and melted. Beat in the butter and vanilla essence, pour into the tartlets and leave to cool.

Beat the lemon curd until soft and spoon a thick layer over the chocolate in each tartlet, spreading gently to the edges. Do not chill in the refrigerator or the chocolate will be too firm. Place the prepared custard sauce into a large bowl and gradually whisk in the cream and almond essence until the custard is smooth and runny. To serve, spoon a little custard onto a plate and place a tartlet in the centre. Sprinkle with grated chocolate and almonds, then serve.

# Roasted Vegetable Pie

INGREDIENTS **Serves 4**

225 g/8 oz plain flour
pinch of salt
50 g/2 oz white vegetable fat or lard, cut into squares
50 g/2 oz butter, cut into squares
2 tsp herbes de Provence
1 red pepper, deseeded and halved
1 green pepper, deseeded and halved
1 yellow pepper, deseeded and halved
3 tbsp extra virgin olive oil
1 aubergine, trimmed and sliced
1 courgette, trimmed and halved lengthways
1 leek, trimmed and cut into chunks
1 medium egg, beaten
125 g/4 oz fresh mozzarella cheese, sliced
salt and freshly ground black pepper
sprigs of mixed herbs, to garnish

Preheat the oven to 220°C/425°F/Gas Mark 7. Sift the flour and salt into a large bowl, add the fats and mix lightly. Using the fingertips rub into the flour until the mixture resembles breadcrumbs. Stir in the herbes de Provence. Sprinkle over a tablespoon of cold water and with a knife start bringing the dough together – it may be necessary to use the hands for the final stage. If the dough does not form a ball instantly, add a little more water. Place the pastry in a polythene bag and chill for 30 minutes.

Place the peppers on a baking tray and sprinkle with 1 tablespoon of oil. Roast in the preheated oven for 20 minutes or until the skins start to blacken. Brush the aubergines, courgettes and leeks with oil and place on another baking tray. Roast in the oven with the peppers for 20 minutes. Place the blackened peppers in a polythene bag and leave the skin to loosen for 5 minutes. When cool enough to handle, peel the skins off the peppers.

Roll out half the pastry on a lightly floured surface and use to line a 20.5 cm/8 inch round pie dish. Line the pastry with greaseproof paper and fill with baking beans or rice and bake blind for about 10 minutes. Remove the beans and the paper, then brush the base with a little of the beaten egg. Return to the oven for 5 minutes. Layer the cooked vegetables and the cheese in the pastry case, seasoning each layer. Roll out the remaining pastry on a lightly floured surface, and cut out the lid 5 mm/¼ inch wider than the dish. Brush the rim with the beaten egg, lay the pastry lid on top and press to seal. Knock the edges with the back of a knife, then cut a slit in the lid and brush with the beaten egg. Bake for 30 minutes. Transfer to a large serving dish, garnish with sprigs of mixed herbs and serve immediately.

HEALTH RATING

**WINTER ALTERNATIVE**
Vegetable Cassoulet

**SUGGESTED ACCOMPANIMENT**
Carrot, Celeriac & Sesame Seed Salad

INGREDIENTS **Serves 6**

125 g/4 oz dried haricot beans, soaked overnight
2 tbsp olive oil
2 garlic cloves, peeled and chopped
225 g/8 oz baby onions, peeled and halved
2 carrots, peeled and diced
2 celery sticks, trimmed and finely chopped
1 red pepper, deseeded and chopped
175 g/6 oz mixed mushrooms, sliced
1 tbsp each freshly chopped rosemary, thyme and sage
150 ml/¼ pint red wine
4 tbsp tomato purée
1 tbsp dark soy sauce
salt and freshly ground black pepper
50 g/2 oz fresh breadcrumbs
1 tbsp freshly chopped parsley
basil sprigs, to garnish

**WINTER ALTERNATIVE**
## Vegetable Cassoulet

Preheat the oven to 190°C/375°F/Gas Mark 5. Drain the haricot beans and place in a saucepan with 1.1 litres/2 pints of fresh water. Bring to the boil and boil rapidly for 10 minutes. Reduce the heat and simmer gently for 45 minutes. Drain the beans, reserving 300 ml/½ pint of the liquid.

Heat 1 tablespoon of the oil in a flameproof casserole dish and add the garlic, onions, carrot, celery and red pepper. Cook gently for 10–12 minutes until tender and starting to brown. Add a little water if the vegetables start to stick. Add the mushrooms and cook for a further 5 minutes until softened. Add the herbs and stir briefly.

Stir in the red wine and boil rapidly for about 5 minutes until reduced and syrupy. Stir in the reserved beans and their liquid, tomato purée and soy sauce. Season to taste with salt and pepper.

Mix together the breadcrumbs and parsley with the remaining 1 tablespoon of oil. Scatter this mixture evenly over the top of the stew. Cover loosely with foil, transfer to the preheated oven and cook for 30 minutes. Carefully remove the foil and cook for a further 15–20 minutes until the topping is crisp and golden. Serve immediately, garnished with basil sprigs.

INGREDIENTS **Serves 6**

225 g/8 oz celeriac
225 g/8 oz carrots, peeled
50 g/2 oz seedless raisins
2 tbsp sesame seeds
freshly chopped parsley, to garnish

**Lemon & chilli dressing:**

grated rind of 1 lemon
4 tbsp lemon juice
2 tbsp sunflower oil
2 tbsp clear honey
1 red bird's eye chilli, deseeded and finely chopped
salt and freshly ground black pepper

**SUGGESTED ACCOMPANIMENT**
## Carrot, Celeriac & Sesame Seed Salad

Slice the celeriac into thin matchsticks. Place in a small saucepan of boiling salted water and boil for 2 minutes.

Drain and rinse the celeriac in cold water and place in a mixing bowl. Finely grate the carrot. Add the carrot and the raisins to the celeriac in the bowl.

Place the sesame seeds under a hot grill or dry-fry in a frying pan for 1–2 minutes until golden brown, then leave to cool.

Make the dressing by whisking together the lemon rind, lemon juice, oil, honey, chilli and seasoning or by shaking thoroughly in a screw-topped jar.

Pour 2 tablespoons of the dressing over the salad and toss well. Turn into a serving dish and sprinkle over the toasted sesame seeds and chopped parsley. Serve the remaining dressing separately.

# Spiced Couscous & Vegetables

INGREDIENTS **Serves 4**

1 tbsp olive oil
1 large shallot, peeled and finely chopped
1 garlic clove, peeled and finely chopped
1 small red pepper, deseeded and cut into strips
1 small yellow pepper, deseeded and cut into strips
1 small aubergine, diced
1 tsp each turmeric, ground cumin, ground cinnamon and paprika
2 tsp ground coriander
large pinch saffron strands
2 tomatoes, peeled, deseeded and diced
2 tbsp lemon juice
225 g/8 oz couscous
225 ml/8 fl oz vegetable stock
2 tbsp raisins
2 tbsp whole almonds
2 tbsp freshly chopped parsley
2 tbsp freshly chopped coriander
salt and freshly ground black pepper

Heat the oil in a large frying pan, add the shallot and garlic and cook for 2–3 minutes until softened. Add the peppers and aubergine and reduce the heat.

Cook for 8–10 minutes until the vegetables are tender, adding a little water if necessary.

Test a piece of aubergine to ensure it is cooked through. Add all the spices and cook for a further minute, stirring.

Increase the heat and add the tomatoes and lemon juice. Cook for 2–3 minutes until the tomatoes have started to break down. Remove from the heat and leave to cool slightly.

Meanwhile, put the couscous into a large bowl. Bring the stock to the boil in a saucepan, then pour over the couscous. Stir well and cover with a clean tea towel.

Leave to stand for 7–8 minutes until all the stock is absorbed and the couscous is tender.

Uncover the couscous and fluff with a fork. Stir in the vegetable and spice mixture along with the raisins, almonds, parsley and coriander. Season to taste with salt and pepper and serve.

HEALTH RATING 🍎🍎🍎🍎

**SPICY ALTERNATIVE**
Black Bean Chilli with Avocado Salsa

**ENTERTAINING ALTERNATIVE**
Baby Onion Risotto

## PICY ALTERNATIVE
# 3lack Bean Chilli with Avocado Salsa

NGREDIENTS **Serves 4**

50 g/9 oz black beans
and black-eye beans,
soaked overnight
tbsp olive oil
large onion, peeled and
finely chopped
red pepper, deseeded and diced
garlic cloves, peeled and
finely chopped
red chilli, deseeded and
finely chopped

2 tsp chilli powder
1 tsp ground cumin
2 tsp ground coriander
400 g can chopped tomatoes
450 ml/¾ pint
vegetable stock
1 small ripe avocado, diced
½ small red onion, peeled
and finely chopped
2 tbsp freshly
chopped coriander

juice of 1 lime
1 small tomato, peeled,
deseeded and diced
salt and freshly ground
black pepper
25 g/1 oz dark chocolate

**To garnish:**
crème fraîche
lime slices
sprigs of coriander

)rain the beans and place in a large saucepan with at least twice their volume of fresh water. Bring lowly to the boil, skimming off any froth that rises to the surface. Boil rapidly for 10 minutes, then educe the heat and simmer for about 45 minutes, adding more water if necessary. Drain and reserve.

Heat the oil in a large saucepan and add the onion and pepper. Cook for 3–4 minutes until softened. Add the garlic and chilli. Cook for 5 minutes, or until the onion and pepper have softened. Add the :hilli powder, cumin and coriander and cook for 30 seconds. Add the beans along with the tomatoes ınd stock. Bring to the boil and simmer uncovered for 40–45 minutes until the beans and /egetables are tender and the sauce has reduced.

Mix together the avocado, onion, fresh coriander, lime juice and tomato. Season with salt and pepper and set aside. Remove the chilli from the heat. Break the chocolate into pieces and sprinkle over the chilli. Leave for 2 minutes then stir well. Garnish with crème fraîche, lime and coriander. Serve with the avocado salsa.

## ENTERTAINING ALTERNATIVE
# Baby Onion Risotto

INGREDIENTS **Serves 4**

**For the baby onions:**
1 tbsp olive oil
450 g/1 lb baby onions, peeled and
halved if large
pinch of sugar
1 tbsp freshly chopped thyme

**For the risotto:**
1 tbsp olive oil
1 small onion, peeled and finely chopped
2 garlic cloves, peeled and finely chopped
350 g/12 oz risotto rice
150 ml/¼ pint red wine
1 litre/1¾ pint hot vegetable stock
125 g/4 oz low-fat soft goat's cheese
salt and freshly ground black pepper

For the baby onions, heat the olive oil in a saucepan and add the onions with the sugar. Cover and cook over a low heat, stirring occasionally, for 20–25 minutes until caramelised. Uncover during the last 10 minutes of cooking.

Meanwhile, for the risotto, heat the oil in a large frying pan and add the onion. Cook over a medium heat for 5 minutes until softened. Add the garlic and cook for a further 30 seconds. Add the risotto rice and stir well. Add the red wine and stir constantly until the wine is almost completely absorbed by the rice. Begin adding the stock a ladleful at a time, stirring well and waiting until the last ladleful has been absorbed before stirring in the next. It will take 20–25 minutes to add all the stock by which time the rice should be just cooked but still firm. Remove from the heat.

Add the thyme to the onions and cook briefly. Increase the heat and allow the onion mixture to bubble for 2–3 minutes until almost evaporated. Add the onion mixture to the risotto along with the goat's cheese. Stir well and season to taste with salt and pepper. Serve with rocket leaves.

**SUGGESTED ACCOMPANIMENT**
## Roasted Butternut Squash

Preheat the oven to 200°C/400°F/Gas Mark 6. Cut the butternut squash in half lengthwise and scoop out all of the seeds.

Score the squash in a diamond pattern with a sharp knife. Mix the garlic with the olive oil and brush over the cut surfaces of the squash. Season well with salt and pepper. Put on a baking sheet and roast for 40 minutes until tender.

Heat the walnut oil in a saucepan and fry the leeks and mustard seeds for 5 minutes. Add the drained cannellini beans, French beans and vegetable stock. Bring to the boil and simmer gently for 5 minutes until the French beans are tender.

Remove from the heat and stir in the rocket and chives. Season well. Remove the squash from the oven and allow to cool for 5 minutes. Spoon in the bean mixture. Garnish with a few snipped chives and serve immediately with the fromage frais and a mixed salad.

INGREDIENTS **Serves 4**

2 small butternut squash
4 garlic cloves, peeled and crushed
1 tbsp olive oil
salt and freshly ground black pepper
1 tbsp walnut oil
4 medium-sized leeks, trimmed, cleaned and thinly sliced
1 tbsp black mustard seeds
300 g can cannellini beans, drained and rinsed
125 g/4 oz fine French beans, halved
150 ml/¼ pint vegetable stock
50 g/2 oz rocket
2 tbsp freshly snipped chives
fresh chives, to garnish

**To serve:**
4 tbsp fromage frais
mixed salad

**ENTERTAINING ALTERNATIVE**
## Fennel & Caramelised Shallot Tartlets

Preheat the oven to 200°C/400°F/Gas Mark 6. Sift the flour into a bowl, then rub in the butter using your fingertips. Stir in the cheese, then add the egg yolk with about 2 tablespoons of cold water. Mix to a firm dough, then knead lightly. Wrap in clingfilm and chill in the refrigerator for 30 minutes.

Roll out the pastry on a lightly floured surface and use to line 6 x 10 cm/4 inch individual flan tins or patty tins which are about 2 cm/¾ inch deep. Line the pastry cases with greaseproof paper and fill with baking beans or rice. Bake blind in the preheated oven for about 10 minutes, then remove the paper and beans.

Heat the oil in a frying pan, add the shallots and fennel and fry gently for 5 minutes. Sprinkle with the sugar and cook for a further 10 minutes, stirring occasionally until lightly caramelised. Reserve until cooled.

Beat together the egg and cream and season to taste with salt and pepper. Divide the shallot mixture between the pastry cases. Pour over the egg mixture and sprinkle with the cheese and cinnamon. Bake for 20 minutes, until golden and set. Serve with the salad leaves.

INGREDIENTS **Serves 6**

**Cheese pastry:**
176 g/6 oz plain white flour
75 g/3 oz slightly salted butter
50 g/2 oz Gruyère cheese, grated
1 small egg yolk

**For the filling:**
2 tbsp olive oil
225 g/8 oz shallots, peeled and halved
1 fennel bulb, trimmed and sliced
1 tsp soft brown sugar
1 medium egg
150 ml/¼ pint double cream
salt and freshly ground black pepper
25 g/1 oz Gruyère cheese, grated
½ tsp ground cinnamon
mixed salad leaves, to serve

# Mushroom Stew

INGREDIENTS **Serves 4**

15 g/½ oz dried porcini mushrooms
900 g/2 lb assorted fresh mushrooms, wiped
2 tbsp good quality virgin olive oil
1 onion, peeled and finely chopped
2 garlic cloves, peeled and finely chopped
1 tbsp fresh thyme leaves
pinch of ground cloves
salt and freshly ground black pepper
700 g/1½ lb tomatoes, peeled, deseeded and chopped
225 g/8 oz instant polenta
600ml/1 pint vegetable stock
3 tbsp freshly chopped mixed herbs
sprigs of parsley, to garnish

Soak the porcini mushrooms in a small bowl of hot water for 20 minutes.

Drain, reserving the porcini mushrooms and their soaking liquid. Cut the fresh mushrooms in half and reserve.

In a saucepan, heat the oil and add the onion.

Cook gently for 5–7 minutes until softened. Add the garlic, thyme and cloves and continue cooking for 2 minutes.

Add all the mushrooms and cook for 8–10 minutes until the mushrooms have softened, stirring often. Season to taste with salt and pepper and add the tomatoes and the reserved soaking liquid.

Simmer, partly covered, over a low heat for about 20 minutes until thickened. Adjust the seasoning to taste.

Meanwhile, cook the polenta according to the packet instructions using the vegetable stock. Stir in the herbs and divide between four dishes.

Ladle the mushrooms over the polenta, garnish with the parsley and serve immediately.

HEALTH RATING 🍎🍎🍎

**SUGGESTED ACCOMPANIMENT**
Roasted Butternut Squash

**ENTERTAINING ALTERNATIVE**
Fennel & Caramelised Shallot Tartlets

# Creamy Vegetable Korma

INGREDIENTS **Serves 4–6**

2 tbsp ghee or vegetable oil
1 large onion, peeled and chopped
2 garlic cloves, peeled and crushed
2.5 cm/1 inch piece of root ginger, peeled and grated
4 cardamom pods
2 tsp ground coriander
1 tsp ground cumin
1 tsp ground turmeric
finely grated rind and juice of ½ lemon
50 g/2 oz ground almonds
400 ml/14 fl oz vegetable stock
450 g/1 lb potatoes, peeled and diced
450 g/1 lb mixed vegetables, such as cauliflower, carrots and turnip, cut into chunks
150 ml/¼ pint double cream
3 tbsp freshly chopped coriander
salt and freshly ground black pepper
naan bread, to serve

Heat the ghee or oil in a large saucepan. Add the onion and cook for 5 minutes. Stir in the garlic and ginger and cook for a further 5 minutes, or until soft and just beginning to colour.

Stir in the cardamom, ground coriander, cumin and turmeric. Continue cooking over a low heat for 1 minute, stirring.

Stir in the lemon rind and juice and almonds. Blend in the vegetable stock. Slowly bring to the boil, stirring occasionally.

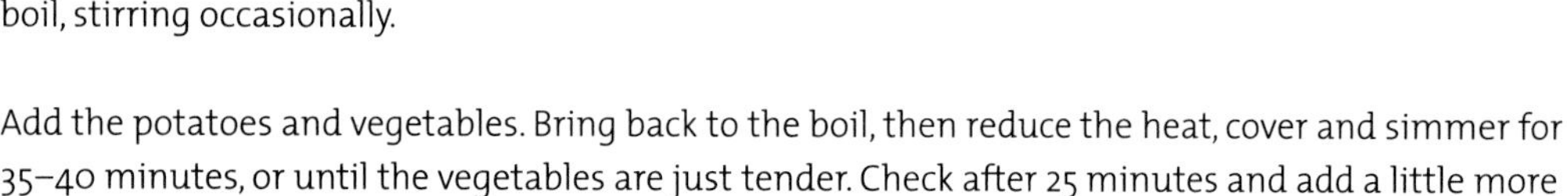

Add the potatoes and vegetables. Bring back to the boil, then reduce the heat, cover and simmer for 35–40 minutes, or until the vegetables are just tender. Check after 25 minutes and add a little more stock if needed.

Slowly stir in the cream and chopped coriander. Season to taste with salt and pepper. Cook very gently until heated through, but do not boil. Serve immediately with naan bread.

HEALTH RATING 🍎🍎🍎

**SUGGESTED ACCOMPANIMENT**

Sweet Potato Cakes with Mango & Tomato Salsa

**STARTER SUGGESTION**

Coriander Chicken & Soy Sauce Cakes

**SUGGESTED ACCOMPANIMENT**

## Sweet Potato Cakes with Mango & Tomato Salsa

INGREDIENTS **Serves 4**

- 700 g/1½ lb sweet potatoes, peeled and cut into large chunks
- salt and freshly ground black pepper
- 25 g/1 oz butter
- 1 onion, peeled and chopped
- 1 garlic clove, peeled and crushed
- pinch of freshly grated nutmeg
- 1 medium egg, beaten
- 50 g/2 oz quick-cook polenta
- 2 tbsp sunflower oil

**For the salsa:**

- 1 ripe mango, peeled, stoned and diced
- 6 cherry tomatoes, cut in wedges
- 4 spring onions, trimmed and thinly sliced
- 1 red chilli, deseeded and finely chopped
- finely grated rind and juice of ½ lime
- 2 tbsp freshly chopped mint
- 1 tsp clear honey
- salad leaves, to serve

Steam or cook the sweet potatoes in lightly salted boiling water for 15–20 minutes, until tender. Drain well, then mash until smooth.

Melt the butter in a saucepan. Add the onion and garlic and cook gently for 10 minutes until soft. Add to the mashed sweet potato and season with the nutmeg, salt and pepper. Stir together until mixed thoroughly. Leave to cool.

Shape the mixture into four oval potato cakes, about 2.5 cm/1 inch thick. Dip first in the beaten egg, allowing the excess to fall back into the bowl, then coat in the polenta. Refrigerate for at least 30 minutes.

Meanwhile, mix together all the ingredients for the salsa. Spoon into a serving bowl, cover with clingfilm and leave at room temperature to allow the flavours to develop.

Heat the oil in a frying pan and cook the potato cakes for 4–5 minutes on each side. Serve with the salsa and salad leaves.

**STARTER SUGGESTION**

## Coriander Chicken & Soy Sauce Cakes

INGREDIENTS **Serves 4**

- ¼ cucumber, peeled
- 1 shallot, peeled and thinly sliced
- 6 radishes, trimmed and sliced
- 350 g/12 oz skinless, boneless chicken thigh
- 4 tbsp roughly chopped fresh coriander
- 2 spring onions, trimmed and roughly chopped
- 1 red chilli, deseeded and chopped
- finely grated rind of ½ lime
- 2 tbsp soy sauce
- 1 tbsp caster sugar
- 2 tbsp rice vinegar
- 1 red chilli, deseeded and finely sliced
- freshly chopped coriander, to garnish

Preheat the oven to 190°C/375°F/Gas Mark 5. Halve the cucumber lengthwise, deseed and dice. In a bowl mix the shallot and radishes. Chill until ready to serve with the diced cucumber.

Place the chicken thighs in a food processor and blend until coarsely chopped. Add the coriander and spring onions to the chicken with the chilli, lime rind and soy sauce. Blend again until mixed.

Using slightly damp hands, shape the chicken mixture into 12 small rounds. Place the rounds on a lightly oiled baking tray and bake in the preheated for 15 minutes, until golden.

In a small pan heat the sugar with 2 tablespoons of water until dissolved. Simmer until syrupy.

Remove from the heat and allow to cool a little, then stir in the vinegar and chilli slices. Pour over the cucumber and the radish and shallot salad. Garnish with the chopped coriander and serve the chicken cakes with the salad immediately.

# Crispy Pancake Rolls

INGREDIENTS **Makes 8**

250 g/9 oz plain flour
pinch of salt
1 medium egg
4 tsp sunflower oil
2 tbsp light olive oil
2 cm/¾ inch piece fresh root ginger, peeled and grated
1 garlic clove, peeled and crushed
225 g/8 oz tofu, drained and cut into small cubes
2 tbsp soy sauce
1 tbsp dry sherry
175 g/6 oz button mushrooms, wiped and chopped
1 celery stalk, trimmed and finely chopped
2 spring onions, trimmed and finely chopped
2 tbsp groundnut oil
fresh coriander sprig and sliced spring onion, to garnish

Sift 225 g/8 oz of the flour with the salt into a large bowl, make a well in the centre and drop in the egg. Beat to form a smooth, thin batter, gradually adding 300 ml/½ pint of water and drawing in the flour from the sides of the bowl. Mix the remaining flour with 1–2 tablespoons of water to make a thick paste. Reserve.

Heat a little sunflower oil in a 20.5 cm/8 inch omelette or frying pan and pour in 2 tablespoons of the batter. Cook for 1–2 minutes, flip over and cook for a further 1–2 minutes, or until firm. Slide from the pan and keep warm. Make more pancakes with the remaining batter.

Heat a wok or large frying pan, add the olive oil and when hot, add the ginger, garlic and tofu, stir-fry for 30 seconds, then pour in the soy sauce and sherry. Add the mushrooms, celery and spring onions. Stir-fry for 1–2 minutes, then remove from the wok and leave to cool.

Place a little filling in the centre of each pancake. Brush the edges with the reserved flour paste, fold in the edges, then roll up into parcels. Heat the groundnut oil to 180°C/350°F in the wok. Fry the pancake rolls for 2–3 minutes or until golden. Serve immediately, garnished with chopped spring onions and a sprig of coriander.

HEALTH RATING ●●●

**SPEEDY ALTERNATIVE**
Chinese Omelette

**SUGGESTED ACCOMPANIMENT**
Bean & Cashew Stir Fry

**SPEEDY ALTERNATIVE**
## Chinese Omelette

INGREDIENTS **For 1 omelette**

50 g/2 oz beansprouts
50 g/2 oz carrots, peeled and cut into matchsticks
1 cm/½ inch piece fresh root ginger, peeled and grated
1 tsp soy sauce
2 large eggs
salt and freshly ground black pepper
1 tbsp dark sesame oil

**To serve:**
tossed green salad
Special Fried Rice (see page 287)
soy sauce

Lightly rinse the beansprouts, then place in the top of a bamboo steamer with the carrots. Add the grated ginger and soy sauce. Set the steamer over a pan or wok half-filled with gently simmering water and steam for 10 minutes, or until the vegetables are tender but still crisp. Reserve and keep warm.

Whisk the eggs in a bowl until frothy and season to taste with salt and pepper. Heat a 20.5 cm/ 8 inch omelette or frying pan, add the sesame oil and when very hot, pour in the beaten eggs. Whisk the eggs around with a fork, then allow them to cook and start to set. When the top surface starts to bubble, tilt the edges to allow the uncooked egg to run underneath.

Spoon the beansprout and carrot mixture over the top of the omelette and allow it to cook a little longer. When it has set, slide the omelette on to a warmed serving dish and carefully roll up. Serve immediately with a tossed green salad, special fried rice and extra soy sauce.

**SUGGESTED ACCOMPANIMENT**
## Bean & Cashew Stir Fry

INGREDIENTS **Serves 4**

3 tbsp sunflower oil
1 onion, peeled and finely chopped
1 celery stalk, trimmed and chopped
2.5 cm/1 inch piece fresh root ginger, peeled and grated
2 garlic cloves, peeled and crushed
1 red chilli, deseeded and finely chopped
175 g/6 oz fine French beans, trimmed and halved
175 g/6 oz mangetout, sliced diagonally into thirds
75 g/3 oz unsalted cashew nuts
1 tsp brown sugar
125 ml/4 fl oz vegetable stock
2 tbsp dry sherry
1 tbsp light soy sauce
1 tsp red wine vinegar
salt and freshly ground black pepper
freshly chopped coriander, to garnish

Heat a wok or large frying pan, add the oil and when hot, add the onion and celery and stir-fry gently for 3–4 minutes or until softened. Add the ginger, garlic and chilli to the wok and stir-fry for 30 seconds. Stir in the French beans and mangetout together with the cashew nuts and continue to stir-fry for 1–2 minutes, or until the nuts are golden brown.

Dissolve the sugar in the stock, then blend with the sherry, soy sauce and vinegar. Stir into the bean mixture and bring to the boil. Simmer gently, stirring occasionally for 3–4 minutes, or until the beans and mangetout are tender but still crisp and the sauce has thickened slightly. Season to taste with salt and pepper. Transfer to a warmed serving bowl or spoon on to individual plates. Sprinkle with freshly chopped coriander and serve immediately.

# Supreme Baked Potatoes

INGREDIENTS **Serves 4**

4 large baking potatoes
40 g/1½ oz butter
1 tbsp sunflower oil
1 carrot, peeled and chopped
2 celery stalks, trimmed and finely chopped
200 g can white crab meat
2 spring onions, trimmed and finely chopped
salt and freshly ground black pepper
50 g/2 oz Cheddar cheese, grated
tomato salad, to serve

Preheat the oven to 200°C/400°F/Gas Mark 6. Scrub the potatoes and prick all over with a fork, or thread two potatoes onto two long metal skewers. Place in the preheated oven for 1–1½ hours, or until soft to the touch. Allow to cool a little, then cut in half.

Scoop out the cooked potato and turn into a bowl, leaving a reasonably firm potato shell. Mash the cooked potato flesh, then mix in the butter and mash until the butter has melted.

While the potatoes are cooking, heat the oil in a frying pan and cook the carrot and celery for 2 minutes. Cover the pan tightly and continue to cook for another 5 minutes, or until the vegetables are tender.

Add the cooked vegetables to the bowl of mashed potato and mix well. Fold in the crab meat and the spring onions, then season to taste with salt and pepper.

Pile the mixture back into the potato shells and press in firmly. Sprinkle the grated cheese over the top and return the potato halves to the oven for 12–15 minutes until hot, golden and bubbling. Serve immediately with a tomato salad.

## HEALTH RATING 🍎🍎

**ENTERTAINING ALTERNATIVE**

Crispy Baked Potatoes with Serrano Ham

**SUGGESTED ACCOMPANIMENT**

Winter Coleslaw

**ENTERTAINING ALTERNATIVE**
## Crispy Baked Potatoes with Serrano Ham

INGREDIENTS **Serves 4**

4 large baking potatoes
4 tsp half-fat crème fraîche
salt and freshly ground black pepper
50 g/2 oz lean serrano ham or prosciutto, with fat removed
50 g/2 oz cooked baby broad beans
50 g/2 oz cooked carrots, diced
50 g/2 oz cooked peas
50 g/2 oz hard cheese such as Edam or Cheddar, grated
fresh green salad, to serve

Preheat the oven to 200°C/400°F/Gas Mark 6. Scrub the potatoes dry. Prick with a fork and place on a baking sheet. Cook for 1–1½ hours or until tender when squeezed. (Use oven gloves or a kitchen towel to pick up the potatoes as they will be very hot.)

Cut the potatoes in half horizontally and scoop out all the flesh into a bowl.

Spoon the crème fraîche into the bowl and mix thoroughly with the potatoes. Season to taste with a little salt and pepper. Cut the ham into strips and carefully stir into the potato mixture with the broad beans, carrots and peas.

Pile the mixture back into the eight potato shells and sprinkle a little grated cheese on top. Place under a hot grill and cook until golden and heated through. Serve immediately with a fresh green salad.

**SUGGESTED ACCOMPANIMENT**
## Winter Coleslaw

INGREDIENTS **Serves 6**

175 g/6 oz white cabbage
1 medium red onion, peeled
175 g/6 oz carrot, peeled
175 g/6 oz celeriac, peeled
2 celery stalks, trimmed
75 g/3 oz golden sultanas

**Yogurt & herb dressing:**

150 ml/¼ pint natural yogurt
1 garlic clove, peeled and crushed
1 tbsp lemon juice
1 tsp clear honey
1 tbsp freshly snipped chives

Remove the hard core from the cabbage with a small knife and shred the cabbage finely. Slice the onion finely and coarsely grate the carrot. Place the raw vegetables in a large bowl and mix together.

Cut the celeriac into thin strips and simmer in boiling water for about 2 minutes. Drain the celeriac and rinse thoroughly with cold water. Chop the celery and add to the bowl with the celeriac and sultanas and mix well.

Make the yogurt and herb dressing by briskly whisking the yogurt, garlic, lemon juice, honey and chives together.

Pour the dressing over the top of the salad. Stir the vegetables thoroughly to coat evenly and serve.

ENTERTAINING ALTERNATIVE

## Peperonata (Braised Mixed Peppers)

INGREDIENTS **Serves 4**

2 green peppers
1 red pepper
1 yellow pepper
1 orange pepper
1 onion, peeled
2 garlic cloves, peeled
2 tbsp olive oil
4 very ripe tomatoes
1 tbsp freshly chopped oregano
salt and freshly ground black pepper
150 ml/¼ pint light chicken or vegetable stock
sprigs of fresh oregano, to garnish
focaccia or flat bread, to serve

Remove the seeds from the peppers and cut into thin strips. Slice the onion into rings and chop the garlic cloves finely.

Heat the olive oil in a frying pan and fry the peppers, onions and garlic for 5–10 minutes, or until soft and lightly coloured. Stir continuously.

Make a cross on the top of the tomatoes then place in a bowl and cover with boiling water. Allow to stand for about 2 minutes. Drain, then remove the skins and seeds and chop the tomato flesh into cubes.

Add the tomatoes and oregano to the peppers and onion and season to taste with salt and pepper. Cover the pan and bring to the boil. Simmer gently for about 30 minutes, or until tender, adding the chicken or vegetable stock halfway through the cooking time.

Garnish with sprigs of oregano and serve hot with plenty of freshly baked focaccia bread or lightly toasted slices of flat bread and pile a spoonful of peperonata on to each plate.

SUGGESTED ACCOMPANIMENT

## Corn Fritters with Hot & Spicy Relish

To make the relish, heat a wok, add the sunflower oil and when hot, add the onion and stir-fry for 3–4 minutes or until softened. Add the chillies and garlic, stir-fry for 1 minute, then leave to cool slightly. Stir in the plum sauce, transfer to a food processor and blend to the consistency of chutney. Reserve.

Place the sweetcorn in a food processor and blend briefly until just mashed. Transfer to a bowl with the onions, chilli powder, coriander, flour, baking powder and egg. Season to taste with salt and pepper and mix together.

Heat a wok, add the oil and heat to 180°C/350°F. Working in batches, drop a few spoonfuls of the sweetcorn mixture into the oil and deep-fry for 3–4 minutes, or until golden and crispy, turning occasionally. Using a slotted spoon, remove and drain on absorbent kitchen paper. Arrange on a warmed serving platter, garnish with sprigs of coriander and serve immediately with the relish.

INGREDIENTS **Makes 16–20**

325 g can sweetcorn kernels, drained
1 onion, peeled and very finely chopped
1 spring onion, trimmed and very finely chopped
½ tsp chilli powder
1 tsp ground coriander
4 tbsp plain flour
1 tsp baking powder
1 medium egg
salt and freshly ground black pepper
300 ml/½ pint groundnut oil
sprigs of fresh coriander, to garnish

**For the spicy relish:**

3 tbsp sunflower oil
1 onion, peeled and very finely chopped
¼ tsp dried crushed chillies
2 garlic cloves, peeled and crushed
2 tbsp plum sauce

# Light Ratatouille

INGREDIENTS **Serves 4**

1 red pepper
2 courgettes, trimmed
1 small aubergine, trimmed
1 onion, peeled
2 ripe tomatoes
50 g/2 oz button mushrooms, wiped and halved or quartered
200 ml/7 fl oz tomato juice
1 tbsp freshly chopped basil
salt and freshly ground black pepper

Deseed the peppers, remove the membrane with a sharp knife and cut into small cubes. Thickly slice the courgettes and cut the aubergine into small cubes. Slice the onion into rings.

Place the tomatoes in boiling water until their skins begin to peel away.

Remove the skins from the tomatoes, cut into quarters and remove the seeds.

Place all the vegetables in a saucepan with the tomato juice and basil. Season to taste with salt and pepper.

Bring to the boil, then cover and simmer for 15 minutes, or until the vegetables are tender.

Remove the vegetables with a slotted spoon and arrange in a serving dish.

Bring the liquid in the pan to the boil and boil for 20 seconds until it is slightly thickened. Season the sauce to taste with salt and pepper.

Pass the sauce through a sieve to remove some of the seeds and pour over the vegetables. Serve the ratatouille hot or cold.

HEALTH RATING

**ENTERTAINING ALTERNATIVE**
Peperonata (Braised Mixed Peppers)

**SUGGESTED ACCOMPANIMENT**
Corn Fritters with Hot & Spicy Relish

# Spanish Baked Tomatoes

INGREDIENTS **Serves 4**

175 g/6 oz whole-grain rice
600 ml/1 pint vegetable stock
2 tsp sunflower oil
2 shallots, peeled and finely chopped
1 garlic clove, peeled and crushed
1 green pepper, deseeded and cut into small cubes
1 red chilli, deseeded and finely chopped
50 g/2 oz button mushrooms, finely chopped
1 tbsp freshly chopped oregano
salt and freshly ground black pepper
4 large ripe beef tomatoes
1 large egg, beaten
1 tsp caster sugar
basil leaves, to garnish
crusty bread, to serve

Preheat the oven to 180°C/350°F/Gas Mark 4. Place the rice in a saucepan, pour over the vegetable stock and bring to the boil. Simmer for 30 minutes or until the rice is tender. Drain and turn into a mixing bowl.

Add 1 teaspoon of sunflower oil to a small non-stick pan and gently fry the shallots, garlic, pepper, chilli and mushrooms for 2 minutes. Add to the rice with the chopped oregano. Season with plenty of salt and pepper.

Slice the top off each tomato. Cut and scoop out the flesh, removing the hard core. Pass the tomato flesh through a sieve and add 1 tablespoon of the juice to the rice mixture. Stir in the beaten egg and mix. Sprinkle a little sugar in the base of each tomato, then pile the rice mixture into the shells.

Place the tomatoes in a baking dish and pour a little cold water around them. Replace their lids and drizzle a few drops of sunflower oil over the tops.

Bake in the preheated oven for about 25 minutes. Garnish with the basil leaves and season with black pepper and serve immediately with crusty bread.

HEALTH RATING 🍎🍎🍎🍎🍎

**ENTERTAINING ALTERNATIVE**
Coconut-baked Courgettes

**SUGGESTED ACCOMPANIMENT**
Boston-style Baked Beans

**ENTERTAINING ALTERNATIVE**
## Coconut-baked Courgettes

INGREDIENTS **Serves 4**

3 tbsp groundnut oil
1 onion, peeled and finely sliced
4 garlic cloves, peeled and crushed
½ tsp chilli powder
1 tsp ground coriander
6–8 tbsp desiccated coconut
1 tbsp tomato purée
700 g/1½ lb courgettes, thinly sliced
freshly chopped parsley, to garnish

Preheat the oven to 180°C/350°F/Gas Mark 4, 10 minutes before cooking. Lightly oil a 1.4 litre/2½ pint ovenproof gratin dish. Heat a wok, add the oil and when hot, add the onion and stir-fry for 2–3 minutes or until softened. Add the garlic, chilli powder and coriander and stir-fry for 1–2 minutes.

Pour 300 ml/½ pint cold water into the wok and bring to the boil. Add the coconut and tomato purée and simmer for 3–4 minutes; most of the water will evaporate at this stage. Spoon 4 tablespoons of the spice and coconut mixture into a small bowl and reserve.

Stir the courgettes into the remaining spice and coconut mixture, coating well. Spoon the courgettes into the oiled gratin dish and sprinkle the reserved spice and coconut mixture evenly over the top. Bake, uncovered, in the preheated oven for 15–20 minutes, or until golden. Garnish with chopped parsley and serve immediately.

**SUGGESTED ACCOMPANIMENT**
## Boston-style Baked Beans

INGREDIENTS **Serves 8**

350 g/12 oz mixed dried pulses, e.g. haricot, flageolet, cannellini, chickpeas or pinto beans
1 large onion, peeled and finely chopped
125 g/4 oz black treacle or molasses
2 tbsp Dijon mustard
2 tbsp light brown soft sugar
125 g/4 oz plain flour
150 g/5 oz fine cornmeal
2 tbsp caster sugar
21/2 tsp baking powder
½ tsp salt
2 tbsp freshly chopped thyme
2 medium eggs
200 ml/7 fl oz milk
2 tbsp melted butter
salt and freshly ground black pepper
parsley sprigs, to garnish

Preheat the oven to 130°C/250°F/Gas Mark ½. Put the pulses into a large saucepan and cover with at least twice their volume of water. Bring to the boil and simmer for 2 minutes. Leave to stand for 1 hour. Return to the boil and boil rapidly for about 10 minutes. Drain and reserve.

Mix together the onion, treacle or molasses, mustard and sugar in a large mixing bowl. Add the drained beans and 300 ml/½ pint fresh water. Stir well, bring to the boil, cover and transfer to the preheated oven for 4 hours in an ovenproof dish, stirring once every hour and adding more water if necessary.

When the beans are cooked, remove from the oven and keep warm. Increase the oven temperature to 200°C/400°F/Gas Mark 6. Mix together the plain flour, cornmeal, caster sugar, baking powder, salt and most of the thyme, reserving about one third for garnish. In a separate bowl beat the eggs, then stir in the milk and butter. Pour the wet ingredients on to the dry ones and stir just enough to combine.

Pour into a buttered 18 cm/7 inch square cake tin. Sprinkle over the remaining thyme. Bake for 30 minutes until golden and risen or until a toothpick inserted into the centre comes out clean. Cut into squares, then reheat the beans. Season to taste with salt and pepper and serve immediately, garnished with parsley sprigs.

# Melanzane Parmigiana

INGREDIENTS **Serves 4**

900 g/2 lb aubergines
salt and freshly ground black pepper
5 tbsp olive oil
1 red onion, peeled and chopped
½ tsp mild paprika pepper
150 ml/¼ pint dry red wine
150 ml/¼ pint vegetable stock
400 g can chopped tomatoes
1 tsp tomato purée
1 tbsp freshly chopped oregano
175 g/6 oz mozzarella cheese, thinly sliced
40 g/1½ oz Parmesan cheese, coarsely grated
sprig of fresh basil, to garnish

Preheat the oven to 200°C/400°F/Gas Mark 6, 15 minutes before cooking. Cut the aubergines lengthways into thin slices. Sprinkle with salt and leave to drain in a colander over a bowl for 30 minutes.

Meanwhile, heat 1 tablespoon of the olive oil in a saucepan and fry the onion for 10 minutes, until softened. Add the paprika and cook for 1 minute. Stir in the wine, stock, tomatoes and tomato purée. Simmer, uncovered, for 25 minutes, or until fairly thick. Stir in the oregano and season to taste with salt and pepper. Remove from the heat.

Rinse the aubergine slices thoroughly under cold water and pat dry on absorbent kitchen paper. Heat 2 tablespoons of the oil in a griddle pan and cook the aubergines in batches, for 3 minutes on each side, until golden. Drain well on absorbent kitchen paper.

Pour half of the tomato sauce into the base of a large ovenproof dish. Cover with half the aubergine slices, then top with the mozzarella. Cover with the remaining aubergine slices and pour over the remaining tomato sauce. Sprinkle with the grated Parmesan cheese.

Bake in the preheated oven for 30 minutes, or until the aubergines are tender and the sauce is bubbling. Garnish with a sprig of fresh basil and cool for a few minutes before serving.

HEALTH RATING

**ENTERTAINING ALTERNATIVE**

Aubergine Cannelloni with Watercress Sauce

**SUGGESTED ACCOMPANIMENT**

Vegetable Frittata

**ENTERTAINING ALTERNATIVE**
## Aubergine Cannelloni with Watercress Sauce

INGREDIENTS **Serves 4**

4 large aubergines, about 250 g/9 oz each
5–6 tbsp olive oil
350 g/12 oz ricotta cheese
75 g/3 oz Parmesan cheese, grated
3 tbsp freshly chopped basil
salt and freshly ground black pepper

**For the watercress sauce:**

75 g/3 oz watercress, trimmed
200 ml/⅓ pint vegetable stock
1 shallot, peeled and sliced
pared strip of lemon rind
1 large sprig of thyme
3 tbsp crème fraîche
1 tsp lemon juice

**To garnish:**

sprigs of watercress
lemon zest

Preheat the oven to 190°C/375°F/Gas Mark 5, 10 minutes before cooking. Cut the aubergines lengthways into thin slices, discarding the side pieces. Heat 2 tablespoons of oil in a frying pan and cook the aubergine slices in a single layer in several batches, turning once, until golden on both sides.

Mix the cheeses, basil and seasoning together. Lay the aubergine slices on a clean surface and spread the cheese mixture evenly between them.

Roll up the slices from one of the short ends to enclose the filling. Place seam-side down in a single layer in an ovenproof dish. Bake in the preheated oven for 15 minutes, or until golden.

To make the watercress sauce, blanch the watercress leaves in boiling water for about 30 seconds. Drain well, then rinse in a sieve under cold running water and squeeze dry. Put the stock, shallot, lemon rind and thyme in a small saucepan. Boil rapidly until reduced by half, then remove from the heat and strain.

Put the watercress and strained stock in a food processor and blend until fairly smooth. Return to the saucepan, stir in the crème fraîche, lemon juice and season to taste with salt and pepper. Heat gently until the sauce is piping hot.

Serve a little of the sauce drizzled over the aubergines and the rest separately in a jug. Garnish the aubergine cannelloni with sprigs of watercress and lemon zest and serve immediately.

**SUGGESTED ACCOMPANIMENT**
## Vegetable Frittata

INGREDIENTS **Serves 2**

6 medium eggs
2 tbsp freshly chopped parsley
1 tbsp freshly chopped tarragon
25 g/1 oz pecorino or Parmesan cheese, finely grated
freshly ground black pepper
175 g/6 oz tiny new potatoes
2 small carrots, peeled and sliced
125 g/4 oz broccoli, cut into small florets
1 courgette, about 125 g/4 oz, sliced
2 tbsp olive oil
4 spring onions, trimmed and thinly sliced

**To serve:**

mixed green salad
crusty Italian bread

Preheat grill just before cooking. Lightly beat the eggs with the parsley, tarragon and half the cheese. Season to taste with black pepper and reserve. (Salt is not needed as the pecorino is very salty.)

Bring a large saucepan of lightly salted water to the boil. Add the new potatoes and cook for 8 minutes. Add the carrots and cook for 4 minutes, then add the broccoli florets and the courgettes and cook for a further 3–4 minutes, or until all the vegetables are barely tender. Drain well.

Heat the oil in a 20.5 cm/8 inch heavy-based frying pan. Add the spring onions and cook for 3–4 minutes, or until softened. Add all the vegetables and cook for a few seconds, then pour in the beaten egg mixture.

Stir gently for about a minute, then cook for a further 1–2 minutes, or until the bottom of the frittata is set and golden brown.

Place the pan under a hot grill for 1 minute, or until almost set and just beginning to brown. Sprinkle with the remaining cheese and grill for a further 1 minute, or until it is lightly browned.

Loosen the edges and slide out of the pan. Cut into wedges and serve hot or warm with a mixed green salad and crusty Italian bread.

# Fresh Tuna Salad

INGREDIENTS **Serves 4**

225 g/8 oz mixed salad leaves
225 g/8 oz baby cherry tomatoes, halved lengthways
125 g/4 oz rocket leaves, washed
2 tbsp groundnut oil
550 g/1¼ lb boned tuna steaks, each cut into 4 small pieces
50 g/2 oz piece fresh Parmesan cheese

**For the dressing:**

8 tbsp olive oil
grated zest and juice of 2 small lemons
1 tbsp wholegrain mustard
salt and freshly ground black pepper

Wash the salad leaves and place in a large salad bowl with the cherry tomatoes and rocket and reserve.

Heat the wok, then add the oil and heat until almost smoking. Add the tuna, skin-side down, and cook for 4–6 minutes, turning once during cooking, until the fish is cooked and the flesh flakes easily. Remove from the heat and leave to stand in the juices for 2 minutes before removing.

Meanwhile, to make the dressing, place the olive oil, lemon zest and juice and mustard in a small bowl or screw-topped jar and whisk or shake until well blended. Season to taste with salt and pepper.

Transfer the tuna to a clean chopping board and flake, then add it to the salad and toss lightly.

Using a swivel blade vegetable peeler, peel the piece of Parmesan cheese into shavings. Divide the salad between four large serving plates, drizzle the dressing over the salad, then scatter with the Parmesan shavings and serve.

HEALTH RATING 🍎🍎🍎

**ENTERTAINING ALTERNATIVE**
Smoked Mackerel & Potato Salad

**SUGGESTED ACCOMPANIMENT**
Creamy Puy Lentils

**ENTERTAINING ALTERNATIVE**
## Smoked Mackerel & Potato Salad

INGREDIENTS **Serves 4**

½ tsp dry mustard powder
1 large egg yolk
salt and freshly ground black pepper
150 ml/¼ pint sunflower oil
1–2 tbsp lemon juice
450 g/1 lb baby new potatoes
25 g/1 oz butter
350 g/12 oz smoked mackerel fillets
4 celery stalks, trimmed and finely chopped
3 tbsp creamed horseradish
150 ml/¼ pint crème fraîche
1 little gem lettuce, rinsed and roughly torn
8 cherry tomatoes, halved

Place the mustard powder and egg yolk in a small bowl with salt and pepper and whisk until blended. Add the oil, drop by drop, into the egg mixture, whisking continuously. When the mayonnaise is thick, add the lemon juice, drop by drop, until a smooth, glossy consistency is formed. Reserve.

Cook the potatoes in boiling salted water until tender, then drain. Cool slightly, then cut into halves or quarters, depending on size. Return to the saucepan and toss in the butter.

Remove the skin from the mackerel fillets and flake into pieces. Add to the potatoes in the saucepan, together with the celery.

Blend 4 tablespoons of the mayonnaise with the horseradish and crème fraîche. Season to taste with salt and pepper, then add to the potato and mackerel mixture and stir lightly.

Arrange the lettuce and tomatoes on four serving plates. Pile the smoked mackerel mixture on top of the lettuce, grind over a little pepper and serve with the remaining mayonnaise.

**SUGGESTED ACCOMPANIMENT**
## Creamy Puy Lentils

INGREDIENTS **Serves 4**

225 g/8 oz puy lentils
1 tbsp olive oil
1 garlic clove, peeled and finely chopped
zest and juice of 1 lemon
1 tsp whole grain mustard
1 tbsp freshly chopped tarragon
3 tbsp crème fraîche
salt and freshly ground black pepper
2 small tomatoes, deseeded and chopped
50 g/2 oz pitted black olives
1 tbsp freshly chopped parsley

**To garnish:**
sprigs of fresh tarragon
lemon wedges

Put the lentils in a saucepan with plenty of cold water and bring to the boil. Boil rapidly for 10 minutes, reduce the heat and simmer gently for a further 20 minutes until just tender. Drain well.

Meanwhile, prepare the dressing. Heat the oil in a frying pan over a medium heat. Add the garlic and cook for about a minute until just beginning to brown. Add the lemon zest and juice.

Add the mustard and cook for a further 30 seconds.

Add the tarragon and crème fraîche and season to taste with salt and pepper.

Simmer and add the drained lentils, tomatoes and olives.

Transfer to a serving dish and sprinkle the chopped parsley on top.

Garnish the lentils with the tarragon sprigs and the lemon wedges and serve immediately.

**SPICY ALTERNATIVE**
## Indonesian Salad with Peanut Dressing

Cook the potatoes in a saucepan of boiling salted water for 15–20 minutes until tender. Remove with a slotted spoon and thickly slice into a large bowl. Keep the saucepan of water boiling.

Add the carrot, French beans and cauliflower to the water, return to the boil and cook for 2 minutes, or until just tender. Drain and refresh under cold running water, then drain well. Add to the potatoes with the cucumber and bean sprouts.

To make the dressing, gently heat the sesame oil in a small saucepan. Add the garlic and chilli and cook for a few seconds, then remove from the heat. Stir in the peanut butter.

Stir in the stock, a little at a time. Add the remaining ingredients and mix together to make a thick, creamy dressing.

Divide the vegetables between four plates and arrange the eggs on top. Drizzle the dressing over the salad and serve immediately.

INGREDIENTS **Serves 4**

225 g/8 oz new potatoes, scrubbed
1 large carrot, peeled and cut into matchsticks
125 g/4 oz French beans, trimmed
225 g/8 oz tiny cauliflower florets
125 g/4 oz cucumber, cut into matchsticks
75 g/3 oz fresh bean sprouts
3 medium eggs, hard-boiled and quartered

**For the peanut dressing:**
2 tbsp sesame oil
1 garlic clove, peeled and crushed
1 red chilli, deseeded and finely chopped
150 g/5 oz crunchy peanut butter
6 tbsp hot vegetable stock
2 tsp soft light brown sugar
2 tsp dark soy sauce
1 tbsp lime juice

**SUGGESTED ACCOMPANIMENT**
## Chunky Vegetable & Fennel Goulash with Dumplings

Cut the fennel bulbs in half widthways. Thickly slice the stalks and cut the bulbs into eight wedges. Heat the oil in a large saucepan or flameproof casserole dish. Add the onion and fennel and cook gently for 10 minutes until soft. Stir in the paprika and flour.

Remove from the heat and gradually stir in the stock. Add the chopped tomatoes, potatoes and mushrooms. Season to taste with salt and pepper. Bring to the boil, reduce the heat and simmer for 20 minutes.

Meanwhile, make the dumplings. Heat the oil in a frying pan and gently cook the onion for 10 minutes, until soft. Leave to cool for a few minutes.

In a bowl, beat the egg and milk together, then add the onion, parsley and breadcrumbs and season to taste. With damp hands form the breadcrumb mixture into 12 round dumplings, each about the size of a walnut.

Arrange the dumplings on top of the goulash. Cover and cook for a further 15 minutes, until the dumplings are cooked and the vegetables are tender. Serve immediately.

INGREDIENTS **Serves 4**

2 fennel bulbs, weighing about 450 g/1 lb
2 tbsp sunflower oil
1 large onion, peeled and sliced
1½ tbsp paprika
1 tbsp plain flour
300 ml/½ pint vegetable stock
400 g can chopped tomatoes
450 g/1 lb potatoes, peeled and cut into 2.5 cm/1 inch chunks
125 g/4 oz small button mushrooms
salt and freshly ground black pepper

**For the dumplings:**
1 tbsp sunflower oil
1 small onion, peeled and finely chopped
1 medium egg
3 tbsp milk
3 tbsp freshly chopped parsley
125 g/4 oz fresh white breadcrumbs

# Mediterranean Potato Salad

INGREDIENTS **Serves 4**

700 g/1½ lb small waxy potatoes
2 red onions, peeled and roughly chopped
1 yellow pepper, deseeded and roughly chopped
1 green pepper, deseeded and roughly chopped
5 tbsp extra virgin olive oil
125 g/4 oz ripe tomatoes, chopped
50 g/2 oz pitted black olives, sliced
125 g/4 oz feta cheese
3 tbsp freshly chopped parsley
2 tbsp white wine vinegar
1 tsp Dijon mustard
1 tsp clear honey
salt and freshly ground black pepper
sprigs of fresh parsley, to garnish

Preheat the oven to 200°C/400°F/Gas Mark 6. Place the potatoes in a large saucepan of salted water, bring to the boil and simmer until just tender. Do not overcook. Drain and plunge into cold water, to stop them from cooking further.

Place the onions in a bowl with the yellow and green peppers, then pour over 2 tablespoons of the olive oil. Stir and spoon onto a large baking tray. Cook in the preheated oven for 25–30 minutes, or until the vegetables are tender and lightly charred in places, stirring occasionally. Remove from the oven and transfer to a large bowl.

Cut the potatoes into bite-sized pieces and mix with the roasted onions and peppers. Add the tomatoes and olives to the potatoes. Crumble over the feta cheese and sprinkle with the chopped parsley.

Whisk together the remaining olive oil, vinegar, mustard and honey, then season to taste with salt and pepper. Pour the dressing over the potatoes and toss gently together. Garnish with parsley sprigs and serve immediately.

## HEALTH RATING ●●●

**SPICY ALTERNATIVE**
Indonesian Salad with Peanut Dressing

**SUGGESTED ACCOMPANIMENT**
Chunky Vegetable & Fennel Goulash with Dumplings

# Warm Chicken & Potato Salad with Peas & Mint

INGREDIENTS **Serves 4–6**

450 g/1 lb new potatoes, peeled or scrubbed and cut into bite-sized pieces
salt and freshly ground black pepper
2 tbsp cider vinegar
175 g/6 oz frozen garden peas, thawed
1 small ripe avocado
4 cooked chicken breasts, about 450 g/1 lb in weight, skinned and diced
2 tbsp freshly chopped mint
2 heads little gem lettuce
fresh mint sprigs, to garnish

**For the dressing:**

2 tbsp raspberry or sherry vinegar
2 tsp Dijon mustard
1 tsp clear honey
50 ml/2 fl oz sunflower oil
50 ml/2 fl oz extra virgin olive oil

Cook the potatoes in lightly salted boiling water for 15 minutes, or until just tender when pierced with the tip of a sharp knife; do not overcook. Rinse under cold running water to cool slightly, then drain and turn into a large bowl. Sprinkle with the cider vinegar and toss gently.

Run the peas under hot water to ensure that they are thawed, pat dry with absorbent kitchen paper and add to the potatoes.

Cut the avocado in half lengthways and remove the stone. Peel and cut the avocado into cubes and add to the potatoes and peas. Add the chicken and stir together lightly.

To make the dressing, place all the ingredients in a screw-top jar with a little salt and pepper and shake well to mix – add a little more oil if the flavour is too sharp. Pour over the salad and toss gently to coat. Sprinkle over half the mint and stir lightly.

Separate the lettuce leaves and spread onto a large, shallow serving plate. Spoon the salad on top and sprinkle with the remaining mint. Garnish with mint sprigs and serve.

HEALTH RATING ★★★

**VEGETARIAN ALTERNATIVE**

Warm Potato, Pear & Pecan Salad

**SUGGESTED ACCOMPANIMENT**

Pumpkin Pâté

**VEGETARIAN ALTERNATIVE**

## Warm Potato, Pear & Pecan Salad

INGREDIENTS **Serves 4**

900 g/2 lb new potatoes, preferably red-skinned, unpeeled
salt and freshly ground black pepper
1 tsp Dijon mustard
2 tsp white wine vinegar
3 tbsp groundnut oil
1 tbsp hazelnut or walnut oil
2 tsp poppy seeds
2 firm, ripe dessert pears
2 tsp lemon juice
175 g/6 oz baby spinach leaves
75 g/3 oz toasted pecan nuts

Scrub the potatoes, then cook in a saucepan of lightly salted boiling water for 15 minutes, or until tender. Drain, cut into halves, or quarters if large, and place in a serving bowl.

In a small bowl or jug, whisk together the mustard and vinegar. Gradually add the oils until the mixture begins to thicken. Stir in the poppy seeds and season to taste with salt and pepper.

Pour about two-thirds of the dressing over the hot potatoes and toss gently to coat. Leave until the potatoes have soaked up the dressing and are just warm.

Meanwhile, quarter and core the pears. Cut into thin slices, then sprinkle with the lemon juice to prevent them from going brown. Add to the potatoes with the spinach leaves and toasted pecan nuts. Gently mix together.

Drizzle the remaining dressing over the salad. Serve immediately before the spinach starts to wilt.

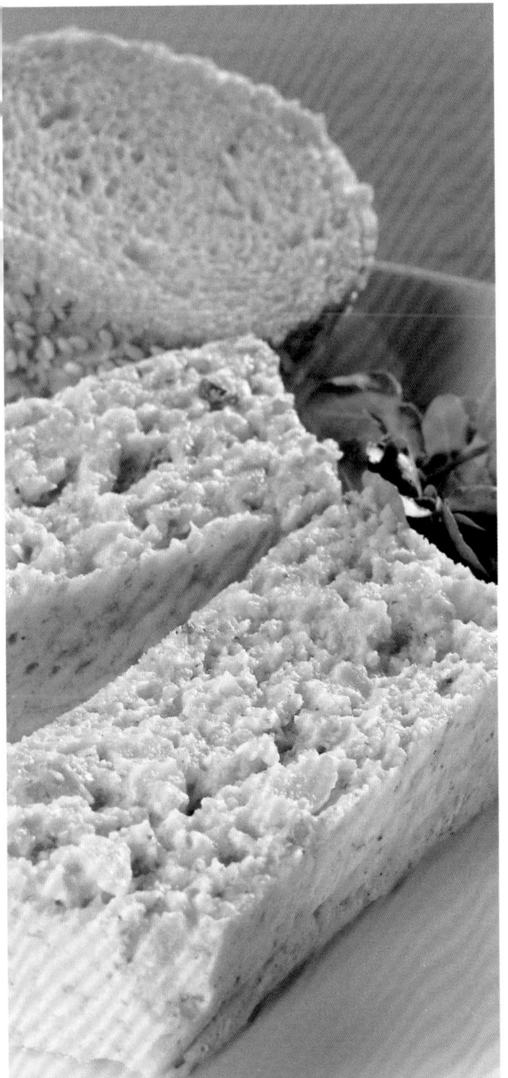

**SUGGESTED ACCOMPANIMENT**

## Pumpkin Pâté

INGREDIENTS **Serves 8–10**

450 g/1 lb fresh pumpkin flesh (when in season), peeled, or 425 g can pumpkin purée
1 tsp sunflower oil
1 small onion, peeled and finely chopped
½ orange pepper, deseeded and finely chopped
2 medium eggs, beaten
3 tbsp natural yogurt
125 g/4 oz hard cheese (such as Edam or Gouda), grated
50 g/2 oz wheatgerm
1 tbsp freshly chopped oregano
salt and freshly ground black pepper
fresh salad leaves and crusty bread, to serve

Preheat the oven to 180°C/350°F/Gas Mark 4. Oil and line a 900 ml/1½ pint oblong dish or loaf tin. Cut the pumpkin flesh into cubes and place in a pan of boiling water. Simmer for 20 minutes or until the pumpkin is very tender. Drain and leave to cool, then mash well to form a purée.

Heat the oil in a non-stick frying pan and cook the chopped onion and pepper for about 4 minutes, until softened.

Mix together the puréed pumpkin, softened vegetables, eggs and yogurt. Add the cheese, wheatgerm and chopped oregano. Season well with salt and pepper.

When the pumpkin mixture is well blended, spoon it into the prepared tin and stand in a baking dish. Fill the tray with hot water to come halfway up the sides of the tin and carefully place in the preheated oven.

Bake for about 1 hour or until firm, then leave to cool. Chill for 30 minutes before turning out on to a serving plate. Serve with crusty bread and a fresh salad.

# Pasta & Pepper Salad

INGREDIENTS **Serves 4**

4 tbsp olive oil
1 each red, orange and yellow pepper, deseeded and cut into chunks
1 large courgette, trimmed and cut into chunks
1 medium aubergine, trimmed and diced
275 g/10 oz fusilli pasta
4 plum tomatoes, quartered
1 bunch fresh basil leaves, roughly chopped
2 tbsp pesto
2 garlic cloves, peeled and roughly chopped
1 tbsp lemon juice
225 g/8 oz boneless and skinless roasted chicken breast
salt and freshly ground black pepper
125 g/4 oz feta cheese, crumbled
crusty bread, to serve

Preheat the oven to 200°C/400°F/Gas Mark 6. Spoon the olive oil into a roasting tin and heat in the oven for 2 minutes, or until almost smoking. Remove from the oven, add the peppers, courgette and aubergine and stir until coated. Bake for 30 minutes, or until charred, stirring occasionally.

Bring a large pan of lightly salted water to a rolling boil. Add the pasta and cook according to the packet instructions, or until 'al dente'. Drain and refresh under cold running water. Drain thoroughly, place in a large salad bowl and reserve.

Remove the cooked vegetables from the oven and allow to cool. Add to the cooled pasta, together with the quartered tomatoes, chopped basil leaves, pesto, garlic and lemon juice. Toss lightly to mix.

Shred the chicken roughly into small pieces and stir into the pasta and vegetable mixture. Season to taste with salt and pepper, then sprinkle the crumbled feta cheese over the pasta and stir gently. Cover the dish and leave to marinate for 30 minutes, stirring occasionally. Serve the salad with fresh crusty bread.

HEALTH RATING 🍎🍎🍎

**MEAT ALTERNATIVE**
Spicy Chicken & Pasta Salad

**ENTERTAINING ALTERNATIVE**
Pastini-stuffed Peppers

**MEAT ALTERNATIVE**
## Spicy Chicken & Pasta Salad

INGREDIENTS **Serves 6**

450 g/1 lb pasta shells
25 g/1 oz butter
1 onion, peeled and chopped
2 tbsp mild curry paste
125 g/4 oz ready-to-eat dried apricots, chopped
2 tbsp tomato purée
3 tbsp mango chutney
300 ml/½ pint mayonnaise
425 g can pineapple slices in fruit juice
salt and freshly ground black pepper
450 g/1 lb skinned and boned cooked chicken, cut into bite-sized pieces
25 g/1 oz flaked toasted almond slivers
coriander sprigs, to garnish

Bring a large pan of lightly salted water to a rolling boil. Add the pasta shells and cook according to the packet instructions, or until 'al dente'. Drain and refresh under cold running water then drain thoroughly and place in a large serving bowl.

Meanwhile, melt the butter in a heavy-based pan, add the onion and cook for 5 minutes, or until softened. Add the curry paste and cook, stirring, for 2 minutes. Stir in the apricots and tomato purée, then cook for 1 minute. Remove from the heat and allow to cool.

Blend the mango chutney and mayonnaise together in a small bowl. Drain the pineapple slices, adding 2 tablespoons of the pineapple juice to the mayonnaise mixture; reserve the pineapple slices. Season the mayonnaise to taste with salt and pepper.

Cut the pineapple slices into chunks and stir into the pasta together with the mayonnaise mixture, curry paste and cooked chicken pieces. Toss lightly together to coat the pasta. Sprinkle with the almond slivers, garnish with coriander sprigs and serve.

**ENTERTAINING ALTERNATIVE**
## Pastini-stuffed Peppers

INGREDIENTS **Serves 6**

6 red, yellow or orange peppers, tops cut off and deseeded
salt and freshly ground black pepper
175 g/6 oz pastini
4 tbsp olive oil
1 onion, peeled and finely chopped
2 garlic cloves, peeled and finely chopped
3 ripe plum tomatoes, skinned, deseeded and chopped
50 ml/2 fl oz dry white wine
8 pitted black olives, chopped
4 tbsp freshly chopped mixed herbs, such as parsley, basil, oregano or marjoram
125 g/4 oz mozzarella cheese, diced
4 tbsp grated Parmesan cheese
fresh tomato sauce, preferably home-made, to serve

Preheat the oven to 190°C/375°F/Gas Mark 5, 10 minutes before cooking. Bring a pan of water to the boil. Trim the bottom of each pepper so it sits straight. Blanch the peppers for 2–3 minutes, then drain on absorbent kitchen paper.

Return the water to the boil, add ½ teaspoon of salt and the pastini and cook for 3–4 minutes, or until 'al dente'. Drain thoroughly, rinse under cold running water, drain again and reserve.

Heat 2 tablespoons of the olive oil in a large frying pan, add the onion and cook for 3–4 minutes. Add the garlic and cook for 1 minute. Stir in the tomatoes and wine and cook for 5 minutes, stirring frequently. Add the olives, herbs, mozzarella cheese and half the Parmesan cheese. Season to taste with salt and pepper. Remove from the heat and stir in the pastini.

Dry the insides of the peppers with absorbent kitchen paper, then season lightly. Arrange the peppers in a lightly oiled shallow baking dish and fill with the pastini mixture. Sprinkle with the remaining Parmesan cheese and drizzle over the remaining oil. Pour in boiling water to come 1 cm/½ inch up the sides of the dish. Cook in the preheated oven for 25 minutes, or until cooked. Serve immediately with freshly made tomato sauce.

# Rice

Endlessly versatile as an accompaniment, a meal in it's own right or even a pudding, rice forms the basis of these delicious recipes. From Risottos, Paella and Egg Fried Rice, to Thai Rice Cakes, Rice-filled Peppers and even Rice Soup, your family will love these tasty dishes. And for those with a sweet tooth, there's a Chocolate Rice Pudding that will banish school meal memories forever.

# Leek & Ham Risotto

INGREDIENTS **Serves 4**

1 tbsp olive oil
25 g/1 oz butter
1 medium onion, peeled and finely chopped
4 leeks, trimmed and thinly sliced
1½ tbsp freshly chopped thyme
350 g/12 oz Arborio rice
1.4 litres/2¼ pints vegetable or chicken stock, heated
225 g/8 oz cooked ham
175 g/6 oz peas, thawed if frozen
50 g/2 oz Parmesan cheese, grated
salt and freshly ground black pepper

Heat the oil and half the butter together in a large saucepan. Add the onion and leeks and cook over a medium heat for 6–8 minutes, stirring occasionally, until soft and beginning to colour. Stir in the thyme and cook briefly.

Add the rice and stir well. Continue stirring over a medium heat for about 1 minute until the rice is glossy. Add a ladleful or two of the stock and stir well until the stock is absorbed. Continue adding stock, a ladleful at a time and stirring well between additions, until about two-thirds of the stock has been added.

Meanwhile, either chop or finely shred the ham, then add to the saucepan of rice together with the peas. Continue adding ladlefuls of stock, as described above, until the rice is tender and the ham is heated through thoroughly.

Add the remaining butter, sprinkle over the Parmesan cheese and season to taste with salt and pepper. When the butter has melted and the cheese has softened, stir well to incorporate. Taste and adjust the seasoning, then serve immediately.

HEALTH RATING 🍏🍏

**VEGETARIAN ALTERNATIVE**
Wild Mushroom Risotto

**SEAFOOD ALTERNATIVE**
Seafood Risotto

## VEGETARIAN ALTERNATIVE
# Wild Mushroom Risotto

INGREDIENTS **Serves 4**

15 g/½ oz dried porcini
1.1 litres/2 pints vegetable stock
75 g/3 oz butter
1 tbsp olive oil
1 onion, peeled and chopped
2–4 garlic cloves, peeled and chopped
1–2 red chillies, deseeded and chopped
225 g/8 oz wild mushrooms, wiped and halved, if large
125 g/4 oz button mushrooms, wiped and sliced
350 g/12 oz Arborio rice
175 g/6 oz cooked prawns, peeled (optional)
150 ml/¼ pint white wine
salt and freshly ground black pepper
1 tbsp lemon zest
1 tbsp freshly snipped chives
2 tbsp freshly chopped parsley

Soak the porcini in 300 ml/½ pint of very hot, but not boiling water for 30 minutes. Drain, reserving the mushrooms and the soaking liquid. Pour the stock into a saucepan and bring to the boil, then reduce the heat to keep it simmering.

Melt the butter and oil in a large, deep frying pan, add the onion, garlic and chillies and cook gently for 5 minutes. Add the wild and button mushrooms with the drained porcini, and continue to cook for 4–5 minutes, stirring frequently.

Stir in the rice and cook for 1 minute. Strain the reserved soaking liquid and stir into the rice with a little of the hot stock. Cook gently, stirring frequently, until the liquid is absorbed.

Continue to add most of the stock, a ladleful at a time, cooking after each addition, until the rice is tender and the risotto looks creamy.

Add the prawns, if using, and wine along with the last additions of stock. When the prawns are hot and all the liquid is absorbed, season to taste with salt and pepper. Remove from the heat and stir in the lemon zest, chives and parsley, reserving some for the garnish. Garnish and serve.

## SEAFOOD ALTERNATIVE
# Seafood Risotto

INGREDIENTS **Serves 4**

50 g/2 oz butter
2 shallots, peeled and finely chopped
1 garlic clove, peeled and crushed
350 g/12 oz Arborio rice
150 ml/¼ pint white wine
600 ml/1 pint fish or vegetable stock, heated
125 g/4 oz large prawns
290 g can baby clams
50 g/2 oz smoked salmon trimmings
2 tbsp freshly chopped parsley

**To serve:**
green salad
crusty bread

Melt the butter in a large, heavy-based saucepan, add the shallots and garlic and cook for 2 minutes until slightly softened. Add the rice and cook for 1–2 minutes, stirring continuously, then pour in the wine and boil for 1 minute.

Pour in half the hot stock, bring to the boil, cover the saucepan and simmer gently for 15 minutes, adding the remaining stock a little at a time. Continue to simmer for 5 minutes, or until the rice is cooked and all the liquid is absorbed.

Meanwhile, prepare the fish by peeling the prawns and removing the heads and tails. Drain the clams and discard the liquid. Cut the smoked salmon trimmings into thin strips.

When the rice has cooked, stir in the prawns, clams, smoked salmon strips and half the chopped parsley, then heat through for 1–2 minutes until everything is piping hot. Turn into a serving dish, sprinkle with the remaining parsley and the Parmesan cheese and serve immediately with a green salad and crusty bread.

# Risi e Bisi

INGREDIENTS **Serves 4**

700 g/1½ lb young peas in pods or 175 g/6 oz frozen petits pois, thawed
25 g/1 oz unsalted butter
1 tsp olive oil
3 rashers pancetta or unsmoked back bacon, chopped
1 small onion, peeled and finely chopped
1 garlic clove, peeled and finely chopped
1.3 litres/2¼ pints vegetable stock
pinch of caster sugar
1 tsp lemon juice
1 bay leaf
200 g/7 oz Arborio rice
3 tbsp freshly chopped parsley
50 g/2 oz Parmesan cheese, finely grated
salt and freshly ground black pepper

**To garnish:**
sprig of fresh parsley
julienne strips of orange rind

Shell the peas, if using fresh ones. Melt the butter and olive oil together in a large, heavy-based saucepan. Add the chopped pancetta or bacon, the chopped onion and garlic and gently fry for about 10 minutes, or until the onion is softened and is just beginning to colour.

Pour in the vegetable stock, then add the caster sugar, lemon juice and bay leaf. Add the fresh peas if using. Bring the mixture to a fast boil.

Add the rice, stir and simmer, uncovered, for about 20 minutes or until the rice is tender. Occasionally stir the mixture gently while it cooks. If using frozen petits pois, stir them into the rice about 2 minutes before the end of the cooking time.

When the rice is cooked, remove the bay leaf and discard. Stir in 2½ tablespoons of the chopped parsley and the grated Parmesan cheese. Season to taste with salt and pepper.

Transfer the rice to a large serving dish. Garnish with the remaining chopped parsley, a sprig of fresh parsley and julienne strips of orange rind. Serve immediately while piping hot.

HEALTH RATING ●●●

**ENTERTAINING ALTERNATIVE**
Italian Risotto

**SEAFOOD ALTERNATIVE**
Paella

## ENTERTAINING ALTERNATIVE
# Italian Risotto

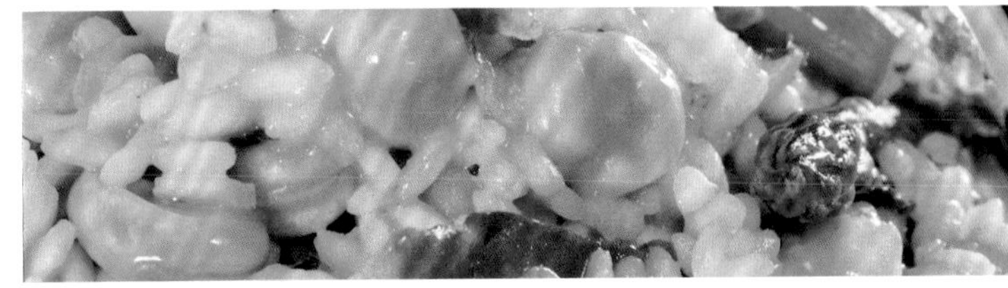

Chop the onion and garlic and reserve. Heat the olive oil in a large frying pan and cook the salami for 3–5 minutes, or until golden. Using a slotted spoon, transfer to a plate and keep warm. Add the asparagus and stir-fry for 2–3 minutes, until just wilted. Transfer to the plate with the salami. Add the onion and garlic to the pan and cook for 5 minutes, or until softened.

Add the rice to the pan and cook for about 2 minutes. Add the wine, bring to the boil, then simmer, stirring until the wine has been absorbed. Add half the stock and return to the boil. Simmer, stirring until the liquid has been absorbed.

Add half of the remaining stock and the broad beans to the rice mixture. Bring to the boil, then simmer for a further 5–10 minutes, or until all of the liquid has been absorbed.

Add the remaining stock, bring to the boil, then simmer until all the liquid is absorbed and the rice is tender. Stir in the remaining ingredients until the cheese has just melted. Serve immediately.

INGREDIENTS **Serves 4**

- 1 onion, peeled
- 2 garlic cloves, peeled
- 1 tbsp olive oil
- 125 g/4 oz Italian salami or speck, chopped
- 125 g/4 oz asparagus
- 350 g/12 oz risotto rice
- 300 ml/½ pt dry white wine
- 1 litre/1¾ pints chicken stock, warmed
- 125 g/4 oz frozen broad beans, thawed
- 125 g/4 oz Dolcelatte cheese, diced
- 3 tbsp freshly chopped mixed herbs, such as parsley and basil
- salt and freshly ground black pepper

## SEAFOOD ALTERNATIVE
# Paella

Rinse the mussels under cold running water, scrubbing well to remove any grit and barnacles, then pull off the hairy 'beards'. Tap any open mussels sharply with a knife, and discard if they refuse to close. Heat the oil in a paella pan or large, heavy-based frying pan and cook the chicken thighs for 10–15 minutes until golden. Remove and keep warm.

Fry the onion and garlic in the remaining oil in the pan for 2–3 minutes, then add the tomatoes, peppers, peas and paprika and cook for a further 3 minutes. Add the rice to the pan and return the chicken with the turmeric and half the stock. Bring to the boil and simmer, gradually adding more stock as it is absorbed. Cook for 20 minutes, or until most of the stock has been absorbed and the rice is almost tender.

Put the mussels in a large saucepan with 5 cm/2 inches boiling salted water, cover and steam for 5 minutes. Discard any with shells that have not opened, then stir into the rice with the prawns. Season to taste with salt and pepper. Heat through for 2–3 minutes until piping hot. Squeeze the juice from one of the limes over the paella. Cut the remaining limes and the lemon into wedges and arrange on top of the paella. Sprinkle with the basil, garnish with the prawns and serve.

INGREDIENTS **Serves 6**

- 450 g/1 lb live mussels
- 4 tbsp olive oil
- 6 medium chicken thighs
- 1 medium onion, peeled and finely chopped
- 1 garlic clove, peeled and crushed
- 225 g/8 oz tomatoes, skinned, deseeded and chopped
- 1 red pepper, deseeded and chopped
- 1 green pepper, deseeded and chopped
- 125 g/4 oz frozen peas
- 1 tsp paprika
- 450 g/1 lb Arborio rice
- ½ tsp turmeric
- 900 ml/1½ pints chicken stock, warmed
- 175 g/6 oz large peeled prawns
- salt and freshly ground black pepper
- 2 limes
- 1 lemon
- 1 tbsp freshly chopped basil
- whole cooked unpeeled prawns, to garnish

# Spring Vegetable & Herb Risotto

INGREDIENTS **Serves 2–3**

1 litre/1¾ pints vegetable stock
125 g/4 oz asparagus tips, trimmed
125 g/4 oz baby carrots, scrubbed
50 g/2 oz peas, fresh or frozen
50 g/2 oz fine French beans, trimmed
1 tbsp olive oil
1 onion, peeled and finely chopped
1 garlic clove, peeled and finely chopped
2 tsp freshly chopped thyme
225 g/8 oz risotto rice
150 ml/¼ pint white wine
1 tbsp each freshly chopped basil, chives and parsley
zest of ½ lemon
3 tbsp crème fraîche
salt and freshly ground black pepper

Bring the vegetable stock to the boil in a large saucepan and add the asparagus, baby carrots, peas and beans. Bring the stock back to the boil and remove the vegetables at once using a slotted spoon. Rinse under cold running water. Drain again and reserve. Keep the stock hot.

Heat the oil in a large, deep frying pan and add the onion. Cook over a medium heat for 4–5 minutes until starting to brown. Add the garlic and thyme and cook for a further few seconds. Add the rice and stir well for a minute until the rice is hot and coated in oil.

Add the white wine and stir constantly until the wine is almost completely absorbed by the rice. Begin adding the stock a ladleful at a time, stirring well and waiting until the last ladleful has been absorbed before stirring in the next. Add the vegetables after using about half of the stock. Continue until all the stock is used. This will take 20–25 minutes. The rice and vegetables should both be tender.

Remove the pan from the heat. Stir in the herbs, lemon zest and crème fraîche. Season to taste with salt and pepper and serve immediately.

HEALTH RATING 🍎🍎🍎

**MEAT ALTERNATIVE**

Chicken & Summer Vegetable Risotto

**CHILDREN'S ALTERNATIVE**

Sausage & Bacon Risotto

**MEAT ALTERNATIVE**
## Chicken & Summer Vegetable Risotto

INGREDIENTS **Serves 4**

- 1 litre/1¾ pints chicken or vegetable stock
- 225 g/8 oz baby asparagus spears
- 125 g/4 oz French beans
- 15 g/½ oz butter
- 1 small onion, peeled and finely chopped
- 150 ml/¼ pint dry white wine
- 275 g/10 oz Arborio rice
- pinch of saffron strands
- 75 g/3 oz frozen peas, thawed
- 225 g/8 oz cooked chicken, skinned and diced
- juice of ½ lemon
- salt and freshly ground black pepper
- 25 g/1 oz Parmesan, shaved

Bring the stock to the boil in a large saucepan. Trim the asparagus and cut into 4 cm/1½ inch lengths. Blanch the asparagus in the stock for 1–2 minutes or until tender, then remove with a slotted spoon and reserve.

Halve the green beans and cook in the boiling stock for 4 minutes. Remove and reserve. Turn down the heat and keep the stock barely simmering.

Melt the butter in a heavy-based saucepan. Add the onion and cook gently for about 5 minutes. Pour the wine into the pan and boil rapidly until the liquid has almost reduced. Add the rice and cook, stirring for 1 minute until the grains are coated and look translucent. Add the saffron and a ladle of the stock. Simmer, stirring all the time, until the stock has absorbed. Continue adding the stock, a ladle at a time, until it has all been absorbed.

After 15 minutes the risotto should be creamy with a slight bite to it. If not add a little more stock and cook for a few more minutes, or until it is of the correct texture and consistency. Add the peas, reserved vegetables, chicken and lemon juice. Season to taste with salt and pepper and cook for 3–4 minutes or until the chicken is thoroughly heated and piping hot. Spoon the risotto on to warmed serving plates. Scatter each portion with a few shavings of Parmesan cheese and serve immediately.

**CHILDREN'S ALTERNATIVE**
## Sausage & Bacon Risotto

INGREDIENTS **Serves 4**

- 225 g/8 oz long-grain rice
- 1 tbsp olive oil
- 25 g/1 oz butter
- 175 g/6 oz cocktail sausages
- 1 shallot, peeled and finely chopped
- 75 g/3 oz bacon lardons or thick slices of streaky bacon, chopped
- 150 g/5 oz chorizo or similar spicy sausage, cut into chunks
- 1 green pepper, deseeded and cut into strips
- 197 g can of sweetcorn, drained
- 2 tbsp freshly chopped parsley
- 50 g/2 oz mozzarella cheese, grated

Cook the rice in a saucepan of boiling salted water for 15 minutes or until tender, or according to packet instructions. Drain and rinse in cold water. Drain again and leave until completely cold.

Meanwhile, heat the wok, pour in the oil and melt the butter. Cook the cocktail sausages, turning continuously until cooked. Remove with a slotted spoon, cut in half and keep warm.

Add the chopped shallot and bacon to the wok and cook for 2–3 minutes until cooked but not browned. Add the spicy sausage and green pepper and stir-fry for a further 3 minutes.

Add the cold rice and the sweetcorn to the wok and stir-fry for 2 minutes, then return the cooked sausages to the wok and stir over the heat until everything is piping hot.

Garnish with the freshly chopped parsley and serve immediately with a little grated mozzarella cheese.

**ORIENTAL ALTERNATIVE**
## Sweet-&-Sour Rice with Chicken

Trim the spring onions, then cut lengthways into fine strips. Drop into a large bowl of iced water and reserve.

Mix together the sesame oil and Chinese five spice powder and use to rub into the cubed chicken. Heat the wok, then add the oil and when hot, cook the garlic and onion for 2–3 minutes, or until transparent and softened.

Add the chicken and stir-fry over a medium-high heat until the chicken is golden and cooked through. Using a slotted spoon, remove from the wok and keep warm.

Stir the rice into the wok and add the water, tomato ketchup, tomato purée, honey, vinegar and soy sauce. Stir well to mix.

Bring to the boil, then simmer until almost all of the liquid is absorbed. Stir in the carrot and reserved chicken and continue to cook for 3–4 minutes.

Drain the spring onions, which will have become curly. Garnish with the spring onion curls and serve immediately with the rice and chicken.

INGREDIENTS **Serves 4**

4 spring onions
2 tsp sesame oil
1 tsp Chinese five spice powder
450 g/1 lb chicken breast, cut into cubes
1 tbsp oil
1 garlic clove, peeled and crushed
1 medium onion, peeled and sliced into thin wedges
225 g/8 oz long-grain white rice
600 ml/1 pint water
4 tbsp tomato ketchup
1 tbsp tomato purée
2 tbsp honey
1 tbsp vinegar
1 tbsp dark soy sauce
1 carrot, peeled and cut into matchsticks

**ENTERTAINING ALTERNATIVE**
## Red Prawn Curry with Jasmine-scented rice

Using a pestle and mortar or a spice grinder, grind the coriander and cumin seeds, peppercorns and salt to a fine powder. Add the dried chillies one at a time and grind to a fine powder. Place the shallots, garlic, galangal or ginger, kaffir lime leaf or rind, chilli powder and shrimp paste in a food processor. Add the ground spices and process until a thick paste forms. Scrape down the bowl once or twice, adding a few drops of water if the mixture is too thick and not forming a paste. Stir in the lemon grass.

Transfer the paste to a large wok and cook over a medium heat for 2–3 minutes or until fragrant. Stir in the coconut milk, bring to the boil, then lower the heat and simmer for about 10 minutes. Add the chilli, fish sauce, sugar and red pepper and simmer for 15 minutes. Stir in the prawns and cook for 5 minutes, or until the prawns are pink and tender. Stir in the shredded herbs, heat for a further minute and serve immediately with the cooked rice.

INGREDIENTS **Serves 4**

½ tbsp coriander seeds
1 tsp cumin seeds
1 tsp black peppercorns
½ tsp salt
1–2 dried red chillies
2 shallots, peeled and chopped
3–4 garlic cloves
2.5 cm/1 inch piece fresh galangal or root ginger, peeled and chopped
1 kaffir lime leaf or 1 tsp kaffir lime rind
½ tsp red chilli powder
½ tbsp shrimp paste
1–1½ lemon grass stalks, outer leaves removed and thinly sliced
750 ml/1¼ pints coconut milk
1 red chilli deseeded and thinly sliced
2 tbsp Thai fish sauce
2 tsp soft brown sugar
1 red pepper, deseeded and thinly sliced
550 g/1¼ lb large peeled tiger prawns
2 fresh lime leaves, shredded (optional)
2 tbsp fresh mint leaves, shredded
2 tbsp Thai or Italian basil leaves, shredded
freshly cooked Thai fragrant rice, to serve

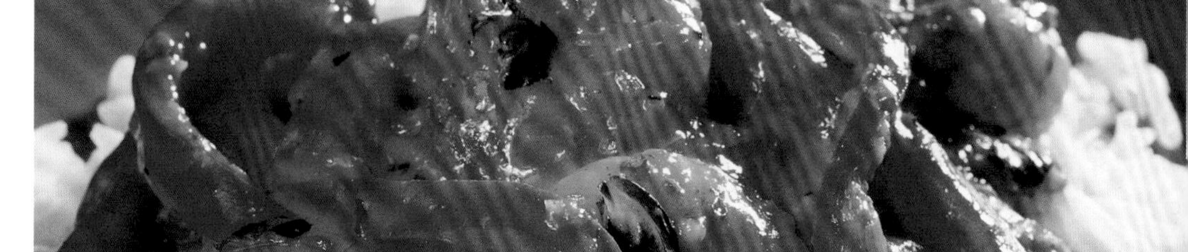

# Creamy Chicken & Rice Pilau

INGREDIENTS **Serves 4–6**

- 350 g/12 oz basmati rice
- salt and freshly ground black pepper
- 50 g/2 oz butter
- 100 g/3½ oz flaked almonds
- 75 g/3 oz unsalted shelled pistachio nuts
- 4–6 skinless chicken breast fillets, each cut into 4 pieces
- 2 tbsp vegetable oil
- 2 medium onions, peeled and thinly sliced
- 2 garlic cloves, peeled and finely chopped
- 2.5 cm/1 inch piece of fresh root ginger, finely chopped
- 6 green cardamom pods, lightly crushed
- 4–6 whole cloves
- 2 bay leaves
- 1 tsp ground coriander
- ½ tsp cayenne pepper, or to taste
- 225 ml/8 fl oz natural yogurt
- 225 ml/8 fl oz double cream
- 225 g/8 oz seedless green grapes, halved if large
- 2 tbsp freshly chopped coriander or mint

Bring a saucepan of lightly salted water to the boil. Gradually pour in the rice, return to the boil, then simmer for about 12 minutes until tender. Drain, rinse under cold water and reserve.

Heat the butter in a large, deep frying pan over a medium-high heat. Add the almonds and pistachios and cook for about 2 minutes, stirring constantly, until golden. Using a slotted spoon, transfer to a plate.

Add the chicken pieces to the pan and cook for about 5 minutes, or until golden, turning once. Remove from the pan and reserve. Add the oil to the pan and cook the onions for 10 minutes, or until golden, stirring frequently. Stir in the garlic, ginger and spices and cook for 2–3 minutes, stirring.

Add 2–3 tablespoons of the yogurt and cook, stirring until the moisture evaporates. Continue adding the yogurt in this way until it is used up.

Return the chicken and nuts to the pan and stir. Stir in 125 ml/4 fl oz of boiling water and season to taste with salt and pepper. Cook, covered, over a low heat for 10 minutes until the chicken is tender. Stir in the cream, grapes and half the herbs. Gently fold in the rice. Heat through for 5 minutes and sprinkle with the remaining herbs, then serve.

HEALTH RATING 🍎🍎

**ORIENTAL ALTERNATIVE**

Sweet-&-Sour Rice with Chicken

**ENTERTAINING ALTERNATIVE**

Red Prawn Curry with Jasmine-scented Rice

# Thai Chicken Fried Rice

INGREDIENTS **Serves 4**

175 g/6 oz boneless, chicken breast
2 tbsp vegetable oil
2 garlic cloves, peeled and finely chopped
2 tsp medium curry paste
450 g/1 lb cold cooked rice
1 tbsp light soy sauce
2 tbsp Thai fish sauce
large pinch of sugar
freshly ground black pepper

**To garnish:**

2 spring onions, trimmed and shredded lengthways
½ small onion, peeled and very finely sliced

Using a sharp knife, trim the chicken, discarding any sinew or fat and cut into small cubes. Reserve.

Heat a wok or large frying pan, add the oil and when hot, add the garlic and cook for 10–20 seconds or until just golden. Add the curry paste and stir-fry for a few seconds. Add the chicken and stir-fry for 3–4 minutes, or until tender and the chicken has turned white.

Stir the cold cooked rice into the chicken mixture, then add the soy sauce, fish sauce and sugar, stirring well after each addition. Stir-fry for 2–3 minutes, or until the chicken is cooked through and the rice is piping hot.

Check the seasoning and, if necessary, add a little extra soy sauce. Turn the rice and chicken mixture into a warmed serving dish. Season lightly with black pepper and garnish with shredded spring onion and onion slices. Serve immediately.

## HEALTH RATING

**MILD ALTERNATIVE**

Lemon Chicken Rice

**ENTERTAINING ALTERNATIVE**

Chicken & Red Pepper Curried Rice

**MILD ALTERNATIVE**
## Lemon Chicken Rice

INGREDIENTS **Serves 4**

- 2 tbsp sunflower oil
- 4 chicken leg portions
- 1 medium onion, peeled and chopped
- 1–2 garlic cloves, peeled and crushed
- 1 tbsp curry powder
- 25 g/1 oz butter
- 225 g/8 oz long-grain white rice
- 1 lemon, preferably unwaxed, sliced
- 600 ml/1 pint chicken stock
- salt and freshly ground black pepper
- 2 tbsp flaked, toasted almonds
- sprigs of fresh coriander, to garnish

Preheat the oven to 180°C/350°F/Gas Mark 4, about 10 minutes before required. Heat the oil in a large frying pan, add the chicken legs and cook, turning, until sealed and golden all over. Using a slotted spoon, remove from the pan and reserve.

Add the onion and garlic to the oil remaining in the frying pan and cook for 5–7 minutes, or until just beginning to brown. Sprinkle in the curry powder and cook, stirring, for a further 1 minute. Return the chicken to the pan and stir well, then remove from the heat.

Melt the butter in a large, heavy-based saucepan. Add the rice and cook, stirring, to ensure that all the grains are coated in the melted butter, then remove from the heat.

Stir the lemon slices into the chicken mixture, then spoon the mixture onto the rice and pour over the stock. Season to taste with salt and pepper. Cover with a tight fitting lid and cook in the preheated oven for 45 minutes, or until the rice is tender and the chicken is thoroughly cooked. Serve sprinkled with the toasted flaked almonds and sprigs of coriander.

**ENTERTAINING ALTERNATIVE**
## Chicken & Red Pepper Curried Rice

INGREDIENTS **Serves 4**

- 350 g/12 oz long-grain rice
- salt
- 1 large egg white
- 1 tbsp cornflour
- 300 g/11 oz skinless chicken breast fillets, cut into chunks
- 3 tbsp groundnut oil
- 1 red pepper, deseeded and roughly chopped
- 1 tbsp curry powder or paste
- 125 ml/4 fl oz chicken stock
- 1 tsp sugar
- 1 tbsp Chinese rice wine or dry sherry
- 1 tbsp light soy sauce
- sprigs of fresh coriander, to garnish

Wash the rice in several changes of water until the water remains relatively clear. Drain well. Put into a saucepan and cover with fresh water. Add a little salt and bring to the boil. Cook for 7–8 minutes until tender. Drain and refresh under cold running water, then drain again and reserve.

Lightly whisk the egg white with 1 teaspoon of salt and 2 teaspoons of cornflour until smooth. Add the chicken and mix together well. Cover and chill in the refrigerator for 20 minutes.

Heat the oil in a wok until moderately hot. Add the chicken mixture to the wok and stir-fry for 2–3 minutes until all the chicken has turned white. Using a slotted spoon, lift the cubes of chicken from the wok, then drain on absorbent kitchen paper. Add the red peppers to the wok and stir-fry for 1 minute over a high heat. Add the curry powder or paste and cook for a further 30 seconds, then add the chicken stock, sugar, Chinese rice wine and soy sauce.

Mix the remaining cornflour with 1 teaspoon of cold water and add to the wok, stirring. Bring to the boil and simmer gently for 1 minute. Return the chicken to the wok, then simmer for a further 1 minute before adding the rice. Stir over a medium heat for another 2 minutes until heated through. Garnish with the sprigs of coriander and serve.

# Turkey & Pesto Rice Roulades

INGREDIENTS **Serves 4**

125 g/4 oz cooked white rice, at room temperature
1 garlic clove, peeled and crushed
1–2 tbsp Parmesan cheese, grated
2 tbsp prepared pesto sauce
2 tbsp pine nuts, lightly toasted and chopped
4 turkey steaks, each weighing about 150 g/5 oz
salt and freshly ground black pepper
4 slices Parma ham
2 tbsp olive oil
50 ml/2 fl oz white wine
25 g/1 oz unsalted butter, chilled

**To serve:**
freshly cooked spinach
freshly cooked pasta

Put the rice in a bowl and add the garlic, Parmesan cheese, pesto and pine nuts. Stir to combine the ingredients, then reserve.

Place the turkey steaks on a chopping board and, using a sharp knife, cut horizontally through each steak, without cutting right through. Open up the steaks and cover with baking parchment. Flatten slightly by pounding with a meat mallet or rolling pin.

Season each steak with salt and pepper. Divide the stuffing equally among the steaks, spreading evenly over one half. Fold the steaks in half to enclose the filling,then wrap each steak in a slice of Parma ham and secure with cocktail sticks.

Heat the oil in a large frying pan over a medium heat. Cook the steaks for 5 minutes, or until golden on one side. Turn and cook for a further 2 minutes. Push the steaks to the side and pour in the wine. Allow the wine to bubble and evaporate. Add the butter, a little at a time, whisking constantly until the sauce is smooth. Discard the cocktail sticks, then serve the steaks drizzled with the sauce and serve with spinach and pasta.

HEALTH RATING

**VEGETARIAN ALTERNATIVE**
Rice-filled Peppers

**SEAFOOD ALTERNATIVE**
Seafood Rice Ring

**VEGETARIAN ALTERNATIVE**

## Rice-filled Peppers

INGREDIENTS **Serves 4**

- 8 ripe tomatoes
- 2 tbsp olive oil
- 1 onion, peeled and chopped
- 1 garlic clove, peeled and crushed
- ½ tsp dark muscovado sugar
- 125 g/4 oz cooked long-grain rice
- 50 g/2 oz pine nuts, toasted
- 1 tbsp freshly chopped oregano
- salt and freshly ground black pepper
- 2 large red peppers
- 2 large yellow peppers

**To serve:**

- mixed salad
- crusty bread

Preheat the oven to 200°C/400°F/Gas Mark 6. Put the tomatoes in a small bowl and pour over boiling water to cover. Leave for 1 minute, then drain. Plunge the tomatoes into cold water to cool, then peel off the skins. Quarter, remove the seeds and chop.

Heat the olive oil in a frying pan, and cook the onion gently for 10 minutes until softened. Add the garlic, chopped tomatoes and sugar.

Gently cook the tomato mixture for 10 minutes until thickened. Remove from the heat and stir the rice, pine nuts and oregano into the sauce. Season to taste with salt and pepper.

Halve the peppers lengthways, cutting through and leaving the stem on. Remove the seeds and cores, then put the peppers in a lightly oiled roasting tin, cut-side down and cook in the preheated oven for about 10 minutes.

Turn the peppers so they are cut side up. Spoon in the filling, then cover with tinfoil. Return to the oven for 15 minutes, or until the peppers are very tender, removing the tinfoil for the last 5 minutes to allow the tops to brown a little.

Serve one red pepper half and one yellow pepper half per person with a mixed salad and plenty of warmed, crusty bread.

**SEAFOOD ALTERNATIVE**

## Seafood Rice Ring

INGREDIENTS **Serves 4**

- 350 g/12 oz long-grain rice
- ½ tsp turmeric
- 5 tbsp sunflower oil
- 2 tbsp white wine vinegar
- 1 tsp Dijon mustard
- 1 tsp caster sugar
- 1 tbsp mild curry paste
- 4 shallots, peeled and finely chopped
- salt and freshly ground black pepper
- 125 g/4 oz peeled prawns, thawed if frozen
- 2 tbsp freshly chopped coriander
- 8 fresh crevettes or large tiger prawns, with shells on
- 4 sprigs of fresh coriander, to garnish
- lemon wedges, to serve

Lightly oil a 1.1 litre/2 pint ring mould, or line the mould with clingfilm. Cook the rice in boiling salted water with the turmeric for 15 minutes, or until tender. Drain thoroughly. Whisk 4 tablespoons of the oil with the vinegar, mustard and sugar to form a dressing and pour over the warm rice. Reserve.

Heat the remaining oil in a saucepan, add the curry paste and shallots and cook for 5 minutes, or until the shallots are just softened. Fold into the dressed rice, season to taste with salt and pepper and mix well. Leave to cool completely.

Stir in the prawns and the chopped coriander and turn into the prepared ring mould. Press the mixture down firmly with a spoon, then chill in the refrigerator for at least 1 hour.

Invert the ring onto a serving plate and fill the centre with the crevettes or tiger prawns. Arrange the cooked mussels around the edge of the ring and garnish with sprigs of fresh coriander. Serve immediately with lemon wedges.

# Thai Rice Cakes with Mango Salsa

INGREDIENTS **Serves 4**

225 g/8 oz Thai fragrant rice
400 g can of coconut milk
1 lemon grass stalk, bruised
2 kaffir lime leaves, shredded
1 tbsp vegetable oil, plus extra for deep frying
1 garlic clove, peeled and finely chopped
1 tsp freshly grated root ginger
1 red pepper, deseeded and finely chopped
2 red chillies, deseeded and finely chopped
1 medium egg, beaten
25 g/1 oz dried breadcrumbs

**For the mango salsa:**

1 large mango, peeled, stoned and finely chopped
1 small red onion, peeled and finely chopped
2 tbsp freshly chopped coriander
2 tbsp freshly chopped basil
juice of 1 lime

Wash the rice in several changes of water until the water stays relatively clear. Drain, place in a saucepan with a tight fitting lid and add the coconut milk, lemon grass and lime leaves. Bring to the boil, cover and cook over the lowest possible heat for 10 minutes. Turn off the heat and leave to stand for 10 minutes, without lifting the lid.

Heat the wok, then add 1 tablespoon of oil and when hot, add the garlic, ginger, red pepper and half the chilli. Stir-fry for 1–2 minutes until just softened then place in a large bowl.

When the rice is cooked, turn into the mixing bowl and add the egg. Season to taste with salt and pepper and mix together well. Put the breadcrumbs into a shallow dish. Form the rice mixture into eight cakes and coat them in the breadcrumbs. Chill the cakes in the refrigerator for 30 minutes.

Meanwhile, make the mango salsa. In a bowl, mix together the mango, red onion, coriander, basil, lime juice and remaining red chilli and reserve.

Fill a clean wok about one-third full of vegetable oil. Heat to 190°C/375°F, or until a cube of bread browns in 30 seconds. Cook the rice cakes, 1 or 2 at a time, for 2–3 minutes until golden and crisp. Drain on absorbent kitchen paper. Serve with the mango salsa.

HEALTH RATING 

**SPEEDY ALTERNATIVE**
Rice Nuggets in Herby Tomato Sauce

**STARTER SUGGESTION**
Bread & Tomato Soup

**SPEEDY ALTERNATIVE**

## Rice Nuggets in Herby Tomato Sauce

INGREDIENTS **Serves 4**

600 ml/1 pint vegetable stock
1 bay leaf
175 g/6 oz Arborio rice
50 g/2 oz Cheddar cheese, grated
1 medium egg yolk
1 tbsp plain flour
2 tbsp freshly chopped parsley
salt and freshly ground black pepper
grated Parmesan cheese, to serve

**For the herby tomato sauce:**

1 tbsp olive oil
1 onion, peeled and thinly sliced
1 garlic clove, peeled and crushed
1 small yellow pepper, deseeded and diced
400 g can chopped tomatoes
1 tbsp freshly chopped basil

Pour the stock into a large saucepan. Add the bay leaf. Bring to the boil, add the rice, stir, then cover and simmer for 15 minutes.

Uncover, reduce the heat to low and cook for a further 5 minutes until the rice is tender and all the stock is absorbed, stirring frequently towards the end of cooking time. Leave to cool.

Stir the cheese, egg yolk, flour and parsley into the rice. Season to taste, then shape into 20 walnut-sized balls. Cover and refrigerate.

To make the sauce, heat the oil in a large frying pan and cook the onion for 5 minutes. Add the garlic and yellow pepper and cook for a further 5 minutes, until soft.

Stir in the chopped tomatoes and simmer gently for 3 minutes. Stir in the chopped basil and season to taste.

Add the rice nuggets to the sauce and simmer for a further 10 minutes, or until the rice nuggets are cooked through and the sauce has reduced a little.

Spoon onto serving plates and serve hot, sprinkled with grated Parmesan cheese.

**STARTER SUGGESTION**

## Bread & Tomato Soup

INGREDIENTS **Serves 4**

900 g/2 lb very ripe tomatoes
4 tbsp olive oil
1 onion, peeled and finely chopped
1 tbsp freshly chopped basil
3 garlic cloves, peeled and crushed
¼ tsp hot chilli powder
salt and freshly ground black pepper
600 ml/1 pint chicken stock
175 g/6 oz stale white bread
50 g/2 oz cucumber, cut into small dice
4 whole basil leaves

Make a small cross in the base of each tomato, then place in a bowl and cover with boiling water. Allow to stand for 2 minutes, or until the skins have started to peel away, then drain, remove the skins and seeds and chop into large pieces.

Heat 3 tablespoons of the olive oil in a saucepan and gently cook the onion until softened. Add the skinned tomatoes, chopped basil, garlic and chilli powder and season to taste with salt and pepper. Pour in the stock, cover the saucepan, bring to the boil and simmer gently for 15–20 minutes.

Remove the crusts from the bread and break into small pieces. Remove the tomato mixture from the heat and stir in the bread. Cover and leave to stand for 10 minutes, or until the bread has blended with the tomatoes. Season to taste.

Serve warm or cold with a swirl of olive oil on the top, garnished with a spoonful of chopped cucumber and basil leaves.

**SPICY ALTERNATIVE**
## Brown Rice Spiced Pilaf

INGREDIENTS **Serves 4**

1 tbsp vegetable oil
1 tbsp blanched almonds, flaked or chopped
1 onion, peeled and chopped
1 carrot, peeled and diced
225 g/8 oz flat mushrooms, sliced thickly
¼ tsp cinnamon
large pinch dried chilli flakes
50 g/2 oz dried apricots, roughly chopped
25 g/1 oz currants
zest of 1 orange
350 g/12 oz brown basmati rice
900 ml/1½ pints vegetable stock
2 tbsp freshly chopped coriander
2 tbsp freshly snipped chives
salt and freshly ground black pepper
snipped chives, to garnish

Preheat the oven to 200°C/400°F/Gas Mark 6. Heat the oil in a large flameproof casserole and add the almonds. Cook for 1–2 minutes until just browning – be careful as the nuts will burn very easily.

Add the onion and carrot. Cook for 5 minutes until softened and starting to turn brown. Add the mushrooms and cook for a further 5 minutes, stirring often.

Add the cinnamon and chilli flakes and cook for about 30 seconds before adding the apricots, currants, orange zest and rice.

Stir together well and add the stock. Bring to the boil, cover tightly and transfer to the preheated oven. Cook for 45 minutes until the rice and vegetables are tender.

Stir the coriander and chives into the pilaf and season to taste with salt and pepper. Garnish with the extra chives and serve immediately.

**SUMMER ALTERNATIVE**
## Chef's Rice Salad

INGREDIENTS **Serves 4**

225 g/8 oz wild rice
½ cucumber
175 g/6 oz cherry tomatoes
6 spring onions, trimmed
5 tbsp extra virgin olive oil
2 tbsp balsamic vinegar
1 tsp Dijon mustard
1 tsp caster sugar
salt and freshly ground black pepper
125 g/4 oz rocket
125 g/4 oz back bacon
125 g/4 oz cooked chicken meat, finely diced
125 g/4 oz Emmenthal cheese, grated
125 g/4 oz large cooked prawns, peeled
1 avocado, stoned, peeled and sliced, to garnish
warm crusty bread, to serve

Put the rice in in a saucepan of water and bring to the boil, stirring once or twice. Reduce the heat, cover and simmer gently for 30–50 minutes, depending on the texture you prefer. Drain well and reserve.

Thinly peel the cucumber, cut in half, then using a teaspoon, remove the seeds. Cut the cucumber into thin slices. Cut the tomatoes in quarters. Cut the spring onions into diagonal slices.

Whisk the olive oil with the vinegar, then whisk in the mustard and sugar. Season to taste with salt and pepper.

In a large bowl, gently toss together the cooled rice with the tomatoes, cucumber, spring onions and the rocket. Pour over the dressing and toss lightly together.

Heat a griddle pan and, when hot, cook the bacon on both sides for 4–6 minutes or until crisp. Remove and chop. Arrange the prepared rice salad on a platter, then arrange the bacon, chicken, cheese and prawns on top. Toss, if wished. Garnish with avocado slices and serve with plenty of warm, crusty bread.

# Mixed Grain Pilaf

INGREDIENTS **Serves 4**

2 tbsp olive oil
1 garlic clove, peeled and crushed
½ tsp ground turmeric
125 g/4 oz mixed long-grain and wild rice
50 g/2 oz red split lentils
300 ml/½ pint vegetable stock
200 g can chopped tomatoes
5 cm/2 inch piece cinnamon stick
salt and freshly ground black pepper
400 g can mixed beans, drained and rinsed
15 g/½ oz butter
1 bunch spring onions, trimmed and finely sliced
3 medium eggs
4 tbsp freshly chopped herbs, such as parsley and chervil
sprigs of fresh dill, to garnish

Heat 1 tablespoon of the oil in a saucepan. Add the garlic and turmeric and cook for a few seconds. Stir in the rice and lentils.

Add the stock, tomatoes and cinnamon. Season to taste with salt and pepper. Stir once and bring to the boil. Lower the heat, cover and simmer for 20 minutes, until most of the stock is absorbed and the rice and lentils are tender.

Stir in the beans, replace the lid and leave to stand for 2–3 minutes to allow the beans to heat through.

While the rice is cooking, heat the remaining oil and butter in a frying pan. Add the spring onions and cook for 4–5 minutes, until soft. Lightly beat the eggs with 2 tablespoons of the herbs, then season with salt and pepper.

Pour the egg mixture over the spring onions. Stir gently with a spatula over a low heat, drawing the mixture from the sides to the centre as the omelette sets. When almost set, stop stirring and cook for about 30 seconds until golden underneath.

Remove the omelette from the pan, roll up and slice into thin strips. Fluff the rice up with a fork and remove the cinnamon stick. Spoon onto serving plates, top with strips of omelette and the remaining chopped herbs. Garnish with sprigs of dill and serve.

HEALTH RATING ●●●

**SPICY ALTERNATIVE**

Brown Rice Spiced Pilaf

**SUMMER ALTERNATIVE**

Chef's Rice Salad

# Wild Rice & Bacon Salad with Smoked Chicken

INGREDIENTS **Serves 4**

150 g/5 oz wild rice
50 g/2 oz pecan or walnut halves
1 tbsp vegetable oil
4 slices smoked bacon, diced
3–4 shallots, peeled and finely chopped
75 ml/3 fl oz walnut oil
2–3 tbsp sherry or cider vinegar
2 tbsp freshly chopped dill
salt and freshly ground black pepper
275 g/10 oz smoked chicken or duck breast, thinly sliced
dill sprigs, to garnish

Put the wild rice in a medium saucepan with 600 ml/1 pint water and bring to the boil, stirring once or twice. Reduce the heat, cover and simmer gently for 30–50 minutes, depending on the texture you prefer, chewy or tender. Using a fork, gently fluff into a large bowl and leave to cool slightly.

Meanwhile, toast the nuts in a frying pan over a medium heat for 2 minutes, or until they are fragrant and lightly coloured, stirring and tossing frequently. Cool, then chop coarsely and add to the rice.

Heat the oil in the frying pan over a medium heat. Add the bacon and cook, stirring from time to time, for 3–4 minutes or until crisp and brown. Remove from the pan and drain on absorbent kitchen paper. Add the shallots to the pan and cook for 4 minutes or until just softened, stirring from time to time. Stir into the rice and nuts, with the drained bacon pieces.

Whisk the walnut oil, vinegar, half the dill and salt and pepper in a small bowl until combined. Pour the dressing over the rice mixture and toss well to combine. Mix the chicken and the remaining chopped dill into the rice, then spoon into bowls and garnish each serving with a dill sprig. Serve slightly warm, or at room temperature.

HEALTH RATING 🍎🍎🍎

**ENTERTAINING ALTERNATIVE**
Brown Rice & Lentil Salad with Duck

**SPICY ALTERNATIVE**
Rice & Papaya Salad

## ENTERTAINING ALTERNATIVE
# Brown Rice & Lentil Salad with Duck

Bring a large saucepan of water to the boil, sprinkle in the lentils, return to the boil, then simmer over a low heat for 30 minutes or until tender – do not overcook. Drain and rinse under cold running water, then drain again and reserve.

Heat 2 tablespoons of the oil in a saucepan. Add the onion and cook for 2 minutes until it begins to soften. Stir in the rice with the thyme and stock. Season to taste with salt and pepper and bring to the boil. Cover and simmer for 40 minutes, or until tender and the liquid is absorbed.

Heat the remaining oil in a large frying pan and add the mushrooms. Cook for 5 minutes until golden. Stir in the duck and garlic and cook for 2–3 minutes to heat through. Season well.

To make the dressing, whisk the vinegars, mustard and honey in a large serving bowl, then gradually whisk in the oils. Add the lentils and the rice, then stir lightly together. Gently stir in the ham, blanched courgettes, spring onions and parsley. Season to taste and sprinkle with the walnuts. Serve topped with the duck and mushrooms.

INGREDIENTS **Serves 6**

- 225 g/8 oz puy lentils, rinsed
- 4 tbsp olive oil
- 1 medium onion, peeled and finely chopped
- 200 g/7 oz long-grain brown rice
- ½ tsp dried thyme
- 450 ml/¾ pint chicken stock
- salt and freshly ground black pepper
- 350 g/12 oz shiitake or portabella mushrooms, trimmed and sliced
- 375 g/13 oz cooked Chinese-style spicy duck or roasted duck, sliced into chunks
- 2 garlic cloves, peeled and finely chopped
- 125 g/4 oz cooked smoked ham, diced
- 2 small courgettes, trimmed, diced and blanched
- 6 spring onions, trimmed and thinly sliced
- 2 tbsp freshly chopped parsley
- 2 tbsp walnut halves, toasted and chopped

**For the dressing:**

- 2 tbsp red or white wine vinegar
- 1 tbsp balsamic vinegar
- 1 tsp Dijon mustard
- 1 tsp clear honey
- 75 ml/3 fl oz extra virgin olive oil
- 2–3 tbsp walnut oil

## SPICY ALTERNATIVE
# Rice & Papaya Salad

Rinse and drain the rice and pour into a saucepan. Add 450 ml/¾ pint boiling salted water and the cinnamon stick. Bring to the boil, reduce the heat to very low, then cover and cook without stirring for 15–18 minutes or until all the liquid is absorbed. The rice should be light and fluffy and have steam holes on the surface. Remove the cinnamon stick and stir in the rind from 1 lime.

To make the dressing, place the bird's-eye chilli, remaining rind and lime and lemon juice, fish sauce and sugar in a food processor and mix for a few minutes until blended. Alternatively, place all these ingredients in a screw-top jar and shake until well blended. Pour half the dressing over the hot rice and toss until the rice glistens.

Slice the papaya and mango into thin slices, then place in a bowl. Add the chopped green chilli, coriander and mint. Place the cooked chicken on a chopping board and remove and discard any skin or sinews. Cut into fine shreds and add to the bowl with the chopped peanuts.

Add the remaining dressing to the chicken mixture and stir until all the ingredients are lightly coated. Spoon the rice onto a platter, pile the chicken mixture on top and serve with warm strips of pitta bread.

INGREDIENTS **Serves 4**

- 175 g/6 oz easy-cook basmati rice
- 1 cinnamon stick, bruised
- 1 bird's-eye chilli, deseeded and finely chopped
- rind and juice of 2 limes
- rind and juice of 2 lemons
- 2 tbsp Thai fish sauce
- 1 tbsp soft light brown sugar
- 1 papaya, peeled and seeds removed
- 1 mango, peeled and stone removed
- 1 green chilli, deseeded and finely chopped
- 2 tbsp freshly chopped coriander
- 1 tbsp freshly chopped mint
- 250 g/9 oz cooked chicken
- 50 g/2 oz roasted peanuts, chopped
- strips of pitta bread, to serve

# Rice Soup with Potato Sticks

INGREDIENTS **Serves 4**

175 g/6 oz butter
1 tsp olive oil
1 large onion, peeled and finely chopped
4 slices Parma ham, chopped
100 g/3½ oz Arborio rice
1.1 litres/2 pints chicken stock
350 g/12 oz frozen peas
salt and freshly ground black pepper
1 medium egg
125 g/4 oz self-raising flour
175 g/6 oz mashed potato
1 tbsp milk
1 tbsp poppy seeds
1 tbsp Parmesan cheese, finely grated
1 tbsp freshly chopped parsley

Preheat the oven to 190°C/375°F/Gas Mark 5. Heat 25 g/1 oz of the butter and the olive oil in a saucepan and cook the onion for 4–5 minutes until softened, then add the Parma ham and cook for about 1 minute. Stir in the rice, the stock and the peas. Season to taste with salt and pepper and simmer for 10–15 minutes, or until the rice is tender.

Beat the egg and 125 g/4 oz of the butter together until smooth, then beat in the flour, a pinch of salt and the potato. Work the ingredients together to form a soft, pliable dough, adding a little more flour if necessary.

Roll the dough out on a lightly floured surface into a rectangle 1 cm/½ inch thick and cut into 12 long, thin sticks. Brush with milk and sprinkle on the poppy seeds. Place the sticks on a lightly oiled baking tray and bake in the preheated oven for 15 minutes, or until golden.

When the rice is cooked, stir the remaining butter and Parmesan cheese into the soup and sprinkle the chopped parsley over the top. Serve immediately with the warm potato sticks.

HEALTH RATING 🍎🍎

**SPEEDY ALTERNATIVE**
Rice & Tomato Soup

**SUGGESTED ACCOMPANIMENT**
Daktyla-style Bread

**SPEEDY ALTERNATIVE**
## Rice & Tomato Soup

INGREDIENTS **Serves 4**

- 150 g/5 oz easy-cook basmati rice
- 400 g can chopped tomatoes
- 2 garlic cloves, peeled and crushed
- grated rind of ½ lime
- 2 tbsp extra virgin olive oil
- 1 tsp sugar
- salt and freshly ground pepper
- 300 ml/½ pint vegetable stock or water

**For the croûtons:**

- 2 tbsp prepared pesto sauce
- 2 tbsp olive oil
- 6 thin slices ciabatta bread, cut into 1 cm/½ inch cubes

Preheat the oven to 220°C/425°F/Gas Mark 7. Rinse and drain the basmati rice. Place the canned tomatoes with their juice in a large, heavy-based saucepan with the garlic, lime rind, oil and sugar. Season to taste with salt and pepper. Bring to the boil, then reduce the heat, cover and simmer for 10 minutes.

Add the boiling vegetable stock or water and the rice, then cook, uncovered, for a further 15–20 minutes or until the rice is tender. If the soup is too thick, add a little more water. Reserve and keep warm, if the croutons are not ready.

Meanwhile, to make the croutons, mix the pesto and olive oil in a large bowl. Add the bread cubes and toss until they are coated completely with the mixture. Spread on a baking sheet and bake in the preheated oven for 10–15 minutes, until golden and crisp, turning them over halfway through cooking. Serve the soup immediately sprinkled with the warm croutons.

**SUGGESTED ACCOMPANIMENT**
## Daktyla-style Bread

INGREDIENTS **Makes 1 loaf**

- 350 g/12 oz strong white flour
- 125 g/4 oz wholemeal flour
- 1 tsp salt
- 50 g/2 oz fine cornmeal
- 2 tsp easy-blend dried yeast
- 2 tsp clear honey
- 1 tbsp olive oil
- 4 tbsp milk
- 250 ml/9 fl oz water

**To glaze & finish:**

- 4 tbsp milk
- 4 tbsp sesame seeds

Preheat the oven to 220°C/425°F/Gas Mark 7, 15 minutes before baking. Sift the white and wholemeal flours and salt into a large bowl, adding the bran left in the sieve. Stir in the cornmeal and yeast. Make a well in the centre.

Put the honey, oil, milk and water in a saucepan and heat gently until tepid. Add to the dry ingredients and mix to a soft dough, adding a little more water if needed.

Knead the dough on a lightly floured surface for 10 minutes, until smooth and elastic. Put in an oiled bowl, cover with clingfilm and leave to rise in a warm place for 1½ hours or until it has doubled in size.

Turn the dough out and knead for a minute or two. Shape into a long oval about 25.5 cm/10 inches long. Cut the oval into six equal pieces. Shape each piece into an oblong, then on an oiled baking sheet arrange in a row so that all the pieces of dough are touching.

Cover with oiled clingfilm and leave for 45 minutes, or until doubled in size.

Brush the bread with milk, then scatter with sesame seeds.

Bake the bread in the preheated oven for 40–45 minutes, or until golden brown and hollow-sounding when tapped underneath. Cool on a wire rack and serve.

# Chinese Egg Fried Rice

INGREDIENTS **Serves 4**

250 g/9 oz long-grain rice
1 tbsp dark sesame oil
2 large eggs
1 tbsp sunflower oil
2 garlic cloves, peeled and crushed
2.5 cm/1 inch piece fresh root ginger, peeled and grated
1 carrot, peeled and cut into matchsticks
125 g/4 oz mangetout, halved
220 g can water chestnuts, drained and halved
1 yellow pepper, deseeded and diced
4 spring onions, trimmed and finely shredded
2 tbsp light soy sauce
½ tsp paprika
salt and freshly ground black pepper

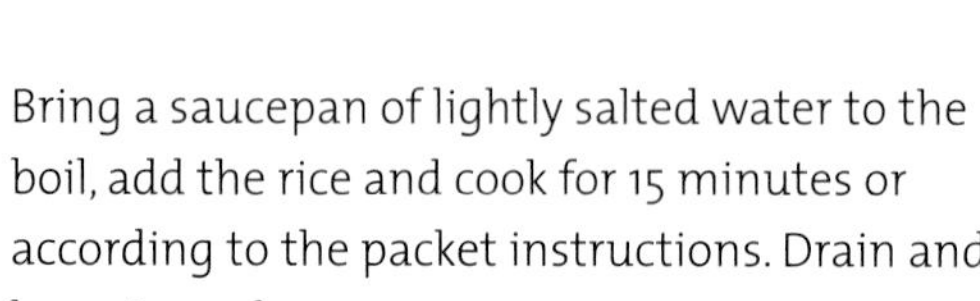

Bring a saucepan of lightly salted water to the boil, add the rice and cook for 15 minutes or according to the packet instructions. Drain and leave to cool.

Heat a wok or large frying pan and add the sesame oil. Beat the eggs in a small bowl and pour into the hot wok. Using a fork, draw the egg in from the sides of the pan to the centre until it sets, then turn over and cook the other side. When set and golden turn out on to a board. Leave to cool, then cut into very thin strips.

Wipe the wok clean with absorbent kitchen paper, return to the heat and add the sunflower oil. When hot add the garlic and ginger and stir-fry for 30 seconds. Add the remaining vegetables and continue to stir-fry for 3–4 minutes, or until tender but still crisp.

Stir the reserved cooked rice into the wok with the soy sauce and paprika and season to taste with salt and pepper. Fold in the cooked egg strips and heat through. Tip into a warmed serving dish and serve immediately.

HEALTH RATING

**ENTERTAINING ALTERNATIVE**

Special Fried Rice

**STARTER SUGGESTION**

Chicken & Lamb Satay

## ENTERTAINING ALTERNATIVE
# Special Fried Rice

INGREDIENTS **Serves 4**

1 large egg

1 tsp sesame oil

350 g/8 oz long-grain white rice

1 tbsp groundnut oil

450 g/1 lb boneless, skinless chicken breast, diced

8 spring onions, trimmed and sliced

2 large carrots, trimmed and cut into matchsticks

125 g/4 oz sugar snap peas

125 g/4 oz raw tiger prawns, peeled

2 tsp Chinese five spice powder

1 tbsp soy sauce

1 tbsp Thai fish sauce

1 tbsp rice wine vinegar

Beat the egg in a bowl with ½ teaspoon of the sesame oil and 2 teaspoons of water. Heat a frying pan over a medium-high heat and swirl in 2 tablespoons of the egg mixture to form a paper-thin omelette. Remove and reserve. Repeat this process until all the egg has been used.

Cook the rice in lightly salted boiling water for 12 minutes, or until tender. Drain and reserve.

Heat a wok, then add the remaining sesame oil with the groundnut oil and stir-fry the chicken for 5 minutes until cooked through. Using a slotted spoon, remove from the wok and keep warm.

Add the spring onions, carrot and sugar snap peas to the wok and stir-fry for 2–3 minutes. Add the prawns and stir-fry for 2–3 minutes, or until pink. Return the chicken to the wok with the Chinese five spice powder and stir-fry for 1 minute. Stir in the drained rice.

Mix together the soy sauce, fish sauce and vinegar. Pour into the wok and continue to stir-fry for 2–3 minutes. Roll the papery omelettes into tight rolls and slice to form thin strips. Stir into the rice and serve immediately.

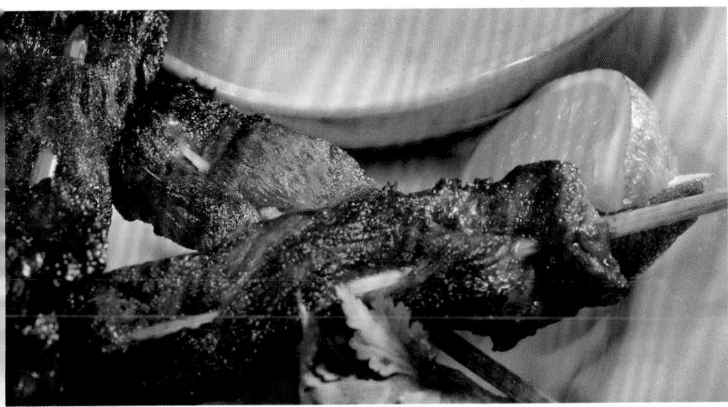

## STARTER SUGGESTION
# Chicken & Lamb Satay

INGREDIENTS **Makes 16**

225 g/8 oz skinless, boneless chicken

225 g/8 oz lean lamb

**For the marinade:**

1 small onion, peeled and finely chopped

2 garlic cloves, peeled and crushed

2.5 cm/1 inch piece fresh root ginger, peeled and grated

4 tbsp soy sauce

1 tsp ground coriander

2 tsp dark brown sugar

2 tbsp lime juice

1 tbsp vegetable oil

**For the peanut sauce:**

300 ml/½ pint coconut milk

4 tbsp crunchy peanut butter

1 tbsp Thai fish sauce

1 tsp lime juice

1 tbsp chilli powder

1 tbsp brown sugar

salt and freshly ground black pepper

**To garnish:**

sprigs of fresh coriander

lime wedges

Preheat the grill just before cooking. Soak the bamboo skewers for 30 minutes before required. Cut the chicken and lamb into thin strips, about 7.5 cm/ 3 inches long and place in two shallow dishes. Blend all the marinade ingredients together, then pour half over the chicken and half over the lamb.

Stir until lightly coated, then cover with clingfilm and leave to marinate in the refrigerator for at least 2 hours, turning occasionally.

Remove the chicken and lamb from the marinade and thread on to the skewers. Reserve the marinade. Cook under the preheated grill for 8–10 minutes or until cooked, turning and brushing with the marinade.

Meanwhile, make the peanut sauce. Blend the coconut milk with the peanut butter, fish sauce, lime juice, chilli powder and sugar. Pour into a saucepan and cook gently for 5 minutes, stirring occasionally, then season to taste with salt and pepper. Garnish with coriander sprigs and lime wedges and serve the satays with the prepared sauce.

**CHILDREN'S ALTERNATIVE**
## Chocolate Rice Pudding

INGREDIENTS **Serves 6–8**

60 g/2½ oz pudding rice
75 g/3 oz caster sugar
410 g can evaporated milk
600 ml/1 pint milk
pinch of freshly grated nutmeg
¼ tsp ground cinnamon, optional
50 g/2 oz plain chocolate chips
25 g/1 oz butter
freshly sliced strawberries, to decorate
crème fraîche, to serve

Preheat the oven to 170°C/325°F/Gas Mark 3, 10 minutes before cooking. Lightly butter a large ovenproof dish. Rinse the pudding rice, then place in the base of the buttered dish and sprinkle over the caster sugar.

Pour the evaporated milk and milk into a heavy-based saucepan and bring slowly to the boil over a low heat, stirring occasionally to avoid sticking. Pour the milk over the rice and sugar and stir well until well mixed and the sugar has dissolved.

Grate a little nutmeg over the top, then sprinkle with the ground cinnamon, if liked. Cover tightly with tinfoil and bake in the preheated oven for 30 minutes.

Remove the pudding from the oven and stir well to break up any lumps that may have formed. Cover with tinfoil and return to the oven for a further 30 minutes. Remove the pudding from the oven once again and stir to break up any more lumps.

Stir the chocolate chips into the rice pudding and then dot with the butter. Continue to bake, uncovered, in the oven for a further 45 minutes–1 hour, or until the rice is tender and the skin is golden brown. Serve warm, with or without the skin, according to personal preference. Serve with a few sliced strawberries and a spoonful of crème fraîche.

**ENTERTAINING ALTERNATIVE**
## Coconut Rice Served with Stewed Ginger Fruits

INGREDIENTS **Serves 6–8**

1 vanilla pod
450 ml/¾ pint coconut milk
1.1 litres/2 pints semi-skimmed milk
600 ml/1 pint double cream
100 g/3½ oz caster sugar
2 star anise
8 tbsp toasted desiccated coconut
250 g/9 oz short-grain pudding rice
1 tsp melted butter
2 mandarin oranges, peeled and pith removed
1 star fruit, sliced
50 g/2 oz stem ginger, finely diced
300 ml/½ pint sweet white wine
caster sugar, to taste

Preheat the oven to 160°C/325°F/Gas Mark 3. Using a sharp knife, split the vanilla pod in half lengthways, scrape out the seeds from the pods and place both the pod and seeds in a large, heavy-based casserole dish. Pour in the coconut milk, the semi-skimmed milk and the double cream and stir in the sugar, star anise and 4 tablespoons of the toasted coconut. Bring to the boil, then simmer for 10 minutes, stirring occasionally. Remove the vanilla pod and star anise.

Wash the rice and add to the milk. Simmer gently for 25–30 minutes or until the rice is tender, stirring frequently. Stir in the melted butter.

Divide the mandarins into segments and place in a saucepan with the sliced star fruit and stem ginger. Pour in the white wine and 300 ml/½ pint water, bring to the boil, then reduce the heat and simmer for 20 minutes or until the liquid has reduced and the fruits softened. Add sugar to taste. Serve the rice, topped with the stewed fruits and the remaining toasted coconut.

# Rice Pudding

NGREDIENTS **Serves 4**

- o g/2½ oz pudding rice
- o g/2 oz granulated sugar
- 10 g can light evaporated milk
- oo ml/½ pint semi-skimmed milk
- inch of freshly grated nutmeg
- 5 g/1 oz butter
- am, to serve

reheat the oven to 150°C/300°F/Gas Mark 2. Lightly oil a arge ovenproof dish.

prinkle the rice and the sugar into the dish and mix.

Bring the evaporated milk and milk to the boil in a small pan, stirring occasionally.

Stir the milks into the rice and mix well until the rice is coated thoroughly.

Sprinkle over the nutmeg, cover with tinfoil and bake in the preheated oven for 30 minutes.

Remove the pudding from the oven and stir well, breaking up any lumps.

Cover with the same tinfoil. Bake in the preheated oven for a further 30 minutes. Remove from the oven and stir well again.

Dot the pudding with butter and bake for a further 45–60 minutes, until the rice is tender and the skin is browned.

Divide the pudding into four individual serving bowls. Top with a large spoonful of the jam and serve immediately.

## HEALTH RATING

**CHILDREN'S ALTERNATIVE**

Chocolate Rice Pudding

**ENTERTAINING ALTERNATIVE**

Coconut Rice Served with Stewed Ginger Fruits

# Pasta

When it comes to quick and simple dishes, nothing beats pasta for speed and convenience. You'll find something to tempt everyone here, from delicious family favourites such as Macaroni Cheese and Spaghetti with Meatballs, to the more sophisticated Parma Ham-wrapped Chicken with Ribbon Pasta and Fettuccini with Wild Mushrooms & Prosciutto.

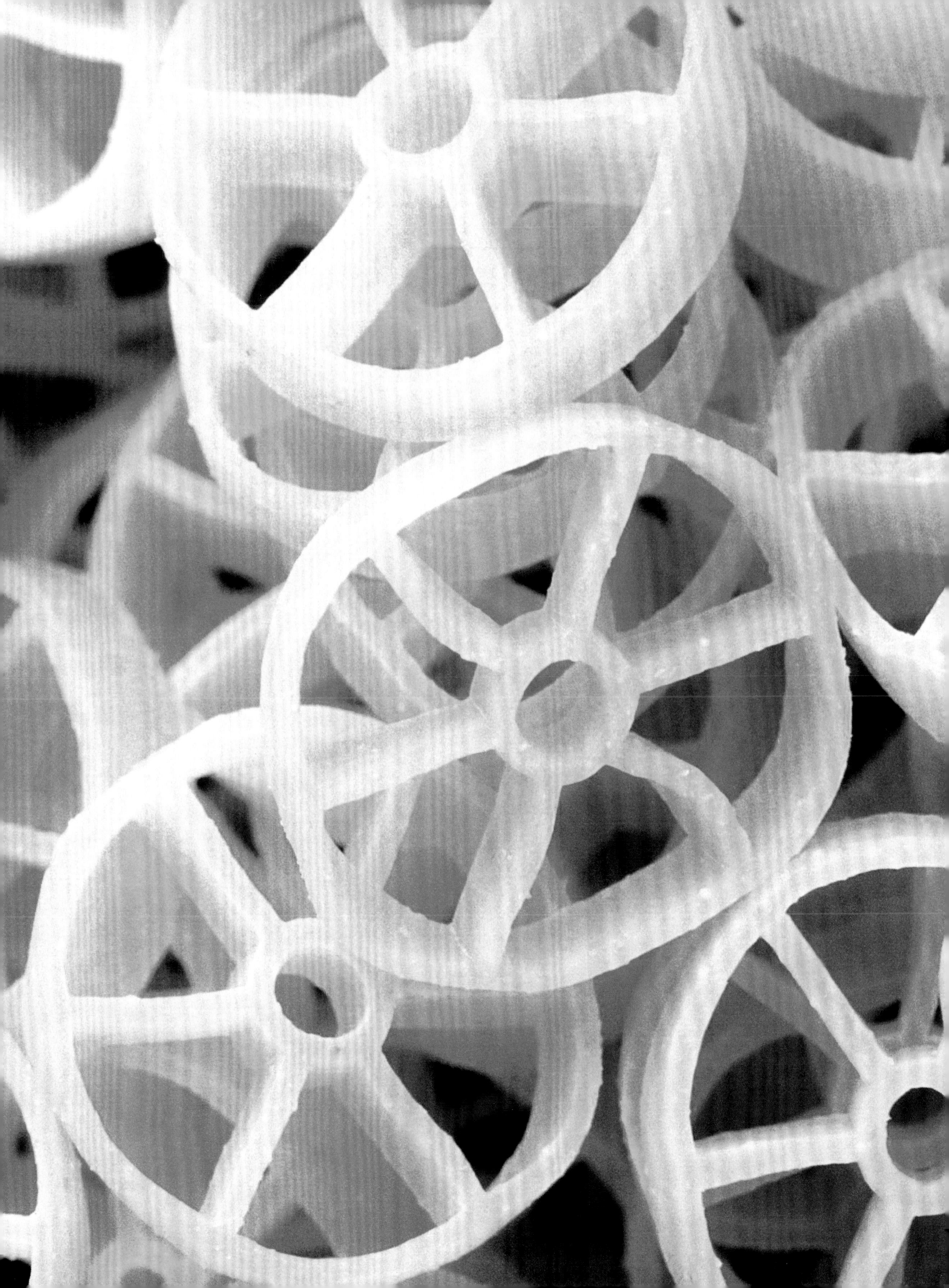

# Creamy Turkey & Tomato Pasta

INGREDIENTS **Serves 4**

4 tbsp olive oil
450 g/1 lb turkey breasts, cut into bite-sized pieces
550 g/1¼ lb cherry tomatoes, on the vine
2 garlic cloves, peeled and chopped
4 tbsp balsamic vinegar
4 tbsp freshly chopped basil
salt and freshly ground black pepper
200 ml tub crème fraîche
350 g/12 oz tagliatelle
shaved Parmesan cheese, to garnish

Preheat the oven to 200°C/400°F/Gas Mark 6. Heat 2 tablespoons of the olive oil in a large frying pan. Add the turkey and cook for 5 minutes, or until sealed, turning occasionally. Transfer to a roasting tin and add the remaining olive oil, the vine tomatoes, garlic and balsamic vinegar. Stir well and season to taste with salt and pepper. Cook in the preheated oven for 30 minutes, or until the turkey is tender, turning the tomatoes and turkey once.

Meanwhile, bring a large pan of lightly salted water to a rolling boil. Add the pasta and cook according to the packet instructions, or until 'al dente'. Drain, return to the pan and keep warm. Stir the basil and seasoning into the crème fraîche.

Remove the roasting tin from the oven and discard the vines. Stir the crème fraîche and basil mix into the turkey and tomato mixture and return to the oven for 1–2 minutes, or until thoroughly heated through.

Stir the turkey and tomato mixture into the pasta and toss lightly together. Tip into a warmed serving dish. Garnish with Parmesan cheese shavings and serve immediately.

HEALTH RATING

**VEGETARIAN ALTERNATIVE**
Fusilli with Courgettes & Sun-dried Tomatoes

**ENTERTAINING ALTERNATIVE**
Rigatoni with Oven-dried Cherry Tomatoes & Mascarpone

**VEGETARIAN ALTERNATIVE**

## Fusilli with Courgettes & Sun-dried Tomatoes

INGREDIENTS **Serves 6**

5 tbsp olive oil
1 large onion, peeled and thinly sliced
2 garlic cloves, peeled and finely chopped
700 g/1½ lb courgettes, trimmed and sliced
400 g can chopped plum tomatoes
12 sun-dried tomatoes, cut into thin strips
salt and freshly ground black pepper
450 g/1 lb fusilli
25 g/1 oz butter, diced
2 tbsp freshly chopped basil or flat leaf parsley
grated Parmesan or pecorino cheese, for serving

Heat 2 tablespoons of the olive oil in a large frying pan, add the onion and cook for 5-7 minutes or until softened. Add the chopped garlic and courgette slices and cook for a further 5 minutes, stirring occasionally.

Stir the chopped tomatoes and the sun-dried tomatoes into the frying pan and season to taste with salt and pepper. Cook until the courgettes are just tender and the sauce is slightly thickened.

Bring a large pan of lightly salted water to a rolling boil. Add the fusilli and cook according to the packet instructions, or until 'al dente'.

Drain the fusilli thoroughly and return to the pan. Add the butter and remaining oil and toss to coat. Stir the chopped basil or parsley into the courgette mixture and pour over the fusilli. Toss and tip into a warmed serving dish. Serve with grated Parmesan or pecorino cheese.

**ENTERTAINING ALTERNATIVE**

## Rigatoni with Oven-dried Cherry Tomatoes & Mascarpone

INGREDIENTS **Serves 4**

350 g/12 oz red cherry tomatoes
1 tsp caster sugar
salt and freshly ground black pepper
2 tbsp olive oil
400 g/14 oz dried rigatoni
125 g/4 oz petits pois
2 tbsp mascarpone cheese
1 tbsp freshly chopped mint
1 tbsp freshly chopped parsley
sprigs of fresh mint, to garnish

Preheat the oven to 140°C/275°F/Gas Mark 1. Halve the cherry tomatoes and place close together on a non-stick baking tray, cut-side up. Sprinkle lightly with the sugar, then with a little salt and pepper. Bake in the preheated oven for 1¼ hours, or until dry, but not beginning to colour. Leave to cool on the baking tray. Put in a bowl, drizzle over the olive oil and toss to coat.

Bring a large saucepan of lightly salted water to the boil and cook the pasta for about 10 minutes or until 'al dente'. Add the petits pois, 2–3 minutes before the end of the cooking time. Drain thoroughly and return the pasta and the petits pois to the saucepan.

Add the mascarpone to the saucepan. When melted, add the tomatoes, mint, parsley and a little black pepper. Toss gently together, then transfer to a warmed serving dish or individual plates and garnish with sprigs of fresh mint. Serve immediately.

# Chorizo with Pasta in a Tomato Sauce

INGREDIENTS **Serves 4**

25 g/1 oz butter
2 tbsp olive oil
2 large onions, peeled and finely sliced
1 tsp soft brown sugar
2 garlic cloves, peeled and crushed
225 g/8 oz chorizo, sliced
1 chilli, deseeded and finely sliced
400g can of chopped tomatoes
1 tbsp sun-dried tomato paste
150 ml/¼ pint red wine
salt and freshly ground black pepper
450 g/1 lb rigatoni
freshly chopped parsley, to garnish

Melt the butter with the olive oil in a large, heavy-based pan. Add the onions and sugar and cook over a very low heat, stirring occasionally, for 15 minutes or until soft and starting to caramelize.

Add the garlic and chorizo to the pan and cook for 5 minutes. Stir in the chilli, chopped tomatoes and tomato paste, and pour in the wine. Season well with salt and pepper. Bring to the boil, cover, reduce the heat and simmer for 30 minutes, stirring occasionally. Remove the lid and simmer for a further 10 minutes, or until the sauce starts to thicken.

Meanwhile, bring a large pan of lightly salted water to a rolling boil. Add the pasta and cook according to the packet instructions, or until 'al dente'.

Drain the pasta, reserving 2 tablespoons of the water, and return to the pan. Add the chorizo sauce with the reserved cooking water and toss gently until the pasta is evenly covered. Tip into a warmed serving dish, sprinkle with the parsley and serve immediately.

HEALTH RATING

**VEGETARIAN ALTERNATIVE**
Pasta with Spicy Red Pepper Sauce

**PUDDING SUGGESTION**
Almond & Pine Nut Tart

INGREDIENTS **Serves 6**

2 red peppers
2 tbsp olive oil
1 onion, peeled and chopped
2 garlic cloves, peeled and crushed
4 anchovy fillets (optional)
1 red chilli, deseeded and finely chopped
200 g/7 oz can of chopped tomatoes
finely grated rind and juice of ½ lemon
salt and freshly ground black pepper
2–3 tbsp vegetable stock (optional)
400 g/14 oz dried pasta, such as tagliatelle, linguine or shells

**To garnish:**
shaved Parmesan cheese
fresh basil leaves

**VEGETARIAN ALTERNATIVE**
## Pasta with Spicy Red Pepper Sauce

Preheat the grill. Set the whole peppers on the grill rack about 10 cm/4 inches away from the heat, then grill, turning frequently, for 10 minutes until the skins are blackened and blistered.

Put the peppers in a plastic bag and leave until cool enough to handle. Peel off the skin, then halve the peppers and scrape away the seeds. Chop the pepper flesh roughly and put in a food processor or blender.

Heat the olive oil in a large saucepan and gently fry the onion for 5 minutes. Stir in the garlic, anchovy fillets (if using) and chilli and cook for a further 5 minutes, stirring. Add to the food processor and blend until fairly smooth.

Return the mixture to the saucepan with the tomatoes and stir in the lemon rind and juice. Season to taste with salt and pepper. Add 2–3 tablespoons of vegetable stock if the sauce is a little thick. Bring to the boil and bubble for 1–2 minutes.

Meanwhile, bring a large saucepan of lightly salted water to the boil and cook the pasta for 10 minutes, or until 'al dente'. Drain thoroughly. Add the sauce and toss well to coat.

Tip into a warmed serving dish or on to individual plates. Scatter with shavings of Parmesan cheese and a few basil leaves before serving.

**PUDDING SUGGESTION**
## Almond & Pine Nut Tart

INGREDIENTS **Serves 6**

250 g/9 oz ready-made sweet shortcrust pastry (see page 10)
75 g/3 oz blanched almonds
75 g/3 oz caster sugar
pinch of salt
2 medium eggs
1 tsp vanilla essence
2–3 drops almond essence
125 g/4 oz unsalted butter, softened
2 tbsp flour
½ tsp baking powder
3–4 tbsp raspberry jam
50 g/2 oz pine nuts
icing sugar, to decorate
whipped cream, to serve

Preheat the oven to 200°C/400°F/Gas Mark 6. Roll out the pastry and use to line a 23 cm/9 inch fluted flan tin. Chill in the refrigerator for 10 minutes, then line with greaseproof paper and baking beans and bake blind in the preheated oven for 10 minutes. Remove the paper and beans and bake for a further 10–12 minutes until cooked. Leave to cool. Reduce the temperature to 190°C/375°F/Gas Mark 5.

Grind the almonds in a food processor until fine. Add the sugar, salt, eggs, vanilla and almond essences and blend. Add the butter, flour and baking powder and blend until smooth.

Spread a thick layer of the raspberry jam over the cooled pastry case, then pour in the almond filling. Sprinkle the pine nuts evenly over the top and bake for 30 minutes, until firm and browned.

Remove the tart from the oven and leave to cool. Dust generously with icing sugar and serve cut into wedges with whipped cream.

# Antipasto Penne

INGREDIENTS **Serves 4**

3 medium courgettes, trimmed
4 plum tomatoes
175 g/6 oz Italian ham
2 tbsp olive oil
salt and freshly ground black pepper
350 g/12 oz dried penne pasta
285 g jar antipasto
125 g/4 oz mozzarella cheese, drained and diced
125 g/4 oz Gorgonzola cheese, crumbled
3 tbsp freshly chopped flat leaf parsley

Preheat the grill just before cooking. Cut the courgettes into thick slices. Rinse the tomatoes and cut into quarters, then cut the ham into strips. Pour the oil into a baking dish and place under the grill for 2 minutes, or until almost smoking. Remove from the grill and stir in the courgettes. Return to the grill and cook for 8 minutes, stirring occasionally. Remove from the grill and add the tomatoes and cook for a further 3 minutes.

Add the ham to the baking dish and cook under the grill for 4 minutes, until all the vegetables are charred and the ham is brown. Season to taste with salt and pepper.

Meanwhile, plunge the pasta into a large saucepan of lightly salted, boiling water, return to a rolling boil, stir and cook for 8 minutes or until 'al dente'. Drain well and return to the saucepan.

Stir the antipasto into the vegetables and cook under the grill for 2 minutes, or until heated through. Add the cooked pasta and toss together gently with the remaining ingredients. Grill for a further 4 minutes, then serve immediately.

## HEALTH RATING 🍎🍎

**VEGETARIAN ALTERNATIVE**
Pasta Primavera

**PUDDING SUGGESTION**
Goats' Cheese & Lemon Tart

**VEGETARIAN ALTERNATIVE**
## Pasta Primavera

INGREDIENTS **Serves 4**

150 g/5 oz French beans
150 g/5 oz sugar snap peas
40 g/1½ oz butter
1 tsp olive oil
225 g/8 oz baby carrots, scrubbed
2 courgettes, trimmed and thinly sliced
175 g/6 oz baby leeks, trimmed and cut into 2.5 cm/1 inch lengths
200 ml/7 fl oz double cream
1 tsp finely grated lemon rind
350 g/12 oz dried tagliatelle
25 g/1 oz Parmesan cheese, grated
1 tbsp freshly snipped chives
1 tbsp freshly chopped dill
salt and freshly ground black pepper
sprigs of fresh dill, to garnish

Trim and halve the French beans. Bring a large saucepan of lightly salted water to the boil and cook the beans for 4–5 minutes, adding the sugar snap peas after 2 minutes so that both are tender at the same time. Drain the beans and sugar snap peas and briefly rinse under cold running water.

Heat the butter and oil in a large, non-stick frying pan. Add the baby carrots and cook for 2 minutes, then stir in the courgettes and leeks and cook for 10 minutes, stirring, until the vegetables are almost tender.

Stir the cream and lemon rind into the vegetables and bubble over a gentle heat until the sauce is slightly reduced and the vegetables are cooked.

Meanwhile, bring a large saucepan of lightly salted water to the boil and cook the tagliatelle for 10 minutes or until 'al dente'.

Add the beans, sugar snaps, Parmesan cheese and herbs to the sauce. Stir for 30 seconds, or until the cheese has melted and the vegetables are hot.

Drain the tagliatelle, add the vegetables and sauce, then toss gently to mix and season to taste with salt and pepper. Spoon into a warmed serving bowl and garnish with a few sprigs of dill and serve immediately.

**PUDDING SUGGESTION**
## Goats' Cheese & Lemon Tart

INGREDIENTS **Serves 4**

**For the pastry:**
125 g/4 oz butter, cut into small pieces
225 g/8 oz plain flour
pinch of salt
50 g/2 oz caster sugar
1 medium egg yolk

**For the filling:**
350 g/12 oz mild fresh goats' cheese, e.g. Chavroux
3 medium eggs, beaten
150 g/5 oz caster sugar
grated rind and juice of 3 lemons
450 ml/¾ pint double cream
fresh raspberries, to decorate

Preheat the oven to 200°C/400°F/Gas Mark 6, 15 minutes before cooking. Rub the butter into the plain flour and salt until the mixture resembles breadcrumbs, then stir in the sugar. Beat the egg yolk with 2 tablespoons of cold water and add to the mixture. Mix together until a dough is formed, then turn the dough out on to a lightly floured surface and knead until smooth. Chill in the refrigerator for 30 minutes.

Roll the dough out thinly on a lightly floured surface and use to line a 4 cm/1½ inch deep 23 cm/9 inch fluted flan tin. Chill in the refrigerator for 10 minutes. Line the pastry case with greaseproof paper and baking beans or tinfoil and bake blind in the preheated oven for 10 minutes. Remove the paper and beans or tinfoil. Return to the oven for a further 12–15 minutes until cooked. Leave to cool slightly, then reduce the oven temperature to 150°C/300°F/Gas Mark 2.

Beat the goats' cheese until smooth. Whisk in the eggs, sugar, lemon rind and juice. Add the cream and mix well. Carefully pour the cheese mixture into the pastry case and return to the oven. Bake in the oven for 35–40 minutes, or until just set. If it begins to brown or swell, open the oven door for 2 minutes, then reduce the temperature to 120°C/250°F/Gas Mark ½ and leave the tart to cool in the oven. Chill in the refrigerator until cold. Decorate and serve with fresh raspberries.

**SPICY ALTERNATIVE**
## Tagliatelle with Broccoli & Sesame

INGREDIENTS **Serves 2**

225 g/8 oz broccoli, cut into florets
125 g/4 oz baby corn
175 g/6 oz dried tagliatelle
1½ tbsp tahini paste
1 tbsp dark soy sauce
1 tbsp dark muscovado sugar
1 tbsp red wine vinegar
1 tbsp sunflower oil
1 garlic clove, peeled and finely chopped
2.5 cm/1 inch piece fresh root ginger, peeled and shredded
½ tsp dried chilli flakes
salt and freshly ground black pepper
1 tbsp toasted sesame seeds
slices of radish, to garnish

Bring a large saucepan of salted water to the boil and add the broccoli and corn. Return the water to the boil then remove the vegetables at once using a slotted spoon, reserving the water. Plunge them into cold water and drain well. Dry on kitchen paper and reserve.

Return the water to the boil. Add the tagliatelle and cook until 'al dente' or according to the packet instructions. Drain well. Run under cold water until cold, then drain well again.

Place the tahini, soy sauce, sugar and vinegar into a bowl. Mix well, then reserve. Heat the oil in a wok or large frying pan over a high heat and add the garlic, ginger and chilli flakes and stir-fry for about 30 seconds. Add the broccoli and baby corn and continue to stir-fry for about 3 minutes.

Add the tagliatelle to the wok along with the tahini mixture and stir together for a further 1–2 minutes until heated through. Season to taste with salt and pepper.

Sprinkle with sesame seeds, garnish with the radish slices and serve immediately.

**PUDDING SUGGESTION**
## Sauternes & Olive Oil Cake

INGREDIENTS **Serves 8–10**

125 g/4 oz plain flour, plus extra for dusting
4 medium eggs
125 g/4 oz caster sugar
grated zest of ½ lemon
grated zest of ½ orange
2 tbsp Sauternes or other sweet dessert wine
3 tbsp very best quality extra virgin olive oil
4 ripe peaches
1–2 tsp soft brown sugar, or to taste
1 tbsp lemon juice
icing sugar, to dust

Preheat the oven to 140°C/275°F/Gas Mark 1. Oil and line a 25.5 cm/10 inch springform tin. Sift the flour on to a large sheet of greaseproof paper and reserve. Using a freestanding electric mixer, if possible, whisk the eggs and sugar together until pale and stiff. Add the lemon and orange zest.

Turn the speed to low and pour the flour from the paper in a slow, steady stream on to the eggs and sugar mixture. Immediately add the wine and olive oil and switch the machine off as the olive oil should not be incorporated completely.

Using a rubber spatula, fold the mixture very gently 3 or 4 times so that the ingredients are just incorporated. Pour the mixture immediately into the prepared tin and bake in the preheated oven for 20–25 minutes, without opening the door for at least 15 minutes. Test if cooked by pressing the top lightly with a clean finger – if it springs back, remove from the oven. If not, bake for a little longer.

Leave the cake to cool in the tin on a wire rack. Remove the cake from the tin when cool enough to handle. Meanwhile, skin the peaches and cut into segments. Toss with the brown sugar and lemon juice and reserve. When the cake is cold, dust generously with icing sugar, cut into wedges and serve with the peaches.

# Farfalle with Courgettes & Mushrooms

INGREDIENTS **Serves 4**

25 g/1 oz butter
2 tsp olive oil
1 small onion, peeled and finely chopped
2 garlic cloves, peeled and crushed
125 g/4 oz bacon lardons
450 g/1 lb courgettes, trimmed and diced
125 g/4 oz button mushrooms, wiped and roughly chopped
350 g/12 oz farfalle
salt and freshly ground black pepper
250 ml carton crème fraîche
2 tbsp freshly chopped parsley
shaved pecorino cheese, to garnish

**To serve:**
mixed salad
crusty bread

Heat the butter and olive oil in a large pan, add the onion, garlic and bacon lardons and cook for 3–4 minutes, or until the onion has softened. Add the courgettes and cook, stirring, for 3–4 minutes. Add the mushrooms, lower the heat and cook, covered, for 4–5 minutes.

Meanwhile, bring a large pan of lightly salted water to a rolling boil. Add the farfalle and cook according to the packet instructions or until 'al dente'. Drain thoroughly, return to the pan and keep warm.

Season the mushroom mixture to taste with salt and pepper, then stir in the crème fraîche and half the chopped parsley. Simmer for 2–3 minutes, or until the sauce is thick and creamy.

Pour the sauce over the cooked pasta, toss lightly, then reheat for 2 minutes or until piping hot. Tip into a warmed serving dish and sprinkle over the chopped parsley. Garnish with pecorino cheese shavings and serve immediately with a mixed salad and crusty bread.

HEALTH RATING 🍎🍎

**SPICY ALTERNATIVE**
Tagliatelle with Broccoli & Sesame

**PUDDING SUGGESTION**
Sauternes & Olive Oil Cake

# Chicken Tagliatelle

INGREDIENTS **Serves 4**

350 g/12 oz tagliatelle
125 g/4 oz frozen peas
4 boneless and skinless chicken breasts
2 tbsp olive oil
¼ cucumber, cut into strips
150 ml/¼ pint dry vermouth
150 ml/¼ pint double cream
125 g/4 oz Stilton cheese, crumbled
3 tbsp freshly snipped chives, plus extra to garnish
salt and freshly ground black pepper
fresh herbs, to garnish

Bring a large pan of lightly salted water to a rolling boil. Add the pasta and cook according to the packet instructions, or until 'al dente'. Add the peas to the pan 5 minutes before the end of cooking time and cook until tender. Drain the pasta and peas, return to the pan and keep warm.

Trim the chicken if necessary, then cut into bite-sized pieces. Heat the olive oil in a large frying pan, add the chicken and cook for 8 minutes, or until golden, stirring occasionally.

Add the cucumber and cook for 2 minutes, or until slightly softened, stirring occasionally. Stir in the vermouth, bring to the boil, then lower the heat and simmer for 3 minutes, or until reduced slightly.

Add the cream to the pan, bring to the boil, stirring constantly, then stir in the Stilton cheese and snipped chives. Season to taste with salt and pepper. Heat through thoroughly, stirring occasionally, until the cheese is just beginning to melt.

Toss the chicken mixture into the pasta. Tip into a warmed serving dish or on to individual plates. Garnish and serve immediately.

HEALTH RATING 🍎🍎

**ENTERTAINING ALTERNATIVE**
Pesto Chicken Tagliatelle

**VEGETARIAN ALTERNATIVE**
Four-cheese Tagliatelle

**ENTERTAINING ALTERNATIVE**
## Pesto Chicken Tagliatelle

INGREDIENTS **Serves 4**

2 tbsp olive oil
350 g/12 oz boneless and skinless chicken breasts, cut into chunks
75 g/3 oz butter
2 medium leeks, trimmed and sliced thinly
125 g/4 oz oyster mushrooms, trimmed and halved
200 g/7 oz small open chestnut mushrooms, wiped and halved
450 g/1lb fresh tagliatelle
4–6 tbsp red pesto
200 ml/7 fl oz crème fraîche
50 g/2 oz freshly grated Parmesan cheese
salt and freshly ground black pepper

Heat the oil in a large frying pan, add the chicken and cook for 8 minutes, or until golden brown, stirring occasionally. Using a slotted spoon, remove the chicken from the pan, drain on absorbent kitchen paper and reserve.

Melt the butter in the pan. Add the leeks and cook for 3–5 minutes, or until slightly softened, stirring occasionally.

Add the oyster and chestnut mushrooms and cook for 5 minutes, or until browned, stirring occasionally.

Bring a large pan of lightly salted water to the boil, add the tagliatelle, return to the boil and cook for 4 minutes, or until 'al dente'.

Add the chicken, pesto and crème fraîche to the mushroom mixture. Stir, then heat through thoroughly. Stir in the grated Parmesan cheese and season to taste with salt and pepper.

Drain the tagliatelle thoroughly and pile on to warmed plates. Spoon over the sauce and serve immediately.

**VEGETARIAN ALTERNATIVE**
## Four-cheese Tagliatelle

INGREDIENTS **Serves 4**

300 ml/½ pint whipping cream
4 garlic cloves, peeled and lightly bruised
75 g/3 oz fontina cheese, diced
75 g/3 oz Gruyère cheese, grated
75 g/3 oz mozzarella cheese, diced
50 g/2 oz Parmesan cheese, grated, plus extra to serve
salt and freshly ground black pepper
275 g/10 oz fresh green tagliatelle
1–2 tbsp freshly snipped chives
fresh basil leaves, to garnish

Place the whipping cream with the garlic cloves in a medium pan and heat gently until small bubbles begin to form around the edge of the pan. Using a slotted spoon, remove and discard the garlic cloves.

Add all the cheeses to the pan and stir until melted. Season with a little salt and a lot of black pepper. Keep the sauce warm over a low heat, but do not allow to boil.

Meanwhile, bring a large pan of lightly salted water to the boil. Add the taglietelle, return to the boil and cook for 2–3 minutes or until 'al dente'.

Drain the pasta thoroughly and return to the pan. Pour the sauce over the pasta, add the chives then toss lightly until well coated. Tip into a warmed serving dish or spoon on to individual plates. Garnish with a few basil leaves and serve immediately with extra Parmesan cheese.

# Creamy Chicken Cannelloni

INGREDIENTS **Serves 6**

50 g/2 oz butter
2 garlic cloves, peeled and finely crushed
225 g/8 oz button mushrooms, thinly sliced
2 tbsp freshly chopped basil
450 g/1 lb fresh spinach, blanched
salt and freshly ground black pepper
2 tbsp plain flour
300 ml/½ pint chicken stock
150 ml/¼ pint dry white wine
150 ml/¼ pint double cream
350 g/12 oz skinless, boneless, cooked chicken, chopped
175 g/6 oz Parma ham, finely chopped
½ tsp dried thyme
225 g/8 oz pre-cooked cannelloni tubes
175 g/6 oz Gruyère cheese, grated
40 g/1½ oz Parmesan cheese, grated
sprig of fresh basil, to garnish

Preheat the oven to 190°C/375°F/Gas Mark 5, 10 minutes before cooking. Lightly butter a 28 x 23 cm/11 x 9 inch ovenproof baking dish. Heat half the butter in a large, heavy-based frying pan, then add the garlic and mushrooms and cook gently for 5 minutes. Stir in the basil and the spinach and cook, covered, until the spinach is wilted and just tender, stirring frequently. Season to taste with salt and pepper, then spoon into the dish and reserve.

Melt the remaining butter in a small saucepan, then stir in the flour and cook for about 2 minutes, stirring constantly. Remove from the heat, stir in the stock, then the wine and the cream. Return to the heat, bring to the boil and simmer, until the sauce is thick and smooth, then season to taste.

Measure 125 ml/4 fl oz of the cream sauce into a bowl. Add the chopped chicken, Parma ham and the dried thyme. Season to taste, then spoon the chicken mixture into the cannelloni tubes, arranging them in 2 long rows on top of the spinach layer.

Add half the Gruyère cheese to the cream sauce and heat, stirring, until the cheese melts. Pour over the sauce and top with the remaining Gruyère and the Parmesan cheeses. Bake in the preheated oven for 35 minutes, or until golden and bubbling. Garnish with a sprig of fresh basil and serve immediately.

HEALTH RATING 

**SPEEDY ALTERNATIVE**

Chicken & Asparagus with Tagliatelle

**SUMMER ALTERNATIVE**

Chicken & Pasta Salad

**SPEEDY ALTERNATIVE**
## Chicken & Asparagus with Tagliatelle

INGREDIENTS **Serves 4**

275 g/10 oz fresh asparagus
50 g/2 oz butter
4 spring onions, trimmed and coarsely chopped
350 g/12 oz boneless, skinless chicken breast, thinly sliced
2 tbsp white vermouth
300 ml/½ pint double cream
2 tbsp freshly chopped chives
400 g/14 oz fresh tagliatelle
50 g/2 oz Parmesan or pecorino cheese, grated
snipped chives, to garnish
extra Parmesan cheese (optional), to serve

Using a swivel-bladed vegetable peeler, lightly peel the asparagus stalks and then cook in lightly salted, boiling water for 2–3 minutes, or until just tender. Drain and refresh in cold water, then cut into 4 cm/1½ inch pieces and reserve.

Melt the butter in a large frying pan then add the spring onions and the chicken and fry for 4 minutes. Add the vermouth and allow to reduce until the liquid has evaporated. Pour in the cream and half the chives. Cook gently for 5–7 minutes, until the sauce has thickened and slightly reduced and the chicken is tender.

Bring a large saucepan of lightly salted water to the boil and cook the tagliatelle for 4–5 minutes, or until 'al dente'. Drain and immediately add to the chicken and cream sauce.

Using a pair of spaghetti tongs or kitchen forks, lightly toss the sauce and pasta until it is mixed thoroughly. Add the remaining chives and the Parmesan cheese and toss gently. Garnish with snipped chives and serve immediately, with extra Parmesan cheese, if wanted.

**SUMMER ALTERNATIVE**
## Chicken & Pasta Salad

INGREDIENTS **Serves 6**

450 g/1 lb short pasta
2–3 tbsp extra virgin olive oil
300 g/11 oz cold cooked chicken, cut into bite-sized pieces (preferably roasted)
1 red pepper, deseeded and diced
1 yellow pepper, deseeded and diced
4–5 sun-dried tomatoes, sliced
2 tbsp capers, rinsed and drained
125 g/4 oz pitted black Italian olives
4 spring onions, chopped
225 g/8 oz mozzarella cheese, preferably buffalo, diced
salt and freshly ground black pepper

**For the dressing:**

50 ml/2 fl oz red or white wine vinegar
1 tbsp mild mustard
1 tsp sugar
75–125 ml/3–4 fl oz extra virgin olive oil
125 ml/4 fl oz mayonnaise

Bring a large saucepan of lightly salted water to the boil. Add the pasta and cook for 10 minutes, or until 'al dente'. Drain the pasta and rinse under cold running water, then drain again. Place in a large serving bowl and toss with the olive oil.

Add the chicken, diced red and yellow peppers, sliced sun-dried tomatoes, capers, olives, spring onions and mozzarella to the pasta and toss gently until mixed. Season to taste with salt and pepper.

To make the dressing, put the vinegar, mustard and sugar into a small bowl or jug and whisk until well blended and the sugar is dissolved. Season with some pepper, then gradually whisk in the olive oil in a slow, steady stream until a thickened vinaigrette forms.

Put the mayonnaise in a bowl and gradually whisk in the dressing until smooth. Pour over the pasta mixture and mix gently until all the ingredients are coated. Turn into a large, shallow serving bowl and serve at room temperature.

# Fettuccine with Wild Mushrooms & Prosciutto

INGREDIENTS **Serves 6**

15 g/½ oz dried porcini mushrooms
150 ml/¼ pint hot chicken stock
2 tbsp olive oil
1 small onion, peeled and finely chopped
2 garlic cloves, peeled and finely chopped
4 slices prosciutto, chopped or torn
225 g/8 oz mixed wild or cultivated mushrooms, wiped and sliced if necessary
450 g/1 lb fettuccine
3 tbsp crème fraîche
2 tbsp freshly chopped parsley
salt and freshly ground black pepper
freshly grated Parmesan cheese, to serve

Place the dried mushrooms in a small bowl and pour over the hot chicken stock. Leave to soak for 15–20 minutes, or until the mushrooms have softened.

Meanwhile, heat the olive oil in a large frying pan. Add the onion and cook for 5 minutes over a medium heat, or until softened. Add the garlic and cook for 1 minute, then add the prosciutto and cook for a further minute.

Drain the dried mushrooms, reserving the soaking liquid. Roughly chop and add to the frying pan together with the fresh mushrooms. Cook over a high heat for 5 minutes, stirring often until softened. Strain the mushroom soaking liquid into the pan.

Meanwhile, bring a large pan of lightly salted water to a rolling boil. Add the pasta and cook according to the packet instructions, or until 'al dente'.

Stir the crème fraîche and chopped parsley into the mushroom mixture and heat through gently. Season to taste with salt and pepper. Drain the pasta well, transfer to a large warmed serving dish and pour over the sauce. Serve immediately with grated Parmesan cheese.

HEALTH RATING 🍎🍎🍎

**CHILDREN'S ALTERNATIVE**

Penne with Artichokes, Bacon & Mushrooms

**VEGETARIAN ALTERNATIVE**

Tagliatelle with Brown Butter, Asparagus & Parmesan

**CHILDREN'S ALTERNATIVE**
## Penne with Artichokes, Bacon & Mushrooms

INGREDIENTS **Serves 6**

2 tbsp olive oil
75 g/3 oz smoked bacon or pancetta, chopped
1 small onion, peeled and finely sliced
125 g/4 oz chestnut mushrooms, wiped and sliced
2 garlic cloves, peeled and finely chopped
400 g/14 oz can artichoke hearts, drained and halved or quartered if large
100 ml/3½ fl oz dry white wine
100 ml/3½ fl oz chicken stock
3 tbsp double cream
50 g/2 oz freshly grated Parmesan cheese, plus extra to serve
salt and freshly ground black pepper
450 g/1 lb penne
shredded basil leaves, to garnish

Heat the olive oil in a frying pan and add the pancetta or bacon and the onion. Cook over a medium heat for 8–10 minutes, or until the bacon is crisp and the onion is just golden. Add the mushrooms and garlic and cook for a further 5 minutes, or until softened.

Add the artichoke hearts to the mushroom mixture and cook for 3–4 minutes. Pour in the wine, bring to the boil then simmer rapidly until the liquid is reduced and syrupy.

Pour in the chicken stock, bring to the boil then simmer rapidly for about 5 minutes, or until slightly reduced. Reduce the heat slightly, then slowly stir in the double cream and Parmesan cheese. Season the sauce to taste with salt and pepper.

Meanwhile, bring a large pan of lightly salted water to a rolling boil. Add the pasta and cook according to the packet instructions, or until 'al dente'. Drain the pasta thoroughly and transfer to a large, warmed serving dish. Pour over the sauce and toss together. Garnish with shredded basil and serve with extra Parmesan cheese.

**VEGETARIAN ALTERNATIVE**
## Tagliatelle with Brown Butter, Asparagus & Parmesan

INGREDIENTS **Serves 6**

450 g/1 lb fresh or dried tagliatelle nests, such as the white and green variety
350 g/12 oz asparagus, trimmed and cut into short lengths
75 g/3 oz unsalted butter
1 garlic clove, peeled and sliced
25 g/1 oz flaked hazelnuts or whole hazelnuts, roughly chopped
1 tbsp freshly chopped parsley
1 tbsp freshly snipped chives
salt and freshly ground black pepper
50 g/2 oz freshly grated Parmesan cheese, to serve

Bring a pan of lightly salted water to the boil. Add the asparagus and cook for 1 minute. Drain immediately, refresh under cold running water and drain again. Pat dry and reserve.

Melt the butter in a large frying pan, then add the garlic and hazelnuts and cook over a medium heat until the butter turns golden. Immediately remove from the heat and add the parsley, chives and asparagus. Leave for 2–3 minutes, until the asparagus is heated through.

Meanwhile, bring a large pan of lightly salted water to a rolling boil, then add the pasta nests. Cook until 'al dente': 2–3 minutes for fresh pasta and according to the packet instructions for dried pasta. Drain the pasta thoroughly and return to the pan.

Add the asparagus mixture and toss together. Season to taste with salt and pepper and tip into a warmed serving dish. Serve immediately with grated Parmesan cheese.

## SPEEDY ALTERNATIVE
## Pasta Provençale

INGREDIENTS **Serves 4**

- 2 tbsp olive oil
- 1 garlic clove, peeled and crushed
- 1 onion, peeled and finely chopped
- 1 small fennel bulb, trimmed, halved and thinly sliced
- 400 g can chopped tomatoes
- 1 rosemary sprig, plus extra sprig to garnish
- 350 g/12 oz monkfish, skinned
- 2 tsp lemon juice
- 400 g/14 oz gnocchi
- 50 g/2 oz pitted black olives
- 200 g can flageolet beans, drained and rinsed
- 1 tbsp freshly chopped oregano, plus sprig to garnish
- salt and freshly ground black pepper

Heat the olive oil in a large saucepan, add the garlic and onion and cook gently for 5 minutes. Add the fennel and cook for a further 5 minutes. Stir in the chopped tomatoes and rosemary sprig. Half-cover the pan and simmer for 10 minutes.

Cut the monkfish into bite-sized pieces and sprinkle with the lemon juice. Add to the tomatoes, cover and simmer gently for 5 minutes, or until the fish is opaque.

Meanwhile, bring a large pan of lightly salted water to a rolling boil. Add the pasta and cook according to the packet instructions, or until 'al dente'. Drain the pasta thoroughly and return to the saucepan.

Remove the rosemary from the tomato sauce. Stir in the black olives, flageolet beans and chopped oregano, then season to taste with salt and pepper. Add the sauce to the pasta and toss gently together to coat, taking care not to break up the monkfish. Tip into a warmed serving bowl. Garnish with rosemary and oregano sprigs and serve immediately.

## ENTERTAINING ALTERNATIVE
## Gnocchi with Tuscan Beef Ragù

INGREDIENTS **Serves 4**

- 25 g/1 oz dried porcini
- 3 tbsp olive oil
- 1 small onion, peeled and finely chopped
- 1 carrot, peeled and finely chopped
- 1 celery, trimmed and finely chopped
- 1 fennel bulb, trimmed and sliced
- 2 garlic cloves, peeled and crushed
- 450 g/1 lb fresh beef steak mince
- 4 tbsp red wine
- 50 g/2 oz pine nuts
- 1 tbsp freshly chopped rosemary
- 2 tbsp tomato paste
- 400 g can chopped tomatoes
- 225 g/8 oz fresh gnocchi
- salt and freshly ground black pepper
- 100 g/4 oz mozzarella cheese, cubed

Preheat the oven to 200°C/400°F/Gas Mark 6, 15 minutes before cooking. Place the porcini in a small bowl and cover with almost boiling water. Leave to soak for 30 minutes. Drain, reserving the soaking liquid and straining it through a muslin-lined sieve. Chop the porcini.

Heat the olive oil in a large, heavy-based pan. Add the onion, carrot, celery, fennel and garlic and cook for 8 minutes, stirring, or until soft. Add the minced steak and cook, stirring, for 5–8 minutes, or until sealed and any lumps are broken up.

Pour in the wine, then add the porcini with half the pine nuts, the rosemary and tomato paste. Stir in the porcini soaking liquid then simmer for 5 minutes. Add the chopped tomatoes and simmer gently for about 40 minutes, stirring occasionally.

Meanwhile, bring 1.7 litres/3 pints of lightly salted water to a rolling boil in a large pan. Add the gnocchi and cook for 1–2 minutes, until they rise to the surface.

Drain the gnocchi and place in an ovenproof dish. Stir in three-quarters of the mozzarella cheese with the beef sauce. Top with the remaining mozzarella and pine nuts, then bake in the preheated oven for 20 minutes, until golden brown. Serve immediately.

# Gnocchi & Parma Ham Bake

INGREDIENTS **Serves 4**

3 tbsp olive oil
1 red onion, peeled and sliced
2 garlic cloves, peeled
175 g/6 oz plum tomatoes, skinned and quartered
2 tbsp sun-dried tomato paste
250 g tub mascarpone cheese
salt and freshly ground black pepper
1 tbsp freshly chopped tarragon
300 g/11 oz fresh gnocchi
125 g/4 oz Cheddar or Parmesan cheese, grated
50 g/2 oz fresh white breadcrumbs
50 g/2 oz Parma ham, sliced
10 pitted green olives, halved
sprigs of flat leaf parsley, to garnish

Preheat the oven to 180°C/350°F/Gas Mark 4, 10 minutes before cooking. Heat 2 tablespoons of the olive oil in a large frying pan and cook the onion and garlic for 5 minutes, or until softened. Stir in the tomatoes, sun-dried tomato paste and mascarpone cheese. Season to taste with salt and pepper. Add half the tarragon. Bring to the boil, then lower the heat immediately and simmer for 5 minutes.

Meanwhile, bring 1.7 litres/3 pints water to the boil in a large pan. Add the remaining olive oil and a good pinch of salt. Add the gnocchi and cook for 1–2 minutes, or until they rise to the surface.

Drain the gnocchi thoroughly and transfer to a large ovenproof dish. Add the tomato sauce and toss gently to coat the pasta. Combine the Cheddar or Parmesan cheese with the breadcrumbs and remaining tarragon and scatter over the pasta mixture. Top with the Parma ham and olives and season again.

Cook in the preheated oven for 20–25 minutes, or until golden and bubbling. Serve immediately, garnished with parsley sprigs.

HEALTH RATING

**SPEEDY ALTERNATIVE**
Pasta Provençale

**ENTERTAINING ALTERNATIVE**
Gnocchi with Tuscan Beef Ragù

# Seared Salmon & Lemon Linguine

INGREDIENTS **Serves 4**

4 small skinless salmon fillets, each about 75 g/3 oz
2 tsp sunflower oil
½ tsp mixed or black peppercorns, crushed
400 g/14 oz linguine
15 g/½ oz unsalted butter
1 bunch spring onions, trimmed and shredded
300 ml/½ pint soured cream
zest of 1 lemon, finely grated
50 g/2 oz freshly grated Parmesan cheese
1 tbsp lemon juice
pinch of salt

**To garnish:**
dill sprigs
lemon slices

Brush the salmon fillets with the sunflower oil, sprinkle with crushed peppercorns and press on firmly and reserve.

Bring a large pan of lightly salted water to a rolling boil. Add the linguine and cook according to the packet instructions, or until 'al dente'.

Meanwhile, melt the butter in a saucepan and cook the shredded spring onions gently for 2–3 minutes, or until soft. Stir in the soured cream and the lemon zest and remove from the heat.

Preheat a griddle or heavy-based frying pan until very hot. Add the salmon and sear for 1½–2 minutes on each side. Remove from the pan and allow to cool slightly.

Bring the soured cream sauce to the boil and stir in the Parmesan cheese and lemon juice. Drain the pasta thoroughly and return to the pan. Pour over the sauce and toss gently to coat.

Spoon the pasta on to warmed serving plates and top with the salmon fillets. Serve immediately with sprigs of dill and lemon slices.

HEALTH RATING 🍎🍎

**SPEEDY ALTERNATIVE**
Tagliatelle with Tuna & Anchovy Tapenade

**ENTERTAINING ALTERNATIVE**
Warm Swordfish Niçoise

INGREDIENTS **Serves 4**

400 g/14 oz tagliatelle
125 g can tuna fish in oil, drained
45 g/1¾ oz can anchovy fillets, drained
150 g/5 oz pitted black olives
2 tbsp capers in brine, drained
2 tsp lemon juice
100 ml/3½ fl oz olive oil
2 tbsp freshly chopped parsley
freshly ground black pepper
sprigs of flat leaf parsley, to garnish

**SPEEDY ALTERNATIVE**
## Tagliatelle with Tuna & Anchovy Tapenade

Bring a large pan of lightly salted water to a rolling boil. Add the tagliatelle and cook according to the packet instructions, or until 'al dente'.

Meanwhile, place the tuna fish, anchovy fillets, olives and capers in a food processor with the lemon juice and 2 tablespoons of the olive oil and blend for a few seconds until roughly chopped.

With the motor running, pour in the remaining olive oil in a steady stream; the resulting mixture should be slightly chunky rather than smooth.

Spoon the sauce into a bowl, stir in the chopped parsley and season to taste with black pepper. Check the taste of the sauce and add a little more lemon juice, if required.

Drain the pasta thoroughly. Pour the sauce into the pan and cook over a low heat for 1–2 minutes to warm through.

Return the drained pasta to the pan and mix together with the sauce. Tip into a warmed serving bowl or spoon on to warm individual plates.

Garnish with sprigs of flat leaf parsley and serve immediately.

**ENTERTAINING ALTERNATIVE**
## Warm Swordfish Niçoise

Place the swordfish steaks in a shallow dish. Mix the lime juice with the oil, season to taste with salt and pepper and spoon over the steaks. Turn the steaks to coat them evenly. Cover and place in the refrigerator to marinate for 1 hour.

Bring a large pan of lightly salted water to a rolling boil. Add the farfalle and cook according to the packet instructions, or until 'al dente'. Add the French beans about 4 minutes before the end of cooking time.

Mix the mustard, vinegar and sugar together in a small jug. Gradually whisk in the olive oil to make a thick dressing.

Cook the swordfish in a griddle pan or under a hot preheated grill for 2 minutes on each side, or until just cooked through; overcooking will make it tough and dry. Remove and cut into 2 cm/¾ inch chunks.

Drain the pasta and beans thoroughly and place in a large bowl. Pour over the dressing and toss to coat. Add the cooked swordfish, tomatoes, olives, hard-boiled eggs and anchovy fillets. Gently toss together, taking care not to break up the eggs. Tip into a warmed serving bowl or divide the pasta between individual plates. Serve immediately.

INGREDIENTS **Serves 4**

4 swordfish steaks, about 2.5 cm/1 inch thick, weighing about 175 g/6 oz each
juice of 1 lime
2 tbsp olive oil
salt and freshly ground black pepper
400 g/14 oz farfalle
225 g/8 oz French beans, topped and cut in half
1 tsp Dijon mustard
2 tsp white wine vinegar
pinch caster sugar
3 tbsp olive oil
225 g/8 oz ripe tomatoes, quartered
50 g/2 oz pitted black olives
2 medium eggs, hard boiled and quartered
8 anchovy fillets, drained and cut in half lengthways

# Salmon & Spaghetti in a Creamy Egg Sauce

INGREDIENTS **Serves 4**

3 medium eggs
1 tbsp freshly chopped parsley
1 tbsp freshly chopped dill
40 g/1½ oz freshly grated Parmesan cheese
40 g/1½ oz freshly grated pecorino cheese
2 tbsp dry white wine
freshly ground black pepper
400 g/14 oz spaghetti
350 g/12 oz salmon fillet, skinned
25 g/1 oz butter
1 tsp olive oil
flat leaf parsley sprigs, to garnish

Beat the eggs in a bowl with the parsley, dill, half of the Parmesan and pecorino cheeses and the white wine. Season to taste with freshly ground black pepper and reserve.

Bring a large pan of lightly salted water to a rolling boil. Add the spaghetti and cook according to the packet instructions, or until 'al dente'.

Meanwhile, cut the salmon into bite-sized pieces. Melt the butter in a large frying pan with the oil and cook the salmon pieces for 3–4 minutes, or until opaque.

Drain the spaghetti thoroughly, return to the pan and immediately add the egg mixture. Remove from the heat and toss well – the eggs will cook in the heat of the spaghetti to make a creamy sauce.

Stir in the remaining cheeses and the cooked pieces of salmon and toss again. Tip into a warmed serving bowl or on to individual plates. Garnish with sprigs of flat leaf parsley and serve immediately.

## HEALTH RATING 🍎🍎🍎

**ENTERTAINING ALTERNATIVE**
Creamy Coconut Seafood Pasta

**VEGETARIAN ALTERNATIVE**
Tagliarini with Broad Beans, Saffron & Crème Fraîche

**ENTERTAINING ALTERNATIVE**
## Creamy Coconut Seafood Pasta

INGREDIENTS **Serves 2–3**

400 g/14 oz egg tagliatelle
1 tsp sunflower oil
1 tsp sesame oil
4 spring onions, trimmed and sliced diagonally
1 garlic clove, peeled and crushed
1 red chilli, deseeded and finely chopped
2.5 cm/1 inch piece fresh root ginger, peeled and grated
150 ml/¼ pint coconut milk
100 ml/3½ fl oz double cream
225 g/8 oz cooked, peeled tiger prawns
185 g/6½ oz fresh white crab meat
2 tbsp freshly chopped coriander, plus sprigs to garnish
salt and freshly ground black pepper

Bring a large pan of lightly salted water to a rolling boil. Add the pasta and cook according to the packet instructions, or until 'al dente'.

Meanwhile, heat the sunflower and sesame oils together in a saucepan. Add the spring onions, garlic, chilli and ginger and cook for 3–4 minutes, or until softened.

Blend the coconut milk and cream together in a jug. Add the prawns and crab meat to the pan and stir over a low heat for a few seconds to heat through. Gradually pour in the coconut cream, stirring all the time.

Stir the chopped coriander into the seafood sauce and season to taste with salt and pepper. Continue heating the sauce gently until piping hot, but do not allow to boil.

Drain the pasta thoroughly and return to the pan. Add the seafood sauce and gently toss together to coat the pasta.

Tip into a warmed serving dish or spoon on to individual plates. Serve immediately, garnished with fresh coriander sprigs.

**VEGETARIAN ALTERNATIVE**
## Tagliarini with Broad Beans, Saffron & Crème Fraîche

INGREDIENTS **Serves 2–3**

225 g/8 oz fresh young broad beans in pods or 100 g/3½ oz frozen broad beans, thawed
1 tbsp olive oil
1 garlic clove, peeled and chopped
small handful basil leaves, shredded
200 ml/7 fl oz crème fraîche
large pinch saffron strands
350 g/12 oz tagliarini
salt and freshly ground black pepper
1 tbsp freshly snipped chives
freshly grated Parmesan cheese, to serve

If using fresh broad beans, bring a pan of lightly salted water to the boil. Pod the beans and drop them into the boiling water for 1 minute. Drain and refresh under cold water. Drain again. Remove the outer skin of the beans and discard. If using thawed frozen broad beans, remove and discard the skins. Reserve the peeled beans.

Heat the olive oil in a saucepan. Add the peeled broad beans and the garlic and cook gently for 2–3 minutes. Stir in the basil, the crème fraîche and the pinch of saffron strands and simmer for 1 minute.

Meanwhile, bring a large pan of lightly salted water to a rolling boil. Add the pasta and cook according to the packet instructions, or until 'al dente'. Drain the pasta well and add to the sauce. Toss together and season to taste with salt and pepper.

Transfer the pasta and sauce to a warmed serving dish. Sprinkle with snipped chives and serve immediately with Parmesan cheese.

# Mixed Vegetable & Chicken Pasta

INGREDIENTS **Serves 4**

3 boneless and skinless chicken breasts
2 leeks
1 red onion
350 g/12 oz pasta shells
25 g/1 oz butter
2 tbsp olive oil
1 garlic clove, peeled and chopped
175 g/6 oz cherry tomatoes, halved
200 ml/7 fl oz double cream
425 g can asparagus tips, drained
salt and freshly ground black pepper
125 g/4 oz double Gloucester cheese with chives, crumbled
green salad, to serve

Preheat the grill just before using. Cut the chicken into thin strips. Trim the leeks, leaving some of the dark green tops, then shred and wash thoroughly in plenty of cold water. Peel the onion and cut into thin wedges.

Bring a large pan of lightly salted water to a rolling boil. Add the pasta and cook according to the packet instructions, or until 'al dente'.

Meanwhile, melt the butter with the olive oil in a large, heavy-based pan. Add the chicken and cook, stirring occasionally, for 8 minutes or until browned all over. Add the leeks and onion and cook for 5 minutes, or until softened. Add the garlic and cherry tomatoes and cook for a further 2 minutes.

Stir the cream and asparagus tips into the chicken and vegetable mixture, bring to the boil slowly, then remove from the heat. Drain the pasta thoroughly and return to the pan. Pour the sauce over the pasta, season to taste with salt and pepper, then toss lightly.

Tip the pasta mixture into a gratin dish and sprinkle with the cheese. Cook under the preheated grill for 5 minutes, or until bubbling and golden, turning the dish occasionally. Serve immediately with a green salad.

HEALTH RATING

**ENTERTAINING ALTERNATIVE**
Salmon & Mushroom Linguine

**PUDDING SUGGESTION**
Coffee Ricotta

**ENTERTAINING ALTERNATIVE**
## Salmon & Mushroom Linguine

INGREDIENTS **Serves 4**

450 g/1 lb salmon fillets, skinned
salt and freshly ground black pepper
75 g/3 oz butter
40 g/1½ oz flour
300 ml/½ pint chicken stock
150 ml/¼ pint whipping cream
225 g/8 oz mushrooms, wiped and sliced
350 g/12 oz linguine
50 g/2 oz Cheddar cheese, grated
50 g/2 oz fresh white breadcrumbs
2 tbsp freshly chopped parsley, to garnish

Preheat the oven to 190°C/375°F/Gas Mark 5, 10 minutes before cooking. Place the salmon in a shallow pan and cover with water. Season well with salt and pepper and bring to the boil, then lower the heat and simmer for 6–8 minutes, or until cooked. Drain and keep warm.

Melt 50 g/2 oz of the butter in a heavy-based pan, stir in the flour, cook for 1 minute then whisk in the chicken stock. Simmer gently until thickened. Stir in the cream and season to taste. Keep the sauce warm.

Melt the remaining butter in a pan, add the sliced mushrooms and cook for 2–3 minutes. Stir the mushrooms into the white sauce.

Bring a large pan of lightly salted water to a rolling boil. Add the linguine and cook according to the packet instructions, or until 'al dente'.

Drain the pasta thoroughly and return to the pan. Stir in half the sauce, then spoon into a lightly oiled 1.4 litre/2½ pint shallow ovenproof dish. Flake the salmon, add to the remaining sauce then pour over the pasta. Sprinkle with the cheese and breadcrumbs, then bake in the preheated for 15–20 minutes, or until golden. Garnish with the parsley and serve immediately.

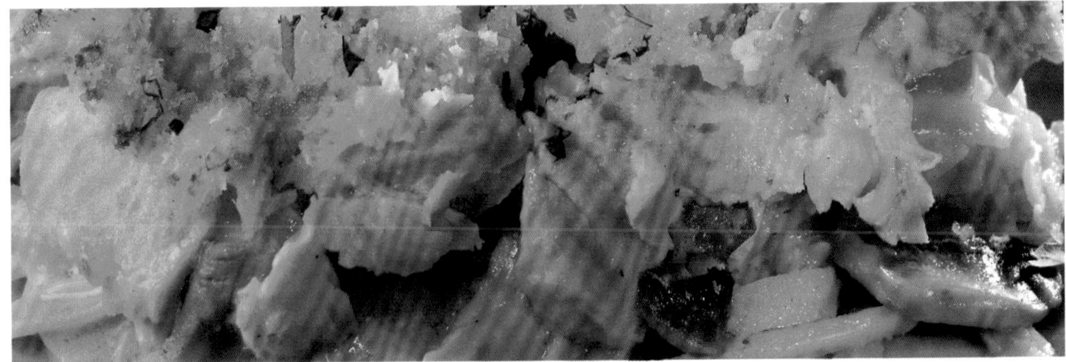

**PUDDING SUGGESTION**
## Coffee Ricotta

INGREDIENTS **Serves 6**

700 g/1½ lb fresh ricotta cheese
125 ml/4 fl oz double cream
25 g/1 oz espresso beans, freshly ground
4 tbsp caster sugar
3 tbsp brandy
50 g/2 oz butter, softened
75 g/3 oz caster sugar
1 medium egg, beaten
50 g/2 oz plain flour

Preheat the oven to 220°C/425°F/Gas Mark 7, 15 minutes before baking. Beat the ricotta and cream together until smooth. Stir in the ground coffee beans, sugar and brandy. Cover and refrigerate for at least 2 hours (the flavour improves the longer it stands). Meanwhile, oil two baking sheets and line with non-stick baking parchment.

Cream together the butter and sugar until fluffy. Gradually beat in the egg, a little at a time. In a bowl, sift the flour then fold into the butter mixture to form a soft dough. Spoon the mixture into a piping bag fitted with a 1 cm/½ inch plain nozzle. Pipe 7.5 cm/3 inch lengths of the mixture spaced well apart on to the baking sheet. Use a sharp knife to cut the dough off cleanly at the nozzle.

Bake in the preheated oven for 6–8 minutes, until just golden at the edges. Cool on the baking sheet for 5 minutes before transferring to a wire rack to cool completely.

To serve, spoon the coffee and ricotta mixture into small coffee cups. Serve with the biscuits.

**ORIENTAL ALTERNATIVE**

## Singapore Noodles

INGREDIENTS **Serves 4**

225 g/8 oz thin round egg noodles
3 tbsp groundnut or vegetable oil
125 g/4 oz field mushrooms, wiped and thinly sliced
2.5 cm/1 inch piece root ginger, peeled and finely chopped
1 red chilli, deseeded and thinly sliced
1 red pepper, deseeded and thinly sliced
2 garlic cloves, peeled and crushed
1 medium courgette, cut in half lengthwise and diagonally sliced
4-6 spring onions, trimmed and thinly sliced
50 g/2 oz frozen garden peas, thawed
1 tbsp curry paste
2 tbsp tomato ketchup
salt or soy sauce
125 g/4 oz beansprouts, rinsed and drained

**To garnish:**

sesame seeds
fresh coriander leaves

Bring a large pan of lightly salted water to a rolling boil. Add the noodles and cook according to the packet instructions, or until 'al dente'. Drain thoroughly and toss with 1 tablespoon of the oil.

Heat the remaining oil in a wok or large frying pan over high heat. Add the mushrooms, ginger, chilli and red pepper and stir-fry for 2 minutes. Add the garlic, courgettes, spring onions and garden peas and stir lightly.

Push the vegetables to one side and add the curry paste, tomato ketchup and about 125 ml/4 fl oz hot water. Season to taste with salt or a few drops of soy sauce and allow to boil vigorously, stirring, until the paste is smooth. Stir the reserved egg noodles and the beansprouts into the vegetable mixture and stir-fry until coated with the paste and thoroughly heated through.

Season with more soy sauce if necessary, then turn into a large warmed serving bowl or spoon on to individual plates. Garnish with sesame seeds and coriander leaves and serve immediately.

**STARTER SUGGESTION**

## Italian Baked Tomatoes with Curly Endive & Radicchio

INGREDIENTS **Serves 4**

1 tsp olive oil
4 beef tomatoes
salt
50 g/2 oz fresh white breadcrumbs
1 tbsp freshly snipped chives
1 tbsp freshly chopped parsley
125 g/4 oz button mushrooms, finely chopped
salt and freshly ground black pepper
25 g/1 oz fresh Parmesan cheese, grated

**For the salad:**

½ curly endive lettuce
½ small piece of radicchio
2 tbsp olive oil
1 tsp balsamic vinegar
salt and freshly ground black pepper

Preheat the oven to 190°C/375°F/Gas Mark 5. Lightly oil a baking tray with the teaspoon of oil. Slice the tops off the tomatoes, remove all the tomato flesh and sieve into a large bowl. Sprinkle a little salt inside the tomato shells and place them upside down on a plate while the filling is prepared.

Mix the sieved tomato with the breadcrumbs, fresh herbs and mushrooms and season well with salt and pepper. Place the tomato shells on the prepared baking tray and fill with the tomato and mushroom mixture. Sprinkle the cheese on top and bake in the preheated oven for 15–20 minutes, until golden brown.

Meanwhile, prepare the salad. Arrange the endive and radicchio on individual serving plates and mix the remaining ingredients together in a small bowl to make the dressing. Season to taste.

When the tomatoes are cooked, allow to rest for 5 minutes then place on the prepared plates and drizzle over a little dressing. Serve warm.

# Parma Ham-wrapped Chicken with Ribbon Pasta

INGREDIENTS **Serves 4**

4 boneless and skinless chicken breasts
salt and freshly ground black pepper
12 slices Parma ham
2 tbsp olive oil
350 g/12 oz ribbon pasta
1 garlic clove, peeled and chopped
1 bunch spring onions, trimmed and diagonally sliced
400 g can chopped tomatoes
juice of 1 lemon
150 ml/¼ pint crème fraîche
3 tbsp freshly chopped parsley
pinch of sugar
freshly grated Parmesan cheese, to garnish

Cut each chicken breast into three pieces and season well with salt and pepper. Wrap each chicken piece in a slice of Parma ham to enclose completely, securing if necessary with either fine twine or cocktail sticks.

Heat the oil in a large frying pan and cook the chicken, turning occasionally, for 12–15 minutes or until thoroughly cooked. Remove from the pan with a slotted spoon and reserve.

Meanwhile, bring a large pan of lightly salted water to a rolling boil. Add the pasta and cook according to the packet instructions, or until 'al dente'.

Add the garlic and spring onions to the frying pan and cook, stirring occasionally, for 2 minutes, or until softened. Stir in the tomatoes, lemon juice and crème fraîche. Bring to the boil, lower the heat and simmer, covered, for 3 minutes. Stir in the parsley and sugar, season to taste, then return the chicken to the pan and heat for 2–3 minutes until piping hot.

Drain the pasta thoroughly and mix in the chopped parsley, then spoon on to a warmed serving dish or individual plates. Arrange the chicken and sauce over the pasta. Garnish and serve immediately.

HEALTH RATING

**ORIENTAL ALTERNATIVE**
Singapore Noodles

**STARTER SUGGESTION**
Italian Baked Tomatoes with Curly Endive & Radicchio

# Herb-baked Chicken with Tagliatelle

INGREDIENTS **Serves 4**

75 g/3 oz fresh white breadcrumbs
3 tbsp olive oil
1 tsp dried oregano
2 tbsp sun-dried tomato paste
salt and freshly ground black pepper
4 boneless and skinless chicken breasts, each about 150 g/5 oz
2 x 400 g cans plum tomatoes
4 tbsp freshly chopped basil
2 tbsp dry white wine
350 g/12 oz tagliatelle
fresh basil sprigs, to garnish

Preheat the oven to 200°C/400°F/Gas Mark 6, 15 minutes before cooking. Mix together the breadcrumbs, 1 tablespoon of the olive oil, the oregano and tomato paste. Season to taste with salt and pepper. Place the chicken breasts well apart in a roasting tin and coat with the breadcrumb mixture.

Mix the plum tomatoes with the chopped basil and white wine. Season to taste, then spoon evenly round the chicken.

Drizzle the remaining olive oil over the chicken breasts and cook in the preheated oven for 20–30 minutes, or until the chicken is golden and the juices run clear when a skewer is inserted into the flesh.

Meanwhile, bring a large pan of lightly salted water to a rolling boil. Add the pasta and cook according to the packet instructions, or until 'al dente'.

Drain the pasta thoroughly and transfer to warmed serving plates. Arrange the chicken breasts on top of the pasta and spoon over the sauce. Garnish with sprigs of basil and serve immediately.

HEALTH RATING 🍎🍎🍎

**CHILDREN'S ALTERNATIVE**
Creamy Chicken & Sausage Penne

**SPICY ALTERNATIVE**
Spicy Mexican Chicken

**CHILDREN'S ALTERNATIVE**
## Creamy Chicken & Sausage Penne

Heat the olive oil in a large frying pan, add the shallots and cook for 3 minutes, or until golden. Remove and drain on absorbent kitchen paper. Add the chicken thighs to the pan and cook for 5 minutes, turning frequently until browned. Drain on absorbent kitchen paper.

Add the smoked sausage and chestnut mushrooms to the pan and cook for 3 minutes, or until browned. Drain separately on absorbent kitchen paper.

Return the shallots, chicken and sausage to the pan, then add the garlic, paprika and thyme and cook for 1 minute, stirring. Pour in the water and stock and season to taste with black pepper. Bring to the boil, lower the heat and simmer, covered, for 15 minutes. Add the mushrooms to the pan and simmer, covered, for 15 minutes, or until the chicken is tender.

Meanwhile, bring a large pan of lightly salted water to a rolling boil. Add the penne and cook according to the packet instructions, or until 'al dente'. Drain thoroughly.

Stir the mascarpone cheese into the chicken sauce and heat through, stirring gently. Spoon the pasta on to a warmed serving dish, top with the sauce, garnish and serve immediately.

INGREDIENTS **Serves 4**

2 tbsp olive oil
225 g/8 oz shallots, peeled
8 chicken thighs
175 g/6 oz smoked sausage, thickly sliced
125 g/4 oz chestnut mushrooms, wiped and halved
2 garlic cloves, peeled and chopped
1 tbsp paprika
1 small bunch fresh thyme, chopped, plus leaves to garnish
150 ml/¼ pint water
300 ml/½ pint chicken stock
freshly ground black pepper
350 g/12 oz penne
250 g tub mascarpone cheese

**SPICY ALTERNATIVE**
## Spicy Mexican Chicken

Heat the oil in a large frying pan, add the chicken mince and cook for 5 minutes, stirring frequently with a wooden spoon to break up any lumps. Add the onion, garlic and pepper and cook for 3 minutes, stirring occasionally. Stir in the chilli powder and cook for a further 2 minutes.

Stir in the tomato paste, pour in the chicken stock and season to taste with salt and pepper. Bring to the boil, reduce the heat, and simmer, covered, for 20 minutes. Add the kidney and chilli beans and cook, stirring occasionally, for 10 minutes, or until the chicken is tender.

Meanwhile, bring a large pan of lightly salted water to a rolling boil. Add the spaghetti and cook according to the packet instructions, or until 'al dente'.

Drain the spaghetti thoroughly, arrange on warmed plates and spoon over the chicken and bean mixture. Serve with the grated cheese, guacamole and salsa.

INGREDIENTS **Serves 4**

2 tbsp olive oil
450 g/1 lb chicken mince
1 red onion, peeled and chopped
2 garlic cloves, peeled and chopped
1 red pepper, deseeded and chopped
1–2 tsp hot chilli powder
2 tbsp tomato paste
225 ml/8 fl oz chicken stock
salt and freshly ground black pepper
420 g can red kidney beans, drained
420 g can chilli beans, drained
350 g/12 oz spaghetti

**To serve:**
Monterey Jack or Cheddar cheese, grated
guacamole
hot chilli salsa

# Chicken Gorgonzola & Mushroom Macaroni

INGREDIENTS **Serves 4**

450 g/1 lb macaroni
75 g/3 oz butter
225 g/8 oz chestnut mushrooms, wiped and sliced
225 g/8 oz baby button mushrooms, wiped and halved
350 g/12 oz cooked chicken, skinned and chopped
2 tsp cornflour
300 ml/½ pint semi-skimmed milk
50 g/2 oz Gorgonzola cheese, chopped, plus extra to serve
2 tbsp freshly chopped sage
1 tbsp freshly chopped chives, plus extra chive leaves to garnish
salt and freshly ground black pepper

Bring a large pan of lightly salted water to a rolling boil. Add the macaroni and cook according to the packet instructions, or until 'al dente'.

Meanwhile, melt the butter in a large frying pan, add the chestnut and button mushrooms and cook for 5 minutes, or until golden, stirring occasionally. Add the chicken to the pan and cook for 4 minutes, or until heated through thoroughly and slightly golden, stirring occasionally.

Blend the cornflour with a little of the milk in a jug to form a smooth paste, then gradually blend in the remaining milk and pour into the frying pan. Bring to the boil slowly, stirring constantly. Add the cheese and cook for 1 minute, stirring frequently until melted.

Stir the sage and chives into the frying pan. Season to taste with salt and pepper then heat through. Drain the macaroni thoroughly and return to the pan. Pour the chicken and mushroom sauce over the macaroni and toss lightly to coat. Tip into a warmed serving dish, and serve immediately with extra Gorgonzola cheese.

HEALTH RATING ⬤⬤

**VEGETARIAN ALTERNATIVE**

Pasta with Courgettes, Rosemary & Lemon

**ENTERTAINING ALTERNATIVE**

Chicken & Prawn-stacked Ravioli

## VEGETARIAN ALTERNATIVE
## Pasta with Courgettes, Rosemary & Lemon

Bring a large saucepan of salted water to the boil and add the pasta. Return to the boil and cook until 'al dente' or according to the packet instructions.

When the pasta is almost done, heat the oil in a large frying pan and add the garlic. Cook over a medium heat until the garlic just begins to brown. Be careful not to overcook the garlic at this stage or it will become bitter.

Add the courgettes, rosemary, parsley and lemon zest and juice. Cook for 3–4 minutes until the courgettes are just tender.

Add the olives to the frying pan and stir well. Season to taste with salt and pepper and remove from the heat.

Drain the pasta well and add to the frying pan. Stir until thoroughly combined. Garnish with lemon and sprigs of fresh rosemary and serve immediately.

INGREDIENTS **Serves 4**

- 350 g/12 oz dried pasta shapes, e.g. rigatoni
- 1½ tbsp good quality extra virgin olive oil
- 2 garlic cloves, peeled and finely chopped
- 4 medium courgettes, thinly sliced
- 1 tbsp freshly chopped rosemary
- 1 tbsp freshly chopped parsley
- zest and juice of 2 lemons
- 25 g/1 oz pitted black olives, roughly chopped
- 25 g/1 oz pitted green olives, roughly chopped
- salt and freshly ground black pepper

**To garnish:**

- lemon slices
- sprigs of fresh rosemary

## ENTERTAINING ALTERNATIVE
## Chicken & Prawn-stacked Ravioli

INGREDIENTS **Serves 4**

- 1 tbsp olive oil
- 1 onion, peeled and chopped
- 1 garlic clove, peeled and chopped
- 450 g/1 lb boned and skinned cooked chicken, cut into large pieces
- 1 beefsteak tomato, deseeded and chopped
- 150 ml/¼ pint dry white wine
- 150 ml/¼ pint double cream
- 250 g/9 oz peeled cooked prawns, thawed if frozen
- 2 tbsp freshly chopped tarragon, plus sprigs to garnish
- salt and freshly ground black pepper
- 8 sheets fresh lasagne

Heat the olive oil in a large frying pan, add the onion and garlic and cook for 5 minutes, or until softened, stirring occasionally. Add the chicken pieces and fry for 4 minutes, or until heated through, turning occasionally.

Stir in the chopped tomato, wine and cream and bring to the boil. Lower the heat and simmer for about 5 minutes, or until reduced and thickened. Stir in the prawns and tarragon and season to taste with salt and pepper. Heat the sauce through gently.

Meanwhile, bring a large pan of lightly salted water to the boil and add 2 lasagne sheets. Return to the boil and cook for 2 minutes, stirring gently to avoid sticking. Remove from the pan using a slotted spoon and keep warm. Repeat with the remaining sheets.

Cut each sheet of lasagne in half. Place two pieces on each of the warmed plates and divide half of the chicken mixture among them. Top each serving with a second sheet of lasagne and divide the remainder of the chicken mixture among them. Top with a final layer of lasagne. Garnish with tarragon sprigs and serve immediately.

# Spaghetti with Turkey & Bacon Sauce

INGREDIENTS **Serves 4**

450 g/1 lb spaghetti
25 g /1 oz butter
225 g/8 oz smoked streaky bacon, rind removed
350 g/12 oz fresh turkey strips
1 onion, peeled and chopped
1 garlic clove, peeled and chopped
3 medium eggs, beaten
300 ml/½ pint double cream
salt and freshly ground black pepper
50 g/2 oz freshly grated Parmesan cheese
2–3 tbsp freshly chopped coriander, to garnish

Bring a large pan of lightly salted water to a rolling boil. Add the spaghetti and cook according to the packet instructions, or until 'al dente'.

Meanwhile, melt the butter in a large frying pan. Using scissors, cut the streaky bacon into small pieces. Add the bacon to the pan with the turkey strips and cook for 8 minutes, or until browned, stirring occasionally to prevent sticking. Add the onion and garlic and cook for 5 minutes or until softened, stirring occasionally.

Place the eggs and cream in a bowl and season to taste with salt and pepper. Beat together then pour into the frying pan and cook, stirring, for 2 minutes or until the mixture begins to thicken but does not scramble.

Drain the spaghetti thoroughly and return to the pan. Pour over the sauce, add the grated Parmesan cheese and toss lightly. Heat through for 2 minutes, or until piping hot. Tip into a warmed serving dish and sprinkle with freshly chopped coriander. Serve immediately.

## HEALTH RATING 🍎

**VEGETARIAN ALTERNATIVE**

Spaghetti with Pesto

**ENTERTAINING ALTERNATIVE**

Spaghetti alla Puttanesca

**VEGETARIAN ALTERNATIVE**
## Spaghetti with Pesto

To make the pesto, place the Parmesan cheese in a food processor with the basil leaves, pine nuts and garlic and process until well blended.

With the motor running, gradually pour in the extra virgin olive oil until a thick sauce forms. Add a little more oil if the sauce seems too thick. Season to taste with salt and pepper. Transfer to a bowl, cover and store in the refrigerator until required.

Bring a large pan of lightly salted water to a rolling boil. Add the spaghetti and cook according to the packet instructions, or until 'al dente'.

Drain the spaghetti thoroughly and return to the pan. Stir in the pesto and toss lightly. Heat through gently, then tip the pasta into a warmed serving dish or spoon on to individual plates. Garnish with basil leaves and serve immediately with extra Parmesan cheese.

INGREDIENTS **Serves 4**

200 g/7 oz freshly grated Parmesan cheese, plus extra to serve
25 g/1 oz fresh basil leaves, plus extra to garnish
6 tbsp pine nuts
3 large garlic cloves, peeled
200 ml/7 fl oz extra virgin olive oil, plus more if necessary
salt and freshly ground pepper
400 g/14 oz spaghetti

**ENTERTAINING ALTERNATIVE**
## Spaghetti alla Puttanesca

Heat the olive oil in a large frying pan, add the anchovies and cook, stirring with a wooden spoon and crushing the anchovies until they disintegrate. Add the garlic and dried chillies and cook for 1 minute, stirring frequently.

Add the tomatoes, olives, capers, oregano and tomato paste and cook, stirring occasionally, for 15 minutes, or until the liquid has evaporated and the sauce is thickened. Season the tomato sauce to taste with salt and pepper.

Meanwhile, bring a large pan of lightly salted water to a rolling boil. Add the spaghetti and cook according to the packet instructions, or until 'al dente'.

Drain the spaghetti thoroughly, reserving 1–2 tablespoons of the the cooking water. Return the spaghetti with the reserved water to the pan. Pour the tomato sauce over the spaghetti, add the chopped parsley and toss to coat. Tip into a warmed serving dish or spoon on to individual plates and serve immediately.

INGREDIENTS **Serves 4**

4 tbsp olive oil
50 g/2 oz anchovy fillets in olive oil, drained and coarsely chopped
2 garlic cloves, peeled and finely chopped
½ tsp crushed dried chillies
400 g can chopped plum tomatoes
125 g/4 oz pitted black olives, cut in half
2 tbsp capers, rinsed and drained
1 tsp freshly chopped oregano
1 tbsp tomato paste
salt and freshly ground black pepper
400 g/14 oz spaghetti
2 tbsp freshly chopped parsley

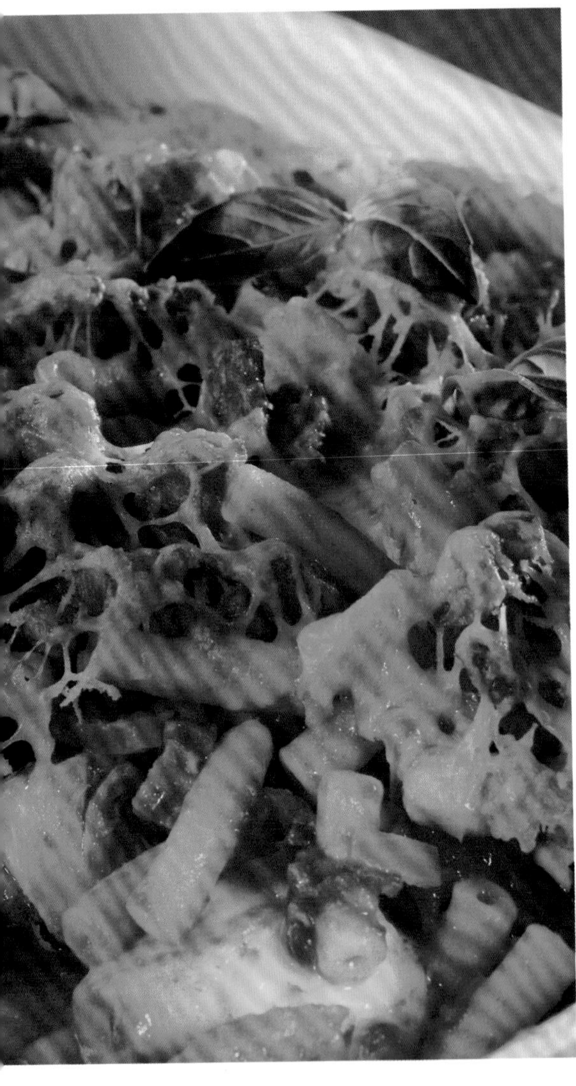

**MEAT ALTERNATIVE**
## Cheesy Baked Chicken Macaroni

INGREDIENTS **Serves 4**

1 tbsp olive oil
350 g/12 oz boneless and skinless chicken breasts, diced
75 g/3 oz pancetta, diced
1 onion, peeled and chopped
1 garlic clove, peeled and chopped
350 g packet or jar of fresh tomato sauce
400 g can chopped tomatoes
2 tbsp freshly chopped basil, plus leaves to garnish
salt and freshly ground black pepper
350 g/12 oz macaroni
150 g/5oz mozzarella cheese, drained and chopped
50 g/2 oz Gruyère cheese, grated
50 g/2 oz freshly grated Parmesan cheese

Preheat the grill just before cooking. Heat the oil in large frying pan and cook the chicken for 8 minutes, or until browned, stirring occasionally. Drain on absorbent kitchen paper and reserve. Add the pancetta slices to the pan and fry on both sides until crispy. Remove from the pan and reserve.

Add the onion and garlic to the frying pan and cook for 5 minutes, or until softened. Stir in the tomato sauce, chopped tomatoes and basil and season to taste with salt and pepper. Bring to the boil, lower the heat and simmer the sauce for 5 minutes.

Meanwhile, bring a large pan of lightly salted water to a rolling boil. Add the macaroni and cook according to the packet instructions, or until 'al dente'.

Drain the macaroni thoroughly, return to the pan and stir in the sauce, chicken and mozzarella cheese. Spoon into a shallow ovenproof dish.

Sprinkle the pancetta over the macaroni. Sprinkle over the Gruyère and Parmesan cheeses. Place under the preheated grill and cook for 5–10 minutes, or until golden brown, turning the dish occasionally. Garnish and serve immediately.

**ENTERTAINING ALTERNATIVE**
## Baked Macaroni with Mushrooms & Leeks

INGREDIENTS **Serves 4**

2 tbsp olive oil
1 onion, peeled and finely chopped
1 garlic clove, peeled and crushed
2 small leeks, trimmed and chopped
450 g/1 lb assorted wild mushrooms, trimmed
50 ml/2 fl oz white wine
75 g/3 oz butter
150 ml/¼ pint crème fraîche or whipping cream
salt and freshly ground black pepper
75 g/3 oz fresh white breadcrumbs
350 g/12 oz short cut macaroni
1 tbsp freshly chopped parsley, to garnish

Preheat the oven to 220°C/425°F/Gas Mark 7, 15 minutes before cooking. Heat 1 tablespoon of the olive oil in a large frying pan, add the onion and garlic and cook for 2 minutes. Add the leeks, mushrooms and 25 g/1 oz of the butter then cook for 5 minutes. Pour in the white wine, cook for 2 minutes then stir in the crème fraîche or cream. Season to taste with salt and pepper.

Meanwhile, bring a large pan of lightly salted water to a rolling boil. Add the macaroni and cook according to the packet instructions, or until 'al dente'.

Melt 25 g/1 oz of the butter with the remaining oil in a small frying pan. Add the breadcrumbs and fry until just beginning to turn golden brown. Drain on absorbent kitchen paper.

Drain the pasta thoroughly, toss in the remaining butter then tip into a lightly oiled, 1.4 litre/2½ pint shallow baking dish. Cover the pasta with the leek and mushroom mixture then sprinkle with the fried breadcrumbs. Bake in the preheated oven for 5–10 minutes, or until golden and crisp. Garnish with chopped parsley and serve.

# Baked Macaroni Cheese

INGREDIENTS **Serves 8**

450 g/1 lb macaroni
75 g/3 oz butter
1 onion, peeled and finely chopped
40 g/1½ oz plain flour
1 litre/1¾ pints milk
1–2 dried bay leaves
½ tsp dried thyme
salt and freshly ground black pepper
cayenne pepper
freshly grated nutmeg
2 small leeks, trimmed, finely chopped, cooked and drained
1 tbsp Dijon mustard
200 g/8 oz mature Cheddar cheese, grated
2 tbsp dried breadcrumbs
2 tbsp freshly grated Parmesan cheese
basil sprig, to garnish

Preheat the oven to 190°C/375°F/Gas Mark 5, 10 minutes before cooking. Bring a large pan of lightly salted water to a rolling boil. Add the macaroni and cook according to the packet instructions, or until 'al dente'. Drain thoroughly and reserve.

Meanwhile, melt 50 g/2 oz of the butter in a large, heavy-based saucepan, add the onion and cook, stirring frequently, for 5–7 minutes, or until softened. Sprinkle in the flour and cook, stirring constantly, for 2 minutes. Remove the pan from the heat, stir in the milk, return to the heat and cook, stirring, until a smooth sauce has formed.

Add the bay leaf and thyme to the sauce and season to taste with salt, pepper, cayenne pepper and freshly grated nutmeg. Simmer for about 15 minutes, stirring frequently, until thickened and smooth.

Remove the sauce from the heat. Add the cooked leeks, mustard and Cheddar cheese and stir until the cheese has melted. Stir in the macaroni then tip into a lightly oiled baking dish.

Sprinkle the breadcrumbs and Parmesan cheese over the macaroni. Dot with the remaining butter, then bake in the preheated oven for 1 hour, or until golden. Garnish with a basil sprig and serve immediately.

HEALTH RATING

**MEAT ALTERNATIVE**
Cheesy Baked Chicken Macaroni

**ENTERTAINING ALTERNATIVE**
Baked Macaroni with Mushrooms & Leeks

# Cannelloni with Tomato & Red Wine Sauce

INGREDIENTS **Serves 6**

2 tbsp olive oil
1 onion, peeled and finely chopped
1 garlic clove, peeled and crushed
250 g carton ricotta cheese
50 g/2 oz pine nuts
salt and freshly ground black pepper
pinch freshly grated nutmeg
250 g/9 oz fresh spinach lasagne
25 g/1 oz butter
1 shallot, peeled and finely chopped
150 ml/¼ pint red wine
400 g can chopped tomatoes
½ tsp sugar
50 g/2 oz mozzarella cheese, grated, plus extra to serve
1 tbsp freshly chopped parsley, to garnish
fresh green salad, to serve

Preheat the oven to 200°C/400°F/Gas Mark 6, 15 minutes before cooking. Heat the oil in a heavy-based pan, add the onion and garlic and cook for 2–3 minutes. Cool slightly, then stir in the ricotta cheese and pine nuts. Season the filling to taste with salt, pepper and the nutmeg.

Cut each lasagne sheet in half, put a little of the ricotta filling on each piece and roll up like a cigar to resemble cannelloni tubes. Arrange the cannelloni seam-side down in a single layer, in a lightly oiled, 2.3 litre/4 pint shallow ovenproof dish.

Melt the butter in a pan, add the shallot and cook for 2 minutes. Pour in the red wine, tomatoes and sugar and season well. Bring to the boil, lower the heat and simmer for about 20 minutes, or until thickened. Add a little more sugar if desired. Transfer to a food processor and blend until a smooth sauce is formed.

Pour the warm tomato sauce over the cannelloni and sprinkle with the grated mozzarella cheese. Bake in the preheated oven for about 30 minutes, or until golden and bubbling. Garnish and serve immediately with a green salad.

HEALTH RATING

**SEAFOOD ALTERNATIVE**
Tuna Cannelloni

**ENTERTAINING ALTERNATIVE**
Cannelloni with Gorgonzola Sauce

**SEAFOOD ALTERNATIVE**
## Tuna Cannelloni

INGREDIENTS **Serves 4**

1 tbsp olive oil
6 spring onions, trimmed and finely sliced
1 sweet Mediterranean red pepper, deseeded and finely chopped
200 g can tuna in brine
250 g tub ricotta cheese
zest and juice of 1 lemon
1 tbsp freshly snipped chives
salt and freshly ground black pepper
8 dried cannelloni tubes
1 medium egg, beaten
125 g/4 oz cottage cheese
150 ml/¼ pint natural yogurt
pinch of freshly grated nutmeg
50 g/2 oz mozzarella cheese, grated
tossed green salad, to serve

Preheat the oven to 180°C/375°F/Gas Mark 5, 10 minutes before cooking. Heat the olive oil in a frying pan and cook the spring onions and pepper until soft. Remove from the pan with a slotted draining spoon and place in large bowl.

Drain the tuna, then stir into the spring onions and pepper. Beat the ricotta cheese with the lemon zest and juice and the snipped chives until soft and blended and season to taste with salt and pepper. Add to the tuna and mix together. If the mixture is still a little stiff, add a little extra lemon juice.

With a teaspoon, carefully spoon the mixture into the cannelloni tubes, then lay the filled tubes in a lightly oiled shallow ovenproof dish. Beat the egg, cottage cheese, natural yogurt and nutmeg together and pour over the cannelloni. Sprinkle with the grated mozzarella cheese and bake in the preheated oven for 15–20 minutes, or until the topping is golden brown and bubbling. Serve immediately with a tossed green salad.

**ENTERTAINING ALTERNATIVE**
## Cannelloni with Gorgonzola Sauce

INGREDIENTS **Serves 2–3**

50 g/2 oz salted butter
1 shallot, peeled and finely chopped
2 rashers streaky bacon, rind removed and chopped
225 g/8 oz mushrooms, wiped and finely chopped
25 g/1 oz plain flour
120 ml/4 fl oz double cream
125 g/4 oz fresh egg lasagne, 6 sheets in total
40 g/1½ oz unsalted butter
150 g/5 oz Gorgonzola cheese, diced
150 ml/¼ pint whipping cream
assorted salad leaves, to serve

Preheat the oven to 190°C/375°F/Gas Mark 5, 10 minutes before cooking. Melt the salted butter in a heavy-based pan, add the shallot and bacon and cook for about 4–5 minutes. Add the mushrooms to the pan and cook for 5–6 minutes, or until the mushrooms are very soft. Stir in the flour, cook for 1 minute, then stir in the double cream and cook gently for 2 minutes. Allow to cool.

Cut each sheet of lasagne in half. Spoon some filling on to each piece and roll up from the longest side to resemble cannelloni. Arrange the cannelloni in a lightly oiled, shallow 1.4 litre/2½ pint ovenproof dish.

Heat the unsalted butter very slowly in a pan and when melted, add the Gorgonzola cheese. Stir until the cheese has melted, then stir in the whipping cream. Bring to the boil slowly, then simmer gently for about 5 minutes, or until thickened. Pour the cream sauce over the cannelloni. Place in the preheated oven and bake for 20 minutes, or until golden and thoroughly heated through. Serve immediately with assorted salad leaves.

# Ratatouille & Pasta Bake

INGREDIENTS **Serves 4**

1 tbsp olive oil
2 large onions, peeled and finely chopped
400 g can chopped tomatoes
100 ml/3½ fl oz white wine
½ tsp caster sugar
salt and freshly ground black pepper
40 g/1½ oz butter
2 garlic cloves, peeled and crushed
125 g/4 oz mushrooms, wiped and thickly sliced
700 g/1½ lb courgettes, trimmed and thickly sliced
125 g/4 oz fresh spinach lasagne
2 large eggs
2 tbsp double cream
75 g/3 oz mozzarella cheese, grated
25 g/1 oz pecorino cheese, grated
green salad, to serve

Preheat the oven to 190°C/375°F/Gas Mark 5, 10 minutes before cooking. Heat the olive oil in a heavy-based pan, add half the onion and cook gently for 2–3 minutes. Stir in the tomatoes and wine, then simmer for 20 minutes, or until a thick consistency is formed. Add the sugar and season to taste with salt and pepper. Reserve.

Meanwhile, melt the butter in another pan, add the remaining onion, the garlic, mushrooms and courgettes and cook for 10 minutes, or until softened.

Spread a little tomato sauce in the base of a lightly oiled, 1.4 litre/2 ½ pint baking dish. Top with a layer of lasagne and spoon over half the mushroom and courgette mixture. Repeat the layers, finishing with a layer of lasagne.

Beat the eggs and cream together, then pour over the lasagne. Mix the mozzarella and pecorino cheeses together then sprinkle on top of the lasagne. Place in the preheated oven and cook for 20 minutes, or until golden-brown. Serve immediately with a green salad.

HEALTH RATING 🍎🍎

**SEAFOOD ALTERNATIVE**
Saucy Cod & Pasta Bake

**PUDDING SUGGESTION**
Zabaglione with Rum-soaked Raisin Compote

INGREDIENTS **Serves 4**

450 g/1 lb cod fillets, skinned
2 tbsp sunflower oil
1 onion, peeled and chopped
4 rashers smoked streaky bacon, rind removed and chopped
150 g/5 oz baby button mushrooms, wiped
2 celery sticks, trimmed and thinly sliced
2 small courgettes, halved lengthwise and sliced
400 g can chopped tomatoes
100 ml/3½ fl oz fish stock or dry white wine
1 tbsp freshly chopped tarragon
salt and freshly ground black pepper

**For the pasta topping:**

225–275 g/8–10 oz pasta shells
25 g/1 oz butter
4 tbsp plain flour
450 ml/¾ pint milk

## SEAFOOD ALTERNATIVE
# Saucy Cod & Pasta Bake

Preheat the oven to 200°C/400°F/Gas Mark 6, 15 minutes before cooking. Cut the cod into bite-sized pieces and reserve.

Heat the sunflower oil in a large saucepan, add the onion and bacon and cook for 7–8 minutes. Add the mushrooms and celery and cook for 5 minutes, or until fairly soft.

Add the courgettes and tomatoes to the bacon mixture and pour in the fish stock or wine. Bring to the boil, then simmer uncovered for 5 minutes or until the sauce has thickened slightly. Remove from the heat and stir in the cod pieces and the tarragon. Season to taste with salt and pepper, then spoon into a large oiled baking dish.

Meanwhile, bring a large pan of lightly salted water to a rolling boil. Add the pasta shells and cook according to the packet instructions, or until 'al dente'.

For the topping, place the butter and flour in a saucepan and pour in the milk. Bring to the boil slowly, whisking until thickened and smooth.

Drain the pasta thoroughly, and stir into the sauce. Spoon carefully over the fish and vegetables. Place in the preheated oven and bake for 20–25 minutes, or until the top is lightly browned and bubbling.

## PUDDING SUGGESTION
# Zabaglione with Rum-soaked Raisin Compote

Put the raisins in a small bowl with the lemon zest and ground cinnamon. Pour over the Marsala wine to cover and leave to macerate for at least one hour. When the raisins are plump, lift out of the Marsala wine and reserve the raisins and wine, discarding the lemon zest.

In a large heatproof bowl, mix together the egg yolks and sugar. Add the white wine and Marsala wine and stir well to combine. Put the bowl over a saucepan of simmering water, ensuring that the bottom of the bowl does not touch the water. Whisk constantly until the mixture doubles in bulk.

Remove from the heat and continue whisking for about 5 minutes until the mixture has cooled slightly. Fold in the raisins and then immediately fold in the whipped cream. Spoon into dessert glasses or goblets and serve with crisp biscuits.

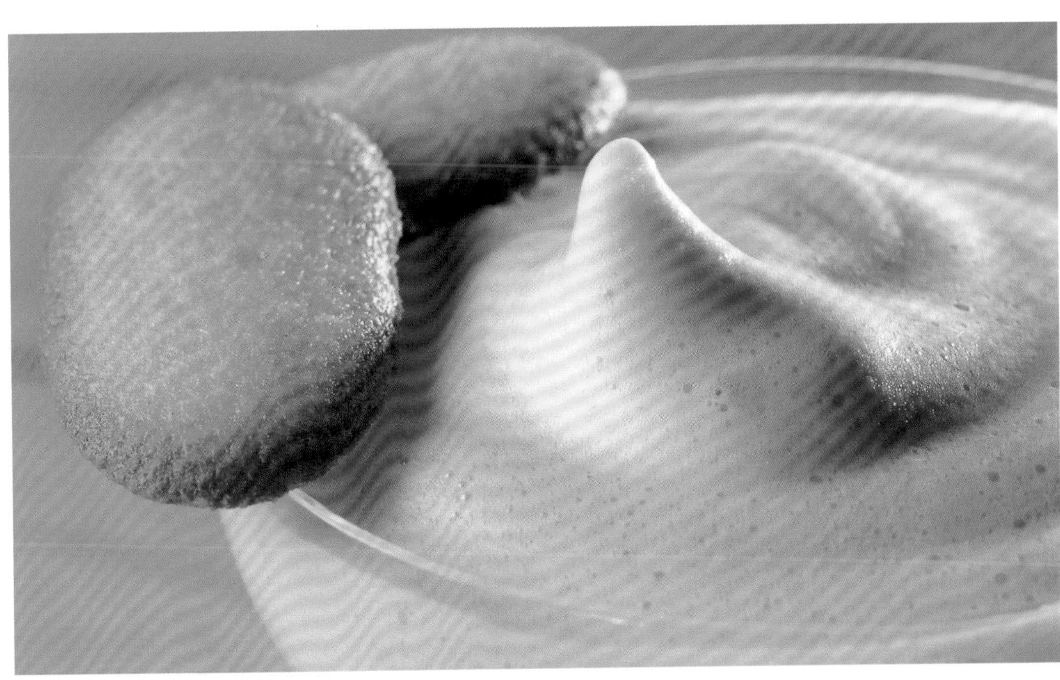

INGREDIENTS **Serves 6**

2 tbsp raisins
1 strip thinly pared lemon zest
½ tsp ground cinnamon
3 tbsp Marsala wine
3 medium egg yolks
3 tbsp caster sugar
125 ml/4 fl oz dry white wine
150 ml/¼ pint double cream, lightly whipped
crisp biscuits, to serve

# Aubergine & Tomato Layer

INGREDIENTS **Serves 4**

2 aubergines, about 700 g/1½ lb, trimmed and thinly sliced
6 tbsp olive oil
1 onion, peeled and finely sliced
1 garlic clove, peeled and crushed
400 g can chopped tomatoes
50 ml/2 fl oz red wine
½ tsp sugar
salt and freshly ground black pepper
50 g/2 oz butter
40 g/1½ oz flour
450 ml/¾ pint milk
225 g/8 oz fresh egg lasagne
2 medium eggs, beaten
200 ml/7 fl oz Greek yogurt
125 g/3 oz mozzarella cheese, grated
fresh basil leaves, to garnish

Preheat the oven to 190°C/375°F/Gas Mark 5, 10 minutes before cooking. Brush the aubergine slices with 5 tablespoons of the olive oil and place on a baking sheet. Bake in the preheated oven for 20 minutes, or until tender. Remove from the oven and increase the temperature to 200°C/400°F/Gas Mark 6.

Heat the remaining oil in a heavy-based pan. Add the onion and garlic, cook for 2–3 minutes then add the tomatoes, wine and sugar. Season to taste with salt and pepper, then simmer for 20 minutes.

Melt the butter in another pan. Stir in the flour, cook for 2 minutes, then whisk in the milk. Cook for 2–3 minutes, or until thickened. Season to taste.

Pour a little white sauce into a lightly oiled, 1.7 litre/3 pint baking dish. Cover with a layer of lasagne, spread with tomato sauce, then add some of the aubergines. Cover thinly with white sauce and sprinkle with a little cheese. Continue to layer in this way, finishing with a layer of lasagne.

Beat together the eggs and yogurt. Season, then pour over the lasagne. Sprinkle with the remaining cheese and bake in the preheated oven for 25–30 minutes, or until golden. Garnish with basil leaves and serve.

HEALTH RATING 🍎🍎

**MEAT ALTERNATIVE**

Baked Aubergines with Tomato & Mozzarella

**ENTERTAINING ALTERNATIVE**

Aubergine & Ravioli Parmigiana

## MEAT ALTERNATIVE
# Baked Aubergines with Tomato & Mozzarella

INGREDIENTS **Serves 4**

3 medium aubergines, trimmed and sliced
salt and freshly ground black pepper
4–6 tbsp olive oil
450 g/1 lb fresh turkey mince
1 onion, peeled and chopped
2 garlic cloves, peeled and chopped
2 x 400 g cans chopped tomatoes
1 tbsp fresh mixed herbs
200 ml/7 fl oz red wine
350 g/12 oz macaroni
5 tbsp freshly chopped basil
125 g/4 oz mozzarella cheese, drained and chopped
50 g/2 oz freshly grated Parmesan cheese

Preheat the oven to 200°C/400°F/Gas Mark 6, 15 minutes before cooking. Place the aubergine slices in a colander and sprinkle with salt. Leave for 1 hour or until the juices run clear. Rinse and dry on absorbent kitchen paper.

Heat 3–5 tablespoons of the olive oil in a large frying pan and cook the prepared aubergines in batches for 2 minutes on each side, or until softened. Remove and drain on absorbent kitchen paper.

Heat 1 tablespoon of olive oil in a saucepan, add the turkey mince and cook for 5 minutes, or until browned and sealed.

Add the onion to the pan and cook for 5 minutes, or until softened. Add the chopped garlic, the tomatoes and mixed herbs. Pour in the wine and season to taste with salt and pepper. Bring to the boil, lower the heat and simmer for 15 minutes, or until thickened.

Meanwhile, bring a large pan of lightly salted water to a rolling boil. Add the macaroni and cook according to the packet instructions, or until 'al dente'. Drain thoroughly.

Spoon half the tomato mixture into a lightly oiled ovenproof dish. Top with half the aubergine, pasta and chopped basil, then season lightly. Repeat the layers, finishing with a layer of aubergine. Sprinkle with the mozzarella and Parmesan cheeses, then bake in the preheated oven for 30 minutes or until golden and bubbling. Serve immediately.

## ENTERTAINING ALTERNATIVE
# Aubergine & Ravioli Parmigiana

INGREDIENTS **Serves 6**

4 tbsp olive oil
1 large onion, peeled and finely chopped
2–3 garlic cloves, peeled and crushed
2 x 400 g cans chopped tomatoes
2 tsp brown sugar
1 dried bay leaf
1 tsp dried oregano
1 tsp dried basil
2 tbsp freshly shredded basil
salt and freshly ground black pepper
2–3 medium aubergines, sliced crosswise 1 cm/½ inch thick
2 medium eggs, beaten with 1 tbsp water
125 g/4 oz dried breadcrumbs
75 g/3 oz freshly grated Parmesan cheese
400 g/14 oz mozzarella cheese, thinly sliced
250 g/9 oz cheese-filled ravioli, cooked and drained

Preheat the oven to 180°C/350°F/Gas Mark 4, about 15 minutes before cooking. Heat 2 tablespoons of the olive oil in a large, heavy-based pan, add the onion and cook for 6–7 minutes, or until softened.

Add the garlic, cook for 1 minute then stir in the tomatoes, sugar, bay leaf, dried oregano and basil, then bring to the boil, stirring frequently. Simmer for 30–35 minutes, or until thickened and reduced, stirring occasionally.

Stir in the fresh basil and season to taste with salt and pepper. Remove the tomato sauce from the heat and reserve.

Heat the remaining olive oil in a large, heavy-based frying pan over a high heat. Dip the aubergine slices in the egg mixture then in the breadcrumbs. Cook in batches until golden on both sides. Drain on absorbent kitchen paper. Add more oil between batches if necessary.

Spoon a little tomato sauce into the base of a lightly oiled large baking dish. Cover with a layer of aubergine slices, a sprinkling of Parmesan cheese, a layer of mozzarella cheese, then more sauce. Repeat the layers then cover the sauce with a layer of cooked ravioli. Continue to layer in this way, ending with a layer of mozzarella cheese. Sprinkle the top with Parmesan cheese.

Drizzle with a little extra olive oil if liked, then bake in the preheated oven for 30 minutes, or until golden brown and bubbling. Serve immediately.

## ENTERTAINING ALTERNATIVE
## Mini Chicken Balls with Tagliatelle

INGREDIENTS **Serves 4**

450 g/1 lb fresh chicken mince
50 g/2 oz sun-dried tomatoes, drained and finely chopped
salt and freshly ground black pepper
25 g/1 oz butter
1 tbsp oil
350 g/12 oz leeks, trimmed and diagonally sliced
125 g/4 oz frozen broad beans
300 ml/½ pint single cream
50 g/2 oz freshly grated Parmesan cheese
350 g/12 oz tagliatelle
4 medium eggs
fresh herbs, to garnish

Mix the chicken and tomatoes together and season to taste with salt and pepper. Divide the mixture into 32 pieces and roll into balls. Transfer to a baking sheet, cover and leave in the refrigerator for 1 hour.

Melt the butter in a large frying pan, add the chicken balls and cook for 5 minutes, or until golden, turning occasionally. Remove, drain on absorbent kitchen paper and keep warm. Add the leeks and broad beans to the frying pan and cook, stirring, for 10 minutes or until cooked and tender. Return the chicken balls to the pan, then stir in the cream and Parmesan cheese and heat through.

Meanwhile, bring a large pan of lightly salted water to a rolling boil. Add the pasta and cook according to the packet instructions, or until 'al dente'.

Bring a separate frying pan full of water to the boil, crack in the eggs and simmer for 2–4 minutes, or until poached to personal preference.

Meanwhile, drain the pasta thoroughly and return to the pan. Pour the chicken balls and vegetable sauce over the pasta, toss lightly and heat through for 1–2 minutes. Arrange on warmed individual plates and top with the poached eggs. Garnish with fresh herbs and serve immediately.

## PUDDING SUGGESTION
## Chocolate Pancakes

INGREDIENTS **Serves 6**

**For the pancakes:**
75 g/3 oz plain flour
1 tbsp cocoa powder
1 tsp caster sugar
½ tsp freshly grated nutmeg
2 medium eggs
175 ml/6 fl oz milk
75 g/3 oz unsalted butter, melted

**For the mango sauce:**
1 ripe mango, peeled and diced
50 ml/2 fl oz white wine
2 tbsp golden caster sugar
2 tbsp rum

**For the filling:**
225 g/8 oz plain dark chocolate
75 ml/3 fl oz double cream
3 eggs, separated
25 g/1 oz golden caster sugar

Preheat the oven to 200°C/400°F/Gas Mark 6, 15 minutes before cooking. To make the pancakes, sift the flour, cocoa powder, sugar and nutmeg into a bowl and make a well in the centre. Beat the eggs and milk together, then gradually beat into the flour mixture to form a batter. Stir in 50 g/2 oz of the melted butter and leave to stand for 1 hour.

Heat an 18 cm/7 inch non-stick frying pan and brush with a little melted butter. Add about 3 tablespoons of the batter and swirl to cover the base of the pan. Cook over a medium heat for 1–2 minutes, flip over and cook for a further 40 seconds. Repeat with the remaining batter. Stack the pancakes interleaving with greaseproof paper.

To make the sauce, place the mango, white wine and sugar in a saucepan and bring to the boil over a medium heat, then simmer for 2–3 minutes, stirring constantly. When the mixture has thickened add the rum. Chill in the refrigerator.

For the filling, melt the chocolate and cream in a small heavy-based saucepan over a medium heat. Stir until smooth, then leave to cool. Beat the egg yolks with the caster sugar for 3–5 minutes, or until the mixture is pale and creamy, then beat in the chocolate mixture.

Beat the egg whites until stiff, then add a little to the chocolate mixture. Stir in the remainder. Spoon a little of the mixture onto a pancake. Fold in half, then fold in half again, forming a triangle. Repeat with the remaining pancakes. Brush the pancakes with a little melted butter and bake in the preheated oven for 15–20 minutes or until the filling is set. Serve hot or cold with the mango sauce.

# Spaghetti & Meatballs

INGREDIENTS **Serves 4**

- 400 g can of chopped tomatoes
- 1 tbsp tomato paste
- 1 tsp chilli sauce
- ¼ tsp brown sugar
- salt and freshly ground black pepper
- 350 g/12 oz spaghetti
- 75g/3 oz Cheddar cheese, grated, plus extra to serve
- freshly chopped parsley, to garnish

**For the meatballs:**

- 450 g/1 lb lean pork or beef mince
- 125 g/4 oz fresh breadcrumbs
- 1 large onion, peeled and finely chopped
- 1 medium egg, beaten
- 1 tbsp tomato paste
- 2 tbsp freshly chopped parsley
- 1 tbsp freshly chopped oregano

Preheat the oven to 200°C/400°F/Gas Mark 6, 15 minutes before using. Place the chopped tomatoes, tomato paste, chilli sauce and sugar in a saucepan. Season to taste with salt and pepper and bring to the boil. Cover and simmer for 15 minutes, then cook, uncovered, for a further 10 minutes, or until the sauce has reduced and thickened.

Meanwhile, make the meatballs. Place the meat, breadcrumbs and onion in a food processor. Blend until all the ingredients are well mixed. Add the beaten egg, tomato paste, parsley and oregano and season to taste. Blend again.

Shape the mixture into small balls, about the size of a plum, and place on an oiled baking tray. Cook in the preheated oven for 25–30 minutes, or until browned and cooked.

Meanwhile, bring a large pan of lightly salted water to a rolling boil. Add the pasta and cook according to the packet instructions, or until 'al dente'.

Drain the pasta and return to the pan. Pour over the tomato sauce and toss gently to coat the spaghetti. Tip into a warmed serving dish and top with the meatballs. Garnish with chopped parsley and serve immediately with grated cheese.

HEALTH RATING 

**ENTERTAINING ALTERNATIVE**
Mini Chicken Balls with Tagliatelle

**PUDDING SUGGESTION**
Chocolate Pancakes

# Spicy Chilli Beef

INGREDIENTS **Serves 4**

2 tbsp olive oil
1 onion, peeled and finely chopped
1 red pepper, deseeded and sliced
450 g/1 lb minced beef steak
2 garlic cloves, peeled and crushed
2 red chillies, deseeded and finely sliced
salt and freshly ground black pepper
400 g can chopped tomatoes
2 tbsp tomato paste
400 g can red kidney beans, drained
50 g/2 oz good quality, plain dark chocolate, grated
350 g/12 oz dried fusilli
knob of butter
2 tbsp freshly chopped flat leaf parsley
paprika, to garnish
soured cream, to serve

Heat the olive oil in a large, heavy-based pan. Add the onion and red pepper and cook for 5 minutes, or until beginning to soften. Add the minced beef and cook over a high heat for 5–8 minutes, or until the meat is browned. Stir with a wooden spoon during cooking to break up any lumps in the meat. Add the garlic and chilli, fry for 1 minute then season to taste with salt and pepper.

Add the chopped tomatoes, tomato paste and the kidney beans to the pan. Bring to the boil, lower the heat, and simmer, covered, for at least 40 minutes, stirring occasionally. Stir in the grated chocolate and cook for 3 minutes, or until melted.

Meanwhile, bring a large pan of lightly salted water to a rolling boil. Add the fusilli and cook according to the packet instructions, or until 'al dente'.

Drain the pasta, return to the pan and toss with the butter and parsley. Tip into a warmed serving dish or spoon on to individual plates. Spoon the sauce over the pasta. Sprinkle with paprika and serve immediately with spoonfuls of soured cream.

HEALTH RATING 🍎🍎

**SPEEDY ALTERNATIVE**

Pasta with Beef, Capers & Olives

**ORIENTAL ALTERNATIVE**

Chinese Beef with Angel Hair Pasta

**SPEEDY ALTERNATIVE**

## Pasta with Beef, Capers & Olives

INGREDIENTS **Serves 4**

- 2 tbsp olive oil
- 300 g/11 oz rump steak, trimmed and cut into strips
- 4 spring onions, trimmed and sliced
- 2 garlic cloves, peeled and chopped
- 2 courgettes, trimmed and cut into strips
- 1 red pepper, deseeded and cut into strips
- 2 tsp freshly chopped oregano
- 2 tbsp capers, drained and rinsed
- 4 tbsp pitted black olives, sliced
- 400 g can chopped tomatoes
- salt and freshly ground black pepper
- 450 g/1 lb fettuccine
- 1 tbsp freshly chopped parsley, to garnish

Heat the olive oil in a large frying pan over a high heat. Add the steak and cook, stirring, for 3–4 minutes, or until browned. Remove from the pan using a slotted spoon and reserve.

Lower the heat, add the spring onions and garlic to the pan and cook for 1 minute. Add the courgettes and pepper and cook for 3–4 minutes.

Add the oregano, capers and olives to the pan with the chopped tomatoes. Season to taste with salt and pepper, then simmer for 7 minutes, stirring occasionally. Return the beef to the pan and simmer for 3–5 minutes, or until the sauce has thickened slightly.

Meanwhile, bring a large pan of lightly salted water to a rolling boil. Add the pasta and cook according to the packet instructions, or until 'al dente'.

Drain the pasta thoroughly. Return to the pan and add the beef sauce. Toss gently until the pasta is lightly coated. Tip into a warmed serving dish or on to individual plates. Sprinkle with chopped parsley and serve immediately.

**ORIENTAL ALTERNATIVE**

## Chinese Beef with Angel Hair Pasta

INGREDIENTS **Serves 4**

- 1 tbsp pink peppercorns
- 1 tbsp chilli powder
- 1 tbsp Szechuan pepper
- 3 tbsp light soy sauce
- 3 tbsp dry sherry
- 450 g/1 lb sirloin steak, cut into strips
- 350 g/12 oz angel hair pasta
- 1 tbsp sesame oil
- 1 tbsp sunflower oil
- 1 bunch spring onions, trimmed and finely shredded, plus extra to garnish
- 1 red pepper, deseeded and thinly sliced
- 1 green pepper, deseeded and thinly sliced
- 1 tbsp toasted sesame seeds, to garnish

Crush the peppercorns, using a pestle and mortar. Transfer to a shallow bowl and combine with the chilli powder, Szechuan pepper, light soy sauce and sherry. Add the beef strips and stir until lightly coated. Cover and place in the refrigerator to marinate for 3 hours. Stir occasionally during this time.

When ready to cook, bring a large pan of lightly salted water to a rolling boil. Add the pasta and cook according to the packet instructions, or until 'al dente'. Drain thoroughly and return to the pan. Add the sesame oil and toss lightly. Keep the pasta warm.

Heat a wok or large frying pan, add the sunflower oil and heat until very hot. Add the shredded spring onions with the sliced red and green peppers and stir-fry for 2 minutes.

Drain the beef, reserving the marinade, then add the beef to the wok or pan and stir-fry for 3 minutes. Pour the marinade and stir-fry for 1–2 minutes, until the steak is tender.

Pile the pasta on to four warmed plates. Top with the stir-fried beef and peppers and garnish with toasted sesame seeds and shredded spring onions. Serve immediately.

# Moroccan Penne

INGREDIENTS **Serves 4**

1 tbsp sunflower oil
1 red onion, peeled and chopped
2 cloves garlic, peeled and crushed
1 tbsp coriander seeds
¼ tsp cumin seeds
¼ tsp freshly grated nutmeg
450 g/1 lb lean lamb mince
1 aubergine, trimmed and diced
400 g can chopped tomatoes
300 ml/½ pint vegetable stock
125 g/4 oz ready-to-eat apricots, chopped
12 black olives, pitted
salt and freshly ground black pepper
350 g/12 oz penne
1 tbsp toasted pine nuts, to garnish

Preheat the oven to 200°C/400°F/Gas Mark 6, 15 minutes before using. Heat the sunflower oil in a large flameproof casserole dish. Add the chopped onion and fry for 5 minutes, or until softened.

Using a pestle and mortar, pound the garlic, coriander seeds, cumin seeds and grated nutmeg together into a paste. Add to the onion and cook for 3 minutes.

Add the lamb mince to the casserole and fry, stirring with a wooden spoon, for 4–5 minutes, or until the mince has broken up and browned.

Add the aubergine to the mince and fry for 5 minutes. Stir in the chopped tomatoes and vegetable stock and bring to the boil. Add the apricots and olives, then season well with salt and pepper. Return to the boil, lower the heat and simmer for 15 minutes.

Add the penne to the casserole, stir well, then cover and place in the preheated oven. Cook for 10 minutes then stir and return to the oven, uncovered, for a further 15–20 minutes, or until the pasta is 'al dente'. Remove from the oven, sprinkle with toasted pine nuts and serve immediately.

HEALTH RATING ●●●

**CHILDREN'S ALTERNATIVE**
Penne with Mixed Peppers & Garlic

**ENTERTAINING ALTERNATIVE**
Penne with Pan-fried Chicken & Capers

**CHILDREN'S ALTERNATIVE**
## Penne with Mixed Peppers & Garlic

INGREDIENTS **Serves 4**

450 g/1 lb green, red and yellow peppers
2 tbsp olive oil
1 large onion, peeled and sliced
1 celery stick, trimmed and finely chopped
2 garlic cloves, peeled and crushed
4 rashers smoked streaky bacon, finely chopped
300 ml/½ pint chicken stock
salt and freshly ground black pepper
350 g/12 oz fresh penne
2 tbsp freshly chopped parsley
2 tbsp pecorino cheese, finely grated

**To serve:**
green salad
warm granary bread

Preheat the grill and line the grill rack with tinfoil. Cut the peppers in half, deseed and place cut-side down on the grill rack. Cook under the grill until the skins become blistered and black all over.

Place the peppers in a polythene bag and allow to cool, then discard the skin and slice thinly.

Heat the oil in a heavy-based pan. Add the onion, celery, garlic and bacon and cook for 4–5 minutes, or until the onion has softened.

Add the peppers and cook for 1 minute. Pour in the stock and season to taste with salt and pepper. Cover and simmer for 20 minutes.

Meanwhile, bring a large pan of lightly salted water to a rolling boil. Add the penne and cook according to the packet instructions, about 3–4 minutes, or until 'al dente'. Drain thoroughly and return to the pan.

Pour the pepper sauce over the pasta and toss lightly. Tip into a warmed serving dish and sprinkle with the chopped parsley and grated pecorino cheese. Serve immediately with a green salad and warm granary bread.

**ENTERTAINING ALTERNATIVE**
## Penne with Pan-fried Chicken & Capers

INGREDIENTS **Serves 4**

4 boneless and skinless chicken breasts
25 g/1 oz plain flour
salt and freshly ground black pepper
350 g/12 oz penne
2 tbsp olive oil
25 g/1 oz butter
1 red onion, peeled and sliced
1 garlic clove, peeled and chopped
4–6 tbsp pesto
250 g carton of mascarpone cheese
1 tsp wholegrain mustard
1 tbsp lemon juice
2 tbsp freshly chopped basil
3 tbsp capers in brine, rinsed and drained
freshly shaved pecorino cheese, to garnish

Trim the chicken and cut into bite-sized pieces. Season the flour with salt and pepper then toss the chicken in the seasoned flour and reserve.

Bring a large saucepan of lightly salted water to a rolling boil. Add the penne and cook according to the packet instructions, or until 'al dente'.

Meanwhile, heat the olive oil in a large frying pan. Add the chicken to the pan and cook for 8 minutes, or until golden on all sides, stirring frequently. Transfer the chicken to a plate and reserve.

Add the onion and garlic to the oil remaining in the frying pan and cook for 5 minutes, or until softened, stirring frequently.

Return the chicken to the frying pan. Stir in the pesto and mascarpone cheese and heat through, stirring gently, until smooth.

Stir in the wholegrain mustard, lemon juice, basil and capers. Season to taste, then continue to heat through until piping hot.

Drain the penne thoroughly and return to the saucepan. Pour over the sauce and toss well to coat. Arrange the pasta on individual warmed plates. Scatter with the cheese and serve immediately.

# Puddings

No matter how good the main course, there's always room for pudding! With these delicious recipes, old-fashioned favourites such as Jam Roly Poly are made easy, and no one will be able to resist Chocolate Sponge Pudding with Fudge Sauce. Dieters need not despair, though – low fat recipes such as Summer Pavlova and Oaty Fruit Puddings mean that everyone can indulge.

# Crunchy Rhubarb Crumble

INGREDIENTS **Serves 6**

125 g/4 oz plain flour
50 g/2 oz softened butter
50 g/2 oz rolled oats
50 g/2 oz demerara sugar
1 tbsp sesame seeds
½ tsp ground cinnamon
450 g/1 lb fresh rhubarb
50 g/2 oz caster sugar
custard or cream, to serve

Preheat the oven to 180°C/350°F/Gas Mark 4. Place the flour in a large bowl and cut the butter into cubes. Add to the flour and rub in with the fingertips until the mixture looks like fine breadcrumbs, or blend for a few seconds in a food processor.

Stir in the rolled oats, demerara sugar, sesame seeds and cinnamon. Mix well and reserve.

Prepare the rhubarb by removing the thick ends of the stalks and cut diagonally into 2.5 cm/1 inch chunks. Wash thoroughly and pat dry with a clean tea towel. Place the rhubarb in a 1.1 litre/2 pint pie dish.

Sprinkle the caster sugar over the rhubarb and top with the reserved crumble mixture. Level the top of the crumble so that all the fruit is well covered and press down firmly. If liked, sprinkle the top with a little extra caster sugar.

Place on a baking sheet and bake in the preheated oven for 40–50 minutes, or until the fruit is soft and the topping is golden brown. Sprinkle the pudding with some more caster sugar and serve hot with custard or cream.

## HEALTH RATING 🍎🍎

**ENTERTAINING ALTERNATIVE**

Chocolate & Fruit Crumble

**LOW FAT ALTERNATIVE**

Oaty Fruit Puddings

**:NTERTAINING ALTERNATIVE**
## :hocolate & Fruit Crumble

INGREDIENTS **Serves 4**

**For the crumble:**

125 g/4 oz plain flour
125 g/4 oz butter
75 g/3 oz soft light brown sugar
50 g/2 oz rolled porridge oats
50 g/2 oz hazelnuts, chopped

**For the filling:**

450 g/1 lb Bramley apples
1 tbsp lemon juice
50 g/2 oz sultanas
50 g/2 oz seedless raisins
50 g/2 oz soft light brown sugar
350 g/12 oz pears, peeled, cored and chopped
1 tsp ground cinnamon
125 g/4 oz plain dark chocolate, very roughly chopped
2 tsp caster sugar for sprinkling

'reheat the oven to 190°C/375°F/Gas Mark 5, 10 minutes before baking. Lightly oil an ovenproof dish.

or the crumble, sift the flour into a large bowl. Cut the butter into small cubes and add to the flour. ₹ub the butter into the flour until the mixture resembles fine breadcrumbs.

.tir the sugar, porridge oats and the chopped hazelnuts into the mixture and reserve.

'or the filling, peel the apples, core and slice thickly. Place in a large heavy-based saucepan with the emon juice and 3 tablespoons of water. Add the sultanas, raisins and the soft brown sugar. Bring ,lowly to the boil, cover and simmer over a gentle heat for 8–10 minutes, stirring occasionally, or ıntil the apples are slightly softened.

₹emove the saucepan from the heat and leave to cool slightly before stirring in the pears, ground :innamon and the chopped chocolate.

ƽpoon into the prepared ovenproof dish. Sprinkle the crumble evenly over the top, then bake in the preheated oven for 35–40 minutes or until the top is golden. Remove from the oven, sprinkle with the caster sugar and serve immediately.

**LOW FAT ALTERNATIVE**
## Oaty Fruit Puddings

INGREDIENTS **Serves 4**

125 g/4 oz rolled oats
50 g/2 oz low-fat margarine, melted
2 tbsp chopped almonds
1 tbsp clear honey
pinch of ground cinnamon
2 pears, peeled, cored and finely chopped
1 tbsp marmalade
orange zest, to decorate
low-fat custard or fruit-flavoured yogurt, to serve

Preheat the oven to 200°C/400°F/Gas Mark 6. Lightly oil and line the bases of four individual pudding bowls or muffin tins with a small circle of greaseproof paper.

Mix together the oats, low-fat margarine, nuts, honey and cinnamon in a small bowl.

Using a spoon, spread two thirds of the oaty mixture over the base and around the sides of the pudding bowls or muffin tins.

Toss together the pears and marmalade and spoon into the oaty cases.

Scatter over the remaining oaty mixture to cover the pears and marmalade.

Bake in the preheated oven for 15–20 minutes, until cooked and the tops of the puddings are golden and crisp.

Leave for 5 minutes before removing the pudding bowls or the muffin tins. Decorate with orange zest and serve hot with low-fat custard or low-fat fruit-flavoured yogurt.

**FRUITY ALTERNATIVE**
## Eve's Pudding

INGREDIENTS **Serves 6**

- 450 g/1 lb cooking apples
- 175 g/6 oz blackberries
- 75 g/3 oz demerara sugar
- grated rind of 1 lemon
- 125 g/4 oz caster sugar
- 125 g/4 oz butter
- few drops of vanilla essence
- 2 medium eggs, beaten
- 125 g/4 oz self-raising flour
- 1 tbsp icing sugar
- ready-made custard, to serve

Preheat the oven to 180°C/350°F/Gas Mark 4. Oil a 1.1 litre/2 pint baking dish. Peel, core and slice the apples and place a layer in the base of the prepared dish. Sprinkle over some of the blackberries, a little demerara sugar and lemon zest. Continue to layer the apple and blackberries in this way until all the ingredients have been used.

Cream the sugar and butter together until light and fluffy. Beat in the vanilla essence and then the eggs a little at a time, adding a spoonful of flour after each addition. Fold in the extra flour with a metal spoon or rubber spatula and mix well. Spread the sponge mixture over the top of the fruit and level with the back of a spoon.

Place the dish on a baking sheet and bake in the preheated oven for 35–40 minutes, or until well risen and golden brown. To test if the pudding is cooked, press the cooked sponge lightly with a clean finger – if it springs back, the sponge is cooked. Dust the pudding with a little icing sugar and serve immediately with custard.

**LIGHT ALTERNATIVE**
## Queen of Puddings

INGREDIENTS **Serves 4**

- 75 g/3 oz fresh white breadcrumbs
- 25 g/1 oz granulated sugar
- 450 ml/¾ pint full-cream milk
- 25 g/1 oz butter
- grated rind of 1 small lemon
- 2 medium eggs, separated
- 2 tbsp seedless raspberry jam
- 50 g/2 oz caster sugar

Preheat the oven to 170°C/325°F/Gas Mark 3. Oil a 900 ml/1½ pint ovenproof baking dish and reserve. Mix the breadcrumbs and sugar together in a bowl.

Pour the milk into a small saucepan and heat gently with the butter and lemon rind until the butter has melted. Allow the mixture to cool a little, then pour over the breadcrumbs. Stir well and leave to soak for 30 minutes.

Whisk the egg yolks into the cooled breadcrumb mixture and pour into the prepared dish. Place the dish on a baking sheet and bake in the preheated oven for about 30 minutes, or until firm and set. Remove from the oven.

Allow to cool slightly, then spread the jam over the pudding. Whisk the egg whites until stiff and standing in peaks.

Gently fold in the caster sugar with a metal spoon or rubber spatula. Pile the meringue over the top of the pudding.

Return the dish to the oven for a further 25–30 minutes, or until the meringue is crisp and slightly coloured. Serve hot or cold.

# Jam Roly Poly

INGREDIENTS **Serves 6**

25 g/8 oz self-raising flour
¼ tsp salt
25 g/4 oz shredded suet
about 150 ml/¼ pint water
3 tbsp strawberry jam
tbsp milk, to glaze
tsp caster sugar
ready-made jam sauce, to serve

Preheat the oven to 200°C/400°F/Gas Mark 6. Make the pastry by sifting the flour and salt into a large bowl.

Add the suet and mix lightly, then add the water a little at a time and mix to form a soft and pliable dough. Take care not to make the dough too wet.

Turn the dough out on to a lightly floured board and knead gently until smooth.

Roll the dough out into a 23 x 28 cm/9 x 11 inch rectangle.

Spread the jam over the pastry leaving a border of 1 cm/½ inch all round. Fold the border over the jam and brush the edges with water.

Lightly roll the rectangle up from one of the short sides, seal the top edge and press the ends together. Do not roll the pudding up too tightly.

Turn the pudding upside down on to a large piece of greaseproof paper large enough to come halfway up the sides. If using non-stick paper, then oil lightly beforehand.

Tie the ends of the paper to make a boat-shaped paper case for the pudding to sit in, leaving plenty of room for the roly poly to expand.

Brush the pudding lightly with milk and sprinkle with the sugar. Bake in the preheated oven for 30–40 minutes, or until well risen and golden. Serve immediately with the jam sauce.

HEALTH RATING

**FRUITY ALTERNATIVE**
Eve's Pudding

**LIGHT ALTERNATIVE**
Queen of Puddings

# Golden Castle Pudding

INGREDIENTS **Serves 4–6**

125 g/4 oz butter
125 g/4 oz caster sugar
a few drops of vanilla essence
2 medium eggs, beaten
125 g/4 oz self-raising flour
4 tbsp golden syrup
crème fraîche or ready-made custard, to serve

Preheat the oven to 180°C/350°F/Gas Mark 4. Lightly oil 4–6 individual pudding bowls and place a small circle of lightly oiled non-stick baking or greaseproof paper in the base of each one.

Place the butter and caster sugar in a large bowl, then beat together until the mixture is pale and creamy. Stir in the vanilla essence and gradually add the beaten eggs, a little at a time. Add a tablespoon of flour after each addition of egg and beat well.

When the mixture is smooth, add the remaining flour and fold in gently. Add a tablespoon of water and mix to form a soft mixture that will drop easily off a spoon.

Spoon enough mixture into each basin to come halfway up the tin, allowing enough space for the puddings to rise. Place on a baking sheet and bake in the preheated oven for about 25 minutes until firm and golden brown.

Allow the puddings to stand for 5 minutes. Discard the paper circle and turn out on to individual serving plates.

Warm the golden syrup in a small saucepan and pour a little over each pudding. Serve hot with the crème fraîche or custard.

HEALTH RATING 

**FRUITY ALTERNATIVE**
College Pudding

**SUMMER ALTERNATIVE**
Lemon Surprise

## FRUITY ALTERNATIVE
# College Pudding

INGREDIENTS **Serves 4**

- 125 g/4 oz shredded suet
- 125 g/4 oz fresh white breadcrumbs
- 50 g/2 oz sultanas
- 50 g/2 oz seedless raisins
- ½ tsp ground cinnamon
- ¼ tsp freshly grated nutmeg
- ¼ tsp mixed spice
- 50 g/2 oz caster sugar
- ½ tsp baking powder
- 2 medium eggs, beaten
- orange zest, to garnish

Preheat the oven to 180°C/350°F/Gas Mark 4. Lightly oil a 900 ml/1½ pint ovenproof pudding basin and place a small circle of greaseproof paper in the base.

Mix the shredded suet and breadcrumbs together and rub lightly together with the fingertips to remove any lumps.

Stir in the dried fruit, spices, sugar and baking powder. Add the eggs and beat lightly together until the mixture is well blended and the fruit is evenly distributed.

Spoon the mixture into the prepared pudding basin and level the surface. Place on a baking tray and cover lightly with some greaseproof paper.

Bake in the preheated oven for 20 minutes, then remove the paper and continue to bake for a further 10–15 minutes, or until the top is firm.

When the pudding is cooked, remove from the oven and carefully turn out on to a warmed serving dish. Decorate with the orange zest and serve immediately.

## SUMMER ALTERNATIVE
# Lemon Surprise

INGREDIENTS **Serves 4**

- 75 g/3 oz low-fat margarine
- 175 g/6 oz caster sugar
- 3 medium eggs, separated
- 75 g/3 oz self-raising flour
- 450 ml/¾ pint semi-skimmed milk
- juice of 2 lemons
- juice of 1 orange
- 2 tsp icing sugar
- lemon zest, to decorate
- sliced strawberries, to serve

Preheat the oven to 190°C/375°F/Gas Mark 5. Lightly oil a deep ovenproof dish.

Beat together the margarine and sugar until pale and fluffy. Add the egg yolks, one at a time, with 1 tablespoon of the flour and beat well after each addition. Once added, stir in the remaining flour. Stir in the milk, 4 tablespoons of the lemon juice and 3 tablespoons of the orange juice.

Whisk the egg whites until stiff and fold into the pudding mixture with a metal spoon or rubber spatula until well combined. Pour into the prepared dish.

Stand the dish in a roasting tin and pour in just enough boiling water to come halfway up the sides of the dish. Bake in the preheated oven for 45 minutes, until well risen and spongy to the touch.

Remove the pudding from the oven and sprinkle with the icing sugar. Decorate with the lemon zest and serve immediately with the strawberries.

# Cherry Batter Pudding

INGREDIENTS **Serves 4**

450 g/1 lb fresh cherries (or 425 g can of pitted cherries)
50 g/2 oz plain flour
pinch of salt
3 tbsp caster sugar
2 medium eggs
300 ml/½ pint milk
40 g/1½ oz butter
1 tbsp rum
extra caster sugar, to decorate
fresh cream, to serve

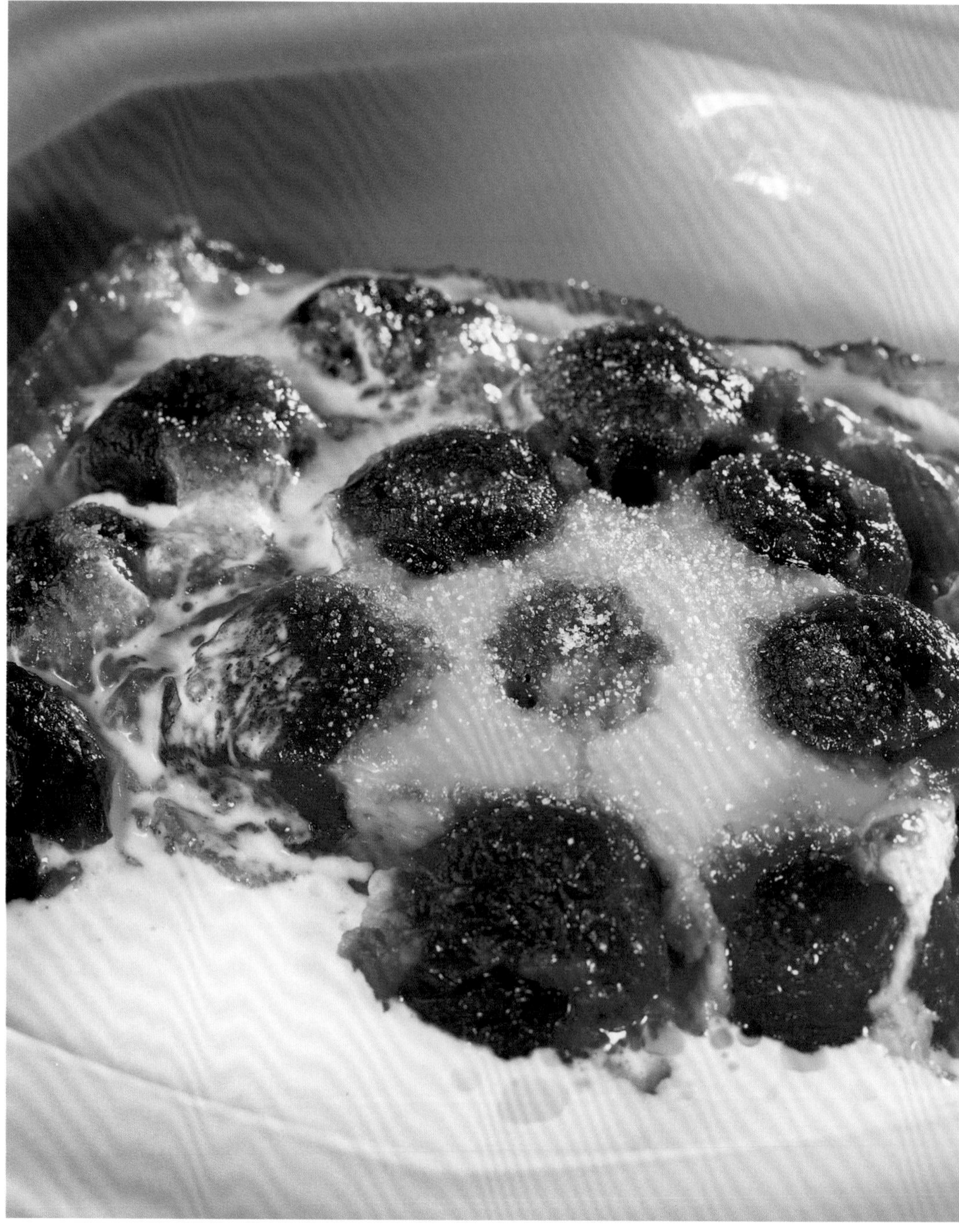

Preheat the oven to 220°C/425°F/Gas Mark 7. Lightly oil a 900 ml/1½ pint shallow baking dish.

Rinse the cherries, drain well and remove the stones (using a cherry stoner if possible). If using canned cherries, drain well, discard the juice and place in the prepared dish.

Sift the flour and salt into a large bowl. Stir in 2 tablespoons of the caster sugar and make a well in the centre. Beat the eggs, then pour into the well.

Warm the milk and slowly pour into the well, beating throughout and gradually drawing in the flour from the sides of the bowl. Continue until a smooth batter has formed.

Melt the butter in a small saucepan over a low heat, then stir into the batter with the rum. Reserve for 15 minutes, then beat again until smooth and easy to pour.

Pour into the prepared baking dish and bake in the preheated oven for 30–35 minutes, or until golden brown and set.

Remove the pudding from the oven, sprinkle with the remaining sugar and serve hot with plenty of fresh cream.

HEALTH RATING 🍎🍎

**BAKING ALTERNATIVE**

Rich Double-crust Plum Pie

**BAKING ALTERNATIVE**

Autumn Bramley Apple Cake

**BAKING ALTERNATIVE**
## Rich Double-crust Plum Pie

INGREDIENTS **Serves 6**

**For the pastry:**

75 g/3 oz butter
75 g/3 oz white vegetable fat
225 g/8 oz plain flour
2 medium egg yolks

**For the filling:**

450 g/1 lb fresh plums, preferably Victoria
50 g/2 oz caster sugar
1 tbsp milk
a little extra caster sugar

Preheat the oven to 200°C/400°F/Gas Mark 6. Make the pastry by rubbing the butter and white vegetable fat into the flour until it resembles fine breadcrumbs or blend in a food processor. Add the egg yolks and enough water to make a soft dough. Knead lightly, then wrap and leave in the refrigerator for about 30 minutes.

Meanwhile, prepare the fruit. Rinse and dry the plums, then cut in half and remove the stones. Slice the plums into chunks and cook in a saucepan with 25 g/1 oz of the sugar and 2 tablespoons of water for 5–7 minutes, or until slightly softened. Remove from the heat and add the remaining sugar to taste and allow to cool.

Roll out half the chilled pastry on a lightly floured surface and use to line the base and sides of a 1.1 litre/2 pint pie dish. Allow the pastry to hang over the edge of the dish. Spoon in the prepared plums.

Roll out the remaining pastry to use as the lid and brush the edge with a little water. Wrap the pastry around the rolling pin and place over the plums.

Press the edges together to seal and mark a decorative edge around the rim of the pastry by pinching with the thumb and forefinger or using the back of a fork.

Brush the lid with milk, and make a few slits in the top. Use any trimmings to decorate the top of the pie with pastry leaves. Place on a baking tray and bake in the preheated oven for 30 minutes, or until golden brown. Sprinkle with a little caster sugar and serve hot or cold.

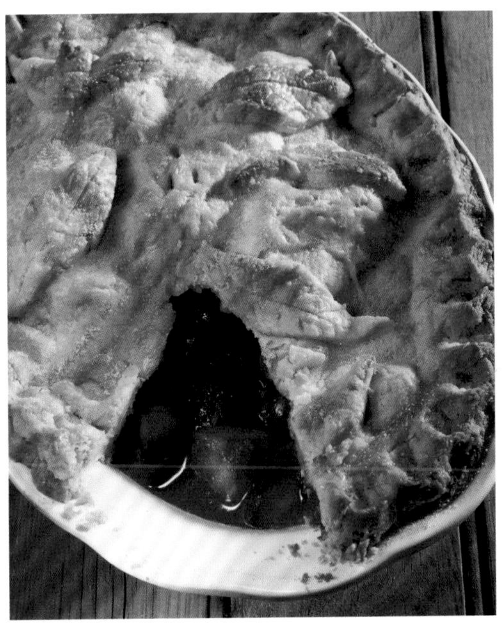

**BAKING ALTERNATIVE**
## Autumn Bramley Apple Cake

INGREDIENTS **Cuts into 8–10 slices**

225 g/8 oz self-raising flour
1½ tsp baking powder
150 g/5 oz margarine, softened
150 g/5 oz caster sugar, plus extra for sprinkling
1 tsp vanilla essence
2 large eggs, beaten
1.1 kg/2½ lbs Bramley cooking apples, peeled, cored and sliced
1 tbsp lemon juice
½ tsp ground cinnamon
fresh custard sauce or cream, to serve

Preheat the oven to 170°C/325°F/Gas Mark 3, 10 minutes before baking. Lightly oil and line the base of a 20.5 cm/8 inch deep cake tin with non-stick baking or greaseproof paper.

Sift the flour and baking powder into a small bowl. Beat the margarine, sugar and vanilla essence in a larger bowl until light and fluffy. Gradually beat in the eggs a little at a time, beating well after each addition. Stir in the flour.

Spoon about one-third of the mixture into the tin, smoothing the surface. Toss the apple slices in the lemon juice and cinnamon and spoon over the cake mixture, making a thick even layer. Spread the remaining mixture over the apple layer to the edge of the tin, making sure the apples are covered. Smooth the top with the back of a wet spoon and sprinkle generously with sugar.

Bake in the preheated oven for 1½ hours, or until well risen and golden, the apples are tender and the centre of the cake springs back when lightly pressed. If the top browns too quickly, reduce the oven temperature slightly and cover the cake loosely with tinfoil.

Transfer to a wire rack and cool for about 20 minutes in the tin. Run a thin knife blade between the cake and the the tin to loosen the cake and invert on to a paper-lined rack. Turn the cake the right way up and cool. Serve with the custard sauce or cream.

# Iced Bakewell Tart

INGREDIENTS **Cuts into 8 slices**

**For the pastry:**

175 g/6 oz plain flour
pinch of salt
60 g/2½ oz butter, cut into small pieces
50 g/2 oz white vegetable fat, cut into small pieces
2 small egg yolks, beaten

**For the filling:**

125 g/4 oz butter, melted
125 g/4 oz caster sugar
125 g/4 oz ground almonds
2 large eggs, beaten
few drops of almond essence
2 tbsp seedless raspberry jam

**For the icing:**

125 g/4 oz icing sugar, sifted
6–8 tsp fresh lemon juice
25 g/1 oz toasted flaked almonds

Preheat the oven to 200°C/400°F/Gas Mark 6. Place the flour and salt in a bowl and rub in the butter and vegetable fat until the mixture resembles breadcrumbs. Alternatively blend in short bursts in a food processor.

Add the eggs with sufficient water to make a soft, pliable dough. Knead lightly on a floured board then chill in the refrigerator for about 30 minutes. Roll out the pastry and use to line a 23 cm/9 inch loose-bottomed flan tin.

For the filling, mix together the melted butter, sugar, almonds and beaten eggs and add a few drops of almond essence. Spread the base of the pastry case with the raspberry jam and spoon over the egg mixture.

Bake in the preheated oven for about 30 minutes, or until the filling is firm and golden brown. Remove from the oven and allow to cool completely.

When the tart is cold, make the icing by mixing together the icing sugar and lemon juice, a little at a time, until the icing is smooth and of a spreadable consistency. Spread the icing over the tart, leave to set for 2–3 minutes and sprinkle with the almonds. Chill in the refrigerator for about 10 minutes and serve.

HEALTH RATING

**CHILDREN'S ALTERNATIVE**
Lattice Treacle Tart

**FRUITY ALTERNATIVE**
Raspberry & Almond Tart

INGREDIENTS **Serves 6–8**

**For the pastry:**

175 g/6 oz plain flour

40 g/1½ oz butter

40 g/1½ oz white vegetable fat

**For the filling:**

225 g/8 oz golden syrup

finely grated rind and juice of 1 lemon

75 g/3 oz fresh white breadcrumbs

1 small egg, beaten

**CHILDREN'S ALTERNATIVE**

## Lattice Treacle Tart

Preheat the oven to 190°C/375°F/Gas Mark 5. Make the pastry by placing the flour, butter and white vegetable fat in a food processor. Blend in short, sharp bursts until the mixture resembles fine breadcrumbs. Remove from the processor and place on a pastry board or in a large bowl. Stir in enough cold water to make a dough and knead in a large bowl or on a floured surface until smooth and pliable.

Roll out the pastry and use to line a 20.5 cm/8 inch loose-bottomed fluted flan dish or tin. Reserve the pastry trimmings for decoration. Chill for 30 minutes.

Meanwhile, to make the filling, place the golden syrup in a saucepan and warm gently with the lemon rind and juice. Tip the breadcrumbs into the pastry case and pour the syrup mixture over the top.

Roll the pastry trimmings out on a lightly floured surface and cut into 6–8 thin strips. Lightly dampen the pastry edge of the tart, then place the strips across the filling in a lattice pattern. Brush the ends of the strips with water and seal to the edge of the tart. Brush a little beaten egg over the pastry and bake in the preheated oven for 25 minutes or until the filling is just set. Serve hot or cold.

**FRUITY ALTERNATIVE**

## Raspberry & Almond Tart

INGREDIENTS **Serves 6–8**

**For the pastry:**

225 g/8 oz plain flour

pinch of salt

125 g/4 oz butter, cut into pieces

50 g/2 oz caster sugar

grated zest of ½ lemon

1 medium egg yolk

**For the filling:**

75 g/3 oz butter

75 g/3 oz caster sugar

75 g/3 oz ground almonds

2 medium eggs

225 g/8 oz raspberries, thawed if frozen

2 tbsp slivered or flaked almonds

icing sugar for dusting

Preheat the oven to 200°C/400°F/Gas Mark 6, 15 minutes before cooking. Blend the flour, salt and butter in a food processor until the mixture resembles breadcrumbs. Add the sugar and lemon zest and blend again for 1 minute. Mix the egg yolk with 2 tablespoons of cold water and add to the mixture. Blend until the mixture starts to come together, adding a little more water if necessary, then tip out on to a lightly floured surface. Knead until smooth, wrap in clingfilm and chill in the refrigerator for 30 minutes.

Roll the dough out thinly on a lightly floured surface and use to line a 23 cm/9 inch fluted tart tin. Chill in the refrigerator for 10 minutes. Line the pastry case with greaseproof paper and baking beans. Bake for 10 minutes, then remove the paper and beans and return to the oven for a further 10–12 minutes until cooked. Allow to cool slightly, then reduce the oven temperature to 190°C/375°F/Gas Mark 5.

Blend together the butter, sugar, ground almonds and eggs until smooth. Spread the raspberries over the base of the pastry, then cover with the almond mixture. Bake for 15 minutes. Remove from the oven and sprinkle with the slivered or flaked almonds and dust generously with icing sugar. Bake for a further 15–20 minutes until firm and golden brown. Leave to cool, then serve.

**CHILDREN'S ALTERNATIVE**
## Steamed Chocolate Chip Pudding

INGREDIENTS **Serves 6**

175 g/6 oz self-raising flour
½ tsp baking powder
75 g/3 oz fresh white breadcrumbs
125 g/4 oz shredded suet
125 g/4 oz golden caster sugar
2 medium eggs, lightly beaten
1 tsp vanilla essence
125 g/4 oz chocolate chips
150 ml/¼ pint cold milk
grated chocolate, to decorate

**For the chocolate custard:**

300 ml/½ pint milk
1 tbsp cornflour
1 tbsp cocoa powder
1 tbsp caster sugar
½ tsp vanilla essence
1 medium egg yolk

Lightly oil a 1.1 litre/2 pint pudding basin and line the base with a small circle of non-stick baking parchment. Sift the flour and baking powder into a bowl, add the breadcrumbs, suet and sugar and mix well.

Stir in the eggs and vanilla essence with the chocolate chips and mix with sufficient cold milk to form a smooth dropping consistency.

Spoon the mixture into the prepared basin and cover the pudding with a double sheet of baking parchment and then either a double sheet of tinfoil or a pudding cloth, with a pleat in the centre to allow for expansion. Secure tightly with string.

Place in the top of a steamer, set over a saucepan of simmering water and steam for 1½–2 hours, or until the pudding is cooked and firm to the touch – replenish the water as necessary. Remove and leave to rest for 5 minutes before turning out on to a warmed serving plate.

Meanwhile, make the custard. Blend a little of the milk with the cornflour and cocoa powder to form a paste. Stir in the remaining milk with the sugar and vanilla essence.

Pour into a saucepan and bring to the boil, stirring. Whisk in the egg yolk and cook for 1 minute. Decorate the pudding with grated chocolate and serve with the sauce.

**ENTERTAINING ALTERNATIVE**
## Individual Steamed Chocolate Puddings

Preheat the oven to 180°C/350°F/Gas Mark 4, 10 minutes before baking. Lightly oil and line the bases of 8 individual 175 ml/6 fl oz pudding basins with a small circle of non-stick baking parchment. Cream the butter with 50 g/2 oz of the sugar and the nutmeg until light and fluffy.

Sift the flour and cocoa powder together, then stir into the creamed mixture. Beat in the egg yolks and mix well, then fold in the ground almonds and the breadcrumbs.

Whisk the egg whites in a clean, grease-free bowl until stiff and standing in peaks then gradually whisk in the remaining sugar. Using a metal spoon, fold a quarter of the egg whites into the chocolate mixture and mix well, then fold in the remaining egg whites.

Spoon the mixture into the prepared basins, filling them two-thirds full to allow for expansion. Cover with a double sheet of tinfoil and secure tightly with string. Stand the pudding basins in a roasting tin and pour in sufficient water to come halfway up the sides of the basins.

Bake in the centre of the preheated oven for 30 minutes or until the puddings are firm to the touch. Remove from the oven, loosen around the edges and invert on to warmed plates. Serve with Greek yogurt and chocolate curls.

INGREDIENTS **Serves 8**

150 g/5 oz unsalted butter, softened
175 g/6 oz light muscovado sugar
½ tsp freshly grated nutmeg
25 g/1 oz plain white flour, sifted
4 tbsp cocoa powder, sifted
5 medium eggs, separated
125 g/4 oz ground almonds
50 g/2 oz fresh white breadcrumbs

**To serve:**

Greek yogurt
orange-flavoured chocolate curls

# Chocolate Sponge Pudding with Fudge Sauce

INGREDIENTS **Serves 4**

75 g/3 oz butter
75 g/3 oz caster sugar
50 g/2 oz plain dark chocolate, melted
50 g/2 oz self-raising flour
25 g/1 oz drinking chocolate
1 large egg
1 tbsp icing sugar, to dust
crème fraîche, to serve

**For the fudge sauce:**

50 g/2 oz soft light brown sugar
1 tbsp cocoa powder
40 g/1½ oz pecan nuts, roughly chopped
25 g/1 oz caster sugar
300 ml/½ pint hot, strong black coffee

Preheat the oven to 170°C/325°F/Gas Mark 3. Oil a 900 ml/1½ pint pie dish.

Cream the butter and sugar together in a large bowl until light and fluffy.

Stir in the melted chocolate, flour, drinking chocolate and egg and mix together. Turn the mixture into the prepared dish and level the surface.

To make the fudge sauce, blend the brown sugar, cocoa powder and pecan nuts together and sprinkle evenly over the top of the pudding.

Stir the caster sugar into the hot black coffee until it has dissolved. Carefully pour the coffee over the top of the pudding.

Bake in the preheated oven for 50–60 minutes, until the top is firm to touch. There will now be a rich sauce underneath the sponge.

Remove from the oven, dust with icing sugar and serve hot with crème fraîche.

HEALTH RATING

**CHILDREN'S ALTERNATIVE**
Steamed Chocolate Chip Pudding

**ENTERTAINING ALTERNATIVE**
Individual Steamed Chocolate Puddings

# Frozen Mississippi Mud Pie

INGREDIENTS **Cuts into 6–8 slices**

24–26 gingernut biscuits, roughly crushed
100 g/3½ oz butter, melted
1–2 tbsp sugar, or to taste
½ tsp ground ginger
600 ml/1 pint chocolate ice cream
600 ml/1 pint coffee-flavoured ice cream

**For the chocolate topping:**

175 g/6 oz plain dark chocolate, chopped
50 ml/2 fl oz single cream
1 tbsp golden syrup
1 tsp vanilla essence
50 g/2 oz coarsely grated white and milk chocolate

To make the crust, place the biscuits with the melted butter, sugar and ginger in a food processor and blend together. Press into the sides and base of a 23 cm/9 inch loose-based flan tin and freeze for 30 minutes.

Soften the ice creams at room temperature for about 25 minutes. Spoon the chocolate ice cream into the crumb crust, spreading it evenly over the base, then spoon the coffee ice cream on top. Return to the freezer to re-freeze the ice cream.

For the topping, heat the chocolate with the cream, golden syrup and vanilla essence in a saucepan. Stir until the chocolate has melted and is smooth. Pour into a bowl and chill in the refrigerator, stirring occasionally until cold but not set.

Spread the cooled chocolate mixture over the top of the frozen pie. Sprinkle with the chocolate and return to the freezer for 1½ hours or until firm. Serve at room temperature.

## HEALTH RATING

**BAKING ALTERNATIVE**
Chocolate Pecan Pie

**ENTERTAINING ALTERNATIVE**
Mocha Pie

INGREDIENTS **Cuts into 8–10 slices**

- 225 g/8 oz prepared shortcrust pastry (see page 8)
- 200 g/7 oz pecan halves
- 125 g/4 oz plain dark chocolate, chopped
- 25 g/1 oz butter, diced
- 3 medium eggs
- 125 g/4 oz light brown sugar
- 175 ml/6 fl oz golden syrup
- 2 tsp vanilla essence
- vanilla ice cream, to serve

**BAKING ALTERNATIVE**

## Chocolate Pecan Pie

Preheat the oven to 180°C/350°F/Gas Mark 4, 10 minutes before baking. Roll the prepared pastry out on a lightly floured surface and use to line a 25.5 cm/10 inch pie tin. Roll the trimmings out and use to make a decorative edge around the pie, then chill in the refrigerator for 1 hour.

Reserve about 60 perfect pecan halves, or enough to cover the top of the pie, then coarsely chop the remainder and reserve. Melt the chocolate and butter in a small saucepan over a low heat or in the microwave and reserve.

Beat the eggs and brush the base and sides of the pastry with a little of the beaten egg. Beat the sugar, golden syrup and vanilla essence into the beaten eggs. Add the pecans, then beat in the chocolate mixture.

Pour the filling into the pastry case and arrange the reserved pecan halves in concentric circles over the top. Bake in the preheated oven for 45–55 minutes, or until the filling is well risen and just set. If the pastry edge begins to brown too quickly, cover with strips of tinfoil. Remove from the oven and serve with ice cream.

**ENTERTAINING ALTERNATIVE**

## Mocha Pie

Place the prepared pastry case on a large serving plate and reserve. Melt the chocolate in a heatproof bowl set over a saucepan of simmering water. Ensure the water is not touching the base of the bowl.

Remove from the heat, stir until smooth and leave to cool.

Cream the butter, soft brown sugar and vanilla essence until light and fluffy, then beat in the cooled chocolate.

Add the strong black coffee, pour into the pastry case and chill in the refrigerator for about 30 minutes.

For the topping, whisk the cream until beginning to thicken, then whisk in the sugar and vanilla essence.

Continue to whisk until the cream is softly peaking. Spoon just under half of the cream into a separate bowl and fold in the dissolved coffee.

Spread the remaining cream over the filling in the pastry case. Spoon the coffee-flavoured whipped cream evenly over the top, then swirl it decoratively with a palate knife.

Sprinkle with grated chocolate and chill in the refrigerator until ready to serve.

INGREDIENTS **Serves 4–6**

1 x 23 cm/9 inch ready-made sweet pastry case

**For the filling:**

- 125 g/4 oz plain dark chocolate, broken into pieces
- 175g/6 oz unsalted butter
- 225 g/8 oz soft brown sugar
- 1 tsp vanilla essence
- 3 tbsp strong black coffee

**For the topping:**

- 600 ml/1 pint double cream
- 50 g/2 oz icing sugar
- 2 tsp vanilla essence
- 1 tsp instant coffee dissolved in 1 tsp boiling water and cooled
- grated plain and white chocolate, to decorate

# White Chocolate Cheesecake

INGREDIENTS **Cuts into 16 slices**

**For the base:**

150 g/5 oz digestive biscuits
50 g/2 oz whole almonds, lightly toasted
50 g/2 oz butter, melted
½ tsp almond essence

**For the topping:**

450 ml/¾ pint soured cream
50 g/2 oz caster sugar
½ tsp almond or vanilla essence
white chocolate curls, to decorate

**For the filling:**

350 g/12 oz good quality white chocolate, chopped
125 ml/4 fl oz double cream
700 g/1½ lb cream cheese, softened
50 g/2 oz caster sugar
4 large eggs
2 tbsp Amaretto or almond-flavour liqueur

Preheat the oven to 180°C/350°F/Gas Mark 4, 10 minutes before baking. Lightly oil a 23 x 7.5 cm/9 x 3 inch springform tin. Crush the biscuits and almonds in a food processor to form fine crumbs.

Pour in the butter and almond essence and blend. Pour the crumbs into the tin and using the back of a spoon, press on to the bottom and up the sides to within 1 cm/½ inch of the top of the tin edge.

Bake in the preheated oven for 5 minutes to set. Remove and transfer to a wire rack. Reduce the oven temperature to 150°C/300°F/Gas Mark 2.

Heat the white chocolate and cream in a saucepan over a low heat, stirring constantly until melted. Remove and cool.

Beat the cream cheese and sugar until smooth. Add the eggs, one at a time, beating well after each addition. Slowly beat in the cooled white chocolate cream and the Amaretto and pour into the baked crust. Place on a baking tray and bake for 45–55 minutes, until the edge of the cake is firm, but the centre is slightly soft. Reduce the oven temperature if the top begins to brown. Remove to a wire rack and increase the temperature to 200°C/400°F/Gas Mark 6.

To make the topping, beat the soured cream, sugar and almond or vanilla essence until smooth and gently pour over the cheesecake, tilting the pan to distribute the topping evenly. Alternatively spread with a metal palette knife.

Bake for another 5 minutes to set. Turn off the oven and leave the door halfway open for about 1 hour. Transfer to a wire rack and run a sharp knife around the edge of the crust to separate from the tin. Cool and refrigerate until chilled. Remove from the tin, decorate with white chocolate curls and serve.

HEALTH RATING 

**CHOCOHOLICS ALTERNATIVE**

Triple Chocolate Cheesecake

**NON-CHOCOLATE ALTERNATIVE**

Baked Lemon & Sultana Cheesecake

INGREDIENTS **Serves 6**

**For the base:**

150 g/5 oz digestive biscuits, crushed
50 g/2 oz butter, melted

**For the cheesecake:**

75 g/3 oz white chocolate, roughly chopped
300 ml/½ pint double cream
50 g/2 oz caster sugar
3 medium eggs, beaten
400 g/14 oz full-fat soft cream cheese
2 tbsp cornflour
75 g/3 oz plain dark chocolate, roughly chopped
75 g/3 oz milk chocolate, roughly chopped
fromage frais, to serve

## CHOCOHOLICS ALTERNATIVE
## Triple Chocolate Cheesecake

Preheat the oven to 180°C/350°F/Gas Mark 4, 10 minutes before baking. Lightly oil a 23 x 7.5 cm/9 x 3 inch springform tin.

To make the base, mix together the crushed biscuits and the melted butter. Press into the base of the tin and leave to set. Chill in the refrigerator.

Place the white chocolate and cream in a small, heavy-based saucepan and heat gently until the chocolate has melted. Stir until smooth and reserve.

Beat the sugar and eggs together until light and creamy in colour, add the cream cheese and beat until the mixture is smooth and free from lumps.

Stir the reserved white chocolate cream together with the cornflour into the soft cream cheese mixture. Add the dark and milk chocolate to the soft cream cheese mixture and mix lightly together until blended.

Spoon over the chilled base, place on a baking sheet and bake in the preheated oven for 1 hour.

Switch off the heat, open the oven door and leave the cheesecake to cool in the oven. Chill in the refrigerator for at least 6 hours before removing from the tin. Cut into slices, transfer to serving plates and serve with fromage frais.

INGREDIENTS **Cuts into 10 slices**

275 g/10 oz caster sugar
50 g/2 oz butter
50 g/2 oz self-raising flour
½ level tsp baking powder
5 large eggs
450 g/1 lb cream cheese
40 g/1½ oz plain flour
grated rind of 1 lemon
3 tbsp fresh lemon juice
150 ml/¼ pint crème fraîche
75 g/3 oz sultanas

**To decorate:**

1 tbsp icing sugar
fresh blackcurrants or blueberries
mint leaves

## NON-CHOCOLATE ALTERNATIVE
## Baked Lemon & Sultana Cheesecake

Preheat the oven to 170°C/325°F/Gas Mark 3. Oil a 20.5 cm/8 inch loose-bottomed round cake tin with non-stick baking paper.

Beat 50 g/2 oz of the sugar and the butter together until light and creamy, then stir in the self-raising flour, baking powder and 1 egg.

Mix lightly together until well blended. Spoon into the prepared tin and spread the mixture over the base. Separate the 4 remaining eggs and reserve.

Blend the cheese in a food processor until soft. Gradually add the eggs yolks and sugar and blend until smooth. Turn into a bowl and stir in the rest of the flour, lemon rind and juice. Mix lightly before adding the crème fraîche and sultanas, stirring well.

Whisk the egg whites until stiff, fold into the cheese mixture and pour into the tin. Tap lightly on the work surface to remove any air bubbles. Bake in the preheated oven for about 1 hour, or until golden and firm. Cover lightly if browning too much. Switch the oven off and leave in the oven to cool for 2–3 hours.

Remove the cheesecake from the oven and, when completely cold, remove from the tin. Sprinkle with the icing sugar, decorate with the blackcurrants or blueberries and mint leaves and serve.

# Tiramisu

INGREDIENTS **Serves 4**

225 g/8 oz mascarpone cheese
25 g/1 oz icing sugar, sifted
150 ml/¼ pint strong brewed coffee, chilled
300 ml/½ pint double cream
3 tbsp coffee liqueur
125 g/4 oz Savoiardi or sponge finger biscuits
50 g/2 oz plain dark chocolate, grated or made into small curls
cocoa powder, for dusting
assorted summer berries, to serve

Lightly oil and line a 900 g/2 lb loaf tin with a piece of clingfilm. Put the mascarpone cheese and icing sugar into a large bowl and using a rubber spatula, beat until smooth. Stir in 2 tablespoons of chilled coffee and mix thoroughly.

Whip the cream with 1 tablespoon of the coffee liqueur until just thickened. Stir a spoonful of the whipped cream into the mascarpone mixture, then fold in the rest. Spoon half of the the mascarpone mixture into the prepared loaf tin and smooth the top.

Put the remaining coffee and coffee liqueur into a shallow dish just bigger than the biscuits. Using half of the biscuits, dip one side of each biscuit into the coffee mixture, then arrange on top of the mascarpone mixture in a single layer. Spoon the rest of the mascarpone mixture over the biscuits and smooth the top.

Dip the remaining biscuits in the coffee mixture and arrange on top of the mascarpone mixture. Drizzle with any remaining coffee mixture. Cover with clingfilm and chill in the refrigerator for 4 hours.

Carefully turn the tiramisu out on to a large serving plate and sprinkle with the grated chocolate or chocolate curls. Dust with cocoa powder, cut into slices and serve with a few summer berries.

HEALTH RATING 

**ENTERTAINING ALTERNATIVE**
Chocolate Fruit Tiramisu

**CHILDREN'S ALTERNATIVE**
Chocolate Mousse

**ENTERTAINING ALTERNATIVE**
## Chocolate Fruit Tiramisu

INGREDIENTS **Serves 4**

2 ripe passion fruit
2 fresh nectarines or peaches
75 g/3 oz sponge finger biscuits
125 g/4 oz amaretti biscuits
5 tbsp amaretti liqueur
6 tbsp prepared black coffee
250 g tub mascarpone cheese
450 ml/¾ pint fresh custard
200 g/7 oz plain dark chocolate, finely chopped or grated
2 tbsp cocoa powder, sifted

Cut the passion fruit, scoop out the seeds and reserve. Plunge the nectarines or peaches into boiling water and leave for 2–3 minutes.

Carefully remove the nectarines or peaches from the water, cut in half and remove the stones. Peel off the skin, chop the flesh finely and reserve.

Break the sponge finger biscuits and amaretti biscuits in half. Place the amaretti liqueur and prepared black coffee into a shallow dish and stir well. Place half the sponge fingers and amaretti biscuits into the amaretti and coffee mixture and soak for 30 seconds. Lift out the biscuits from the liquor and arrange in the bases of four deep individual glass dishes.

Cream the mascarpone cheese until soft and creamy, then slowly beat in the fresh custard and mix well together.

Spoon half the mascarpone mixture over the biscuits in the dishes and sprinkle with 125 g/4 oz of the finely chopped or grated dark chocolate.

Arrange half the passion fruit seeds and the chopped nectarine or peaches over the chocolate and sprinkle with half the sifted cocoa powder.

Place the remaining biscuits in the remaining coffee liqueur mixture and soak for 30 seconds, then arrange on top of the fruit and cocoa powder. Top with the remaining chopped or grated chocolate, the nectarines or peaches and the mascarpone cheese mixture, piling the mascarpone high in the dishes.

Chill in the refrigerator for 1½ hours, then spoon the remaining passion fruit seeds and cocoa powder over the desserts. Chill in the refrigerator for 30 minutes and serve.

**CHILDREN'S ALTERNATIVE**
## Chocolate Mousse

INGREDIENTS **Serves 6**

175 g/6 oz milk or plain chocolate orange
535 g carton ready-made custard
450 ml/¾ pint half-fat double cream
12 Cape gooseberries, to decorate
sweet biscuits, to serve

Break the chocolate into segments and place in a bowl set over a saucepan of simmering water. Leave until melted, stirring occasionally. Remove the bowl in the pan from the heat and allow the melted chocolate to cool slightly.

Place the custard in a bowl and fold the melted chocolate into it using a metal spoon or rubber spatula. Stir well until completely combined.

Pour the cream into a small bowl and whip until the cream forms soft peaks. Using a metal spoon or rubber spatula, fold in most of the whipped cream into the chocolate mixture.

Spoon into six tall glasses and carefully top with the remaining cream. Leave the desserts to chill in the refrigerator for at least 1 hour or preferably overnight.

Peel back the skins from the gooseberries to form petal shapes and use to decorate the chocolate desserts. Serve with sweet biscuits.

**ENTERTAINING ALTERNATIVE**

## Crème Brûlée with Sugared Raspberries

INGREDIENTS **Serves 6**

600 ml/1 pint fresh whipping cream
4 medium egg yolks
75 g/3 oz caster sugar
½ tsp vanilla essence
25 g/1 oz demerara sugar
175 g/6 oz fresh raspberries

Preheat the oven to 150°C/300°F/Gas Mark 2. Pour the cream into a bowl and place over a saucepan of gently simmering water. Heat gently but do not allow to boil.

Meanwhile, whisk together the egg yolks, 50 g/2 oz of the caster sugar and the vanilla essence. When the cream is warm, pour it over the egg mixture, whisking briskly until it is completely mixed.

Pour into six individual ramekin dishes and place in a roasting tin. Fill the tin with sufficient water to come halfway up the sides of the dishes. Bake in the preheated oven for about 1 hour, or until the puddings are set. To test if set, carefully insert a round-bladed knife into the centre. If the knife comes out clean, they are set. Remove the puddings from the roasting tin and allow to cool. Chill in the refrigerator, preferably overnight.

Sprinkle the demerara sugar over the top of each dish and place the puddings under a preheated hot grill. When the sugar has caramelised and turned deep brown, remove from the heat and cool. Chill the puddings in the refrigerator for 2–3 hours before serving.

Toss the raspberries in the remaining caster sugar and sprinkle over the top of each dish. Serve with a little extra cream if liked.

**CHILDREN'S ALTERNATIVE**

## Creamy Puddings with Mixed Berry Compote

INGREDIENTS **Serves 6**

300 ml/½ pint half-fat double cream
1 x 250 g carton ricotta cheese
50 g/2 oz caster sugar
125 g/4 oz white chocolate, broken into pieces
350 g/12 oz mixed summer fruits such as strawberries, blueberries and raspberries
2 tbsp Cointreau

Set the freezer to rapid freeze. Whip the cream until soft peaks form. Fold in the ricotta cheese and half the sugar.

Place the chocolate in a bowl set over a saucepan of simmering water. Stir until melted. Remove from the heat and leave to cool, stirring occasionally. Stir into the cheese mixture until well blended. Spoon the mixture into six individual pudding moulds and level the surface of each pudding with the back of a spoon. Place in the freezer and freeze for 4 hours.

Place the fruits and the remaining sugar in a pan and heat gently, stirring occasionally until the sugar has dissolved and the juices are just beginning to run. Stir in the Cointreau to taste.

Dip the pudding moulds in hot water for 30 seconds and invert on to six serving plates. Spoon the fruit compote over the puddings and serve immediately. Remember to return the freezer to its normal setting.

# Vanilla & Lemon Panna Cotta with Raspberry Sauce

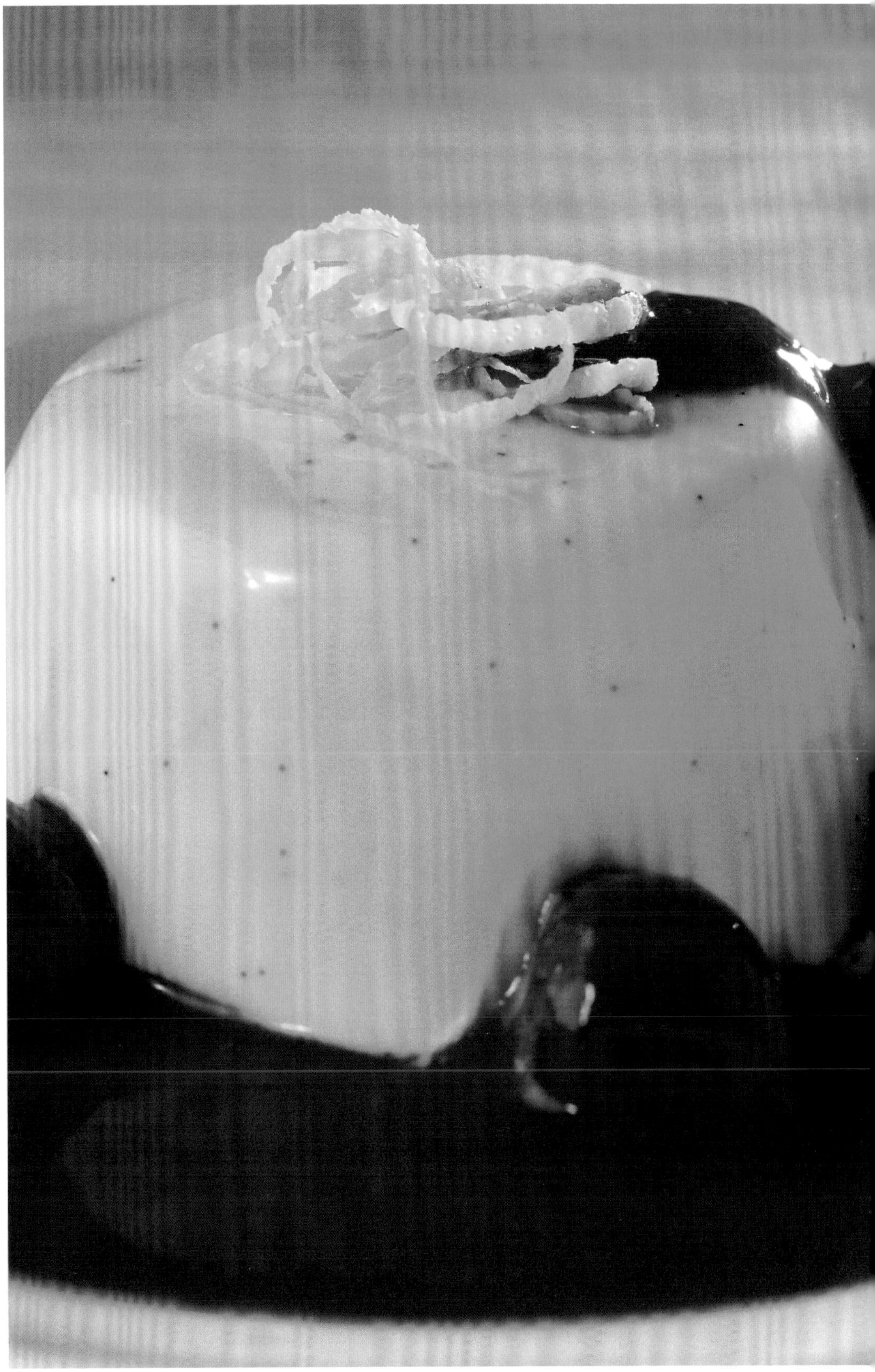

INGREDIENTS **Serves 6**

900 ml/1½ pints double cream
1 vanilla pod, split
100 g/3½ oz caster sugar
zest of 1 lemon
3 sheets gelatine
5 tbsp milk
450 g/1 lb raspberries
3–4 tbsp icing sugar, to taste
1 tbsp lemon juice
extra lemon zest, to decorate

Put the cream, vanilla pod and sugar into a saucepan. Bring to the boil, then simmer for 10 minutes until slightly reduced, stirring to prevent scalding. Remove from the heat, stir in the lemon zest and remove the vanilla pod.

Soak the gelatine in the milk for 5 minutes, or until softened. Squeeze out any excess milk and add to the hot cream. Stir well until dissolved.

Pour the cream mixture into six ramekins or mini pudding moulds and leave in the refrigerator for 4 hours, or until set.

Meanwhile, put 175 g/6 oz of the raspberries in a food processor with the icing sugar and lemon juice. Blend to a purée then pass the mixture through a sieve. Stir in the remaining raspberries with a metal spoon or rubber spatula and chill in the refrigerator until ready to serve.

To serve, dip each of the moulds into hot water for a few seconds then turn out on to individual serving plates. Spoon some of the raspberry sauce over and around the panna cotta, decorate with extra lemon zest and serve.

## HEALTH RATING ●

**ENTERTAINING ALTERNATIVE**
Crème Brûlée with Sugared Raspberries

**CHILDREN'S ALTERNATIVE**
Creamy Puddings with Mixed Berry Compote

# Summer Pavlova

INGREDIENTS **Serves 6–8**

4 medium egg whites
225 g/8 oz caster sugar
1 tsp vanilla essence
2 tsp white wine vinegar
1½ tsp cornflour
300 ml/½ pint half-fat Greek-set yogurt
2 tbsp honey
225 g/8 oz strawberries, hulled
125 g/4 oz raspberries
125 g/4 oz blueberries
4 kiwis, peeled and sliced
icing sugar, to decorate

Preheat the oven to 150°C/300°F/Gas Mark 2. Line a baking tray with a sheet of greaseproof or baking parchment paper.

Place the egg whites in a clean, grease-free bowl and whisk until very stiff.

Whisk in half the sugar, vanilla essence, vinegar and cornflour and continue whisking until stiff.

Gradually whisk in the remaining sugar, a teaspoonful at a time, until the mixture is very stiff and glossy.

Using a large spoon, arrange the meringue in a circle on the greaseproof paper or baking parchment paper.

Bake in the preheated oven for 1 hour until crisp and dry. Turn the oven off and leave the meringue in the oven to cool completely.

Remove the meringue from the baking sheet and peel away the parchment paper. Mix together the yogurt and honey. Place the pavlova on a serving plate and spoon the yogurt into the centre.

Scatter over the strawberries, raspberries, blueberries and kiwis. Dust with the icing sugar and serve.

HEALTH RATING ●●●

**ENTERTAINING ALTERNATIVE**
Summer Pudding

**ENTERTAINING ALTERNATIVE**
Summer Fruit Semifreddo

## ENTERTAINING ALTERNATIVE
## Summer Pudding

INGREDIENTS **Serves 6–8**

450 g/1 lb redcurrants
125 g/4 oz caster sugar
350 g/12 oz strawberries, hulled and halved
125 g/4 oz raspberries
2 tbsp Grand Marnier or Cointreau
8–10 medium slices white bread, crusts removed
mint sprigs, to decorate
low-fat Greek-set yogurt or low-fat fromage frais, to serve

Place the redcurrants, sugar and 1 tablespoon of water in a large saucepan. Heat gently until the sugar has just dissolved and the juices have just begun to run. Remove the saucepan from the heat and stir in the strawberries, raspberries and the Grand Marnier or Cointreau.

Line the base and sides of a 1.1 litre/2 pint pudding basin with two-thirds of the bread, making sure that the slices overlap each other slightly.

Spoon the fruit with their juices into the bread-lined pudding basin, then top with the remaining bread slices.

Place a small plate on top of the pudding inside the pudding basin. Ensure the plate fits tightly, then weigh down with a clean can or some weights and chill in the refrigerator overnight.

When ready to serve, remove the weights and plate. Carefully loosen round the sides of the basin with a round-bladed knife. Invert the pudding on to a serving plate, decorate with the mint sprigs and serve with the yogurt or fromage frais.

## ENTERTAINING ALTERNATIVE
## Summer Fruit Semifreddo

INGREDIENTS **Serves 6–8**

225 g/8 oz raspberries
125 g/4 oz blueberries
125 g/4 oz redcurrants
50 g/2 oz icing sugar
juice of 1 lemon
1 vanilla pod, split
50 g/2 oz sugar
4 large eggs, separated
600 ml/1 pint double cream
pinch of salt
fresh redcurrants, to decorate

Wash and hull or remove stalks from the fruits, as necessary, then put them into a food processor or blender with the icing sugar and lemon juice. Blend to a purée, pour into a jug and chill in the refrigerator until needed.

Remove the seeds from the vanilla pod by opening the pod and scraping with the back of a knife. Add the seeds to the sugar and whisk with the egg yolks until pale and thick.

In another bowl, whip the cream until soft peaks form. Do not overwhip. In a third bowl, whip the egg whites with the salt until stiff peaks form.

Using a large metal spoon (to avoid knocking any air from the mixture) fold together the fruit purée, egg yolk mixture, the cream and egg whites. Transfer the mixture to a round, shallow, lidded freezer box and put into the freezer until almost frozen. If the mixture freezes solid, thaw in the refrigerator until semi-frozen. Turn out the semi-frozen mixture, cut into wedges and serve decorated with a few fresh redcurrants. If the mixture thaws completely, eat immediately and do not re-freeze.

# Baking

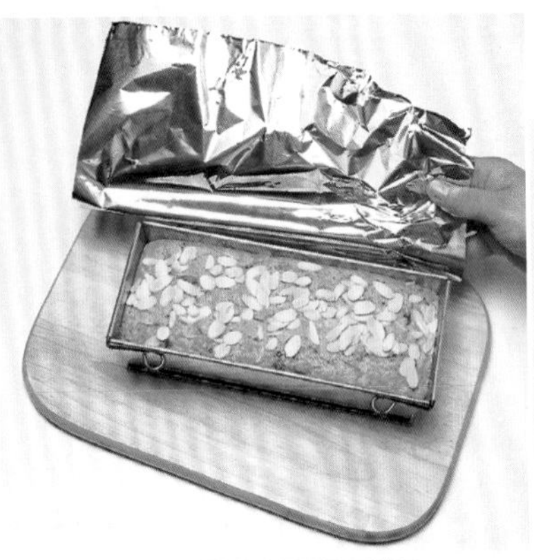

Whether you're making delicious homemade bread and rolls or tasty tea-time treats, nothing beats the smell of baking. Children will love to eat these delicious cakes and biscuits, and the simplicity of the recipes means that they can even help to make them. Breads and savoury baking are just as easy with these foolproof, step-by-step recipes.

# Classic White Loaf

INGREDIENTS **Serves 4**

700 g/1½ lb strong white flour
1 tbsp salt
25 g/1 oz butter, cubed
1 tsp caster sugar
2 tsp easy-blend dried yeast
150 ml/¼ pint milk
300 ml/½ pint warm water
1 tbsp plain flour, to dust

**Light wholemeal variation:**

450 g/1 lb strong wholemeal flour
225 g/8 oz strong white flour
beaten egg, to glaze
1 tbsp kibbled wheat, to finish

Preheat the oven to 220°C/425°F/Gas Mark 7, 15 minutes before baking. Oil and line the base of a 900 g/2 lb loaf tin with greaseproof paper. Sift the flour and salt into a large bowl. Rub in the butter, then stir in the sugar and yeast. Make a well in the centre.

Add the milk and the warm water to the dry ingredients. Mix to a soft dough, adding a little more water if needed. Turn out the dough and knead on a lightly floured surface for 10 minutes, or until smooth and elastic.

Place the dough in an oiled bowl, cover with clingfilm or a clean tea towel and leave in a warm place to rise for 1 hour, or until doubled in size. Knead again for a minute or two to knock out the air.

Shape the dough into an oblong and place in the prepared tin. Cover with oiled clingfilm and leave to rise for a further 30 minutes or until the dough reaches the top of the tin. Dust the top of the loaf with flour or brush with the egg glaze and scatter with kibbled wheat if making the wholemeal version. Bake the loaf on the middle shelf of the preheated oven for 15 minutes.

Turn down the oven to 200°C/400°F/Gas Mark 6. Bake the loaf for a further 20–25 minutes, or until well risen and hollow sounding when tapped underneath. Turn out, cool on a wire rack and serve.

HEALTH RATING 🍎🍎

**ALTERNATIVE**
Mixed Grain Bread

**ALTERNATIVE**
Quick Brown Bread

**ALTERNATIVE**
## Mixed Grain Bread

INGREDIENTS **Makes 1 large loaf**

350 g/12 oz strong white flour
2 tsp salt
225 g/8 oz granary flour
125 g/4 oz rye flour
25 g/1 oz butter, diced
2 tsp easy-blend dried yeast
25 g/1 oz rolled oats
2 tbsp sunflower seeds
1 tbsp malt extract
450 ml/¾ pint warm water
1 medium egg, beaten

Preheat the oven to 220°C/425°F/Gas Mark 7, 15 minutes before baking. Sift the white flour and salt into a large bowl. Stir in the granary and rye flours, then rub in the butter until the mixture resembles breadcrumbs. Stir in the yeast, oats and seeds and make a well in the centre.

Stir the malt extract into the warm water until dissolved. Add the malt water to the dry ingredients. Mix to a soft dough.

Turn the dough out on to a lightly floured surface and knead for 10 minutes, until smooth and elastic. Put in an oiled bowl, cover with clingfilm and leave to rise in a warm place for 1½ hours or until doubled in size.

Turn out and knead again for a minute or two to knock out the air. Shape into an oval loaf about 30.5 cm/12 inches long and place on a well-oiled baking sheet. Cover with oiled clingfilm and leave to rise for 40 minutes, or until doubled in size

Brush the loaf with beaten egg and bake in the preheated oven for 35–45 minutes, or until the bread is well risen, browned and sounds hollow when the base is tapped. Leave to cool on a wire rack, then serve.

**ALTERNATIVE**
## Quick Brown Bread

INGREDIENTS **Makes 2 x 450 g/1 lb loaves**

700 g/1½ lb strong wholemeal flour
2 tsp salt
½ tsp caster sugar
7 g/¼ oz sachet easy-blend dried yeast
450 ml/¾ pint warm water

**To finish:**
beaten egg, to glaze
1 tbsp plain white flour, to dust

**Onion & Caraway Seed Rolls:**
1 small onion, peeled and finely chopped
1 tbsp olive oil
2 tbsp caraway seeds
milk, to glaze

Preheat the oven to 200°C/400°F/Gas Mark 6, 15 minutes before baking. Oil 2 x 450 g/1 lb loaf tins. Sift the flour, salt and sugar into a large bowl, adding the remaining bran in the sieve. Stir in the yeast, then make a well in the centre.

Pour the warm water into the dry ingredients and mix to form a soft dough, adding a little more water if needed. Knead on a lightly floured surface for 10 minutes, until smooth and elastic.

Divide in half, shape into two oblongs and place in the tins. Cover with oiled clingfilm and leave in a warm place for 40 minutes, or until risen to the top of the tins.

Glaze one loaf with the beaten egg and dust the other loaf generously with the plain flour.

Bake the loaves in the preheated oven for 35 minutes or until well risen and lightly browned. Turn out of the tins and return to the oven for 5 minutes to crisp the sides. Cool on a wire rack.

This recipe can also be used to make onion and caraway seed rolls. For these, gently fry the onion in the oil until soft. Reserve until the onions are cool, then stir into the dry ingredients with 1 tablespoon of the caraway seeds. Make the dough as before.

Divide the dough into 16 pieces and shape into rolls. Put on two oiled baking trays, cover with oiled clingfilm and leave for 30 minutes.

Glaze the rolls with milk and sprinkle with the rest of the seeds. Bake for 25–30 minutes, cool on a wire rack and serve.

# Irish Soda Bread

INGREDIENTS **Makes 1 loaf**

400 g/14 oz plain white flour, plus 1 tbsp for dusting
1 tsp salt
2 tsp bicarbonate of soda
15 g/½ oz butter
50 g/2 oz coarse oatmeal
1 tsp clear honey
300 ml/½ pint buttermilk
2 tbsp milk

**Wholemeal variation:**

400 g/14 oz plain wholemeal flour, plus 1 tbsp for dusting
1 tbsp milk

Preheat the oven to 200°C/400°F/Gas Mark 6, 15 minutes before baking. Sift the flour, salt and bicarbonate of soda into a large bowl. Rub in the butter until the mixture resembles fine breadcrumbs. Stir in the oatmeal and make a well in the centre.

Mix the honey, buttermilk and milk together and add to the dry ingredients. Mix to a soft dough.

Knead the dough on a lightly floured surface for 2–3 minutes, until the dough is smooth. Shape into a 20.5 cm/8 inch round and place on an oiled baking sheet.

Thickly dust the top of the bread with flour. Using a sharp knife, cut a deep cross on top, going about halfway through the loaf.

Bake in the preheated oven on the middle shelf for 30–35 minutes or until the bread is slightly risen, golden and sounds hollow when tapped underneath. Cool on a wire rack. Eat on the day of making.

For a wholemeal soda bread, use all the wholemeal flour instead of the white flour and add an extra tablespoon of milk when mixing together. Dust the top with wholemeal flour and bake.

HEALTH RATING

**ALTERNATIVE**

Rosemary & Olive Focaccia

**ALTERNATIVE**

Soft Dinner Rolls

**ALTERNATIVE**
## Rosemary & Olive Focaccia

INGREDIENTS **Makes 2 loaves**

700 g/1½ lb strong white flour
pinch of salt
pinch of caster sugar
7 g/¼ oz sachet easy-blend dried yeast
2 tsp freshly chopped rosemary
450 ml/¾ pint warm water
3 tbsp olive oil
75 g/3 oz pitted black olives, roughly chopped
sprigs of rosemary, to garnish

**To finish:**
3 tbsp olive oil
coarse sea salt
freshly ground black pepper

Preheat the oven to 200°C/400°F/Gas Mark 6, 15 minutes before baking. Sift the flour, salt and sugar into a large bowl. Stir in the yeast and rosemary and make a well in the centre.

Pour in the warm water and the oil and mix to a soft dough. Turn out on to a lightly floured surface and knead for about 10 minutes, until smooth and elastic.

Pat the olives dry on kitchen paper, then gently knead into the dough. Put in an oiled bowl, cover with clingfilm and leave to rise in a warm place for 1½ hours, or until it has doubled in size.

Turn out the dough and knead again for a minute or two. Divide in half and roll out each piece to a 25.5 cm/10 inch circle.

Transfer to oiled baking sheets, cover with oiled clingfilm and leave to rise for 30 minutes.

Using the fingertips, make deep dimples all over the the dough. Drizzle with the oil and sprinkle with sea salt. Bake in the preheated oven for 20–25 minutes, or until risen and golden.

Cool on a wire rack and garnish with sprigs of rosemary. Grind over a little black pepper before serving.

INGREDIENTS **Makes 16**

50 g/2 oz butter
1 tbsp caster sugar
225 ml/8 fl oz milk
550 g/1¼ lb strong white flour
1½ tsp salt
2 tsp easy-blend dried yeast
2 medium eggs, beaten

**To glaze & finish:**
2 tbsp milk
1 tsp sea salt
2 tsp poppy seeds

**ALTERNATIVE**
## Soft Dinner Rolls

Preheat the oven to 220°C/425°F/Gas Mark 7, 15 minutes before baking. Gently heat the butter, sugar and milk in a saucepan until the butter has melted and the sugar has dissolved. Cool until tepid. Sift the flour and salt into a bowl, stir in the yeast and make a well in the centre. Reserve 1 tablespoon of the beaten eggs. Add the rest to the dry ingredients with the milk mixture. Mix to form a soft dough.

Knead the dough on a lightly floured surface for 10 minutes until smooth and elastic. Put in an oiled bowl, cover with clingfilm and leave in a warm place to rise for 1 hour, or until doubled in size. Knead again for a minute or two, then divide into 16 pieces. Shape into balls, plaits, coils, cottage buns or whatever shape you want. Place on two oiled baking sheets, cover with oiled clingfilm and leave to rise for 30 minutes, until doubled in size.

Mix the reserved beaten egg with the milk and brush over the rolls. Sprinkle some with sea salt, others with poppy seeds and leave some plain. Bake in the preheated oven for about 20 minutes, or until golden and hollow sounding when tapped underneath. Transfer to a wire rack. Cover with a clean tea towel while cooling to keep the rolls soft and serve.

# Traditional Oven Scones

INGREDIENTS **Makes 8**

225 g/8 oz self-raising flour
1 tsp baking powder
pinch of salt
40 g/1½ oz butter, cubed
15 g/½ oz caster sugar
150 ml/¼ pint milk, plus 1 tbsp for brushing
1 tbsp plain flour, to dust

**Lemon & Sultana Scone variation:**

50 g/2 oz sultanas
finely grated rind of ½ lemon
beaten egg, to glaze

Preheat the oven to 220°C/425°F/Gas Mark 7, 15 minutes before baking. Sift the flour, baking powder and salt into a large bowl. Rub in the butter until the mixture resembles fine breadcrumbs. Stir in the sugar and mix in enough milk to give a fairly soft dough.

Knead the dough on a lightly floured surface for a few seconds until smooth. Roll out until 2 cm/¾ inches thick and stamp out 6.5 cm/2½ inch rounds with a floured plain cutter.

Place on an oiled baking sheet and brush the tops with milk – do not brush it over the sides or the scones will not rise properly. Dust with a little plain flour.

Bake in the preheated oven for 12–15 minutes, or until well risen and golden brown. Transfer to a wire rack and serve warm or leave to cool completely. The scones are best eaten on the day of baking, but may be kept in an airtight tin for up to two days.

For lemon and sultana scones, stir in the sultanas and lemon rind with the sugar. Roll out until 2 cm/¾ inches thick and cut into 8 fingers, 10 x 2.5 cm/4 x 1 inches in size. Bake the scones as before.

HEALTH RATING

**ALTERNATIVE**
Cheese-crusted Potato Scones

**ALTERNATIVE**
Bacon, Mushroom & Cheese Puffs

**ALTERNATIVE**
## Cheese-crusted Potato Scones

INGREDIENTS **Serves 4**

200 g/7 oz self-raising flour
25 g/1 oz wholemeal flour
½ tsp salt
1½ tsp baking powder
25 g/1 oz butter, cubed
5 tbsp milk
175 g/6 oz cold mashed potato
freshly ground black pepper

**To finish:**

2 tbsp milk
40 g/1½ oz mature Cheddar cheese, finely grated
paprika, to dust
sprig of basil, to garnish

Preheat the oven to 220°C/425°F/Gas Mark 7, 15 minutes before baking. Sift the flours, salt and baking powder into a large bowl. Rub in the butter until the mixture resembles fine breadcrumbs.

Stir 4 tablespoons of the milk into the mashed potato and season with black pepper. Add the dry ingredients to the potato mixture, mixing together with a fork and adding the remaining 1 tablespoon of milk if needed.

Knead the dough on a lightly floured surface for a few seconds until smooth. Roll out to a 15 cm/6 inch round and transfer to an oiled baking sheet.

Mark the scone round into six wedges, cutting about halfway through with a small sharp knife. Brush with milk, then sprinkle with the cheese and a faint dusting of paprika.

Bake on the middle shelf of the preheated oven for 15 minutes, or until well risen and golden brown. Transfer to a wire rack and leave to cool for 5 minutes before breaking into wedges.

Serve warm or leave to cool completely. Once cool, store the scones in an airtight tin. Garnish with a sprig of basil and serve split and buttered.

**ALTERNATIVE**
## Bacon, Mushroom & Cheese Puffs

INGREDIENTS **Serves 4**

1 tbsp olive oil
225 g/8 oz field mushrooms, wiped and roughly chopped
225 g/8 oz rindless streaky bacon, roughly chopped
2 tbsp freshly chopped parsley
salt and freshly ground black pepper
350 g/12 oz ready-rolled puff pastry sheets, thawed if frozen
25 g/1 oz Emmenthal cheese, grated
1 medium egg, beaten
salad leaves such as rocket or watercress, to garnish
tomatoes, to serve

Preheat the oven to 200°C/400°F/Gas Mark 6. Heat the olive oil in a large frying pan. Add the mushrooms and bacon and fry for 6–8 minutes until golden in colour. Stir in the parsley, season to taste with salt and pepper and allow to cool.

Roll the sheet of pastry a little thinner on a lightly floured surface until you have a 30.5 cm/12 inch square. Cut the pastry into four equal squares.

Stir the grated emmenthal cheese into the mushroom mixture. Spoon a quarter of the mixture on to one half of each square. Brush the edges of the square with a little of the beaten egg.

Fold over the pastry to form a triangular parcel. Seal the edges well and place on a lightly oiled baking sheet. Repeat until the squares are done.

Make shallow slashes in the top of the pastry with a knife.

Brush the parcels with the remaining beaten egg and cook in the preheated oven for 20 minutes, or until puffy and golden brown.

Serve warm or cold, garnished with the salad leaves and served with tomatoes.

**ALTERNATIVE**
## Roquefort, Parma & Rocket Pizza

INGREDIENTS **Serves 2–4**

1 quantity pizza dough (see opposite page)

**Basic tomato sauce:**

400 g can chopped tomatoes
2 garlic cloves, peeled and crushed
grated rind of ½ lime
2 tbsp extra virgin olive oil
2 tbsp freshly chopped basil
½ tsp sugar
salt and freshly ground black pepper

**For the topping:**

125 g/4 oz Roquefort cheese, cut into chunks
6 slices Parma ham
50 g/2 oz rocket leaves, rinsed
1 tbsp extra virgin olive oil
50 g/2 oz Parmesan cheese, freshly shaved

Preheat the oven to 220°C/425°F/Gas Mark 7. Roll the pizza dough out on a lightly floured board to form a 25.5 cm/10 inch round.

Lightly cover the dough and reserve while making the sauce. Place a baking sheet in the preheated oven to heat up.

Place all of the tomato sauce ingredients in a large, heavy-based saucepan and slowly bring to the boil. Cover and simmer for 15 minutes, uncover and cook for a further 10 minutes until the sauce has thickened and reduced by half.

Spoon the tomato sauce over the shaped pizza dough. Place on the hot baking sheet and bake for 10 minutes.

Remove the pizza from the oven and top with the Roquefort and Parma ham, then bake for a further 10 minutes.

Toss the rocket in the olive oil and pile on to the pizza. Sprinkle with the Parmesan cheese and serve immediately.

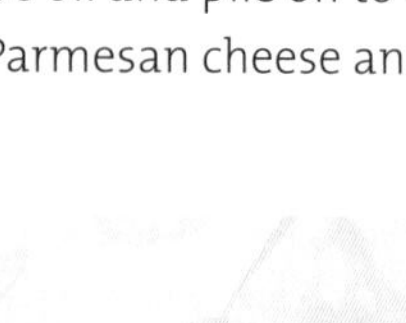

**ALTERNATIVE**
## Spinach, Pine Nut & Mascarpone Pizza

INGREDIENTS **Serves 2–4**

1 quantity pizza dough (see opposite page)

**For the topping:**

3 tbsp olive oil
1 large red onion, peeled and chopped
2 garlic cloves, peeled and finely sliced
450 g/1 lb frozen spinach, thawed and drained
salt and freshly ground black pepper
3 tbsp passata
125 g/4 oz mascarpone cheese
1 tbsp toasted pine nuts

Preheat the oven to 220°C/425°F/Gas Mark 7. Make the pizza dough as before, then shape and roll out thinly on a lightly floured board. Place on a lightly floured baking sheet and lift the edge to make a little rim. Place another baking sheet into the preheated oven to heat up. Heat half the oil in a frying pan and gently fry the onion and garlic until soft and starting to change colour.

Squeeze out any excess water from the spinach and finely chop. Add to the onion and garlic with the remaining olive oil. Season to taste with salt and pepper.

Spread the passata on the pizza dough and top with the spinach mixture. Mix the mascarpone with the pine nuts and dot over the pizza. Slide the pizza on to the hot baking sheet and bake for 15–20 minutes. Transfer to a large plate and serve immediately.

# Three Tomato Pizza

INGREDIENTS **Serves 2–4**

**Basic pizza dough:**

225 g/8 oz strong plain flour

½ tsp salt

¼ tsp quick-acting dried yeast

150 ml/¼ pint warm water

1 tbsp extra-virgin olive oil

**For the topping:**

3 plum tomatoes

8 cherry tomatoes

6 sun-dried tomatoes

pinch of sea salt

1 tbsp freshly chopped basil

2 tbsp extra-virgin olive oil

125 g/4 oz buffalo mozzarella cheese, sliced

freshly ground black pepper

fresh basil leaves, to garnish

Preheat the oven to 220°C/425°F/Gas Mark 7 and place a baking sheet in the oven to heat up. Sift the flour and salt into a bowl and stir in the yeast. Make a well in the centre and gradually add the water and oil to form a soft dough. Knead the dough on a floured surface for about 5 minutes until smooth and elastic. Place in a lightly oiled bowl and cover with clingfilm. Leave to rise in a warm place for 1 hour.

Knock the pizza dough with your fist a few times, then divide into four equal pieces. Roll out one-quarter of the pizza dough on a lightly floured board to form a 20.5 cm/ 8 inch round. Roll out the other three pieces into rounds, one at a time. While rolling out any piece of dough, keep the others lightly covered with clingfilm.

Slice the plum tomatoes, halve the cherry tomatoes and chop the sun-dried tomatoes into small pieces. Place a few pieces of each type of tomato on each pizza base then season to taste with the sea salt. Sprinkle with the chopped basil and drizzle with the olive oil. Place a few slices of mozzarella on each pizza and season with black pepper. Transfer the pizza on to the heated baking sheet and cook for 15–20 minutes, or until the cheese is golden brown and bubbling. Garnish with the basil leaves and serve immediately.

HEALTH RATING 🍎🍎

**ALTERNATIVE**

Roquefort, Parma Ham & Rocket Pizza

**ALTERNATIVE**

Spinach, Pine Nut & Mascarpone Pizza

# Fish Puff Tart

INGREDIENTS **Serves 4**

350 g/12 oz prepared puff pastry, thawed if frozen
150 g/5 oz smoked haddock
150 g/5 oz cod fillet
1 tbsp pesto sauce
2 tomatoes, sliced
125 g/4 oz goats' cheese, sliced
1 medium egg, beaten
freshly chopped parsley, to garnish

Preheat the oven to 220°C/425°F/Gas Mark 7. On a lightly floured surface roll out the pastry into a 20.5 x 25.5 cm/8 x 10 inch rectangle.

Draw a 18 x 23 cm/7 x 9 inch rectangle in the centre of the pastry, to form a 2.5 cm/1 inch border. Be careful not to cut through the pastry.

Lightly cut criss-cross patterns in the border of the pastry with a knife.

Place the fish on a chopping board and with a sharp knife skin the cod and smoked haddock. Cut into thin slices.

Spread the pesto evenly over the bottom of the pastry case with the back of a spoon.

Arrange the fish, tomatoes and cheese in the pastry case and brush the pastry with the beaten egg.

Bake the tart in the preheated oven for 20–25 minutes, until the pastry is well risen, puffed and golden brown. Garnish with the chopped parsley and serve immediately.

## HEALTH RATING

**ALTERNATIVE**
Smoked Haddock Tart

**ALTERNATIVE**
Luxury Fish Pasties

INGREDIENTS **Serves 6**

**Shortcrust pastry:**

150 g/5 oz plain flour
pinch of salt
25 g/1 oz lard or white vegetable fat, cut into small cubes
40 g/1½ oz butter or hard margarine, cut into small cubes

**For the filling:**

225 g/8 oz smoked haddock, skinned and cubed
2 large eggs, beaten
300 ml/½ pint double cream
1 tsp Dijon mustard
freshly ground black pepper
125 g/4 oz Gruyère cheese, grated
1 tbsp freshly snipped chives

**To serve:**

lemon wedges
tomato wedges
fresh green salad leaves

**ALTERNATIVE**
## Smoked Haddock Tart

Preheat the oven to 190°C/375°F/Gas Mark 5. Sift the flour and salt into a large bowl. Add the fats and mix lightly. Using the fingertips rub into the flour until the mixture resembles breadcrumbs. Sprinkle 1 tablespoon of cold water into the mixture and with a knife, start bringing the dough together, using your hands if necessary. If the dough does not form a ball instantly, add a little more water. Put the pastry in a polythene bag and chill for at least 30 minutes.

On a lightly floured surface, roll out the pastry and use to line a 18 cm/7 inch lightly oiled quiche or flan tin. Prick the base all over with a fork and bake blind in the preheated oven for 15 minutes. Carefully remove the pastry from the oven and brush with a little of the beaten egg. Return to the oven for a further 5 minutes, then place the fish in the pastry case. For the filling, beat together the eggs and cream. Add the mustard, black pepper and cheese and pour over the fish. Sprinkle with the chives and bake for 35–40 minutes or until the filling is golden brown and set in the centre. Serve hot or cold with the lemon and tomato wedges and salad leaves.

**ALTERNATIVE**
## Luxury Fish Pasties

Preheat the oven to 200°C/400°F/Gas Mark 6. Place the butter in a saucepan and slowly heat until melted. Add the flour and cook, stirring for 1 minute. Remove from the heat and gradually add the milk a little at a time, stirring between each addition.

Return to the heat and simmer, stirring continuously until thickened. Remove from the heat and add the salmon, parsley, dill, lime rind, lime juice, prawns and seasoning.

Roll out the pastry on a lightly floured surface and cut out six 12.5 cm/5 inch circles and six 15 cm/6 inch circles. Brush the edges of the smaller circles with the beaten egg and place two tablespoons of filling in the centre of each one.

Place the larger circles over the filling and press the edges together to seal. Pinch the edge of the pastry between the forefinger and thumb to ensure a firm seal and decorative edge. Cut a slit in each parcel, brush with the beaten egg and sprinkle with sea salt.

Transfer to a baking sheet and cook in the preheated oven for 20 minutes, or until golden brown. Serve immediately with some fresh green salad leaves.

INGREDIENTS **Serves 6**

2 quantities of quick flaky pastry (see French Onion Tart, page 234), chilled
125 g/4 oz butter
125 g/4 oz plain flour
300 ml/½ pint milk
225 g/8 oz salmon fillet, skinned and cut into chunks
1 tbsp freshly chopped parsley
1 tbsp freshly chopped dill
grated rind and juice of 1 lime
225 g/8 oz peeled prawns
salt and freshly ground black pepper
1 small egg, beaten
1 tsp sea salt
fresh green salad leaves, to serve

# Moist Mincemeat Tea Loaf

INGREDIENTS **Cuts into 10**

225 g/8 oz self-raising flour
½ tsp ground mixed spice
125 g/4 oz cold butter, cubed
75 g/3 oz flaked almonds
25 g/1 oz glacé cherries, rinsed, dried and quartered
75 g/3 oz light muscovado sugar
2 medium eggs
250 g/9 oz prepared mincemeat
1 tsp lemon zest
2 tsp brandy or milk

Preheat the oven to 180°C/350°F/Gas Mark 4, 10 minutes before cooking. Oil and line the base of a 900 g/2 lb loaf tin with non-stick baking paper.

Sift the flour and mixed spice into a large bowl. Add the butter and rub in until the mixture resembles breadcrumbs.

Reserve 2 tablespoons of the flaked almonds and stir in the rest with the glacé cherries and sugar.

Make a well in the centre of the dry ingredients. Lightly whisk the eggs, then stir in the mincemeat, lemon zest and brandy or milk.

Add the egg mixture and fold together until blended. Spoon into the prepared loaf tin, smooth the top with the back of a spoon, then sprinkle over the reserved flaked almonds.

Bake on the middle shelf of the preheated oven for 30 minutes. Cover with tinfoil to prevent the almonds browning too much. Bake for a further 30 minutes, or until well risen and a skewer inserted into the centre comes out clean. Leave the tea loaf in the tin for 10 minutes before removing and cooling on a wire rack. Remove the lining paper, slice thickly and serve.

HEALTH RATING 

**ALTERNATIVE**

Fruity Apple Tea Bread

**ALTERNATIVE**

Marbled Chocolate & Orange Loaf

## ALTERNATIVE
# Fruity Apple Tea Bread

INGREDIENTS **Cuts into 12 slices**

125 g/4 oz butter

125 g/4 oz soft light brown sugar

275 g/10 oz sultanas

150 ml/¼ pint apple juice

1 eating apple, peeled cored and chopped

2 medium eggs, beaten

275 g/10 oz plain flour

½ tsp ground cinnamon

½ tsp ground ginger

2 tsp bicarbonate of soda

curls of butter, to serve

**To decorate:**

1 eating apple, cored and sliced

1 tsp lemon juice

1 tbsp golden syrup, warmed

Preheat the oven to 180°C/350°F/Gas Mark 4. Oil and line the base of a 900 g/2 lb loaf tin with non-stick baking paper.

Put the butter, sugar, sultanas and apple juice in a small saucepan. Heat gently, stirring occasionally until the butter has melted. Tip into a bowl and leave to cool.

Stir in the chopped apple and beaten eggs. Sift the flour, spices and bicarbonate of soda over the apple mixture. Stir into the sultana mixture, spoon into the prepared loaf tin and smooth the top level with the back of a spoon.

Toss the apple slices in lemon juice and arrange on top. Bake in the preheated oven for 50 minutes or until a skewer inserted into the centre comes out clean. Cover with tinfoil to prevent the top from browning too much.

Leave in the tin for 10 minutes before turning out to cool on to a wire rack.

Brush the top with golden syrup and leave to cool. Remove the lining paper, cut into thick slices and serve with curls of butter.

## ALTERNATIVE
# Marbled Chocolate & Orange Loaf

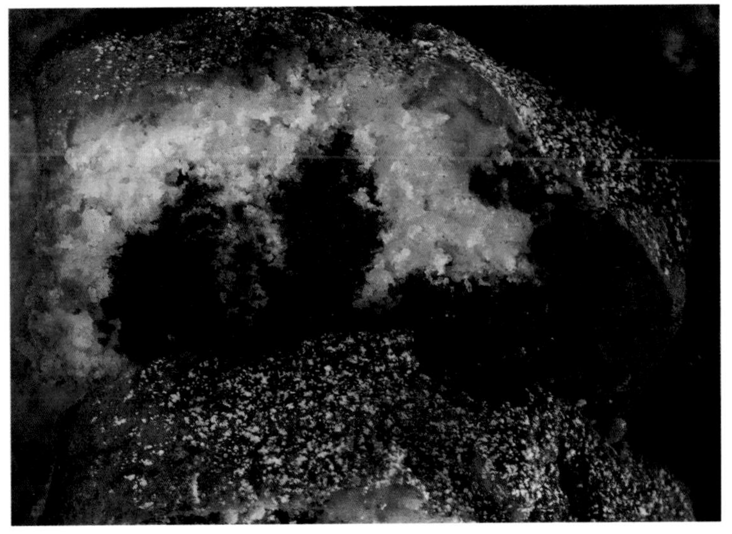

INGREDIENTS **Cuts into 6 slices**

50 g/2 oz plain dark chocolate, broken into squares

125 g/4 oz butter, softened

125 g/4 oz caster sugar

zest of 1 orange

2 medium eggs, beaten

125 g/4 oz self-raising flour

2 tsp orange juice

1 tbsp cocoa powder, sifted

**To finish:**

1 tbsp icing sugar

1 tsp cocoa powder

Preheat the oven to 180°C/350°F/Gas Mark 4. Lightly oil a 450 g/1 lb loaf tin and line the base with a layer of non-stick baking paper.

Put the chocolate in a bowl over a saucepan of very hot water. Stir occasionally until melted. Remove and leave until just cool, but not starting to reset.

Meanwhile, cream together the butter, sugar and orange zest until pale and fluffy. Gradually add the beaten eggs, beating well after each addition.

Sift in the flour, add the orange juice and fold with a metal spoon or rubber spatula. Divide the mixture by half into two separate bowls. Gently fold the cocoa powder and chocolate into one half of the mixture.

Drop tablespoonfuls of each cake mixture into the prepared tin, alternating between the orange and chocolate mixtures. Briefly swirl the colours together with a knife to give a marbled effect.

Bake in the preheated oven for 40 minutes, or until firm and a fine skewer inserted into the centre comes out clean. Leave in the tin for 5 minutes, then turn out and cool on a wire rack. Carefully remove the lining paper.

Dust the cake with the icing sugar and then with the cocoa powder. Cut into thick slices and serve.

# Apple & Cinnamon Crumble-top Cake

INGREDIENTS **Cuts into 8 slices**

**For the topping:**

350 g/12 oz eating apples, peeled
1 tbsp lemon juice
125 g/4 oz self-raising flour
1 tsp ground cinnamon
75 g/3 oz butter or margarine
75 g/3 oz demerara sugar
1 tbsp milk

**For the base:**

125 g/4 oz butter or margarine
125 g/4 oz caster sugar
2 medium eggs
150 g/5 oz self-raising flour
cream or freshly made custard, to serve

Preheat the oven to 180°C/350°F/Gas Mark 4, 10 minutes before baking. Lightly oil and line the base of a 20.5 cm/8 inch deep round cake tin with greaseproof or baking paper.

Finely chop the apples and mix with the lemon juice. Reserve while making the cake.

For the crumble topping, sift the flour and cinnamon together into a large bowl.

Rub the butter or margarine into the flour and cinnamon until the mixture resembles coarse breadcrumbs. Stir the sugar into the breadcrumbs and reserve.

For the base, cream the butter or margarine and sugar together until light and fluffy. Gradually beat the eggs into the sugar and butter mixture a little at a time until all the egg has been added. Sift the flour and gently fold in with a metal spoon or rubber spatula.

Spoon into the base of the prepared cake tin. Arrange the apple pieces on top, then lightly stir the milk into the crumble mixture.

Scatter the crumble mixture over the apples and bake in the preheated oven for 1½ hours. Serve cold with cream or custard.

HEALTH RATING

**ALTERNATIVE**
Toffee Apple Cake

**ALTERNATIVE**
Honey Cake

**ALTERNATIVE**
## Toffee Apple Cake

INGREDIENTS **Cuts into 6–8 slices**

2 small eating apples, peeled
4 tbsp soft dark brown sugar
175 g/6 oz butter or margarine
175 g/6 oz caster sugar
3 medium eggs
175 g/6 oz self-raising flour
150 ml/¼ pint double cream
2 tbsp icing sugar
½ tsp vanilla essence
½ tsp ground cinnamon

Preheat the oven to 180°C/350°F/Gas Mark 4, 10 minutes before baking time. Lightly oil and line the bases of two 20.5 cm/8 inch sandwich tins with greaseproof or baking paper.

Thinly slice the apples and toss in the brown sugar until well coated. Arrange them over the base of the prepared tins and reserve. Cream together the butter or margarine and caster sugar until light and fluffy.

Beat the eggs together in a small bowl and gradually beat them into the creamed mixture, beating well between each addition. Sift the flour into the mixture and using a metal spoon or rubber spatula, fold in. Divide the mixture between the two cake tins and level the surface. Bake in the preheated oven for 25–30 minutes, until golden and well risen. Leave in the tins to cool.

Lightly whip the cream with 1 tablespoon of the icing sugar and vanilla essence. Sandwich the cakes together with the cream. Mix the remaining icing sugar and ground cinnamon together, sprinkle over the top of the cake and serve.

**ALTERNATIVE**
## Honey Cake

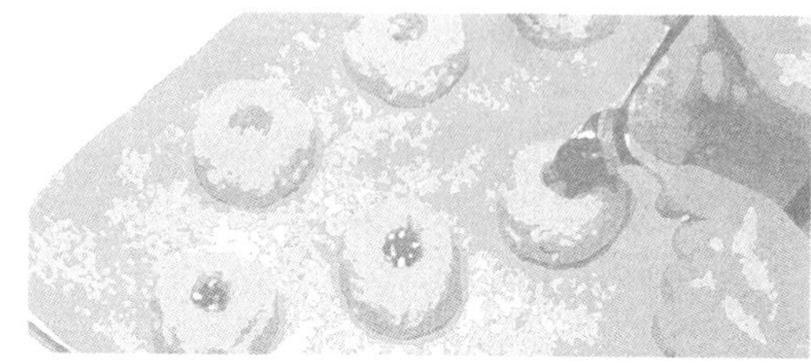

INGREDIENTS **Cuts into 6–8 slices**

50 g/2 oz butter
25 g/1 oz caster sugar
125 g/4 oz clear honey
175 g/6 oz plain flour
½ tsp bicarbonate of soda
½ tsp mixed spice
1 medium egg
2 tbsp milk
25 g/1 oz flaked almonds
1 tbsp clear honey, to drizzle

Preheat the oven to 180°C/350°F/Gas Mark 4, 10 minutes before baking. Lightly oil and line the base of an 18 cm/7 inch deep round cake tin with lightly oiled greaseproof or baking paper.

In a saucepan gently heat the butter, sugar and honey until the butter has just melted. Sift the flour, bicarbonate of soda and mixed spice together into a bowl.

Beat the egg and the milk until mixed thoroughly.

Make a well in the centre of the sifted flour and pour in the melted butter and honey. Using a wooden spoon, beat well, gradually drawing in the flour from the sides of the bowl. When all the flour has been beaten in, add the egg mixture and mix thoroughly. Pour into the prepared tin and sprinkle with the flaked almonds.

Bake in the preheated oven for 30–35 minutes, or until well risen and golden brown and a skewer inserted into the centre of the cake comes out clean. Remove from the oven, then cool for a few minutes in the tin before turning out and leaving to cool on a wire rack. Drizzle with the remaining tablespoon of honey and serve.

**ALTERNATIVE**
## Victoria Sponge with Mango & Mascarpone

INGREDIENTS **Cuts into 8 slices**

175 g/6 oz caster sugar, plus extra for dusting
175 g/6 oz self-raising flour, plus extra for dusting
175 g/6 oz butter or margarine
3 large eggs
1 tsp vanilla essence
25 g/1 oz icing sugar
250 g tub mascarpone cheese
1 large ripe mango, peeled

Preheat the oven to 190°C/375°F/Gas Mark 5, 10 minutes before baking. Lightly oil two 18 cm/7 inch sandwich tins and lightly dust with caster sugar and flour, tapping the tins to remove any excess.

In a large bowl, cream the butter or margarine and sugar together with a wooden spoon until light and creamy. In another bowl mix the eggs and vanilla essence together. Sift the flour several times on to a plate. Beat a little egg into the butter and sugar, then a little flour and beat well.

Continue adding the flour and eggs alternately, beating between each addition, until the mixture is well mixed and smooth. Divide the mixture between the two prepared cake tins, level the surface, then using the back of a large spoon, make a slight dip in the centre of each cake.

Bake in the preheated oven for 25–30 minutes, until the centre of the cake springs back when gently pressed with a clean finger. Turn out on to a wire rack and leave the cakes until cold.

Beat the icing sugar and mascarpone cheese together, then chop the mango into small cubes. Use half the mascarpone and mango to sandwich the cakes together. Spread the rest of the mascarpone on top, decorate with the remaining mango and serve. Otherwise lightly cover and store in the refrigerator. Use within 3–4 days.

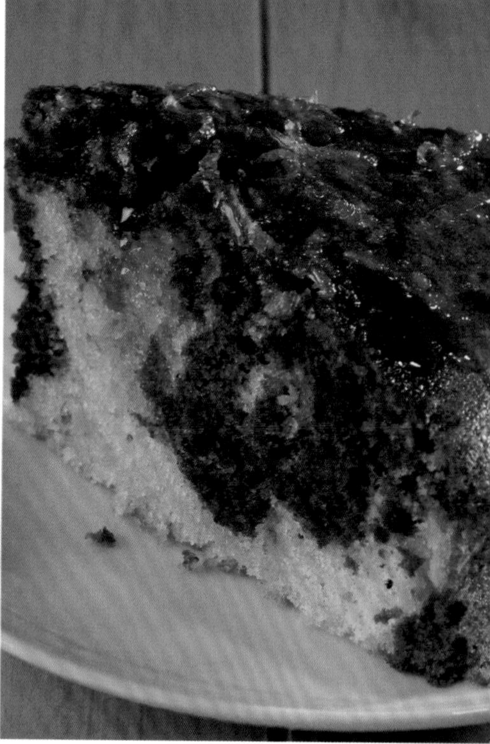

**ALTERNATIVE**
## Marble Cake

INGREDIENTS **Cuts into 8 slices**

225 g/8 oz butter or margarine
225 g/8 oz caster sugar
4 medium eggs
225 g/8 oz self-raising flour, sifted
finely grated rind and juice of 1 orange
25 g/1 oz cocoa powder, sifted

**For the topping:**
zest and juice of 1 orange
1 tbsp granulated sugar

Preheat the oven to 190°C/375°F/Gas Mark 5, 10 minutes before baking. Lightly oil and line the base of a 20.5 cm/8 inch deep round cake tin with greaseproof or baking paper.

In a large bowl, cream the butter or margarine and sugar together until light and fluffy. Beat the eggs together. Beat into the creamed mixture a little at a time, beating well between each addition. When all the egg has been added, fold in the flour with a metal spoon or rubber spatula.

Divide the mixture equally between two bowls. Beat the grated orange rind into one of the bowls with a little of the orange juice. Mix the cocoa powder with the remaining orange juice until smooth, then add to the other bowl and beat well.

Spoon the mixture into the prepared tin, in alternate spoonfuls. When all the cake mixture is in the tin, take a skewer and swirl it in the two mixtures.

Tap the base of the tin on the work surface to level the mixture. Bake in the preheated oven for 50 minutes, or until cooked and a skewer inserted into the centre of the cake comes out clean. Remove from the oven and leave in the tin for a few minutes before cooling on a wire rack. Discard the lining paper.

For the topping, place the orange zest and juice with the granulated sugar in a small saucepan and heat gently until the sugar has dissolved. Bring to the boil and simmer gently for 3–4 minutes, until the juice is syrupy. Pour over the cooled cake and serve when cool. Otherwise, store in an airtight tin.

# Lemon Drizzle Cake

INGREDIENTS **Cuts into 16 squares**

125 g/4 oz butter or margarine

175 g/6 oz caster sugar

2 large eggs

175 g/6 oz self-raising flour

2 lemons, preferably unwaxed

50 g/2 oz granulated sugar

Preheat the oven to 180°C/350°F/Gas Mark 4, 10 minutes before baking. Lightly oil and line the base of an 18 cm/7 inch square cake tin with baking paper.

In a large bowl, cream the butter or margarine and sugar together until soft and fluffy.

Beat the eggs, then gradually add a little of the egg to the creamed mixture, adding 1 tablespoon of flour after each addition.

Finely grate the rind from 1 of the lemons and stir into the creamed mixture, beating well until smooth. Squeeze the juice from the lemon, strain, then stir into the mixture.

Spoon into the prepared tin, level the surface and bake in the preheated oven for 25–30 minutes. Using a zester, remove the peel from the last lemon and mix with 25 g/1 oz of the granulated sugar and reserve.

Squeeze the juice into a small saucepan. Add the rest of the granulated sugar to the lemon juice in the saucepan and heat gently, stirring occasionally.

When the sugar has dissolved, simmer gently for 3–4 minutes until syrupy.

Prick the cake all over with a cocktail stick or fine skewer, to allow to the syrup to soak in.

Sprinkle the lemon zest and sugar over the top of the cake, drizzle over the syrup and leave to cool in the tin. Cut the cake into squares and serve.

HEALTH RATING

**ALTERNATIVE**

Victoria Sponge with Mango & Mascarpone

**ALTERNATIVE**

Marble Cake

# Carrot Cake

INGREDIENTS **Cuts into 8 slices**

200 g/7 oz plain flour
½ tsp ground cinnamon
½ tsp freshly grated nutmeg
1 tsp baking powder
1 tsp bicarbonate of soda
150 g/5 oz dark muscovado sugar
200 ml/7 fl oz vegetable oil
3 medium eggs
225 g/8 oz carrots, peeled and roughly grated
50 g/2 oz chopped walnuts

**For the icing:**

175 g/6 oz cream cheese
finely grated rind of 1 orange
1 tbsp orange juice
1 tsp vanilla essence
125 g/4 oz icing sugar

Preheat the oven to 150°C/300°F/Gas Mark 2, 10 minutes before baking. Lightly oil and line the base of a 15 cm/6 inch deep square cake tin with greaseproof or baking paper.

Sift the flour, spices, baking powder and bicarbonate of soda together into a large bowl. Stir in the dark muscovado sugar and mix together.

Lightly whisk the oil and eggs together, then gradually stir into the flour and sugar mixture. Stir well.

Add the carrots and walnuts. Mix thoroughly, then pour into the prepared cake tin. Bake in the preheated oven for 1¼ hours, or until light and springy to the touch and a skewer inserted into the centre of the cake comes out clean. Remove from the oven and allow to cool in the tin for 5 minutes before turning out on to a wire rack. Leave until cold.

To make the icing, beat together the cream cheese, orange rind, orange juice and vanilla essence. Sift the icing sugar and stir into the cream cheese mixture.

When cold, discard the lining paper, spread the cream cheese icing over the top and serve cut into squares.

HEALTH RATING

**ALTERNATIVE**

Banana Cake

**ALTERNATIVE**

Fruit Cake

INGREDIENTS **Cuts into 8 slices**

3 medium-sized ripe bananas
1 tsp lemon juice
150 g/5 oz soft brown sugar
75 g/3 oz butter or margarine
250 g/9 oz self-raising flour
1 tsp ground cinnamon
3 medium eggs
50 g/2 oz walnuts, chopped
1 tsp each ground cinnamon and caster sugar, to decorate
fresh cream, to serve

**ALTERNATIVE**
## Banana Cake

Preheat the oven to 190°C/375°F/Gas Mark 5, 10 minutes before baking. Lightly oil and line the base of an 18 cm/7 inch deep round cake tin with greaseproof or baking paper.

Mash two of the bananas in a small bowl, sprinkle with the lemon juice and a heaped tablespoon of the sugar. Mix together lightly and reserve.

Gently heat the remaining sugar and butter or margarine in a small saucepan until the butter has just melted.

Pour into a small bowl, then allow to cool slightly. Sift the flour and cinnamon into a large bowl and make a well in the centre.

Beat the eggs into the cooled sugar mixture, pour into the well of flour and mix thoroughly.

Gently stir in the mashed banana mixture. Pour half of the mixture into the prepared tin. Thinly slice the remaining banana and arrange over the cake mixture. Sprinkle over the chopped walnuts, then cover with the remaining cake mixture.

Bake in the preheated oven for 50–55 minutes, or until well risen and golden brown. Allow to cool in the tin, turn out and sprinkle with the ground cinnamon and caster sugar. Serve hot or cold with a jug of fresh cream for pouring.

INGREDIENTS **Cuts into 10 slices**

225 g/8 oz butter or margarine
200 g/7 oz soft brown sugar
finely grated rind of 1 orange
1 tbsp black treacle
3 large eggs, beaten
275 g/10 oz plain flour
¼ tsp ground cinnamon
½ tsp mixed spice
pinch of freshly grated nutmeg
¼ tsp bicarbonate of soda
75 g/3 oz mixed peel
50 g/2 oz glacé cherries
125 g/4 oz raisins
125 g/4 oz sultanas
125 g/4 oz ready-to-eat dried apricots, chopped

**ALTERNATIVE**
## Fruit Cake

Preheat the oven to 150°C/300°C/Gas Mark 2, 10 minutes before baking. Lightly oil and line a 23 cm/9 inch deep round cake tin with a double thickness of greaseproof paper.

In a large bowl, cream together the butter or margarine, sugar and orange rind until light and fluffy, then beat in the treacle. Beat in the eggs a little at a time, beating well between each addition.

Reserve 1 tablespoon of the flour. Sift the remaining flour, the spices and bicarbonate of soda into the mixture.

Mix all the fruits and the reserved flour together, then stir into the cake mixture.

Turn into the prepared tin and smooth the top, making a small hollow in the centre of the cake mixture.

Bake in the preheated oven for 1 hour, then reduce the heat to 140°C/275°F/Gas Mark 1. Bake for a further 1½ hours, or until cooked and a skewer inserted into the centre comes out clean. Leave to cool in the tin, then turn the cake out and serve. Store in an airtight tin when cold.

# Gingerbread

INGREDIENTS **Cuts into 8 slices**

175 g/6 oz butter or margarine
225 g/8 oz black treacle
50 g/2 oz dark muscovado sugar
350 g/12 oz plain flour
2 tsp ground ginger
150 ml/¼ pint milk, warmed
2 medium eggs
1 tsp bicarbonate of soda
1 piece of stem ginger in syrup
1 tbsp stem ginger syrup

Preheat the oven to 150°C/300°C/Gas Mark 2, 10 minutes before baking. Lightly oil and line the base of a 20.5 cm/8 inch deep round cake tin with greaseproof or baking paper.

In a saucepan gently heat the butter or margarine, black treacle and sugar, stirring occasionally until the butter melts. Leave to cool slightly.

Sift the flour and ground ginger into a large bowl.

Make a well in the centre, then pour in the treacle mixture. Reserve 1 tablespoon of the milk, then pour the rest into the treacle mixture. Stir together lightly until mixed.

Beat the eggs together, then stir into the mixture.

Dissolve the bicarbonate of soda in the remaining 1 tablespoon of warmed milk and add to the mixture.

Beat the mixture until well combined and free of lumps.

Pour into the prepared tin and bake in the preheated oven for 1 hour, or until well risen and a skewer inserted into the centre comes out clean.

Cool in the tin, then remove. Slice the stem ginger into thin slivers and sprinkle over the cake. Drizzle with the syrup and serve.

HEALTH RATING

**ALTERNATIVE**
Lemon-iced Ginger Squares

**ALTERNATIVE**
Ginger Snaps

**ALTERNATIVE**
## Lemon-iced Ginger Squares

INGREDIENTS **Makes 12**

225 g/8 oz caster sugar
50 g/2 oz butter, melted
2 tbsp black treacle
2 medium egg whites, lightly whisked
225 g/8 oz plain flour
1 tsp bicarbonate of soda
½ tsp ground cloves
1 tsp ground cinnamon
¼ tsp ground ginger
pinch of salt
225 ml/8 fl oz buttermilk
175 g/6 oz icing sugar
lemon juice

Preheat the oven to 200°C/400°F/Gas Mark 6, 15 minutes before baking. Lightly oil a 20.5 cm/8 inch square cake tin and sprinkle with a little flour.

Mix together the caster sugar, butter and treacle. Stir in the egg whites.

Mix together the flour, bicarbonate of soda, cloves, cinnamon, ginger and salt.

Stir the flour mixture and buttermilk alternately into the butter mixture until well blended.

Spoon into the prepared tin and bake in the preheated oven for 35 minutes, or until a skewer inserted into the centre of the cake comes out clean.

Remove from the oven and allow to cool for 5 minutes in the tin before turning out on to a wire rack over a large plate. Using a cocktail stick, make holes on the top of the cake.

Mix together the icing sugar with enough lemon juice to make a smooth, pourable icing.

Carefully pour the icing over the hot cake, then leave until cold. Cut the ginger cake into squares and serve.

**ALTERNATIVE**
## Ginger Snaps

INGREDIENTS **Makes 40**

300 g/11 oz butter or margarine, softened
225 g/8 oz soft light brown sugar
75 g/3 oz black treacle
1 medium egg
400 g/14 oz plain flour
2 tsp bicarbonate of soda
½ tsp salt
1 tsp ground ginger
1 tsp ground cloves
1 tsp ground cinnamon
50 g/2 oz granulated sugar

Preheat the oven to 190°C/375°F/Gas Mark 5, 10 minutes before baking. Lightly oil a baking sheet.

Cream together the butter or margarine and the sugar until light and fluffy.

Warm the treacle in the microwave for 30–40 seconds, then add gradually to the butter mixture with the egg. Beat until combined well.

In a separate bowl, sift the flour, bicarbonate of soda, salt, ground ginger, ground cloves and ground cinnamon. Add to the butter mixture and mix together to form a firm dough.

Chill in the refrigerator for 1 hour. Shape the dough into small balls and roll in the granulated sugar. Place well apart on the oiled baking sheet.

Sprinkle the baking sheet with a little water and transfer to the preheated oven. Bake for 12 minutes, until golden and crisp. Transfer to a wire rack to cool and serve.

# Jammy Buns

INGREDIENTS **Makes 12**

175 g/6 oz plain flour
175 g/6 oz wholemeal flour
2 tsp baking powder
150 g/5 oz butter or margarine
125 g/4 oz golden caster sugar
50 g/2 oz dried cranberries
1 large egg, beaten
1 tbsp milk
4–5 tbsp seedless raspberry jam

Preheat the oven to 190°C/375°F/Gas Mark 5, 10 minutes before baking. Lightly oil a large baking sheet.

Sift the flours and baking powder together into a large bowl, then tip in the grains remaining in the sieve.

Cut the butter or margarine into small pieces. It is easier to do this when the butter is in the flour as it helps stop the butter from sticking to the knife.

Rub the butter into the flours until it resembles coarse breadcrumbs. Stir in the sugar and cranberries.

Using a round-bladed knife stir in the beaten egg and milk. Mix to form a firm dough. Divide the mixture into 12 and roll into balls.

Place the dough balls on the baking tray, leaving enough space for expansion. Press your thumb into the centre of each ball to make a small hollow.

Spoon a little of the jam in each hollow. Pinch lightly to seal the tops.

Bake in the preheated oven for 20–25 minutes or until golden brown. Cool on a wire rack and serve.

HEALTH RATING 🍎

**ALTERNATIVE**
Lemon & Ginger Buns

**ALTERNATIVE**
Chocolate & Orange Rock Buns

**ALTERNATIVE**
## Lemon & Ginger Buns

INGREDIENTS **Makes 15**

175 g/6 oz butter or margarine
350 g/12 oz plain flour
2 tsp baking powder
½ tsp ground ginger
pinch of salt
finely grated rind of 1 lemon
175 g/6 oz soft light brown sugar
125 g/4 oz sultanas
75 g/3 oz chopped mixed peel
25 g/1 oz stem ginger, finely chopped
1 medium egg
juice of 1 lemon

Preheat the oven to 220°C/425°F/Gas Mark 7, 15 minutes before baking. Cut the butter or margarine into small pieces and place in a large bowl.

Sift the flour, baking powder, ginger and salt together and add to the butter with the lemon rind. Using your fingertips, rub the butter into the flour and spice mixture until it resembles coarse breadcrumbs. Stir in the sugar, sultanas, chopped mixed peel and stem ginger.

Add the egg and lemon juice to the mixture, then using a round -bladed knife stir well to mix. The mixture should be quite stiff and just holding together. Place heaped tablespoons of the mixture on to a lightly oiled baking tray, making sure that the dollops of mixture are well apart.

Using a fork, rough up the edges of the buns and bake in the preheated oven for 12–15 minutes. Leave the buns to cool for 5 minutes before transferring to a wire rack until cold, then serve. Otherwise store the buns in an airtight tin and eat within 3–5 days.

**ALTERNATIVE**
## Chocolate & Orange Rock Buns

INGREDIENTS **Makes 12**

200 g/7 oz self-raising flour
25 g/1 oz cocoa powder
½ tsp baking powder
125 g/4 oz butter
40 g/1 ½ oz granulated sugar
50 g/2 oz candied pineapple, chopped
50 g/2 oz ready-to-eat dried apricots, chopped
50 g/2 oz glacé cherries, quartered
1 medium egg
finely grated rind of ½ orange
1 tbsp orange juice
2 tbsp demerara sugar

Preheat the oven to 200°C/400°F/Gas Mark 6, 15 minutes before baking. Lightly oil two baking sheets, or line them with non-stick baking parchment. Sift the flour, cocoa powder and baking powder into a bowl. Cut the butter into small squares. Add to the dry ingredients, then, using your hands, rub in until the mixture resembles fine breadcrumbs.

Add the granulated sugar, pineapple, apricots and cherries to the bowl and stir to mix. Lightly beat the egg together with the grated orange rind and juice. Drizzle the egg mixture over the dry ingredients and stir to combine. The mixture should be fairly stiff but not too dry – add a little more orange juice, if needed.

Using two teaspoons, shape the mixture into 12 rough heaps on the prepared baking sheets. Sprinkle generously with the demerara sugar. Bake in the preheated oven for 15 minutes, switching the baking sheets around after 10 minutes. Leave on the baking sheets for 5 minutes to cool slightly, then transfer to a wire rack to cool. Serve warm or cold.

ALTERNATIVE
## White Chocolate Cookies

INGREDIENTS **Makes about 24**

140 g/4½ oz butter
40 g/1½ oz caster sugar
60 g/2½ oz soft dark brown sugar
1 medium egg
125 g/4 oz plain flour
½ tsp bicarbonate of soda
few drops of vanilla essence
150 g/5 oz white chocolate
50 g/2 oz whole hazelnuts, shelled

Preheat the oven to 180°C/350°F/Gas Mark 4, 10 minutes before baking. Lightly butter several baking sheets with 15 g/½ oz of the butter.

Place the remaining butter with both sugars into a large bowl and beat with a wooden spoon or an electric mixer until soft and fluffy.

Beat the egg, then gradually beat into the creamed mixture. Sift the flour and the bicarbonate of soda together, then carefully fold into the creamed mixture with a few drops of vanilla essence.

Roughly chop the chocolate and hazelnuts into small pieces, add to the bowl and gently stir into the mixture. Mix together lightly to blend.

Spoon heaped teaspoons of the mixture on to the prepared baking sheets, making sure that there is plenty of space in between each one as they will spread a lot during cooking.

Bake the cookies in the preheated oven for 10 minutes or until golden, then remove from the oven and leave to cool for 1 minute.

Using a spatula, carefully transfer to a wire rack and leave to cool completely. These cookies are best eaten on the day they are made.

ALTERNATIVE
## Chocolate Orange Biscuits

INGREDIENTS **Makes 30**

100 g/3½ oz plain dark chocolate
125 g/4 oz butter
125 g/4 oz caster sugar
pinch of salt
1 medium egg, beaten
grated zest of 2 oranges
200 g/7 oz plain flour
1 tsp baking powder
125 g/4 oz icing sugar
1–2 tbsp orange juice

Preheat the oven to 200°C/400°F/Gas Mark 6, 15 minutes before baking. Lightly oil several baking sheets. Coarsely grate the chocolate and reserve. Beat the butter and sugar together until creamy. Add the salt, beaten egg and half the orange zest and beat again.

Sift the flour and baking powder, add to the bowl with the grated chocolate and beat to form a dough. Shape into a ball, wrap in clingfilm and chill in the refrigerator for 2 hours.

Roll the dough out on a lightly floured surface to 5 mm/¼ inch thickness and cut into 5 cm/2 inch rounds. Place the rounds on the prepared baking sheets, allowing room for expansion.

Bake in the preheated oven for 10–12 minutes or until firm. Remove the biscuits from the oven and leave to cool slightly. Transfer to a wire rack and leave to cool.

Sift the icing sugar into a small bowl and stir in sufficient orange juice to make a smooth, spreadable icing. Spread the icing over the biscuits, leave until almost set, then sprinkle on the remaining grated orange zest before serving.

# Chocolate Chip Cookies

INGREDIENTS **Make 36**

175 g/6 oz plain flour

pinch of salt

1 tsp baking powder

¼ tsp bicarbonate of soda

75 g/3 oz butter or margarine

50 g/2 oz soft light brown sugar

3 tbsp golden syrup

125 g/4 oz chocolate chips

Preheat the oven to 190°C/375°F/Gas Mark 5, 10 minutes before baking. Lightly oil a large baking sheet.

In a large bowl, sift together the flour, salt, baking powder and bicarbonate of soda.

Cut the butter or margarine into small pieces and add to the flour mixture.

Using two knives or your fingertips, rub in the butter or margarine until the mixture resembles coarse breadcrumbs.

Add the light brown sugar, golden syrup and chocolate chips. Mix together until a smooth dough forms.

Shape the mixture into small balls and arrange on the baking sheet, leaving enough space to allow them to expand. These cookies do not increase in size by a great deal, but allow a little space for expansion.

Flatten the mixture slightly with your fingertips or the heel of your hand.

Bake in the preheated oven for 12–15 minutes, or until golden and cooked through.

Allow to cool slightly, then transfer the biscuits on to a wire rack to cool. Serve when cold or otherwise store in an airtight tin.

HEALTH RATING

**ALTERNATIVE**

White Chocolate Cookies

**ALTERNATIVE**

Chocolate Orange Biscuits

# Shortbread Thumbs

INGREDIENTS **Makes 12**

125 g/4 oz self-raising flour
125 g/4 oz butter, softened
25 g/1 oz white vegetable fat
50 g/2 oz granulated sugar
25 g/1 oz cornflour, sifted
5 tbsp cocoa powder, sifted
125 g/4 oz icing sugar
6 assorted colour glacé cherries, rinsed, dried and halved

Preheat the oven to 150°C/300°F/Gas Mark 2, 10 minutes before baking. Lightly oil two baking sheets. Sift the flour into a large bowl, cut 75 g/3 oz of the butter and the white vegetable fat into small cubes and add to the flour. Then, using your fingertips, rub in until the mixture resembles fine breadcrumbs.

Stir in the granulated sugar, sifted cornflour and 4 tablespoons of cocoa powder and bring the mixture together with your hands to form a soft and pliable dough.

Place on a lightly floured surface and shape into 12 small balls. Place onto the baking sheets at least 5 cm/2 inches apart, then press each one with a clean thumb to make a dent.

Bake in the preheated oven for 20–25 minutes or until light golden brown. Remove from the oven and leave for 1–2 minutes to cool. Transfer to a wire rack and leave until cold.

Sift the icing sugar and the remaining cocoa powder into a bowl and add the remaining softened butter. Blend to form a smooth and spreadable icing with 1–2 tablespoons of hot water. Spread a little icing over the top of each biscuit and place half a cherry on each. Leave until set before serving.

## HEALTH RATING 🍎

**ALTERNATIVE**
Whipped Shortbread

**ALTERNATIVE**
Marbled Toffee Shortbread

**ALTERNATIVE**
## Whipped Shortbread

INGREDIENTS **Makes 36**

- 225 g/8 oz butter, softened
- 75 g/3 oz icing sugar
- 175 g/6 oz plain flour
- hundreds and thousands
- sugar strands
- chocolate drops
- silver balls
- 50 g/2 oz icing sugar
- 2–3 tsp lemon juice

Preheat the oven to 180°C/350°F/Gas Mark 4, 10 minutes before baking. Lightly oil a baking sheet. Cream the butter and icing sugar until fluffy. Gradually add the flour and continue beating for a further 2–3 minutes until it is smooth and light.

Roll into balls and place on a baking sheet. Cover half of the dough mixture with hundreds and thousands, sugar strands, chocolate drops or silver balls. . Keep the other half plain.

Bake in the preheated oven for 6–8 minutes, until the bottoms are lightly browned. Remove from the oven and transfer to a wire rack to cool.

Sift the icing sugar into a small bowl. Add the lemon juice and blend until a smooth icing forms.

Using a small spoon, swirl the icing over the cooled plain cookies. Decorate with either the extra hundreds and thousands, chocolate drops or silver balls and serve.

**ALTERNATIVE**
## Marbled Toffee Shortbread

INGREDIENTS **Makes 12**

- 175 g/6 oz butter
- 75 g/3 oz caster sugar
- 175 g/6 oz plain flour
- 25 g/1 oz cocoa powder
- 75 g/3 oz fine semolina

**For the toffee filling:**

- 50 g/2 oz butter
- 50 g/2 oz soft light brown sugar
- 397 g can condensed milk

**For the chocolate topping:**

- 75 g/3 oz plain dark chocolate
- 75 g/3 oz milk chocolate
- 75 g/3 oz white chocolate

Preheat the oven to 180°C/350°F/Gas Mark 4, 10 minutes before baking. Oil and line a 20.5 cm/8 inch square cake tin with non-stick baking parchment. Cream the butter and sugar until light and fluffy then sift in the flour and cocoa powder. Add the semolina and mix together to form a soft dough. Press into the base of the prepared tin. Prick all over with a fork, then bake in the preheated oven for 25 minutes. Leave to cool.

To make the toffee filling, gently heat the butter, sugar and condensed milk together until the sugar has dissolved. Bring to the boil, then simmer for 5 minutes, stirring constantly. Leave for 1 minute, then spread over the shortbread and leave to cool.

For the topping, place the different chocolates in separate heatproof bowls and melt one at a time, set over a saucepan of almost boiling water. Drop spoonfuls of each on top of the toffee and tilt the tin to cover evenly. Swirl with a knife for a marbled effect.

Leave the chocolate to cool. When just set, mark into bars using a sharp knife. Leave for at least 1 hour to harden before cutting into bars.

# Oatmeal Raisin Cookies

INGREDIENTS **Makes 24**

175 g/6 oz plain flour
150 g/5 oz rolled oats
1 tsp ground ginger
½ tsp baking powder
½ tsp bicarbonate of soda
125 g/4 oz soft light brown sugar
50 g/2 oz raisins
1 medium egg, lightly beaten
150 ml/¼ pint vegetable or sunflower oil
4 tbsp milk

Preheat the oven to 200°C/400°F/Gas Mark 6, 15 minutes before baking. Lightly oil a baking sheet.

Mix together the flour, oats, ground ginger, baking powder, bicarbonate of soda, sugar and the raisins in a large bowl.

In another bowl, mix the egg, oil and milk together. Make a well in the centre of the dry ingredients and pour in the egg mixture.

Mix together well with either a fork or a wooden spoon to make a soft but not sticky dough.

Place spoonfuls of the dough well apart on the oiled baking sheet and flatten the tops down slightly with the tines of a fork.

Transfer the biscuits to the preheated oven and bake for 10–12 minutes until golden.

Remove from the oven, leave to cool for 2–3 minutes, then transfer the biscuits to a wire rack to cool. Serve when cold or otherwise store in an airtight tin.

HEALTH RATING

**ALTERNATIVE**
Oatmeal Coconut Cookies

**ALTERNATIVE**
Chewy Choc & Nut Cookies

**ALTERNATIVE**
## Oatmeal Coconut Cookies

INGREDIENTS **Makes 30**

225 g/8 oz butter or margarine
125 g/4 oz soft light brown sugar
125 g/4 oz caster sugar
1 large egg, lightly beaten
1 tsp vanilla essence
225 g/8 oz plain flour
1 tsp baking powder
½ tsp bicarbonate of soda
125 g/4 oz rolled oats
75 g/3 oz desiccated coconut

Preheat the oven to 180°C/350°F/Gas Mark 4, 10 minutes before baking. Lightly oil a baking sheet. Cream together the butter or margarine and sugars until light and fluffy. Gradually stir in the egg and vanilla essence and beat until well blended.

Sift together the flour, baking powder and bicarbonate of soda in another bowl. Add to the butter and sugar mixture and beat together until smooth. Fold in the rolled oats and coconut with a metal spoon or rubber spatula.

Roll heaped teaspoonfuls of the mixture into balls and place on the baking sheet about 5 cm/2 inches apart and flatten each ball slightly with the heel of your hand. Transfer to the preheated oven and bake for 12–15 minutes, until just golden. Remove from the oven and transfer the biscuits to a wire rack to completely cool and serve.

**ALTERNATIVE**
## Chewy Choc & Nut Cookies

INGREDIENTS **Makes 18**

15 g/½ oz butter
4 medium egg whites
350 g/12 oz icing sugar
75 g/3 oz cocoa powder
2 tbsp plain flour
1 tsp instant coffee powder
125 g/4 oz walnuts, finely chopped

Preheat the oven to 180°C/350°F/Gas Mark 4, 10 minutes before baking. Lightly butter several baking sheets with the butter and line with a sheet of non-stick baking parchment. Place the egg whites in a large, grease-free bowl and whisk with an electric mixer until the egg whites are very frothy.

Add the sugar, with the cocoa powder, the flour and coffee powder and whisk again until the ingredients are blended thoroughly. Add 1 tablespoon of water and continue to whisk on the highest speed until the mixture is very thick. Fold in the chopped walnuts.

Place tablespoons of the mixture onto the prepared baking sheets, leaving plenty of space between them, as they expand greatly during cooking.

Bake in the preheated oven for 12–15 minutes, or until the tops are firm, golden and quite cracked. Leave to cool for 30 seconds, then using a spatula, transfer to a wire rack and leave to cool. Store in an airtight tin.

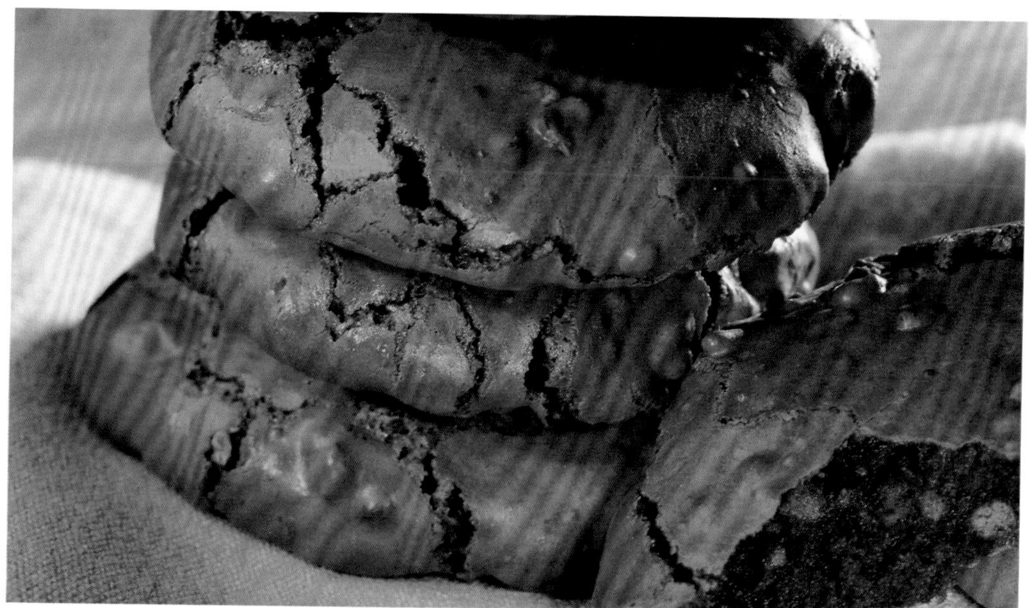

# Chunky Chocolate Muffins

INGREDIENTS **Makes 7**

50 g/2 oz plain dark chocolate, roughly chopped
50 g/2 oz light muscovado sugar
25 g/1 oz butter, melted
125 ml/4 fl oz milk, heated to room temperature
½ tsp vanilla essence
1 medium egg, lightly beaten
150 g/5 oz self-raising flour
½ tsp baking powder
pinch of salt
75 g/3 oz white chocolate, chopped
2 tsp icing sugar (optional)

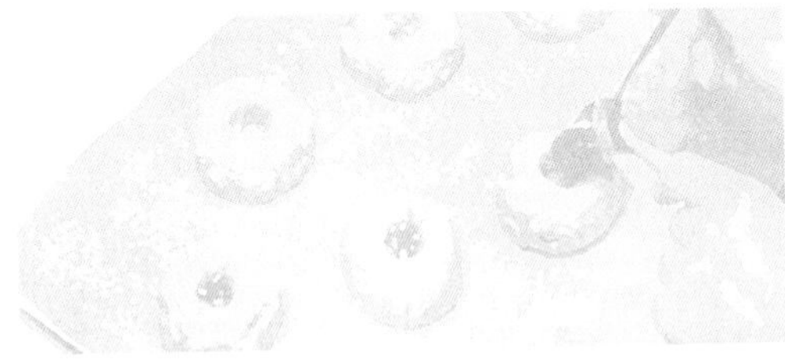

Preheat the oven to 200°C/400°F/Gas Mark 6, 15 minutes before baking. Line a muffin or deep bun tin tray with seven paper muffin cases or oil the individual compartments well. Place the plain chocolate in a large heatproof bowl set over a saucepan of very hot water and stir occasionally until melted. Remove the bowl and leave to cool for a few minutes.

Stir the sugar and butter into the melted chocolate, then the milk, vanilla essence and egg. Sift the flour, baking powder and salt in together. Add the chopped white chocolate then using a metal spoon, fold together quickly, taking care not to overmix.

Divide the mixture between the paper cases, piling it up in the centre. Bake on the centre shelf of the preheated oven for 20–25 minutes, or until well risen and firm to the touch.

Lightly dust the tops of the muffins with icing sugar as soon as they come out of the oven, if wanted. Leave the muffins in the tins for a few minutes, then transfer to a wire rack. Serve warm or cold.

HEALTH RATING

**ALTERNATIVE**
Rich Chocolate Cup Cakes

**ALTERNATIVE**
Fudgy & Top Hat Chocolate Buns

**ALTERNATIVE**
## Rich Chocolate Cup Cakes

Preheat the oven to 180°C/350°F/Gas Mark 4, 10 minutes before baking. Line a 12 hole muffin or deep bun tin tray with paper muffin cases. Sift the flour and cocoa powder into a bowl. Stir in the sugar, then add the melted butter, eggs and vanilla essence. Beat together with a wooden spoon for 3 minutes or until well blended.

Divide half the mixture between six of the paper cases. Dry the cherries thoroughly on absorbent kitchen paper, then fold into the remaining mixture and spoon into the rest of the paper cases.

Bake on the shelf above the centre of the preheated oven for 20 minutes, or until a skewer inserted into the centre of a cake comes out clean. Transfer to a wire rack and leave to cool.

For the chocolate icing, melt the chocolate and butter in a heatproof bowl set over a saucepan of hot water. Remove from the heat and leave to cool for 3 minutes, stirring occasionally. Stir in the icing sugar. Spoon over the six plain chocolate cakes and leave to set.

For the cherry icing, sift the icing sugar into a bowl and stir in 1 tablespoon of boiling water, the butter and cherry syrup. Spoon the icing over the remaining six cakes, decorate each with a halved cherry and leave to set.

INGREDIENTS **Makes 12**

175 g/6 oz self-raising flour
25 g/1 oz cocoa powder
175 g/6 oz soft light brown sugar
75 g/3 oz butter, melted
2 medium eggs, lightly beaten
1 tsp vanilla essence
40 g/1½ oz maraschino cherries, drained and chopped

**For the chocolate icing:**

50 g/2 oz plain dark chocolate
25 g/1 oz unsalted butter
25 g/1 oz icing sugar, sifted

**For the cherry icing:**

125 g/4 oz icing sugar
7 g/¼ oz unsalted butter, melted
1 tsp syrup from the maraschino cherries
3 maraschino cherries, halved, to decorate

**ALTERNATIVE**
## Fudgy & Top Hat Chocolate Buns

Preheat the oven to 190°C/375°F/Gas Mark 5, 10 minutes before baking. Sift the flour, cocoa powder and baking powder into a bowl. Add the butter, sugar, egg and milk. Beat for 2–3 minutes or until light and fluffy.

Divide the mixture equally between 12 paper cases arranged in a bun tin tray. Bake on the shelf above the centre in the preheated oven for 15–20 minutes, or until well risen and firm to the touch. Leave in the bun tin for a few minutes, then transfer to a wire rack and leave to cool completely.

For the fudgy icing, mix together the melted butter, milk, cocoa powder and icing sugar. Place a spoonful of icing on the top of six of the buns, spreading out to a circle with the back of the spoon. Sprinkle with grated chocolate.

To make the top hats, use a sharp knife to cut and remove a circle of sponge, about 3 cm/1¼ inch across from each of the six remaining cakes. Whip the cream, orange liqueur and 1 teaspoon of icing sugar together until soft peaks form.

Spoon the filling into a piping bag fitted with a large star nozzle and pipe a swirl in the centre of each cake. Replace the tops, then dust with the remaining icing sugar and serve with the other buns.

INGREDIENTS **Makes 12**

50 g/2 oz self-raising flour
25 g/1 oz cocoa powder
½ tsp baking powder
75 g/3 oz butter, softened
75 g/3 oz soft light brown sugar
1 medium egg, lightly beaten
1 tbsp milk

**For the fudgy icing:**

15 g/½ oz unsalted butter, melted
1 tbsp milk
15 g/½ oz cocoa powder, sifted
40 g/1½ oz icing sugar, sifted
25 g/1 oz plain dark chocolate, coarsely grated

**For the top hat filling:**

150 ml/¼ pint whipping cream
2 tsp orange liqueur
1 tbsp icing sugar, sifted

# Pecan Caramel Millionaire's Shortbread

INGREDIENTS **Makes 20**

125 g/4 oz butter, softened
2 tbsp smooth peanut butter
75 g/3 oz caster sugar
75 g/3 oz cornflour
175 g/6 oz plain flour

**For the topping:**

200 g/7 oz caster sugar
125 g/4 oz butter
2 tbsp golden syrup
75 g/3 oz liquid glucose
75 ml/3 fl oz water
400 g can sweetened condensed milk
175 g/6 oz pecans, roughly chopped
75 g/3 oz plain dark chocolate
1 tbsp butter

Preheat the oven to 180°C/350°F/Gas Mark 4, 10 minutes before baking. Lightly oil and line an 18 cm x 28 cm/7 x 11 inch tin with greaseproof or baking paper.

Cream together the butter, peanut butter and sugar until light. Sift in the cornflour and flour together and mix in to make a smooth dough. Press the mixture into the prepared tin and prick all over with a fork. Bake in the preheated oven for 20 minutes, until just golden. Remove from the oven.

Meanwhile, for the topping, combine the sugar, butter, golden syrup, glucose, water and milk in a heavy-based saucepan. Stir constantly over a low heat without boiling until the sugar has dissolved. Increase the heat and boil steadily, stirring constantly for about 10 minutes until the mixture turns a golden caramel colour. Remove the saucepan from the heat and add the pecans. Pour over the shortbread base immediately. Allow to cool, then refrigerate for at least 1 hour.

Break the chocolate into small pieces and put into a heatproof bowl with the butter. Place over a saucepan of barely simmering water, ensuring that the bowl does not come into contact with the water. Leave until melted, then stir together well. Remove the shortbread from the refrigerator and pour the chocolate evenly over the top, spreading thinly to cover. Leave to set, cut into squares and serve.

HEALTH RATING

**ALTERNATIVE**

Chocolate Biscuit Bars

**ALTERNATIVE**

Fudgy Chocolate Bars

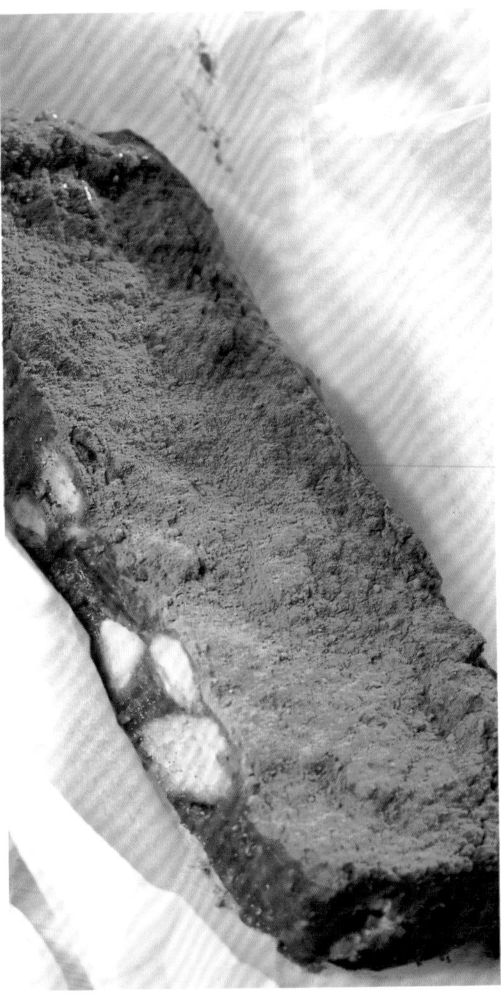

## ALTERNATIVE
# Chocolate Biscuit Bars

INGREDIENTS **Makes 20**

50 g/2 oz sultanas
3–4 tbsp brandy (optional)
100 g/3½ oz plain dark chocolate
125 g/4 oz unsalted butter
2 tbsp golden syrup
90 ml/3 fl oz double cream
6 digestive biscuits, roughly crushed
50 g/2 oz shelled pistachio nuts, toasted and roughly chopped
50 g/2 oz blanched almonds, toasted and roughly chopped
50 g/2 oz glacé cherries, roughly chopped
grated zest of 1 orange
cocoa powder, sifted

Lightly oil a 20.5 cm/8 inch square tin and line with clingfilm. Place the sultanas in a small bowl and pour over the brandy, if using. Leave to soak for 20–30 minutes.

Meanwhile, break the chocolate into small pieces and put into a heatproof bowl. Place the bowl over a saucepan of simmering water, making sure that the bottom of the bowl does not touch the water. Leave the chocolate until melted, stirring occasionally. Remove from the heat.

Add the butter, golden syrup and double cream to a small saucepan and heat until the butter has melted. Remove the saucepan from the heat and add the melted chocolate, biscuits, nuts, cherries, orange zest, sultanas and the brandy mixture.

Mix thoroughly and pour into the prepared tin. Smooth the top and chill in the refrigerator for at least 4 hours, or until firm.

Turn out the cake and remove the clingfilm. Dust liberally with the cocoa powder then cut into bars to serve. Store lightly covered in the refrigerator.

## ALTERNATIVE
# Fudgy Chocolate Bars

INGREDIENTS **Makes 14**

25 g/1 oz glacé cherries
60 g/2½ oz shelled hazelnuts
150 g/5 oz plain dark chocolate
150 g/5 oz unsalted butter
¼ tsp salt
150 g/5 oz digestive biscuits
1 tbsp icing sugar, sifted, optional

Preheat the oven to 180°C/350°F/Gas Mark 4, 10 minutes before baking. Lightly oil a 18 cm/7 inch square tin and line the base with non-stick baking parchment. Rinse the glacé cherries thoroughly, dry well on absorbent kitchen paper and reserve.

Place the nuts on a baking tray and roast in the preheated oven for 10 minutes, or until light golden brown. Leave to cool slightly, then chop roughly and reserve.

Break the chocolate into small pieces, place with the butter and salt into the top of a double boiler or in a bowl set over a saucepan of gently simmering water. Heat gently, stirring until melted and smooth. Alternatively, melt the chocolate in the microwave, according to the manufacturer's instructions. Chop the biscuits into 5 mm/¼ inch pieces and cut the cherries in half. Add to the chocolate mixture with the nuts and stir well. Spoon the mixture into the prepared tin and level the top.

Chill in the refrigerator for 30 minutes, remove from the tin, discard the baking parchment and cut into 14 bars. Cover lightly, return to the refrigerator and keep chilled until ready to serve. To serve, lightly sprinkle the bars with sifted icing sugar if using. Store covered in the refrigerator.

**ALTERNATIVE**
## Apple & Cinnamon Crumble Bars

INGREDIENTS **Makes 16**

450 g/1 lb Bramley cooking apples, roughly chopped
50 g/2 oz raisins
50 g/2 oz caster sugar
1 tsp ground cinnamon
zest of 1 lemon
200 g/7 oz plain flour
250 g/9 oz soft light brown sugar
½ tsp bicarbonate of soda
150 g/5 oz rolled oats
150 g/5 oz butter, melted
crème fraîche or whipped cream, to serve

Preheat the oven to 190°C/375°F/Gas Mark 5, 10 minutes before baking. Place the apples, raisins, sugar, cinnamon and lemon zest into a saucepan over a low heat.

Cover and cook for about 15 minutes, stirring occasionally, until the apple is cooked through. Remove the cover and stir well with a wooden spoon to break up the apple completely.

Cook for a further 15–30 minutes over a very low heat until reduced, thickened and slightly darkened. Allow to cool. Lightly oil and line a 20.5 cm/8 inch square cake tin with greaseproof or baking paper.

Mix together the flour, sugar, bicarbonate of soda, rolled oats and butter until well combined and crumbly. Spread half of the flour mixture into the bottom of the prepared tin and press down. Pour over the apple mixture.

Sprinkle over the remaining flour mixture and press down lightly. Bake in the preheated oven for 30–35 minutes, until golden brown.

Remove from the oven and allow to cool before cutting into slices. Serve the bars warm or cold with crème fraîche or whipped cream.

**ALTERNATIVE**
## Crunchy-topped Citrus Chocolate Slices

INGREDIENTS **Makes 12 slices**

175 g/6 oz butter
175 g/6 oz soft light brown sugar
finely grated rind of 1 orange
3 medium eggs, lightly beaten
1 tbsp ground almonds
175 g/6 oz self-raising flour
¼ tsp baking powder
125 g/4 oz plain dark chocolate, coarsely grated
2 tsp milk

**For the crunchy topping:**
125 g/4 oz granulated sugar
juice of 2 limes
juice of 1 orange

Preheat the oven to 170°C/325°F/Gas Mark 3, 10 minutes before baking. Oil and line a 28 x 18 x 2.5 cm/11 x 7 x 1 inch cake tin with non-stick baking parchment. Place the butter, sugar and orange rind into a large bowl and cream together until light and fluffy. Gradually add the eggs, beating after each addition, then beat in the ground almonds.

Sift the flour and baking powder into the creamed mixture. Add the grated chocolate and milk, then gently fold in using a metal spoon. Spoon the mixture into the prepared tin.

Bake on the centre shelf of the preheated oven for 35–40 minutes, or until well risen and firm to the touch. Leave in the tin for a few minutes to cool slightly. Turn out onto a wire rack and remove the baking parchment.

To make the crunchy topping, place the sugar with the lime and orange juices into a small jug and stir together. Drizzle the sugar mixture over the hot cake, ensuring the whole surface is covered. Leave until completely cold, then cut into 12 slices and serve.

# Lemon Bars

INGREDIENTS **Makes 24**

175 g/6 oz flour
125 g/4 oz butter
50 g/2 oz granulated sugar
200 g/7 oz caster sugar
2 tbsp flour
½ tsp baking powder
¼ tsp salt
2 medium eggs, lightly beaten
juice and finely grated rind of 1 lemon
sifted icing sugar, to decorate

Preheat the oven to 170°C/325°F/Gas Mark 3, 10 minutes before baking. Lightly oil and line a 20.5 cm/8 inch square cake tin with greaseproof or baking paper.

Rub together the flour and butter until the mixture resembles breadcrumbs. Stir in the granulated sugar and mix.

Turn the mixture into the prepared tin and press down firmly. Bake in the preheated oven for 20 minutes, until pale golden.

Meanwhile, in a food processor, mix together the caster sugar, flour, baking powder, salt, eggs, lemon juice and rind until smooth. Pour over the prepared base.

Transfer to the preheated oven and bake for a further 20–25 minutes, until nearly set but still a bit wobbly in the centre. Remove from the oven and cool in the tin on a wire rack. Dust with icing sugar and cut into squares. Serve cold or store in an airtight tin.

HEALTH RATING 

**ALTERNATIVE**
Apple & Cinnamon Crumble Bars

**ALTERNATIVE**
Crunchy-topped Citrus Chocolate Slices

# Triple Chocolate Brownies

INGREDIENTS **Serves 4**

350 g/12 oz plain dark chocolate, broken into pieces
225 g/8 oz butter, cubed
225 g/8 oz caster sugar
3 large eggs, lightly beaten
1 tsp vanilla essence
2 tbsp very strong black coffee
100 g/3½ oz self-raising flour
125 g/4 oz pecans, roughly chopped
75 g/3 oz white chocolate, roughly chopped
75 g/3 oz milk chocolate, roughly chopped

Preheat the oven to 190°C/375°F/Gas Mark 5, 10 minutes before baking. Oil and line a 28 x 18 x 2.5 cm/11 x 7 x 1 inch cake tin with non-stick baking parchment. Place the plain chocolate in a heatproof bowl with the butter over a saucepan of almost boiling water and stir occasionally until melted. Remove from the heat and leave until just cool, but not beginning to set.

Place the caster sugar, eggs, vanilla essence and coffee in a large bowl and beat together until smooth. Gradually beat in the chocolate mixture. Sift the flour into the chocolate mixture. Add the pecans and the white and milk chocolate and gently fold in until mixed thoroughly.

Spoon the mixture into the prepared tin and level the top. Bake on the centre shelf of the preheated oven for 45 minutes, or until just firm to the touch in the centre and crusty on top. Leave to cool in the tin, then turn out onto a wire rack. Trim off the crusty edges and cut into 15 squares. Store in an airtight container.

HEALTH RATING 

**ALTERNATIVE**

Chocolate Fudge Brownies

**ALTERNATIVE**

Iced Chocolate Nut Brownies

INGREDIENTS **Makes 16**

125 g/4 oz butter
175 g/6 oz plain dark chocolate, roughly chopped or broken
225 g/8 oz caster sugar
2 tsp vanilla essence
2 medium eggs, lightly beaten
150 g/5 oz plain flour
175 g/6 oz icing sugar
2 tbsp cocoa powder
15 g/½ oz butter

**ALTERNATIVE**
## Chocolate Fudge Brownies

Preheat the oven to 180°C/350°F/Gas Mark 4, 10 minutes before baking. Lightly oil and line a 20.5 cm/8 inch square cake tin with greaseproof or baking paper.

Slowly melt the butter and chocolate together in a heatproof bowl set over a saucepan of simmering water. Transfer the mixture to a large bowl. Stir in the sugar and vanilla essence, then stir in the eggs. Sift over the flour and fold together well with a metal spoon or rubber spatula. Pour into the prepared tin.

Transfer to the preheated oven and bake for 30 minutes until just set. Remove the cooked mixture from the oven and leave to cool in the tin before turning it out on to a wire rack.

Sift the icing sugar and cocoa powder into a small bowl and make a well in the centre. Place the butter in the well then gradually add about 2 tablespoons of hot water. Mix to form a smooth spreadable icing.

Pour the icing over the cooked mixture. Allow the icing to set before cutting into squares. Serve the brownies when they are cold.

**ALTERNATIVE**
## Iced Chocolate Nut Brownies

INGREDIENTS **Makes 16**

125 g/4 oz butter
150 g/5 oz soft light brown sugar
50 g/2 oz plain dark chocolate, roughly chopped or broken
2 tbsp smooth peanut butter
2 medium eggs
50 g/2 oz unsalted roasted peanuts, finely chopped
100 g/3½ oz self-raising flour

**For the topping:**
125 g/4 oz plain dark chocolate, roughly chopped or broken
50 ml/2 fl oz soured cream

Preheat the oven to 180°C/350°F/Gas Mark 4, 10 minutes before baking. Lightly oil and line a 20.5 cm/8 inch square cake tin with greaseproof or baking paper.

Combine the butter, sugar and chocolate in a small saucepan and heat gently until the sugar and chocolate have melted, stirring constantly. Reserve and cool slightly.

Mix together the peanut butter, eggs and peanuts in a large bowl. Stir in the cooled chocolate mixture. Sift in the flour and fold together with a metal spoon or rubber spatula until combined. Pour into the prepared tin and bake in the preheated oven for about 30 minutes, or until just firm.

Cool for 5 minutes in the tin before turning out on to a wire rack to cool.

To make the topping, melt the chocolate in a heatproof bowl over a saucepan of simmering water, making sure that the base of the bowl does not touch the water.

Cool slightly, then stir in the soured cream until smooth and glossy. Spread over the brownies, refrigerate until set, then cut into squares. Serve the brownies cold.

# Entertaining

If you're hosting a dinner party and are cooking to impress, or you're just having a few friends round and want to cook something special, these recipes will help you create a delicious meal. Covering everything from starters and main courses to puddings and drinks, whatever the occasion, you'll be ready for anything.

# Crispy Pork Wontons

INGREDIENTS **Makes 20**

1 small onion, peeled and roughly chopped
2 garlic cloves, peeled and crushed
1 green chilli, deseeded and chopped
2.5 cm/1 inch piece fresh root ginger, peeled and roughly chopped
450 g/1 lb lean pork mince
4 tbsp freshly chopped coriander
1 tsp Chinese five spice powder
salt and freshly ground black pepper
20 wonton wrappers
1 medium egg, lightly beaten
vegetable oil for deep-frying
chilli sauce, to serve

Place the onion, garlic, chilli and ginger in a food processor and blend until very finely chopped. Add the pork, coriander and Chinese five spice powder. Season to taste with salt and pepper, then blend again briefly to mix. Divide the mixture into 20 equal portions and with floured hands, shape each into a walnut-sized ball.

Brush the edges of a wonton wrapper with beaten egg, place a pork ball in the centre, then bring the corners to the centre and pinch together to make a money bag. Repeat with the remaining pork balls and wrappers.

Pour sufficient oil into a heavy-based saucepan or deep-fat fryer so that it is one-third full and heat to 180°C/350°F. Deep-fry the wontons in three or four batches for 3–4 minutes, or until cooked through and golden and crisp. Drain on absorbent kitchen paper. Serve the crispy pork wontons immediately, allowing five per person, with some chilli sauce for dipping.

## HEALTH RATING

**SEAFOOD ALTERNATIVE**

Deep-fried Crab Wontons

**VEGETARIAN ALTERNATIVE**

Savoury Wontons

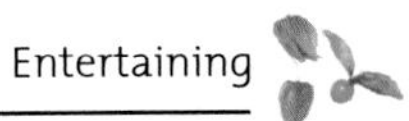

**SEAFOOD ALTERNATIVE**
## Deep-fried Crab Wontons

INGREDIENTS **Makes 24–30**

2 tbsp sesame oil
6–8 water chestnuts, rinsed, drained and chopped
2 spring onions, peeled and finely chopped
1 cm/½ inch piece fresh root ginger, peeled and grated
185 g can white crabmeat, drained
50 ml/2 fl oz soy sauce
2 tbsp rice wine vinegar
½ tsp dried, crushed chillies
2 tsp sugar
½ tsp hot pepper sauce, or to taste
1 tbsp freshly chopped coriander or dill
1 large egg yolk
1 packet wonton skins
vegetable oil for deep-frying
lime wedges, to garnish
dipping sauce, to serve (see Crispy Prawns with Chinese Dipping Sauce, page 139)

Heat a wok or large frying pan, add 1 tablespoon of the sesame oil and when hot, add the water chestnuts, spring onions and ginger and stir-fry for 1 minute. Remove from the heat and leave to cool slightly.

In a bowl, mix the crabmeat with the soy sauce, rice wine vinegar, crushed chillies, sugar, hot pepper sauce, chopped coriander or dill and the egg yolk. Stir in the cooled stir-fried mixture until well blended.

Lay the wonton skins on a work surface and place 1 teaspoonful of the crab mixture on the centre of each. Brush the edges of each wonton skin with a little water and fold up one corner to the opposite corner to form a triangle. Press to seal. Bring the two corners of the triangle together to meet in the centre, brush one with a little water and overlap them, pressing to seal and form a 'tortellini' shape. Place on a baking sheet and continue with the remaining triangles.

Pour enough oil into a large wok to come 5 cm/2 inches up the sides and place over a high heat. Working in batches of five or six, fry the wontons for 3 minutes or until crisp and golden, turning once or twice.

Carefully remove the wontons with a slotted spoon, drain on absorbent kitchen paper and keep warm. Place on individual warmed serving plates, garnish each dish with a lime wedge and serve immediately with the dipping sauce.

**VEGETARIAN ALTERNATIVE**
## Savoury Wontons

INGREDIENTS **Makes 15**

125 g/4 oz filo pastry or wonton skins
15 whole chive leaves
225 g/8 oz spinach
25 g/1 oz butter
½ tsp salt
225 g/8 oz mushrooms, wiped and roughly chopped
1 garlic clove, peeled and crushed
1–2 tbsp dark soy sauce
2.5 cm/1 inch piece fresh root ginger, peeled and grated
salt and freshly ground black pepper
1 small egg, beaten
300 ml/½ pint groundnut oil for deep-frying

**To garnish:**
spring onion curls
radish roses

Cut the filo pastry or wonton skins into 12.5 cm/5 inch squares, stack and cover with clingfilm. Chill in the refrigerator while preparing the filling. Blanch the chive leaves in boiling water for 1 minute, drain and reserve.

Melt the butter in a saucepan, add the spinach and salt and cook for 2–3 minutes or until wilted. Add the mushrooms and garlic and cook for 2–3 minutes or until tender. Transfer the spinach and mushroom mixture to a bowl. Stir in the soy sauce and ginger. Season to taste with salt and pepper.

Place a small spoonful of the spinach and mushroom mixture on to a pastry or wonton square and brush the edges with beaten egg. Gather up the four corners to make a little bag and tie with a chive leaf. Make up the remainder of the wontons.

Heat a wok, add the oil and heat to 180°C/350°F. Deep-fry the wontons in batches for 2–3 minutes, or until golden and crisp. Drain on absorbent kitchen paper and serve immediately, garnished with spring onion curls and radish roses.

# Dim Sum Pork Parcels

INGREDIENTS **Makes about 40**

125 g/4 oz canned water chestnuts, drained and finely chopped
125 g/4 oz raw prawns, peeled, de-veined and coarsely chopped
350 g/12 oz fresh pork mince
2 tbsp smoked bacon, finely chopped
1 tbsp light soy sauce, plus extra to serve
1 tsp dark soy sauce
1 tbsp Chinese rice wine
2 tbsp fresh root ginger, peeled and finely chopped
3 spring onions, trimmed and finely chopped
2 tsp sesame oil
1 medium egg white, lightly beaten
salt and freshly ground black pepper
2 tsp sugar
40 wonton skins, thawed if frozen
toasted sesame seeds, to garnish
soy sauce, to serve

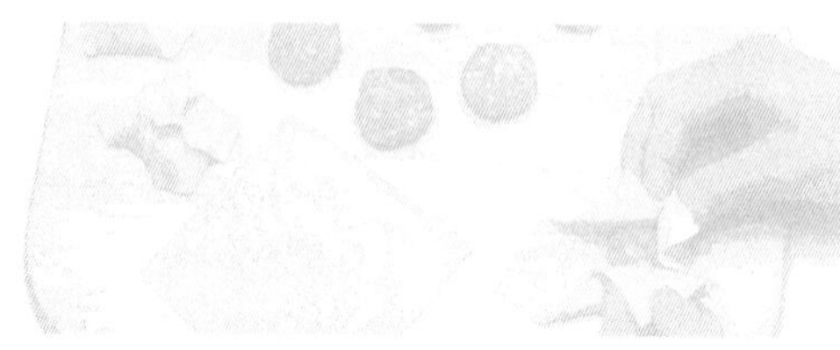

Place the water chestnuts, prawns, pork mince and bacon in a bowl and mix together. Add the soy sauces, Chinese rice wine, ginger, chopped spring onion, sesame oil and egg white. Season to taste with salt and pepper, sprinkle in the sugar and mix the filling thoroughly.

Place a spoonful of filling in the centre of a wonton skin. Bring the sides up and press around the filling to make a basket shape. Flatten the base of the skin, so the wonton stands solid. The top should be wide open, exposing the filling.

Place the parcels on a heatproof plate, either on a wire rack inside a wok or on the base of a muslin-lined bamboo steamer placed over a wok. Half-fill the wok with boiling water, cover, then steam the parcels for about 20 minutes. Do this in two batches. Transfer to a warmed serving plate, sprinkle with toasted sesame seeds, drizzle with soy sauce and serve immediately.

HEALTH RATING

**VEGETARIAN ALTERNATIVE**
Olive & Feta Parcels

**VEGETARIAN ALTERNATIVE**
Mozzarella Parcels with Cranberry Relish

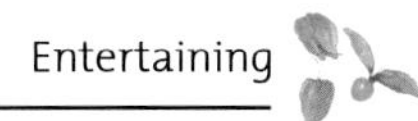

**VEGETARIAN ALTERNATIVE**
## Olive & Feta Parcels

INGREDIENTS **Makes 30**

1 small red pepper
1 small yellow pepper
125 g/4 oz assorted marinated green and black olives
125 g/4 oz feta cheese
2 tbsp pine nuts, lightly toasted
6 sheets filo pastry
3 tbsp olive oil
sour cream and chive dip, to serve

Preheat the oven to 180°C/350°F/Gas Mark 4. Preheat the grill, then line the grill rack with tinfoil.

Cut the peppers into quarters and remove the seeds. Place skin-side up on the foil-lined grill rack and cook under the preheated grill for 10 minutes, turning occasionally until the skins begin to blacken.

Place the peppers in a polythene bag and leave until cool enough to handle, then skin and thinly slice.

Chop the olives and cut the feta cheese into small cubes. Mix together the olives, feta, sliced peppers and pine nuts.

Cut a sheet of filo pastry in half then brush with a little of the oil. Place a spoonful of the olive and feta mix about one -third of the way up the pastry.

Fold over the pastry and wrap to form a square parcel encasing the filling completely.

Place this parcel in the centre of the second half of the pastry sheet. Brush the edges lightly with a little oil, bring up the corners to meet in the centre and twist them loosely to form a purse. Brush with a little more oil and repeat with the remaining filo pastry and filling.

Place the parcels on a lightly oiled baking sheet and bake in the preheated oven for 10–15 minutes, or until crisp and golden brown. Serve with the dip.

**VEGETARIAN ALTERNATIVE**
## Mozzarella Parcels with Cranberry Relish

INGREDIENTS **Serves 4**

125 g/4 oz mozzarella cheese
8 slices of thin white bread
2 medium eggs, beaten
salt and freshly ground black pepper
300 ml/½ pint olive oil

**For the relish:**

125 g/4 oz cranberries
2 tbsp fresh orange juice
grated rind of 1 small orange
50 g/2 oz soft light brown sugar
1 tbsp port

Slice the mozzarella thinly, remove the crusts from the bread and make sandwiches with the bread and cheese. Cut into 5 cm/2 inch squares and squash them quite flat. Season the eggs with salt and pepper, then soak the bread in the seasoned egg for 1 minute on each side until well coated.

Heat the oil in a wok or deep fryer to 190°C/375°F and deep-fry the bread squares for 1–2 minutes, or until crisp and golden brown. Drain on absorbent kitchen paper and keep warm while the cranberry relish is prepared.

Place the cranberries, orange juice, rind, sugar and port into a small saucepan and add 5 tablespoons of water. Bring to the boil, then simmer for 10 minutes until the cranberries have 'popped'. Sweeten with a little more sugar if necessary. Arrange the mozzarella parcels on individual serving plates and serve with a little of the cranberry relish.

# Mixed Satay Sticks

INGREDIENTS **Serves 4**

12 large raw prawns
350 g/12 oz beef rump steak
1 tbsp lemon juice
1 garlic clove, peeled and crushed
salt
2 tsp soft dark brown sugar
1 tsp ground cumin
1 tsp ground coriander
¼ tsp ground turmeric
1 tbsp groundnut oil
fresh coriander leaves, to garnish

**For the spicy peanut sauce:**

1 shallot, peeled and very finely chopped
1 tsp demerara sugar
50 g/2 oz creamed coconut, chopped
pinch of chilli powder
1 tbsp dark soy sauce
125 g/4 oz crunchy peanut butter

Preheat the grill on high just before required. Soak eight bamboo skewers in cold water for at least 30 minutes. Peel the prawns, leaving the tails on. Using a sharp knife, remove the black vein along the back of the prawns. Cut the beef into 1 cm/½ inch wide strips. Place the prawns and beef in separate bowls and sprinkle each with ½ tablespoon of the lemon juice.

Mix together the garlic, pinch of salt, sugar, cumin, coriander, turmeric and groundnut oil to make a paste. Lightly brush over the prawns and beef. Cover and place in the refrigerator to marinate for at least 30 minutes, but for longer if possible.

Meanwhile, make the sauce. Pour 125 ml/4 fl oz of water into a small saucepan, add the shallot and sugar and heat gently until the sugar has dissolved. Stir in the creamed coconut and chilli powder. When melted, remove from the heat and stir in the peanut butter. Leave to cool slightly, then spoon into a serving dish.

Thread three prawns each on to four skewers and divide the sliced beef between the remaining skewers. Cook the skewers under the preheated grill for 4–5 minutes, turning occasionally. The prawns should be opaque and pink and the beef browned on the outside, but still pink in the centre. Transfer to warmed individual serving plates, garnish with a few fresh coriander leaves and serve immediately with the warm peanut sauce.

HEALTH RATING

**SPEEDY ALTERNATIVE**

Mixed Canapés

**VEGETARIAN ALTERNATIVE**

Sweet Potato Crisps with Mango Salsa

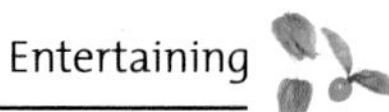

**SPEEDY ALTERNATIVE**
## Mixed Canapés

For the cheese canapés, cut the crusts off the bread, then gently roll with a rolling pin to flatten slightly. Spread thinly with butter, then sprinkle over the mixed cheeses as evenly as possible.

Roll up each slice tightly, then cut into four slices, each about 2.5 cm/1 inch long. Heat the oil in a wok or large frying pan and stir-fry the cheese rolls in two batches, turning them all the time until golden brown and crisp. Drain on absorbent kitchen paper and serve warm or cold.

For the spicy nuts, melt the butter and oil in a wok, then add the nuts and stir-fry over a low heat for about 5 minutes, stirring all the time, or until they begin to colour.

Sprinkle the paprika and cumin over the nuts and continue stir-frying for a further 1–2 minutes, or until the nuts are golden brown.

Remove from the wok and drain on absorbent kitchen paper. Sprinkle with the salt, garnish with sprigs of fresh coriander and serve hot or cold. If serving cold, store both the cheese canapés and the spicy nuts in airtight containers.

INGREDIENTS **Serves 6**

**For the stir-fried cheese canapés:**

6 thick slices white bread
40 g/1½ oz butter, softened
75 g/3 oz mature Cheddar cheese, grated
75 g/3 oz blue cheese such as Stilton or Gorgonzola, crumbled
3 tbsp sunflower oil

**For the spicy nuts:**

25 g/1 oz unsalted butter
2 tbsp light olive oil
450 g/1 lb mixed unsalted nuts
1 tsp ground paprika
½ tsp ground cumin
½ tsp fine sea salt
sprigs of fresh coriander, to garnish

**VEGETARIAN ALTERNATIVE**
## Sweet Potato Crisps with Mango Salsa

To make the salsa, mix the mango with the tomatoes, cucumber and onion. Add the sugar, chilli, vinegar, oil and the lime rind and juice. Mix together thoroughly, cover and leave for 45–50 minutes.

Soak the potatoes in cold water for 40 minutes to remove as much of the excess starch as possible. Drain and dry thoroughly in a clean tea towel, or absorbent kitchen paper.

Heat the oil to 190°C/375°F in a deep fryer. When at the correct temperature, place half the potatoes in the frying basket, then carefully lower the potatoes into the hot oil and cook for 4–5 minutes or until they are golden brown, shaking the basket every minute so that they do not stick together.

Drain the potato crisps on absorbent kitchen paper, sprinkle with sea salt and place under a preheated moderate grill for a few seconds to dry out. Repeat with the remaining potatoes. Stir the mint into the salsa and serve with the potato crisps.

INGREDIENTS **Serves 6**

**For the salsa:**

1 large mango, peeled, stoned and cut into small cubes
8 cherry tomatoes, quartered
½ cucumber, peeled if preferred and finely diced
1 red onion, peeled and finely chopped
pinch of sugar
1 red chilli, deseeded and finely chopped
2 tbsp rice vinegar
2 tbsp olive oil
grated rind and juice of 1 lime

**For the sweet potato crisps:**

450 g/1 lb sweet potatoes, peeled and thinly sliced
vegetable oil, for deep-frying
sea salt
2 tbsp freshly chopped mint

**SPEEDY ALTERNATIVE**

## Pasta Triangles with Pesto & Walnut Dressing

INGREDIENTS **Serves 6**

450 g/1 lb fresh egg lasagne
4 tbsp ricotta cheese
4 tbsp pesto
125 g/4 oz walnuts
1 slice white bread, crusts removed
150 ml/¼ pint soured cream
75 g/3 oz mascarpone cheese
25 g/1 oz pecorino cheese, grated
salt and freshly ground black pepper
1 tbsp olive oil
sprig of dill or freshly chopped basil or parsley, to garnish
tomato and cucumber salad, to serve

Preheat the grill to high. Cut the lasagne sheets in half, then into triangles and reserve. Mix the pesto and ricotta cheese together and warm gently in a pan. Toast the walnuts under the preheated grill until golden. Rub off the papery skins, then place the nuts in a food processor with the bread and grind finely.

Mix the soured cream with the mascarpone cheese in a bowl. Add the ground walnuts and grated pecorino cheese and season to taste with salt and pepper. Whisk in the olive oil, then pour into a pan and warm gently.

Bring a large pan of lightly salted water to a rolling boil. Add the pasta triangles and cook according to the packet instructions, or for about 3–4 minutes until 'al dente'.

Drain the pasta thoroughly and arrange a few triangles on each serving plate. Top each one with a spoonful of the pesto mixture then place another triangle on top. Continue to layer the pasta and pesto mixture, then spoon a little of the walnut sauce on top of each stack. Garnish with dill, basil or parsley and serve immediately with a freshly dressed tomato and cucumber salad.

**ORIENTAL ALTERNATIVE**

## Thai Stuffed Eggs with Spinach & Sesame Seeds

INGREDIENTS **Makes 8**

4 large eggs
salt and freshly ground black pepper
225 g/8 oz baby spinach
2 garlic cloves, peeled and crushed
1 tbsp spring onions, trimmed and finely chopped
1 tbsp sesame seeds
75 g/3 oz plain flour
1 tbsp light olive oil
300 ml/½ pint vegetable oil for frying

**To garnish:**

sliced red chilli
snipped fresh chives

Bring a small saucepan of water to the boil, add the eggs, bring back to the boil and cook for 6–7 minutes. Plunge into cold water, then shell and cut in half lengthways. Using a teaspoon, remove the yolks and place in a bowl. Reserve the whites.

Place 1 teaspoon of water and ½ teaspoon of salt in a saucepan, add the spinach and cook until tender and wilted. Drain, squeeze out the excess moisture and chop. Mix with the egg yolk, then stir in the garlic, spring onions and sesame seeds. Season to taste with salt and pepper. Fill the egg shells with the mixture, smoothing into a mound.

Place the flour in a bowl with the olive oil, a large pinch of salt and 125 ml/4 fl oz warm water. Beat together to make a completely smooth batter.

Heat a wok, add the vegetable oil and heat to 180°C/350°F. Dip the stuffed eggs in the batter, allowing any excess batter to drip back into the bowl, and deep-fry in batches for 3–4 minutes or until golden brown. Place the eggs in the wok filled-side down first, then turn over to finish cooking. Remove from the wok with a slotted spoon and drain on absorbent kitchen paper. Serve hot or cold garnished with snipped chives and chilli rings.

# Wild Rice Dolmades

INGREDIENTS **Serves 4–6**

6 tbsp olive oil
25 g/1 oz pine nuts
175 g/6 oz mushrooms, wiped and finely chopped
4 spring onions, trimmed and finely chopped
1 garlic clove, peeled and crushed
50 g/2 oz cooked wild rice
2 tsp freshly chopped dill
2 tsp freshly chopped mint
salt and freshly ground black pepper
16–24 prepared medium vine leaves
about 300 ml/½ pint vegetable stock

**To garnish:**
lemon wedges
sprigs of fresh dill

Heat 1 tbsp of the oil in a frying pan and gently cook the pine nuts for 2–3 minutes, stirring frequently, until golden. Remove from the pan and reserve.

Add 1½ tablespoons of oil to the pan and gently cook the mushrooms, spring onions and garlic for 7–8 minutes until very soft. Stir in the rice, herbs, salt and pepper.

Put a heaped teaspoon of stuffing in the centre of each leaf (if the leaves are small, put two together, overlapping slightly). Fold over the stalk end, then the sides and roll up to make a neat parcel. Continue until all the stuffing is used.

Arrange the stuffed vine leaves close together seam-side down in a large saucepan, drizzling each with a little of the remaining oil – there will be several layers. Pour over just enough stock to cover.

Put an inverted plate over the dolmades to stop them unrolling during cooking. Bring to the boil, then simmer very gently for 3 minutes. Cool in the saucepan.

Transfer the dolmades to a serving dish. Cover and chill in the refrigerator before serving. Sprinkle with the pine nuts and garnish with lemon and dill. Serve.

HEALTH RATING ●●●

**SPEEDY ALTERNATIVE**
Pasta Triangles with Pesto & Walnut Dressing

**ORIENTAL ALTERNATIVE**
Thai Stuffed Eggs with Spinach & Sesame Seeds

# Potato Pancakes with Smoked Salmon

INGREDIENTS **Serves 4**

450 g/1 lb floury potatoes, peeled and quartered
salt and freshly ground black pepper
1 large egg
1 large egg yolk
25 g/1 oz butter
25 g/1 oz plain flour
150 ml/¼ pint double cream
2 tbsp freshly chopped parsley
5 tbsp crème fraîche
1 tbsp horseradish sauce
225 g/8 oz smoked salmon, sliced
salad leaves, to serve

**To garnish:**
lemon slices
snipped chives

Cook the potatoes in a saucepan of lightly salted boiling water for 15–20 minutes, or until tender. Drain thoroughly, then mash until free of lumps. Beat in the whole egg and egg yolk together with the butter and beat until smooth and creamy. Slowly beat in the flour and cream, then season to taste with salt and pepper. Stir in the chopped parsley.

Beat the crème fraîche and horseradish sauce together in a small bowl, cover with cling-film and reserve.

Heat a lightly oiled, heavy-based frying pan over a medium-high heat. Place a few spoonfuls of the potato mixture in the hot pan and cook for 4–5 minutes or until cooked and golden, turning halfway through cooking time. Remove from the pan, drain on absorbent kitchen paper and keep warm. Repeat with the remaining mixture.

Arrange the pancakes on individual serving plates. Place the smoked salmon on the pancakes and spoon over a little of the horseradish sauce. Serve with salad and the remaining horseradish sauce and garnish with lemon slices and chives.

HEALTH RATING

**LOW FAT ALTERNATIVE**
Smoked Salmon Sushi

**ORIENTAL ALTERNATIVE**
Rice with Smoked Salmon & Ginger

## LOW FAT ALTERNATIVE
## Smoked Salmon Sushi

INGREDIENTS **Serves 4**

175 g/6 oz sushi rice
2 tbsp rice vinegar
4 tsp caster sugar
½ tsp salt
2 sheets sushi nori
60 g/2½ oz smoked salmon
¼ cucumber, cut into fine strips

**To serve:**
wasabi
soy sauce
pickled ginger

Rinse the rice thoroughly in cold water until the water runs clear, then place in a pan with 300 ml/½ pint of water. Bring to the boil and cover with a tight fitting lid. Reduce to a simmer and cook gently for 10 minutes. Turn the heat off, but keep the pan covered to allow the rice to steam for a further 10 minutes.

In a small saucepan, gently heat the rice vinegar, sugar and salt until the sugar has dissolved. When the rice has finished steaming, pour over the vinegar mixture and stir well to mix. Empty the rice out on to a large flat surface – a chopping board or large plate is ideal. Fan the rice to cool and to produce a shinier rice.

Lay one sheet of sushi nori on a sushi mat (if you do not have a sushi mat, improvise with a stiff piece of fabric that is a little larger than the sushi nori) and spread with half the cooled rice. Dampen your hands while doing this – it will help to prevent the rice from sticking to your hands. On the nearest edge place half the salmon and half the cucumber strips.

Roll up the rice and smoked salmon into a tight Swiss roll-like shape. Dampen the blade of a sharp knife and cut the sushi into slices about 2 cm/¾ inch thick. Repeat with the remaining sushi nori, rice, smoked salmon and cucumber. Serve with a little wasabi, soy sauce and pickled ginger.

## ORIENTAL ALTERNATIVE
## Rice with Smoked Salmon & Ginger

INGREDIENTS **Serves 4**

225 g/8 oz basmati rice
600 ml/1 pint fish stock
1 bunch spring onions, trimmed and diagonally sliced
3 tbsp freshly chopped coriander
1 tsp grated fresh root ginger
200 g/7 oz sliced smoked salmon
2 tbsp soy sauce
1 tsp sesame oil
2 tsp lemon juice
4–6 slices pickled ginger
2 tsp sesame seeds
rocket leaves, to serve

Place the rice in a sieve and rinse under cold water until the water runs clear. Drain, then place in a large saucepan with the stock and bring gently to the boil. Reduce to a simmer and cover with a tight fitting lid. Cook for 10 minutes, then remove from the heat and leave, covered, for a further 10 minutes.

Stir the spring onions, coriander and fresh ginger into the cooked rice and mix well.

Spoon the rice into four tartlet tins, each measuring 10 cm/4 inches, and press down firmly with the back of a spoon to form cakes. Invert a tin onto an individual serving plate, then tap the base firmly and remove the tin. Repeat with the rest of the filled tins.

Top the rice with the salmon, folding if necessary, so the sides of the rice can still be seen in places. Mix together the soy sauce, sesame oil and lemon juice to make a dressing, then drizzle over the salmon.

Top with the pickled ginger and a sprinkling of sesame seeds. Scatter the rocket leaves around the edge of the plates and serve immediately.

# Warm Lobster Salad with Hot Thai Dressing

INGREDIENTS **Serves 4**

1 orange
50 g/2 oz granulated sugar
2 cos lettuce hearts, shredded
1 small avocado, peeled and thinly sliced
½ cucumber, peeled, deseeded and thinly sliced
1 ripe mango, peeled, stoned and thinly sliced
1 tbsp butter or vegetable oil
1 large lobster, meat removed and cut into bite-sized pieces
2 tbsp Thai or Italian basil leaves
4 large cooked prawns, peeled with tails left on, to garnish

**For the dressing:**

1 tbsp vegetable oil
4–6 spring onions, trimmed and sliced diagonally into 5 cm/2 inch pieces
2.5 cm/1 inch piece fresh root ginger, peeled and grated
1 garlic clove, peeled and crushed
grated zest of 1 lime
juice of 2–3 small limes
2 tbsp Thai fish sauce
1 tbsp brown sugar
1–2 tsp sweet chilli sauce, or to taste
1 tbsp sesame oil

With a sharp knife, cut the orange rind into thin julienne strips, then cook in boiling water for 2 minutes.

Drain the orange strips, then plunge into cold running water, drain and return to the saucepan with the sugar and 1 cm/ ½ inch of water. Simmer until soft, then add 1 tablespoon of cold water to stop cooking. Remove from the heat and reserve.

Arrange the lettuce on four large plates and arrange the avocado, cucumber and mango slices over the lettuce.

Heat a wok or large frying pan, add the butter or oil and when hot, but not sizzling, add the lobster and stir-fry for 1–2 minutes or until heated through. Remove and drain on absorbent kitchen paper.

To make the dressing, heat the vegetable oil in a wok, then add the spring onions, ginger and garlic and stir-fry for 1 minute. Add the lime zest, lime juice, fish sauce, sugar and chilli sauce. Stir until the sugar dissolves. Remove from the heat, add the sesame oil with the orange rind and liquor.

Arrange the lobster meat over the salad and drizzle with dressing. Sprinkle with basil leaves, garnish with prawns and serve immediately.

HEALTH RATING ●●●

**SPEEDY ALTERNATIVE**

Hot Tiger Prawns with Parma Ham

**ORIENTAL ALTERNATIVE**

Thai Green Fragrant Mussels

**SPEEDY ALTERNATIVE**

## Hot Tiger Prawns with Parma Ham

INGREDIENTS **Serves 4**

½ cucumber, peeled if preferred
4 ripe tomatoes
12 raw tiger prawns
6 tbsp olive oil
4 garlic cloves, peeled and crushed
4 tbsp freshly chopped parsley
salt and freshly ground black pepper
6 slices of Parma ham, cut in half
4 slices flat Italian bread
4 tbsp dry white wine

Preheat the oven to 180°C/350°F/Gas Mark 4. Slice the cucumber and tomatoes thinly, then arrange on four large plates and reserve. Peel the prawns, leaving the tail shell intact and remove the thin black vein running down the back.

Whisk together 4 tablespoons of the olive oil, garlic and chopped parsley in a small bowl and season to taste with plenty of salt and pepper. Add the prawns to the mixture and stir until they are well coated. Remove the prawns, then wrap each one in a piece of Parma ham and secure with a cocktail stick.

Place the prepared prawns on a lightly oiled baking sheet or dish with the slices of bread and cook in the preheated oven for 5 minutes.

Remove the prawns from the oven and spoon the wine over the prawns and bread. Return to the oven and cook for a further 10 minutes until piping hot.

Carefully remove the cocktail sticks and arrange three prawn rolls on each slice of bread. Place on top of the sliced cucumber and tomatoes and serve immediately.

**ORIENTAL ALTERNATIVE**

## Thai Green Fragrant Mussels

INGREDIENTS **Serves 4**

2 kg/4½ lb fresh mussels
4 tbsp olive oil
2 garlic cloves, peeled and finely sliced
3 tbsp fresh root ginger, peeled and finely sliced
3 lemon grass stalks, outer leaves discarded and finely sliced
1–3 red or green chillies, deseeded and chopped
1 green pepper, deseeded and diced
5 spring onions, trimmed and finely sliced
3 tbsp freshly chopped coriander
1 tbsp sesame oil
juice of 3 limes
400 ml can coconut milk
warm crusty bread, to serve

Scrub the mussels under cold running water, removing any barnacles and beards. Discard any that have broken or damaged shells or are opened and do not close when tapped gently.

Heat a wok or large frying pan, add the oil and when hot, add the mussels. Shake gently and cook for 1 minute, then add the garlic, ginger, sliced lemon grass, chillies, green pepper, spring onions, 2 tablespoons of the chopped coriander and the sesame oil.

Stir-fry over a medium heat for 3–4 minutes, or until the mussels are cooked and have opened. Discard any mussels that remain unopened.

Pour the lime juice with the coconut milk into the wok and bring to the boil. Tip the mussels and the cooking liquor into warmed individual bowls. Sprinkle with the remaining chopped coriander and serve immediately with warm crusty bread.

# Scallop & Potato Gratin

INGREDIENTS **Serves 4**

8 fresh scallops in their shells, cleaned
4 tbsp white wine
salt and freshly ground black pepper
50 g/2 oz butter
3 tbsp plain flour
2 tbsp single cream
50 g/2 oz Cheddar cheese, grated
450 g/1 lb potatoes, peeled and cut into chunks
1 tbsp milk

Preheat the oven to 220°C/425°F/Gas Mark 7. Clean four scallop shells to use as serving dishes and reserve. Place the scallops in a small saucepan with the wine, 150 ml/ ¼ pint water and salt and pepper. Cover and simmer very gently for 5 minutes, or until just tender. Remove with a slotted spoon and cut each scallop into three pieces. Reserve the cooking juices.

Melt 25 g/1 oz of the butter in a saucepan, stir in the flour and cook for 1 minute, stirring, then gradually whisk in the reserved cooking juices. Simmer, stirring, for 3–4 minutes until the sauce has thickened. Season to taste with salt and pepper. Remove from the heat and stir in the cream and 25 g/1 oz of the grated cheese. Fold in the scallops.

Boil the potatoes in lightly salted water until tender, then mash with the remaining butter and milk. Spoon or pipe the mashed potato around the edges of the cleaned scallop shells.

Divide the scallop mixture between the four shells, placing the mixture neatly in the centre. Sprinkle with the remaining grated cheese and bake in the preheated oven for about 10–15 minutes until golden brown and bubbling. Serve immediately.

## HEALTH RATING

**ORIENTAL ALTERNATIVE**

Scallops & Prawns Braised in Lemon Grass

**LOW FAT ALTERNATIVE**

Curly Endive & Seafood Salad

## ORIENTAL ALTERNATIVE
## Scallops & Prawns Braised in Lemon Grass

INGREDIENTS **Serves 4–6**

- 450 g/1 lb large raw prawns, peeled with tails left on
- 350 g/12 oz scallops, with coral attached
- 2 red chillies, deseeded and coarsely chopped
- 2 garlic cloves, peeled and coarsely chopped
- 4 shallots, peeled
- 1 tbsp shrimp paste
- 2 tbsp freshly chopped coriander
- 400 ml can of coconut milk
- 2–3 lemon grass stalks, outer leaves discarded and bruised
- 2 tbsp Thai fish sauce
- 1 tbsp sugar
- freshly steamed basmati rice, to serve

Rinse the prawns and scallops and pat dry with absorbent kitchen paper. Using a sharp knife, remove the black vein along the back of the prawns. Reserve.

Place the chillies, garlic, shallots, shrimp paste and 1 tablespoon of the chopped coriander in a food processor. Add 1 tablespoon of the coconut milk and 2 tablespoons of water and blend to form a thick paste. Reserve the chilli paste.

Pour the remaining coconut milk with 3 tablespoons of water into a large wok or frying pan, add the lemon grass and bring to the boil. Simmer over a medium heat for 10 minutes or until reduced slightly.

Stir the chilli paste, fish sauce and sugar into the coconut milk and continue to simmer for 2 minutes, stirring occasionally. Add the prepared prawns and scallops and simmer gently for 3 minutes, stirring occasionally, or until cooked and the prawns are pink and the scallops are opaque.

Remove the lemon grass and stir in the remaining chopped coriander. Serve immediately spooned over freshly steamed basmati rice.

## LOW FAT ALTERNATIVE
## Curly Endive & Seafood Salad

INGREDIENTS **Serves 4**

- 1 head of curly endive lettuce
- 2 green peppers
- 12.5 cm/5 inch piece of cucumber
- 125 g/4 oz squid, cleaned and cut into thin rings
- 225 g/8 oz baby asparagus spears
- 125 g/4 oz smoked salmon slices, cut into wide strips
- 175 g/6 oz freshly cooked mussels in their shells

**For the lemon dressing:**

- 2 tbsp sunflower oil
- 1 tbsp white wine vinegar
- 5 tbsp fresh lemon juice
- 1–2 tsp caster sugar
- 1 tsp mild wholegrain mustard
- salt and freshly ground black pepper

**To garnish:**

- slices of lemon
- sprigs of fresh coriander

Rinse and tear the endive into small pieces and arrange on a serving platter.

Remove the seeds from the peppers and cut the peppers and the cucumber into small cubes. Sprinkle over the endive.

Bring a saucepan of water to the boil and add the squid rings. Bring the pan up to the boil again, then switch off the heat and leave it to stand for 5 minutes. Then drain and rinse thoroughly in cold water.

Cook the asparagus in boiling water for 5 minutes or until tender but still crisp. Arrange with the squid, smoked salmon and mussels on top of the salad.

To make the lemon dressing, put all the ingredients into a screw-topped jar or into a small bowl and mix thoroughly until combined.

Spoon 3 tablespoons of the dressing over the salad and serve the remainder in a small jug.

Garnish the salad with slices of lemon and sprigs of coriander and serve.

**LOW FAT ALTERNATIVE**
## Creamy Salmon with Dill in Filo Baskets

INGREDIENTS **Serves 4**

1 bay leaf
6 black peppercorns
1 large sprig of fresh parsley
175 g/6 oz salmon fillet
4 large sheets filo pastry
fine spray of oil
125 g/4 oz baby spinach leaves
8 tbsp low-fat fromage frais
2 tsp Dijon mustard
2 tbsp freshly chopped dill
salt and freshly ground black pepper

Preheat the oven to 200°C/400°F/Gas Mark 6. Place the bay leaf, peppercorns, parsley and salmon in a frying pan and add enough water to barely cover the fish.

Bring to the boil, reduce the heat and poach the fish for 5 minutes until it flakes easily. Remove it from the pan. Reserve.

Spray each sheet of filo pastry lightly with the oil. Scrunch up the pastry to make a nest shape approximately 12.5 cm/5 inches in diameter.

Place on a lightly oiled baking sheet and cook in the preheated oven for 10 minutes until golden and crisp.

Blanch the spinach in a pan of lightly salted boiling water for 2 minutes. Drain thoroughly and keep warm.

Mix the fromage frais, mustard and dill together, then warm gently. Season to taste with salt and pepper. Divide the spinach between the filo pastry nests and flake the salmon on to the spinach. Spoon the mustard and dill sauce over the filo baskets and serve immediately.

**SPEEDY ALTERNATIVE**
## Salmon with Herbed Potatoes

INGREDIENTS **Serves 4**

450 g/1 lb baby new potatoes
salt and freshly ground black pepper
4 salmon steaks, each weighing about 175 g/6 oz
1 carrot, peeled and cut into fine strips
175 g/6 oz asparagus spears, trimmed
175 g/6 oz sugar snap peas, trimmed
finely grated rind and juice of 1 lemon
25 g/1 oz butter
4 large sprigs of fresh parsley

Preheat the oven to 190°C/375°F/Gas Mark 5, about 10 minutes before required. Parboil the potatoes in lightly salted boiling water for 5–8 minutes until they are barely tender. Drain and reserve.

Cut out four pieces of baking parchment paper, measuring 20.5 cm/8 inches square, and place on the work surface. Arrange the parboiled potatoes on top. Wipe the salmon steaks and place on top of the potatoes.

Place the carrot strips in a bowl with the asparagus spears, sugar snaps and grated lemon rind and juice. Season to taste with salt and pepper. Toss lightly together. Divide the vegetables evenly between the salmon. Dot the top of each parcel with butter and a sprig of parsley.

To wrap a parcel, lift up two opposite sides of the paper and fold the edges together. Twist the paper at the other two ends to seal the parcel well. Repeat with the remaining parcels.

Place the parcels on a baking tray and bake in the preheated oven for 15 minutes. Place an unopened parcel on each plate and open just before eating.

# Salmon & Filo Parcels

INGREDIENTS **Serves 4**

1 tbsp sunflower oil
1 bunch of spring onions, trimmed and finely chopped
1 tsp paprika
175 g/6 oz long-grain white rice
300 ml/½ pint fish stock
salt and freshly ground black pepper
450 g/1 lb salmon fillet, cubed
1 tbsp freshly chopped parsley
grated rind and juice of 1 lemon
150 g/5 oz rocket
150 g/5 oz spinach
12 sheets filo pastry
50 g/2 oz butter, melted

Preheat the oven to 200°C/400°F/Gas Mark 6. Heat the oil in a small frying pan and gently cook the spring onions for 2 minutes. Stir in the paprika and continue to cook for 1 minute, then remove from the heat and reserve.

Put the rice in a sieve, rinse under cold running water until the water runs clear and drain. Put the rice and stock in a saucepan, bring to the boil, then cover and simmer for 10 minutes, or until the liquid is absorbed and the rice is tender. Add the spring onion mixture and fork through. Season to taste with salt and pepper, then leave to cool.

In a non-metallic bowl, mix together the salmon, parsley, lemon rind and juice and salt and pepper. Mix well and reserve. Blanch the rocket and spinach for 30 seconds in a large saucepan of boiling water until just wilted. Drain well in a colander and refresh in plenty of cold water, then squeeze out as much moisture as possible.

Brush three sheets of filo pastry with melted butter and lay them on top of one another. Take a quarter of the rice mixture and arrange it in an oblong in the centre of the pastry. On top of this place a quarter of the salmon followed by a quarter of the rocket and spinach. Draw up the pastry around the filling and twist at the top to create a parcel. Repeat with the remaining pastry and filling until you have four parcels. Brush with the remaining butter. Place the parcels on a lightly oiled baking tray and cook in the preheated oven for 20 minutes, or until golden brown and cooked. Serve immediately.

HEALTH RATING

**LOW FAT ALTERNATIVE**
Creamy Salmon with Dill in Filo Baskets

**SPEEDY ALTERNATIVE**
Salmon with Herbed Potatoes

# Potato-stuffed Roast Poussin

INGREDIENTS **Serves 4**

4 oven-ready poussins
salt and freshly ground black pepper
1 lemon, cut into quarters
450 g/1 lb floury potatoes, peeled and cut into 4 cm/1½ inch pieces
1 tbsp freshly chopped thyme or rosemary
3–4 tbsp olive oil
4 garlic cloves, unpeeled and lightly smashed
8 slices streaky bacon or Parma ham
125 ml/4 fl oz white wine
2 spring onions, trimmed and thinly sliced
2 tbsp double cream or crème fraîche
lemon wedges, to garnish

Preheat the oven to 220°C/425°F/Gas Mark 7. Place a roasting tin in the oven to heat. Rinse the poussin cavities and pat dry with absorbent kitchen paper. Season the cavities with salt and pepper and a squeeze of lemon, and push a lemon quarter into each cavity.

Put the potatoes in a saucepan of lightly salted water and bring to the boil. Reduce the heat to low and simmer until just tender; do not overcook. Drain and cool slightly. Sprinkle the chopped herbs over the potatoes and drizzle with 2–3 tablespoons of the oil.

Spoon half the seasoned potatoes into the poussin cavities; do not pack too tightly. Rub each poussin with a little more oil and season with pepper. Carefully spoon 1 tablespoon of oil into the hot roasting tin and arrange the poussins in the tin. Spoon the remaining potatoes around the edge and sprinkle over the garlic.

Roast the poussins in the preheated oven for 30 minutes, or until the skin is golden and beginning to crisp. Carefully lay the bacon slices over the breast of each poussin and continue to roast for 15–20 minutes until crisp and the poussins are cooked through.

Transfer the poussins and potatoes to a serving platter and cover loosely with tinfoil. Skim off the fat from the juices. Place the tin over a medium heat and add the wine and spring onions. Cook briefly, scraping the bits from the bottom of the tin. Whisk in the cream or crème fraîche and bubble for 1 minute, or until thickened. Garnish the poussins with lemon wedges, and serve with the creamy gravy.

HEALTH RATING 🍎🍎

**ORIENTAL ALTERNATIVE**

Chinese-glazed Poussin with Green & Black Rice

**SPICY ALTERNATIVE**

Chinese Barbecue-style Quails with Aubergines

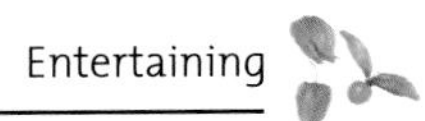

**ORIENTAL ALTERNATIVE**

## Chinese-glazed Poussin with Green & Black Rice

INGREDIENTS **Serves 4**

4 oven-ready poussins
salt and freshly ground black pepper
300 ml/½ pint apple juice
1 cinnamon stick
2 star anise
½ tsp Chinese five spice powder
50 g/2 oz dark muscovado sugar
2 tbsp tomato ketchup
1 tbsp cider vinegar
grated rind of 1 orange
350 g/12 oz mixed basmati white and wild rice
125 g/4 oz mangetout, finely sliced lengthways
1 bunch spring onions, trimmed and finely shredded lengthways
salt and freshly ground black pepper

Preheat the oven to 200°C/400°F/Gas Mark 6, 15 minutes before cooking. Rinse the poussins inside and out and pat dry with absorbent kitchen paper. Using tweezers, remove any feathers. Season well with salt and pepper, then reserve.

Pour the apple juice into a small saucepan and add the cinnamon stick, star anise and Chinese five spice powder. Bring to the boil, then simmer rapidly until reduced by half. Reduce the heat, stir in the sugar, tomato ketchup, vinegar and orange rind and simmer gently until the sugar is dissolved and the glaze is syrupy. Remove from the heat and leave to cool completely. Remove the whole spices. Place the poussins on a wire rack set over a tinfoil-lined roasting tin. Brush generously with the apple glaze. Roast in the preheated oven for 40–45 minutes, or until the juices run clear when the thigh is pierced with a skewer, basting once or twice with the remaining glaze. Remove the poussins from the oven and leave to cool slightly.

Meanwhile, cook the rice according to the packet instructions. Bring a large saucepan of lightly salted water to the boil and add the mangetout. Blanch for 1 minute, then drain thoroughly. As soon as the rice is cooked, drain and transfer to a warmed bowl. Add the mangetout and spring onions, season to taste and stir well. Arrange on warmed dinner plates, place a poussin on top and serve immediately.

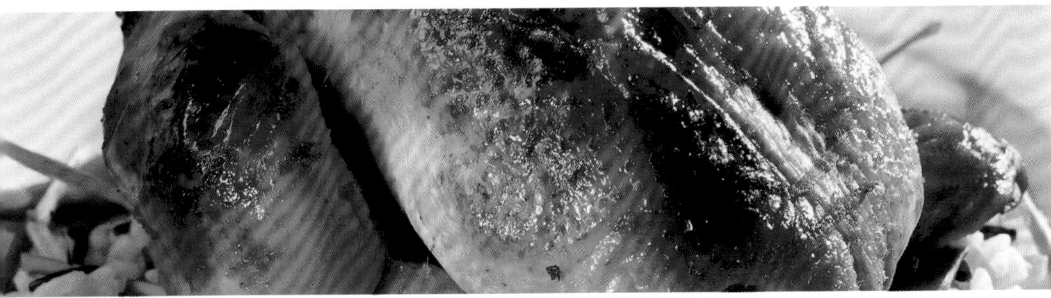

**SPICY ALTERNATIVE**

## Chinese Barbecue-style Quails with Aubergines

INGREDIENTS **Serves 6**

4 quails
2 tbsp salt
3 tbsp hoisin sauce
1 tbsp Chinese rice wine or dry sherry
1 tbsp light soy sauce
700 g/1½ lb aubergines, trimmed and cubed
1 tbsp oil
4 garlic cloves, peeled and finely chopped
1 tbsp freshly chopped root ginger
6 spring onions, trimmed and finely chopped
3 tbsp dark soy sauce
¼ tsp dried chilli flakes
1 tbsp yellow bean sauce
1 tbsp sugar

**To garnish:**
sprigs of fresh coriander
sliced red chilli

Preheat the oven to 240°C/475°F/Gas Mark 9. Rub the quails inside and out with 1 tablespoon of the salt. Mix together the hoisin sauce, Chinese rice wine or sherry and light soy sauce. Rub the quails inside and out with the sauce. Transfer to a small roasting tin and roast in the preheated oven for 5 minutes. Reduce the heat to 180°C/350°F/Gas Mark 4 and continue to roast for 20 minutes. Turn the oven off and leave the quails for 5 minutes, then remove and leave to rest for 10 minutes.

Place the aubergine in a colander and sprinkle with the remaining salt. Leave to drain for 20 minutes, then rinse under cold running water and pat dry with absorbent kitchen paper.

Heat a wok or large frying pan over a moderate heat. Add the oil and when hot, add the aubergines, garlic, ginger and four of the spring onions and cook for 1 minute. Add the dark soy sauce, chilli flakes, yellow bean sauce, sugar and 450 ml/¾ pint of water. Bring to the boil, then simmer uncovered for 10–15 minutes.

Increase the heat to high and continue to cook, stirring occasionally, until the sauce is reduced and slightly thickened. Spoon the aubergine mixture on to warmed individual plates and top with a quail. Garnish with the remaining spring onion, fresh chilli and a sprig of coriander and serve immediately.

# Crispy Roast Duck Legs with Pancakes

INGREDIENTS **Serves 6**

900 g/2 lb plums, halved
25 g/1 oz butter
2 star anise
1 tsp freshly grated root ginger
50 g/2 oz soft brown sugar
zest and juice of 1 orange
salt and freshly ground black pepper
4 duck legs
3 tbsp dark soy sauce
2 tbsp dark brown sugar
½ cucumber, cut into matchsticks
1 small bunch spring onions, trimmed and shredded
18 ready-made Chinese pancakes, warmed

Preheat the oven to 220°C/425°F/Gas Mark 7, 15 minutes before cooking. Discard the stones from the plums and place in a saucepan with the butter, star anise, ginger, brown sugar and orange zest and juice. Season to taste with pepper. Cook over a gentle heat until the sugar has dissolved. Bring to the boil, then reduce the heat and simmer for 15 minutes, stirring occasionally until the plums are soft and the mixture is thick. Remove the star anise and leave to cool.

Using a fork, prick the duck legs all over. Place in a large bowl and pour boiling water over to remove some of the fat. Drain, pat dry on absorbent kitchen paper and leave until cold.

Mix together the soy sauce, dark brown sugar and the ½ teaspoon of salt. Rub this mixture generously over the duck legs. Transfer to a wire rack set over a roasting tin and roast in the preheated oven for 30–40 minutes, or until well cooked and the skin is browned and crisp. Remove from the oven and leave to rest for 10 minutes.

Shred the duck meat using a fork to hold the hot duck leg and another to remove the meat. Transfer to a warmed serving platter with the cucumber and spring onions. Serve immediately with the plum compote and warmed pancakes.

HEALTH RATING

**SPEEDY ALTERNATIVE**

Honey-glazed Duck in Kumquat Sauce

**SPICY ALTERNATIVE**

Seared Duck with Pickled Plums

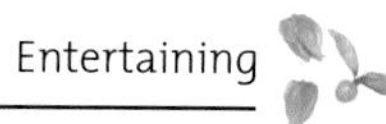

**SPEEDY ALTERNATIVE**

## Honey-glazed Duck in Kumquat Sauce

INGREDIENTS **Serves 4**

4 duck breast fillets
1 tbsp light soy sauce
1 tsp sesame oil
1 tbsp clear honey
3 tbsp brandy
1 tbsp sunflower oil
2 tbsp caster sugar
1 tbsp white wine vinegar
150 ml/¼ pint orange juice
125 g/4 oz kumquats, thinly sliced
2 tsp cornflour
salt and freshly ground black pepper
fresh watercress, to garnish
basmati and wild rice, to serve

Thinly slice the duck breasts and put in a shallow bowl. Mix together the soy sauce, sesame oil, honey and 1 tablespoon of brandy. Pour over the duck, stir well, cover and marinate in the refrigerator for at least 1 hour.

Heat a wok until hot, add the sunflower oil and swirl it round to coat the sides. Drain the duck, reserving the marinade, and stir-fry over a high heat for 2–3 minutes, or until browned. Remove from the wok and reserve.

Wipe the wok clean with absorbent kitchen paper. Add the sugar, vinegar and 1 tablespoon of water. Gently heat until the sugar dissolves, then boil until a rich golden colour. Pour in the orange juice, then the remaining brandy. Stir in the kumquat slices and simmer for 5 minutes.

Blend the cornflour with 1 tablespoon of cold water. Add to the wok and simmer for 2–3 minutes, stirring until thickened. Return the duck to the wok and cook gently for 1–2 minutes, or until warmed through. Season to taste with salt and pepper. Spoon onto warmed plates and garnish with fresh watercress leaves. Serve immediately with freshly cooked basmati and wild rice.

**SPICY ALTERNATIVE**

## Seared Duck with Pickled Plums

INGREDIENTS **Serves 4**

4 small skinless, boneless duck breasts
2 garlic cloves, peeled and crushed
1 tsp hot chilli sauce
2 tsp clear honey
2 tsp dark brown sugar
juice of 1 lime
1 tbsp dark soy sauce
6 large plums, halved and stones removed
50 g/2 oz caster sugar
50 ml/2 fl oz white wine vinegar
¼ tsp dried chilli flakes
¼ tsp ground cinnamon
1 tbsp sunflower oil
150 ml/¼ pint chicken stock
2 tbsp oyster sauce
sprigs of fresh flat leaf parsley, to garnish
freshly cooked noodles, to serve

Cut a few deep slashes in each duck breast and place in a shallow dish. Mix together the garlic, chilli sauce, honey, brown sugar, lime juice and soy sauce. Spread over the duck and leave to marinate in the refrigerator for 4 hours or overnight, if time permits, turning occasionally. Place the plums in a saucepan with the caster sugar, white wine vinegar, chilli flakes and cinnamon and bring to the boil. Simmer gently for 5 minutes, or until the plums have just softened, then leave to cool.

Remove the duck from the marinade and pat dry with absorbent kitchen paper. Reserve the marinade. Heat a wok or large frying pan, add the oil and when hot, brown the duck on both sides. Pour in the stock, oyster sauce and reserved marinade and simmer for 5 minutes. Remove the duck and keep warm.

Remove the plums from their liquid and reserve. Pour the liquid into the duck sauce, bring to the boil, then simmer, uncovered, for 5 minutes, or until reduced and thickened. Arrange the duck on warmed plates. Divide the plums between the plates and spoon over the sauce. Garnish with parsley and serve immediately with noodles.

# Veal Escalopes with Marsala Sauce

INGREDIENTS **Serves 6**

6 veal escalopes, about 125 g/4 oz each
lemon juice
salt and freshly ground black pepper
6 sage leaves
6 slices prosciutto
2 tbsp olive oil
25 g/1 oz butter
1 onion, peeled and sliced
1 garlic clove, peeled and chopped
2 tbsp Marsala wine
4 tbsp double cream
2 tbsp freshly chopped parsley
sage leaves to garnish
selection of freshly cooked vegetables, to serve

Place the veal escalopes between sheets of non-pvc clingfilm and using a mallet or rolling pin, pound lightly to flatten out thinly to about 5 mm/¼ inch thickness. Remove the clingfilm and sprinkle the veal escalopes with lemon juice, salt and black pepper.

Place a sage leaf in the centre of each escalope. Top with a slice of prosciutto, making sure it just fits, then roll up the escalopes enclosing the prosciutto and sage leaves. Secure each escalope with a cocktail stick.

Heat the olive oil and butter in a large, non-stick frying pan and fry the onions for 5 minutes, or until softened. Add the garlic and rolled escalopes and cook for about 8 minutes, turning occasionally, until the escalopes are browned all over.

Add the Marsala wine and cream to the pan and bring to the boil, cover and simmer for 10 minutes, or until the veal is tender. Season to taste and then sprinkle with the parsley. Discard the cocktail sticks and serve immediately with a selection of freshly cooked vegetables.

HEALTH RATING

**BUDGET ALTERNATIVE**

Turkey Escalopes Marsala with Wilted Watercress

**LOW FAT ALTERNATIVE**

Guinea Fowl with Calvados & Apples

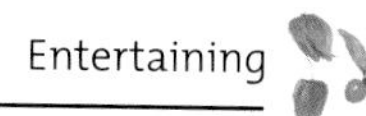

**BUDGET ALTERNATIVE**
## Turkey Escalopes Marsala with Wilted Watercress

INGREDIENTS **Serves 4**

- 4 turkey escalopes, each about 150 g/5 oz
- 25 g/1 oz plain flour
- ½ tsp dried thyme
- salt and freshly ground black pepper
- 1–2 tbsp olive oil
- 125 g/4 oz watercress
- 40 g/1½ oz butter
- 225 g/8 oz mushrooms, wiped and quartered
- 50 ml/2 fl oz dry Marsala wine
- 50 ml/2 fl oz chicken stock or water

Place each turkey escalope between two sheets of non-stick baking parchment and, using a meat mallet or rolling pin, pound until about 3 mm/⅛ inch thick. Put the flour in a shallow dish, add the thyme, season to taste with salt and pepper and stir to blend. Coat each escalope lightly on both sides with the flour mixture, then reserve.

Heat the olive oil in a large frying pan, then add the watercress and stir-fry for about 2 minutes, until just wilted and brightly coloured. Season with salt and pepper. Using a slotted spoon, transfer the watercress to a plate and keep warm.

Add half the butter to the frying pan and when melted, add the mushrooms. Stir-fry for 4 minutes, or until golden and tender. Remove from the pan and reserve.

Add the remaining butter to the pan and, working in batches if necessary, cook the flour-coated escalopes for 2–3 minutes on each side, or until golden and cooked thoroughly, adding the remaining oil, if necessary. Remove from the pan and keep warm. Add the Marsala wine to the pan and stir, scraping up any browned bits from the bottom of the pan. Add the stock or water and bring to the boil over a high heat. Season lightly.

Return the escalopes and mushrooms to the pan and reheat gently until piping hot. Divide the warm watercress between four serving plates.

Arrange an escalope over each serving of wilted watercress and spoon over the mushrooms and Marsala sauce. Serve immediately.

**LOW FAT ALTERNATIVE**
## Guinea Fowl with Calvados & Apples

INGREDIENTS **Serves 4**

- 4 guinea fowl supremes, each about 150 g/5 oz, skinned
- 1 tbsp plain flour
- 1 tbsp sunflower oil
- 1 onion, peeled and finely sliced
- 1 garlic clove, peeled and crushed
- 1 tsp freshly chopped thyme
- 150 ml/¼ pint dry cider
- salt and freshly ground black pepper
- 3 tbsp Calvados brandy
- sprigs of fresh thyme, to garnish

**For the caramelised apples:**

- 15 g/½ oz unsalted butter
- 2 red-skinned eating apples, quartered, cored and sliced
- 1 tsp caster sugar

Lightly dust the guinea fowl supremes with the flour. Heat 2 teaspoons of the oil in a large, non-stick frying pan and cook the meat for 2–3 minutes on each side until browned. Remove from the pan and reserve.

Heat the remaining teaspoon of oil in the pan and add the onion and garlic. Cook over a medium heat for 10 minutes, stirring occasionally until soft and just beginning to colour.

Stir in the chopped thyme and cider. Return the guinea fowl to the pan, season with salt and pepper and bring to a very gentle simmer. Cover and cook over a low heat for 15–20 minutes or until the guinea fowl is tender. Remove the guinea fowl and keep warm. Turn up the heat and boil the sauce until thickened and reduced by half.

Meanwhile, prepare the caramelised apples. Melt the butter in a small, non-stick pan, add the apple slices in a single layer and sprinkle with the sugar. Cook until the apples are tender and beginning to caramelise, turning once.

Put the Calvados in a metal ladle or small saucepan and gently heat until warm. Carefully set alight with a match, let the flames die down, then stir into the sauce. Serve the guinea fowl with the sauce spooned over and garnished with the caramelised apples and sprigs of fresh thyme.

## MEDITERRANEAN ALTERNATIVE
# Pheasant with Portabella Mushrooms & Red Wine Gravy

INGREDIENTS **Serves 4**

- 25 g/1 oz butter
- 1 tbsp olive oil
- 2 small pheasants (preferably hens) rinsed, well dried and halved
- 8 shallots, peeled
- 300 g/11 oz portabella mushrooms, thickly sliced
- 2–3 sprigs of fresh thyme or rosemary, leaves stripped
- 300 ml/½ pint Valpolicella or fruity red wine
- 300 ml/½ pint hot chicken stock
- 1 tbsp cornflour
- 2 tbsp balsamic vinegar
- 2 tbsp redcurrant jelly, or to taste
- 2 tbsp freshly chopped flat leaf parsley
- salt and freshly ground black pepper
- sprigs of fresh thyme, to garnish

Preheat the oven to 180°C/350°F/Gas Mark 4. Heat the butter and oil in a large saucepan or frying pan. Add the pheasant halves and shallots, working in batches if necessary, and cook for 10 minutes or until golden on all sides, shaking the pan to glaze the shallots. Transfer to a casserole dish large enough to hold the pieces in a single layer. Add the mushroom and thyme to the pan and cook for 2–3 minutes, or until beginning to colour. Transfer to the dish with the pheasant halves.

Add the wine to the saucepan, which will bubble and steam. Cook, stirring up any browned bits from the pan and allow to reduce by half. Pour in the stock and bring to the boil, then pour over the pheasant halves. Cover and braise in the preheated oven for 50 minutes, or until tender. Remove the pheasant halves and vegetables to a wide, shallow serving dish and set the casserole or roasting tin over a medium-high heat.

Skim off any surface fat and bring to the boil. Blend the cornflour with the vinegar and stir into the sauce with the redcurrant jelly. Boil until the sauce is reduced and thickened slightly. Stir in the parsley and season to taste with salt and pepper. Pour over the pheasant halves, garnish with sprigs of fresh thyme and serve immediately.

## LOW FAT ALTERNATIVE
# Fruity Rice-stuffed Poussins

INGREDIENTS **Serves 6**

**For the rice stuffing:**

- 225 ml/8 fl oz port
- 125 g/4 oz raisins
- 125 g/4 oz ready-to-eat dried apricots, chopped
- 2 tbsp olive oil
- 1 medium onion, peeled and finely chopped
- 1 celery stalk, trimmed and finely sliced
- 2 garlic cloves, peeled and finely chopped
- 1½ tsp mixed spice
- 1 tsp each dried oregano and mint or basil
- 225 g/8 oz unsweetened canned chestnuts, chopped
- 200 g/7 oz long-grain white rice, cooked
- grated rind and juice of 2 oranges
- 350 ml/12 fl oz chicken stock
- 50 g/2 oz walnut halves, lightly toasted and chopped
- 2 tbsp each freshly chopped mint and parsley
- salt and freshly ground black pepper

- 6 oven-ready poussins
- 50 g/2 oz butter, melted

**To garnish:**

- fresh herbs
- orange wedges

Preheat the oven to 180°C/350°F/Gas Mark 4. To make the stuffing, place the port, raisins and apricots in a bowl and leave for 15 minutes. Heat the oil in a large saucepan. Add the onion and celery and cook for 3–4 minutes. Add the garlic, mixed spice, herbs and chestnuts and cook for 4 minutes, stirring occasionally. Add the rice, half the orange rind and juice and the stock and simmer for 5 minutes until most of the liquid is absorbed.

Drain the raisins and apricots, reserving the port. Stir into the rice with the walnuts, mint, parsley and seasoning and cook for 2 minutes. Remove and cool.

Rinse the poussin cavities, pat dry and season with salt and pepper. Lightly fill the cavities with the stuffing, then tie the legs of together, tucking in the tail. Form any extra stuffing into balls.

Place in roasting tins with the stuffing balls and brush with melted butter. Drizzle over the remaining butter, orange rind and juice and port. Roast in the preheated oven for 50 minutes or until golden and cooked, basting every 15 minutes. Transfer to a platter, cover with tinfoil and rest. Pour over any pan juices. Garnish with herbs and orange wedges and serve with the stuffing.

# Pheasant with Sage & Blueberries

INGREDIENTS **Serves 4**

3 tbsp olive oil
3 shallots, peeled and coarsely chopped
2 sprigs of fresh sage, coarsely chopped
1 bay leaf
1 lemon, halved
salt and freshly ground black pepper
2 pheasants or guinea fowl, rinsed and dried
125 g/4 oz blueberries
4 slices Parma ham or bacon
125 ml/4 fl oz vermouth or dry white wine
200 ml/⅓ pint chicken stock
3 tbsp double cream or butter (optional)
1 tbsp brandy
roast potatoes, to serve

Preheat the oven to 180°C/350°F/Gas Mark 4, 10 minutes before cooking. Place the oil, shallots, sage and bay leaf in a bowl with the juice from the lemon halves. Season with salt and pepper. Tuck each of the squeezed lemon halves into the birds with 75 g/3 oz of the blueberries, then rub the birds with the marinade and leave for 2–3 hours, basting occasionally.

Remove the birds from the marinade and cover each with two slices of Parma ham. Tie the legs of each bird with string and place in a roasting tin. Pour over the marinade and add the vermouth. Roast in the preheated oven for 1 hour, or until tender and golden and the juices run clear when a thigh is pierced with a sharp knife or skewer.

Transfer to a warm serving plate, cover with tinfoil and discard the string. Skim off any surface fat from the tin and set over a medium-high heat.

Add the stock to the tin and bring to the boil, scraping any browned bits from the bottom and mixing in. Boil until slightly reduced. Whisk in the cream or butter, if using, and simmer until thickened, whisking constantly. Stir in the brandy and strain into a gravy jug. Add the remaining blueberries and keep warm.

Using a sharp carving knife, cut each of the birds in half and arrange on the plate with the crispy Parma ham. Serve immediately with roast potatoes and the gravy.

HEALTH RATING

**MEDITERRANEAN ALTERNATIVE**

Pheasant with Portabella Mushrooms & Red Wine Gravy

**LOW FAT ALTERNATIVE**

Fruity Rice-stuffed Poussins

# Spicy Chicken Skewers with Mango Tabbouleh

INGREDIENTS **Serves 4**

400 g/14 oz chicken breast fillet
200 ml/7 fl oz natural low fat yogurt
1 garlic clove, peeled and crushed
1 small red chilli, deseeded and finely chopped
½ tsp ground turmeric
finely grated rind and juice of ½ lemon
sprigs of fresh mint, to garnish

**For the mango tabbouleh:**

175 g/6 oz bulgur wheat
1 tsp olive oil
juice of ½ lemon
½ red onion, finely chopped
1 ripe mango, halved, stoned, peeled and chopped
¼ cucumber, finely diced
2 tbsp freshly chopped parsley
2 tbsp freshly shredded mint
salt and finely ground black pepper

If using wooden skewers, pre-soak them in cold water for at least 30 minutes to stop them from burning whilst grilling. Cut the chicken into 5 x 1 cm/2 x ½ inch strips and place in a shallow dish.

Mix together the yogurt, garlic, chilli, turmeric, lemon rind and juice. Pour over the chicken and toss to coat. Cover and leave to marinate in the refrigerator for up to 8 hours.

To make the tabbouleh, put the bulgur wheat in a bowl. Pour over enough boiling water to cover. Put a plate over the bowl and leave to soak for 20 minutes. Whisk together the oil and lemon juice in another bowl. Add the red onion and leave to marinade for 10 minutes.

Drain the bulgur wheat and squeeze out any excess moisture in a clean tea towel. Add to the red onion with the mango, cucumber and herbs and season to taste with salt and pepper. Toss together. Thread the chicken strips on to eight wooden or metal skewers. Cook under a hot grill for 8 minutes. Turn and brush with the marinade until the chicken is lightly browned and cooked through.Spoon the tabbouleh on to individual plates. Arrange the chicken skewers on top and garnish with the sprigs of mint. Serve warm or cold.

HEALTH RATING

**LOW FAT ALTERNATIVE**
Chilli Roast Chicken

**MILD ALTERNATIVE**
Chicken Baked in a Salt Crust

INGREDIENTS **Serves 4**

3 medium-hot fresh red chillies, deseeded
½ tsp ground turmeric
1 tsp cumin seeds
1 tsp coriander seeds
2 garlic cloves, peeled and crushed
2.5 cm/1 inch piece fresh root ginger, peeled and chopped
1 tbsp lemon juice
1 tbsp olive oil
2 tbsp roughly chopped fresh coriander
½ tsp salt
freshly ground black pepper
1.4 kg/3 lb oven-ready chicken
15 g/½ oz unsalted butter, melted
550 g/1¼ lb butternut squash
fresh parsley and coriander sprigs, to garnish

**To serve:**

4 baked potatoes
seasonal green vegetables

## LOW FAT ALTERNATIVE
## Chilli Roast Chicken

Preheat the oven to 190°C/375°F/Gas Mark 5. Roughly chop the chillies and put in a food processor with the turmeric, cumin seeds, coriander seeds, garlic, ginger, lemon juice, olive oil, coriander, salt, pepper and 2 tablespoons of cold water. Blend to a paste, leaving the ingredients still slightly chunky.

Starting at the neck end of the chicken, gently ease up the skin to loosen it from the breast. Reserve 3 tablespoons of the paste. Push the remaining paste over the chicken breast under the skin, spreading it evenly.

Put the chicken in a large roasting tin. Mix the reserved chilli paste with the melted butter. Use 1 tablespoon to brush evenly over the chicken, then roast in the preheated oven for 20 minutes. Meanwhile, halve, peel and scoop out the seeds from the butternut squash. Cut into large chunks and mix with the remaining chilli paste and butter mixture.

Arrange the butternut squash around the chicken. Roast for a further hour, basting with the cooking juices about every 20 minutes until the chicken is fully cooked and the squash tender. Garnish with parsley and coriander. Serve hot with baked potatoes and green vegetables.

INGREDIENTS **Serves 4**

1.8 kg/4 lb oven-ready chicken
salt and freshly ground black pepper
1 medium onion, peeled
sprig of fresh rosemary
sprig of fresh thyme
1 bay leaf
15 g/½ oz butter, softened
1 garlic clove, peeled and crushed
pinch of ground paprika
finely grated rind of ½ lemon

**To garnish:**

fresh herbs
lemon slices

**For the salt crust:**

900 g/2 lb plain flour
450 g/1 lb fine cooking salt
450 g/1 lb coarse sea salt
2 tbsp oil

## MILD ALTERNATIVE
## Chicken Baked in a Salt Crust

Preheat the oven to 170°C/325°F/Gas Mark 3. Remove the giblets if necessary and rinse the chicken with cold water. Sprinkle the inside with salt and pepper. Put the onion inside with the rosemary, thyme and bay leaf. Mix the butter, garlic, paprika and lemon rind together. Starting at the neck end, gently ease the skin from the chicken and push the mixture under.

To make the salt crust, put the flour and salts in a large mixing bowl and stir together. Make a well in the centre. Pour in 600 ml/1 pint of cold water and the oil. Mix to a stiff dough, then knead on a lightly floured surface for 2–3 minutes. Roll out the pastry to a circle with a diameter of about 51 cm/20 inches. Place the chicken breast-side down in the middle. Lightly brush the edges with water, then fold over to enclose. Pinch the joints together to seal.

Put the chicken join-side down in a roasting tin and cook in the preheated oven for 2¾ hours. Remove from the oven and stand for 20 minutes. Break open the hard crust and remove the chicken. Discard the crust and remove the skin from the chicken. Garnish with the fresh herbs and lemon slices and serve immediately.

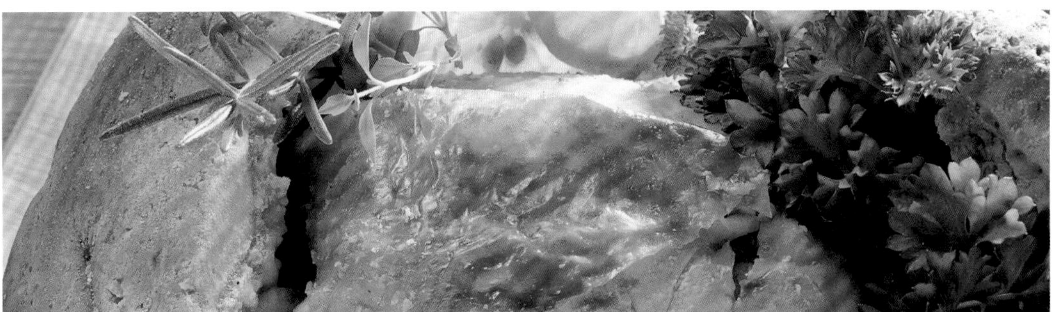

# Seared Pancetta-wrapped Cod

INGREDIENTS **Serves 4**

4 x 175 g/6 oz thick cod fillets
4 very thin slices of pancetta
3 tbsp capers in vinegar
1 tbsp of vegetable or sunflower oil
2 tbsp lemon juice
1 tbsp olive oil
freshly ground black pepper
1 tbsp freshly chopped parsley, to garnish

**To serve:**

freshly cooked vegetables
new potatoes

Wipe the cod fillets and wrap each one with the pancetta. Secure each fillet with a cocktail stick and reserve.

Drain the capers and soak in cold water for 10 minutes to remove any excess salt, then drain and reserve.

Heat the oil in a large frying pan and sear the wrapped pieces of cod fillet for about 3 minutes on each side, turning carefully with a fish slice so as not to break up the fish.

Lower the heat then continue to cook for 2–3 minutes or until the fish is thoroughly cooked.

Meanwhile, place the reserved capers, lemon juice and olive oil into a small saucepan. Grind over some black pepper.

Place the saucepan over a low heat and bring to a gentle simmer, stirring continuously for 2–3 minutes.

Once the fish is cooked, garnish with the parsley and serve with the warm caper dressing, freshly cooked vegetables and new potatoes.

HEALTH RATING ●●●●

**LOW FAT ALTERNATIVE**
Cod with Fennel & Cardamom

**SPICY ALTERNATIVE**
Steamed Monkfish with Chilli & Ginger

**LOW FAT ALTERNATIVE**

## Cod with Fennel & Cardamom

INGREDIENTS **Serves 4**

- 1 garlic clove, peeled and crushed
- finely grated rind of 1 lemon
- 1 tsp lemon juice
- 1 tbsp olive oil
- 1 fennel bulb
- 1 tbsp cardamom pods
- salt and freshly ground black pepper
- 4 x 175 g/6 oz thick cod fillets

Preheat the oven to 190°C/375°F/Gas Mark 5. Place the garlic in a small bowl with the lemon rind, juice and olive oil and stir well.

Cover and leave to infuse for at least 30 minutes. Stir well before using.

Trim the fennel bulb, thinly slice and place in a bowl.

Place the cardamom pods in a pestle and mortar and lightly pound to crack the pods. Alternatively place in a polythene bag and pound gently with a rolling pin. Add the crushed cardamom to the fennel slices.

Season the fish with salt and pepper and place on to four separate 20.5 x 20.5 cm/8 x 8 inch parchment paper squares.

Spoon the fennel mixture over the fish and drizzle with the infused oil.

Place the parcels on a baking sheet and bake in the preheated oven for 8–10 minutes or until cooked. Serve immediately in the paper parcels.

**SPICY ALTERNATIVE**

## Steamed Monkfish with Chilli & Ginger

INGREDIENTS **Serves 4**

- 700 g/1½ lb skinless monkfish tail
- 1–2 red chillies
- 4 cm/1½ inch piece fresh root ginger
- 1 tsp sesame oil
- 4 spring onions, trimmed and thinly sliced diagonally
- 2 tbsp soy sauce
- 2 tbsp Chinese rice wine or dry sherry
- freshly steamed rice, to serve

**To garnish:**

- sprigs of fresh coriander
- lime wedges

Place the monkfish on a chopping board. Using a sharp knife, cut down each side of the central bone and remove. Cut the fish into 2.5cm/1 inch pieces and reserve.

Make a slit down the side of each chilli, remove and discard the seeds and the membrane, then slice thinly. Peel the ginger and either chop finely or grate.

Brush a large heatproof plate with the sesame oil and arrange the monkfish pieces in one layer on the plate. Sprinkle over the spring onions and pour over the soy sauce and Chinese rice wine or sherry.

Place a wire rack or inverted ramekin in a large wok. Pour in enough water to come about 2.5 cm/1 inch up the side of the wok and bring to the boil over a high heat. Fold a long piece of tinfoil lengthways to about 5–7.5 cm/2–3 inches wide and lay it over the rack or ramekin. It must extend beyond the plate edge when it is placed in the wok, so you can use it to remove the hot plate.

Place the plate with the monkfish on the rack or ramekin and cover tightly. Steam over a medium-low heat for 5 minutes, or until the fish is tender and opaque. Using the tinfoil as a hammock, lift out the plate. Garnish with sprigs of coriander and lime wedges and serve immediately with steamed rice.

# Tagliatelle with Stuffed Pork Escalopes

INGREDIENTS **Serves 4**

150 g/5 oz broccoli florets, finely chopped and blanched
125 g/4 oz mozzarella cheese, grated
1 garlic clove, peeled and crushed
2 large eggs, beaten
salt and freshly ground black pepper
4 thin pork escalopes, weighing about
100 g/3½ oz each
1 tbsp olive oil
25 g/1 oz butter
2 tbsp flour
150 ml/¼ pint milk
150 ml/¼ pint chicken stock
1 tbsp Dijon mustard
225 g/8 oz fresh tagliatelle
sage leaves, to garnish

Preheat the oven to 180°C/350°F/Gas Mark 4, 10 minutes before cooking. Mix the broccoli with the mozzarella cheese, garlic and beaten eggs. Season to taste with salt and pepper and reserve.

Using a meat mallet or rolling pin, pound the escalopes on a sheet of greaseproof paper until 5 mm/¼ inch thick. Divide the broccoli mixture between the escalopes and roll each one up from the shortest side. Place the pork rolls in a lightly oiled ovenproof dish, drizzle over the olive oil and bake in the preheated oven for 40–50 minutes, or until cooked.

Meanwhile, melt the butter in a heavy-based pan, stir in the flour and cook for 2 minutes. Remove from the heat and whisk in the milk and stock. Season to taste, stir in the mustard then cook until smooth and thickened. Keep warm.

Bring a large pan of lightly salted water to a rolling boil. Add the taglietelle and cook according to the packet instructions or for about 3–4 minutes until 'al dente'. Drain thoroughly and tip into a warmed serving dish. Slice each pork roll into three, place on top of the pasta and pour the sauce over the top. Garnish with sage leaves and serve immediately.

HEALTH RATING 🍏🍏🍏

**SPEEDY ALTERNATIVE**

Fettuccine with Calves' Liver & Calvados

**SEAFOOD ALTERNATIVE**

Seafood Parcels with Pappardelle & Coriander Pesto

**SPEEDY ALTERNATIVE**
## Fettuccine with Calves' Liver & Calvados

INGREDIENTS **Serves 4**

450 g/1 lb calves' liver, trimmed and thinly sliced
50 g/2 oz plain flour
salt and freshly ground black pepper
1 tsp paprika
50 g/2 oz butter
1½ tbsp olive oil
2 tbsp Calvados
150 ml/¼ pint cider
150 ml/¼ pint whipping cream
350 g/12 oz fresh fettuccine
fresh thyme sprigs, to garnish

Season the flour with the salt, black pepper and paprika, then toss the liver in the flour until well coated.

Melt half the butter and 1 tablespoon of the olive oil in a large frying pan and fry the liver in batches for 1 minute, or until just browned but still slightly pink inside. Remove using a slotted spoon and place in a warmed dish.

Add the remaining butter to the pan, stir in 1 tablespoon of the seasoned flour and cook for 1 minute. Pour in the Calvados and cider and cook over a high heat for 30 seconds.

Stir the cream into the sauce and simmer for 1 minute to thicken slightly, then season to taste. Return the liver to the pan and heat through.

Bring a large pan of lightly salted water to a rolling boil. Add the fettuccine and cook according to the packet instructions, about 3–4 minutes, or until 'al dente'.

Drain the fettuccine thoroughly, return to the pan and toss in the remaining olive oil. Divide among four warmed plates and spoon the liver and sauce over the pasta. Garnish with thyme sprigs and serve immediately.

**SEAFOOD ALTERNATIVE**
## Seafood Parcels with Pappardelle & Coriander Pesto

INGREDIENTS **Serves 4**

300 g/11 oz pappardelle or tagliatelle
8 raw tiger prawns, shelled
12 raw queen scallops
225 g/8oz baby squid, cleaned and cut into rings
4 tbsp dry white wine
4 thin slices of lemon

**For the coriander pesto:**
50 g/2 oz fresh coriander leaves
1 garlic clove, peeled
25 g/1 oz pine nuts, toasted
1 tsp lemon juice
5 tbsp olive oil
1 tbsp grated Parmesan cheese
salt and freshly ground black pepper

Preheat the oven to 180°C/350°F/Gas Mark 4, 10 minutes before cooking. To make the pesto, blend the coriander leaves, garlic, pine nuts and lemon juice with 1 tablespoon of the olive oil to a smooth paste in a food processor. With the motor running slowly, add the remaining oil. Stir the Parmesan cheese into the pesto and season to taste with salt and pepper.

Bring a pan of lightly salted water to a rolling boil. Add the pasta and cook for 3 minutes only. Drain thoroughly, return to the pan and spoon over two-thirds of the pesto. Toss to coat.

Cut out four circles about 30 cm/12 inches in diameter from non-stick baking parchment. Spoon the pasta on to one half of each circle. Top each pile of pasta with 2 prawns, 3 scallops and a few squid rings. Spoon 1 tablespoon of wine over each serving, then drizzle with the remaining coriander pesto and top with a slice of lemon.

Close the parcels by folding over the other half of the paper to make a semi-circle, then turn and twist the edges of the paper to secure.

Place the parcels on a baking tray and bake in the preheated oven for 15 minutes, or until cooked. Serve the parcels immediately, allowing each person to open their own.

**SPICY ALTERNATIVE**
## Conchiglioni with Crab au Gratin

INGREDIENTS **Serves 4**

175 g/6 oz large pasta shells
50 g/2 oz butter
1 shallot, peeled and finely chopped
1 bird's-eye chilli, deseeded and finely chopped
2 x 200 g cans crabmeat, drained
3 tbsp plain flour
50 ml/2 fl oz white wine
50 ml/2 fl oz milk
3 tbsp crème fraîche
15 g/½ oz Cheddar cheese, grated
salt and freshly ground black pepper
1 tbsp oil or melted butter
50 g/2 oz fresh white breadcrumbs

**To serve:**

cheese or tomato sauce
tossed green salad or freshly cooked baby vegetables

Preheat the oven to 200°C/400°F/Gas Mark 6, 15 minutes before cooking. Bring a large pan of lightly salted water to a rolling boil. Add the pasta shells and cook according to the packet instructions, or until 'al dente'. Drain thoroughly and allow to dry completely.

Melt half the butter in a heavy-based pan, add the shallots and chilli and cook for 2 minutes, then stir in the crabmeat. Stuff the cooled shells with the crab mixture and reserve. Melt the remaining butter in a small pan and stir in the flour. Cook for 1 minute, then whisk in the wine and milk and cook, stirring, until thickened. Stir in the crème fraîche and grated cheese and season the sauce to taste with salt and pepper.

Place the crab-filled shells in a lightly oiled, large shallow baking dish or tray and spoon a little of the sauce over. Toss the breadcrumbs in the melted butter or oil, then sprinkle over the pasta shells. Bake in the preheated oven for 10 minutes. Serve immediately with a cheese or tomato sauce and a tossed green salad or cooked baby vegetables.

**SPEEDY ALTERNATIVE**
## Pappardelle with Smoked Haddock & Blue Cheese Sauce

INGREDIENTS **Serves 4**

350 g/12 oz smoked haddock
2 bay leaves
300 ml/½ pint milk
400 g/14 oz pappardelle or tagliatelle
25 g/1 oz butter
25 g/1 oz plain flour
150 ml/¼ pint single cream or extra milk
125 g/4 oz Dolcelatte cheese or Gorgonzola, cut into small pieces
¼ tsp freshly grated nutmeg
salt and freshly ground black pepper
40 g/1½ oz toasted walnuts, chopped
1 tbsp freshly chopped parsley

Place the smoked haddock in a saucepan with 1 bay leaf and pour in the milk. Bring to the boil slowly, cover and simmer for 6–7 minutes, or until the fish is opaque. Remove and roughly flake the fish, discarding the skin and any bones. Strain the milk and reserve. Bring a large pan of lightly salted water to a rolling boil. Add the pasta and cook according to the packet instructions, or until 'al dente'.

Meanwhile, place the butter, flour and single cream or milk if preferred, in a pan and stir to mix. Stir in the reserved warm milk and add the remaining bay leaf. Bring to the boil, whisking all the time until smooth and thick. Gently simmer for 3–4 minutes, stirring frequently. Discard the bay leaf. Add the Dolcelatte or Gorgonzola cheese to the sauce. Heat gently, stirring until melted. Add the flaked haddock and season to taste with nutmeg and salt and pepper.

Drain the pasta thoroughly and return to the pan. Add the sauce and toss gently to coat, taking care not to break up the flakes of fish. Tip into a warmed serving bowl, sprinkle with toasted walnuts and parsley and serve immediately.

# Spaghetti with Smoked Salmon & Tiger Prawns

INGREDIENTS **Serves 4**

225 g/8 oz baby spinach leaves
salt and freshly ground black pepper
pinch freshly grated nutmeg
225 g/8 oz cooked tiger prawns in their shells
450 g/1 lb fresh angel hair spaghetti
50 g/2 oz butter
3 medium eggs
1 tbsp freshly chopped dill, plus extra to garnish
125 g/4 oz smoked salmon, cut into strips
dill sprigs, to garnish
2 tbsp grated Parmesan cheese, to serve

Cook the baby spinach leaves in a large pan with 1 teaspoon of water for 3–4 minutes, or until wilted. Drain thoroughly, season to taste with salt, pepper and nutmeg and keep warm. Remove the shells from all but four of the tiger prawns and reserve.

Bring a large pan of lightly salted water to a rolling boil. Add the pasta and cook according to the packet instructions, about 3–4 minutes, or until 'al dente'. Drain thoroughly and return to the pan. Stir in the butter and the peeled prawns, cover and keep warm.

Beat the eggs with the dill, season well, then stir into the spaghetti and prawns. Return the pan to the heat briefly, just long enough to lightly scramble the eggs, then remove from the heat. Carefully mix in the smoked salmon strips and the cooked spinach. Toss gently to mix. Tip into a warmed serving dish and garnish with the reserved prawns and dill sprigs. Serve immediately with grated Parmesan cheese.

## HEALTH RATING ●●●

**SPICY ALTERNATIVE**
Conchiglioni with Crab au Gratin

**SPEEDY ALTERNATIVE**
Pappardelle with Smoked Haddock & Blue Cheese Sauce

# White Chocolate Terrine with Red Fruit Compote

INGREDIENTS **Serves 4**

225 g/8 oz white chocolate
300 ml/½ pint double cream
225 g/8 oz full fat soft cream cheese
2 tbsp finely grated orange rind
125 g/4 oz caster sugar
350 g/12 oz mixed summer fruits, such as strawberries, blueberries and raspberries
1 tbsp Cointreau
sprigs of fresh mint, to decorate

Set the freezer to rapid freeze at least 2 hours before required. Lightly oil and line a 450 g/1 lb loaf tin with clingfilm, taking care to keep the clingfilm as wrinkle free as possible. Break the white chocolate into small pieces and place in a heatproof bowl set over a saucepan of gently simmering water. Leave for 20 minutes or until melted, then remove from the heat and stir until smooth. Leave to cool.

Whip the cream until soft peaks form. Beat the cream cheese until soft and creamy, then beat in the grated orange rind and 50 g/2 oz of the caster sugar. Mix well, then fold in the whipped cream and then the cooled melted white chocolate.

Spoon the mixture into the prepared loaf tin and level the surface. Place in the freezer and freeze for at least 4 hours or until frozen. Once frozen, remember to return the freezer to its normal setting.

Place the fruits with the remaining sugar in a heavy-based saucepan and heat gently, stirring occasionally, until the sugar has dissolved and the juices from the fruits are just beginning to run. Add the Cointreau.

Dip the loaf tin into hot water for 30 seconds and invert onto a serving plate. Carefully remove the tin and clingfilm. Decorate with sprigs of mint and serve sliced with the prepared red fruit compote.

HEALTH RATING

**ALTERNATIVE**

Iced Chocolate & Raspberry Mousse

**ALTERNATIVE**

Rich Chocolate & Orange Mousse

**ALTERNATIVE**
## Iced Chocolate & Raspberry Mousse

INGREDIENTS **Serves 4**
12 sponge finger biscuits
juice of 2 oranges
2 tbsp Grand Marnier
300 ml/½ pint double cream
175 g/6 oz plain dark chocolate, broken into small pieces
225 g/8 oz frozen raspberries
6 tbsp icing sugar, sifted
cocoa powder, for dusting

**To decorate:**
few fresh whole raspberries
few mint leaves
grated white chocolate

Break the sponge finger biscuits into small pieces and divide between four individual glass dishes. Blend together the orange juice and Grand Marnier, then drizzle evenly over the sponge fingers. Cover with clingfilm and chill in the refrigerator for 30 minutes.

Meanwhile, place the cream in a small, heavy-based saucepan and heat gently, stirring occasionally until boiling. Remove the saucepan from the heat then add the pieces of dark chocolate and leave to stand untouched for about 7 minutes. Using a whisk, whisk the chocolate and cream together, until the chocolate has melted and is well blended and completely smooth. Leave to cool slightly.

Place the frozen raspberries and icing sugar into a food processor or liquidizer and blend until roughly crushed.

Fold the crushed raspberries into the cream and chocolate mixture and mix lightly until well blended. Spoon over the chilled sponge finger biscuits. Lightly dust with a little cocoa powder and decorate with whole raspberries, mint leaves and grated white chocolate. Serve immediately.

**ALTERNATIVE**
## Rich Chocolate & Orange Mousse

INGREDIENTS **Serves 8**
12 sponge finger biscuits
225 g/8 oz plain dark chocolate, broken into pieces
225 g/8 oz unsalted butter
2 tbsp orange flower water
40 g/1½ oz cocoa powder, sifted
125 g/4 oz icing sugar, sifted
5 medium eggs, separated
50 g/2 oz caster sugar
1 orange, thinly sliced
300 ml/½ pint double cream

Oil and line a 900 g/2 lb loaf tin with clingfilm, taking care to keep the clingfilm as wrinkle free as possible. Arrange the sponge finger biscuits around the edge of the loaf tin, trimming the biscuits to fit if necessary.

Place the chocolate, butter and orange flower water in a heavy-based saucepan and heat gently, stirring occasionally, until the chocolate has melted and is smooth. Remove the saucepan from the heat, add the cocoa powder and 50 g/2 oz of the icing sugar. Stir until smooth, then beat in the egg yolks.

In a clean, grease-free bowl whisk the egg whites until stiff but not dry. Sift in the remaining icing sugar and whisk until stiff and glossy. Fold the egg white mixture into the chocolate mixture and, using a metal spoon or rubber spatula, stir until well blended.

Spoon the mousse mixture into the prepared loaf tin and level the surface. Cover and chill in the refrigerator until set.

Meanwhile, place the caster sugar with 150 ml/¼ pint of water in a heavy-based saucepan and heat until the sugar has dissolved. Bring to the boil and boil for 5 minutes. Add the orange slices and simmer for about 2–4 minutes or until the slices become opaque. Drain on absorbent kitchen paper and reserve.

Trim the top of the biscuits to the same level as the mousse. Invert onto a plate and remove the tin and clingfilm.

Whip the cream until soft peaks form and spoon into a piping bag fitted with a star-shaped nozzle. Pipe swirls on top of the mousse and decorate with the orange slices. Chill in the refrigerator before serving.

# Chocolate Profiteroles

INGREDIENTS **Serves 4**

**For the pastry:**

150 ml/¼ pint water
50 g/2 oz butter
65 g/2½ oz plain flour, sifted
2 medium eggs, lightly beaten

**For the custard:**

300 ml/½ pint milk
pinch of freshly grated nutmeg
3 medium egg yolks
50 g/2 oz caster sugar
2 tbsp plain flour, sifted
2 tbsp cornflour, sifted

**For the sauce:**

175 g/6 oz soft brown sugar
150 ml/¼ pint boiling water
1 tsp instant coffee
1 tbsp cocoa powder
1 tbsp brandy
75 g/3 oz butter
1 tbsp golden syrup

Preheat the oven to 220°C/425°F/Gas Mark 7, 15 minutes before cooking. Lightly oil two baking sheets. For the pastry, place the water and the butter in a heavy-based saucepan and bring to the boil. Remove from the heat and beat in the flour. Return to the heat and cook for 1 minute or until the mixture forms a ball in the centre of the saucepan.

Remove from the heat and leave to cool slightly, then gradually beat in the eggs a little at a time, beating well after each addition. Once all the eggs have been added, beat until the paste is smooth and glossy. Pipe or spoon 20 small balls onto the baking sheets, allowing plenty of room for expansion.

Bake in the preheated oven for 25 minutes or until well risen and golden brown. Reduce the oven temperature to 180°C/350°F/Gas Mark 4. Make a hole in each ball and continue to bake for a further 5 minutes. Remove from the oven and leave to cool.

For the custard, place the milk and nutmeg in a heavy-based saucepan and bring to the boil. In another saucepan, whisk together the egg yolks, the sugar and the flours, then beat in the hot milk. Bring to the boil and simmer, whisking constantly for 2 minutes. Cover and leave to cool.

Spoon the custard into the profiteroles and arrange on a large serving dish. Place all the sauce ingredients in a small saucepan and bring to the boil, then simmer for 10 minutes. Remove from the heat and cool slightly before serving with the chocolate profiteroles.

HEALTH RATING

**ALTERNATIVE**

Caramelised Chocolate Tartlets

**ALTERNATIVE**

White Chocolate Raspberry Brûlée

## ALTERNATIVE
## Caramelised Chocolate Tartlets

INGREDIENTS **Serves 6**

350 g/12 oz ready-made shortcrust pastry, thawed if frozen
150 ml/¼ pint coconut milk
40 g/1½ oz demerara sugar
50 g/2 oz plain dark chocolate, melted
1 medium egg, beaten
few drops vanilla essence
1 small mango, peeled, stoned and sliced
1 small papaya, peeled, deseeded and chopped
1 star fruit, sliced
1 kiwi, peeled and sliced, or use fruits of your choice

Preheat the oven to 200°C/400°F/Gas Mark 6, 15 minutes before baking. Lightly oil six individual tartlet tins. Roll out the ready-made pastry on a lightly floured surface and use to line the oiled tins. Prick the bases and sides with a fork and line with non-stick baking parchment and baking beans. Bake blind for 10 minutes in the preheated oven, then remove from the oven and discard the baking beans and the baking parchment.

Reduce the oven temperature to 180°C/350°F/Gas Mark 4. Heat the coconut milk and 15 g/½ oz of the sugar in a heavy-based saucepan, stirring constantly until the sugar has dissolved. Remove the saucepan from the heat and leave to cool.

Stir the melted chocolate, the beaten egg and the vanilla essence into the cooled coconut milk. Stir until well mixed, then strain into the cooked pastry cases.

Place on a baking sheet and bake in the oven for 25 minutes or until set. Remove and leave to cool, then chill in the refrigerator.

Preheat the grill, then arrange the fruits in a decorative pattern on the top of each tartlet. Sprinkle with the remaining demerara sugar and place the tartlets in the grill pan. Grill for 2 minutes or until the sugar bubbles and browns. Turn the tartlets, if necessary and take care not to burn the sugar. Remove from the grill and leave to cool before serving.

## ALTERNATIVE
## White Chocolate Raspberry Brûlée

INGREDIENTS **Serves 6**

175 g/6 oz fresh raspberries
125 g/4 oz caster sugar
5 medium egg yolks
600 ml/1 pint double cream
1 tsp vanilla essence
175 g/6 oz white chocolate, chopped
6 tbsp demerara sugar

Hull and clean the raspberries. Rinse lightly, then leave to dry on absorbent kitchen paper. Once dry, divide the raspberries evenly between six 150 ml/¼ pint ramekins or individual dishes.

Whisk the caster sugar and egg yolks in a large bowl until very thick. Pour the cream into a heavy-based saucepan, place over a medium-high heat and bring to the boil. Remove from the heat and gradually whisk into the egg mixture, then whisk in the vanilla essence.

Place the bowl over a saucepan of simmering water and cook for about 15–20 minutes, stirring frequently, or until thick and the custard coats the back of a wooden spoon.

Remove the bowl from the heat, add the chopped white chocolate and stir until melted and well blended. Pour over the raspberries in the ramekins and leave to cool. Cover with clingfilm and chill in the refrigerator for 6 hours or until firm.

Preheat the grill. Remove the ramekins from the refrigerator and sprinkle 1 tablespoon of the demerara sugar over each, ensuring that the custard is completely covered.

Cook under the preheated grill for 5–6 minutes, or until the sugar has melted and begun to caramelise. Remove from the grill, leave to cool slightly, then chill again in the refrigerator for at least 1 hour. Serve immediately.

# Caramelised Oranges in an Iced Bowl

INGREDIENTS **Serves 4**

**For the iced bowl:**

about 36 ice cubes

fresh flowers and fruits

**For the caramelised oranges:**

8 medium-sized oranges

225 g/8 oz caster sugar

4 tbsp Grand Marnier or Cointreau

Set the freezer to rapid freeze. Place a few ice cubes in the base of a 1.7 litre/3 pint freezable glass bowl. Place a 900 ml /1½ pint glass bowl on top of the ice cubes. Arrange the flower heads and fruits in between the two bowls, wedging in position with the ice cubes.

Weigh down the smaller bowl with some heavy weights, then carefully pour cold water between the two bowls, making sure that the flowers and the fruit are covered. Freeze for at least 6 hours or until the ice is frozen solid.

When ready to use, remove the weights and using a hot, damp cloth rub the inside of the smaller bowl with the cloth until it loosens sufficiently for you to remove the bowl. Place the larger bowl in the sink or washing-up bowl, half filled with very hot water. Leave for about 30 seconds or until the ice loosens. Take care not to leave the bowl in the water for too long otherwise the ice will melt. Remove the bowl and leave in the refrigerator. Return the freezer to its normal setting.

Thinly pare the rind from 2 oranges and then cut into julienne strips. Using a sharp knife, cut away the rind and pith from all the oranges, holding over a bowl to catch the juices. Slice the oranges, discarding any pips and reform each orange back to its original shape. Secure with cocktail sticks, then place in a bowl.

Heat 300 ml/½ pint water with the orange rind and sugar in a pan. Stir the sugar until dissolved and bring to the boil. Boil for 15 minutes until a caramel colour and remove the pan from the heat. Stir in the liqueur and pour over the oranges. Allow to cool. Chill for 3 hours, turning the oranges occasionally. Spoon into the ice bowl and serve.

HEALTH RATING

**ALTERNATIVE**

Orange Freeze

**ALTERNATIVE**

Coconut Sorbet with Mango Sauce

**ALTERNATIVE**
## Orange Freeze

INGREDIENTS **Serves 4**

- 4 large oranges
- about 300 ml/½ pint vanilla ice cream
- 225 g/8 oz raspberries
- 75 g/3 oz icing sugar, sifted
- redcurrant sprigs, to decorate

Set the freezer to rapid freeze. Using a sharp knife, carefully cut the top off each orange. Scoop out the flesh from the orange, discarding any pips and thick pith. Place the shells and lids in the freezer and chop any remaining orange flesh.

Whisk together the orange juice, orange flesh and vanilla ice cream until well blended. Cover and freeze for about 2 hours, occasionally breaking up the ice crystals with a fork or a whisk. Stir the mixture from around the edge of the container into the centre, then level and return to the freezer. Do this two or three times then leave until almost frozen solid.

Place a large scoop of the ice cream mixture into the frozen shells. Add another scoop on top, so that there is plenty outside of the orange shell, and return to the freezer for 1 hour. Arrange the lids on top and freeze for a further 2 hours, until the filled orange shell is completely frozen solid.

Meanwhile, using a nylon sieve, press the raspberries into a bowl using the back of a wooden spoon and mix together with the icing sugar. Spoon the raspberry coulis on to four serving plates and place an orange at the centre of each. Dust with icing sugar and serve decorated with the redcurrants. Remember to return the freezer to its normal setting.

**ALTERNATIVE**
## Coconut Sorbet with Mango Sauce

INGREDIENTS **Serves 4**

- 2 sheets gelatine
- 250 g/9 oz caster sugar
- 600 ml/1 pint coconut milk
- 2 mangos, peeled, pitted and sliced
- 2 tbsp icing sugar
- zest and juice of 1 lime

Set the freezer to rapid freeze 2 hours before freezing the sorbet. Place the sheets of gelatine in a shallow dish, pour over cold water to cover and leave for 15 minutes. Squeeze out excess moisture before use.

Meanwhile, place the caster sugar and 300 ml/½ pint of the coconut milk in a heavy-based saucepan and heat gently, stirring occasionally, until the sugar has dissolved. Remove from the heat.

Add the soaked gelatine to the saucepan and stir gently until dissolved. Stir in the remaining coconut milk and leave until cold.

Pour the gelatine and coconut mixture into a freezable container and place in the freezer. Leave for at least 1 hour, or until the mixture has started to form ice crystals. Remove and beat with a spoon, then return to the freezer and continue to freeze until the mixture is frozen, beating at least twice more during this time.

Meanwhile, make the sauce. Place the sliced mango, icing sugar and the lime zest and juice in a food processor and blend until smooth. Spoon into a small jug.

Leave the sorbet to soften in the refrigerator for at least 30 minutes before serving. Serve scoops of sorbet on individual plates with a little of the mango sauce poured over. Remember to return the freezer to its normal setting.

## ALTERNATIVE
## Raspberry Sorbet Crush

INGREDIENTS **Serves 4**

225 g/8 oz raspberries, thawed if frozen
grated rind and juice of 1 lime
300 ml/½ pint orange juice
225 g/8 oz caster sugar
2 medium egg whites

Set the freezer to rapid freeze. If using fresh raspberries pick over and lightly rinse.

Place the raspberries in a dish and, using a masher, mash to a chunky purée.

Place the lime rind and juice, orange juice and half the caster sugar in a large, heavy-based saucepan. Heat gently, stirring frequently until the sugar is dissolved. Bring to the boil and boil rapidly for about 5 minutes.

Remove the pan from the heat and pour carefully into a freezable container.

Leave to cool, then place in the freezer and freeze for 2 hours, stirring occasionally to break up the ice crystals.

Fold the ice mixture into the raspberry purée with a metal spoon and freeze for a further 2 hours, stirring occasionally.

Whisk the egg whites until stiff. Then gradually whisk in the remaining caster sugar a tablespoonful at a time until the egg white mixture is stiff and glossy.

Fold into the raspberry sorbet with a metal spoon and freeze for 1 hour. Spoon into tall glasses and serve immediately. Remember to return the freezer to its normal setting.

## ALTERNATIVE
## Fruity Roulade

INGREDIENTS **Serves 4**

**For the sponge:**
3 medium eggs
75 g/3 oz caster sugar
75 g/3 oz plain flour, sieved
1–2 tbsp caster sugar for sprinkling

**For the filling:**
125 g/4 oz Quark
125 g/4 oz low fat Greek yogurt
25 g/1 oz caster sugar
1 tbsp orange liqueur (optional)
grated rind of 1 orange
125 g/4 oz strawberries, hulled and cut into quarters

**To decorate:**
strawberries
sifted icing sugar

Preheat the oven to 220°C/425°F/Gas Mark 7. Lightly oil and line a 33 x 23 cm/13 x 9 inch Swiss roll tin with greaseproof or baking parchment paper.

Using an electric whisk, whisk the eggs and sugar until the mixture is double in volume and leaves a trail across the top.

Fold in the flour with a metal spoon or rubber spatula. Pour into the prepared tin and bake in the preheated oven for 10–12 minutes, until well risen and golden.

Place a sheet of greaseproof or baking parchment paper out on a flat work surface and sprinkle evenly with caster sugar.

Turn the cooked sponge out on to the paper, discard the paper, trim the sponge and roll up encasing the paper inside. Reserve until cool.

To make the filling, mix together the Quark, yogurt, caster sugar, liqueur (if using) and orange rind. Unroll the roulade and spread the mixture over the sponge. Scatter over the strawberries and roll up.

Decorate the roulade with the strawberries. Dust with the icing sugar and serve.

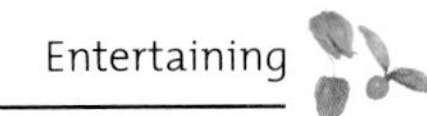

# Raspberry Soufflé

INGREDIENTS **Serves 4**

125 g/4 oz redcurrants
50 g/2 oz caster sugar
1 sachet (3 tsp) powdered gelatine
3 medium eggs, separated
300 g/½ pint low fat Greek yogurt
450 g/1 lb raspberries, thawed if frozen

**To decorate:**

mint sprigs
extra fruits

Wrap a band of double thickness greaseproof paper around the outside of four ramekin dishes, making sure that 5 cm/2 inches of the paper stays above the top of each dish. Secure the paper to the dish with an elastic band or sticky tape.

Place the redcurrants and 1 tablespoon of the sugar in a small saucepan. Cook for 5 minutes until softened. Remove from the heat, press through a sieve and reserve.

Place 3 tablespoons of water in a small bowl and sprinkle over the gelatine. Allow to stand for 5 minutes until spongy. Place the bowl over a pan of simmering water and leave until dissolved. Remove and allow to cool.

Beat together the remaining sugar and egg yolks until thick, pale and creamy, then fold in the yogurt with a metal spoon or rubber spatula until well blended.

Press the raspberries through a sieve and fold into the yogurt mixture with the gelatine. Whisk the egg whites until stiff and fold into the yogurt mixture. Pour into the prepared dishes and chill in the refrigerator for 2 hours until firm.

Remove the paper from the dishes and spread the redcurrant purée over the top of the soufflés. Decorate with mint sprigs and extra fruits and serve.

HEALTH RATING

**ALTERNATIVE**

Raspberry Sorbet Crush

**ALTERNATIVE**

Fruity Roulade

# Drinks

This section includes both alcoholic and non-alcoholic drinks, ranging from making the perfect cup of tea or coffee to fruit smoothies, fruit punches and more sophisticated drinks such as Kir Royale.

## Tea

Most teas drunk in Britain are 'black' tea: this means that the leaves have been fermented before use and come from India and Sri Lanka. China produces 'green' tea which is not fermented and is drunk without milk. There are many types of tea available ranging from everyday breakfast blends to the more exotic Darjeeling, Assam, Ceylon, Earl Grey and Lapsang Suchong, a Chinese tea with a smoky flavour. There are also many fruit, herb and flower-flavoured teas as well as decaffeinated versions.

### The Perfect Cup of Tea

For many, the perfect cup of tea has to be made with the use of tea leaves and a teapot, but whether you use leaves or bags, there are a few guidelines that need to be remembered.

- Only use freshly-drawn water every time. Bring the water to the boil, then warm the pot by pouring a little water into it and swirling the water around and then discarding. Place 1 teaspoon of tea leaves or 1 teabag per person into the pot plus an extra teaspoon or bag. Return the water to a full rolling boil and pour into the teapot. The amount depends on the quantity required (allow about 200 ml/7 fl oz of water per spoonful or bag). Stir, replace the lid and allow to stand for 3–5 minutes.

- Tea can be served either black, with a slice of lemon or with milk. If using leaves, use a tea strainer to pour the tea through.

- Russian tea is strongly-infused China tea. Make it using an extra teaspoon of leaves. Half-fill heatproof glasses with the tea and top up with water. Add sliced lemon and sugar to taste

- For iced tea, make China tea as usual and strain over the back of a spoon into a jug or glasses which are half-filled with crushed ice. Sweeten to taste, adding lemon or mint sprigs if liked.

- Hot, spiced tea can be made by adding 4–6 whole cloves, a small cinnamon stick and some thinly pared strips of orange rind to 900 ml/ 1 ½ pints of water. Bring to the boil then pour onto 15 g/½ oz tea leaves. Add sugar to taste and 3 tablespoons of orange juice. Stir, leave to infuse for 2–3 minutes then strain into heatproof glasses. Serve with long cinnamon sticks to stir.

# Coffee

The varieties of coffee bean that are grown are endless, giving many different flavours, aromas and strengths. Coffee beans comes from many countries in South America, Africa and the West Indies. It is worth trying a good selection in order to discover which suits your palate best. When buying coffee, if possible buy the beans and grind them yourself as it gives the best taste. If you do not have a grinder, buy ready-ground coffee in small amounts and store tightly sealed in an airtight container in the refrigerator.

- There are many methods for making coffee, perhaps the easiest of which is the jug or cafetiere. Simply put 1 scoop (or 40–50 g/ 1–1½ oz per 600 ml/1 pint water) into a jug or cafetiere and fill with freshly drawn boiling water. Stir, place the lid in position and leave to infuse for 2 minutes. Push the plunger down (or use a strainer if using a jug) then pour. Serve black or with warm milk or cream.

- If preferred, there are coffee-making machines available to buy. Filter coffee

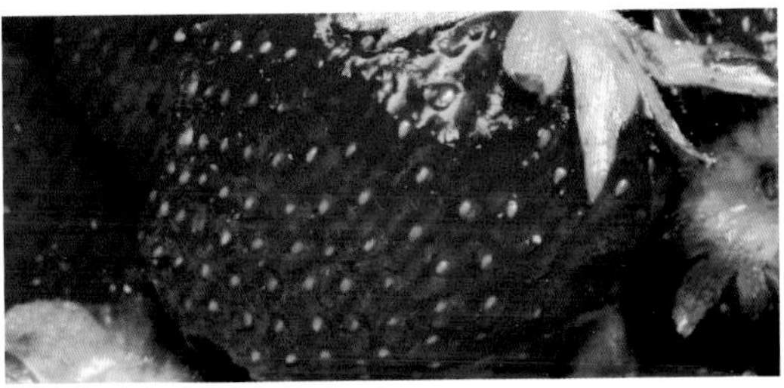

makers can be bought with a heated milk frother, or plain filter machines which use filter papers. Espresso machines produce a wide variety of coffee, from regular coffee to espresso and cappuccino. With all machines, follow the manufacturer's instructions.

- Flavoured and specialist coffees are now extremely popular, from small, very strong espresso to café latte and Americano. Coffees that have a shot of alcohol or flavoured syrup added are also commonly drunk.

**Irish Coffee**
Place a measure of Irish whiskey into a heat-proof glass, add 1 teaspoon of demerara sugar and stir. Pour in freshly brewed black coffee to within 1 cm/½ inch of the rim. Stir until the sugar has dissolved. Pour in chilled double cream over the back of a spoon to the top of the rim. Scottish whisky, Cointreau, rum, brandy, Kirsch, vodka, Tia Maria or Curacao can all be used in place of the whiskey.

**Iced Coffee**
Make strong, black coffee using your preferred bean. Pour into a jug or glasses and sweeten to taste, stirring until the sugar has dissolved. Cool and chill. Just before serving, pour into glasses, add 1–2 ice cubes, top with whipped cream and, if liked, sprinkle with a little grated chocolate.

**Turkish coffee**
Place 50 g/2 oz of finely ground coffee with an equal amount of sugar into a wide based, narrow necked coffee pot. Pour on 500 ml/18 fl oz of water. Bring to the boil, then draw off the heat and allow the coffee to subside. Heat again to boiling point, allowing the coffee to subside again. Repeat once more then serve in small cups.

# Fruit-based Drinks

## Fruity Berry Smoothie

**Serves 4**

225 g/8 oz ripe strawberries
100 g/4 oz fresh or thawed frozen raspberries
1–2 tbsp clear honey
600 ml/1 pint low fat natural yogurt
crushed ice to serve
mint sprigs to decorate

Hull the strawberries and rinse lightly, reserving four for decoration. Chop into evenly-sized pieces and place in a liquidiser or food processor with the raspberries and honey. Blend for 1 minute, then add 85 ml/ 3 fl oz chilled water and the yogurt and blend for 1–2 minutes or until smooth and frothy. Half-fill four tall glasses with crushed ice and add the smoothie. Decorate with strawberries and mint sprigs and serve.

## Tropical Fruit Smoothie

**Serves 4**

1 large ripe mango, peeled, stoned and chopped
1 ripe papaya, peeled, seeded and chopped
1 large banana, peeled and chopped
2 ripe passion fruits
1–2 tbsp light muscovado sugar
450 ml/¾ pint chilled milk
4 scoops vanilla ice cream
2 tsp chopped nuts (optional) to decorate

Place the mango, papaya and banana into a liquidiser and scoop in the passion fruit flesh and seeds. Blend for 1 minute then add the sugar and milk and blend again until smooth and frothy. Half-fill four tall glasses with crushed ice, pour over the smoothie and top each with a scoop of ice cream. Sprinkle with nuts (if using) and serve.

## Spiced Fruit Punch

**Serves 10**

600 ml/1 pt orange and mango juice
thinly pared rind of 2 lemons
150 ml/¼ pint lemon juice
6 whole cloves
1 large cinnamon stick, bruised
½ tsp ground allspice
1.2 litres/2 pint chilled ginger ale
1 small ripe mango, peeled, stoned and finely chopped
crushed ice

Place the fruit juices in a large jug and stir in the spices. Allow to stand in the refrigerator for at least 2 hours, stirring occasionally. When ready to serve, stir in the ginger ale and chopped mango and serve over crushed ice. If liked, the punch can be served warm. Heat the fruit juices with the spices over a very gentle heat. When almost at boiling point, remove from the heat and carefully pour into a punch bowl. Gradually pour in the ginger ale and serve in heatproof glasses with cinnamon sticks to stir.

## Citrus Punch

**Serves 8**

4–5 large oranges, squeezed to yield 300 ml/½ pint juice
juice of 2 lemons, to yield 85 ml/3 fl oz juice
juice of 2 pink grapefruits, to yield 150 ml/¼ pint juice
1–2 tbsp clear honey
1 small orange, thinly sliced
600 ml/1 pint lemonade
crushed ice to serve

Pour all the fruit juices into a jug and stir in the honey. Float the orange slices on top and leave to chill in the refrigerator for at least 1 hour. Top up with the lemonade then serve over crushed ice, ensuring that all glasses get at least one slice of orange.

## Still Lemonade

**Makes about 1.2 litres/2 pints**

3 large ripe lemons, preferably organic or unwaxed
100–175 g/4–6 oz caster sugar, or to taste
900 ml/1 ½ pints freshly boiled water
thinly sliced lemons to serve, optional

Scrub the lemons and thinly pare the rind with a vegetable peeler. Place in a bowl together with the sugar. Squeeze the juice and reserve. Pour the boiling water over the lemon rind, stirring until the sugar has dissolved. Cover and leave until cool then chill for at least 2 hours. Strain the lemonade, discarding the rind, stir in the reserved lemon juice and serve chilled with a lemon slice floating on top.

Orangeade can be made in exactly the same way – simply replace the lemons with oranges. You may wish to add a little lemon juice as well to give a tangier flavour.

## Orange & Lemon Barley Water

**Makes 900 ml/1 ½ pints**

50 g/2 oz pearl barley

50 g/2 oz caster sugar

juice of 2 lemons, strained

juice of 1 large orange, strained

Rinse the pearl barley, place in a saucepan and cover with cold water. Bring to the boil, strain off the liquid and thoroughly rinse the pearl barley. Return to the saucepan, add 600 ml/ 1 pint of cold water and bring to the boil. Cover, reduce the heat and simmer for 1 hour. Strain the liquid into a jug and stir in the sugar. Stir until the sugar has dissolved.

Allow to cool, then chill for 1 hour. Stir in the fruit juices and return to the refrigerator until required.

## Milkshake

**Serves 1**

1 ripe banana, peeled and sliced

300 ml/½ pint chilled milk

1–2 tsp clear honey

1 scoop vanilla ice cream

1 tsp grated chocolate

Place the banana and milk with honey to taste in a liquidiser or food processor. Switch on and blend for 1–2 minutes or until smooth and frothy. Pour into a tall glass, place the scoop of ice cream on top and sprinkle with the grated chocolate.

**Variations:** Try using a variety of different flavours – mixed berries such as strawberries, blueberries or raspberries are good, as are mango and papaya. A little drinking chocolate can be added to the shake before blending and other flavoured ice creams can be used – try chocolate, strawberry or praline and cream.

## Ginger Beer

This takes two weeks before it is ready, although the 'plant', once made, can be used repeatedly.

**For the plant:**

50 g/2 oz fresh yeast

2 tbsp caster sugar

3 tbsp ground ginger

water as required

**For feeding:**

3 tbsp ground ginger

3 tbsp caster sugar plus 500 g/ 18 oz caster sugar

juice of 2 large ripe lemons, strained

Cream the yeast with 1 teaspoon each of sugar and ground ginger until blended, then gradually beat in 300 ml/½ pint cold water, beating well so a smooth runny paste is formed. Place in a bowl or large jar, cover and leave in the dark. The next day, add a further 1 teaspoon each of ground ginger and caster sugar and stir well. Do this for 10 days in total.

After 10 days, heat the 500 g/18 oz caster sugar in 900 ml/1 ½ pints of water and bring slowly to the boil, stirring to dissolve the sugar. Draw off the heat and stir in the strained lemon juice. Strain the ginger beer plant through muslin or a very fine sieve into the lemon juice and water mixture. Stir well until blended then pour into clean, sterilised bottles and screw down tightly. Store in a cool dark place. (Take care: if kept in the warm or light, the bottles will explode.)

To make more ginger beer, take the sediment left on the muslin or in the sieve. To half of this add 300 ml/½ pint cold water and feed with 2 teaspoons of ground ginger and 2 teaspoons of caster sugar. Proceed for the next 10 days as before.

# Alcohol-Based Drinks

## Hot Spiced Cider

**Makes about 1.2 litres/2 pints**

1.2 litres/2 pints cider

6 whole cloves

3 whole star anise

2 cinnamon sticks, lightly bruised

85 g/3 oz light muscovado sugar

Place all the ingredients into either a heavy-based saucepan or a bowl standing over a pan of gently simmering water. Heat gently, stirring until the sugar has dissolved. Strain into heatproof glasses, and serve with whole cinnamon sticks to stir.

## Gluhwein

**Makes about 900 ml/1 ½ pints**

600 ml/1 pint red wine

85 g/3 oz light muscovado sugar

2 cinnamon sticks, lightly bruised

1 lemon, preferably organic, scrubbed and studded with 8 whole cloves

150 ml/¼ pint brandy

Place all the ingredients except the brandy into either a heavy-based saucepan or a bowl standing over a pan of gently simmering water. Heat gently, stirring until the sugar has dissolved. Add the brandy and continue to heat until hot. Strain into heatproof glasses, serving with whole cinnamon sticks to stir.

## Rum Punch

**Makes about 1.2 litres/2 pints**

900 ml/1 ½ pints cold water

225 g/8 oz dark muscovado sugar

1 lemon

2 medium-sized oranges

150 ml/¼ pint freshly brewed strong tea

150 ml/¼ pint dark rum

Pour the water into a heavy-based saucepan and stir in the sugar. Thinly pare the rind from the lemon and 1 of the oranges and add to the pan. Squeeze the juice from all the fruit. Bring to the boil, stirring to dissolve the sugar. When the liquid comes to the boil, strain in the fruit juice then stir in the tea and rum. Heat until hot. Serve in heatproof glasses if serving hot, or over crushed ice if serving cold.

## The Bishop

**Makes about 1.2 litres/2 pints**

1 medium sized orange

10 whole cloves

900 ml/1 ½ pints port

1 tsp ground allspice

50 g/2 oz granulated sugar

Preheat the oven to 180°C/350°F/Gas Mark 4, 10 minutes before cooking. Stud the orange with the cloves and roast in the oven for 30 minutes. Remove and reserve. Place the port with 300 ml/ ½ pint of water in a large heatproof bowl over a pan of gently simmering water and bring to the boil. Meanwhile, blend the allspice with 150 ml/ ¼ pint water in a small pan and bring to the boil, stirring. Add to the port together with the sugar and the roasted orange. Heat until piping hot, and serve as hot as possible.

## Kir Royale

**For each glass**

Pour a measure of crème de cassis into a champagne flute and top up with chilled champagne. If liked a strawberry can be added.

## Bucks Fizz

**For each glass**

Pour equal measures of chilled, freshly-squeezed orange juice and chilled champagne into champagne flutes.

## Whisky Sour

**For each glass**

Mix together the strained juice of 1 small or ½ large lemon with 1 tsp caster sugar. Stir in a measure of whisky and pour over crushed ice. Brandy Sours can be made by substituting the whisky with brandy

## Daiquiri

**For each glass**

Place the strained juice of 1 lime with 1 tsp light muscovado sugar and 1 measure of rum in a cocktail shaker and shake for 1 minute. Pour over crushed ice and serve.

## Pink Gin

**For each glass**

Swirl 2–3 drops of Angostura bitters around a glass until coated. Add a measure of gin and top up with iced water.

## Screwdriver

**For each glass**

Place a few ice cubes in a cocktail shaker and add a measure of vodka, the juice of 1 orange and a dash of Angostura bitters. Shake until blended and pour into a glass.

## Pimms Cup

**Serves 6**

½ small orange
½ small lemon
1 red apple
25 g/1 oz strawberries
small piece cucumber
450 ml/¾ pint Pimms
150 ml/¼ pint gin, optional
3–4 mint sprigs
1.25 litres/2 ¼ pints lemonade
crushed ice

Scrub the fruits (if not using organic) then slice the orange and lemon thinly and cut each slice in half. Core the apple and slice thinly, and rinse the strawberries and slice. Peel the cucumber if preferred and thinly slice. Place all these in a large jug, pour in the Pimms and gin, if using, and stir. Add the ice, then top up with lemonade. Add a few mint sprigs and serve in tall glasses.

# Index



## Picture Credits

**Cephas Picture Library/www.cephas.com:** 19 t © Eising; 23 © FoodPhotographer Eising; 24 © Alack, Chris; 25 br © Studio R. Schmitz; 26 br © Joff Lee Studios; 32 © Skip, Dean; 33 © Jackson, James; 34 © Boyer, Jean-Paul; 36 & 38 © Holsten/Koops; 440 © Bialy, Dorota i Bogdan; 443 l © Shaffer Smith Photography; 444 © Stowell, Roger; 445 l © Studio Bonisolli; 445 m © Schieren, Bodo A.; 445 r © Marcialis, Ren.

**Topham Picturepoint:** 7, 8 b, 17 bl, 28, 30, 31, 44, 52, 55, 85, 123, 173, 361; 8 t & 9 © Rachel Epstein/The Image Works; 29, 46 & 47 © Nancy Richmond/The Images Works; 50 © Larry Kolvoord/The Images Works; 231 © Tiffany M. Herman/ Journal-Courier/The Image Works; 265 © Dion Ogust/The Image Works; 35 r, 291 © Bob Daemmrich/The Image Works; 337 & 399 Marie-Louise Avery

35, 442 Chris Clark © Business AM Survival Guide

All other pictures courtesy of Foundry Arts